T0306147

Forestry Economics

Forestry Economics introduces students and practitioners to the economics of managing forests and forest enterprises. The book adopts the approach of managerial economics textbooks and applies this to the unique problems and production processes faced by managers of forests and forest enterprises.

What many future forest and natural resource managers need is to understand what economic information is and how to use it to make better business and management decisions. John E. Wagner draws on his 30 years of experience teaching and working in the field of forest resource economics to present students with an accessible understanding of the unique production processes and problems faced by forest and other natural resource managers.

The second edition has been updated to include:

- Expanded discussion of compounding, discounting, and capital budgeting, as well as an expanded discussion of when to replace a capital asset that has (i) costs but no direct revenue stream such as a machine; (ii) costs and a direct annual revenue stream such as a solar array; or (iii) costs and a periodic revenue stream illustrated by the forest rotation problem.
- New practical examples to provide students with applications of the concepts being discussed in the text, most notably on New Zealand and a Radiata Pine (*Pinus radiata*) Plantation.
- A brand-new chapter that develops business plans for for-profit businesses to illustrate how a business plan is derived from the economic information contained within the Architectural Plan for Profit and how it can be used to make business decisions about continuing to operate a business or to start a new business.

This textbook is an invaluable source of clear and accessible information on forestry economics and management not only for economics students, but also for students of other disciplines and those already working in forestry and natural resources.

John E. Wagner is Professor of Forest Resource Economics at the State University of New York College of Environmental Science and Forestry in Syracuse, USA.

Routledge Textbooks in Environmental and Agricultural Economics

For more information about this series, please visit: www.routledge.com/Routledge-Textbooks-in-Environmental-and-Agricultural-Economics/book-series/TEAE

Forestry Economics
A Managerial Approach
Second Edition

John E. Wagner

Routledge
Taylor & Francis Group

LONDON AND NEW YORK

Cover image: © John E. Wagner

Second edition published 2024
by Routledge
4 Park Square, Milton Park, Abingdon, Oxon, OX14 4RN

and by Routledge
605 Third Avenue, New York, NY 10158

Routledge is an imprint of the Taylor & Francis Group, an informa business

First edition published by Routledge 2012

British Library Cataloguing-in-Publication Data
A catalogue record for this book is available from the British Library

Library of Congress Cataloging-in-Publication Data
Names: Wagner, John E., author.
Title: Forestry economics : a managerial approach / John E. Wagner.
Description: Second edition. | Abingdon, Oxon; New York : Routledge,
   2024. | Series: Routledge textbooks in environmental and agricultural
   economics | Includes bibliographical references and index. |
   second edition
Identifiers: LCCN 2023035379 | ISBN 9781138933132 (hbk) |
   ISBN 9781138933149 (pbk) | ISBN 9781315678719 (ebk)
Subjects: LCSH: Forests and forestry—Economic aspects. |
   Forest management.
Classification: LCC SD393 .W26 2024 | DDC 333.75—dc23/eng/20230926
LC record available at https://lccn.loc.gov/2023035379

ISBN: 978-1-138-93313-2 (hbk)
ISBN: 978-1-138-93314-9 (pbk)
ISBN: 978-1-315-67871-9 (ebk)

DOI: 10.4324/9781315678719

Typeset in Times New Roman
by Apex CoVantage, LLC

Access the Support Material: www.routledge.com/9781138933149

Contents

Figures

Illustrations

Photos

Tables

Preface

Textbooks that I have used in the past with a focus on forestry or natural resource economics were written from the prospective of an economist to a future economist. However, most students who graduate from environmental, forestry, or natural resource management programs are not going to be economists: They are going to be managers. They will need to understand what economic information is and how they can use it to make better business and management decisions. In this regard, this book takes an approach similar to managerial economics textbooks that are used in business schools at the undergraduate and graduate levels. However, standard business school–type managerial economics textbooks do not address the unique production processes and problems faced by managers of forests and other natural resources. Those issues are addressed in this book.

There are five unique features of the second edition. The first feature is its organization. The introduction develops and describes two common economic models used in the decision-making process: (1) maximization of net benefits and (2) least cost/cost effective. The first four chapters break down each model into its components and identify and critically analyze the economic information each component contains. The fifth chapter reconstitutes the models combining the knowledge gained from the decomposition into useful analysis tools. Chapter 9 discusses techniques commonly used to estimate the demand for nonmarket goods. Chapters 10 and 11 expand business decision modeling to encompass supply, demand, and the market. Chapter 12 examines the impacts of taxes on the decision-making models.

Second, Chapters 6 through 8 further expand the least cost/cost effective and profit models to take into account compounding and discounting, capital budgeting, and risk. New to the second edition, Chapter 6 has been expanded to provide a more detailed discussion of compounding, discounting, and capital budgeting. Also new to the second edition, Chapter 7 has been expanded to examine when to replace a capital asset. This allows for a richer analysis of replacing (i) a capital asset that has costs but no direct revenue stream (for example a car or piece of heavy equipment); (ii) a capital asset that has costs with an annual direct revenue stream (for example a solar array); and (iii) a capital asset that has costs with a periodic direct revenue stream (for example the forest rotation problem).

Third is the use of practical applications from various disciplines such as outdoor and commercial recreation, wood products engineering, forest products, and forestry. New to the second edition is an application from New Zealand based on a Radiata Pine (*Pinus radiata*) Plantation. These applications will be used to illustrate empirically key points.

Fourth is revisiting the statement "How to use economic information to make better business decisions." at the end of each chapter. This ties each chapter to the preceding ones and reinforces the hypothesis that a solid working knowledge of these economic models and the information they contain are necessary for making better business decisions.

Finally, new to the second edition is Chapter 13 that develops business plans for two existing for-profit businesses managed by SUNY – College of Environmental Science and Forestry's Forest Properties Department: A maple syrup operation and a log yard and firewood operation. To illustrate the components of business planning, I will develop a 10-year business plan for a proposed for-profit business: A slab mill. The production levels, cost, and revenue data are the actual data of these businesses. These practical applications are used to illustrate how a business plan is derived from the economic information contained within the Architectural Plan for Profit and can be used to make business decisions about continuing to operate a business, in the cases of the maple syrup operation and the log yard and firewood operation, or to start a new business, in the case of the slab mill. The financial analyses used draw on those presented in Chapters 6 to 8. In addition, I will describe three fundamental financial accounting statements used in developing business plans.

Acknowledgements

There are a few people who should be acknowledged, as without their help this book would have been much harder to complete: First, to my wife Janice and my parents Albert and Mirney. Second, to the following colleagues who provided professional reviews of various chapters of the first and second editions:

Dr. Douglas Carter	University of Florida
Mr. David Feldman	National Renewable Energy Laboratory
Dr. Donald Grebner	Mississippi State University
Dr. Donald Hodges	University of Tennessee
Mr. Michael Kelleher	SUNY – College of Environmental Science and Forestry – Retired
Dr. Don Mead	Lincoln University New Zealand
Dr. John Moore	SCION New Zealand
Dr. David Newman	SUNY – College of Environmental Science and Forestry
Dr. Erik Nordman	Grand Valley State University
Dr. Patrick C. Penfield	Syracuse University
Dr. Jeffery Prestemon	Forest Service – Southern Research Station
Dr. Thomas Stevens	University of Massachusetts – Amherst

Third, the following agencies, professional societies, and business graciously allowed me copyrights to material that I have used: United States Department of Agricultural Forest Service, TimberMart South, Canadian Farm Business Management Council, Ontario Ministry of Agriculture – Food and Rural Affairs, J.W. Sewall, Co., Ohio Sea Grant – The Ohio State University, Society of American Foresters, Forest Products Society, Manomet Center of Conservation Sciences, and Micromill® Systems, Inc. Finally, to the editorial staff at Routledge Press for their help and patience.

Abbreviations

AC	Average cost
ac	Acres
AFC	Average fixed cost
AP	Average product
AR	Average revenue
ARP	Average revenue product
ATC	Average total cost
AVC	Average variable cost
BCR	Benefit-cost ratio
bd.ft.	Board feet
CAI	Current annual increment
CMAI	Culmination of mean annual increment
cu ft	Cubic feet
DBH	Diameter at breast height
FV	Future value
irr	Internal rate of return
LEV	Land expectation value
MAI	Mean annual increment
MC	Marginal cost
MFC	Marginal factor cost
MP	Marginal product
MR	Marginal revenue
MRP	Marginal revenue product
NPV, NPV$_t$, NPV$_T$	Net present value, net present value at
time t,	$t = 0, 1, 2, 3, \ldots, T$
P, PQ, P*	Market price, own-price, market equilibrium price
PAI	Periodic annual increment
PI	Profitability index
PV	Present value
Q, Q*	Market quantity, market equilibrium quantity
ROI	Return on investment
SEV	Soil expectation value
TC	Total cost

TFC	Total fixed costs
TR	Total revenue
TRP	Total revenue product
TVC	Total variable costs
USD	United States dollars
$	Dollars

1 Introduction

Preamble

> I often say that when you can measure what you are speaking about, and express it in numbers, you know something about it; but when you cannot measure it, when you cannot express it in numbers, your knowledge is of a meagre and unsatisfactory kind.
>
> Lord Kelvin (1824–1907; William Thomson),
> Mathematical Physicist and Engineer
> From a Lecture to the Institution of Civil Engineers, 3 May 1883

This quote has often been shortened to: "If you cannot measure it, you cannot improve it." Peter Drucker popularized this idea, within a business management context, in his similar quote: "If you cannot measure it, you cannot manage it." In its most basic form, managing a "system" – a natural resources ecosystem, a renewable or sustainable energy system, a forest ecosystem, or a business system – to produce an owner's desired future condition (e.g., long-term profits) entails measuring and describing analytically the system; determining an appropriate management plan consistent with the owner's desired future condition given the system's measurements; manipulating the system physically based on the management plan; and monitoring and assessing the management results for obtaining the desired future condition. As systems are dynamic and not static, this procedure is repeated as often as required.[1] If systematic changes are needed, the information necessary to make them is available given the owner's desired future condition. Refining this concept further in the specific context of managerial economics, I would assert that managing one of the "systems" mentioned earlier requires identifying alternate ways to achieve an owner's desired future condition and selecting the alternatives that achieves this in, most often, the most resource-efficient manner. Thus, I would also assert that, regardless of the system, using relevant economic information will lead to better business decisions that accomplish this more often than not. Therefore, the purpose of this book is to address the statement: "How to use economic information to make better business and management decisions."

Defining what constitutes economic information as well as developing two analytical constructs to aid management decision making is the purpose of this chapter. I will use a number of practical applications and example systems to illustrate

DOI: 10.4324/9781315678719-1

the concepts discussed in the chapters. The practical applications are drawn from the literature and will be identified at the end of this chapter. I will also use four example systems throughout the book that are based on published and unpublished applied work: (i) maple syrup, (ii) solar array, (iii) natural resource ecosystems contained within the built-to-wildlands continuum,[2] and (iv) schoolwork.

Example Systems

The system for maple syrup starts in the forest and ends in producing and selling various maple syrup products. Some individuals produce maple syrup for individual enjoyment and others produce maple syrup as a commercial enterprise. Managing this system requires describing analytically and measuring the maple stand (typically called a sugarbush) and the process for creating the various maple products. Maple syrup starts as sap obtained by tapping primarily sugar maples (*Acer saccharum* Marsh.). The sap is collected and evaporated to concentrate the sugars creating syrup, which is used to make various products: maple syrup (of course), maple candies, and maple cream (Figure 1.1).

The desired future conditions of this system are (i) a sustainable sugarbush that provides (ii) long-term profits and positive net benefits for the owner.[3] What economic information is necessary for managers to make decisions with respect to resource inputs into and costs of the system? For example, sap can be collected using a vacuum technique potentially reducing costs. A reverse osmosis machine can remove approximately 75% of excess water reducing energy costs (van den Berg et al. 2015). What economic information is necessary for managers to make decisions with respect to outputs and revenues of the system? For example, the same unit of sap cannot be used to make syrup and candies. Tapping a sugar maple leads to a 40% to 60% loss in potential future commercial revenue from selling the trees for lumber. Which output provides a greater net revenue stream? Each management decision represents a tradeoff – something must be given up to gain something else. What additional economic information may be required to manage this system?[4]

The system for a solar array starts with siting the array and ends with converting incoming solar radiation (insolation) to more useable form of energy; namely, electricity as measured in kilowatt-hours or kilowatts-hours used in a day or month (Figure 1.2).

Some individuals have a solar array for personal net benefit (e.g., rooftop unit) and others as a commercial enterprise. Managing this system requires describing analytically and measuring the insolation on the photovoltaic cells to produce energy. An interesting feature of this system relative to the other examples is the greater degree of fixed factors; namely, the solar panels and electrical and structural balance of the system. The desired future conditions of this system are (i) a sustainable source of clean energy that provides (ii) long-term profits and positive net benefits for the owner. What economic information is necessary for managers to make decisions with respect to resource inputs into and costs of the system? For example, sunlight is a critical input for converting energy using solar panels,

Figure 1.1 State University of New York College of Environmental Science and Forestry's Maple Syrup Operation

Photo credit: Jill Rahn

Figure 1.2 State University of New York College of Environmental Science and Forestry's 24.192 Kilowatt Solar Array

Photo credit: John E. Wagner

but a manager has very little control over when the sun shines. The manager does have control over the positioning of the array or using sun-tracking technology to capture the greatest insolation relative to costs. What economic information is necessary for managers to make decisions with respect to outputs and revenues of the system; for example, should a manager sell every kilowatt-hour the solar array can produce? Each management decision represents a tradeoff – something must be given up to gain something else. What additional economic information may be required to manage this system?[5]

Natural resource systems start with an ecosystem along the built-to-wildlands continuum and ends with producing a desired suite of ecosystem output(s) and outcome(s).[6] Figure 1.3 illustrates this continuum that encompasses urban environments (e.g., an area with an increased density of human-created structures) to wildlands environment (e.g., natural environments that have not been significantly modified by humans).

Figure 1.3 also illustrates the various ecosystem output(s) and outcome(s) given various points on or segments of the continuum. Some individuals own land along this continuum for individual net benefits (e.g., aesthetics, privacy, recreation, . . .) and others as a commercial enterprise selling outputs in existing markets ranging from local and regional to global (e.g., timber stumpage,[7] recreation leases, mushrooms, and maple syrup) or in emerging markets (e.g., carbon sequestration credits). Managing this system requires describing analytically and measuring the natural resource ecosystem in terms of structure (e.g., age, species per unit area, trees per unit area by diameter class), density (e.g., richness, abundance, basal area per unit area, crown competition factor, leaf area index), and composition (e.g., percent species per unit area). The desired future conditions of this system are (i) a sustainable natural resource ecosystem that provides (ii) long-term profits and positive net benefits for the owner. What economic information is necessary for managers to make decisions with respect to resource inputs into and costs of the system? In addition to structure, density, and composition, managers need to know how modifying these using appropriate actions (e.g., silvicultural prescriptions) will create a future structure necessary to provide the desired suite of ecosystem output(s) and outcome(s) consistent with the owner's goals and objectives.[8] What economic information is necessary for managers to make decisions with respect to output(s)/outcome(s) and revenues of the system? For example, a forest structure producing softwood trees for lumber (e.g., loblolly pine (*Pinus taeda*) in the Southeast, Douglas fir (*Pseudotsuga menziesii*) in the

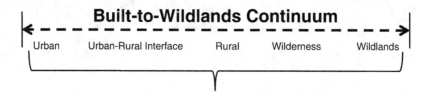

Built-to-Wildlands Continuum

| Urban | Urban-Rural Interface | Rural | Wilderness | Wildlands |

Traditional Outputs: Wood Fiber, Biomass, Forage and Fodder, Aquatic and Terrestrial Wildlife, Water, Recreation, Food, Oils, Chemicals and Compounds, and Energy
Traditional Outcomes: Provisioning, Regulating, and Cultural Services

Figure 1.3 Natural Resources Ecosystem: Built-to-Wildlands Continuum

Pacific Northwest, or Monterey pine (*Pinus radiata*) in New Zealand) generates a periodic revenue stream, but a forest structure providing the necessary conditions for wildlife habitat could generate an annual revenue stream from a recreational lease. Each management decision represents a tradeoff – something must be given up to gain something else. What additional economic information may be required to manage this system?

The system for schoolwork starts with a context and ends with schoolwork accomplished (or maybe not).[9] The context: It is a dark and stormy night, the semester is underway, and you have four hours after supper to spend on one or more activities: (i) study, (ii) spend time with friends, or (iii) watch some television. Managing this system requires describing analytically and measuring the tradeoffs associated with each choice. The desired future condition of this system is allocating the four hours that will lead to the most satisfying outcome. What economic information is necessary for you to decide with respect to resource inputs into and costs of the system? With nothing much to watch on TV this evening, you decide the relevant choices would be either studying or spending time with friends. What economic information is necessary for managers to make decisions with respect to outputs and revenues of the system? Weighing studying – you have some reading from two classes to finish – versus meeting friends, you decide that for this evening you will use the first two hours studying and spend the rest of the time with friends. Each management decision represents a tradeoff – something must be given up to gain something else. What additional economic information may be required to manage this system?

Let's examine the schoolwork system a little more in depth: How did you go about making the decision to allocate those four hours among the different uses? What tradeoffs did you make? Studying implied that you gave up watching television, as reading and studying school material is an activity best done with few distractions (Foerde et al. 2006).[10] Simply, if you are not efficient with the time allotted to studying, the cost is having to spend more time studying, resulting in less time to relax and reducing your overall satisfaction. You also know that reading school material usually takes a lot of concentration and after about two hours you need a rest. As a result, you decided to study for the first two hours (giving up spending the entire time with friends), then spend the remaining time with your friends (giving up two hours of study time). If it were a sunny warm afternoon rather than a stormy night, you probably would have opted to spend more than two hours outside with your friends because you could have then studied all evening. As the semester comes to a close there always seems to be more work due – term papers and projects, etc. – in addition to the normal reading and homework. You might have spent the entire four hours studying. Having a test tomorrow tends to focus your attention on preparing for the test, especially if you did not spend as much time earlier in the week preparing. Again, you might have spent the entire four hours studying. So, while we are talking about a four-hour block of time, to analyze the tradeoffs between studying and relaxing requires economic information concerning how much studying or relaxing would add to your overall satisfaction in a given context.

A re-examining the forest system would seem straightforward: Selling softwood trees (referred to as stumpage) to be milled for dimension lumber. However, selling your trees to be milled for dimension lumber requires that they be defined as merchantable and suitable to be used for that purpose. Who defined what is merchantable? If those trees are sold, where did the price the buyer offered come from? The answer to the latter question is straightforward: The price offered by the buyer is based on what the primary processor (e.g., sawmill, pulp or paper mill, etc.) is willing to pay. The answer to the former question is also straightforward. The primary processor defines what is merchantable.[11] Interestingly, a similar set of relationships can be described among primary, secondary, and final processors.[12] Consequently, the owner's desired future condition (i.e., long-term profits) is not only dependent on the structure, density, and composition, but also on the supply and demand of the stumpage and wood fiber markets and the supply and demand of the secondary and primary markets.

What if the owner's desired future condition is not the production of timber or wood fiber to generate profits but the creation of wildlife habitat for personal use? This would require managing structure, density, and composition to create the conditions necessary for creating the habitat structures. Again, in its most basic form, managing a forest entails measuring and describing analytically the resource, determining an appropriate management plan given the owner's desired future condition, and manipulating the forest based on the management plan. Describing the desired future condition physically seems straightforward (e.g., creating edge and openings to increase deer habitat), but how is this desired future condition described economically? The desired future conditions of this system are (i) a sustainable forest ecosystem that provides (ii) long-term positive net benefits from the wildlife habitat for the owner with an additional proviso that the management costs do not exceed the owner's budget. What if the owner's management plan could be described as neglect, benign or otherwise? As forests grow without any human intervention, does this latter example imply there is no economic information the owner can use to inform their choice to take no management action? Or, is the owner ignoring or ignorant of the relevant economic information surrounding their choice to take no management action?

What if the example was a recreational charter boat fishing system; a wind turbine or biomass energy generating system; a local, regional, national park/natural area system; or an urban forest system (e.g., Escobedo et al. 2006, 2008, 2010; Szantio et al. 2012)? In terms of managerial economics, what do all of these different systems have in common?

- In all cases, the owner's goals for the desired future conditions of these systems can be characterized as (i) a sustainable system that provides (ii) long-term profits or positive net benefits.
- In all cases, describing analytically and measuring the system is a required precursor to managing the system.
- In all cases, a logical process of measurements and analytical descriptions $\Rightarrow$ least cost $\Rightarrow$ profit/net benefit provides a flexible method to manage any system regardless of the context.

A curiosity of the first and third bullet is the distinction between "profits" and "positive net benefits." In the maple syrup system, if the owner is producing syrup for their own use (not selling to anyone), there are no revenues generated. However, there still are costs. The owner is receiving a "benefit" from producing and consuming their own maple syrup minus their production costs. Therefore, the owner is receiving a net benefit, and if the benefit is greater than the production costs, they are receiving a positive net benefit. In the forest system, a similar argument could be made: The owner is receiving a benefit from producing and consuming their own privacy, aesthetics, and recreation minus their production costs from their forest; therefore, the owner is receiving a net benefit, and if the benefit is greater than the production costs, they are receiving a positive net benefit. In the solar array system, a similar argument could be made: A residential owner is receiving a benefit from producing and consuming their own clean energy. Part of this benefit is their satisfaction from producing clean energy and part is the result of net metering.[13] Therefore, the owner is receiving a net benefit, and if the benefit is greater than the solar array costs, they are receiving a positive net benefit.[14] In all cases, minimizing the production costs relative to the benefits will make the positive net benefit stream as large as possible.

The second bullet recognizes that measuring and describing analytically a natural resource, forested, or renewable energy system builds on knowledge of the fundamental input–output relationships gained from studying biology, ecology, chemistry, and physics. These relationships are probably the most familiar as they are some of the earliest courses taken. However, these input–output relationships are also a fundamental component of defining and using economic information.

By the end of this chapter, I will define what exactly constitutes "economic information" and will provide two analytical constructs to achieve an entrepreneur's desired future condition. The remaining chapters will build on this definition and the constructs to address the statement of "How to use economic information to make better business decisions."

What Is Economics?

Economics textbooks, some with greater effectiveness than others, regularly provide a definition of economics. As I believe it is necessary to define and describe important terms, I will also provide one. The following is based on a definition used by Samuelson (1976a):

> Economics is the study of how individuals choose, with or without money, to employ scarce productive resources that have alternative uses, to produce various commodities and services and distribute them for current or future consumption and investment among various persons in society.

There are four key concepts in this definition that need further clarification. The first is scarcity. Pearce (1994) defines scarcity as "usually reserved for situations in which the resources available for producing outputs are insufficient to satisfy wants." Scarcity is often cited as the fundamental reason why economics exists. There are two types of scarcity: absolute and relative. Absolute scarcity implies that there is a finite quantity of a resource. For example, oil and coal are often referred to as absolutely scarce. Relative scarcity implies that sacrifices must be made to keep the resource in its current use or to obtain it. These resources have alternative uses. A barrel of oil can be refined into gasoline and other petrochemicals or can be held in the ground or in barrels for future uses. On the other hand, I have an obsolete calculus and analytical geometry textbook published in 1951. This textbook is, for all practical purposes, absolutely scarce. There exist a finite number of these books. However, it is not useful as a reference, while it is old it is not a collectable item, and I have not had to make any sacrifices to keep it in my bookshelf. There are, for all practical purposes, no alternative uses of this book. In fact, I have not made sacrifices of any kind with respect to this book. Consequently, it is not relatively scarce. The fact that the book is absolutely scarce is less important than the fact that it is not relatively scarce. Oil on the other hand is absolutely scarce; but more importantly, also relatively scarce. I must make sacrifices to obtain it (now or in the future) and keep it in its current use. Thus, in terms of the comparative importance, relative scarcity is more important than absolute scarcity.[15]

The second key concept is choice. Only individuals choose and, therefore, only the individual is responsible for the choices they make. While it may appear that organizations and institutions choose, it is the individuals in the organizations and institutions who make the decisions and are ultimately held responsible (Heyne et al. 2006). The reason individuals must choose is because of scarcity, more specifically, relative scarcity. Relative scarcity implies choice, or

Relative Scarcity $\leftrightarrow$ Choice

On that dark and stormy night, you had four hours to spend. Spending time with your friends was the alternative you gave up or sacrificed to study. On the other hand, spending time studying was the alternative you gave up or sacrificed to spend time with your friends. Stated differently, relative scarcity implies choice, and choice implies an opportunity cost:

Relative Scarcity $\leftrightarrow$ Choice $\leftrightarrow$ Opportunity Cost

The first two key concepts lead to one of the fundamental building blocks of economics, and that is "opportunity cost." Opportunity cost is defined as the highest-valued alternative forgone. This implies an incremental decision-making process.[16] As described by Ferraro and Taylor (2005) and Potter and Sanders (2012), the highest-valued alternative is defined as a "net" benefit forgone as there are benefits but also potential costs to any decision. The key is to identify the relevant incremental benefits and costs given the context of the decision.[17] In the schoolwork system, studying implied that you gave up watching TV and seeing your friends. As you valued being with your friends more than watching TV, the opportunity cost of an additional hour studying was relaxing with your friends. In the maple syrup system, sap is concentrated by removing water. This concentrated sap is used to produce maple syrup, candies, or cream. Maple cream and candies are produced using maple syrup. So, a unit of maple syrup can be sold or processed further to produce maple cream or candies. What is the opportunity cost of not selling a unit of maple syrup and processing it into maple cream? The relevant incremental costs are the lost net revenues from not selling the maple syrup plus the additional processing costs. The incremental revenues are selling the unit of maple cream produced. In the commercial solar array system, the opportunity cost of providing a kilowatt-hour of energy is not providing it to the electrical grid. This opportunity cost is a function of any contractual agreements, the electrical grid's system constraints, and locational based marginal price.[18] Opportunity cost is the "What if" question: What am I giving up or what sacrifices are made to continue what I am doing now and in the future?[19] Learning to ask and answer this question explicitly is vital to comprehending the economic way of reasoning about scarcity. Ignoring the choices associated with scarcity does not make the opportunity cost of those choices go away. You can be either ignorant or informed.

The third key concept is "with or without money." There are basically three functions of money: (1) medium of exchange, (2) unit of account, and (3) store of value. As a medium of exchange, money is a convenient way to exchange goods that allows individuals to gain the advantages of geographic and human specialization (Heyne et al. 2006; McConnell and Brue 2005). As a unit of account it is a standard for measuring relative value; it aids an individual by making it easy to compare the prices of goods, services, and resources (Heyne et al. 2006; McConnell and Brue 2005). Finally, as a store of value it enables individuals to transfer purchasing power from the present to the future (Heyne et al. 2006; McConnell and Brue 2005). Anything widely accepted as a medium of exchange, unit of account, and store of value can serve as money. The USA dollar can serve as a medium of exchange, but salt was once used as the medium of exchange, most notably in the Roman Empire. If you do not like dollars, change to some other medium of exchange. However, changing to some other medium of exchange, even a barter system, does not make relative scarcity or the opportunity costs of choices associated with relative scarcity go away.

The fourth key concept is consumption of the resource now versus investing for future consumption. Just as there is an opportunity cost of using a tree now to produce various commodities, there is also the choice of investing; namely, not cutting the tree and letting it grow to produce more valuable outputs or outcomes at a future date. This illustrates a time component within an opportunity. Your use of a credit card to purchase a commodity for current consumption is also an illustration of this. You buy the commodity using the credit card company's money with the promise of paying back the purchase amount at a future date plus, if necessary, a premium.

What Is the Economy?

As with the definition of economics, there are many definitions of the economy. The definition I prefer is:

> The economy is a collection of technological, legal, and social arrangements through which individuals in society seek to increase their material and spiritual well-being.
>
> Field and Field (2002: 23)

This definition highlights two important concepts. The first concept is the importance of "technical, legal, and social arrangements" or institutions necessary to allow individuals to realize gains from trading. These institutions include (1) property rights – without a system of property rights, gains from trading are difficult to realize.[20] (2) A legal system – without a legal system, there is no established rule for contracts property rights, and so forth; nor is a means of redress available if a wrong has been committed. (3) Money – without money, transactions are more expensive. To serve as a medium of exchange, unit of account, and store of value, money must be stable. (4) Governments (local, state, and national) – without governments, the conditions for these institutions to function and evolve will not exist (Heyne et al. 2006).

The second concept is individuals seeking to "increase their material and spiritual well-being"; other authors use the terminology "increase their wealth" (Heyne et al. 2006; Silberberg and Suen 2001). The economic concept of wealth is the accumulation of whatever people value (Heyne et al. 2006; Klemperer 1996; Pearce 1994). People value material goods (monetary), they also value mental and spiritual well-being (nonmonetary), and they value these things now and in the future. Thus, the goal of the economy is to increase individual wealth now and in the future. Obviously, one way wealth can increase is by producing physical commodities. However, it does not follow logically that only producing physical commodities increases wealth.[21] Trade, a voluntary exchange of goods or services, increases the wealth of those involved in the exchange.[22] For example, Kyle McDonald started on 12 July 2005 with one red paper clip and 14 trades later on 15 July 2006 traded for a house on 503 Main Street in the Town of Kipling, Saskatchewan, Canada (http://oneredpaperclip.blogspot.com/2005/07/about-one-red-paperclip.html, accessed 13 October 2016).

Economic Reasoning

Economics, like physics or biology, is a science. More specifically, economics is a social science. As a science, economic theories can be used to hypothesize cause-and-effect relationships that can be tested empirically (Silberberg and Suen 2001; Friedman 1953). Facts without a theory are useless, because one set of facts cannot be shown to cause another set of facts. There are no means of separating the irrelevant from relevant facts (Heyne et al. 2006; Silberberg and Suen 2001). For example, if you throw a ball straight up in the air, it will rise rapidly, then less rapidly, and finally reach a point where it stops rising, stops, and descends toward you, slowly at first but gaining speed. Fact A: You toss a ball in the air nightly. Fact B: A week before your economics exam you study economics at least two hours a night. Fact C: You receive an A on your economics test. There are no theories that can be identified to show a cause-and-effect relationship between Fact A and Fact C. Stated differently, Fact A is irrelevant in explaining Fact C as Fact C cannot be inferred from Fact A. There are, however, theories that can be identified to show a cause-and-effect relationship between Fact B and Fact C. Thus, Fact B is relevant in explaining Fact C as Fact C can be inferred from Fact B.

Economic theories can help systematically analyze the costs and benefits of different resource allocation decisions made by individuals. That is, economic theories will not identify what to choose but will examine the tradeoffs or opportunity costs associated with the choices. If the context in which the analysis was done holds in the future, it allows the development of testable statements about the individual's future choices. Economic reasoning is thus about systematically examining the choices or tradeoffs individuals make in a given context. This requires developing a consistent set of terminology, models, and methods (Silberberg and Suen 2001; Friedman 1953). The rest of the chapter will be devoted to introducing the minimum set of terminology, models, and methods necessary to reason economically. Subsequent chapters will build on these.

Individual Decision-Making Behavioral Assertions

In a nutshell, economics is the study of individual choice given scarcity and the resulting opportunity costs of those choices. Because the principal agent of interest is the individual, if we are to study individual choice we need to develop two assertions or postulates concerning their decision-making behavior.[23] First, individuals are asserted to be maximizers; in terms of voluntary exchanges, individuals will seek to maximize their satisfaction, net benefit, utility, profit, or smiles-per-minute, and so forth. Consistent with relative scarcity, net benefits are defined as benefits associated with the choice minus opportunity costs of the choice. Second, individuals have preferences for goods and services. They can order these preferences, and they are consistent in that ordering. For example, if an individual prefers Coke® to Pepsi®, and Pepsi® to all other carbonated cola beverages, and if given a choice of Coke® or Pepsi®, they will always choose Coke® voluntarily. Further, if given a choice between Pepsi® and all other carbonated cola beverages, they will always choose Pepsi® voluntarily. Finally, if given a choice between Coke® and all other carbonated cola beverages, they will always choose Coke® voluntarily.[24]

The assertions that individuals are maximizers of net benefits (i.e., benefits minus opportunity costs) and can order their preferences are often not well understood and lead to confusion. McKenzie and Lee (2006: 108–109) provide the clearest and concise discussion of what these assertions imply that I will paraphrase. Being a maximizer does not imply an individual is selfish. People receive pleasure from others' happiness; however, if the objective is improve their or others' well-being, people are motivated to make decisions that do the most to accomplish this objective. These assertions do not mean that individuals never make mistakes. Individuals do not have perfect knowledge or can fully control the future, thus they base their choices on what they expect to happen, not on what does happen. Given the plethora of possible choices (e.g., breakfast cereal), individuals may make choices based on habit. While a better choice may be made if individuals collect and examine all information, the opportunity cost of spending the time to collect and examine all this information is too high relative to the benefit. Individuals do maximize their net benefits and order their preferences; however, anyone who equates rational behavior with what *they* would do will have no trouble concluding that others are irrational. Do not make the assumption that everyone has the same set of preferences. Do not make the assumption that everyone has *your* set of preferences.

While the principal agent of interest is the individual, economic theories are not designed or intended to develop hypotheses about an identified individual's choices; for example, the person sitting next to you. The individual referenced is a representative or average individual in a given context.

Value Versus Price

One of the fundamental building blocks of economics is opportunity cost, and interestingly the term value is in its definition. Thus being able to answer the "What if" question requires an understanding of value.

Value can have many different meanings; as economics is a social science and the principal agent of interest is the individual, I will be concerned with preference-related concepts of value. According to a seminal work on the economic concept of value by Brown (1984), an assigned value is the expressed relative importance or worth of an object to an individual in a given context. Therefore, an assigned value is observable based on the choices an individual makes. Assigned values are relative; it is not the intrinsic nature of the object but the object relative to all other objects that gives rise to an assigned value (Brown 1984). Assigned values are relative, not absolute; assigned values depend on the context surrounding an individual's choice. If the context changes now or in the future, the value an individual assigns to an object will also change. As can be seen, the preference-related concept of value is tied to the assertions concerning individual decision-making behavior.

Price is defined as a per unit measure of assigned value and thus a measure of relative scarcity. As the price of a good or service increases relative to other goods and service, this particular good or service is scarcer relative to the other goods and services. It bears repeating that the concept of relative scarcity is a function of an individual's preference for goods and services (Silberberg and Suen 2001). It is left to the reader to draw the relationship between price and opportunity cost through answering the following question: If the price of a resource is zero, what is its opportunity cost?

Market price is economic information that consumers use in examining their opportunity cost of purchasing a good or service. That same market price is economic information that suppliers use in examining their opportunity cost of producing or providing a good or service. As with value, price is not a measure of the intrinsic value of the good; it is information individuals employ to allocate a scarce good or service to a specific use. If a person purchases a good, we know the minimum assigned value they place on that good, other things being equal. Although price is usually denoted in monetary terms, it need not be.

To illustrate the relationship between value and price, the market price of a 500-milliliter bottle of maple syrup is $22.00. This maple syrup is produced from a sugarbush and processing facilities owned by the College of Environmental Science and Forestry in Syracuse, NY, and sold in the college's bookstore (Figure 1.1). If you bought one bottle, then the observed assigned value you place on that bottle would be

$$\$22.00 = 22.00 \frac{\$}{\text{bottle}} \cdot 1 \text{ bottle}$$

as you could have spent that $22.00 on another item (an opportunity cost). If you bought two bottles, the observed assigned value would be

$$\$44.00 = 44.00 \frac{\$}{\text{bottle}} \cdot 2 \text{ bottles}$$

as you could have taken that $44.00 and purchased something else (an opportunity cost).

According to Maital (1994), assigned value is the degree to which buyers think goods and services make them better off than if they did without. The language of economics insists that when choices are made, the value of the option must be weighed against their price or "opportunity" cost. No decision can be made unless our knowledge of values is at least as extensive and accurate as our understanding of output price and input wage (Maital 1994). An often-made mistake is to think about value only in terms of a consumer purchasing your output; for example, a bottle of maple syrup. However, as an entrepreneur you are also a buyer; namely, a buyer of inputs. Maital's entrepreneurial description of "assigned" value is relevant in both cases.

Assumptions Concerning the Market and Workable Competition

The economic concepts of value and price are based on a given context. The market provides a place where information concerning the relative scarcity of a good or service is revealed and the choices individuals make are observed. Given the information generated by the market, an individual can choose to provide or produce a particular good or service and another individual can choose to purchase that particular good or service. A market can be a physical place like a grocery store or local farmers market, or it can be a place like eBay® where individuals offer to sell Les Paul Gibson guitars, bamboo fly rods, or one red paperclip and others can choose to purchase the item or make a counter offer.

Price is a key piece of information generated by the markets and used by buyers and sellers. Generally speaking, the more sellers of a good or service in a market, the greater the inability of a single seller to have control over the price. Similarly, the more buyers of a good or service in the market, the greater the inability of a single buyer to have control over price. Thus if the market price is to only reflect how scarce a good or service is relative to other goods and services, no one buyer or group of buyers and no one seller or group of sellers can influence price. This is the characteristic of workable competition. Deviations from workable competition imply that the resulting price reflects not only some concept of relative scarcity but also an individual's market power. In the terminology of economic reasoning, deviations from workable competition imply a market imperfection.

Economics Versus Accounting

When an accountant discusses costs, it is in term of actual dollar outlays (e.g., debits, credits, income statements, and balance sheets). For example, if you look at the debit column of your checkbook, you can tell me the amount of money you spent last month and what you purchased. These are explicit costs. When an economist discusses costs, it is in terms of opportunity cost: What am I giving up to continue what I am doing? Opportunity costs obviously include explicit costs or actual dollar outlays. In addition, there are other costs that may not be included in explicit costs.

Table 1.1 gives the annual costs and revenues associated with owning and operating a small hardwood sawmill. Total receipts of $1,100,000 are the sum of selling dimension lumber and chips. The accounting or explicit costs of $1,050,000 include employee wages, employee benefits, taxes, utilities, purchasing delivered logs, and fixed costs. At the end of the year net receipts total $50,000. For the sawmill's owner, net receipts are salary. Accounting profits are $000.00.

In order to own and operate this sawmill you are giving up working as the manager of another sawmill in a different county. The owner of that sawmill would have paid you $60,000 per year as a manager. You are forgoing or giving up $10,000 in salary to own and operate your own mill. This implicit cost cannot be found on any accounting sheet; nonetheless, it is a cost to you. To operate this mill you have used some of your savings as a down payment to buy equipment. You are forgoing or giving up interest that you could have earned by investing that savings in a financial instrument such as a mutual fund. Again, this implicit cost cannot be found on any accounting sheet but is a cost to you. The sum of these forgone alternatives is $15,000. The opportunity cost of owning and operating the sawmill is then $1,050,000 + $15,000 = 1,065,000 or the sum of explicit and implicit costs.[25] If explicit and implicit costs are included in the analysis, the economic profit of owning and operating your sawmill is −$15,000.

Table 1.1 Economics Versus Accounting – Hardwood Sawmill Example

Sale: Dimension Lumber	$1,000,000	
Sale: Chips	100,000	
Total Revenue		$1,100,000[†]
Cost: Employee Wages	$120,000	
Cost: Employee Benefits	60,000	
Cost: Delivered Logs	320,000	
Cost: Fuel, Oil, etc.	190,000	
Cost: Utilities and Maintenance	170,000	
Cost: Fixed Costs (i.e., Depreciation, Interest, Rent, Taxes, Insurance, etc.)	190,000	
Total (Explicit) Costs		$1,050,000[†]
Net Receipts		$50,000[†]
Cost: Salary Sawmill Owner	$50,000	
Accounting Profit		$000[†]
Forgone: Salary ($60,000 you could have earned elsewhere; $60,000 − $50,000 = $10,000)	$10,000	
Forgone: Interest on Capital	$5,000	
Total (Implicit) Costs		$15,000[†]
Economic Profit		−$15,000[†]

[†]Shaded values represent the sum

Efficiency Versus Equity

Efficiency in economics has to do with producing and facilitating as much production and consumption as possible with available resources (Just et al. 1982). The focus of economics and managerial economics is on efficiency or the optimal "efficient" allocation of resources to achieve an entrepreneur's objective of, for example, profit maximization. This is an objective analysis, and an improvement in economic efficiency can be determined by a simple and unambiguous criterion – an increase in total net benefits; that is, marginal analysis (Fullerton and Stavins 1998).

Equity has to do with how goods are distributed among individuals (Just et al. 1982). Equity denotes the concept of a just or fair (not necessarily equal) distribution of goods, services, output, income, and so on among all consumers. This is a subjective analysis. However, what constitutes an improvement in distributional equity, on the other hand, is inevitably the subject of considerable dispute (Fullerton and Stavins 1998). Thus the focus of this book will not be on equity.

More recently the concept of equality has been described as a measure of fairness: The property of distributing economic prosperity uniformly among the members of society. As opposed to equity, what constitutes an improvement in distributional equality is seemingly simple and can provide an unambiguous decision criterion. While equity refers to rewarding individuals in proportion to some measure of their contributions, equality refers to equal allocations irrespective of contributions. The public, in general, have expressed growing concern in recent years about rising economic inequality; for example, income distribution. There is evidence that people accept inequalities due to factors people control (e.g., effort – equity), but reject inequalities resulting from factors people do not control (e.g., luck, opportunities, etc. – equality). Thus, what constitutes an unambiguous improvement in equality is inevitably the subject of considerable dispute: Is effort due to luck? Research findings suggest fairness preferences move progressively toward equality with greater proximity, that is, as relationships become more personal through belonging to a group and being non-anonymous (Konow et al. 2016).

In a broader context, efficiency objectives cannot be pursued independently of equity or equality objectives. It is important to note that the objectives of efficiency and equity or equality often conflict, and it may become necessary to compromise one for another. As noted by Fullerton and Stavins (1998), how to combine efficiency and distributional issues in a unified analysis is a more difficult problem that has yet to be solved in a satisfactory manner. For example, measures that could expand output relative to the amount of input used (i.e., increased efficiency) might create unwanted changes in the distribution of income (i.e., decreased equity), and vice versa, illustrating the tradeoff between improvements in equity and efficiency. The relative weights placed on equity versus efficiency and the appropriate compromises are not matters that can be solved by economic analysis. Political and electoral processes must be used to reconcile divergent opinion about equity and efficiency.

Managerial Analytical Method: Economic Models

Reality is complex, and trying to model this complexity could lead to intractable models that are not very helpful to describe, model, explain, and predict efficient allocations of relatively scarce resources. Economic models, which are succinct representations of complex systems, focus on describing the underlying fundamental characteristics of the system that are critical for systematically examining individual resource allocation choices within a given context (Field and Field 2002; Silberberg and Suen 2001; Kay 1996; Pearce 1994; Friedman 1953). I have asserted that managing any system requires identifying alternate ways to achieve the owner's desired future condition (e.g., long-term profits) and selecting the alternatives that achieves this in, most often, the most resource-efficient (i.e., least cost) manner. And, that using relevant economic information will lead to better business decisions that accomplish this more often than not. This leads to three interconnected economic models and their efficiency measures. This is given in Figure 1.4 and is the first analytical construct to aid management decision making.

I will discuss each model and its outcomes briefly.

Production System

The production system is the fundamental input(s)–output(s) relationship that must be measured and described analytically. Managing the maple syrup system requires

Managerial Economic Model	Analytical/Managerial Outcome(s)
I. Production System	Technical Efficiency
II. Least Cost/Cost Effective	Technical Efficiency
	Production Cost Efficiency
III. Profit	Technical Efficiency
	Production Cost Efficiency
	Economic Efficiency

Figure 1.4 Managerial Analytic Method

Inputs(s)	⇨ Production Process ⇨	Output(s)
Sugarbush (ecology, biology, silvics)	Sap collection	Syrup
	Reverse osmosis	Candies
Equipment (sap collection, reverse osmosis, evaporator, packaging)	Evaporator	Cream
	Packaging	Demineralized water
Labor		
Energy		

Figure 1.5a Production System – State University of New York College of Environmental Science and Forestry's Maple Syrup Operation

Inputs(s)	⇨ Production Process ⇨	Output(s)
Insolation	Physics and chemistry of photovoltaic cells	Energy (kilowatt-hours, kWh)
Photovoltaic cells (power, kilowatt kW)		
Electrical balance of the system (inverter, transformers, switches, etc.)		
Structural balance of the system (mounting system)		
Time		
Labor		

Figure 1.5b Production System – State University of New York College of Environmental Science and Forestry's 24.192-Kilowatt Solar Array. Power (kW) × Time (hours) = Energy (kWh)

describing analytically and measuring the sugarbush and the process for collecting sap and producing the various maple products. This is illustrated in Figure 1.5a. Managing the solar array system requires describing analytically and measuring insolation on the photovoltaic cells and their ability to convert it to produce energy. This is illustrated in Figure 1.5b.

The definition of efficiency requires that the analytical descriptions and measurements have a specific purpose: Provide the manager with information to minimize wasted resource input use. Production systems define the technical and physical relationship between combinations of inputs and the maximum outputs that each combination can produce (i.e., technical efficiency). While Figures 1.5a and 1.5b are conceptual models of production systems, they do not provide enough detail to discuss technical efficiency for each system in any consequential way with respect to decision making. This will be provided in Chapter 2 – Production Systems.

Least Cost/Cost Effective Models

Production systems define technical efficiency. Unfortunately, a purely technical and physical description of an input–output relationship ignores the fact that individuals assign values to inputs and outputs in a given context (i.e., individuals are maximizers and workable competition). The logical next step given technical efficiency would be to determine the cheapest way to produce a given level of output (i.e., production cost efficiency). This leads to the second economic model from Figure 1.4 and is given in equation (1.1):

$$\text{Min Cost} = \text{TVC}$$
$$\text{s.t.} \tag{1.1}$$
$$Q(x) = Q^0$$

where
Min Cost denotes the objective of minimizing costs;
TVC denotes Total Variable Costs (e.g., what the entrepreneur must pay for the variable inputs used in the production process);
s.t. denotes "subject to" and what follows is a constraint placed on the objective;
$Q(x)$ denotes the production system of using inputs, x, to produce or provide a good or service at given quantity or quality;
$Q(x) = Q^0$ defines the required quantity or quality of the good or service, Q^0, from the production system, $Q(x)$.

Equation (1.1) describes a least cost model; in other words, determining the least cost means of producing or providing a given level of a good or service. Using the schoolwork system, studying is one of the jobs you must perform while at school. You use various inputs when studying, but I will focus on your time. The more time you spend studying, the less time you can spend on doing anything else (the opportunity cost of your time). Therefore, you want to use as little time as possible studying (total variable costs in equation (1.1)) while maintaining a given quality of understanding (Q^0 in equation (1.1)). If you do not maintain the quality, that means you have wasted your time because you will have to spend additional time to redo what you should have done in the first place. Using the forest ecosystem, forest landowners whose primary ownership goals are weighted heavily towards aesthetics, recreation, and privacy are minimizing their ownership costs (total variable costs in equation (1.1)) relative to all the benefits (aesthetics, recreation, privacy, and perhaps timber – Q^0 in equation (1.1)) they receive from their land over time (Wagner 2012, 2020; Brazee and Amacher 2000). The maple syrup system provides an interesting least cost problem. Sap flow is due to warm periods when temperatures rise above freezing (causing positive pressure) and cold periods when temperatures fall below freezing (causing negative pressure) (https://monroe.cce.cornell.edu/agriculture/seasonal-produce-highlights/maple-syrup-season-what-causes-the-sap-to-flow-out-of-the-trees accessed 29 August 2023). This results in sap flows coming in waves. Sap not collected cannot become syrup. Sap is generally stored in tanks for a short period until it can be processed through the reverse osmosis contraption and evaporator. The least cost problem is if the storage tanks are too large there is excess storage capacity and if storage tanks are too small there is sap loss.[26]

An alternative form of a least cost model is the cost-effective model given in equation (1.2):

$$\text{Max } Q(x)$$
$$\text{s.t.} \qquad\qquad\qquad\qquad\qquad\qquad\qquad\qquad\qquad (1.2)$$
$$\text{TVC} = C^0$$

where

Max $Q(x)$ denotes the objective of providing or producing the maximizing quantity or quality of a good or service using inputs, x;

s.t. denotes "subject to";

TVC $= C^0$ denotes that the Total Variable Costs of using variable inputs x to produce or provide the good or service cannot exceed a given budget, C^0.

Equation (1.2) states for any given budget level, your objective is to produce the most output. Using the stormy-night example, you have a given amount of time you want to spend studying on any given day (C^0 in equation (1.2)). For that given amount of time you want to be as productive (or efficient) as possible in terms of quality of studying ($Q(x)$ in equation (1.2)). If you are not, then you have wasted the time budgeted to this activity. Using the forest ecosystem, forest landowners whose primary ownership goals are weighted heavily towards aesthetics, recreation, and privacy are looking to create a desired future condition ($Q(x)$ in equation (1.2)) that will provide for aesthetics, recreation, and privacy. However, these landowners do not have unlimited resources to create this desired future condition (the budget constraint C^0 in equation (1.2)).

The least cost (equation (1.1)) and cost effective (equation 1.2)) model formulations show that production cost efficiency requires technical efficiency. If you are not technically efficient, you are wasting an input. If you are wasting an input, your costs cannot be minimized. In addition, equations (1.1) and (1.2) plus the examples show that the least cost and cost effective models are heads and tails of the same coin.[27] The solution for the least cost (cost effective) model is also the solution for the cost effective (least cost) model.

Profit Model

The third economic model identified in Figure 1.4 follows directly from the assertion that individuals are maximizers and is given in equation (1.3):

$$\text{Max NB} = \text{B} - \text{C}$$

or

$$\text{Max } \Pi = \text{TR} - \text{TC}$$
$$= \text{P} \cdot \text{Q}(x) - \text{TVC} - \text{TFC} \qquad (1.3)$$

where
Max NB denotes maximization of Net Benefit (NB);
B denotes Benefits;
C denotes Costs;
Max Π denotes maximization of profit (Π);
TR denotes Total Revenue, TR = P·Q(x);
P denotes market price;
Q(x) denotes market output (as measured by quantity and quality) produced by inputs, x;
TC denotes Total Cost, TC = TVC + TFC;
TVC denotes Total Variable Costs;
TFC denotes Total Fixed Costs.

Individuals, regardless of whether they are buyers or sellers, seek to maximize their net benefits or profits given a market context. Basically, equation (1.3) compares the benefits received from obtaining a good or service with what you gave up to obtain it or its opportunity cost. Simply, individuals search to find the greatest positive difference between benefits and costs or total revenue and total cost. The solution to equation (1.3) defines economic efficiency. The solution to equation (1.3) also defines the optimally efficient resource allocation rule.

Equation (1.3) implies that maximizing profit or net benefit requires management decisions that make total revenue as large as possible while simultaneously making total costs as small as possible for any given input(s)–output(s) combination. Thus, a solution to the profit maximization model is also a solution for the least cost or cost effective models (Silberberg and Suen 2001). Entrepreneurs generally have more control over their costs than revenues. Simply put, if you do not manage costs, you will lose control of profits. As described by Andersch et al. (2013), analyzing product costs (i.e., least cost/cost effective) are critically important for businesses because they help reduce costs, price products at competitive prices, and enable strategic, tactical, and operational decision making. Thus, least cost/cost effective analysis does not replace profit maximization but complements it.[28] Consequently, economic efficiency requires production cost efficiency, which requires technical efficiency as defined by the Managerial Analytical Method (Figure 1.4).

While individuals provide some of what they need with their own labor, individuals do not generally increase their net benefit or profit in isolation: Net benefit

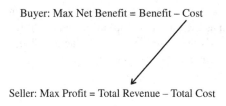

Buyer: Max Net Benefit = Benefit – Cost

Seller: Max Profit = Total Revenue – Total Cost

Figure 1.6 Gains From Trade

or profit is increased by trade. This has been recognized by many economists, from Adam Smith (1776) to the present. Figure 1.6 illustrates this using equation (1.3).

The buyer's objective is to maximize their net benefit. For example, many individuals enjoy maple syrup on their breakfast waffles or pancakes. However, the vast majority of these individuals do not want to own or manage a sugarbush, sap collection, evaporation, and packaging. The buyer will instead seek a seller who is offering to provide them maple syrup. The seller's objective is to maximize their profit by offering to sell maple syrup. The buyer's cost of the maple syrup is the seller's total revenue. The buyer's benefit is using the maple syrup on their waffles or pancakes. As we observe the choice to purchase maple syrup, the buyer's net benefit is positive (i.e., their benefits are greater than their opportunity cost). And the seller's profit is as large as possible if their costs are minimized.

Marginal Analysis

Marginal analysis allows for an objective, scientific, and fact-based systematic examination of observable choices by individuals resulting from observable market conditions. A margin denotes an incremental change from any defined starting point; for example, the amount of output you produce or provide is a variable you control, and an incremental change in what you pay for inputs or what consumers pay for your output will change the amount you produce. Marginal analysis is the tool used to systematically examine if, for example, production is predicted to increase or decrease given a price change. Following the Managerial Analytical Method (Figure 1.4), I will start with the least cost model.

Least Cost or Cost Effective Models

The least cost model is used to determine the minimum expenditures to produce or provide a given quantity or quality of a good or service. The problem being addressed is determining the optimal mix of variable inputs with respect to cost to produce a defined quantity or quality of a good or service. The cost effective model is used to determine the maximum production possible for a given budget. The problem being addressed is determining the optimal mix of variable inputs to use in the production process for a defined production cost budget. The solution defines the optimal variable input mix such that no marginal change in the variable input mix yields a smaller production cost. Using the schoolwork system, given the four hours, the least cost or cost effective solution produces no time allocation, yielding a greater satisfaction as the marginal hour allocated to studying and spending time with your friends yields the same level of satisfaction. This solution is defined as the equimarginal principle and is developed in greater detail in Chapter 3 – Costs.

Profit Model

If I assert that you are a profit maximizer and are consistent in your behavior with respect to profit maximization, then you will increase the amount of output you provide as long as the incremental or marginal revenue of doing so is greater than its incremental or marginal cost. And you will decrease the amount of output you provide as long as marginal costs are greater than marginal revenue. Stated differently, profits increase as long as marginal revenue is greater than marginal cost and decrease when marginal cost is greater than marginal revenue. Finally, profits are maximized when marginal revenue equals marginal cost. The condition of marginal revenue equals marginal cost also defines the optimally efficient resource allocation rule.

Using the schoolwork system in deciding how to spend a four-hour time block, you determined that you would study for two hours. You have some reading in two classes to finish, and from experience you know that for this material one hour is not long enough and three hours are too long. The incremental benefit from studying for the initial hour is greater than the incremental cost. The incremental benefit from studying for the second hour is also greater than the incremental cost. However, the incremental cost of studying for the third hour is greater than the incremental benefit, because this type of reading usually takes a lot of concentration and after about two hours you need a rest. As long as the incremental benefit is greater than the incremental cost, you will continue to study because your net benefits from studying are increasing.

Using the solar array system, operators of commercial solar arrays do so to generate profits. Their profit-maximizing decision is whether to provide an additional kilowatt-hour to the electrical grid. They will do so if the marginal revenue from providing an additional kilowatt-hour is greater than its marginal cost. A uniqueness of the solar array system is that a large proportion of the total costs are fixed; this leads to marginal costs of providing an additional kilowatt-hour being small. In New York State, marginal revenue is defined by locational based marginal price (LBMP). The New York State Independent System Operator (NYISO) provides real-time zonal market LBMP data in five-minute intervals for any given day (http://mis.nyiso.com/public/ accessed 17 October 2016). The column titled LBMP ($/MWHr – dollars per megawatt-hour) is the real-time market energy price for one of the 11 zones in New York State. There are instances of negative LBMPs. In this case, it would cost the solar array owners to provide energy to the electrical grid. The profit-maximizing owners of the solar array would choose not to provide electricity to the grid.[29]

Marginal analysis will not prove if in fact you are maximizing profits or prove if the output level you are producing is "optimal." Marginal analysis allows for statements concerning a direction of change; for example, increasing or decreasing the amount of output you provide. Continuing with the profit maximization model, marginal analysis will also allow for a testable statement concerning whether you will use more or less of an input if the price you pay for that input increases. As a manager you will always seek for ways to increase your profits. Marginal analysis provides you with a systematic method to examine choices that are consistent with the assertion of profit maximization.

Positive, Normative, and Advocacy

Positive analysis attempts to be objective and science- and fact-based and addresses "what is." In principle, all positive analytical statements should be reducible to some form that is testable using technical, production cost, and economic efficiency by reference to empirical evidence using observable choices reflecting assigned value. For example, positive economic analysis is used to model, explain, and predict individual decision-making behavior using the optimal efficient resource allocation rule described earlier. Normative analysis is subjective and addresses "what should be." In principle, normative statements are of the form "X is bad (good)" or "What is best." Distinguishing between describing, modeling, explaining, and predicting observed individual decision-making behavior and what that decision-making behavior "should be" (e.g., what should be the level of carbon dioxide emissions) is the difference between positive and normative economics. Advocacy, on the other hand, is information that is developed, presented, or interpreted based on an assumed, usually unstated, preference for a particular policy or class of policy choices (Lackey 2004). It is often hard to distinguish among positive, normative, and advocacy in certain contexts. The ability to distinguish among them develops over time. The focus of this book is on positive analysis.[30]

Variability

The example systems used to illustrate technical, production cost, and economic efficiency are not static. All the example systems can be described as dynamic with respect to the production system and input and output prices. That is, they can change with time. For example, sunlight is not the same for every hour of the day, day of the month, month of a year, or year to year. Sap flows are not the same for every hour of the day, day of the month, month of a season, or season to season. Kilowatt-hour prices change every hour of the day, day of the month, month of a year, and year to year (http://mis.nyiso.com/public/ accessed 17 October 2016). Tree species' stumpage changes over time (Sendak 1991, 1994; Howard and Chase 1995; Wagner and Sendak 2005; Smith et al. 2012).

The mathematical structure of the models defined in the Managerial Analytical Method (Figure 1.4) allows for changing model parameters to examine their impacts on resource allocation decisions and helps with understanding the dynamics of a system. This procedure to address uncertainty is termed sensitivity analysis. While a more detailed discussion of sensitivity analysis is given in Chapter 6 – Capital

Theory: Investment Analysis, I will provide a brief introduction. To examine the impact of an individual parameter on the system, change one model parameter at a time. To examine the impacts of interactions among parameters simultaneously, change two parameters of the model. The parameters that cause the most significant changes should be determined with a greater level of accuracy than those that do not. Generally, the ranges used to change model parameters are based on the manager's expert knowledge of the system or historic variations.

The Architectural Plan for Profit

Maital (1994) defines the three Pillars of Profit as Price, Value, and Cost.

> Business decisions are built on three pillars – cost, value and price. Cost is what businesses pay out to their workers and suppliers in order to make and market goods and services. Value is the degree to which buyers think those goods and services make them better off, than if they did without. And Price is what buyers pay. Those are the three essential elements in the day-to-day choices managers make. Juggling those three elements is what managers are paid for.
>
> Managers who know what their products cost and what they are worth to customers – and who also know the costs, values, and prices of competing products – will build good businesses, because their decisions will rest on sound foundations. Businesses run by managers who have only fuzzy knowledge of one of those three pillars will eventually stumble. It is deceptively difficult to build them, precisely because they have to be built – the information required is often incomplete or not readily at hand.
>
> (Maital 1994: 6–7)

While I agree with his assessment in terms of the three Pillars of Profit, I would include an additional component: the production system. While Maital implies that managers must have knowledge of production systems – managers should know "their production costs" – I believe this component should be explicit. This leads to the second analytical construct: The Architectural Plan for Profit (Figure 1.7).

The Architectural Plan for Profit defines explicitly what constitutes economic information: production system, cost, value, price, and profit. The Managerial Analytical Method (Figure 1.4) describes the three economic models that pair with the Architectural Plan for Profit to provide a complete systematic approach for making better business decisions.

Figure 1.7 illustrates that the production system is the foundation on which the three Pillars of Profit are set. On top of the three pillars rests Profit. Profits cannot be held up if the foundation or one or more of the three pillars are weak. Economic efficiency (profit model) requires production cost efficiency (least cost model) which requires technical efficiency (production system model). This holds whether you are producing, for example, schoolwork, maple syrup, natural resource and forest ecosystem output(s) and outcome(s), or electricity from solar arrays.

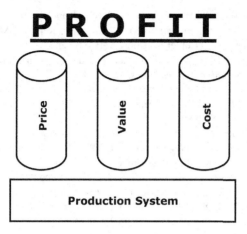

Figure 1.7 The Architectural Plan for Profit

Figure 1.7 also provides a road map for the first seven chapters of this book, starting with the production system, moving onto the pillars that represent cost (cost and value) and revenue (price and value), ending with profits (including time as a relevant variable input). While the first seven chapters are focused narrowly, the next five chapters provide a broader view, and the last chapter is an example of how to apply the information presented to create a business plan. The businesses used in this chapter are for-profit business run by the College of Environmental Sciences and Forestry in Syracuse, NY. The beginning of each of these chapters will have a graphic tying Figures 1.4 and 1.7 together.

Practical Applications

I will use the following articles throughout the book to illustrate economic concepts. They are drawn from various disciplines such as outdoor and commercial recreation, wood products engineering, forest products, maple syrup, and forestry. The information presented in these articles reflects actual economic information that managers or entrepreneurs of the representative business can use to make resource-efficient decisions. The following is a list of the practical applications.

Becker, D.R., Hjerpe, E.E., and Lowell, E.C. (2004) *Economic Assessment of Using a Mobile Micromill® for Processing Small-Diameter Ponderosa Pine, Gen. Tech. Rpt. PNW-GTR-623*, Portland, OR: US Dept. of Agriculture, Forest Service, Pacific Northwest Research Station.

Burdurlu, E., Ciritcioğlu, H.H., Bakir, K., and Özdemir, M. (2006) Analysis of the most suitable fitting type for the assembly of knockdown panel furniture, *Forest Products Journal*, 56(1):46–52.

Graham, W.G., Goebel, P.C., Heiligmann, R.B., and Bumgardner, M.S. (2006) Maple syrup in Ohio and the impact of Ohio State University (OSU) extension program, *Journal of Forestry*, 104(2):94–100.

Hagan, J.M., Irland, L.C. and Whitman, A.A. (2005) *Changing Timberland Ownership in the Northern Forest and Implications for Biodiversity.* Report # MCCS-FCP-2005–1, Brunswick, ME: Manomet Center for Conservation Science.

Hahn, J.T., and Hansen, M.H. (1991) Cubic and board foot volume models for the central states, *Northern Journal of Applied Forestry*, 8(2):47–57.

Huyler, N.K. (2000) *Cost of Maple Map Production for Various Size Tubing Operations, Research Paper NE-RP-712*, Newtown Square, PA: US Dept. of Agriculture, Forest Service, Northeastern Research Station.

Lichtkoppler, F.R. and Kuehn, D. (2003) *New York's Great Lakes Charter Fishing Industry in 2002, Ohio Sea Grant College Program OHSU-TS-039*, Columbus, OH: Sea Grant Great Lakes Network, The Ohio State University.

Patterson, D.W., Kluender, R.A., and Granskog, J.E. (2002) Economic feasibility of producing inside-out beams from small-diameter logs, *Forest Products Journal*, 52(1):23–26.

Patterson, D.W. and Xie, X. (1998) Inside-out beams from small-diameter Appalachian hardwood logs, *Forest Products Journal*, 48(1):76–80.

How to Use Economic Information to Make Better Business Decisions

The purpose of this book is to address the statement: "How to use economic information to make better business decisions." This statement will be revisited at the end of each chapter. The answer will become more complex as additional knowledge is obtained by examining critically each model of the Managerial Analytical Method relative to the economic information given in the Architectural Plan for Profit. I will address this question briefly given the material presented in this chapter. To do so, I will re-examine the three economic models identified in the Managerial Analytical Method (Figure 1.4), tying them directly to economic information defined in the Architectural Plan for Profit (Figure 1.7).

The first economic model is the production system, which measures and describes analytically the technically efficient relationships to convert input(s) to the desired quantity and quality of output(s). This is the foundation of the Architectural Plan for Profit. The second economic model is given by equations (1.1) and (1.2), which define the least cost and cost effective models, respectively. The variables included in this model are total variable cost – what the entrepreneur must pay for inputs used in the production process – and the production system. The economic information required by this model is the production system (technical efficiency) and the Pillars of Cost and Value. The Pillar of Cost represents the entrepreneur's opportunity cost of buying input(s) used in the production process. These inputs are purchased in a market. Thus, the entrepreneur's knowledge of their input markets must be just as strong as their knowledge of their output markets. This detail will be discussed in Chapters 3 – Costs, Chapter 10 – Supply and Demand, and Chapter 11 – Market Equilibrium and Structure. The Pillar of Value represents the degree to which the entrepreneur thinks buying the input makes them better off than if they did without; namely, the value added by the input to the output(s) in terms of quantity and quality. The second economic model defines production cost efficiency for any given output level (quality or quantity) or budget (total variable cost).

The third economic model is maximizing profit or net benefit, which is given by equation (1.3). The difference between a net benefit and profit model is that total revenues are replaced with benefits. Traditionally total revenues are associated with monetary flows (e.g., selling maple syrup, energy from a solar array, or trees for lumber). Benefits are associated with nonmonetary and monetary flows. For example, net metering from a residential solar array is a monetary flow to the individual, and individual satisfaction of producing and consuming your own clean energy is a nonmonetary flow. Benefits, in the net benefit model, are comprised of both flows. Chapter 9 – Estimating Nonmarket Values will discuss this topic in more detail. However, for the purposes of this brief discussion, I will focus only on profits.

There are three variables included in the profit model: (1) production system, (2) total revenue, and (3) total cost. The economic information contained in the production system, $Q(x)$ – technical efficiency, has been discussed previously in the first and second economic models and is required for maximizing profit. Total revenue is a function of three terms: price (P), output ($Q(x)$), and value ($P·Q(x)$). Price is a per unit measure of assigned value, reflects the output's relative scarcity with respect to quantity and quality and the market structure for the output, and is what consumers pay for the output. This economic information is reflected in the Pillar of Price and will be discussed in detail in Chapter 4 – Revenue, Chapter 10 – Supply and Demand, and Chapter 11 – Market Equilibrium and Structure. Value represents the degree to which consumers think buying the output makes them better off than if they did without. This economic information is reflected in the Pillar of Value. The economic information contained in total revenue is reflected in the Pillars of Price and Value.

Total cost is a function of two terms: (1) total variable cost and (2) total fixed cost. The economic information contained in total variable cost is defined by the Pillars of Cost and Value as given by the second economic model – production cost efficiency – and is required for maximizing profit. At this time, I will assert that the economic information contained in total fixed cost is also contained in the Pillars of Cost and Value.

Profit maximization is the culmination of the other two economic models and their economic information. It is a simple idea: Make the total revenues as large as possible (the Pillars of Price and Value for outputs) relative to the costs (the Pillars of Cost and Value for inputs) for any given input(s)–output(s) combination (the production system). Thus, to address the statement posed earlier, you first need to identify the required economic information and then obtain it at the appropriate level of detail. As Maital (1994: 7) stated previously, and it bears repeating: "It is deceptively difficult to build them [the three Pillars of Profit], precisely because they have to be built – the information required is often incomplete or not readily at hand." I have identified broad categories of economic information required and a systematic modeling procedure to use the information. Unfortunately, not enough detail is given in the preceding discussion to use economic information to make better business decisions. This detail will be provided in the rest of the book.

Final Thoughts

While this work is my own (as well as the errors), I would be truly negligent if I did not acknowledge those books and authors that provided the foundation upon which I have built my theoretical background: Amacher et al. (2009), Buongiorno and Gilles (2003), Davis et al. (2001 and earlier additions), Rideout and Hesseln (2001), Klemperer (1996), Pearce (1990), Gregory (1987), Johansson and Löfgren (1985), Leuschner (1984), Clutter et al. (1983), and Duerr (1960 and later editions).

Notes

1 This management procedure is often attributed to Frederick Taylor's Monograph: Taylor, F. W. 1911. Principles of Scientific Management. Harper & Brothers Publishers, New York, New York.

2 The built environment is defined as the human-made space in which people live, work, and recreate on a day-to-day basis. It includes the buildings and spaces people create or modify. It can extend overhead in the form of electric transmission lines and underground in the form of landfills (Roof and Oleru 2008). Wildland is a natural environment that has not been significantly modified by human activity. It is an area in which development is essentially non-existent, except for roads, railroads, power lines, and similar transportation facilities. Structures, if found, are widely scattered (Ledec and Goodlands 1988). This continuum includes the wildland-urban interface, which is the area were houses meet or intermingle with undeveloped wildland vegetation (Radeloff et al. 2005).

3 You will notice that in the upcoming examples one future condition will be consistent: "long-term profits and positive net benefits for the owner." A question worth asking is why I have made a distinction between "profits" and "positive net benefits." I will start to answer this question shortly and in more detail in upcoming chapters. However, I would like you to think about the context of this system. The maple syruping operation is a for-profit business run by the College of Environmental Science and Forestry whose mission includes teaching, research, and outreach. Thus, are all the outputs from this system monetary? Are there nonmonetary outputs that might be weighted equally with profits?

4 Would economic information regarding the market price per unit of syrup relative to candies be useful? Where would one obtain this information?

5 Once insolation passes the array and is not captured by the array, its energy-generating capacity is lost to the system forever. Is solar energy generation dependent on time of year? Is solar energy dispatchable or not dispatchable? How is the market price of energy determined?

6 I adopt the definition of a final ecosystem service as an output or outcome from the ecosystem that affects human well-being most directly (Sexton et al. 1999; Escobedo et al. 2011; Haines-Young and Potschin 2013; Common International Classification of Ecosystem Services https://cices.eu/ accessed 15 March 2021). These can be further classified as biotic and abiotic provisioning services, regulating and maintenance services, and cultural services (Common International Classification of Ecosystem Services https://cices.eu/ accessed 15 March 2021 for a detailed descriptions of these classifications). For expositional ease, I will use *outputs* to describe commodity goods such as wood fiber, biomass, forage, aquatic and terrestrial wildlife, water, recreation, and energy from primarily the provisioning ecosystem service classification. Many provisioning service outputs are traded in markets. However, in many regions, rural households also directly depend on provisioning services for their livelihoods (www.fao.org/ecosystem-services-biodiversity/background/provisioning-services/en/ accessed 2 January 2023). I will use

outcomes to describe final ecosystem services such as wildlife habitat, aesthetics, nutrient cycling, and so on from primarily the regulating and maintenance and cultural services. There may be an overlap between outputs and outcomes from the provisioning services.

7 Stumpage is the value of the merchantable volume – as measured by quantity (thousand board feet or cubic meters) and quality (log grade) – of a standing tree.

8 This could be creating habitat for game and nongame wildlife, creating forest conditions to store snow for controlled release of water, or creating forest conditions to provide trees to sell for lumber.

9 While this is a standard example, I am indebted to Dr. Klemperer for providing a concise numerical analysis of this problem (Klemperer 1996).

10 Foerde et al. (2006) found that active multitasking, such as watching television while studying, is less efficient than focusing only on studying. Thus, active multitasking comes at a cost of efficiency.

11 Is there a similar "merchantable" characteristic with respect to the schoolwork system? If a homework assignment is an output of the system: (i) who decides if it is of sufficient quality, and (ii) what is the price of a "merchantable" homework assignment?

12 Wagner et al. (2004) examines this issue using hardwood logs.

13 Net metering allows residential and commercial customers who generate their own electricity from solar power to feed electricity they do not use back into the grid (https://crsreports.congress.gov/product/pdf/R/R46010#:~:text=Net%20metering%20is%20a%20policy,DG)%2C%20especially%20solar%20energy accessed 28 August 2023). The Energy Information Agency provides information on net metering programs (www.eia.gov/renewable/annual/greenpricing/ accessed 13 October 2016).

14 If the context were changed from a residential owner to a business owner, how would net metering impact their profits and would there be any possible tax implications?

15 The treatment of absolute versus relative scarcity is described for those resources, commodities, or services traded in the formal marketplace (Wagner and Newman 2013). Simpson et al. (2004) discuss the concept of the "New Scarcity" or the "limitations on the environment to absorb and neutralize the unprecedented waste streams of humanity." While the concept of New Scarcity is important, I have chosen to limit my discussion to the traditional concepts of absolute and relative scarcity.

16 Incremental decision making or marginal analysis will be discussed in detail later in this chapter.

17 When determining the relevant incremental benefits and costs in a given context, an avoided benefit is a cost, and an avoided cost is a benefit.

18 The uniqueness of the energy markets located in the United States will be discussed in Chapter 11 – Market Equilibrium and Structure.

19 For an interesting intradisciplinary discussion on defining opportunity costs see Ferraro and Taylor (2005) and Potter and Sanders (2012).

20 More information on property rights can be found by reading De Soto (2003), Cole and Grossman (2002), Bromley (1998, 1992, 1991), Hanna et al. (1995), Hardin (1968), and Coase (1960).

21 This can be shown through the use of symbolic logic and the invalid deductive argument form known as the fallacy of affirming the consequent (Copi and Cohen 1998).

22 A discussion of the effects of positive and negative externalities on market equilibrium, also known as a market failure, is in Chapter 11 – Market Equilibrium and Structure.

23 An often-heard criticism is that the development of cause-and-effect relationships in economics is, or economic theories are, not based on realistic assumptions. Silberberg and Suen (2001) provide a nice concise discussion of this criticism that will not be repeated here.

24 An interesting example of the transitive preference ordering was the results from a survey dealing with Brexit (www.motherjones.com/kevin-drum/2018/11/preferences-are-not-transitive/ accessed 29 November 2018).

25 Implicit costs can be described as entrepreneurial and social. Entrepreneurial implicit costs are opportunity costs of the time and other resources a firm's owners make available for production with no direct cash outlay (Field and Field 2002; Henderson and Quandt 1980). Social costs are the effects of pollution or negative externalities (Field and Field 2002; Henderson and Quandt 1980).

26 An interesting least cost problem and solution from the remote sensing literature can be found in Wagner and Stehman (2015).

27 In the terminology of operations research, the least cost and cost effective models describe a primal–dual relationship (Winston 1994).

28 It is up to the reader, however, to determine if a solution to the least cost or cost effective model does or does not imply a profit maximization solution.

29 A more detailed analysis of this decision will be covered in Chapter 5 – Profit and Chapter 11– Market Equilibrium and Structure.

30 In the reader is interested in this topic, I would suggest starting with Lackey (2004, 2007), Mills (2000), Colander (1992), and Friedman (1953).

2 Production Systems

Preamble

Chapter 1 argued that describing and measuring the production system analytically is a required precursor to managing the system. Managing the maple syrup system requires describing and measuring the sugarbush and the process for collecting sap and producing the various maple products analytically. Managing a solar array system requires describing and measuring the infrastructure of converting insolation to energy analytically. Managing a natural resource system, such as forested ecosystems, requires describing and measuring structure and density, and diversity and composition analytically. This chapter will provide approaches that can be used on any system to measure and describe analytically the fundamental input(s)–output(s) relationship. These relationships are the foundation of the Architectural Plan for Profit and the first model of the Managerial Analytical Method.

Why Is Knowledge of the Production System Important?

Producing goods and providing services may take many forms. It could be manufacturing one or more outputs (e.g., renewable clean energy, maple syrup, school homework assignment, mushrooms, recreational leases, stumpage,[1] and carbon sequestration) by combining inputs such as land, labor, capital, materials, and energy. It could be providing a service (e.g., by a renewable resource, natural resources, or forestry consultant; charter boat fishing captain; medical doctor; tax accountant; and lawyer), again by combining inputs such as labor, capital, materials, and energy. Whether it is producing a good or providing a service, the production system describes the transformation of inputs into outputs:

Production System
Input(s) $\Rightarrow$ Production Process $\Rightarrow$ Output(s)

A competent manager, or for that matter a competent employee, of *any* business system – for profit or not-for-profit – will usually search for ways to do this in the most resource-efficient manner.

DOI: 10.4324/9781315678719-2

A solid understanding of the production system is necessary for seeking opportunities to minimize costs and ultimately maximize profits. Thus, the production
system is the foundation upon which profits rest. This is illustrated by the Architectural Plan for Profit in Figure 2.1a.

Huyler (2000) confirms this observation:

> The key to a successful maple syrup operation is controlling production to
> maintain an acceptable profit margin. It is important that sugarbush operators
> keep accurate records so that areas of high cost can be identified and steps
> taken to reduce them.
>
> (Huyler 2000: 5)

Figure 2.1a also builds upon the descriptions provided earlier and the Architectural
Plan for Profit given in Figure 1.7 by providing additional detail with respect to
the inputs and outputs. I will highlight three important features. First, while I have
described the inputs as land, labor, and capital previously, there are two additional
general input characteristics that are important for any manager to consider. The
first, and often the most obvious, is quantity – namely, the amount of input used; for
example, the number of laborers used and the hours each worked. However, entrepreneurs must also recognize the quality of the inputs used. Following the labor
example, there is a difference between skilled and unskilled labor in completing
a required component of the production process. While skilled labor is generally

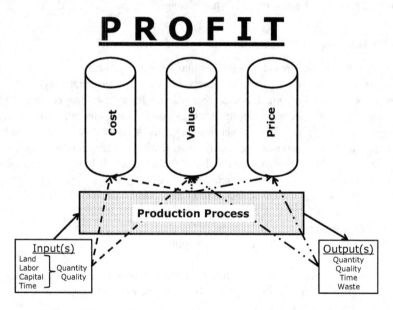

Figure 2.1a The Architectural Plan for Profit

more expensive than unskilled labor, a manager needs economic information to allocate each to completing a required component and minimize costs. Second, I can use the same general quantity and quality characteristics to describe the outputs. While consumers may enjoy maple syrup, they may prefer and are willing to pay for a specific quality of maple syrup. Third, these general quantity and quality characteristics are critical for linking input economic information to the Pillars of Cost and Value and linking output economic information the Pillars of Value and Price.

Although the purpose of this chapter is to focus on the production system, the entrepreneur must understand how this information will be used to ultimately maximize profits. I believe it is instructive to provide a sense of how this fits into managing the whole business systems using the remaining two models of the Managerial Analytical Method. In addition, as production systems range from simple to complex, how can we integrate production systems from the Managerial Analytical Method (Figure 1.4) into the Architectural Plan for Profit? And how this can be done so the entrepreneur will have the necessary economic information useful to search for ways to be resource efficient? This is the purpose of this chapter.

Least Cost/Cost Effective Models[2]

The least cost and cost effective models were introduced in Chapter 1 in a cursory manner. I will now present these models with more analytical detail and provide graphics to show the direct connection to the production system. The least cost model is defined as minimizing the variable production costs to produce a given output and is given in equation (2.1):

$$\text{Min TVC} = \sum_j w_j \cdot x_j$$

s.t. $\hspace{8cm}$ (2.1)

$$Q\left(x_1, x_2, ..., x_j\right) = Q^0$$

where

Min TVC denotes minimizing Total Variable Costs. These costs are what the entrepreneur must pay for inputs used in the production process and are depicted as $\text{TVC} = \sum_j w_j \cdot x_j$;

$\sum_j$ denotes the summation operator;

w_j denotes the jth wage or price paid by the entrepreneur for j^{th} input x_j;

x_j denotes the amount (quantity and quality) of the jth input;

s.t. denotes "subject to" and what follows is a constraint placed on the system;

$Q(x_1, x_2, \ldots, x_j)$ denotes the production system for producing a good or providing a service, Q, using inputs the manager has direct control over, $x_1, x_2, \ldots, x_j$;

$Q(x_1, x_2, \ldots, x_j) = Q^0$ defines the required quantity or quality of the good or service, Q^0, from the production system.

The cost effective model is defined as producing the most output in terms of quantity or quality for a given budget and is given in equation (2.2):

$$\text{Max } Q\left(x_1, x_2, \ldots, x_j\right)$$

s.t.   (2.2)

$$\sum_j w_j \cdot x_j = C^0$$

where

$\sum_j w_j x_j = C^0$ denotes that the total variable costs for using inputs $x_1, x_2, \ldots, x_j$ to produce the good or provide the service cannot exceed a given budget, C^0.

All other variables are defined previously in equation (2.1). As can be seen by equations (2.1) and (2.2), the production system and the economic information it contains is necessary to solving the least cost or cost effective problem. Simply put: How can you minimize costs of producing a given output level (quantity and quality) if you don't know how to produce the required output? Or how can you maximize the amount of output you produce for a given budget, if you don't know how to produce the required output quantity and quality? This is illustrated graphically in Figure 2.1b by building on the maple syrup system example described in Chapter 1.

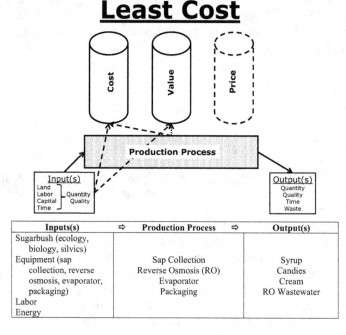

Inputs(s)	⇨	Production Process	⇨	Output(s)
Sugarbush (ecology, biology, silvics) Equipment (sap collection, reverse osmosis, evaporator, packaging) Labor Energy		Sap Collection Reverse Osmosis (RO) Evaporator Packaging		Syrup Candies Cream RO Wastewater

Figure 2.1b The Architectural Plan for Profit: Production System ⇒ Least Cost State University of New York College of Environmental Science and Forestry's Maple Syrup Operation

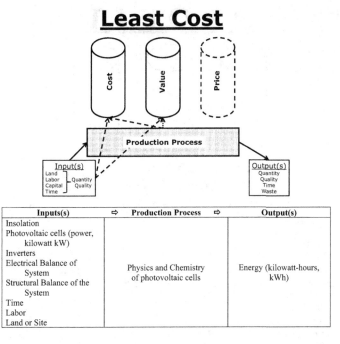

Inputs(s)	⇨	Production Process	⇨	Output(s)

Insolation
Photovoltaic cells (power,
    kilowatt kW)
Inverters
Electrical Balance of
    System
Structural Balance of the
    System
Time
Labor
Land or Site
		Physics and Chemistry
		of photovoltaic cells
				Energy (kilowatt-hours,
				kWh)

Figure 2.1c Architectural Plan for Profit: Production System ⇒ Least Cost. State University of New York College of Environmental Science and Forestry's 24.192 Kilowatt Solar Array

This is also illustrated graphically in Figure 2.1c by building on the solar array system example described in Chapter 1.

These graphics directly illustrate the tie between the production system inputs and production process and the Pillars of Value and Cost.

Profit Model

The profit model was introduced in Chapter 1 in a cursory manner. I will now present this model with more mathematical detail and provide graphics to show the direct connection to the production system. The profit model is given in equation (2.3):

$$\text{Max } \Pi = \text{TR} - \text{TC} = P \cdot Q(x) - \text{TVC} - \text{TFC}$$
$$= P \cdot Q(x_1, x_2, ..., x_j) - \sum_j w_j \cdot x_j - \text{TFC} \tag{2.3}$$

where
Max Π denotes maximization of profit (Π);
TR denotes Total Revenue, $\text{TR} = P \cdot Q(x_1, x_2, \ldots, x_j)$;
P denotes the market price of the good or service;

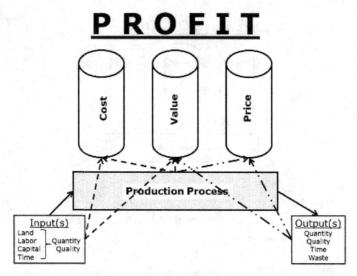

Inputs(s)	⇨	Production Process	⇨	Output(s)
Sugarbush (ecology, biology, silvics) Equipment (sap collection, reverse osmosis, evaporator, packaging) Labor Energy		Sap Collection Reverse Osmosis (RO) Evaporator Packaging		Syrup Candies Cream RO Wastewater

Figure 2.1d The Architectural Plan for Profit: Production System ⇒ Least Cost ⇒ Profit State University of New York College of Environmental Science and Forestry's Maple Syrup Operation

TC denotes Total Cost, TC = TVC + TFC;
TVC denotes Total Variable Costs, $TVC = \sum_j w_j \cdot x_j$;
TFC denotes Total Fixed Costs.

All other variables are defined previously. Maximizing profit is a simple idea: Make the total revenues as large as possible (the Pillars of Price and Value for outputs) relative to the costs (the Pillars of Cost and Value for inputs) for any given input(s)–output(s) combination (from the production system). As can be seen by equation (2.3), the production system and the economic information it contains is necessary for estimating total revenue and total variable cost. This is illustrated graphically in Figure 2.1d by building on the maple syrup system example described in Chapter 1.

This is also illustrated graphically in Figure 2.1e by building on the solar array system example described in Chapter 1.

These graphics illustrate the direct tie between the inputs and production process and the Pillars of Value and Cost and the production process and outputs and the Pillars of Value and Price.

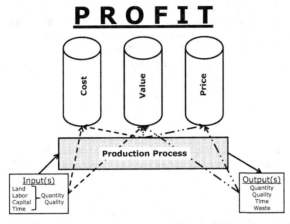

Inputs(s)	⇨	Production Process	⇨	Output(s)
Insolation Photovoltaic cells (power, 　kilowatt kW) Inverters Electrical Balance of 　System Structural Balance of the 　System Time Labor Land or Site		Physics and Chemistry of photovoltaic cells		Energy (kilowatt-hours, kWh)

Figure 2.1e Architectural Plan for Profit: Production System ⇒ Least Cost ⇒ Profit State University of New York College of Environmental Science and Forestry's 24.192 kilowatt Solar Array

Three Fundamental Questions to Examine Any Production System Systematically

Figures 2.1a to 2.1e, equations (2.1) to (2.3), and the accompanying text provide an argument that solid knowledge of the production system is necessary for seeking opportunities to minimize costs and ultimately maximize profits. The problem then is to determine an efficient means of collecting economic information on any production system. I will posit that there are three fundamental questions that if asked, answered correctly, and with sufficient detail can be used to examine any production function systematically. I will use the example systems from Chapter 1 to develop them and then selected practical application articles to examine these questions in more detail.

Becker et al. (2004) recognized the production system as the foundation for minimizing costs and maximizing profits with respect to the Mobile Micromill®:[3]

The number of productive machine hours will not only significantly affect operation and maintenance costs but will also determine the annual investment costs and ultimate mill profitability. To maximize the number of productive hours for each scheduled period of operation, it is imperative that mill owners and operators have a good understanding of how to process different

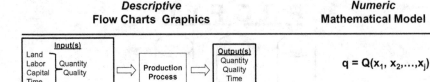

Figure 2.2 Production System Analytical Continuum

tree species and have the ability to maximize the product potential from each size of log with given characteristics such as taper or amount of defect.

Becker et al. (2004: 14)

Production systems can be described from many different viewpoints and can take many forms. Figure 2.2 illustrates an analytical continuum ranging from a combination of verbal and graphics to the numerical approach of the classic production function as described by Carlson (1974), Henderson and Quandt (1980), and Silberberg and Suen (2001).

As a manager, you will need production system descriptions that focus on identifying the underlying fundamental characteristics of the system that are critical to following the Architectural Plan for Profit (Figures 2.1a to 2.1e). Figures 2.1d and 2.1e lead to the three fundamental questions needed to examine any production system systematically: (1) What are the relevant fixed and variable inputs? (2) What are the outputs? and (3) How do you describe the production process analytically? The importance of answering these questions with sufficient detail is also illustrated in Figures 2.1d and 2.1e. Without sufficient economic information on the inputs and production process, you as a manager will not be able to build the Pillars of Cost and Value. Without sufficient economic information on the production process and outputs, you as a manager will not be able to build the Pillars of Price and Value. Again, I am reminded of the quote by Maital (1994: 7): "It is deceptively difficult to build them [the Pillars of Cost, Value, and Price], precisely because they have to be built – the information required is often incomplete or not readily at hand."

The illustrations of the maple syrup and the solar array system examples given in Figures 2.1d and 2.1e provide a means to study the three questions before working through some of the practical applications.

What Are the Relevant Fixed and Variable Inputs?

There are three key concepts in this question that need further clarification. First, fixed inputs are those resources or factors of production that do not vary as output level (quantity or quality) changes. Examples of fixed inputs from Figure 2.1d are land or capital equipment such as sap collection paraphernalia, reverse osmosis machine, and evaporator. Second, variable inputs are those resources or factors of production that change as output level (quantity or quality) changes. Examples of variable inputs from Figure 2.1c are labor and insolation.[4] Identifying *all* the inputs of producing or providing an output could create a very extensive list. Thus, relevant inputs are those resources or factors of production that a manager controls directly and impact output production decisions in terms of quantity and quality directly. You might argue that even though Figure 2.1d (or Figure 2.1e) provides a brief list of inputs, nature would seem to be an important input that was left off the list. Weather or insolation is an important variable factor in the maple syrup and solar array system examples, respectively. The temperature changes – cold nights and warm days – cause sap to flow, and insolation on the surface of the photovoltaic cells is required to convert energy. However, neither of these important variable factors are under the manager's direct control. The manager may use capital inputs to account for variable states of nature; for example, sun-tracking technology for the solar array or storage tanks for the sap to account for peak sap flows.

If an input is identified as a relevant fixed or variable input, then how it is used in the production process must be measured numerically in terms of quantity and/or quality. These measurements are purposeful as they will be tied to the Pillars of Cost and Value for the inputs, technical efficiency, and ultimately management decisions with respect to production.

What Are the Outputs?

In the solar array system example, the output seems very straightforward; namely, clean energy in the form of electricity converted by a solar panel.[5] This can be determined using equation (2.4)

$$E = A \times r \times H \times PR \quad (2.4)$$

where
E denotes energy (Wh, kWh, MWh or Wh/time, kWh/time, MWh/time);
A denotes total solar panel area square meters (m²);
r denotes solar panel efficiency (%) given Standard Testing Conditions of radiation = 1,000 W/m², temperature = 25° centigrade (77° Fahrenheit), wind speed = 1 meter per second, and an air mass spectrum of 1.5

$$r = \frac{\text{Solar panel power rating } (W)}{\left(1{,}000 \left(\frac{W}{m^2}\right)\right) \times \left(\text{Solar panel area } (m^2)\right)}$$

H denotes insolation (Wh/m², kWh/m², Wh/m²/time, or kWh/m²/time) given a solar array installation; and
PR denotes Performance Ratio and is the percent energy losses from cables, transformers, dust, shading, heat, and so forth.

However, the context is important. For a commercial solar array, estimating output solely using equation (2.4) would be reasonable. On the other hand, for a residential solar array, there could be two outputs: (i) the conversion and consumption of clean energy and (ii) the satisfaction the homeowner receives from having their own solar array. For the natural resources system example, the output is a suite of ecosystem goods and services. This suite depends on the owner's desired future condition (Figure 1.3). In the maple syrup system example, Figure 2.1d lists four outputs. The first three are obvious, but the fourth is worth discussing further. Using reverse osmosis to remove excess water does reduce the amount of energy required by the evaporator. But the reverse osmosis process creates waste; namely, demineralized water. All production process will create waste, and disposing of waste can be costly.[6] In some cases waste like the demineralized water can be disposed of at relatively little to no cost to the entrepreneur. This is not the case for all waste products depending on its amount, type, and toxicity.

If an output is identified, then it must be measured numerically in terms of quantity and/or quality. These measurements are purposeful as they will be eventually tied to the Pillars of Price and Value for the output, technical efficiency, and ultimately management decisions with respect to production.

How Do You Describe the Production Process Analytically?

This description must define the technical and physical relationships between combinations of the relevant fixed and variable inputs (from the first question) and the maximum outputs (from the second question) that each combination can produce.[7] In terms of economic information, this description must allow identifying input–output combinations that are technically efficient. A technically efficient input–output combination is when it is not possible to increase output without increasing input or when the maximum output is produced with the least amount of input. Maital (1994) describes the difference between technical inefficiency and technical efficiency as what is produced relative to what could be produced feasibly given the existing resources, knowledge, and ability. Technical efficiency is measured with respect to the relevant fixed and variable inputs.

Solar arrays convert insolation into a more useable energy form; namely, direct or alternating electric current. A solar panel is comprised of photovoltaic cells that are semiconductors made of materials such as silicon. Basically, when light strikes the cell, the portion that is not reflected is absorbed within the semiconductor material. This means that the energy of the absorbed light (kWh/m^2) is transferred to the semiconductor. The energy knocks electrons loose, allowing them to flow freely. Photovoltaic cells also all have one or more electric fields that act to force electrons freed by light absorption to flow in a certain direction. This flow of electrons is a current, and by placing metal contacts on the top and bottom of the photovoltaic cell, that current is drawn off for external use as electricity.

The production process of a natural resources system can best be described as a multi-input and multi-period $\Rightarrow$ multi-output joint production process (Figure 1.3). For example, managing a forest system's structure by thinning out subdominant trees may be integral to meeting landowner goals and objectives because most of their objectives are structure dependent (O'Hara and Gersonde 2004). Management actions are tied to the landowner's goals and objectives and the metrics used to describe structure described in Chapter 1. Some of the metrics could be outputs within a suite of desired outputs/outcomes. For example, for a landowner whose objectives include profit from selling the output stumpage, the metrics could include trees per diameter class, species, and quantity (as measured by (i) volume per unit area – thousand board feet per acre or cubic meters per hectare or (ii) weight per unit area – tons per acre or kilograms per square meter) and quality (as measured by log grade). For other landowners whose primary goals and objectives consist of privacy, aesthetics, wildlife habitat, and biodiversity (Butler and Leatherberry 2004; Butler et al. 2007, 2016; Butler 2008, 2010), metrics such as number of trees per diameter class, diversity of species per unit area, density per unit area, foliage arrangement, and understory vegetation describe the necessary conditions for providing these desired outputs/outcomes. This point bears repeating and makes this production system unique: Management actions create a structure necessary for producing some outputs/outcomes. Some output levels are controlled more directly by management actions than others (Touza et al. 2008). For example, management actions can control volume per unit area (e.g., thousand board feet per acre or cubic meters per hectare) and log grade more directly than some bird species populations, while deer populations may fall somewhere in between. Management can create a habitat structure to increase the probability of producing wildlife output(s), but these variable management inputs do not produce wildlife output(s) directly (Touza et al. 2008).

Referring back to Figure 2.2, the answer to how to describe the production process analytically requires being able to demonstrate the relationship between the numeric input measurements with the numeric output measurements.[8] Thus, does the analytical description provide enough information to allow identifying input–output combinations that are technically efficient?

The production process is also a mechanism to add value to the inputs reflected in the Pillar of Value. For example, dry torrefaction of woody biomass uses high temperatures in an inert environment to remove moisture and volatile compounds to create a bio-coal or biochar product. Wet torrefaction uses steam or hot pressurized liquid water in an inert atmosphere to remove moisture and sugars to create a similar product called hydrochar. This is illustrated using the Architectural Plan for Profit in Figure 2.1f.

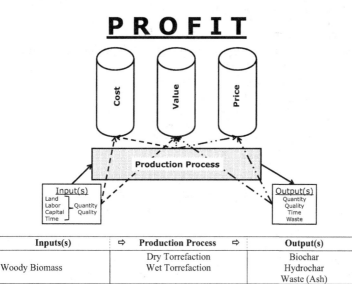

Inputs(s)	⇨	Production Process	⇨	Output(s)
Woody Biomass		Dry Torrefaction Wet Torrefaction		Biochar Hydrochar Waste (Ash)

Figure 2.1f Architectural Plan for Profit: Production System ⇒ Least Cost ⇒ Profit Biochar or Hydorchar

The wet torrefaction process allows the degraded hemicellulose sugars to be recovered and used as a by-product. The ash content of hydrochar is less than that of biochar because of the elements removed in the wet torrefaction process. The dry torrefaction process actually increases ash concentration (Nhuchhen et al. 2014; Acharya et al. 2015). Both processes produce an output that has higher energy content and is more hydrophobic than standard wood pellets and is easier to manipulate than the raw biomass (Nhuchhen et al. 2014; Acharya et al. 2015). Consequently, torrefaction produces a higher quality output using the same woody biomass input with respect to the Pillar of Value. However, the Pillar of Value is also associated with a consumer's willingness and ability to pay for the product as reflected by the market. Are consumers willing and able to pay a higher price for this torrefied pellet? The market for torrefied pellets currently is limited to Asia (primarily Japan and Korea) and France. Thus, while the torrefaction process does add value in terms of output quality, there is a very limited market for this unique output. Just because the ability to produce a higher quality output is available, the entrepreneur needs to tie the economic information available from the production system to the Pillars of Cost, Value, and Price. As just illustrated by this discussion, it is important to remember that production systems do not produce values, they produce outputs that individuals assign value to in a given context. Production decisions are based on the completed Architectural Plan for Profit, not just the production system.

Practical Application Production Systems

In addition to the example systems used to explain the three fundamental questions, the following practical applications reflect published economic information that managers or entrepreneurs can (and do) use to make resource-efficient decisions.

Select Red Oak (Hahn and Hansen 1991)

This production system estimates the gross and net board foot volume measured in International 1/4 log rule, Vol_{gross} and Vol_{net} respectively, of an individual red oak tree using the following two equations:

$$Vol_{gross} = 744.2 \cdot S^{0.2627} \cdot \left(1 - e^{-0.00003487 \cdot D^{2.804}}\right) \tag{2.5}$$

$$Vol_{net} = Vol_{gross} \cdot \left[1 - \left(\frac{-6.696 + 1.077D}{100}\right)\right] \tag{2.6}$$

where
S = site index ($25 \leq S \leq 99$, with the average S being 66.5);[9] and
D = diameter at breast height (maximum D is 51.2 inches for sawtimber).[10]

The difference between gross and net board foot volume is a deduction for cull or non-merchantable volume. Thus, net board foot volume is a measure of merchantable volume. This production process description is on the right-hand side of the continuum given in Figure 2.2.

*Radiata Pine (*Pinus radiata*) Plantations in New Zealand*

Radiata pine or Monterrey pine is a versatile, fast-growing, medium-density soft-wood that is very suitable for a wide range of local, regional, and exported end uses (e.g., sawlogs, pulp logs, posts and poles, energy, and erosion control). Globally, there are just over 4 million hectares of radiata pine plantations, mainly in Australia, Chile, New Zealand, South Africa, Italy, and Spain, making this the most widely planted exotic conifer (Mead 2013). The general management regime calls for plantation establishment (site preparation, planting, and weeding), tending (pruning, thinning, fertilizer, and disease and pest control), and clear felling or clearcutting (Mead 2013). This example illustrates the use of an advanced computer model to describe a production system.

Various radiata pine management regimes can be simulated using Forecaster, which is a system for predicting forest growth and yield in terms of volume (quantity) and log yield (quality). Forecaster was developed by Scion and Future Forests Research, a New Zealand Crown Research Institute specializing in research, science, and technology development for forestry, wood products, and wood-derived materials and other biomaterials.[11] An overview of the biometric equations for estimating radiata pine growth and yield, product characteristics in terms of quantity and quality, and allometric equations for carbon sequestration can be found in West et al. (2013).

Two management regimes were simulated for an average site: Pruned vs. unpruned stands, planting 1-year old nursery plants, and intermediate treatments. The objective of both management regimes is to produce trees for dimension or structural lumber at a profit.

Inside-Out Beams (Patterson et al. 2002 and Patterson and Xie 1998)

This production system uses small-diameter trees (e.g., 6- to 9-inch diameter at breast height) to manufacture 8-foot, 10-foot, 12-foot, 14-foot, or 16-foot 4 × 4 inside-out (ISO) beams depending on the length of the small-diameter tree input. Figure 2.3 illustrates the procedure for manufacturing an ISO beam.

Mobile Micromill® (Becker et al. 2004)

The Micromill® will produce four-sided cants, rough-cut lumber (i.e., 1 × 4, 1 × 6, 2 × 4, 2 × 6, 4 × 4, 6 × 6), and chips using a single-pass system. The mill can process 4- to 20-foot logs with a maximum large-end diameter (outside bark) of 13 inches and a minimum small-end diameter (outside bark) of 4 inches. Figure 2.4 illustrates the single-pass system.

What Are the Relevant Fixed and Variable Inputs?

In the Select Red Oak application (Hahn and Hansen 1991), the explicit mathematical models, equations (2.5) and (2.6), define two inputs. For the ISO Beams (Patterson et al. 2002 and Patterson and Xie 1998) and the Mobile Micromill® (Becker

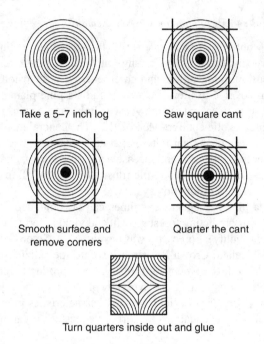

Take a 5–7 inch log   Saw square cant

Smooth surface and   Quarter the cant
remove corners

Turn quarters inside out and glue

Figure 2.3 Production System Inside-Out Beam Illustration

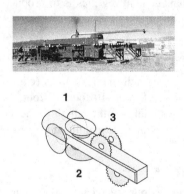

Figure 2.4 Single-Pass Production System Used by the Mobile Micromill®

et al. 2004) applications, the graphics given in Figures 2.3 and 2.4 illustrate the production processes and Table 2.1 gives a list of their inputs.

The left-hand columns of Table 2.1 have the inputs categorized as fixed and variable, while the right-hand column does not. It is left as an exercise for the reader to categorize the inputs in the right-hand column as fixed and variable. For example, logs delivered to both mills are variable inputs if no logs are available, then no beams or dimension lumber can be produced. However, the production of beams

Table 2.1 Input Lists for the ISO Beams and Mobile Micromill® Applications

ISO Beams (Patterson et al. 2002)	Mobile Micromill® (Becker et al. 2004)
Fixed Inputs	Mobile Micromill®
Land, buildings, scale	Support equipment:
Lift trucks (2)	Tractor-loader
Log deck and conveyor	Forklift
Debarker	Maintenance vehicle
Cut-off saw	Chainsaw
Chipper	Mobile Micromill® siting
Skrag mill	Operation and maintenance – Micromill®
Moulder (2)	Operation and maintenance – support equipment
Quartering saw	Labor
ISO clamping	Delivered raw logs
Boiler and kiln(s)	Inventory
Pre-dryer (hardwoods)	Relocation and equipment setup
Trim saw	
Utilities (office)	
Variable Inputs	
Labor	
8- to 14-foot logs	
Utilities (manufacturing)	

or dimension lumber requires fixed inputs such as capital equipment (e.g., the machines listed in Table 2.1). These inputs are required in the production process, but there is a period of time in which they cannot be varied and define the scale or size of the business. For example, Patterson et al. (2002) examines three differ-ent ISO beam daily output levels: 464 ISO beams, 696 ISO beams, and 928 ISO beams. Based on the data provided by Patterson et al. (2002), the boiler, kiln(s), and the pre-dryer are the limiting fixed capital equipment inputs. Thus, to increase output levels from 464 to 696 (or 696 to 928) ISO beams daily, the size of the busi-ness must also increase by purchasing additional capital equipment. Purchasing and installing larger boilers, kiln(s), and pre-dryers is not as easy as varying the number of logs run through the mill daily; for example, 0 to 400 logs to produce to 464 ISO beams.[12] For the radiata pine practical application, the inputs are derived from the description of the management regime: Medium site quality, site prepara-tion and planting 1-year old nursery plants, precommercial thinning, a regeneration harvest using clear felling, and the labor to complete these management actions.

Mathematical models used to depict the production system in the Select Red Oak practical application can be intimidating (as would those used in the Fore-caster model for radiata pine).[13] However, does the input list for Select Red Oak given by equations (2.5) and (2.6) describe the underlying fundamental character-istics of the production system that you, as a manager, can directly control? Are these inputs critical for systematically following the Architectural Plan for Profit – specifically constructing the Pillars of Cost and Value? The simple answers are no. The input diameter at breast height (D) can be managed by manipulating the forest structure and density. While diameter growth changes over time regardless of any management input, the purpose of a precommercial thinning management input is to increase future diameter growth, quality, and growth of the residual trees (Nyland 2016).[14] Although the input variable D, as given in equations (2.5) and (2.6), has no direct link to the Pillar of Cost, the management input thinning does have a direct link to the Pillar of Cost in that thinning costs are defined as dollars per unit area and the Pillar of Value in that thinning concentrates the quantity and quality growth on the residual trees. Equations (2.5) and (2.6) for Select Red Oak were developed by biometricians to estimate volume.[15] These biometricians recognized the importance of gross versus net or merchantable volume but did not have the Architectural Plan for Profit in mind directly when developing them.

For the radiata pine practical application, the desired output – volume (cubic meters per hectare) by log grade – is obtained by managing forest structure directly. The inputs are derived from describing the pruned and unpruned management regimes given a medium site quality. The pruning regime's management inputs are

  i. planting 1,000 1-year old nursery plants per hectare;
 ii. a quality control planting survey;
iii. two herbicides treatments in years 1 and 2 post planting;
 iv. two spray treatments to control *Dothistroma septosporum*, a significant needle disease, in years 5 and 6;
  v. two prunings in years 6 and 8;
 vi. a precommercial thinning (or thinning-to-waste) in year 8; and
vii. a clearcut (or clearfelling) in year 30.

The unpruned regime's management inputs are

  i. planting 833 1-year old nursery plants per hectare;
 ii. a quality control planting survey;
iii. two herbicides treatments in years 1 and 2 post planting;
 iv. two spray treatments to control *Dothistroma septosporum* in years 5 and 6;
  v. a precommercial thinning (or thinning-to-waste) in year 8; and
 vi. a clearcut (or clearfelling) in year 30.

The Forecaster model allows the manager to define the relevant bounds of these management inputs for simulating the desired output of trees for dimension or structural lumber at a profit (West et al. 2013).

While no explicit mathematical models were given in the radiata pine, ISO Beam, and Mobile Micromill® applications, these authors had the Architectural Plan for Profit in mind when developing the list of inputs; namely, a direct link to the Pillars of Cost and Value for the inputs. It bears repeating that in creating the list of relevant fixed and variable inputs, you must decide which inputs depict the underlying fundamental characteristics of the production system that will be critical for following the Architectural Plan for Profit systematically (Figures 2.1a to 2.1f).

What Are the Outputs?

Identifying *all* the outputs of a production system seems deceptively simple. For example, in the Select Red Oak application, the output is volume. Specifically, volume is the gross and net board foot volume (International 1/4 log rule) of an *individual* tree. As before, this list must also depict the underlying fundamental characteristics of the production system that will be critical for following the Architectural Plan for Profit systematically (Figure 2.1a). Specifically, this list should make constructing the Pillar of Price and Value for the output much easier. Hardwood trees, such as red oak (as well as softwood trees), are characterized by an index of quality. A tree designated as a Grade 1 denotes the highest quality, Grade 2 is next in quality followed by Grade 3 and so on. Diameter at breast height is one attribute – of many – used to distinguish between tree grades. Other things being equal, the larger the diameter the better the tree grade.[16] Individuals who purchase red oak stumpage place a higher value on Grade 1 trees, then Grade 2, and so on. The difference between the stumpage price of a Grade 1 tree versus a Grade 2 tree versus a Grade 3 tree can be substantial (Stier 2003). Thus, the output for red oak should include volume (as measured by board foot) as well as quality as defined by Grades 1, 2, or 3. Diameter at breast height from equations (2.5) and (2.6) does not provide information to help in constructing the Pillars of Cost and Value as a relevant variable input, but it does provide some information to help construct the Pillar of Price and Value for the output.

Output for the Radiata Pine application, as provided by the Forecaster simulator, is defined in terms of quantity (cubic meters per hectare (m^3/ha)) and quality (logs and log grades). User-defined log grades are characterized by product class (e.g., large vs. small sawlogs, pruned vs. unpruned sawlogs, and pulp logs), diameter and length of each product class, and sweep (as measured by the maximum deviation of the log's centerline) (West et al. 2013).

The output from the Mobile Micromill® is the most variable, depending on the inputs available. For example, Table 2.2 shows the percentage of lumber size and grade given inputs available in the study area.

Table 2.2 Percentage of Lumber Size and Grade Recovery for Ponderosa Pine

Lumber Size	Lumber Grade	Log Small-End Diameter (in)				
		3	4	5	6	7
Inches		Percent				
1 by 4	Common mid better	0	0	0	38	62
1 by 4	3, 4, and 5 Common	0	0	2	71	2
3 by 3	Standard and better	1	46	52	1	0
3 by 3	Economy	6	64	28	2	0
4 by 4	Standard and better	0	2	42	51	5
4 by 4	Economy			51	30	8

Data from Lowell.
(Used with permission from the USDA Forest Service)

In the case of the Mobile Micromill®, it bears repeating that the list of outputs should depict the underlying fundamental characteristics of the production system that will be critical for following the Architectural Plan for Profit systematically (Figures 2.1a to 2.1f). This list should make it much easier to construct the Pillars of Price and Value. For example, other things being equal, lumber of the same size (e.g., 1 × 4) but of better quality is valued more by the consumer. In addition, kiln drying adds value to lumber. This is illustrated by Table 2.3.

The trick is to saw the most valuable lumber from any given input. Thus, output for the Mobile Micromill® application should be described in terms of quality and quantity of the various different outputs for a given period of time.

The obvious output from the ISO Beam application are 8-foot, 10-foot, 12-foot, 14-foot, or 16-foot 4 × 4 ISO beams depending on the length of the small-end diameter of the tree input. Based on prices for solid wood 4 × 4 beams, consumers will place greater value on longer rather than shorter ISO beams (Patterson et al. 2002). However, creating the cants produces slabs (Figure 2.3). These slabs can be chipped and sold to local pulp mills. Quartering the cants and molding and smoothing the quarters create sawdust and other residuals. These residuals are used as boiler fuel to heat the kilns. This practical application shows production process waste as an output (Figure 2.1a). This practical application also shows that slabs

Table 2.3 Output Price by Lumber Size and Grade for Ponderosa Pine

Product Size	Finished Product Grade	Market Scenario[a]			
		Observed	Low	Average	High
In		*Dollars per thousand board feet*			
Kiln dried, surfaced:[b]					
1 by 4, 6	2 Common and better	530	453	500	548
1 by 4, 6	3 and 4 Common	275	201	245	278
4 by 4	Standard	350	_c	_c	_c
4 by 4	Economy	300	_c	_c	_c
Green, rough sawn:					
4 by 4	Standard, Economy	200	_c	_c	_c
1 by 4	3 Common, Utility	220	164	190	219
1 by 4	5 Common, Economy	150	110	134	155
By-products[d]					
Wood chips	Dirty, including bark	4–20/BDT	_c	_c	_c

Notes
[a] Observed markets are for ponderosa pine products sold in the Four Corners region in October 2003. Low, average, and high market prices were compiled by the Western Wood Products Association and reported by Haynes (2003).
[b] Kiln-dried, planed products will require additional manufacturing and transportation to a secondary processing facility independent of Mobile Micromill® operations.
[c] The Western Wood Products Association does not compile price data for this category.
[d] Chip by-products are "dirty" owing to bark and other impurities. Chip prices are based on biomass purchases for bioenergy powerplants and pellet manufacturing in the Southwest (per bone dry ton [BDT], zero percent moisture). Prices will differ significantly based on distance to market.
(Used with permission from the USDA Forest Service)

and residual waste are (i) turned into a saleable output (i.e., chips) and (ii) heat for the kiln (i.e., residuals), respectively. Nonetheless, using residuals in boilers to generate heat will create a waste product – ash – that must be disposed of in some manner.

What are the waste outputs from the other practical applications? Can they be turned into a saleable output? What is the cost of waste disposal?

How Do I Describe the Production Process Analytically?

The description of the production process is what ties the numeric input measurements with the numeric output measurements so that the entrepreneur can determine technically efficient input–output combinations. The ISO Beam and the Mobile Micromill® manuscripts provide written descriptions and a graphical illustration of the production process. For the ISO Beam case study, step-by-step directions to manufacture ISO beams are given in the Procedures section of Patterson and Xie (1998) and briefly summarized by Patterson et al. (2002) and illustrated in Figure 2.3:

> Small trees (6- to 9-in. diameter at breast height) were cut into 8-foot logs. These logs were cut in to 4–1/4-inch square cants with sides parallel to the pith. The sides of the cants were smoothed on a moulder and the corners chamfered. The cants were quartered, the exterior surfaces heat treated, resorcinol adhesive was applied, and the quarters turned inside-out and clamped together. After the adhesive cured, the new beams were kiln-dried and moulded to the final size of 3–1/2 by 3–1/2 inches.
>
> (Patterson et al. 2002: 24)

For the Mobile Micromill®, descriptions of the production process are scattered throughout Becker et al.'s (2004) document. However, a brief description of the single-pass production process is given by Becker et al. (2004) and illustrated in Figure 2.4:

> The Micromill® is a 300-horsepower dimension sawmill capable of processing 4- to 20-ft logs with a maximum large-end diameter (outside bark) of 13 in and a minimum small-end diameter (outside bark) of 4 in. Designed to cut about 850,000 to 3,500,000 ft^3 per year, depending on tree species and desired product, the mill produces four-sided cants, rough-cut lumber, and chips in a single-pass, automatic-feed system.
>
> (Becker et al. 2004: 1)

The published production rates are provided by Micromill Systems, Inc. The observed production rates were those collected as part of the study conducted by Becker et al. (2004). To compare the observed and published production rates given the difference in the logs used as inputs is described in the footnotes of Table 2.4. Becker et al. (2004) recommends using hourly production rates for a 4-inch square cant. Based on this recommendation, Table 2.4 shows that the observed production

Table 2.4 Observed and Published Production Rates for the Micromill® SLP5000D

Specification	Production Rate					
	Observed[a]	Published[b]				
Average butt-end log diameter (in)	8	12	10	8	6	4
Square cant size (in)	4	8	7	6	4	3
Estimated feed rate (ft/minute)	55	50	55	60	65	70
Hourly production (board feet)	3,000	12,250	10,375	6,500	3,250	2,125
Monthly production (thousand board feet)	504	2,050	1,750	1,100	550	350

Notes
[a] Based on 8 ft log length, 21 working days/month, and one 8-hour shift per day. Figures are based on a continuous run of presorted ponderosa pine with an average butt-end diameter of 8 in.
[b] Based on 12 ft log length, 21 working days/month, and one 8-hour shift per day. All figures are based on a continuous run of presorted, uniform-sized spruce, pine, or fir logs.
(Used with permission from the USDA Forest Service and Micromill Systems, Inc.)

rates for a 4-inch square cant are lower than the published rates for a 4-inch square cant. Becker et al. (2004: 22) state differences between observed and published production rates "will result from variability in operator experience, average log diameter, and cant size." Based on the information provided in Table 2.4, I would conclude that there are some technical inefficiencies that have the potential of being reduced as labor becomes more skilled with the production process.

Technical efficiency cannot be measured directly for the ISO Beam application because no information relating inputs to outputs directly is given in either Patterson et al. (2002) or Patterson and Xie (1998). However, Patterson et al. (2002) provides information about three daily production levels (i.e., 464 ISO beams per day, 696 ISO beams per day, and 928 ISO beams per day) and a list of the machines required (Table 2.1). Pre-drying of each quarter's exterior surfaces is required before the resorcinol adhesive is applied according to the production process description provided by Patterson et al. (2002). The quarters are turned inside-out and clamped and the new beams are dried in kilns. This would lead me to infer that while most of the machines listed in Table 2.1 (e.g., the cut-off saw) are not running at capacity nor are they constraining the product system in any manner, the capacity of the boilers, kiln(s), and pre-dryers are the limiting capital inputs in this production process and define its scale. In other words, to produce more than 464 ISO beams per day more capital equipment – larger capacity boilers, kilns, and pre-dryers – are required. A similar argument can be made for producing more than 696 ISO beams per day. Based on Maital's (1994) definition of technical efficiency, I would assert that each different daily production level, given the production system, is technically efficient.

Economic Descriptors of the Production System

The three classic economic descriptors of the production system – total product, average product, and marginal product – provide additional economic information about the production system primarily with respect to the relevant variable inputs impact on production. In addition, the economic information they provide should not be viewed in isolation of the Architectural Plan for Profit. The relative value of the economic information is its use in helping to constructing the Pillars of Cost and Value for the inputs and Price and Value for the outputs.

Total Product (TP)

Total product defines the most efficient production levels given the production system. That is, total product defines the greatest combination of outputs for a given combination of inputs or the least amount of inputs needed to produce a given level of outputs or technical efficiency.

There are three means of depicting total product: tables, graphs, and mathematical equations. In the Select Red Oak application, the production process is described using mathematical equations (2.5) and (2.6) and total product is given as gross and net International 1/4 board feet volume per tree. An advantage of the mathematical equations is being able to generate yield tables given ranges for site index of $25 \leq S \leq 99$ and diameter at breast height of $1 \leq D \leq 51.2$ inches. Table 2.5 depicts the gross and net volume (International 1/4 board feet per tree) at three levels of site index and varying diameters.

D denotes diameter at breast height measured in inches. Site Index is the height of the dominant and co-dominant trees measured in feet at an index age of 50 years; e.g., Site Index = 66 denotes the height of the dominant and co-dominant trees are 66 feet at tree age of 50 years. Gross and Net Volume, equations (2.5) and (2.6) respectively, are measured as board foot volume (International 1/4) per tree.

Table 2.5 Select Red Oak Board Foot Volume per Tree (International 1/4)

	Site Index 25		Site Index 66		Site Index 99	
	Volume	Volume	Volume	Volume	Volume	Volume
D	Gross	Net	Gross	Net	Gross	Net
1	0	0	0	0	0	0
5	6	6	7	7	8	8
10	38	37	49	47	55	52
15	116	105	150	135	166	151
20	249	212	321	274˙	357	304
25	436	348	563	449	626	499
30	664	494	857	638	954	709
35	910	628	1175	810	1,307	902
40	1,146	729	1,479	941	1,646	1,047
45	1,349	786	1,741	1,014	1,937	1,128
50	1,504	795	1,941	1,026	2,159	1,141
55	1,610	764	2,078	986	2,311	1,097

My first note of caution when using equations to calculate total product: As context is important, equations (2.5) and (2.6) summarize a complex biological process using only two variable inputs. So be very careful of the overconfidence in the precision that is possible when calculating total product using equations or in the forestry case computer growth and yield models. For example, using equation (2.5) with a diameter of 15 inches and a site index of 66, the gross board foot volume of a select red oak tree can be calculated as 149.566871 board feet. However, this level of precision is not defensible nor reasonable given what is being measured and managed.

The yield date in Table 2.5 can also be illustrated graphically. Figure 2.5 is a two-dimensional view of total product for Select Red Oak. In Figure 2.5, site index is held constant at 66 feet and diameter is allowed to vary. A three-dimensional view of total product can also be generated given the information in Table 2.5. Figure 2.6 shows total product or yield as a surface allowing both diameter and site index to vary.

The yield table and graphics also describe an efficiency frontier for the various input levels.[17] For example, you have a select red oak tree with a diameter at breast height of 25 inches growing on a site with a site index of 66. If the net volume of your tree is greater (less) than 563 International 1/4 board feet, then your tree is more (less) productive than a red oak on a similar site with the same diameter at breast height modeled using equations (2.5) and (2.6). *My second note of caution*

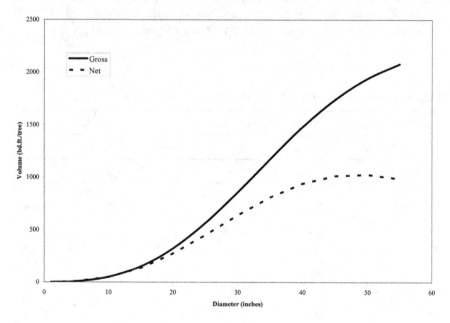

Figure 2.5 Gross and Net Yields for Select Red Oak

Note: Volume is measured as board foot, International 1/4, per tree (bd.ft./tree) given S = 66

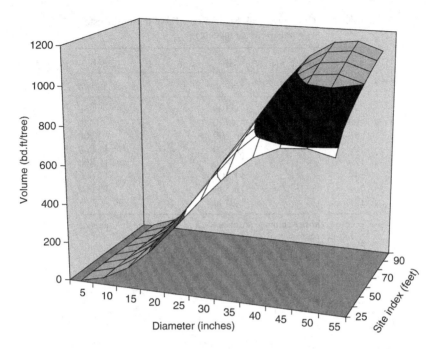

Figure 2.6 Net Volume for Select Red Oak

Note: Volume is measured as board feet per tree (bd.ft./tree)

when using equations like (2.5) and (2.6) to calculate total product: The coefficients of these equations were estimated statistically. Thus, there is a confidence interval associated with each volume estimate given in Table 2.5. It is important when using these volumes to build the Pillar of Value for determining total revenue. Instead of a scalar estimate of total revenue, your estimate will be a range. This range will have important consequences when estimating profit. This topic will be revisited at the end of the chapter in the discussion of variability. Hahn and Hansen (1991) provide information on the confidence intervals for the volume estimates.

Gevorkiantz and Scholz (1948) sampled 385 oak plots in southwestern Wisconsin. These samples were used to develop the gross and net volumes per acre – total product – shown in Table 2.6 and illustrated graphically in Figure 2.7.

The difference between gross and net volumes is determined by subtracting mortality and non-merchantable or cull volume from the gross volume. Thus, net volumes represent merchantable volumes. Figure 2.7 is a graphic of the gross and net volume per acre versus stand age. Both Table 2.6 and Figure 2.7 show that in terms of gross volume, the stand has reached a physiological maximum at an age of 160. In terms of net volume, the stand reaches a maximum at age 120. Gevorkiantz and Scholz (1948) provide a graphic that shows that after age 160, losses due to mortality and cull are greater than growth. Again, these volumes were estimated

Table 2.6 Unthinned Oak Stand Yield Table in Southwestern Wisconsin (Medium Site)‡

	Gross	*Net*
Age	*Volume*	*Volume*
40	300	250
60	4700	4050
80	10,200	8700
100	13,600	11,000
120	15,800	11,800
140	17,300	11,600
160	18,500	10,900
180	18,500	

‡ Gross and net volumes are measured as board foot (International 1/4) per acre

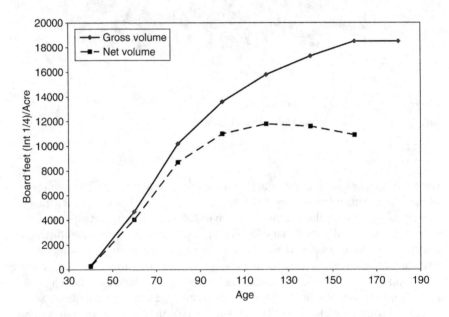

Figure 2.7 Unthinned Oak Stand Yields in Southwestern Wisconsin (Medium Site)

using statistical techniques, and each estimate has an associated confidence interval that must be part of the analysis of the production system and the Pillar of Value.

The yields for the Radiata Pine application are given in Table 2.7a. Volume is measured as cubic meters per hectare (m³/ha) and is calculated based on the simulated management regime described previously and illustrated graphically in Figure 2.8.

As part of the defined management regimes, there were precommercial thinnings (thin-to-waste) to reduce the number of stems per hectare. This is shown in

Table 2.7a Radiata Pine Plantation Yield Table

Plantation Age	Unpruned Total Volume[†] (m³/ha)	Management Action[‡]	Plantation Age	Pruned Total Volume[†] (m³/ha)	Management Action[‡]
0		Planting	0		Planting
1		Herbicide	1		Herbicide
2		Herbicide	2		Herbicide
3	1.2		3	1.4	
4	4.8		4	5.7	
5	13.1	DS	5	15.5	DS
6	27.7	DS	6	32.7	DS+Pruning
7	49.8		7	57.3	PCT
8	79.5	PCT	7	34.2	
8	51.2		8	53.2	Pruning+PCT
9	74.7		8	40.3	
10	102.4		9	55.5	
11	133.9		10	73.6	
12	168.5		11	97.3	
13	205.5		12	126.8	
14	244.6		13	159.2	
15	285.2		14	194.0	
16	327.0		15	230.7	
17	369.6		16	268.9	
18	412.8		17	308.3	
19	456.1		18	348.6	
20	499.0		19	389.4	
21	542.4		20	430.4	
22	585.9		21	471.2	
23	629.5		22	512.4	
24	673.0		23	553.9	
25	716.2		24	595.5	
26	759.0		25	637.1	
27	801.3		26	678.6	
28	842.9		27	719.8	
29	883.8		28	760.5	
30	923.9		29	800.7	
			30	840.4	

[†] Total Volume is measured as cubic meters per hectare (m³/ha) and is calculated based on the simulated management regime described previously.

[‡] DS – *Dothistroma septosporum* spray. PCT – Precommercial Thinning

Table 2.7a and seen in Figure 2.8. Comparing the total volumes of the pruned versus unpruned radiata pine plantations shows they are less for the pruned plantation. The management inputs associated with the pruning regime included an additional precommercial thinning and two prunings (Table 2.7a). The purpose of these management inputs, combined with the other management inputs, is to increase the quality of the output. Table 2.7b shows the yield by product class at plantation age 30 for the pruned and unpruned management regime.

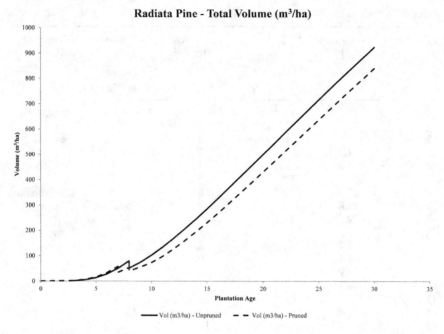

Figure 2.8 Yields for the Radiata Pine Plantation

Note: Volume is measured as cubic meters per hectare (m3/ha) given the management regime described previously

Table 2.7b Radiata Pine Yield at Plantation Age 30 by Product Class

Product Class	Product Description[†]	Pruned Volume	Unpruned Volume
		(m³/ha)	(m³/ha)
Pulpwood		192.2	241.5
L1	Large, large-branched sawlog	26.9	45.0
L2	Small sawlog	62.7	49.5
P1	Large pruned sawlog	77.2	
P2	Small pruned sawlog	105.8	
S1	Large, small-branched sawlog	84.0	138.5
S2	Medium, small-branched sawlog	206.0	367.6
	Sum	754.8	842
	Harvest waste	85.6	81.8
	Total volume (Table 2.7a)	840.4	923.9

[†] Radiata pine output is defined in terms of quantity (cubic meters per hectare (m³/ha)) and quality (logs and log grades). User-defined log grades are characterized by product class (e.g., large vs. small sawlogs, pruned vs. unpruned sawlogs, and pulpwood), diameter and length of each product class, and sweep (as measured by the maximum deviation of the log's centerline) (West et al. 2013).

A cursory look at Table 2.7b would seem to show that the additional manage-ment inputs may not have been effective. However, this is not the case. The man-agement actions will be tied to the Pillars of Cost and Value in Chapter 3 – Costs. The output quantity and quality volumes will be tied to the Pillars of Value and Price in Chapter 4 – Revenue.

Figures 2.5, 2.6, and 2.7 are comparable even given the obvious differences (i.e., species, geographic area, volume units, and inputs). These figures' shapes reflect the classic sigmoidal curves associated with natural production systems. To illustrate why, the shapes in Figures 2.5, 2.6, and 2.7 take as given a fixed land area; for example, an acre or hectare. The land starts with no vegetation and is seeded, relatively uniformly, by the surrounding trees. The seeds germinate within a reasonable period of time and the seedlings can be considered all of the same age or even-aged. At this young age, there is very little if any competition for the fixed quantities of area, sunlight, water, and nutrients. And while there may be some mortality, there is positive net volume growth per unit area for the surviving trees. This positive net volume growth per acre for the surviving trees will prob-ably increase for a number of years, and the measure of volume per unit area will increase. Competition for the fixed quantities of sunlight, water, and nutrients plus physiological changes will eventually cause an increase in mortality resulting in a decline in positive net volume growth per unit area for the surviving trees. But the measure of total volume per unit area will still increase. In time, again due to resource constraints plus stand dynamic and physiological changes, the volume loss due to mortality will be greater than the volume growth of any surviving trees and the measure of total volume per unit area will decrease. This results in the sigmoidal curves illustrated in Figures 2.5, 2.6, and 2.7 with volume per unit area increasing until mortality is greater than growth of the surviving trees and volume per unit area will decline.[18]

Graphical depictions of total product curves for physical or manufacturing sys-tems will also follow a shape similar to Figures 2.5, 2.6, and 2.7. The reasoning is analogous; namely, changing the amount of a variable input given a constrain-ing resource or some fixed capacity. In the ISO Beam application, Patterson et al. (2002) describes a production line. Each machine performs a specific task in pro-ducing an ISO beam and has a physical limit or a fixed capacity. Labor is a variable input. As labor is added initially, output produced per unit labor will increase but there will be a point when adding additional labor will cause output produced per unit labor to decrease. The reason for this is the Law of Diminishing Returns:[19]

When increasing quantities of a given variable input are added to fixed quan-tities of some other factors, first the change in output per unit change of the identified input and then the output per input for the identified input will eventually decrease.

In fact any natural, physical, or manufacturing production process must follow the Law of Diminishing Returns, *ceteris paribus*.[20] The reason total product graphs of the Select Red Oak and Radiata Pine applications have similar shapes is due to the Law of Diminishing Returns and physiological changes in the forest (Mead 2013).

In 2011 the State University of New York College of Environmental Science and Forestry installed 108 Sharp 224BX 224-Watt (W) panels in a two-array system (Figure 1.2) in Tully, NY. The 24.192-kilowatt solar array came online in January 2012. Figure 2.9a shows the total product as measured by total monthly energy converted – kilowatt-hours (kWh) – from 2012 to 2014.[21]

Figure 2.9b shows the total product as measured by hourly energy converted – kilowatt-hours (kWh) –on 1 February and 1 July 2012 and 2014.

Do these graphs reflect the nature of this production system? Obviously, solar arrays will only convert insolation into a more usable energy form when the sun shines. *Ceteris paribus*, insolation is the strongest during the summer months (Figure 2.9a) and midday (Figure 2.9b). Longer days allow for more energy conversion (Figure 2.9b). Thus, the empirical data shown in Figures 2.9a and 2.9b agree with our understanding of the production process. While Figures 2.9a and 2.9b agree with our understanding of the production process, the horizontal axes of these figures – months in Figure 2.9a and hours in Figure 2.9b – is not an explicit input in equation (2.4). As stated previously, insolation is not an input controlled by a manager; however, what is important to the manager is how much energy is being

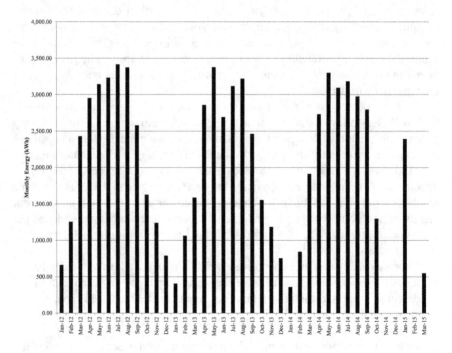

Figure 2.9a State University of New York College of Environmental Science and Forestry's 24.192-Kilowatt Solar Array Monthly Energy Conversion: 2012–2014

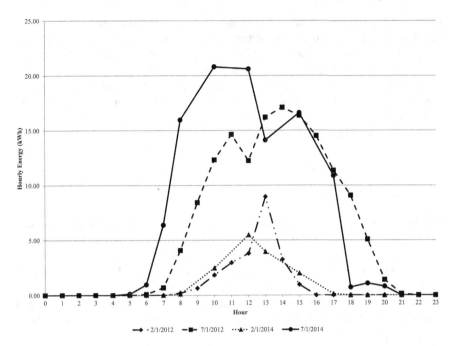

Figure 2.9b State University of New York College of Environmental Science and Forestry's 24.192-Kilowatt Solar Array Hourly Energy Conversion: 1 February and 1 July 2012 and 2014

converted and when.[22] In general, residential energy consumption has two peak periods – summer (July or August) and winter (January), with summer generally having a higher peak (Electric Power Monthly – www.eia.gov/electricity/monthly/ accessed 22 November 2016). In addition, residential hourly energy consumption ramps up starting between 5:00am and 7:00am with a second surge starting at around 4:00pm and peaking around 7:00pm to 8:00pm (Demand for electricity changes through the day – www.eia.gov/todayinenergy/detail.php?id=830 accessed 22 November 2016). Examining Figures 2.9a and 2.9b shows how energy conversion from the Tully Solar Array matches with energy consumption, which is of concern; namely, the Pillars of Value and Price for the output.

I made the following statement earlier: In fact, *any* production process must follow the Law of Diminishing Returns. Figures 2.9a and 2.9b look quite different from Figures 2.5 and 2.6 and seem to show this solar array does not follow the Law of Diminishing Returns.[23] For the purpose of this discussion the solar panel area, photovoltaic material, and power rating are fixed inputs and insolation is the variable input. A solar array converts insolation into electrical energy as shown by equation (2.4). It would seem as insolation increases, energy conversion would also increase. However, as insolation increases, so does solar panel and ambient air temperature as insolation also contains heat. According to the chemical properties of the photovoltaic materials and the physics of the conversion process, as panel temperature increases conversion efficiency decreases and less energy is converted.[24] So while converting insolation to energy using solar must follow the Law of Diminishing Returns, the empirical data presented in Figures 2.9a and 2.9b would not reflect it as dramatically as in Figures 2.5 and 2.6 given the insolation levels available in Tully, NY. What is of more concern for solar is power loss in general (not just loss from heat). For example, each 39.1-inch × 64.6-inch Sharp ND-224UC1BX 224 W solar module in Tully, NY (Figure 1.2) has an efficiency of 13.7% given standard test conditions:

$$0.137 = \frac{224 \text{ W}}{\left(1000 \text{ } W\!/_{\!m^2} \times 1.6296 \text{ m}^2\right)}$$

In addition, according to the panel label of these Sharp modules, power decreases by 5% for every 1° centigrade (1.8° Fahrenheit) increase in panel temperature.[25]

Revisiting the Law of Diminishing Returns' definition, shows it includes two key concepts of the production process: (1) the change in output per unit change of the identified input and (2) output per input for the identified input. These are in fact the next two descriptors of the production system. The first defines marginal product and the second defines average product. Each will be discussed, starting with average product.

Average Product (AP)

Average product is calculated by dividing total output by the level of a variable input necessary to produce that level of output and is given in equation (2.7):

$$AP = \frac{Q(x_j)}{x_j} \tag{2.7}$$

where
$Q(x_j)$ denotes the production system output holding all other inputs and factors constant or fixed except the jth variable input, x_j.

Table 2.8 shows the AP for Select Red Oak.

$$\frac{638 \dfrac{bd.ft.}{tree}}{30 \text{ } inch} = 21.3 \dfrac{bd.ft.}{\dfrac{tree}{inch}}$$

There are three important points which need to be highlighted about this calculation. First, the input site index is held constant – in this case the site index is equal to 66. Second, the units given to AP must be determined correctly or the interpretation of AP will be meaningless in terms of economic information. The units on

Table 2.8 Select Red Oak Net Total, Average, and Marginal Product[‡]

D	Total Product	Average Product	Mid-D	Marginal Product
1	0			
5	7	1.4	2.5	1.8
10	47	4.7	7.5	8.0
15	135	9.0	12.5	17.7
20	274	13.7	17.5	27.6
25	449	18.0	22.5	35.1
30	638	21.3	27.5	37.7
35	810	23.2	32.5	34.5
40	941	23.5	37.5	26.1
45	1014	22.5	42.5	14.5
50	1026	20.5	47.5	2.4
55	986	17.9	52.5	−8.0

[‡] D denotes diameter at breast height measured in inches
Total Product is measured as net board foot volume per tree – International 1/4 (bd.ft./tree) given a site
index of 66
Mid-D denotes the reference diameter for marginal product
Average Product is measured as bd.ft./tree/inch
Marginal Product is measured as bd.ft./tree/inch
For example, the AP for a 30-inch diameter Select Red Oak is

output are defined as net board feet per tree – International 1/4 (bd.ft./tree). The units on the input diameter are measured in inches. Therefore, the units on any AP given in Table 2.8 are bd.ft./tree/inch. Third, the interpretation of the preceding AP calculation is that for every inch in diameter the tree grew between 0 and 30 inches, the tree gained 21.3 net board feet of volume.

Given the information in Table 2.5 and equation (2.7), calculate AP for the Select Red Oak holding diameter constant at 25 inches and allowing site index to vary. What are the units on the results? What is the interpretation of AP?

A form of AP unique to forest management is mean annual increment (MAI) given by equation (2.8)

$$AP = \frac{Q(x_j)}{x_j} = \frac{Volume}{year} = MAI \tag{2.8}$$

Table 2.9a shows the AP or MAI calculations for the Radiata Pine application.

$$\frac{499\frac{m^3}{ha}}{20\,years} = 25.0\,\frac{\frac{m^3}{ha}}{year}$$
$$= 25.0\,m^3 ha^{-1} yr^{-1}$$

As before, there are three important points that must be highlighted about this calculation. First, the fixed input site index is held constant. Second, the units given to MAI must be determined correctly or the interpretation of MAI will be meaningless in terms of economic information. The units on output are defined as cubic meters per hectare (m³/ha). The units on the input are plantation age measured in years. Therefore, the units on any MAI given in Table 2.9a are m³/ha/year or m³ha⁻¹year⁻¹.

Table 2.9a Annual Radiata Pine Plantation Data – Total Product or Total Volume; Average Product (AP) or Mean Annual Increment (MAI); and Marginal Product (MP) or Current Annual Increment (CAI)

	Unpruned				Pruned				
Planta-tion Age	Total Volume[†] MAI (m³/ha)	AP MAI (m³/ha/yr)	MP CAI (m³/ha/ yr)	Manage-ment Action[‡]	Planta-tion Age	Total Volume[†] (m³/ha)	AP MAI (m³/ha/ yr)	MP CAI (m³/ha/ yr)	Management Action[‡]
0				Planting	0				Planting
1				Herbicide	1				Herbicide
2				Herbicide	2				Herbicide
3	1.2	0.4			3	1.4	0.5		
4	4.8	1.2	3.7		4	5.7	1.4	4.4	
5	13.1	2.6	8.3	DS	5	15.5	3.1	9.8	DS
6	27.7	4.6	14.6	DS	6	32.7	5.4	17.2	DS+Pruning
7	49.8	7.1	22.1		7	57.3	8.2	24.6	PCT
8	79.5	9.9	29.7	PCT	7	34.2	4.9		
8	51.2	6.4			8	53.2	6.7	19.0	Pruning+PCT
9	74.7	8.3	23.5		8	40.3	5.0		
10	102.4	10.2	27.7		9	55.5	6.2	15.2	
11	133.9	12.2	31.5		10	73.6	7.4	18.1	
12	168.5	14.0	34.6		11	97.3	8.8	23.7	
13	205.5	15.8	37.1		12	126.8	10.6	29.5	
14	244.6	17.5	39.1		13	159.2	12.2	32.4	
15	285.2	19.0	40.6		14	194.0	13.9	34.8	
16	327.0	20.4	41.8		15	230.7	15.4	36.7	
17	369.6	21.7	42.6		16	268.9	16.8	38.2	
18	412.8	22.9	43.1		17	308.3	18.1	39.4	
19	456.1	24.0	43.3		18	348.6	19.4	40.3	
20	499.0	25.0	43.3		19	389.4	20.5	40.8	
21	542.4	25.8	43.3		20	430.4	21.5	41.0	
22	585.9	26.6	43.6		21	471.2	22.4	40.7	
23	629.5	27.4	43.6		22	512.4	23.3	41.2	
24	673.0	28.0	43.5		23	553.9	24.1	41.5	
25	716.2	28.6	43.2		24	595.5	24.8	41.6	
26	759.0	29.2	42.8		25	637.1	25.5	41.6	
27	801.3	29.7	42.2		26	678.6	26.1	41.5	
28	842.9	30.1	41.6		27	719.8	26.7	41.2	
29	883.8	30.5	40.9		28	760.5	27.2	40.7	
30	923.9	30.8	40.1		29	800.7	27.6	40.2	
					30	840.4	28.0	39.7	

For example, the MAI for the 20-year old radiata unpruned pine plantation is
[†] Total Volume is measured as cubic meters per hectare (m³/ha) and is calculated based on the simulated management regime described previously.
[‡] DS – *Dothistroma septosporum* spray. PCT – Precommercial Thinning

Third, the interpretation of the preceding MAI calculation is that between the plantation ages of 0 and 20, the plantation grew 24.95 cubic meters per hectare per year. However, the column entitled Average Product in Table 2.8 is *not* equivalent to MAI as the measure of volume was *not* divided by time or year.

The Law of Diminishing Returns states that AP will decline at some point. This can be seen in Table 2.8 and graphically in Figure 2.10 for Select Red Oak.

For Select Red Oak the decline occurs at a diameter of 45 inches. Table 2.9b provides the simulation results of the unpruned Radiata Pine Plantation for 50 years. Figure 2.11 shows that AP or MAI will decline starting at plantation age of 40 years.

Examining Figure 2.11 also shows that at plantation age 8 a precommercial thinning was completed. This is illustrated by a drop in MAI at stand age 8. As would be expected, this same management action was also illustrated in the graph of yield (or total volume) in Figure 2.8 at plantation age 8.

Comparing Figure 2.12 with Figure 2.9a reveals that they have the same shape. Basically, average daily energy conversion by month is monthly total energy conversion divided by the number of days in the month. As the denominator is basically a constant, the shape of the average daily energy conversion is the same as the monthly total energy conversion.[26] Basically, Figure 2.12 does not provide any additional understanding of this production system. The reason why is important. Figure 2.1e provides a list of the relevant inputs and output. Equation (2.4) describes the technical relationship between inputs and the output. As discussed previously, insolation is basically the only variable input, with the rest being fixed.

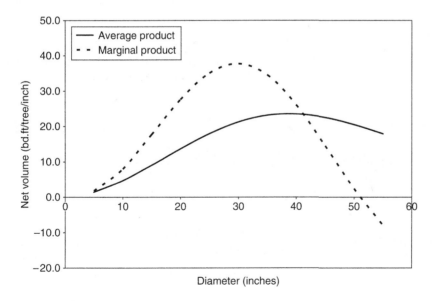

Figure 2.10 Select Red Oak Average and Marginal Product

Given site index (S) = 66 feet

Table 2.9b Five-Year Unpruned Radiata Pine Plantation Data – Total Product or Total Volume; Average Product (AP) or Mean Annual Increment (MAI); and Marginal Product (MP) or Five-Year Periodic Annual Increment (PAI)

Plantation Age	Total Volume[†] (m³/ha)	AP MAI (m³/ha/yr)	PAI Age	MP PAI (m³/ha/yr)
0	0			
5	13.1	2.6	2.5	2.6
10	102.4	10.2	7.5	17.9
15	285.2	19.0	12.5	36.6
20	499.0	25.0	17.5	42.8
25	716.2	28.6	22.5	43.4
30	923.9	30.8	27.5	41.5
35	1111.5	31.8	32.5	37.5
40	1278.5	32.0	37.5	33.4
45	1424.9	31.7	42.5	29.3
50	1550.9	31.0	47.5	25.2

[†] Total Volume is measured as cubic meters per hectare (m³/ha) and is calculated based on the simulated management regime described previously.

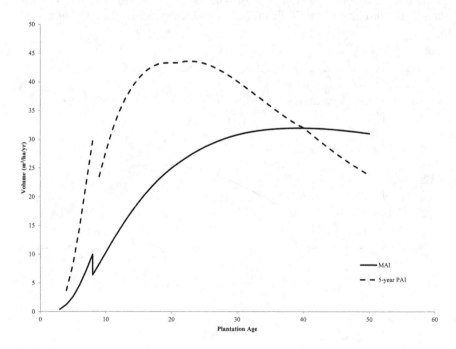

Figure 2.11 Unpruned Radiata Pine Plantation Mean Annual Increment (MAI) and Five-Year Periodic Annual Increment (PAI), Given the Management Regime Defined Previously

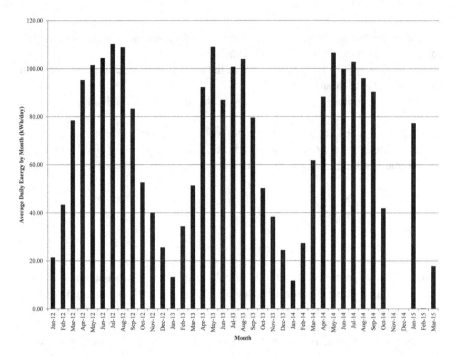

Figure 2.12 State University of New York College of Environmental Science and Forest-ry's 24.192-Kilowatt Solar Array Average Daily Energy Conversion by Month: 2012–2014

Furthermore, insolation is not under the control of the manager, and what is impor-tant to the manager is how much energy is being converted and when (Figures 2.9a and 2.9b). Consequently, just because you can estimate an average product for a production system mathematically does not mean it will provide you with any additional insight into the production system or economic information for follow-ing the Architectural Plan for Profit. Be cognizant of how the economic informa-tion will be used – do not just focus on how to calculate the economic information.

Marginal Product (MP)

Marginal product is defined as the change in output per unit change of the identified variable input and is given by equation (2.9)

$$MP = \frac{\Delta Q(x_j)}{\Delta x_j} = \frac{Q(x_j) - Q(x_{j-1})}{x_j - x_{j-1}}$$
(2.9)

where

$Q(x_j)$ denotes the production system output holding all other inputs and factors constant or fixed except the jth variable input, x_j;

$\Delta Q(x_j) = Q(x_j) - Q(x_{j-1})$ denotes change in the output given a per unit change in the identified variable input x_j; and

$\Delta x_j = x_j - x_{j-1}$ denotes the per unit change in the identified variable input x_j.[27]

The fifth column of Table 2.8 shows the MP of diameter on net volume per tree given site index set at 66 for Select Red Oak. For example, the MP of a change in net volume resulting from changing diameter from 20 to 25 inches is:

$$\frac{(449-274)\dfrac{bd.ft.}{tree}}{(25-20)\,inches} = 35.1\,\dfrac{bd.ft.}{\dfrac{tree}{inch}}$$

Three points are important about this calculation. First, the input site index is held constant – in this case site index is equal to 66 feet. Second, the units given to MP must be determined correctly or the interpretation of MP will be meaningless in terms of economic information. The units on output are defined as net board feet per tree – International 1/4 (bd.ft./tree). The units on the input diameter are measured in inches. Therefore, the units on any MP given in Table 2.8 are bd.ft./tree/inch. Third, the interpretation of the preceding MP calculation is that for every inch in diameter the tree grew between 20 and 25 inches, the tree gained 35.1 net board feet of volume. Given the information in Table 2.5 and equation (2.9), calculate MP for the Select Red Oak, holding diameter constant at 25 inches and allowing site index to vary. What are the units on the results? What is the interpretation of MP?

A form of MP unique to forest management is current annual increment (CAI) and periodic annual increment (PAI) and is given by equation (2.10):

$$MP = \frac{Q(x_j) - Q(x_{j-1})}{x_j - x_{j-1}} = \frac{\Delta Q(x_j)}{\Delta x_j} = \frac{\Delta Volume}{\Delta year} \tag{2.10}$$

By convention, if $\Delta x_j = \Delta year = 1$ then

$$MP = \frac{Q(x_j) - Q(x_{j-1})}{x_j - x_{j-1}} = \frac{"Q(x_j)}{"x_j} = \frac{\Delta Volume}{\Delta year} = \frac{\Delta Volume}{1} = CAI$$

and if $\Delta x_j = \Delta year > 1$ then

$$MP = \frac{Q(x_j) - Q(x_{j-1})}{x_j - x_{j-1}} = \frac{\Delta Q(x_j)}{\Delta x_j} = \frac{\Delta Volume}{\Delta year} = PAI$$

Table 2.9a shows the CAI calculations for the pruned and unpruned Radiata Pine applications. For example, the CAI for plantation age 23 is

$$\mathrm{CAI}_{23} = \frac{(629.5 - 585.9)\dfrac{m^3}{ha}}{(23 - 22)\,year} = 43.6\,\frac{\dfrac{m^3}{ha}}{year}$$

$$= 43.6\ m^3 ha^{-1} yr^{-1}$$

Table 2.9b shows the PAI calculations for the Radiata Pine application. For example the PAI for plantation age between 20 and 25 years old (or a reference plantation age of 22.5) is

$$\mathrm{PAI}_{22.5} = \frac{(716.2 - 499.0)\dfrac{m^3}{ha}}{(25 - 20)\,year} = 43.4\,\frac{\dfrac{m^3}{ha}}{year}$$

$$= 43.4\ m^3 ha^{-1} yr^{-1}$$

There are four important points about interpreting these calculations. First, the input site index is held constant with site index defined as a medium site. Second, the units of CAI and PAI must be determined correctly or their interpretation will be meaningless in terms of economic information. The units on output are defined as cubic meters per hectare (m³/ha or m³ha⁻¹). The units on the input are plantation age measured in years. Therefore, the units on any CAI or PAI given in Tables 2.9a and 2.9b, respectively, are m³/ha/year or m³ha⁻¹yr⁻¹, which are the same as on MAI. Third, the interpretation of the PAI calculation is that between the plantation ages of 20 and 25 or for that specific five-year period, the plantation grew 43.4 cubic meters per hectare per year. For the one-year period between plantation ages 22 and 23, the plantation grew 43.6 cubic meters per hectare per year. The smaller the periodicity (Δx_j or Δyear), the more accurate the growth estimates. Finally, the column entitled Marginal Product in Table 2.8 is *not* equivalent to CAI or PAI as the measure of volume was *not* divided by time or year.

The Law of Diminishing Returns states that MP, CAI, or PAI product will decline at some point. This can be seen in Tables 2.8, 2.9a, and 2.9b; however, Figures 2.10 and 2.11 show this decline readily. For Select Red Oak the decline occurs at a diameter of 35 inches, and for unpruned and pruned Radiata Pine application the decline occurs at plantation age 23 and 25, respectively.

Examining Figure 2.11 also shows that at plantation age 8, a precommercial thinning was completed on the unpruned Radiata Pine Plantation. This is illustrated by a drop in total volume (Figure 2.8), a drop in MAI (Figure 2.11), and a discontinuous drop in CAI at plantation age 8.

Revisiting the definition of MP in equations (2.9) and (2.10) (and for that matter AP in equations (2.7) and 2.8)) shows it is calculated using a relevant variable input. In the Select Red Oak and Radiata Pine practical applications, this is the case. However, for the solar array system example most of the inputs are fixed and total and average product are displayed using months, hours, and days. Moreover months, hours, and days are not inputs in this example production system nor used in estimating energy conversion using equation (2.4). Furthermore, calculating marginal product with respect to months, days, or hours would provide the manager with no additional useful economic information, as these are not controlled by the manager directly. In addition, calculating marginal product with respect to insolation would also not provide any useful economic information as the manager cannot make incremental production decisions using this critical input. A similar conclusion was reached in the discussion of average product. As it has broader implications, it bears repeating:

The economic descriptors of total, average, and marginal product are meant to provide additional economic information about the production system with respect to the Architectural Plan for Profit (Figures 2.1a to 2.1f). Just because they could be calculated does not mean they should be calculated. If calculating any of these descriptors provides the entrepreneur no useful economic information then do not calculate them.

Total Versus Average Versus Marginal Product

Comparing and contrasting the graphs of TP versus AP and MP is instructive.[28] Figure 2.13 shows the graphs of TP, AP, and MP for the Select Red Oak application. Figure 2.14 shows the graphs of yield, MAI, and CAI for the unpruned Radiata Pine application.[29]

Four points follow from this analysis. First, the horizontal axes on the graphs of TP and AP and MP have the same scale. For example, in Figure 2.13 the horizontal scale of TP, AP, and MP is diameter (inches), and in Figures 2.14 the horizontal scale of yield, MAI, and CAI is plantation age (years). The vertical axes on the graphs of TP and AP and MP have different scales. In Figure 2.13, the vertical scale of the TP graph is bd.ft./tree while the vertical scale of the AP and MP graph is bd.ft./tree/inch. In Figure 2.14, the vertical scale of the yield graph is m³/ha while the vertical scale of MAI and CAI is m³/ha/year. This difference in scale is important in interpreting each graph.

Second, according to the Law of Diminishing Returns, "first the change in output per unit change of the identified input and then the output per input for the identified input will eventually decrease." In other words, MP (CAI or PAI) will be the first to decrease followed by AP (MAI). This can also be seen in Figures 2.13 and 2.14. Analyzing Figure 2.14, at a young age when there was little competition for area, sunlight, water, and nutrients the trees grew rapidly and volume per hectare increased quickly. This is illustrated in Figure 2.14 by examining the total volume (TP) curve and CAI (MP) curve. Between stand ages of 0 and 25, the Radiata Pine Plantation is growing rapidly as shown by the CAI curve, and total volume is

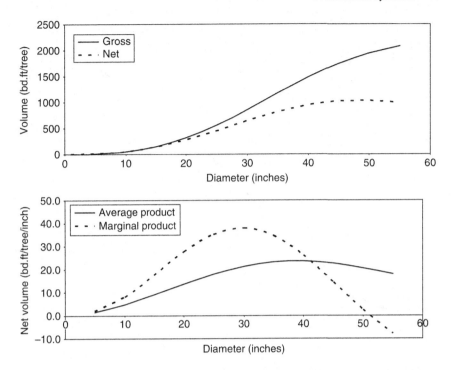

Figure 2.13 Select Red Oak Total, Average, and Marginal Product, Given Site Index (S) = 66 Feet

also increasing quickly. After stand age 25, mortality due to competition increases and while there is still positive net growth, the net growth has slowed as has the increase in total volume. Again, by examining the CAI and total volume curves in Figure 2.14, you can see that after stand age 25 the net growth is still positive, though it is decreasing, as illustrated by the CAI curve. And while total volume is increasing it is increasing more slowly, illustrated by the total volume curve. It is left to the reader to develop a similar argument for describing the relationship between TP and MP for Select Red Oak given in Figure 2.13.

Third, examining Figure 2.14 shows that whenever MP (CAI or PAI) is greater (less) than AP (MAI), AP (MAI) is increasing (decreasing). In the case of the unpruned Radiata Pine application, CAI describes the growth of trees at a given point in time and MAI describes the growth of the trees from when they were planted to a point in time. If the current growth of the trees is greater than the average growth, then the average growth will increase. If the current growth of the trees is less than the average growth, then the average growth will decrease.[30] It is left to the reader to develop a similar argument for describing the relationship between MP and AP for Select Red Oak given in Figure 2.13. An additional relationship between margins and averages also apparent by examining Figures 2.13 and 2.14 – when AP is at its maximum value MP equals AP (MAI = PAI or MAI = CAI). In

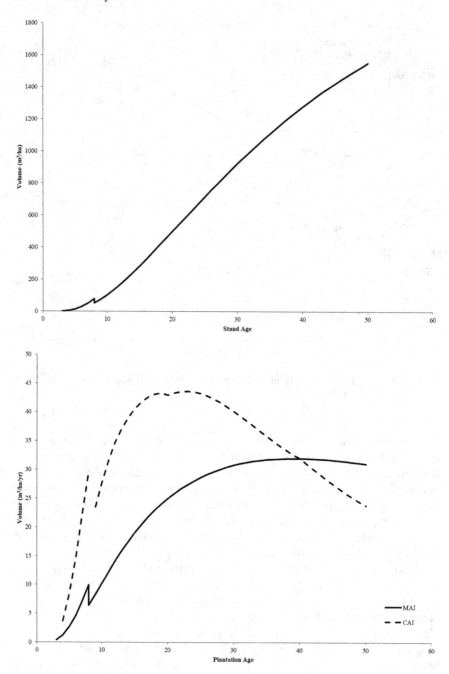

Figure 2.14 Unpruned Radiata Pine Yield, Mean Annual Increment (MAI), and Current Annual Increment (CAI), Given the Management Regime as Defined Previously

Given the management regime as defined previously

forest management, when CAI or PAI equals MAI, this is called the culmination of mean annual increment (CMAI) or the maximum sustained yield rotation (Johansson and Löfgren 1985; Samuelson 1976b). A rotation age defined by CMAI would give the maximum volume or biomass production per acre over multiple rotations.

Fourth, while it seems obvious, every point on the TP curve has a corresponding point on the AP and MP curves. This can be observed in Figure 2.14 with respect to the precommercial thinning. To better illustrate this concept, I will use the Wisconsin Oak data from Gevorkiantz and Scholz (1948). The net yields (TP), mean annual increment (AP), and periodic annual increment (MP) are given in Table 2.7 and graphically in Figure 2.15.

As both the net yields (TP) graph and the MAI (AP) and PAI (MP) graph have the same vertical axis, a vertical line can be drawn between the two graphs to illustrate this analytically. I will highlight three such points. The first point is where PAI (MP) is maximized. This is shown by the vertical line labeled *A*. To the left of this line net volume is increasing at an increasing rate. A rotation aged defined by maximizing PAI would give the maximum growth of the stand. The second point is where MAI (AP) is maximized and MAI = PAI (AP = MP). This is shown by the vertical line labeled *B*. A rotation aged defined at this point is maximum sustained yield. The third point is where yield (TP) is maximized and where PAI = 0 (MP = 0). This is shown by the vertical line labeled *C*. A rotation age defined by this point would give the maximum volume production for a single rotation. A final observation possible with Figure 2.15 is that between lines *A* and *C* net volume is

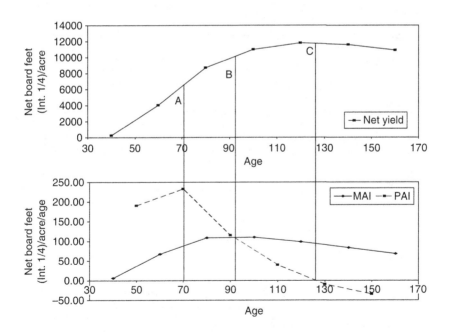

Figure 2.15 Unthinned Oak Stand in Southwestern Wisconsin (Medium Site)

increasing but at a decreasing rate. To the right of line *C* net volume is decreasing at an increasing rate.

Noncontinuous Production Systems

Not every production process can be depicted with a smooth graph as with the Select Red Oak application. For example, the Micromill® and ISO Beam practical applications describe production processes that require a production line or a series of sequential steps to convert a log into a final product. Each step must be completed before the input can move to the next step. I will concentrate on the ISO Beam application and the production process described by Patterson et al. (2002). Given the fixed nature of the existing capital equipment (e.g., the machines listed in Table 2.1), labor, and the sequential steps required by the production process as defined by Patterson et al. (2002), the ISO Beam mill's daily total product with respect to the variable input stems per day is limited to three feasible output levels. This is shown in Figure 2.16.

While it would be possible to draw a line between the points shown in Figure 2.16, this line would imply that technically efficient production levels between the two points are possible by varying the input level. The production levels are either 464, 696, or 928 beams per day, not 580 or 812 ISO beams per day.

There are three possible reasons for a noncontinuous production process. First is the binary nature of the technology of one or more machines used in the production

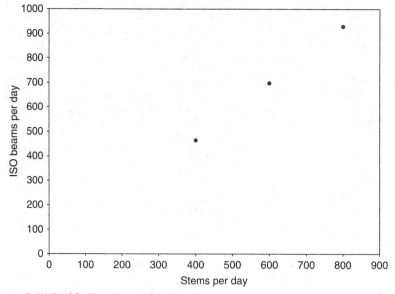

Figure 2.16 Inside-Out Beam Total Product
Based on data from Patterson et al. (2002)

process; it is either on or off. If it is on, the technically efficient point is to run the machine at its physical capacity due to the high fixed resource costs. Zudak (1970) uses the example of an open-hearth furnace in steel fabrication to illustrate this idea:

> They cannot in general be started and stopped at random because the cost is too high. Failure to cool or heat the furnaces very gradually (over a period of several weeks) causes severe damage to their linings. Even after being correctly cooled, several days are required to rebrick certain parts of the system damaged by cooling. During a production period, furnaces are run at capacity or not used at all.
>
> Zudak (1970: 257–258)

A kiln is similar, in some respects, to an open-hearth furnace. Drying schedules prescribe the time required to dry commercial wood safely (e.g., Boone et al. 1988). These schedules should be followed regardless of whether the kiln is full. Thus, for example, splitting a load in half does not reduce the drying time by half, but doubles the drying time for the whole load. While splitting the load in half will reduce the amount of energy used per half load, the total energy required to dry both halves is greater than if the load is dried as a single unit. Consequently, it is more efficient to run kilns at full capacity. This implies that total product is a point as shown in Figure 2.16.

Second, the production process requires several steps to produce the finished product. Figure 2.3 illustrates the steps of the production process for manufacturing an ISO beam. Each step must be completed before the next step can be started. Some machines (e.g., cut-off saw, moulder, quarter and trim saws) will take a minimum amount of time to complete a step. For example, a quarter saw has a maximum feed rate defined by its physical characteristics (e.g., motor power and speed, band saw or circular saw, etc.). These physical characteristics define the minimum amount of time required to, for example, quarter a cant of a given species and length. Thus, total product is always a point defining the minimum amount of time required to complete a step.[31]

Third, some inputs (e.g., labor) are not homogenous in the production process. Each step may require a different set of skills and/or a minimum number of employees per step. In this case increasing the input labor by a single homogenous employee will not increase output. This conclusion is similar to that discussed by Zudak (1970). According to Patterson et al. (2002), new capital equipment (i.e., boiler, kilns, and pre-dryers) is required to increase output. Again, total product is defined as a point. In addition, average and marginal product have no meaning. While it is true that adding a single homogenous employee will decrease average product – from equation (2.7), the numerator is constant while the denominator increases, the decrease is due to an increase in technical inefficiency, not the Law of Diminishing Returns. Thus, due to the noncontinuous nature of the production process, marginal produce may also not reflect the Law of Diminishing Returns accurately.[32]

As a result of the prior three reasons, the total product for the ISO Beam case study is defined as three input–output combinations; that is, 400, 600, and 800 stems per day producing 464, 696, and 928 beams per day, respectively (see Figure 2.16). Given the series of sequential steps required in the production process, the fixed nature of the capital equipment, the kilns, and nonhomogeneous labor, total product is increasing as the number of stems per day increases until it is constrained physically by the capacities of the boiler, kiln, and pre-dryer. Thus, technical efficiency would logically be described as a point, and marginal and average product have no meaning. The only way to increase production to greater than 464 beams per day, for example, is to purchase more capital equipment in terms of boilers, kilns, and pre-dryers. As a manager, you will need to recognize a noncontinuous production process and what is causing the process to be noncontinuous. It is the causes of the noncontinuity that the manager should focus their attention on initially.

Production System – Variability

A reader could get the impression, perhaps based on what I have presented so far, that production systems once defined systematically (i.e., by answering the three fundamental questions with sufficient detail) are constant or static. This is far from the truth. As the capital equipment described in the Mobile Micromill® and the ISO Beam practical applications are used, they wear out. As discussed previously, nature is not constant: Maple sap flows, insolation varies year to year, and tree growth is not constant (as seems to be implied by equations (2.5) and (2.6) and Figures (2.5) and (2.6)). Assessing variability requires the entrepreneur to have numerical measurements on the inputs that can be tied to numerical measurements on the outputs. I will illustrate this using the solar array system.

The conversion of insolation into a more usable energy form is dependent on the amount of insolation (Wh/m^2) that reaches the array (refer to equation (2.4)). As stated previously, the amount of insolation that reaches the array is not an input the entrepreneur can control directly. Basically, there is a degree of variability associated with this input. To illustrate this variability, I will use the National Solar Radiation Data Base (https://nsrdb.nrel.gov/data-sets/tmy accessed 29 August 2023) developed by the National Renewable Energy Laboratory describing the typical meteorological year (TMY).[33] The global horizontal irradiance data collected at Syracuse International Airport in Syracuse, NY, is converted to kilowatt-hours (kWh) using a 13.7% efficiency for the Sharp solar modules and a default performance ratio of 0.75. These estimated energy values are overlaid on the hourly conversion graphs for the Tully Solar Array in Figures 2.17a and 2.17b.

Examining Figure 2.17a illustrates that observed energy converted on 1 February 2012 and 2014 was less than the estimated energy converted from 1 February of a TMY. Examining Figure 2.17b illustrates the observed energy converted on 1 July 2012 and 2014 was greater than the estimated energy converted from 1 July of a TMY. The vertical distance between the observed and the estimated hour energy points in Figures 2.17a and 2.17b illustrates a measure of variability.

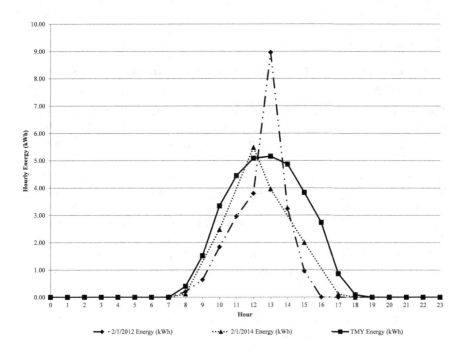

Figure 2.17a State University of New York College of Environmental Science and Forestry's 24.192-Kilowatt Solar Array Hourly Energy Conversion: 1 February 2012 and 2014, Compared to the Typical Insolation Input Based on Data From https://nsrdb.nrel.gov/data-sets/tmy (accessed 29 August 2023)

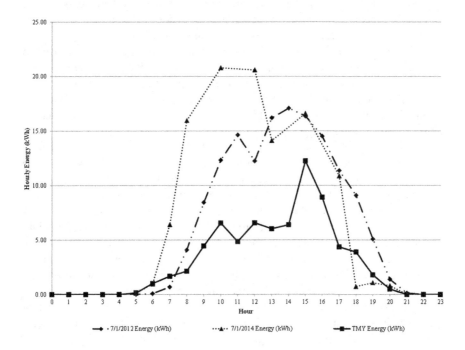

Figure 2.17b State University of New York College of Environmental Science and Forestry's 24.192-Kilowatt Solar Array Hourly Energy Conversion: 1 July 2012 and 2014, Compared to the Typical Insolation Input Based on Data From https://nsrdb.nrel.gov/data-sets/tmy (accessed 29 August 2023)

How to Use Economic Information – Production Systems – to Make Better Business Decisions

The following non-forestry example taken from the news illustrates the important relationship between measurement and management. In December 1998, the National Aeronautics and Space Administration (NASA) launched the Mars Climate Orbiter. The purpose of the orbiter was to collect information about the atmospheric temperature on Mars and the dust, water vapor, clouds, and the amount of carbon dioxide (CO_2) that is added and removed from the poles each Martian year. In addition, the orbiter was to assist in data transmission to and from the Mars Polar Lander. On September 23, 1999, the orbiter burned up in the Mars atmosphere. A review of the incident showed that one team of scientists used English units (e.g., inches, feet, and pounds) while another team used metric units (e.g., centimeters, meters, and kilograms). Incorrect information was given to the orbiter during the critical maneuvers required to place it in the proper Mars orbit. As a result NASA lost the $125 million Mars Climate Orbiter (https://www.jpl.nasa.gov/missions/mars-climate-orbiter accessed 29 August 2023; https://mars.nasa.gov/mars-exploration/missions/polar-lander/ accessed 29 August 2023).

Lord Kelvin (1825–1907) recognized the relationship between measurement and management: "If you cannot measure it, you cannot improve it." Maital (1994: 8) built on this idea by stating: "What you cannot measure, you cannot effectively understand, control, or alter." A slight modification of this quote is often given as: "If you cannot measure it, you cannot manage it." If your measurements are not correct (e.g., incorrect units), your management decision based on this information may turn out to be disastrous. So, don't crash the Mars Orbiter.

To address the statement provided in the section's heading, I will first need to identify the economic information obtained from the production system. Simply put, the production system contains the physical input–output relationships necessary to describe technical efficiency leading to minimizing production costs and maximizing profits as illustrated in Figures 1.4 and 2.1a. These are determined by answering the following three questions:

1. What are the relevant fixed and variable inputs? The relevant inputs are those that you the manager have direct control over and are pertinent to production decisions that change output(s) levels in terms of quantity and quality. Answering this question must help you build the Pillars of Cost and Value for the inputs given in the Architectural Plan for Profit (Figure 2.1b). Diameter at breast height in the Select Red Oak practical application and insolation in the solar array system example could be considered critical inputs, but neither will help the entrepreneur build the Pillars of Cost and Value, as there are no observable opportunity costs associated with either the quantity or quality of these inputs. While it is obvious that these inputs add value to the output given the production process (review equations (2.4), (2.5), and (2.6)) for building the Pillars of Price and Value for the output, again they are not controlled directly by the entrepreneur with respect to changing output levels in terms quality and quantity. If

labor is involved in managing either the Select Red Oak stand or solar array, is this input included in equations (2.4), (2.5), or (2.6)?

2. What are the outputs? Answering this question must help you build the Pillars of Value and Price for the output given in the Architectural Plan for Profit (Figures 2.1a, 2.1d, 2.1e, and 2.1f).[34] The output characteristics of quantity and quality have a direct correlation with how consumers value the output (Pillar of Value) and their willingness and ability to pay for the output and your pricing decisions (Pillar of Price). For example, select red oak trees with larger diameters are valued more highly by consumers. Consumers' willingness and ability to pay and your pricing decisions will be discussed in more detail in Chapter 10 – Supply and Demand and Chapter 11 – Market Equilibrium and Structure.

3. How do you describe the production process analytically? Economic efficiency (profit model) requires production cost efficiency (least cost model) which requires technical efficiency (production system model). Thus, without a sufficient analytical description of the production process, the foundational economic information necessary to follow the Architectural Plan for Profit is not readily available to help answer future questions dealing with cost, value, price, and profit.

Final Thoughts

A purely physical measure of input(s)–output(s) relationships such as total, average, and marginal product ignores factors such as input costs and values and output prices and values. Production systems do not produce values; rather they produce outputs that individuals assign values to in a given context.

Appendix 2A – Marginal Versus Average Product

Marginal product (MP) is defined as the change in output per unit change of the identified input. In mathematical terms MP defines a rate of change (or slope) at a specific point on the total product curve or production function. The slope of a point on a curve is calculated by taking the first derivative of the function with respect to the identified input. Let $Q(x_1, x_2, \ldots, x_j)$ or $Q(\bullet)$ denote the system of producing a good or providing a service, Q, using inputs that the manager has direct control over, $x_1, x_2, \ldots, x_j$. MP for the ith input is defined as:

$$MP = \frac{\partial Q(x_1, x_2, \ldots, x_j)}{\partial x_i} = \frac{\partial Q(\bullet)}{\partial x_i}; i = 1,2,3,\ldots j \tag{A.1}$$

Mathematically, MP can only be calculated for production processes that are continuous; for example, the Select Red Oak practical application. MP is calculated for a range of outputs, not for just the last unit produced as shown in Tables 2.7 through 2.9.

Figures 2.10 and 2.11 show that when MP is greater than average product (AP), AP is increasing, and when MP is less than AP, AP is decreasing. Finally, these figures show that when MP equals AP, AP is at its maximum. These relationships can be illustrated mathematically by using the definition of AP and its first derivative with respect to an identified input. Equation (A.2) defines AP:

$$AP = \frac{Q(x_1, x_2, x_3, \dots, x_j)}{x_i} = \frac{Q(\bullet)}{x_i}; i = 1, 2, 3, \dots, j \tag{A.2}$$

Taking the first derivative of AP with respect to x_i using the quotient rule and simplifying gives:

$$\frac{\partial AP}{\partial x_i} = \frac{1}{x_i} \frac{\partial Q(\bullet)}{\partial x_i} - \frac{Q(\bullet)}{x_i^2}$$

$$= \frac{1}{x_i} \left(\frac{\partial Q(\bullet)}{\partial x_i} - \frac{Q(\bullet)}{x_i} \right) \tag{A.3}$$

$$= \frac{1}{x_i} (MP - AP)$$

Analyzing the last expression of equation (A.3) shows that if MP > AP then $\partial AP / \partial x_i$ > 0 or AP is increasing. If MP < AP then $\partial AP / \partial x_i$ < 0 or AP is decreasing. Finally, if MP = AP then $\partial AP / \partial x_i$ = 0 and AP is at its maximum.

An additional relationship can be developed using both MP and AP; namely, a production elasticity. A production elasticity defines the relative change in producing a good or providing a service given a relative change from an additional unit of input, or the percentage change in producing a good or providing a service relative to the percentage change in input, holding all else constant. This is given in equation (A.4):

$$\varepsilon_{prod} = \frac{\partial Q(\bullet) / \partial x_i}{Q(\bullet) / x_i} = \frac{MP_i}{AP_i}$$

$$= \frac{\partial Q(\bullet) / Q(\bullet)}{\partial x_i / x_i} = \frac{\% \Delta Q(\bullet)}{\% \Delta x_i} \tag{A.4}$$

where $\% \Delta$ denotes a percentage change. If the production elasticity is greater than one, then $\% \Delta Q(\bullet) > \% \Delta x_i$ and MP > AP. If the production elasticity is equal to one, then $\% \Delta Q(\bullet) = \% \Delta x_i$ and MP = AP. If the production elasticity is less than one, then $\% \Delta Q(\bullet) < \% \Delta x_i$ and MP < AP.

Notes

1 Stumpage is the merchantable volume – as measured by quantity (thousand board feet or cubic meters) and quality (log grade) – of a standing tree.

2 This is a summary of a more detailed discussion contained in the Chapter 1 – Introduction.

3 I would challenge the reader to create a map between this quote from Becker et al. (2004) and (i) the Architectural Plan for Profit, (ii) the Managerial Analytical Method, and (iii) the three fundamental production system questions. Hint: Think about Figures 2.1a to 2.1e and equations (2.1) to (2.3).

4 Fixed inputs such as capital define the scale or size of the business. For example, it's easier to hire and fire labor (a variable input) than it is to significantly change the size of the business by purchasing a new evaporator or additional land for a sugar bush. The time horizon in which the scale of the operation is fixed is defined as the short run (generally one year or less). The time horizon in which the scale of the operation can be changed is defined as the long run (generally greater than one year).

5 The terminology and units associated with solar or wind conversion are power – the "rate" at which energy is generated or used. Power is measured in terms of watts (W), kilowatts (kW = 1,000 W), or megawatts (MW = 1,000 kW).

Energy is a measure of how much "fuel" is contained within something or used by something over a specified time period and is in a form we can use to run the lights, heat homes, and charge cell phone batteries, and so on. Energy is measured in terms of watt-hours (Wh), kilowatt-hours (kWh), or megawatt-hours (MWh).

6 The solar array system example is interesting. Not all the potential insolation is used; some is reflected by the solar array. Is this reflected insolation (including heat) waste? In addition, a life cycle analysis of a solar array from manufacturing to installing to disposing the photovoltaic cells does create toxic waste.

7 This key component has been taken from the definition of a production function as given by Carlson (1974), Henderson and Quandt (1980), and Silberberg and Suen (2001).

8 These quantitative and qualitative relationships are the basis of the popular expression: If you cannot measure it, you cannot manage it. However, I would be remiss if I did not acknowledge the difficulty of identifying metrics for measuring outcomes such as spiritual qualities. For example, New Zealand's local indigenous Maori people speak of preserving or enhancing the life-force (mauri) as their management goal, and this is problematic to measure systematically. I am indebted to Dr. Donald Mead, Professor Emeritus, Lincoln University, Lincoln, New Zealand, for reminding me of this issue.

9 Site index is a species-specific measure of actual or potential forest productivity expressed in terms of the average height of trees included in a specified stand component at a specified index or base age. Site index is often used as an indicator of site quality and productivity. The higher the site index for a given index or base age the better the site quality and productivity. The base age used by Hahn and Hansen is 50 years, and height is measured in feet.

10 Diameter at breast height is the diameter of a tree measured 4.5 feet (1.37 meters) above the ground on the uphill side of the tree.

11 I am indebted to Dr. John Moore of Scion for providing various radiata pine management simulations and Dr. Don Mead, Professor Emeritus, Lincoln University, Lincoln, New Zealand, for guidance on the economics and management of radiata pine.

12 Based on the estimated annual revenue and average price per ISO beam provided by Patterson et al. (2002), I challenge the reader to calculate the total number of ISO beams that must be produced annually and the number of day per year required to produce this number of ISO beams. Finally, does Patterson et al. (2002) provide a reasonable argument that this number of ISO beams can be actually sold annually?

13 Simulation models such as Forecaster, NED (https://www.fs.usda.gov/research/nrs/products/dataandtools/software accessed 29 August 2023), Silva (https://www.fs.usda.gov/research/nrs/products/dataandtools/software accessed 29 August 2023), FVS (https://www.fs.usda.gov/fvs/software/index.shtml accessed 29 August 2023) are very useful management tools. However, I would caution the reader to gain a full understanding of these tools so as to use them properly; as the old saying goes: Garbage in – Garbage out.

14 A precommercial thin (or thin to waste) is done prior to trees reaching merchantable size. A commercial thin is an intermediate harvest removing merchantable volume that covers all or part of the harvesting costs.

15 In geometric terms the volume of a cylinder or cone is a function of diameter and height. Calculating the volume of a tree or log is the same as calculating the volume of a cylinder or cone. Thus, for biometricians whose end goal is to calculate volume (not profit), a measure of diameter – diameter at breast height – and height – site index – are sufficient for describing the system.

16 The USDA Forest Service's *Forest Inventory and Analysis National Core Field Guide* give the grading factors for hardwood and softwood trees (USDA FS FIA 2006).

17 Interpreting the concept of technical efficiency should be done with caution given the production process for the select red oak. The idea of technical efficiency has been defined traditionally with respect to the classical definition of a production function (e.g., see Carlson 1974; Henderson and Quandt 1980; Silberberg and Suen 2001). The inputs given in a classical production function can all be controlled directly by the manager. Thus, the manager can manipulate the use of the inputs to increase efficiency. In the case of the select red oak, the manager cannot manipulate an input such as diameter at breast height directly; therefore, concept of productivity is more appropriate for this application and is analogous to technical efficiency.

18 Figure 2.8 illustrates only the portion of the sigmoidal curve where volume is increasing at an increasing rate. Table 2.9b illustrates these radiata pine will exhibit the sigmoidal curve. In addition, Mead (2013: 71–73) provides more detailed explanation of why total volume curve will have a sigmoidal shape.

19 This definition is based on those provided by Rideout and Hesseln (2001) and Pearce (1994).

20 The Law of Diminishing Returns requires at least one variable and one fixed input; thus, if all inputs are fixed or variable the Law of Diminishing Returns does not hold. In economic analysis, capital is often fixed in the short run (generally one year or less) and thus production processes follow the Law of Diminishing Returns. However, in the long run (generally greater than one year) capital is also variable; namely, an entrepreneur can purchase additional capital changing the production process.

21 The data collection system software failed in November 2014 and the hardware and software are being updated.

22 Insolation is measured in terms of watt-hours per square meter (Wh/m^2). While a manager cannot control the amount of insolation on the array's surface (e.g., cloud cover), based on the market price for the electricity, a manager could decide to convert or not to convert energy.

23 Please note this is not a book on physics, chemistry, or electrochemical processes and concepts are discussed in very general terms.

24 Conversion of insolation into energy must follow the First and Second Laws of Thermodynamics. The maximum efficiency of solar conversion is given by the Shockley–Queisser limit for single positive–negative junction to collect energy and Carnot's theorem on thermodynamics.

25 The efficiency also increases by 10% for every 1° centigrade (1.8° Fahrenheit) decrease in panel temperature.

26 An interesting measure of average product is energy return on energy invested (EROEI/ERoEI). EROEI is the ratio of the useable energy acquired (or output), often measured by Btus or joules, from a particular energy resource to the energy expended (or input), again measured by Btus or joules, to obtain the output energy at a given point in time:

$$EROEI = \frac{\text{Useable Acquired Energy}}{\text{Energy Expended}} = \frac{\text{Output}\left[Q(x)\right]}{\text{Variable Input}\left[x\right]}$$

27 By convention, when using equation (2.9) to estimate marginal product, the midpoint between $x_j - x_{j-1}$ is used as the reference. This is illustrated in Table 2.8 with respect to Select Red Oak.

28 Appendix 2A provides a calculus-based discussion comparing average and marginal product.

29 While the same information is in Tables 2.8 and 2.9, it may be easier to see on the graphs.

30 A different example that you may be more familiar with is if this semester's grade point average is greater than your cumulative grade point average, then your cumulative grade point average will increase. However, if this semester's grade point average is less than your cumulative grade point average, then your cumulative grade point average will decrease.

31 Sourd (2005) has developed a mathematical model that examines this problem in greater detail.

32 For average product to be increasing, MP > AP. Thus, the increased inefficiency is also reflected in marginal product, and marginal product does not reflect the Law of Diminishing Returns.

33 A typical meteorological year (TMY) data set provides designers and other users with a reasonably sized annual data set that holds hourly meteorological values that typify conditions at a specific location over a longer period of time, such as 30 years. TMY data sets are used widely by building designers and others for modeling renewable energy conversion systems. The TMY data set is composed of 12 typical meteorological months (January through December) that are concatenated essentially without modification to form a single year with a serially complete data record for primary measurements. These monthly data sets contain actual time-series meteorological measurements and modeled solar values, although some hourly records may contain filled or interpolated data for periods when original observations are missing from the data archive (www.nrel.gov/docs/fy08osti/43156.pdf accessed 2 December 2016).

34 While I will not discuss the problems that waste can have on profits, you as a manager should also be aware that waste is an output of the production process and must be included in your analyses.

3   Costs

Preamble

A common description of profit is what is left over after all costs have been paid regardless of the revenue from outputs produced or services provided. This common description highlights the significance of costs. In addition, I would posit that an entrepreneur has more managerial control over costs than revenues. For example, revenue depends on a customer purchasing the output. This purchase decision is the customer's; the entrepreneur will influence this decision as discussed in Chapter 10 – Supply and Demand and Chapter 11 – Market Equilibrium and Structure, but it is ultimately the customer's decision. The entrepreneur does make decisions directly about inputs and costs (the Pillars of Cost and Value for inputs). This leads me to the conclusion that if entrepreneurs do not manage or control costs, they will lose control of profits.

This conclusion is supported strongly by the following authors:

> Analyzing product costs are important critically for businesses because they help reduce costs, price products at competitive prices, and enable strategic decision-making.
>
> (Andersch et al. 2013: 623)

> It is critical that loggers understand their costs and production capabilities on a wide spectrum of jobs to negotiate a contract that will allow them to thrive and invest in their businesses over the long term.
>
> (Germain et al. 2016: 104)

> The ability to develop value-added products by using small-diameter ponderosa pine is in part contingent on the ability of finished products to compete in the marketplace. Transportation and processing costs need to be minimized to make processing small-diameter logs more competitive.
>
> (Becker et al. 2004: 3)

> The key to a successful maple syrup operation is controlling production to maintain an acceptable profit margin. It is important that sugarbush operators

DOI: 10.4324/9781315678719-3

keep accurate records so that areas of high cost can be identified and steps taken to reduce them.

(Huyler 2000: 5)

Why Are Costs and Values Important?

The conclusion from the preamble bears repeating: If entrepreneurs do not manage costs, they will lose control of profits. The Pillar of Cost represents the entrepreneur's opportunity cost of buying input(s) used in the production process. Just as there are markets for outputs, there are corresponding markets for inputs. Just as a market price is paid by a customer purchasing a good or service, a market price or wage must be paid by the entrepreneur for inputs used in the production process. Thus, the entrepreneur's knowledge of their input markets must be just as strong as their knowledge of their output markets. The Pillar of Value represents the degree to which the entrepreneur thinks buying the input or production technology makes them better off than if they did without; namely, the value they add to the output's quantity and quality. Simply, if an input does not add value to the output, an entrepreneur will not buy it. Therefore, the Pillars of Cost and Value of the Architectural Plan for Profit will be examined first (see Figures 3.1a and 3.1b).

Figures 3.1a and 3.1b show the Pillars of Cost and Value are built on the foundation of the production system. As described in Chapter 2 – Production Systems, answering the questions What are the relevant fixed and variable inputs? and How do you describe the production process analytically? must help you build these pillars. If an input is identified as relevant, then how it is used in the production process must be measured numerically in terms of quantity and/or quality. First, however, I will discuss how costs are part of the two economic models given in Chapter 1 – Introduction and Chapter 2 – Production Systems and describe the practical applications used in this chapter.

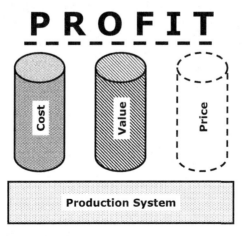

Figure 3.1a Cost: The Architectural Plan for Profit

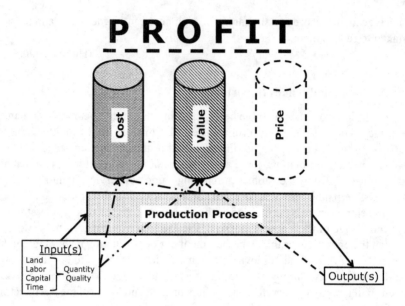

Figure 3.1b Cost: The Expanded Architectural Plan for Profit

Managerial Analytical Models

As shown by the Managerial Analytical Method (Figure 1.4) and the Architectural Plan for Profit (Figures 3.1a and 3.1b), the profit model builds on the least cost/cost effective model. The profit model is given by equation (3.1).

$$\begin{aligned}
\text{Max } \Pi &= \text{TR} - \text{TC} \\
&= P \cdot Q(x_1, x_2, ..., x_j) - \text{TVC} - \text{TFC} \\
&= P \cdot Q(\bullet) - \sum_j w_j \cdot x_j - \text{TFC}
\end{aligned} \tag{3.1}$$

The least cost model is given by equation (3.2).

$$\text{Min TVC} = \sum_j w_j \cdot x_j$$

s.t. $\hspace{5cm}$ (3.2)

$$Q(x_1, x_2, ..., x_j) = Q^0$$

The cost effective model is given by equation (3.3).

$$\text{Max } Q(x_1, x_2, ..., x_j)$$

s.t. $\hspace{5cm}$ (3.3)

$$\sum_j w_j \cdot x_j = C^0$$

The model variables have been defined in detail in Chapter 2 – Production Systems. The relationship between these models has been discussed briefly in Chapter 1 – Introduction and Chapter 2 – Production Systems. I will now build on those discussions.

Profit, as defined in equation (3.1), is a simple but powerful analytical algebraic expression for describing, modeling, explaining, and predicting individual decision-making behavior. These same characteristics provide entrepreneurs and managers analytical tools to help make better business decisions. Given equation (3.1), profit is equal to total revenue minus total cost. Maximizing profit requires decisions that make total revenue as large as possible while simultaneously making total costs as small as possible for any given input(s)–output(s) combination. Therefore, if profits are to increase towards their maximum, then costs must be managed and minimized. Both equation (3.1) and equations (3.2) and (3.3) contain the same concept of costs. The optimal solution for equations (3.2) and (3.3) also requires managing and minimizing costs. Thus, the optimal solution to equation (3.1) is also an optimal solution for equations (3.2) and (3.3). The optimal input–output combinations resulting from solving equations (3.2) and (3.3) for different levels of output or budgets are defined as production cost efficient. Using the Rules of Inference (i.e., Hypothetical Syllogism, see Copi and Cohen (1998)), the optimal input–output combination resulting from equation (3.1) must also be defined as production cost efficient.[1]

Least Cost/Cost Effective Analytical Models – Revisited

Given the prior discussion, if solving the profit maximization problem also solves the least cost/cost effective problem, then why solve the least cost/cost effective problem?

An answer builds on the latter half of the statement: Maximizing profit requires decisions that make total revenue as large as possible *while simultaneously making total costs as small as possible for any given input(s)–output(s) combination.* Modeling this statement algebraically using equation (3.1) would imply that regardless of the total revenue, cost must be managed to be as small as possible in order to make the difference as large as possible in a given market structure: Minimizing costs is similar analytically regardless of market structure (Chapter 11 – Market Equilibrium and Structure). This facilitates analyzing the different fixed and variable input use given different market structures. Figures 3.1a and 3.1b illustrate minimizing costs – equations (3.2) and (3.3) – graphically. Managerially, the economic information you will require to build the Pillars of Cost and Value to minimize cost given different market structures is basically the same. Finally, I would argue that it is easier to think about profit maximization if it is divided into component parts as illustrated by the Managerial Analytical Method (Figure 1.4). Thus, the second and necessary step is minimizing costs (with technical efficiency being the first).

Dividing profits into its component parts implies that you will have to put them back together again to complete the analysis. Managing costs and the potential for cost savings alone will not guarantee profits (Maital 1994). Cost cutting alone without understanding the Pillars of Price and Value for the output will not help in generating the required revenues for profits.

Practical Applications

Two of the five practical applications used in this chapter, Inside-Out (ISO) Beams (Patterson et al. 2002; Patterson and Xie 1998) and the Mobile Micromill® (Becker et al. 2004), were used in Chapter 2 – Production Systems. Their summaries will not be repeated here.

Maple Syrup Operation (Huyler 2000)

The primary focus of this practical appliation will be on the sap collection component of a maple syrup operation as described by Huyler (2000). The secondary focus will be on the processing of sap into syrup and other maple sugar products as described by Heiligmann et al. (2006) and CFBMC (2000).

How Do I Describe the Production Process?

Maple syrup is made primarily from the sap of sugar maples (*Acer saccharum* Marsh.). Other sources of maple sap are black maple (*Acer nigrum* Michx. f.), red maple (*Acer rubrum* L.), and silver maple (*Acer saccharinum* L.) (Graham et al. 2006). The stand of maple trees where the sap is collected is called a sugarbush. Sap is collected starting in the late winter/early spring by tapping the trees (Chapeskie and Koelling 2006). The season length for the maple syrup–producing states has increased in length from 26 to 33 to 37 days for the period 2015 to 2017 (https://www.uvm.edu/sites/default/files/Agriculture/maple-nass-2017.pdf accessed 29 August 2023) and 27 to 29 to 33 days for the period 2020 to 2022 (https://www.nass.usda.gov/Statistics_by_State/New_York/Publications/Latest_Releases/2021/New%20York%20Maple%20Production%20Summary%202021.pdf accessed 29 August 2023; https://www.nass.usda.gov/Statistics_by_State/New_York/Publications/Latest_Releases/2021/New%20York%20Maple%20Production%20Summary%202021.pdf accessed 29 August 2023), illustrating the natural variability associated with maple syrup production. The taps are connected to a storage tank via vacuum tubing.[2] One tap produces approximately 10 to 20 gallons of sap per season depending on weather and the size, age, and health of the tree. The number of gallons of sap required to produce one gallon of syrup depends on the sap's percent sugar content as measured by a Brix scale and can be determined as 86 divided by the percent sap's Brix sugar content (Stowe et al. 2006).[3] The normal sugar content of sap is 1.5% to 3.5% measured using the Brix scale (Sendak and Bennink 1985). In the sugar house, water is evaporated from the sap using either a "batch type" or a "continuous-flow" evaporator concentrating the sugar into syrup (Graham et al. 2006; Stowe et al. 2006).

This leads to two observations. First, the higher the sugar content the fewer gallons of sap are required to produce one gallon of syrup. For example, 57 gallons of sap with a sugar content of 1.5% would be required to produce one gallon of syrup, while only 25 gallons of sap with a sugar content of 3.5% would be required to produce one gallon of syrup. Thus, the higher the sugar content of the sap, the less water has to be evaporated to concentrate the sugar into syrup. Second, for a given quantity of sap, the higher the sugar content, the more syrup can be produced using approximately the same inputs (Sendak and Bennink 1985). For example, the United States Department of Agriculture National Agricultural Statistic Service – Northeastern Regional Field Office provides statistics on syrup yields per tap for Maine, New Hampshire, New York, Pennsylvania, and Vermont. The average annual northeastern regional production was 0.244, 0.309, and 0.287 gallons of syrup per tap for the period 2021–2023 (https://www.nass.usda.gov/Statistics_by_State/New_England_includes/Publications/Current_News_Release/2023/Northeast-2023-Maple-Syrup-Report.pdf accessed 31 August 2023; https://www.nass.usda.gov/Statistics_by_State/New_England_includes/Publications/Annual_Statistical_Bulletin/2021/2021_NewEngland_Annual_Bulletin.pdf accessed 31 August 2023). The annual rates ranged from 0.223 to 0.269, 0.219 to 0.384, and 0.250 to 0.322 gallons of syrup per tap for the period 2021, 2022, and 2023, respectively. Vermont consistently had the highest yields per tap. These data illustrate that sugar content varies by year and by state.

What Are the Relevant Fixed and Variable Inputs?

Besides the sugarbush, Table 3.1 provides a list of the inputs for collecting sap. A similar list can be found in CFBMC (2000) for collecting sap; in addition, the authors of this study provide a list of inputs for further processing the sap. According to Huyler (2000) and CFBMC (2000), there is a fixed proportional relationship between the inputs and the number of taps used to collect the sap (see Table 3.1).

CFBMC (2000) estimates the labor input for collecting sap, maintaining the lines, and so forth at 4.08 minutes per tap, and Huyler (2000) estimates the labor input between 2.92 and 6.93 minutes per tap with an average of 4.74 minutes per tap. In addition to collecting sap, there are the inputs of converting sap into syrup and retail sales. These include, but are not limited to, an evaporator, energy, and a building. CFBMC (2000) estimates the labor input from collecting the sap, converting the sap into final products, and selling the products to range from 8.78 to 27.12 minutes per tap depending on the number of taps and type of evaporator.

What Are the Outputs?

The output can be defined as maple sap, syrup, sugar, cream, and candies. For the purposes of the case study, the output will be defined as either the number of taps, which is consistent with Huyler (2000) and CFBMC (2000), or gallons of syrup. Huyler (2000) and CFBMC (2000) use the following conversion factor: 1 tap produces approximately 10 gallons of sap with a sugar content of 2.15% and 0.25 gallons or 1 liter of syrup.

Table 3.1 Standard Equipment List for a Vacuum Tubing Sap Collection System

Item	Quantity
Nylon sap spout	1 per tap
5-16-inch sap tubing	15 feet per tap
½-inch mainline tubing	2 feet per tap
¾-inch mainline tubing	1.2 feet per tap
1-inch mainline tubing	0.7 feet per tap
5-16-inch connector	0.05 per tap
½-inch connector	0.02 per tap
¾-inch connector	0.012 per tap
1-inch connector	0.007 per tap
5-16-inch end cap	0.04 per tap
5-16-inch tee	1 per tap
4-way wye	0.02 per tap
1-× ¾-inch reducer	0.002 per tap
¾ × ½-inch reducer	0.004 per tap
Quick clamp	0.082 per tap
Aluminum fence wire	0.7 foot per tap
Quick clamp pliers	1 per operation
Wire ties	1 per operation
Wire tier	1 per operation
Fence wire stretcher	1 per operation
Spout puller	1 per operation
Sap vacuum pump	1 per operation
50-gallon vacuum storage tank	1 per operation
Snowshoes (pair)	1 per operation
Power tree tapper with battery pack	1 per operation
Tapping bit, bit file, and spark plug	1 per operation
Hand tool set	1 per operation

(Used with permission from the USDA Forest Service)

Great Lakes Charter Boat Fishing (Lichtkoppler and Kuehn 2003)

How Do I Describe the Production Process?

Charter boat fishing is a commercial recreation enterprise. One or more anglers hire or charter a boat, captain/guide, and maybe a crew for a half or full day of fishing for walleye, lake trout and salmon, steelhead, smallmouth bass, or yellow perch.

What Are the Relevant Fixed and Variable Inputs?

Table 3.2 lists the inputs as either operating or capital.[4]

What Are the Outputs?

The outputs are either a half or full day of a recreational fishing experience.

Table 3.2 Charter Boat Capital and Operating Inputs

Capital Inputs	
Boat	Tackle and Other Equipment

Operating Inputs	
Fuel/Oil	Boat maintenance and repair
Dockage	Office and communications
Labor (hired)	Boat storage fees
Equipment repair	Boat repair not covered by insurance
Advertising	License and fees
Miscellaneous	Drug testing/professional dues
Insurance	Boat launch fees

(Based on information given by Lichtkoppler and Kuehn 2003)

Knockdown Panel Furniture Fittings (Burdurlu et al. 2006)

Knockdown panel furniture (KPF) or "ready-to-assemble" furniture requires no glue or other permanent fastening systems to assemble. KPF is easy to transport and store and can be assembled with relative ease by the consumer. Furniture manufacturers have a choice among a number of different specialized fittings they can use:

> Each fitting requires different machinery and worker-supported processes for the connection of the fitting to the panel and the connection of the panels with fittings to each other. The differences affect processing time, and consequently, the production costs. Processing time could be negligible for a single fitting: however, it could constitute significant annual or long-term cost elements for mass or lot production of large numbers of furniture. Manufacturers should make cost analyses to determine which fitting should be used to lower costs of assembling the panels to each other with the fittings available in the market.
>
> (Burdurlu et al. 2006: 47)

Figure 3.2 illustrates the six different types of fittings used.

What Are the Outputs?

The outputs are not KPF. The focus of this practical application is to determine the least cost fitting to be used in producing a piece of KPF. According to Burdurlu et al. (2006: 48): "The least cost analysis was made using the data obtained to find the least cost fitting." Thus, the outputs are the installed fittings. As this is a least cost analysis, equation (3.2) can be used to express the economic model used by Burdurlu et al. (2006). The Q^0 of equation (3.2) would be equal to 1,000 installed

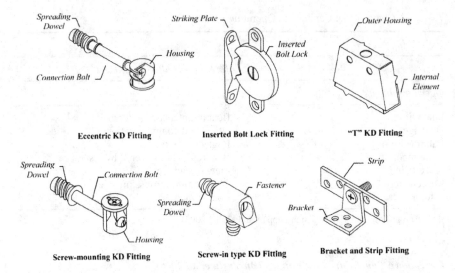

Figure 3.2 Knockdown Panel Furniture Specialized Fittings

Used with permission of the *Forest Products Journal* and Burdurlu et al. 2006

fittings for each of the six different types of fittings examined. The fittings are illustrated in Figure 3.2.

What Are the Relevant Variable Inputs?

Burdurlu et al. (2006) identified the relevant variable inputs as labor, energy, and materials. In terms of equation (3.2), labor, energy, and materials are the inputs for determining total variable cost.

How Do I Describe the Production Process?

The production process of interest describes the steps used to install each of the six fittings. These steps are described in Figure 3.3.

Review: Economics Versus Accounting

Chapter 1 – Introduction provides an example of the distinction between economic costs and accounting costs. The distinction between an accounting and economic cost is important and while I will only summarize the main points of that discussion, I recommend you reread that section in Chapter 1 – Introduction. Table 1.1 lists the annual costs and revenues associated with owning and operating a small hardwood sawmill. The costs are specified as explicit and implicit costs. Explicit accounting costs are those cash outlays that can be found on the cash flow statements, income statements, and balance sheet. The implicit costs are opportunity costs of the time and other resources a sawmill's owner makes available for production with no

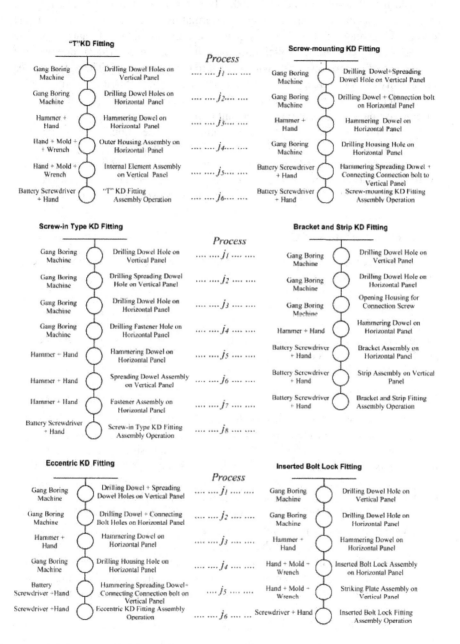

Figure 3.3 Steps to Install Knockdown Panel Furniture Fittings

Used with permission of the *Forest Products Journal* and Burdurlu et al. 2006

direct cash outlay (Field and Field 2002; Henderson and Quandt 1980). Implicit costs are not included in any accounting information. Nonetheless, they are a cost to you. The economic or opportunity cost – the highest-valued alternative forgone – is defined as the sum of explicit and implicit costs. Jensen (1982) reiterates the importance of opportunity costs with respect to management decisions. He defines opportunity costs with respect to production as the sum of explicit cash outlays plus the implicit costs of inputs that might be used in other ways to produce more or different outputs. These define the relevant production costs.

The disciplines of accounting and economics both use some of the same terminology with respect to costs. As shown by Table 1.1, explicit costs by themselves do not represent all that is forgone or given up to continue an action. Thus, the relevant cost information needed to make better management decisions with respect to the Architectural Plan for Profit must include both explicit and implicit costs.

Economic Descriptors of Cost

There are three main descriptors of cost: total cost, average cost, and marginal cost. I will address each in turn.

Total Cost (TC)

Examining equation (3.1) reveals that total cost is the sum of total variable cost (TVC) plus total fixed cost (TFC) or TC = TVC + TFC.

Total Fixed Costs (TFC)

Total fixed costs are costs associated with inputs that are constant, for various reasons, during the production process. In other words, these costs are constant no matter how much is produced or provided in the short run.[5] In the business management literature these fixed costs are described as overhead and sales, general and administrative.

- Overhead costs relate to output production costs such as electricity, cleaning, heating, and depreciation of capital equipment.
- Sales, general, and administrative are all costs that relate to the business entity not directly tied to producing the outputs. These costs are associated with administrative aspects of the business entity; for example, front office and management salaries, non-manufacturing rent, depreciation of non-manufacturing capital, advertising, marketing, accounting, litigation, travel, meals, and bonuses.

In the agricultural farm budgeting literature, these fixed costs are described as the "DIRTI-5":[6]

- Depreciation – Capital equipment wears out as the result of producing or providing an output, age, and obsolescence (Pearce 1994). If allowed by law, depreciation is an "annual noncash expense" that reduces annual taxable net revenue. A purpose of depreciation is to allow the owners of capital the opportunity to save the funds needed to replace the capital. Using depreciation as current income rather than its intended use can have negative consequences with respect to financial loss, equity erosion, and profitability (Germain et al. 2016). The steps to determine an annual straight-line depreciation are

1. Subtract the estimated salvage value from the asset's purchase price.[7]
2. Determine the estimated useful economic life of the asset.
3. Divide the result from Step 1 by the result from Step 2.

- Interest – Payments made to banks or other lenders for the use of money to purchase capital equipment.[8]
- Rent/Repairs – Payments made to the owners of land and capital equipment that are used by, but not owned by, the business, and annual maintenance and repair costs for the upkeep of capital equipment and buildings.
- Taxes – Payments that are usually incurred on capital equipment, land, and buildings.
- Insurance – Costs of protecting the business against fire, weather, theft, and the like.

Managing fixed costs is necessary for managing costs as described in the Preamble. Unnecessary fixed costs are the killer of business. Simply, these are paid whether you produce or not. You want these to be as small as possible. If your equipment, for example, is not right sized for your production system (Pillar of Cost), they will not add sufficient value (Pillar of Value) for their cost. Consequently, think long and hard before committing your organization to any fixed costs.

For the maple syrup operation's practical application, "the annual fixed cost for sap equipment and other fixed costs such as taxes and insurance were included in total fixed costs" (Huyler 2000: 1). The annual equipment fixed costs included a straight-line deprecation schedule and 8.5% interest charge on capital equipment and insurance payments. These costs are reported on an annualized basis.[9] Tables 3.3a and 3.3b give the total fixed costs.

Table 3.3a shows the total fixed costs for different-sized operations. Table 3.3b shows the total fixed costs for a 12,000-tap operation. According to the definition of fixed costs, they should be constant. However, in Table 3.3a, they appear to be increasing. Due to the fixed proportional relationships described in Table 3.1 as the size of the operation increases, the fixed costs will also increase. Table 3.3b shows that if the sugarbush has a 12,000-tap capacity (or producing 3060 gallons or 11,583 liters of syrup per year) and you have the collection equipment necessary for this production level, the fixed costs are constant whether you produce 0, 6000, or 12,000 taps. Thus, for a given sugarbush size, the fixed costs of collecting the sap are constant. The CFBMC (2000) report shows the same pattern for the total fixed costs associated with the processing of the sap into syrup and retailing or wholesaling of the final products.

Table 3.3a Annual Sap Collection Costs by Size of Operation – Maple Syrup Application (1998 USD)[§]

Number of Taps	Gallons of Syrup	Total Variable Costs		Total Fixed Costs		Total Cost ($)
		Labor ($)	Material ($)	Equipment (annual) ($)	Tax ($)	
500	127.5	260	260	1,750	50	2,320
1,000	255	520	370	2,170	100	3,160
2,000	510	1,040	600	3,020	200	4,860
3,000	765	1,560	840	3,870	300	6,570
4,000	1,020	2,080	1,040	4,720	400	8,240
5,000	1,275	2,600	1,300	5,350	500	9,750
6,000	1,530	3,120	1,500	6,420	600	11,640
7,000	1,785	3,640	1,750	7,210	700	13,300
8,000	2,040	4,160	1,920	8,080	800	14,960
9,000	2,295	4,680	2,160	8,910	900	16,650
10,000	2,550	5,200	2,400	9,800	1,000	18,400
11,000	2,805	5,720	3,080	12,650	1,100	22,550
12,000	3,060	6,240	3,360	13,680	1,200	24,480

[§] 1998 USD denotes 1998 US dollars
(Used with permission from the USDA Forest Service)

Table 3.3b Annual Sap Collection Costs for a 12,000-Tap Operation – Maple Syrup Application (1998 USD)[§]

Number of Taps	Gallons of Syrup	Total Variable Costs		Total Fixed Costs		Total Cost ($)
		Labor ($)	Material ($)	Equipment (annual) ($)	Tax ($)	
500	127.5	260	260	13,680	1,200	15,400
1,000	255	520	370	13,680	1,200	15,770
2,000	510	1,040	600	13,680	1,200	16,520
3,000	765	1,560	840	13,680	1,200	17,280
4,000	1,020	2,080	1,040	13,680	1,200	18,000
5,000	1,275	2,600	1,300	13,680	1,200	18,780
6,000	1,530	3,120	1,500	13,680	1,200	19,500
7,000	1,785	3,640	1,750	13,680	1,200	20,270
8,000	2,040	4,160	1,920	13,680	1,200	20,960
9,000	2,295	4,680	2,160	13,680	1,200	21,720
10,000	2,550	5,200	2,400	13,680	1,200	22,480
11,000	2,805	5,720	3,080	13,680	1,200	23,680
12,000	3,060	6,240	3,360	13,680	1,200	24,480

[§] Cost data based on information from Huyler (2000); 1998 USD denotes 1998 US dollars
(Used with permission from the USDA Forest Service)

In the Mobile Micromill® practical application, the fixed costs were made up of financing the Mobile Micromill® and the supporting equipment and the fixed costs associated with siting the mill (Becker et al. 2004).[10]

Table 3.4 and Figure 3.4 show that the fixed costs for the first year included the down payments and the financing costs on the Mobile Micromill® and the supporting equipment and the siting costs. For the next four years, the fixed costs included

Table 3.4 Fixed Costs for the Mobile Micromill®

Item	Year						
	1	2	3	4	5	6	7
Down Payments							
Mobile Micromill	129,956.00						
Tractor-Loader	6,450.00						
Forklift	12,900.00						
Maintenance Vehicle	4,838.00						
Financing							
Mobile Micromill	70,609.00	70,609.00	70,609.00	70,609.00	70,609.00	70,609.00	70,609.00
Tractor-Loader	4,267.00	4,267.00	4,267.00	4,267.00	4,267.00		
Forklift	8,534.00	8,534.00	8,534.00	8,534.00	8,534.00		
Maintenance Vehicle	3,200.00	3,200.00	3,200.00	3,200.00	3,200.00		
Site Lease & Preparation	3,000.00	3,000.00	3,000.00	3,000.00	3,000.00	3,000.00	3,000.00
	243,754.00	89,610.00	89,610.00	89,610.00	89,610.00	73,609.00	73,609.00

Annual production level of 3,600 thousand board (MBF) of product
(Used with permission from the USDA Forest Service)

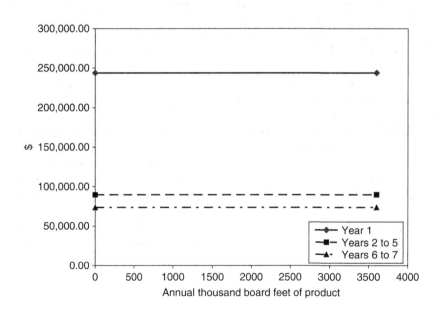

Figure 3.4 Fixed Costs for the Mobile Micromill®

Used with permission from the USDA Forest Service

Table 3.5 Average Annual Operating Costs for New York
Boat-Owning Captains (2002 USD)[§]

Item	Cost
Fuel/Oil	$1,895
Advertising	$1,200
Labor (hired)	$1,168
Equipment repair	$1,115
Dockage	$1,096
Miscellaneous	$901
Insurance	$831
Boat repair and maintenance	$717
Office and communications	$531
Boat storage fees	$429
Boat repair not covered by insurance	$276
Drug testing/Professional dues	$92
License fees	$91
Boat launch fees	$33
Total Operating Cost	$11,093

[§] 2002 USD denotes 2002 US dollars. As the sum of averages
generally does not equal the average of sums, the sum of the
cost column does not equal the total operating cost.
(Based on information given by Lichtkoppler and Kuehn 2003)

the finance costs of the Mobile Micromill® and the supporting equipment and the siting costs. In the final two years of the analysis, the fixed costs included the financing costs of the Mobile Micromill® and the siting costs.[11] Again these costs should be constant. While it is true that there are three levels of fixed costs during an eight-year period, these costs are invariant with respect to how much output is produced or sold. The costs change due to factors not associated with production; namely, contracts signed with the banks for financing capital equipment. In the case of the Mobile Micromill®, the loan period was for eight years while the support equipment was for five years.

Table 3.5 gives the annual operating cost for the Great Lakes Charter Boat Fishing (Lichtkoppler and Kuehn 2003) example. The cost data provided by Lichtkoppler and Kuehn (2003) do not distinguish explicitly between operating expenses that are fixed versus variable. In the Inside-Out Beams example, the capital equipment purchase prices are given but costs are not distinguished as fixed or variable costs per se (Patterson et al. 2002; Patterson and Xie 1998). The primary fixed costs are loan payments on the capital equipment. It is left to the reader to determine why the Knockdown Panel Furniture Fittings application does not include fixed costs.

Total Variable Costs (TVC)

Total variable costs are associated with inputs that the manager can manipulate during the production process. In other words, variable costs change with the level of output produced or provided.[12] As with fixed costs, there is a direct relationship between the answer to the What are the relevant fixed and variable inputs? question from Chapter 2 – Production Systems and TVC. This relationship is illustrated by equations (3.1), (3.2), and (3.3). Specifically, the description of the production system, $Q(x_1, x_2, \ldots, x_j)$, is based on inputs, $x_1, x_2, \ldots, x_j$, the manager controls directly – those inputs that are relevant to following the Architectural Plan for Profit systematically. These same inputs are used in defining TVC or wage (w) times input (x), $\sum_j w_j \cdot x_j$. Given this, it is possible to show this direct relationship between the production system and TVC graphically. Figure 3.5(a) depicts a generic production system using only one input to produce one output; its shape is dictated by the Law of Diminishing Returns as defined in Chapter 2 – Production Systems. Figure 3.5(b) is the same production system with the axes flipped; namely, the Output, $Q(x)$, is now on the horizontal axis and the Input, x, is now on the vertical axis. Finally, as defined TVC $= w \cdot x$, multiplying the vertical axis Input, x, by its wage, w, converts the production system graph into a TVC graph as shown in Figure 3.5(c).

The Knockdown Panel Furniture Fittings example focused solely on the variable production costs which is why there are not fixed costs in the analysis. The three inputs under direct control of the manager were labor, energy, and materials. The unit labor costs were $4.20 per hour. The eccentric fitting used the least hours of labor while the screw-in fitting used the most. The unit energy costs were $0.12 per kilowatt-hour. Two machines – a gang boring machine and chargeable drill/drivers – were used to install the fittings. In terms of energy consumption, inserted bolt lock and T fittings used the least electricity, and the screw-in fitting used the most. The material costs varied with fitting type. The least expensive was the screw-in at $0.022 per fitting and the most expensive was the screw-mounting

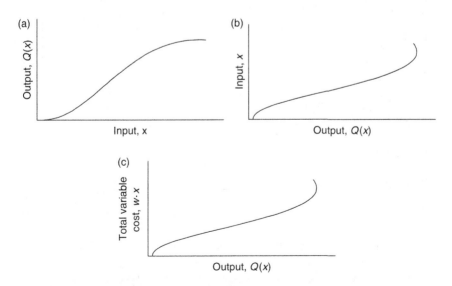

Figure 3.5 The Relationship Between the Production System and Total Variable Cost

at $0.299 per fitting. Total variable costs ranged from a high of $0.387 per fitting for the screw-mounting to a low of $0.146 per fitting for the screw-in type.[13]

For the Maple Syrup Operation application, the "labor, materials, tap rental, and miscellaneous expenses were combined for each operation to determine the variable annual operating cost per tap" (Huyler 2000: 2). Tables 3.3a and 3.3b give the total variable costs of sap collection. In the sap collection component, labor performs four tasks: (1) preparing, (2) tapping, (3) tub checking and repair, and (4) cleanup and storage. According to Huyler (2000), the average labor requirement to perform these four tasks is 4.74 minutes per tap. Assuming a wage of $6.40 per hour as the variable labor cost (Table 3.3a), the variable labor costs for a 12,000-tap operation given in Table 3.3b are the same as those in Table 3.3a. This is due to the fact that the relationship between the time to complete the four tasks does not vary with respect to the number of taps. Thus, if the sugarbush has a 12,000-tap capacity (or producing 3060 gallons or 11,583 liters of syrup per year) and only produces 2000 taps (or 510 gallons or 1931 liters of syrup), the variable labor costs are $1040. The materials costs (e.g., paint, wire, coding tags, gas, oil, etc.) also vary with the level of output, but not in the same fixed manner as with labor. The variable costs are shown graphically in Figure 3.6.

The variable costs of the Mobile Micromill® were operation and maintenance costs of the mill (e.g., sharpening saw knives and blades, maintaining the sawdust blower, in-feed and out-feed decks, and diesel engine) and support equipment, labor (e.g., one operator, one log sorter/loader, two laborers on the green chain handling the outputs), fuel and oil for the Mobile Micromill® and support

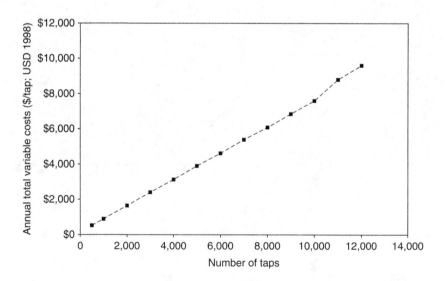

Figure 3.6 Annual Total Variable Sap Collection Costs by Size of Operation – Maple Syrup Application (1998 USD)[§]

[§]1998 USD denotes 1998 US dollars. Used with permission from the USDA Forest Service.

equipment, and delivering and sorting raw logs. Variable costs of operation and maintenance for the Micromill® and the support equipment depend directly on the number of productive machine hours (Becker et al. 2004). Productive machine hours are defined as the time actually spent sawing logs and do not include any downtime for maintenance, labor breaks, cleaning up, resetting saws, and the rest.

Total Cost – Revisited

It is important to think about total costs critically. First, the Pillars of Cost and Value are derived directly from identifying the relevant fixed and variable inputs explicitly (Figure 3.1b). For example, the fixed and variable costs of the management actions for the unpruned and pruned Radiata Pine Plantation, described in Tables 2.7a and 2.9a, are given in Tables 3.6a and 3.6b.

Obviously, there is a direct link between the cost information contained in Tables 3.6a and 3.6b and the Pillar of Cost. The link to the Pillar of Value of these management actions is described in Table 2.7b with respect to the quantity of the products harvested and the product class.

Table 3.6a Unpruned Radiata Pine Plantation Management Action Fixed and Variable Costs

Plantation Age	Management Action[†]	Unit[‡]	Quantity	Unit Cost	Fixed Cost (NZ$/ha)	Variable Cost (NZ$/ha)
0	Planting	Stem/ha	833	0.83		691.39
0	Planting QC	NZ$/ha		40.00	40.00	
1	Herbicide	Stem/ha	833	0.30		249.90
2	Herbicide	Stem/ha	833	0.30		249.90
5	DS	NZ$/ha		40.00	40.00	
6	DS	NZ$/ha		40.00	40.00	
8	PCT	NZ$/ha		500.00		500.00
	PCT QC	NZ$/ha		45.00	45.00	
29	Road	NZ$/ha		1,000.00	1,000.00	
30	Clearcut Harvesting	m³/ha	852.7	35.00		29,844.50
	Equipment	m³/ha	852.7	0.50		426.35
	W&L	m³/ha	852.7	0.50		426.35
	HM	m³/ha	852.7	5.00		4,263.50
Annual	Admin	NZ$/ha		60.00	60.00	

[†] Planting QC – planting quality control audit; DS – *Dothistroma septosporum* spray; PCT – precommercial thinning; PCT QC – precommercial thinning quality control audit; Road – upgrading/building harvest roads; Equipment – moving harvest machinery to the site; W&L – scaling the logs to determine product class (Weights) and yield tax (Levies) for research and development; HM – harvest management; Admin – administration
[‡] Stem/ha – Stems per hectare; NZ$/ha – 2016 New Zealand dollars per hectare; m³/ha – cubic meters per hectare

Table 3.6b Pruned Radiata Pine Plantation Management Action Fixed and Variable Costs

Plantation Age	Management Action[†]	Unit[‡]	Quantity	Unit Cost	Fixed Cost (NZ$/ha)	Variable Cost (NZ$/ha)
0	Planting	Stem/ha	1,000	0.83		830.00
0	Planting QC	NZ$/ha		40.00	40.00	
1	Herbicide	Stem/ha	1,000	0.30		300.00
2	Herbicide	Stem/ha	1,000	0.30		300.00
5	DS	NZ$/ha		40.00		40.00
6	DS	NZ$/ha		40.00		40.00
6	Prune	Stem/ha	500	2.70		1,350.00
6	Prune QC	NZ$/ha		45.00	45.00	
8	Prune	Stem/ha	300	2.25		832.50
8	Prune QC	NZ$/ha		45.00	45.00	
8	PCT	NZ$/ha		300.00		300.00
8	PCT QC	NZ$/ha		45.00	45.00	
29	Road	NZ$/ha		1,000.00	1,000.00	
30	Clearcut					
	Harvesting	m³/ha	765.1	35.00		26,778.50
	Equipment	m³/ha	765.1	0.50		382.55
	W&L	m³/ha	765.1	0.50		382.55
	HM	m³/ha	765.1	5.00		3,825.50
Annual	Admin	NZ$/ha		60.00	60.00	

[†] Planting QC – planting quality control audit; DS – *Dothistroma septosporum* spray; Prune QC – pruning quality control audit; PCT – precommercial thinning; PCT QC – precommercial thinning quality control audit; Road – upgrading/building harvest roads; Equipment – moving harvest machinery to the site; W&L – scaling the logs to determine product class (Weights) and yield tax (Levies) for research and development; HM – harvest management; Admin – administration
[‡] Stem/ha – Stems per hectare; NZ$/ha – 2016 New Zealand dollars per hectare; m³/ha – cubic meters per hectare

Second, depending on the production system, the relative quantities of fixed versus variable inputs impacts the amount of fixed versus variable costs. For example, a solar array production system, illustrated in Figure 2.1e, has an extremely large proportion of the relevant inputs defined as fixed (i.e., capital equipment – photovoltaic cells, transformers, cables, etc.) relative to variable (i.e., labor). Consequently, a higher proportion of total costs are comprised of fixed costs. In the ISO beam example illustrated in Table 2.1, the proportion of variable to fixed costs increases as the annual production of ISO beams increases due to capital equipment purchases. The premise of this chapter is that entrepreneurs have more managerial control over costs than revenues and if they do not manage costs, they will lose control of profits. The solar array versus the ISO beam example illustrates the importance of this point. Most entrepreneurs think about managing variable costs; however, managing fixed costs is equally critical. For example, whether the solar array is converting insolation to energy or not, fixed costs – the largest component of total costs – still must be paid. Thus, managing fixed costs dictates whether the solar array is an economically viable business. In the ISO beam example, the entrepreneurs must also manage fixed costs (Patterson et al. 2002). As will be illustrated later in this chapter, producing more ISO beams decreases the average fixed costs per ISO beam. Capital fixed costs can be reduced by buying used equipment or leasing (Patterson et al. 2002). As with variable costs, fixed cost – overhead and maintenance, sales, general, and administration, or DIRTI-5 – should be as small as possible given the size of your business. Consequently, think long and hard before committing your business to any fixed costs.

Average Cost (AC)

Average cost is defined generically as some measure of production cost divided by the amount of output produced or cost per unit of output. Let's explore briefly the economic information in the general concept of AC before we analyze the specific types of ACs. First, AC is a ratio or fraction. The numerator denotes some measure of production costs, and the denominator is the amount of output produced. If a manager's goal is to maximize profits, then the cost per unit should be minimized or be production cost efficient. Thus, the concept of AC gives the manager information as to whether these costs are increasing or decreasing and to search for ways to make the costs as small as possible per unit output. Second, the units on AC are defined as $/Q. From Chapter 1 – Introduction and examining equation (3.1), the units on price, P, must also be $/Q or value per unit output. Consequently, if output price, P, or average revenue, of the output actually sold is greater than AC, sales revenue will cover some measure of production costs.

The three maindescriptors of AC are (1) average fixed cost (AFC), (2) average variable cost (AVC), and (3) average total cost (ATC). I will discuss each in turn using the Maple Syrup Operation practical application to illustrate the descriptors of AC. Tables 3.7a and 3.7b give the AFC, AVC, and ATC associated with the Maple Syrup case study.

Table 3.7a gives the average annual sap collection costs by size of operation and Table 3.7b gives the average annual sap collection costs for a 12,000-tap operation. These same data are illustrated in Figures 3.7a and 3.7b, respectively.

Average Fixed Cost (AFC)

Average fixed cost is defined as:

$$AFC = \frac{TFC}{Q} \tag{3.4}$$

where the notation used is defined in equation (2.1). As can be seen by equation (3.4), the measures of production costs used in calculating AFC includes only fixed costs. AFC measures the fixed production costs per unit of output.

Table 3.7a shows the AFC by size of operation. As the size or scale of the operations increases, the AFC decreases until a 10,000-tap operation. After this, AFCs

Table 3.7a Total and Average Annual Sap Collection Costs by Size of Operation – Maple Syrup Application (1998 USD)[§]

Number of Taps	Gallons of Syrup	TVC ($)	AVC ($/tap)	TFC ($)	AFC ($/tap)	TC ($)	ATC ($/tap)
500	127.5	520	1.04	1,800	3.60	2,320	4.64
1,000	255	890	0.89	2,270	2.27	3,160	3.16
2,000	510	1,640	0.82	3,220	1.61	4,860	2.43
3,000	765	2,400	0.80	4,170	1.39	6,570	2.19
4,000	1,020	3,120	0.78	5,120	1.28	8,240	2.06
5,000	1,275	3,900	0.78	5,850	1.17	9,750	1.95
6,000	1,530	4,620	0.77	7,020	1.17	11,640	1.94
7,000	1,785	5,390	0.77	7,910	1.13	13,300	1.90
8,000	2,040	6,080	0.76	8,880	1.11	14,960	1.87
9,000	2,295	6,840	0.76	9,810	1.09	16,650	1.85
10,000	2,550	7,600	0.76	10,800	1.08	18,400	1.84
11,000	2,805	8,800	0.80	13,750	1.25	22,550	2.05
12,000	3,060	9,600	0.80	14,880	1.24	24,480	2.04

[§] 1998 USD denotes 1998 US dollars
(Used with permission from the USDA Forest Service)

Table 3.7b Average Annual Sap Collection Costs for a 12,000-Tap Operation – Maple Syrup Application (1998 USD[§])

Number of taps	Gallons of syrup	AVC		AFC		ATC ($/tap)
		Labor ($/tap)	Material ($/tap)	Equipment (annual) ($/tap)	Tax ($/tap)	
500	127.5	0.52	0.52	27.36	2.40	30.80
1,000	255	0.52	0.37	13.68	1.20	15.77
2,000	510	0.52	0.30	6.84	0.60	8.26
3,000	765	0.52	0.28	4.56	0.40	5.76
4,000	1,020	0.52	0.26	3.42	0.30	4.50
5,000	1,275	0.52	0.26	2.74	0.24	3.76
6,000	1,530	0.52	0.25	2.28	0.20	3.25
7,000	1,785	0.52	0.25	1.95	0.17	2.90
8,000	2,040	0.52	0.24	1.71	0.15	2.62
9,000	2,295	0.52	0.24	1.52	0.13	2.41
10,000	2,550	0.52	0.24	1.37	0.12	2.25
11,000	2,805	0.52	0.28	1.24	0.11	2.15
12,000	3,060	0.52	0.28	1.14	0.10	2.04

[§] Cost data based on information from Huyler (2000); 1998 USD denotes 1998 US dollars

start to increase. This is due to additional capital equipment requirements. According to Huyler (2000), capital equipment requirements for operations between 500 and 10,000 taps are very similar and additional capital equipment (e.g., power tree tapper) is required for operations greater than 10,000 taps. In other words, the

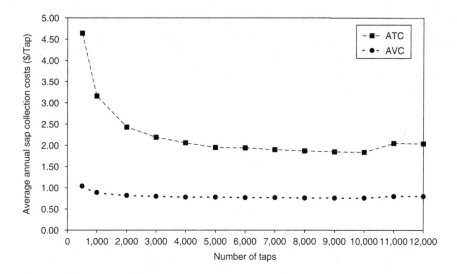

Figure 3.7a Average Annual Sap Collection Costs by Size of Operation – Maple Syrup
Application (1998 USD)[§]

[§]1998 USD denotes 1998 US dollars. Used with permission from the USDA Forest Service.

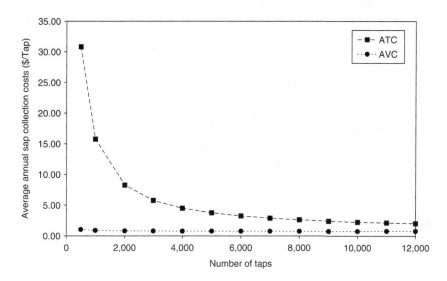

Figure 3.7b Average Annual Sap Collection Costs for a 12,000-Tap Operation – Maple
Syrup Application (1998 USD)[§]

[§]Cost data based on information from Huyler (2000); 1998 USD denotes 1998 US dollars. Used with
permission from the USDA Forest Service.

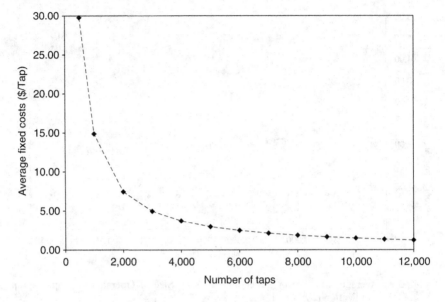

Figure 3.8 Average Fixed Costs for a 12,000-Tap Operation (1998 USD)§

§Cost data based on information from Huyler (2000); 1998 USD denotes 1998 US dollars. Used with permission from the USDA Forest Service.

physical limit of a power tree tapper is to drill approximately 10,000 tap holes per season. While FC for the power tree tapper would be the same regardless if the size of the operation ranged between 500 and 10,000 taps, the AFC would decrease as the size of the operation increased.

Table 3.7b shows the AFCs for a 12,000-tap operation. These data are illustrated in Figure 3.8.

Figure 3.8 illustrates a typical graph of AFC for a firm. As can be seen, AFC decreases quickly and then slowly as output increases. Given equation (3.4), it makes sense that AFC decreases: The numerator is constant (TFC) and the denominator (Q) increases. But what is not obvious is why Figure 3.8 has its shape. The simple answer is that the TFCs are spread out over a larger amount of output, and the change in AFC with respect to output is not constant.[14]

Average Variable Cost (AVC)

Average variable cost is defined as:

$$AVC = \frac{TVC}{Q}$$

$$= \frac{\sum_j w_j \cdot x_j}{Q} \tag{3.5}$$

where the notation used is defined in equation (2.1). As can be seen by equation (3.5), the measures of production costs used in calculating AVC include only variable costs. AVC measures the variable production costs per unit of output.[15]

Table 3.7a and Figure 3.7a show that AVC for all operations decreases until a 10,000-tap operation. They are also relatively constant for 4,000- to 10,000-tap operations. After this AVC costs increase; again, this is due to additional capital equipment requirements. However, the AVCs are still relatively constant. The AVC curve's shape is typical of an industry with relatively fixed capital equipment requirements and a relatively linear relationship between inputs (e.g., labor per tap – 4.74 minutes per tap (Huyler 2000)) and output.

Table 3.7b and Figure 3.7b show the AVC for a 12,000-tap operation. Due to the nature of the data available from Huyler (2000), the AVCs for a 12,000-tap operation are identical to that for all operations.[16] Regardless, the graph of AVC for any individual firm will be U-shaped. There are two reasons for this shape. First is the Law of Diminishing Returns as defined in Chapter 2 – Production Systems and illustrated in Figures 3.5a through 3.5c. Second is mathematical. AVC is a ratio of TVC to output, equation (3.5). AVC can also be defined as the slope of a ray from the origin that intersects the curve depicted in Figure 3.5c. Using a straightedge with one end anchored at the origin, you can show that the slope of this ray will decrease and then start to increase, giving the U-shape. Due to the data provided for the Maple Syrup application, only the left-hand side of the U is shown due to the physical limitations of the fixed capital requirements (i.e., the power tree tapper).

Average Total Cost (ATC)

Average total cost is defined as:

$$
\begin{aligned}
ATC &= \frac{TC}{Q} \\
&= \frac{TVC}{Q} + \frac{TFC}{Q} \\
&= \frac{\sum_j w_j \cdot x_j}{Q} + \frac{TFC}{Q} = AVC + AFC
\end{aligned}
\tag{3.6}
$$

where the notation used is defined in equation (2.1). As can be seen by equation (3.6), the measures of production costs used in calculating ATC include both variable and fixed costs. ATCs are the total production costs per unit of output.

Equation (3.6) also illustrates that

$$AFC = ATC - AVC$$

This relationship is best illustrated by examining Figures 3.7b and 3.8. The vertical distance between the ATC and AVC curve for a given level of output defines AFC. As you move from left to right on the output or horizontal axis of Figure 3.7b, the distance between ATC and AVC – or the number that represents AFC – is large but decreases rapidly. Examining Figure 3.8 illustrates the same concept. As you move from left to right on the output or horizontal axis of Figure 3.8, AFCs are large but decrease rapidly – as does the distance between ATC and AVC.

Tables 3.7a and 3.7b gives the ATC associated with the Maple Syrup practical application. Table 3.7a gives the ATC by size of operation. This table can be used by a maple syrup operation to compare their total production costs per unit to an industry-wide total production costs per unit. For example, if you manage a 6,000-tap operation, the industry-wide ATC is $1.94 per tap; if your ATCs are less than these, you are more production cost effective than the average 6,000-tap operation.

Table 3.7a and Figure 3.7a show that ATCs decrease as the size of the operation increases. The decreasing ATC illustrates economies of scale (or increasing returns to scale), as the size of the operation increases, the total production cost per unit of output decreases.[17] This occurs until an 11,000-tap operation. At this point the ATC starts to increase. The reason is that additional capital equipment (e.g., power tree tapper) is required. CFBMC (2000) describes a similar result.

Table 3.7b illustrates the ATC for a 12,000-tap operation. As with Table 3.7a the ATCs are decreasing as output increases. A closer examination of Tables 3.3b and 3.7b and equation (3.4) provides a clue as to why this occurs. Table 3.3b shows that TVCs are increasing and TFCs are constant as output increases. Table 3.7b shows that while TVCs are increasing, AVCs are decreasing. This is due to the fact that while VCs are increasing, they are not increasing as fast as output. Table 3.7b also shows that AFCs are decreasing as output increases.

Additional Thoughts on ATC, AVC, and AFC

If you have a 12,000-tap operation, the smallest total cost per unit output, or ATC, is to produce all 12,000 taps. The same could be said if you have a 6,000-tap operation, the smallest total cost per unit output is to produce all 6,000 taps. This is due to the nature of the production system – recall the answers to the questions: (1) What are the relevant fixed and variable inputs? (2) What are the outputs? and (3) How do you describe the production process?

It is critical to not confuse output level that minimizes the cost per unit output with the output level that maximizes profits. Figures 3.1a and 3.1b illustrate the Architectural Plan for Profit. Given the economic information we have developed so far, we only have the foundation – the production system – and the Pillars of Cost and Value for the inputs. Profits cannot be held up by only these pillars. There is missing economic information; namely, the Pillars of Value and Price of the output. While the output level that maximizes profits is both technically efficient and production cost efficient, the different output levels that are solutions to the least cost or cost effective models – which are both technically efficient and production cost efficient – are not necessarily what maximizes profit (Silberberg and Suen 2001). In Chapter 5 – Profit, I will discuss this issue in greater detail.

A question a manager is often asked is how much it costs to produce a given output. Png and Lehman (2007) and Silberberg and Suen (2001) define this as the ATC. For example, for a 12,000-tap operation, the cost per tap of producing between 0 and 12,000 taps is $2.04 per tap (Table 3.7b). However, if a 12,000-tap operation is only producing between 0 and 6,000 taps, the cost per tap is $3.25 per tap (Table 3.7b). To compare this to a 6,000-tap operation, the cost per tap of producing between 0 and 6,000 taps is $1.94 per tap (Table 3.7a).

Marginal Cost (MC)

I will use the maple syrup operation practical application to illustrate the concept of MC. Table 3.8 shows the MCs for sap collection.

MC is defined as the change in total cost per unit change in output:

$$MC = \frac{\Delta TC}{\Delta Q(x_1, x_2, ..., x_j)} = \frac{\Delta TVC}{\Delta Q(\bullet)} = \frac{\Delta\left(\sum_j w_j \cdot x_j\right)}{\Delta Q(\bullet)} \tag{3.7}$$

where ΔTC denotes the change in total cost from an incremental change in output. For example, the change in total cost for an incremental change in output from 5,000 to 6,000 taps is $\Delta TC = 19{,}500 - 18{,}780 = \$720$ (Table 3.8);
$\Delta Q(x_1, x_2, ..., x_j) = \Delta Q(\bullet)$ denotes the incremental change in output. For example, the incremental change in output from 5,000 taps to 6,000 taps is 1,000 taps;
$\Delta TVC = \sum_j w_j \cdot x_j$ denotes the change in total variable costs from an incremental change in output. For example, the change in total variable cost for an incremental change in output from 5,000 to 6,000 taps is $\Delta TVC = 4{,}620 - 3{,}900 = \$720$ (Table 3.8).

Table 3.8 Marginal Sap Collection Costs for a 12,000-Tap Operation (1998 USD[§])

Number of Taps	Gallons of Syrup	TVC ($)	TC ($)	Marginal Cost ($/tap)
500	127.5	520	15,400	–
1,000	255	890	15,770	0.74
2,000	510	1,640	16,520	0.75
3,000	765	2,400	17,280	0.76
4,000	1,020	3,120	18,000	0.72
5,000	1,275	3,900	18,780	0.78
6,000	1,530	4,620	19,500	0.72
7,000	1,785	5,390	20,270	0.77
8,000	2,040	6,080	20,960	0.69
9,000	2,295	6,840	21,720	0.76
10,000	2,550	7,600	22,480	0.76
11,000	2,805	8,800	23,680	–
12,000	3,060	9,600	24,480	–

[§] Cost data based on information from Huyler (2000); 1998 USD denotes 1998 US dollars

(Used with permission from the USDA Forest Service)

There are four concepts concerning MC that must be highlighted. First, as can be seen by equation (3.7), the production costs used in calculating MC includes only variable production costs. This is illustrated in equation (3.8):

$$\frac{\Delta TC}{\Delta Q(\bullet)} = \frac{19,500 - 18,780}{6,000 - 5,000} = \frac{720}{1000} = 0.72 \; \$/\text{tap}$$

(3.8)

$$\frac{\Delta TVC}{\Delta Q(\bullet)} = \frac{4,620 - 3,900}{6,000 - 5,000} = \frac{720}{1000} = 0.72 \; \$/\text{tap}$$

According to equations (3.7) and (3.8), TFCs are irrelevant to calculating MC and as such $\Delta TC = \Delta TVC$. The simple explanation for this is that fixed costs do not change with the level of production.[18] Second, MC measures an incremental change. In the case of the maple syrup operation practical application, the changes in output are given in 1,000 tap increments (Table 3.8). As the size of incremental change is decreased, the measure of MC becomes more accurate.[19] Third, MC is interpreted as the incremental variable production cost per unit of output. Thus, for the production of each additional tap between 5,000 and 6,000 taps, the additional cost is 0.72 $/tap. Finally, the units on MC are dollars per output ($/Q) or in the case of the maple syrup operation practical application the units on MC are $/tap. From Chapter 1 – Introduction and examining equation (3.1), the units on price, P, must also be $/Q or revenue per unit output. Thus, if P is greater than MC, sales revenue from selling the incremental production will cover the additional variable cost of its production.

Average and Marginal Cost

As a result of examining the graph of AVC and MC, three observations should be highlighted.[20] Figure 3.9 is the graph of the AVC and MC of sap collection for a 12,000-tap operation.

First, due to the units associated with AVC (and ATC) and MC, they can be put on the same graph. Output (Q) is on the horizontal axis – in this case "number of taps" – and dollars per unit of output ($/Q) is on the vertical axis – in this case $/tap. Both average and marginal cost describe production costs per unit of output. Viewing Figure 3.9 in the larger context of profit given in equation (3.1), revenue is defined as P*Q where price (P) is what consumers pay per unit of output. The units on price are dollars per unit of output ($/Q). From Chapter 1 – Introduction, price is a per unit measure of assigned value, and from equation (3.1) it is half of revenue. Thus, using the graph of average and marginal cost you will be able to compare per unit production costs to a per unit value that consumers place on the output you produce or provide. This will facilitate following the Architectural Plan for Profit.

Second, shapes of the AVC and MC curves in Figure 3.9 and those of AP and MP (Figures 2.12 and 2.13) are similar. While Appendix 3B and notes 15 and 19 provide the mathematical explanation, an alternative logic is as follows: The definition

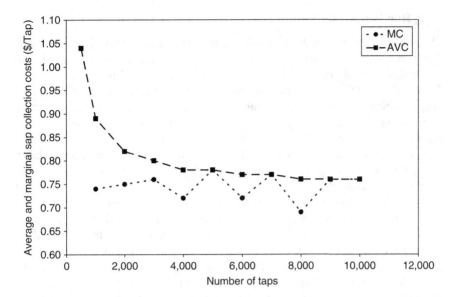

Figure 3.9 Average Variable and Marginal Sap Collection Costs for a 12,000-Tap Operation (1998 USD)[§]

[§]Cost data based on information from Huyler (2000); 1998 USD denotes 1998 US dollars. Used with permission from the USDA Forest Service.

of average cost is some measure of production cost divided by the amount of output produced, and the definition of marginal cost is the incremental variable production cost per unit of output. Both definitions require measuring production costs and outputs. Production costs require measuring how much input is used in producing or providing outputs; e.g., TVC = $\sum_j w_j x_j$. This requires knowledge of the production system and accurate answers to the questions: (1) What are the relevant fixed and variable inputs? (2) What are the outputs? and (3) How do you describe the production process? Consequently, every point on an AVC and MC curve has a corresponding point on an AP and MP curve. The AP and MP curves must follow the Law of Diminishing Returns and thus the AVC and MC must also follow the Law of Diminishing Returns. The reader is encouraged to review Chapter 2 – Production Systems to fully understand these relationships.

Finally, drawing on the relationships between averages and margins from Chapter 2 – Production Systems and Appendix 3B: (1) when the margin is greater (less) than the average, the average is increasing (decreasing); (2) when the margin is equal to the average, the average is either a minimum or maximum. Thus, for relationship between AVC (as well as ATC): (1) when MC < AVC, AVC is decreasing (see Table 3.8 and Figure 3.9); (2) when MC > AVC, AVC is increasing; and (3) when MC = AVC, AVC is at a minimum.[21] A similar result was shown with MP and AP (Figures 2.12 and 2.13).

Long Run Versus Short Run

The universally accepted distinction between the short run and the long run is that the short run is a time period in which one or more inputs are fixed during the production process. In the long run there are no fixed inputs. Thus, in the short run TC = TVC + TFC while in the long run TC = TVC. There is no set time period distinguishing the short from the long run. This depends on the particular firm or industry and the production process. However, a rule of thumb is the short run is one year or less and the long run is greater than one year.

In the case of the Mobile Micromill® and Inside-Out Beam applications, labor and natural resources (e.g., logs delivered to the mills) would be variable in the short run. For example, if consumers are willing to purchase more of their output than is being produced currently, both could potentially increase the number of shifts (labor) and the number of logs delivered to the mills to satisfy the additional demand. However, physical limits of the capital equipment and the skill level of labor provide an upper limit on production, and satisfying any further increase in demand for their outputs beyond this limit would require purchasing and install-ing additional capital equipment and training personal. These changes cannot be accomplished in as short a time (i.e., short run) as just increasing the number of shifts or logs delivered to the mills. In the case of the maple syrup operation practi-cal application, increasing the operation to greater than 10,000 taps requires pur-chasing an additional power tree tapper. The purchase of this additional power tree tapper and training labor can probably happen more quickly than in either the Mobile Micromill® or Inside-Out Beam applications. Thus, the time period defin-ing the difference between the short run and long run would be different between these applications given their defined production systems.

Sunk and Hidden Costs Versus Salvage Value

Sunk Costs

Opportunity cost is defined as the highest-valued alternative forgone. What if the cost has already been paid? For example, you probably rent an apartment during the school year and pay your rent by the first of every month. Until you write the check (and it is cashed), you have alternative uses of the rent money. Once the check is cashed, what are the alternative uses of the rent money by you? What are the opportunity costs? There are absolutely no choices or decisions that you can make concerning that rent money: That money is sunk. Thus, sunk costs measures money that has already been spent. Sunk costs are monies that are forever lost after they have been paid. Sunk costs are *utterly without relevance* for forward-looking decisions that ask: (1) What will the project *cost* from now to completion? (2) What will the project be *worth* from now to completion?

In the preceding definition and description of sunk costs, the phrase "utterly without relevance" was used. I bring your attention to this phrase for two reasons. First, answering the question, What are the relevant fixed and variable inputs? from

Chapter 2 – Production Systems, requires identifying those inputs that a manager controls directly; namely, those inputs that are *relevant* to production decisions and following the Architectural Plan for Profit. Second, those inputs the manager has direct control over are those used in defining the concept of cost (total, variable, fixed, average, marginal, explicit, and implicit) discussed in this chapter. Basically, including sunk costs in any future decision will not provide you the means for seeking ways to improve or increase your profits.

Hidden Costs

Hidden costs are just as problematic as sunk costs. According to Maital (1994: 21), some of your highest business costs "are for things that you have already bought and paid for." Again, think of the definition of an opportunity cost – the highest-valued alternative forgone. The concept of an opportunity cost is answering the "What if" question. If you own capital; for example, a piece of equipment or building: What are you giving up to keep capital in its current use? For example, you own a sawmill that cuts between 10 million board feet (MMBF) and 15 MMBF per year. The sawmill is located on 25 acres of land. The log yard uses about 5 to 7 acres. You have a 15,000 ft^2 building which houses the sawmill, a 15,000 ft^2 building which you use to store the lumber by grade and species, and an old house used as an office for the mill. You own all of this debt-free. The land is zoned for commercial use, has easy access to a major highway, and is on the edge of a medium-sized town. Can you identify the hidden costs in this example?[22]

While sunk costs may or may not show up on one of your cost account ledgers, hidden costs never do. This means that you as a manager must be keenly aware of *all* your opportunity costs.

Salvage Value

While sunk costs never enter into forward-looking decisions, what about the salvage values? The salvage value or residual value of an asset is the estimated value the asset will sell for at the end of its useful life. You just bought a new car for $20,000. However, a month later you realize that your job instead requires a 4x4 pickup that costs $27,000. The check you wrote for $20,000 has been cashed. Is the money spent on the new car a sunk cost in the decision as to whether to buy the pickup? The trade-in value or salvage value of the car is $17,000. Thus, the sunk cost of the car is $3,000. A sunk cost of $20,000 assumes the salvage value is $0.00. The salvage value is important economic information in the decision to buy the pickup. Given this discussion, if you could sublease your apartment that you rent during the school year, what would be your sunk costs?

Salvage value is also important in determining the annual depreciation amount. Recall that:

$$\text{Annual Straight-Line Depreciation} = \frac{\text{Purchase Cost - Salvage Value}}{\text{Useful Life}}$$

As can be seen by the previous equation, a decrease (increase) in a capital asset's salvage value increases (decreases) the annual straight-line depreciation estimate, *ceteris paribus*.

Production Systems – Revisited

It is important to reiterate the direct connection between the cost concepts (total, variable, fixed, average, and marginal) discussed in this chapter and the production system discussed in Chapter 2 – Production Systems. Knowledge of the production system is embodied in the answers to the three questions: (1) What are the relevant fixed and variable inputs? (2) What are the outputs? and (3) How do you describe the production process? In this chapter we focus our attention on the answers to the first and last questions.

The answer to the first question identifies those inputs that the manager controls directly and those inputs that are relevant to production decisions. The definition of total cost given in equation (3.1) includes variable and fixed costs. The variable and fixed costs used in the profit equation and the variable costs used in the least cost/cost effective equations come directly from the variable and fixed inputs that are described in the answer to the first question. Lack of due diligence on your part in identifying these inputs makes it very hard to follow the Architectural Plan for Profit.

The answer to the last question determines how many inputs (variable and fixed) are used to produce various levels of output. Specifically, this answer requires describing input–output combinations where it is not possible to increase output without increasing inputs, or technical efficiency input–output combinations. If input–output combinations are technically efficient, then they will be production cost efficient. Production cost efficient input levels are used in defining total variable costs and are used in solving the least cost/cost efficient decision models described in equations (3.2) and (3.3). Finally, production cost efficient input–output combinations are necessary, but not sufficient, for maximizing profits.

The answers to both questions lead to a final observation. Every point on the TC, TVC, ATC, AVC, and MC curves *must have* corresponding points on TP, AP, and MP curves. Without the TP, AP, and MP curves, the economic information required to define the TC, TVC, ATC, AVC, and MC curves correctly is missing. Calculating costs based on incorrect economic information will not allow you, as the manager, to make decisions to determine ways to improve or increase your profits.

Costs Given Noncontinuous Production Systems

Not every production process can be described using small incremental changes in inputs and outputs. The Micromill® and ISO Beam applications are examples of these types of production systems. In these cases, the technically efficient input–output combinations are described by discrete points. Figure 2.15 in Chapter 2 – Productions Systems shows the ISO Beam mill's daily total product (Patterson et al. 2002). The estimated total cost associated with these three production levels is given in Figure 3.10.

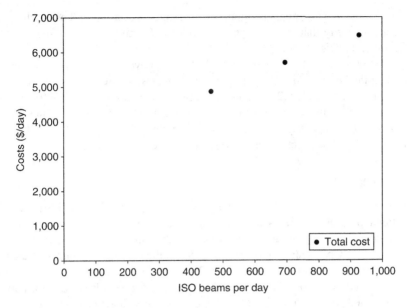

Figure 3.10 Estimated Total Cost for the ISO Beam Application[§]

[§]These total cost estimates are approximations only

Due to the noncontinuous nature of the production system, AP, MP, AC, and MC have no economic meaning. For example, given a daily production of 464 ISO beams, increasing labor in the ISO Beam application by one person per day would have no change on output. The change in output is either 0 or 232 ISO beams per day. The limiting factors are the boilers and kiln(s) and the pre-dryer. Thus, no amount of increases in the variable input labor is going to have any impact on the amount of output produced. Adding an additional person will decrease AP (i.e., the numerator is constant while the denominator increases), but the decrease is due to increased technical inefficiency – not the Law of Diminishing Returns. Adding an additional person will increase AVC (the numerator increases while the denominator is constant), but again this increase is due to technical inefficiency – not the Law of Diminishing Returns. The calculation of MP requires that incremental changes in input and output are feasible. In this case, no such increments are feasible (see Figure 2.15). While you could use equation (2.11) to calculate changes in output relative to changes in input, the result would have no economic meaning. The same argument can be made for MC. While it is possible to calculate changes in cost relative to changes in output using equation (3.7), the result would have no economic meaning. Figure 3.10 shows that incremental changes in cost relative to output are not feasible. This is similar to the discussion presented by Zudak (1970).

In the Micromill® application, Becker et al. (2004) describe the optimal crew size as four people (i.e., one skilled mill operator/supervisor, one log sorter and loader, and two laborers on the green chain). Again, adding an additional person to the crew will have no effect on output. Thus, arguments similar to those earlier can be given to justify that the concepts of AP, MP, AVC, and MC have no economic meaning given this example.

In contrast, increasing the amount of labor employed per season in the maple syrup application would allow a proportional increase in the number of taps (i.e., 4.75 minutes/tap, Huyler (2000)). For example, an increase of 1,000 (500) taps per season would require an additional 79 (39.5) person-hours per season. Thus, given the nature of this production system, increasing output by either 1,000 or 500 taps per season could be described as a marginal change.

Supply-Chain Management

Supply chain management is defined as the systemic, strategic coordination of the traditional business functions and the tactics across these business functions within a particular company and across businesses within the supply chain, for the purposes of improving the long-term performance of the individual companies and the supply chain as a whole (Mentzer et al. 2001: 18). Whether a business uses raw resource inputs and produces a final consumer good (e.g., maple syrup) or is part of a value-added process involving a number of business interacting to produce a final good or service, the profits of all businesses involved could be improved if costs all along this chain are minimized and customer value and satisfaction are maximized (Mentzer et al. 2001). Supply chain management is concerned with improving both efficiency (i.e., cost reduction – Penfield (2007)) and effectiveness (i.e., customer service) in a strategic context (i.e., creating customer value and satisfaction through integrated supply chain management) to obtain competitive advantage that ultimately brings profitability (Mentzer et al. 2001). While the logistics and strategic planning of managing a supply chain are beyond the scope of this book (for example, see Bettinger et al. (2017) for a discussion of this topic), I will focus on the efficiency aspect of supply-chain management as that is the focus of this chapter.

The concept of a supply chain describes an input – transformation – output process depicted in Figure 3.11. Examining Figure 3.11 reveals three points of interest. First is the flow of input to output as input to output as input to output . . . until a final consumer good is produced or provided. While the end result is the final consumer good (output), each intermediate value-added process produces an output that the next value-added process (who are consumers) uses as an input. Along this chain each consumer's value and satisfaction are maximized and costs are minimized. Second, in order for this to occur information, services, finances, and so on should flow in both directions. This requires coordinated strategic and logistic planning across all firms involved in the supply chain. Third, Figure 3.11 can be compared and contrasted with Figure 2.2. The flow chart description of a production system is analogous to the supply chain illustrated in Figure 3.11. There are inputs, transformation processes (i.e., production or value-adding processes), and outputs. The three questions to systematically analyze a production process from Chapter 2 – Production Systems in a very simple case provide a starting point to examine the more complex supply chain.

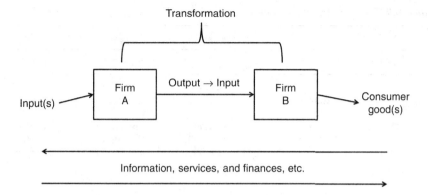

Figure 3.11 Supply Chain

The first Pillars of Architectural Plan for Profit examined have been Cost and Value for the simple reason that managing costs and creating value are paramount for generating the most profits for any given level of output. This is also an explicit goal of supply-chain management and can be illustrated by using a profit margin given in equation (3.9):[23]

$$\text{Profit Margin } (\Pi_M) \;=\; \frac{\Pi}{TR} = \frac{TR - TC}{TR} \tag{3.9}$$

where the terms have been defined in equation (2.1). A profit margin describes the percent of every dollar of total revenue generating profits for the entrepreneur; for example, a profit margin of 5% defines $0.05 of every $1.00 total revenue as profit. A higher profit margin implies a firm has a greater ability to control costs than a lower profit margin. Equation (3.10) illustrates the impacts of controlling costs on total revenue at a given level of output.

$$\begin{aligned}
\Delta TR &= TR_{new} - TR \\
&= \frac{TR - TC + \Delta TC}{\Pi_M} - \frac{TR - TC}{\Pi_M} \\
&= \frac{\Delta TC}{\Pi_M}
\end{aligned} \tag{3.10}$$

with

$$TR = \frac{TR - TC}{\Pi_m}$$

$$TR_{new} = \frac{TR - TC + \Delta TC}{\Pi_m}$$

Table 3.9 The Impact of Cost Savings

Cost		Profit	Margin	
Savings	0.05	0.10	0.15	0.20
		Revenue	Equivalent	
$1.00	$20.00	$10.00	$6.67	$5.00
$10.00	$200.00	$100.00	$66.67	$50.00
$100.00	$2,000.00	$1,000.00	$666.67	$500.00
$1,000.00	$20,000.00	$10,000.00	$6,666.67	$5,000.00

where ΔTC denotes cost savings and ΔTR denotes the cost savings equivalent in terms of total revenue. Table 3.9 illustrates the impact of cost savings given various profit margins.

Table 3.9 shows that cost savings at lower profit margins have a greater equivalence in terms of total revenue than at higher profit margins. Table 3.9 also illustrates the importance of controlling costs in that the potential benefits are magnified many times. For example, the time and effort involved in a $1.00 cost savings is equivalent to a revenue increase of $10.00 given a profit margin of 10%. Would the same amount of time and effort have increased revenue by $10.00? It should be noted that decreasing costs and increasing revenues are not mutually exclusive decisions and are part of building the Architectural Plan for Profit.

Costs – Variability

The Pillar of Cost summarizes the economic information with respect to the wages paid for the inputs. The discussions from Chapter 2 – Production Systems examined the variability associated with the output using the solar array application (Figures 2.17a and 2.17b). A similar discussion could be made with respect to maple syrup production. Given the nature of the production system in the ISO beam example, the greatest variability is not associated with the production process *ceteris paribus*, but with the Pillars of Cost and Price. As this chapter deals with cost, this will be the focus of this discussion; however, the analytical tool introduced here can be used to examine variability throughout the Architectural Plan for Profit.

Sensitivity analysis is the procedure of changing a model parameter and analyzing the impact on the result.[24] For example, the data provided by Patterson et al. (2002) shows that the ISO beam business is not profitable if 464 ISO beams are produced and sold per day but is profitable if 696 or 928 ISO beams are produced and sold per day. Given these data, an implied cost of small-diameter logs is approximately $3.59 per log. The cost per log would have to decrease 72.1% or to $1.00 per log for a production level of 464 ISO beams per day to be profitable, *ceteris paribus*. The cost per log would have to increase 15.6% or to $4.15 per log for a production level of 696 ISO beams per day to not be profitable, *ceteris paribus*. For sensitivity analysis to be a useful tool, the entrepreneur would need to develop reasonable ranges of costs per log based on their knowledge of the input market. Nonetheless, based on the aforementioned input cost sensitivity analysis, a production level of 464 beams per day is probably not going to be profitable.

How to Use Economic Information – Costs – to Make Better Business Decisions

Simply put: If you do not manage or control costs, you will lose control of profits. The Pillars of Cost and Value (see Figures 3.1a and 3.1b) are built on the foundation of the production system. The economic information contained in this foundation is also included in these pillars. The economic information contained in the production system is determined by answering the following three questions: (1) What are the relevant fixed and variable inputs? (2) What are the outputs? and (3) How do you describe the production process? The answer to these three questions should be structured to provide the manager with technically efficient input(s)–output(s) combinations. Answering the question What are the relevant fixed and variable inputs? will identify those inputs that you the manager control directly and thus are relevant to following the Architectural Plan for Profit.

What is the economic information contained in the Pillars of Cost and Value? A cursory look at the definition of total cost shows it comprises three components: wages, variable inputs, and fixed inputs (see equation (3.1)), which can be combined to determine total variable and fixed costs. However, a critical examination of these pillars is more rewarding. First, cost must always be viewed in terms of opportunity cost – the highest-valued alternative forgone. In other words, for what purpose are you using your variable and fixed inputs? Can they be employed to do different parts of the production process? What are you giving up to keep the variable and fixed inputs in their current use? Are your variable and fixed inputs providing the most value they can? Second, you are a consumer of inputs just as there are consumers of the outputs you produce or provide. As a consumer of goods produced by other entrepreneurs, you will only buy the product if you are better off with it than without it. The same logic must hold for purchasing inputs. Are the benefits your variable and fixed inputs providing greater than their costs? Basically, if an input does not add value to the output, you will not purchase it. Third, cost includes the price or wage you pay for your inputs. This implies that you must purchase your inputs from a market. Your knowledge of your input markets must be equal to your knowledge of your output markets. Basically, you want to pay no more than you have to for your inputs. Finally, if profits are to be as large as possible, revenues must be as large as possible at the same time costs must be as small as possible for any given input(s)–output(s) combination. Thus, you are searching for input–output combinations that are production cost efficient. The economic information from the Pillars of Cost and Value must allow you to do this analysis.

Final Thoughts

Despite the importance of managing costs and its potential for cost savings, controlling costs alone cannot guarantee profits. For managing costs to be effective, the sales and revenue end of the business must be analyzed just as critically. Therefore, as will be described in the next chapter, the Pillars of Price and Value define revenue.

Appendix 3A – Technical Efficiency and Production Cost Efficiency

Technical efficiency, as described in Chapter 2 – Production Systems, is combinations of inputs and outputs such that it is not possible to increase output without increasing input or when the most amount of output is produced with the least amount of input. Therefore, all the descriptors of the production system, that is, total product, average product, and marginal product, must reflect technical efficiency. Thus, every point on a graph of total product for which marginal product is greater than or equal to zero must be technically efficient.

Equation (A.1) describes a least cost model; in other words, determining the least cost means of producing or providing a given level of a good or service:

$$\text{Min TVC} = \sum_j w_j \cdot x_j$$

s.t.   (A.1)

$$Q(x_1, x_2, ..., x_j) = Q^0$$

The least cost model, equation (A.1), includes the production system, $Q(x_1, x_2, ..., x_j) = Q(\bullet) = Q^0$, as part of the constraint. By definition any descriptors of the production system must be technically efficient.

Equation (A.1) can be formulated and solved using a Lagrangian equation:[25]

$$\text{Min L} = \sum_j w_j \cdot x_j - \lambda \left[Q(\bullet) - Q^0 \right]$$ (A.2)

where λ is the Lagrangian multiplier. The first order conditions require that:

$$\frac{\partial L}{\partial x_1} = w_1 - \lambda \frac{\partial Q(\bullet)}{\partial x_1} = 0$$

$$\frac{\partial L}{\partial x_2} = w_2 - \lambda \frac{\partial Q(\bullet)}{\partial x_2} = 0$$

$$\vdots \qquad \vdots \qquad \vdots$$ (A.3)

$$\frac{\partial L}{\partial x_j} = w_j - \lambda \frac{\partial Q(\bullet)}{\partial x_j} = 0$$

$$\frac{\partial L}{\partial \lambda} = -\left[Q(x_1, x_2, ..., x_j) - Q^0 \right] = 0$$

I will assume that the production function, $Q(\bullet)$, is twice differentiable with $\partial^2 Q(\bullet)/\partial x_j^2 < 0$ for all j (in other words the production function is consistent with the Law of Diminishing Returns) and the Karush (1939) and Kuhn and Tucker

(1951) conditions are satisfied for optimal values of x_j; $j = 1,2, \ldots$. Solving the first j equations gives:

$$\lambda = \frac{w_1}{\partial Q(\bullet)\big/\partial x_1} = \frac{w_2}{\partial Q(\bullet)\big/\partial x_2} = \ldots = \frac{w_j}{\partial Q(\bullet)\big/\partial x_j}$$

$$\lambda = \frac{w_1}{MP_1} = \frac{w_2}{MP_2} = \ldots = \frac{w_j}{MP_j}$$

(A.4a)

$$\frac{1}{\lambda} = \frac{\partial Q(\bullet)\big/\partial x_1}{w_1} = \frac{\partial Q(\bullet)\big/\partial x_2}{w_2} = \ldots = \frac{\partial Q(\bullet)\big/\partial x_j}{w_j}$$

$$\frac{1}{\lambda} = \frac{MP_1}{w_1} = \frac{MP_2}{w_2} = \ldots = \frac{MP_j}{w_j}$$

Equation (A.4a) also defines the equimarginal principle. The equimarginal principle can also be derived from profit maximization in Appendices 5A and 5B in Chapter 5 – Profit.

An alternative form of a least cost model is the cost effective model. Equation (A.5) describes a cost effective model; in other words, determining the maximizing quantity or quality of a good or service to provide or produce using inputs, x_j, for a given budget:

$$\text{Max } Q(x_1, x_2, \ldots, x_j)$$

s.t.

(A.5)

$$\sum_j w_j \cdot x_j = C^0$$

Equation (A.5) can also be formulated and solved using a Lagrangian equation:

$$\text{Max } L = Q(\bullet) - \mu\left[\sum_j w_j \cdot x_j - C^0\right]$$

(A.6)

where μ is the Lagrangian multiplier. The first order conditions require that:

$$\frac{\partial L}{\partial x_1} = \frac{\partial Q(\bullet)}{\partial x_1} - \mu w_1 = 0$$

$$\frac{\partial L}{\partial x_2} = \frac{\partial Q(\bullet)}{\partial x_2} - \mu w_2 = 0$$

$$\vdots \qquad \vdots \qquad \vdots$$

(A.7)

$$\frac{\partial L}{\partial x_j} = \frac{\partial Q(\bullet)}{\partial x_j} - \mu w_j = 0$$

$$\frac{\partial L}{\partial \mu} = -\left[\sum_j w_j \cdot x_j - C^0\right] = 0$$

Solving the first j equations gives:

$$\mu = \frac{\partial Q(\bullet)\big/\partial x_1}{w_1} = \frac{\partial Q(\bullet)\big/\partial x_2}{w_2} = \ldots = \frac{\partial Q(\bullet)\big/\partial x_j}{w_j}$$

(A.4b)

$$\mu = \frac{MP_1}{w_1} = \frac{MP_2}{w_2} = \ldots = \frac{MP_j}{w_j}$$

Equation (A.4b) again defines the equimarginal principle. This illustrates that the least cost model (A.1) and the cost effective model (A.5) define a primal/dual relationship in that the solution to these two problem formulations are the same. In addition, comparing equations (A.4a) and (A.4b) define the relationship between the Lagrangian multipliers as:

$$\mu = \frac{1}{\lambda}$$

To illustrate the economic interpretation of equations (A.4a) or (A.4b), I will use a production system with only two inputs, x_1 and x_2, and one output, Q. Figure 3A.1a illustrates graphically the relationship between the technically efficient levels of the two inputs required to produce two different levels of output, Q^0 and Q^1.

These curved lines are call isoquants or lines of equal production levels. Given this production system, equation (A.4) reduces to:

$$\frac{\partial Q(\bullet)\big/\partial x_1}{w_1} = \frac{\partial Q(\bullet)\big/\partial x_2}{w_2}$$

$$\frac{MP_1}{w_1} = \frac{MP_2}{w_2}$$

(A.8)

$$\frac{MP_2}{MP_1} = \frac{w_2}{w_1}$$

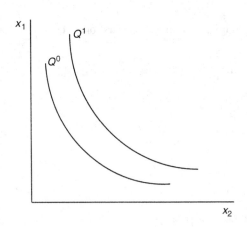

Figure 3A.1a Isoquants

The left-hand side of the last expression in equation (A.8), MP_2/MP_1, defines the marginal rate of technical substitution between inputs x_1 and x_2 in producing a given level of output, Q^0; for example, the substitution of labor for capital. The slope of an isoquant at any given point is defined as MP_2/MP_1 (Silberberg and Suen 2001; Chiang 1984; Henderson and Quandt 1980), and thus defines the marginal rate of technical substitution between inputs x_1 and x_2 for a given level of output, Q^0.

The right-hand side of the same expression, w_2/w_1, defines the slope of the objective function given in equation (A.1):

$$TVC = w_1 x_1 + w_x x_2 \tag{A.9}$$

Solving equation (A.9) for x_1 gives:

$$x_1 = \frac{TVC}{w_1} - \frac{w_2}{w_1} x_2 \tag{A.10}$$

If all the variable costs are used to purchase input x_1, then from equation (A.9) the total amount of x_1 purchased is TVC/w_1. Similarly, if all the variable costs are used to purchase input x_2, then from equation (A.8) the total amount of x_2 purchased is TVC/w_2. Given the prices of the inputs, x_1 and x_2, point A defines the least cost way of producing output level Q^0.

Both points A and B in Figure 3A.1b are technically efficient. At input prices of w_1 and w_2, point A is production cost efficient and technically efficient while point B is only technically efficient. As the price of x_1 increases relative to the price of x_2, less x_1 and more x_2 will be used to produce Q^0. Given the change in prices of the inputs, point B is now production cost efficient and technically efficient while point A is only technically efficient. Technical efficiency requires that the input–output combinations be on the isoquant. Production cost efficiency requires technical efficiency (input–output combinations on the isoquant), and the level of inputs used depends on the prices paid for the inputs.

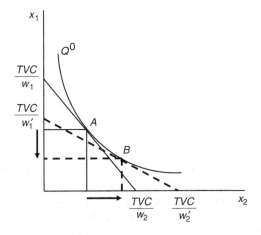

Figure 3A.1b Production Cost Efficiency

The relationship between technical efficiency, production cost efficiency, and economic efficiency will be described in Chapter 5 – Profit.

Appendix 3B – Average and Marginal Cost

Marginal cost (MC) is interpreted as the incremental variable production cost per unit of output. In mathematical terms MC defines a rate of change (or slope) at a specific point on the TC or TVC curves. The slope of a point on a curve is calculated by taking the first derivative of the function with respect to the identified input. As MC is defined with respect to TVC (as TFCs are irrelevant) and output, let $C[Q(x_1, x_2, \ldots, x_j)]$ or $C(\bullet)$ denote the variable cost function. Equation B.1 defines MC:

$$\text{MC} = \frac{dC\left[Q\left(x_1, x_2, \ldots, x_j\right)\right]}{dQ} = \frac{dC(\bullet)}{dQ} \tag{B.1}$$

Equation (B.1) can only be calculated for variable cost functions that are continuous.

Average variable cost measures the variable production costs per unit of output. The mathematical definition of AVC is:

$$\text{AVC} = \frac{C(\bullet)}{Q} \tag{B.2}$$

The mathematical relationship between MC and AVC (or TC) can be illustrated by using the definition of AVC and its first derivative with respect to output. Taking the first derivative of AVC with respect to output using the quotient rules and simplifying gives:

$$
\begin{aligned}
\frac{d\text{AVC}}{dQ} &= \frac{Q\left(\dfrac{dC(\bullet)}{dQ}\right) - C(\bullet)}{Q^2} \\
&= \frac{1}{Q}\left(\frac{dC(\bullet)}{dQ} - \frac{C(\bullet)}{Q}\right) \\
&= \frac{1}{Q}(\text{MC} - \text{AVC})
\end{aligned}
\tag{B.3}
$$

Analyzing the last expression of equation (2.15) shows that if MC < AVC then $d\text{AVC}(\bullet)/dQ < 0$ or AVC (and ATC) is decreasing. If MC > AVC, then $d\text{AVC}(\bullet)/dQ > 0$ or AVC (and ATC) is increasing. Finally if MC = AVC, then $d\text{AVC}(\bullet)/dQ = 0$ and AVC (and ATC) is at its minimum.

Equation (B.3) also identifies two additional important ideas. First, the concepts of average cost (ATC and AVC) and marginal cost are tied to the production system directly. This relationship is based on the definitions of average and marginal cost as illustrated mathematically as $C[Q(x_1, x_2, \ldots, x_j)]$ or $C(\bullet)$ in equations (B.1), (B.2), and (B.3). Thus, it is imperative that you as a manager must answer the questions: (1) What are the relevant fixed and variable inputs? (2) What are the outputs?

and (3) How do you define the production process? to the best of your ability if you want to control your costs. Second, the shapes of the average and marginal cost curves mirror those of AP and MP and equation (B.3) mirrors equation (A.3) of Appendix 2A in Chapter 2 – Production Systems. Again, this is due to the direct tie between average and marginal costs and the production system.

Notes

1 The production system according to Chapter 1 must define input–output combinations that are technically efficient. Appendix 2A develops the relationship between technical efficiency and production cost efficiency.
2 Traditionally, sap was collected in buckets that hung from the taps. This technology has been replaced by vacuum-tubing sap collection systems in commercial operations.
3 This is known as the Rule of 86 or (86)/(% sugar); for example, it would take 43 gallons of sap with 2% sugar content to produce 1 gallon of syrup. The Brix measurement is the ratio of dissolved sugar to water in a liquid; thus, the higher the Brix measurement the higher the dissolved sugar content.
4 An operating input (e.g., hired labor) is described as an input that is bought as part of normal business operations. A capital input is described as a produced good (e.g., a fishing boat or tackle) that is used to produce an output. Capital inputs usually have a useable life span of one year or greater.
5 The difference between the short run and the long run is discussed later in this chapter.
6 The DIRTI-5 are taken from the agricultural farm budgeting literature. American Society of Agricultural Engineers (ASAE) Standards #496, section 6.3.1, and #497, Table 3.
7 The concept of salvage value will be discussed later in this chapter.
8 Interest payments for borrowing money for capital equipment are due to the opportunity cost of time. This will be discussed in more detail in Chapter 6 – Capital Theory: Investment Analysis.
9 Huyler (1982) describes how these fixed equipment costs were annualized.
10 I will revisit how the payments for the Mobile Micromill and support equipment were determined in Chapter 6 – Capital Theory: Investment Analysis.
11 Due to the cost of moving and siting the Mobile Micromill, Becker et al. (2004) assumed the mill would be relocated at most once per year.
12 In addition to fixed and variable costs, some costs can be considered semi-variable. These costs are a mixture of fixed and variable components. Semi-variable costs vary in part with increases or decreases in production, like variable costs, but still exist when production is zero, like fixed costs. Payments for labor overtime are an example of semi-variable costs. Regular wages for workers are generally considered to be fixed costs, as while a company's management can reduce the number of workers and paid work hours, it will always need a workforce of some size to function. Overtime payments are often considered to be variable costs, as the number of overtime hours that a company pays its workers will generally rise with increased production and drop with reduced production. When wages are paid based on conditions of productivity allowing for overtime, the cost has both fixed and variable components and is considered to be a semi-variable cost (www.investopedia.com/terms/o/operating-cost.asp accessed 22 April 2022).
13 If screw-in type fittings have the least variable production costs, does this imply that this fitting is the one that will maximize profit? How do Burdurlu et al. (2006) answer this question?
14 If the change in AFC as output changes is constant, then $\dfrac{d\text{AFC}}{dQ}$ would be constant. However,

$$\frac{d\text{AFC}}{dQ} = \frac{d\left(\dfrac{\text{FC}}{Q}\right)}{dQ} = -\frac{\text{FC}}{Q^2}$$

which is not constant.

15 As defined by equation (3.5), AVC is a relationship between "variable cost" and output. With a production process that uses only one input, AVC can be defined as:

$$AVC = \frac{TVC}{Q} = \frac{wx}{Q} = \frac{w}{\frac{Q}{x}} = \frac{w}{AP}$$

This relationship does not hold if more than one input is used in the production process. Also note that this ties the concept of AVC to the production system directly.

16 I will assume for purposes of illustrating AVC that the information in Table 3.6b represents the production cost efficient variable costs of a 12,000-tap operation.

17 Economies of scale are due to two factors. First, the spreading out of the TFCs over greater output (i.e., AFC decreases as output increases). Second, while TVCs are increasing due to increased production, output is increasing faster. This is due to the nature of the production system. Thus, the ratio of TVC to output (i.e., AVC) is decreasing.

In addition to economies of scale, there are also diseconomies of scale (or decreasing returns to scale) – ATC increases as output production increases – and constant economies of scale (or constant returns to scale) – ATC is constant as output production increases.

18 The fact that TFCs are irrelevant can be shown algebraically:

$$\Delta TC = TC_2 - TC_1$$
$$= TVC_2 + TFC - (TVC_1 + TFC)$$
$$= TVC_2 - TVC_1 + TFC - TFC$$
$$= TVC_2 - TVC_1 = \Delta TVC$$

19 As defined by equation (3.7), MC is a relationship between "variable cost" and output. With a production process that uses only one input, MC can be defined as:

$$MC = \frac{\Delta TVC}{\Delta Q} = \frac{(wx_2 - wx_1)}{\Delta Q}$$
$$= \frac{w(x_2 - x_1)}{\Delta Q} = \frac{w\Delta x}{\Delta Q}$$
$$= \frac{w}{\Delta Q / \Delta x} = \frac{w}{MP}$$

This relationship does not hold if more than one input is used in the production process. Also note that this ties the concept of MC to the production system directly.

20 Appendix 3B provides a calculus-based discussion comparing average and marginal Cost.

21 These last two conditions are not shown in the maple syrup practical application due to limited data presented by Huyler (2000).

22 What about the land? Are you utilizing all of the land? What about the old house? Could you move your office into one of the other buildings and rent the house to another business?

23 Profit margins will be discussed in more detail in an Appendix of Chapter 11 – Market Equilibrium and Structure.

24 A more detailed discussion of sensitivity analysis and other techniques to analyze single and multi-period risk will be discussed in detail in Chapter 8 – Risk.

25 Information concerning using Lagrangian multipliers to solve constrained optimization problems can be found in Lambert (1985) and Chiang (1984).

4 Revenue

Preamble: Why Revenues are Important

A common description of profit is what is left over after all costs have been paid regardless of the revenues generated from outputs or services sold. Profit maximization is a deceptively simple idea: Make the total revenues as large as possible (the Pillars of Price and Value for outputs) relative to the costs (the Pillars of Cost and Value for inputs) for any given input(s)–output(s) combination (the production system). However, according to the Architectural Plan for Profit, revenue does not even appear as one of the pillars.

However, comparing Figures 3.1b and 4.1 shows that the pillars associated with revenue are value and price, implying that revenue is a function of both of these pillars. In Chapter 1 – Introduction, value was defined as the expressed relative importance or worth of an object to an individual in a given context (Brown 1984) and the degree to which buyers think those goods and services make them better off than if they did without (Maital 1994). Both definitions state that individuals have preferences for different outputs and these preferences will be observable given choices individuals make in the market. Based on these definitions, the Pillar of Value contains two elements. The first is the expressed choices that individuals make, or in different terms if consumers choose to buy the outputs that you produce or provide, this is your revenue. The focus of this chapter will be on determining how to measure the revenue concept of value so you can manage it for the purpose of improving profit. The second is modeling the preferences of your consumers so that you produce or provide goods that will make them better off than if they did without. This concept of value will be discussed in Chapter 10 – Supply and Demand.

Also, in Chapter 1 – Introduction, price was defined as a per unit measure of assigned value and a measure of relative scarcity. In the case of output price, it is economic information that both consumers and producers use in their decisions to purchase and produce an output, respectively.[1] The market price is determined when both consumers and producers reveal their choices. Thus far the market has been characterized by workable competition – no one buyer or group of buyers and no one seller or group of sellers can influence price (i.e., neither has market power): That is, output price is constant. In other words, the market sets the price and producers have almost no ability to manipulate the price of their output. In this

DOI: 10.4324/9781315678719-4

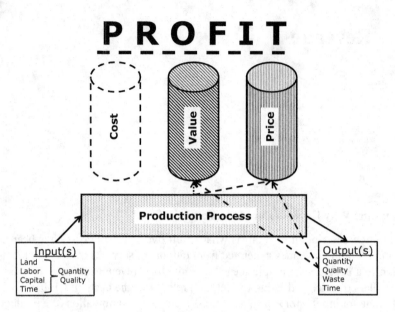

Figure 4.1 Revenue: The Architectural Plan for Profit

chapter I will continue with this market characterization and assume output price is constant. In Chapter 10 – Supply and Demand I will discuss how market price is determined. In Chapter 11 – Market Equilibrium and Structure, I will discuss how market structures other than workable competition impact price and pricing strategies used by producers.

Based on the definition of the profit model (equation (4.1)),

$$
\begin{aligned}
\text{Max } \Pi &= \text{TR - TC} \\
&= P \cdot Q\left(x_1, x_2, \dots, x_j\right) - \text{TVC - TFC} \\
&= P \cdot Q(\bullet) - \sum_j w_j \cdot x_j - \text{TFC}
\end{aligned}
\tag{4.1}
$$

where
Max Π denotes maximization of profit (Π);
TR denotes Total Revenue, TR = $P \cdot Q(x_1, x_2, \dots, x_j)$ = $P \cdot Q(\bullet)$;
P denotes the market price of the good or service;
$Q(x_1, x_2, \dots, x_j)$ = $Q(\bullet)$ denotes the system of producing or providing a good or service, Q, using inputs that the manager has direct control over, $x_1, x_2, \dots, x_j$;
TC denotes Total Cost, TC = TVC + TFC;
TVC denotes Total Variable Costs, TVC = $\sum_j w_j \bullet x_j$;
$\sum_j$ denotes the summation operator;
w_j denotes the jth wage or price paid for j^{th} input x_j;
x_j denotes the jth input, for example, labor; and
TFC denotes Total Fixed Costs.

The most obvious place to start this discussion would seem to be with total revenue. It may seem odd then to start this discussion by reviewing the definition of cost, specifically the definition of opportunity cost – the highest-valued alternative forgone. The basic idea of an opportunity cost is what you are giving up, in terms of explicit and implicit resources, as a result of your current choices. There are opportunity costs or value to be measured and managed in terms of costs: This was done in Chapter 3 – Costs. This chapter will examine the opportunity costs or value to be measured and managed in terms of revenues.

Examining total revenue of equation (4.1) reveals the following three observations. First, TR is half of profit. Second, to improve profits, TRs must be as large as possible while cost must be as small as possible for various input(s)–output(s) combinations. That is, generating revenue and minimizing cost must happen simultaneously. How you create value is equally as important as cost cutting because cost cutting is pointless if the good or service that results is not valued by consumers (Maital 1994): Output produced but not valued by consumers generates cost but no revenues. Finally, TR = P*Q is a measure of assigned value. If a consumer purchases your product then you know (1) the benefit they receive from the product is greater than their cost, and (2) the consumer's cost is your TR. Therefore, your TR depends on your knowledge of consumers' willingness to part with their hard-earned cash for your output. In this chapter I will focus on economic information contained in TR (the combination of Pillars of Price and Value) so you can use it to improve profits.

However, before proceeding, I have two thought questions:

1. In the previous chapters when I introduced the profit model, I also introduced the least cost/cost effective model. Why have I not included it here?[2]
2. What are your predictions of the economic descriptors used to measure value with respect to total revenue? (Hint: Compare and contrast economic descriptors used to measure technical efficiency from Chapter 2 – Production Systems with those used to measure production cost efficiency in Chapter 3 – Costs.

Practical Applications

The practical applications used in this chapter will include the Inside-Out (ISO) Beams (Patterson et al. 2002; Patterson and Xie 1998), Mobile Micromill® (Becker et al. 2004), Maple Syrup Operation (Huyler 2000), Select Red Oak (Hahn and Hansen 1991), Radiata Pine (*Pinus radiata*) Plantations in New Zealand, and Great Lakes Charter Boat Fishing (Lichtkoppler and Kuehn 2003). Their summaries will not be repeated here as they have been used in earlier chapters.

Economic Descriptors of Total Revenue

There are six main descriptors of revenue, three describing revenue with respect to output: total revenue, average revenue, and marginal revenue, and three describing revenue with respect to inputs used in the production process: total revenue product, average revenue product, and marginal revenue product. I will address each in turn.

Total Revenue (TR)

Total revenue is defined by equation (4.2):

$$TR = P \cdot Q\left(x_1, x_2, ..., x_j\right) = P \cdot Q(\bullet) \qquad (4.2)$$

where the notation used is defined in equation (4.1). Given the assumptions about the market (i.e., workable competition), P is constant and TR is linear with respect to output, Q($\bullet$). Total revenue is the output quantity "sold" multiplied by the price you charge. Output produced but not sold generates no revenue *but does generate costs*. Consequently, your analysis of total revenue must also address why you are confident you can sell the output you produce. Finally, as illustrated by Figure 4.1, the quantity (and quality) of output produced may also be a function of time. For example, certain times of the year (as well as times in the day) have more hours and intensity of insolation available for energy conversion. These energy conversion periods also correspond to periods of high energy consumption directly. In the case of the Radiata Pine Plantation example, it takes approximately 30 years to generate a commercial product. While this will be discussed in detail in Chapters 6 – Capital Theory: Investment Analysis and 7 – The Natural Resources Management Puzzle, it is important to recognize that any analysis of total revenue must also be cognizant of time's effect on total revenue.

I will use the practical applications to examine total revenue, starting with the Charter Boat Fishing. Table 4.1 shows the TR for the average charter boat fishing

Table 4.1 Total Revenue for New York's Great Lakes Charter Boat Fishing Industry (2002 USD[§])

Fish Species	Average No. Trips/ Business	Average Charge/Trip	Total Revenue
Lake trout and salmon			
Full day	27.6	$407	$11,233
Half day	6.9	$306	$2,111
Steelhead			
Full day	9.4	$401	$3,769
Half day	1.9	$299	$568
Smallmouth bass			
Full day	7.6	$342	$2,599
Half day	1.7	$251	$427
Walleye			
Full day	5.1	$380	$1,938
Half day	0.6	$273	$164
Yellow perch			
Full day	0.3	$364	$109
Half day	<0.1	$254	$25

[§] 2002 USD denotes 2002 US dollars

(Date used with permission from Lichtkoppler and Kuehn (2003) and Ohio Sea Grant Extension)

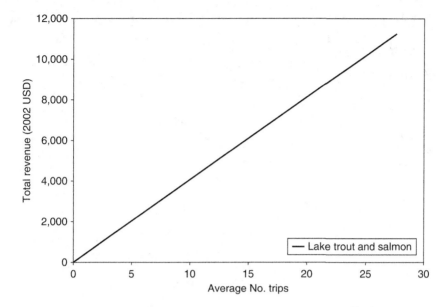

Figure 4.2 Total Revenue From Lake Trout and Salmon Full-Day Charter Boat Fishing on New York's Great Lakes (2002 USD)§

§2002 USD denotes 2002 US dollars

Lichtkoppler and Kuehn (2003) and Ohio Sea Grant Extension

business. Figure 4.2 illustrates the TR for full-day charter fishing trips for lake trout and salmon.

As can be seen by Figure 4.2, TR is in fact linear with respect to output. In other words, if 14 full-day charter fishing trips for lake trout and salmon are provided, the TR would be $5,698 (= 407 × 14) per season. Given the information presented in Table 4.1, what would be the graph of TR for full-day charter fishing trips for steelhead or smallmouth bass look like? What about for half-day charter fishing trips? They would all have the same linear shape as shown in Figure 4.2. Of course, the scales on the axes of the graphs would be different as the magnitudes of the numbers would change. What would be the behavior of a charter boat captain given this data on TR – would they try to book (i.e., sell) more lake trout and salmon full-day excursions or half-day yellow perch excursions? What if the choice were generating no revenue or selling half-day yellow perch excursions? Finally, would the TR of the other practical applications exhibit similar results?

In the ISO Beam application, a weighted price of $7.76 per ISO beam was used to calculate TR (Patterson et al. 2002). Figure 4.3 shows the graph of TR. TR is linear with respect to the amount of output sold. However, the value of an ISO beam would probably vary in a manner similar to solid 4 by 4 beams. Patterson et al. (2002) showed that the market price of solid 4 by 4 beams vary by time of year and length. In general, however, longer solid 4 by 4 beams had a higher market price than short beams. The same could be postulated about ISO beams of

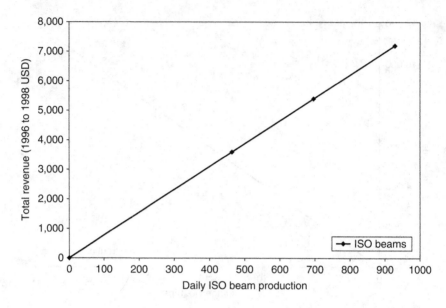

Figure 4.3 Total Revenue for the ISO Beam Case Study (1996–1998 USD)

Patterson et al. (2002)

different length. Thus, TR would behave in a similar manner as the Charter Boat Fishing case study for different fish species and length of excursion. If the market price data showed a variation of ISO beams by time of year and length, what would be the ISO Beam mill owner's behavior?

In the Mobile Micromill® application (Becker et al. 2004), output price by lumber size and grade is given in Table 2.3. However, TR is still linear with respect to the amount of output sold even given the information presented in Table 2.3. Based on the information given in Table 2.3, what do you think the mill owner's behavior will be in terms of producing the various possible outputs described in the table, given the percentage of lumber size and grade recovery of the various sizes of ponderosa pine log (see Table 2.2)? Is this mill owner's behavior similar to that of the charter boat captain or the ISO beam mill owner?

In the maple syrup operation practical application, the output was described as the number of taps by CFBMC (2000) and Huyler (2000). However, for the production system described in Figure 2.1d, consumers do not buy "taps"; they buy syrup or other maple sugar products.[3] Thus in terms of describing TR, taps are awkward in characterizing the retail output. As with the previous practical applications, output has more than one attribute: Maple syrup is graded based primarily on color and taste. The grade that receives the highest consumer price is Grade A Golden with a delicate mild maple flavor, followed in succession by Grade A Amber with a rich maple flavor, Grade A Dark with a robust full-bodied maple flavor, and Grade A Very Dark with a strong maple flavor (www.ams.usda.gov/

sites/default/files/media/MapleSyrupStandards.pdf accessed 29 April 2018 and http://canadagazette.gc.ca/rp-pr/p2/2014/2014-12-31/html/sor-dors297-eng.html accessed 29 April 2018). Variations in grades of maple syrup are due to method of production (e.g., type of evaporator), year of production, season in which the sap was collected, and syrup produced (Marckers et al. 2006). Nonetheless, TR is still linear with respect to the amount of maple syrup sold by grade.

Before, I examine the next two examples, I believe it is important to revisit the three fundamental questions that are needed to examine systematically any production system: (1) What are the relevant fixed and variable inputs? (2) What are the outputs? and (3) How do you describe the production process? It is critical to think about the how the economic information from the answers will be used. In other words, have you provided sufficient detail to help build the Pillars of Cost, Value, and Price? Focusing on answering the question illustrated earlier, What are the outputs? may not provide enough detail to define TR adequately. You may have to revisit the production process description to account for quality and the product classification indicator that impact TR directly. This is true for the Radiata Pine Plantation examples that will be discussed shortly.

In the Select Red Oak example, output is defined as board foot volume International 1/4 per tree (Hahn and Hansen 1991). As described in Chapter 2 – Production Systems, hardwood trees, such as red oak, are characterized by an index of quality. A tree designated as a Grade 1 denotes the highest quality, Grade 2 is next in quality followed by Grade 3 and so on. Diameter at breast height is one – of many – attributes used to distinguish between tree grades.[4] Other things being equal the larger the diameter the better the tree grade. Individuals who purchase red oak place a higher value on Grade 1 trees, then Grade 2 and so on. The difference between the stumpage price of a Grade 1 tree versus a Grade 2 tree versus a Grade 3 tree can be substantial (Stier 2003).[5] The description of the production process (see equations (2.5) and (2.6)) allows volume to be described in terms of diameter at breast height (DBH) (see Table 2.5). Using hardwood tree grading criteria from the US Department of Agricultural Forest Service Forest Inventory and Analysis Handbook (2006) and stumpage price information from New York State Department of Environmental Conservation Winter 2018 Stumpage Price Report (www.dec.ny.gov/lands/5259.html accessed 29 June 2018), Table 4.2 gives the breakdown of stumpage price by tree grade. Figure 4.4 illustrates the TR for select red oak per tree by tree grade using the information in Tables 4.2 and 2.5. As can be seen in Figure 4.4, the TR is linear with respect to tree grade.

In the Radiata Pine Plantation application, the outputs are defined in terms of quantity; namely, cubic meters per hectare, m^3/ha or m^3ha^{-1}. As well as quality or user-defined product class described by dimensions (i.e., minimum and maximum small end diameter, maximum large end diameter, and length); shape (i.e., allowable sweep measured as the maximum deviation of the log's centerline from a line joining the centers of the log's ends); branching (i.e., maximum allowable size and branch angle); pruned vs. not pruned; and the length of clear wood (i.e., the length of the log without knots), the default Forecaster domestic product classes

Table 4.2 Stumpage Price for Select Red Oak by Tree Grade

Tree Grade	DBH Range[§]	Stumpage Price[‡] ($/bd.ft. Int 1/4)
Grade 3	11 inches ≤ DBH ≤ 13 inches	0.32
Grade 2	13 inches ≤ DBH ≤ 16 inches	0.51
Grade 1	16 inches ≤ DBH	0.71

[§] DBH denotes diameter at breast height. DBH ranges are based on hardwood tree grading information found in United States Department of Agriculture, Forest Service (2006).

[‡] The stumpage prices are taken from Bureau of Land Resources Winter (2018) Stumpage Price Report (www.dec.ny.gov/lands/5259.html accessed 29 June 2018). The New York State Department of Environmental Conservation collects and distributes stumpage price data in terms of low, average, and high price range, but not by tree grade. The median price in each range for the Western/Central Region is used for stumpage price by grade; namely, the median price for the low price range is Grade 3, the median price for the average price range is Grade 2, the median price for the high price range is Grade 1. Stumpage price is defined as 2018 US dollars per board feet International 1/4.

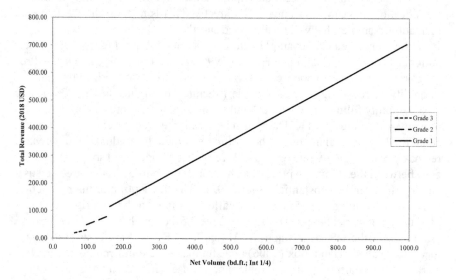

Figure 4.4 Total Revenue for Select Red Oak per Tree by Tree Grade[§]

§2018 USD denotes 2018 US dollars; given S = 66

are Pulpwood, L1 – large, large-branched sawlogs, L2 – small sawlogs, P1 – large pruned sawlogs, P1 – small pruned sawlogs, S1 – large, small-branched sawlogs, and S2 – medium, small-branched sawlogs (West et al. 2013). Table 4.3 provides a summary of the product classes and the 2016 New Zealand stumpage prices (NZ$/m³) for radiata pine.

According to Table 4.3 pulpwood has the lowest value and large pruned sawlogs have the highest value: This illustrates the Pillar of Price; i.e., the stumpage prices, and the Pillar of Value; i.e., the product classes. Tables 4.4a and 4.4b illustrate

Table 4.3 Stumpage Price for Radiata Pine by Product Class

Product Class	Product Description[§]	Stumpage Price[‡] (NZ$/m³)
Pulpwood	Pulpwood	36.00
L1	Large, large-branched sawlog	82.00
L2	Small sawlog	68.00
P1	Large pruned sawlog	147.00
P2	Small pruned sawlog	141.00
S1	Large, small-branched sawlog	94.00
S2	Medium, small-branched sawlog	78.00

[§] Radiata pine output is defined in terms of quantity (cubic meters per hectare (m³/ha)) and quality (logs and log grades). User-defined log grades are characterized by product class (e.g., large vs. small sawlogs, pruned vs. unpruned sawlogs, or pulp logs, etc.), diameter and length of each product class, and sweep (as measured by the maximum deviation of the log's centerline) (West et al. 2013).
[‡] Stumpage prices are 2016 New Zealand dollars per cubic meters (NZ$/m³)

Table 4.4a Radiata Pine Pruned Yield and Revenue at Plantation Age 30

Product Class[§]	Stumpage Price[‡] (NZ$/m³)	Product (m³/ha)	Revenue (NZ$/ha)
Pulpwood	36.00	192.2	6,919.20
L1	82.00	26.9	2,205.80
L2	68.00	62.7	4,263.60
P1	147.00	77.2	11,348.40
P2	141.00	105.8	14,917.80
S1	94.00	84.0	7,896.00
S2	78.00	206.0	16,068.00
	Total	Revenue	63,618.80

[‡] Stumpage prices are 2016 New Zealand dollars per cubic meters (NZ$/m³)
[§] Radiata pine output is defined in terms of quantity (cubic meters per hectare (m³/ha)) and quality (logs and log grades). User-defined log grades are characterized by product class (e.g., large vs. small sawlogs, pruned vs. unpruned sawlogs, pulp logs, etc.), diameter and length of each product class, and sweep (as measured by the maximum deviation of the log's centerline) (West et al. 2013).

combining the Pillars of Price and Value to estimate the total revenue for clearcutting a pruned vs. unpruned 30-year old Radiata Pine Plantation.

The total revenue difference of 6,177.00 NZ$/ha is the value added by changing the management inputs given in Table 2.7a, 2.7b, 3.6a, and 3.6b – the Pillars of Cost and Value for the inputs – and the corresponding revenues in Tables 4.4a and 4.4b – The Pillars of Price and Value for the outputs.

The revenue data by product class given in Table 4.4a for the pruned Radiata Pine Plantation are graphed in Figure 4.5

As with Figure 4.4 based on the data from Tables 4.2 and 2.5, the revenue generated by each product class or tree grade is linear with respect to its price. Tables 4.4a and 4.4b highlight an important concept of total revenue that is not

Table 4.4b Radiata Pine Unpruned Yield and Revenue at Plantation Age 30

Product Class[§]	Stumpage Price[‡] (NZ$/m³)	Product (m³/ha)	Revenue (NZ$/ha)
Pulpwood	36.00	241.5	8,694.00
L1	82.00	45.0	3,690.00
L2	68.00	49.5	3,366.00
S1	94.00	138.5	13,019.00
S2	78.00	367.6	28,672.80
	Total	Revenue	57,441.80

[‡] Stumpage prices are 2016 New Zealand dollars per cubic meters (NZ$/m³)
[§] Radiata pine output is defined in terms of quantity (cubic meters per hectare (m³/ha)) and quality (logs and log grades). User-defined log grades are characterized by product class (e.g., large vs. small sawlogs, pruned vs. unpruned sawlogs, pulp logs, etc.), diameter and length of each product class, and sweep (as measured by the maximum deviation of the log's centerline) (West et al. 2013).

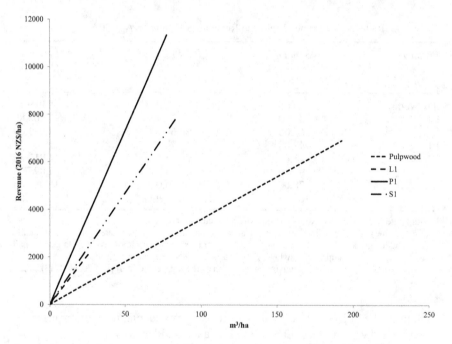

Figure 4.5 Total Revenue for the Pruned Radiata Pine Plantation by Selected Product Class[§]
§2016 NZ$/ha denotes 2016 New Zealand dollars per hectare; m3/ha denotes cubic meters per hectare

readily apparent in Figure 4.4 and equation (4.2); namely, that total revenue could be the sum of multiple outputs each with their unique price:

$$TR = \sum_k P_k Q_k (\bullet)$$

Thus, the total revenue for harvesting a pruned and unpruned Radiata Pine Plantation at age 30 is the column sum given in Tables 4.4a and 4.4b. The same could be said for the daily total revenue from the Charter Boat Fishing example given two half-day trips for the same or different species. Actually, the same could be said for harvesting a unit area of red oak of different diameters.

Average Revenue (AR)

Average revenue is defined by equation (4.3)

$$AR = \frac{TR}{Q(x_1, x_2, \ldots, x_j)} = \frac{P \cdot Q(\bullet)}{Q(\bullet)} = P \cdot \left[\frac{Q(\bullet)}{Q(\bullet)}\right] = P \tag{4.3}$$

where the notation used is defined in equation (4.1). AR is defined as the revenue per unit of output. The units on AR are the same as the units on price, P, that is dollars per unit output, or $/Q.[6] Given the assumptions about the market (i.e., workable competition), P is constant, and AR is linear with respect to output. In fact, AR is a horizontal line and is not a function of the amount of output you sell.

At first glance it may seem odd that AR is constant or does not change as more or less output is produced and sold. To illustrate this, I will use the information from Tables 4.3, 4.4a, and 4.4b for the Radiata Pine Plantation practical application. Table 4.4a and equation (4.4a) define the AR of selling 77.2 m³/ha (m³ha⁻¹) of large pruned sawlogs, P1:

$$AR_{P1} = \frac{TR}{Q(\bullet)} = \frac{11{,}348.40 \dfrac{NZ\$}{ha}}{77.2 \dfrac{m^3}{ha}} = 147.00 \frac{NZ\$}{m^3}$$

$$= \frac{TR}{Q(\bullet)} = \frac{11{,}348.40 \ NZ\$ \ ha^{-1}}{77.2 \ m^3 ha^{-1}} = 147.00 \ NZ\$ \ m^{-3} \tag{4.4a}$$

For every cubic meter of harvested large pruned sawlogs I sell, I will receive 147.00 NZ$ in revenue. This is also the output price listed in Tables 4.3 and 4.4a and is consistent with equation (4.3). Table 4.4b and equation (4.4b) define the AR of selling 45.0 m³/ha (m³ha⁻¹) of large, large-branched sawlogs, L1:

$$AR_{L1} = \frac{TR}{Q(\bullet)} = \frac{3{,}690.00 \dfrac{NZ\$}{ha}}{45.0 \dfrac{m^3}{ha}} = 82.00 \frac{NZ\$}{m^3}$$

$$= \frac{TR}{Q(\bullet)} = \frac{3{,}690.00 \ NZ\$ \ ha^{-1}}{45.0 \ m^3 ha^{-1}} = 82.00 \ NZ\$ \ m^{-3} \tag{4.4b}$$

For every cubic meter of harvested large, large-branched sawlogs I sell, I will receive 82.00 NZ$ in revenue. This is also the output price listed in Tables 4.3 and 4.4b and is consistent with equation (4.3). Similar calculations and interpretations

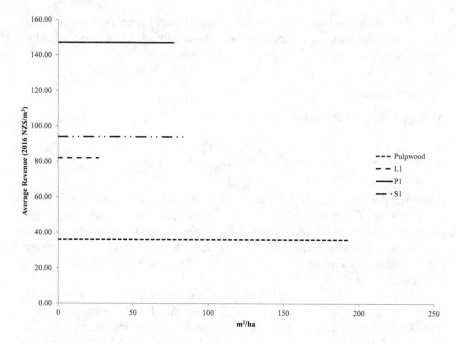

Figure 4.6 Average Revenue for the Radiata Pine Plantation by Selected Product Class[§]

§2016 NZ$/ha denotes 2016 New Zealand dollars per hectare; m3/ha denotes cubic meters per hectare

of AR can be made for the other product classes described in Tables 4.3, 4.4a, and 4.4b. Figure 4.6 shows the AR for each selected product class.

Figure 4.6 shows that AR is in fact linear with respect to output for each product class. In addition, AR is constant for each product class. Based on the prior discussion, I will leave it to you to determine what the tables and graphs of AR look like for rest of the practical applications used in this chapter.

Marginal Revenue (MR)

Marginal revenue is defined as the change in TR from the sale of an additional unit of output

$$MR = \frac{\Delta TR}{\Delta Q(x_1, x_2, ..., x_j)} = \frac{\Delta[P \cdot Q(\bullet)]}{\Delta Q(\bullet)} = P\left[\frac{\Delta Q(\bullet)}{\Delta Q(\bullet)}\right] = P \qquad (4.5)$$

where the notation used is defined in equation (4.1). The units on MR are the same as the units on price, P, that is dollars per unit output, or $/Q.[7] Given the assumptions about the market (i.e., workable competition), P is constant and does not change if the amount of output sold changes. MR is linear with respect to output. In fact, MR is a horizontal line and is not a function of the amount of output you sell.

Again, it may seem odd that MR is constant. I will use the pruned Radiata Pine Plantation to illustrate MR based on the information from Tables 4.3 and 4.4a. Equation (4.6) defines MR for an additional cubic meter per hectare of product class L1 – large, large-branched sawtimber:

$$MR = \frac{\Delta TR}{\Delta Q(\bullet)} = \frac{(2,287.80 - 2,205.80)\dfrac{NZ\$}{ha}}{(27.9 - 26.9)\dfrac{m^3}{ha}} = 82.00 \frac{NZ\$}{m^3}$$

$$= \frac{\Delta TR}{\Delta Q(\bullet)} = \frac{(2,287.80 - 2,205.80)\,NZ\$\,ha^{-1}}{(27.9 - 26.9)\,m^3 ha^{-1}} = 82.00 \; NZ\$m^{-3}$$

(4.6)

Based on equations (4.5) and (4.6), if the pruned management inputs had yielded an additional cubic meter per hectare of L1 product class, an additional 82.00 $NZ/ha of revenue would have been earned. Interestingly, if the unpruned management inputs had yielded an additional cubic meter per hectare of L1 product class, an additional 82.00 $NZ/ha of revenue would have been earned. The same could be said for any of the product classes given in Tables 4.3, 4.4a, and 4.4b. The MRs for selected product class are shown in Figure 4.7.

Examining Tables 4.3, 4.4a, and 4.4b and Figures 4.6 and 4.7 reveals MR = AR, and the units on MR and AR are identical as MR = AR = P given equations (4.3) and (4.5).

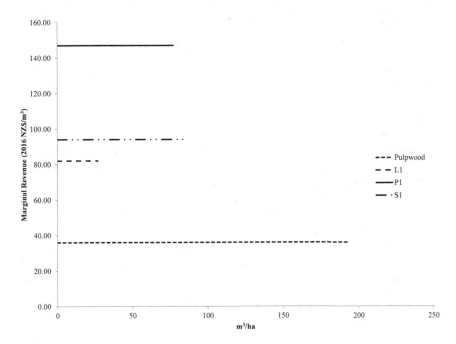

Figure 4.7 Marginal Revenue for the Radiata Pine Plantation by Selected Product Class[§]

§2016 NZ$/ha denotes 2016 New Zealand dollars per hectare; m3/ha denotes cubic meters per hectare

Examining Figure 4.4 reveals a conclusion similar to that associated with a non-continuous production process and AP and MP, and noncontinuous total costs and AVC and MC. Namely, as a red oak tree changes grade there is a noncontinuous change in total revenue for given diameters. Thus, calculating an AR using equation (4.3) and MR from equation (4.4) at these diameters provides no useful economic information.

Based on the prior discussion, I will leave it to you to determine what the tables and graphs of MR look like for rest of the practical applications used in this chapter. The solar array practical application has a unique characteristic with respect to MR that is best discussed in the context of supply and demand curves and market structure. Thus, I will wait to discuss MR with respect to the solar array practical application until Chapter 10 – Supply and Demand and Chapter 11 – Market Equilibrium and Structure.

The next three descriptors of revenue are defined with respect to inputs used in the production process. For the purposes of the following discussion, I will use the Select Red Oak example and DBH as the input.

Total Revenue Product (TRP)

Total revenue product is given in equation (4.7)

$$TRP = P \cdot TP = P \cdot Q(\bullet) \tag{4.7}$$

where the notation used is defined in equation (4.1) with TP denoting total product or the production system. Given the assumptions about the market (i.e., workable competition), P is constant and does not change if the amount of output sold changes. Equations (4.7) and (4.2) appear to be identical. However, I want to draw your attention to the TP term.[8] Table 4.5a gives the TRP for Select Red Oak based on the stumpage price and grade information contained in Table 4.2 and given a site index of 66 feet.

As the focus is on an input, in this circumstance DBH, TRP is graphed with respect to input.

Comparing Figures 4.8 and 4.4 reveals two interesting observations. First, while TR is linear with respect to output, TRP is *not* linear with respect to input. Second, the shape of the TRP curve is similar to the net yield TP curve given in Figure 2.5. The TRP curve (as well as the TP curve) represents a technical efficiency frontier and must also satisfy the Law of Diminishing Returns and in this case stand dynamic and physiological changes as well.

While TR relates output to the revenue it generates, TRP relates the productivity of a variable input (used to produce the output) to the revenue it generates. TRP is used to relate variable input productivity to revenue. Table 4.5a illustrates this relationship between DBH and the revenue it generates (i.e., TRP); for example, a 15-inch select red oak generates a revenue of $69.54 per tree. As with depictions of the TP, TRP for a given variable input assumes that all other inputs are held constant. In the case of the Select Red Oak practical application, the data Table 4.5a

Table 4.5a Select Red Oak Total Revenue Product

DBH[§]	Volume(Net)	Total Revenue Product ($/tree)		
(inches)	(bd.ft./tree)	Grade 3	Grade 2	Grade 1
10	47.1	–	–	–
11	60.7	19.17	–	–
12	76.2	24.09	–	–
13	93.9	29.66	48.20	–
14	113.6	–	58.34	–
15	135.4	–	69.54	–
16	159.3	–	81.78	113.24
17	185.1	–	–	131.61
18	212.8	–	–	151.33
19	242.4	–	–	172.33
20	273.6	–	–	194.52
25	449.0	–	–	319.24
30	637.7	–	–	453.40
35	810.4	–	–	576.21
40	941.0	–	–	669.09
45	1013.7	–	–	720.75
50	1025.8	–	–	729.38
51	1021.6	–	–	726.38

[§] DBH denotes diameter at breast height. Volume(Net) is measured in terms of net board feet (International 1/4) per tree, (bd.ft./tree) for S = 66 feet. Grade and stumpage price are defined in Table 4.2.

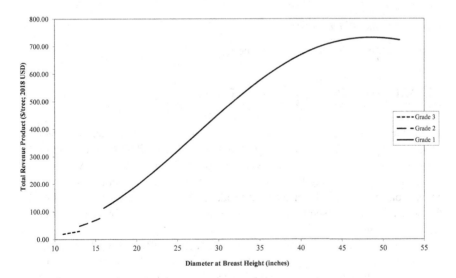

Figure 4.8 Total Revenue Product for Select Red Oak by Grade[§]

§2018 USD denotes 2018 US dollars; given S = 66 feet

assumes a site index of 66 feet. At a site index of 99, the TRP of a 15-inch select red oak would be $77.35 per tree (see Tables 2.5 and 4.2). The difference of $7.81 per tree would be due to the increased site productivity. Finally, DBH generates no revenue until the tree reaches 11 inches (Table 4.2).[9] This is due to the input limitations of a sawmill production system in terms of processing the tree into lumber.

While TRP can be calculated for either DBH or site index, the interpretation of TRP is tricky for two reasons. First, in Chapter 2 – Production Systems, the inputs that are relevant for following the Architectural Plan for Profit are those you have direct control over. However, you do not have direct control over either DBH or site index. You can manipulate them indirectly by thinning or fertilizing. DBH is a proxy used to measure the productivity of natural system in terms of the desired output – volume – and your manipulation of that system to produce the desired volume output. Second, while TP is continuous based on the description of the production system (see equations (2.4) and (2.5) in Chapter 2 – Production Systems), TRP shown in Figure 4.8 is not continuous due to different grades (see Table 4.2). Thus, while the productivity of a variable input changes due to the Law of Diminishing Returns and in this case also stand dynamic and physiological changes, its contribution to revenue can also change due to different prices reflecting different grades of quality.

The labor input in the Charter Boat Fishing, Mobile Micromill®, and ISO Beam applications is under the direct control of the manager; however, not enough data are provided in the descriptions of the production system to calculate TRP in a manner similar to that given above. Nonetheless, the interpretation of an input's productivity in terms of revenue is just as important.

Average Revenue Product (ARP)

Average revenue product is given by equation (4.8)

$$ARP = AR \cdot AP = \frac{P \cdot Q(\bullet)}{Q(\bullet)} \cdot \frac{Q(\bullet)}{x_j} = P \cdot AP \qquad (4.8)$$

where the notation used is defined in equation (4.1) with AP denoting average product. Given the assumptions about the market (i.e., workable competition), P is constant and does not change if the amount of output sold changes. As with TRP, the focus is on measuring the productivity of a variable input in terms of revenue generation. In this case the measure of productivity is AP. Table 4.5b gives the ARP for Select Red Oak based on the stumpage price and grade information contained in Table 4.2 and given a site index of 66 feet.

Figure 4.9 is the graph of ARP with respect to DBH. How does the graph of ARP compare with a graph of AR for the Select Red Oak practical application? If you had drawn the graph of AR as recommended, you would have discovered that it was similar to the graph of AR for the Radiata Pine application (Figure 4.6). While AR is a set of horizontal lines with respect to output, ARP is *not* with respect to input. The shape of the ARP curve is similar to the

Table 4.5b Select Red Oak Average Revenue Product

DBH[§]	AP(Net)	Average Revenue Product ($/tree/inch)		
(inches)	(bd.ft./tree/inch)	Grade 3	Grade 2	Grade 1
10	4.71	–	–	–
11	5.51	1.74	–	–
12	6.35	2.01	–	–
13	7.22	2.28	3.71	–
14	8.11	–	4.17	–
15	9.03	–	4.64	–
16	9.95	–	5.11	7.08
17	10.89	–	–	7.74
18	11.82	–	–	8.41
19	12.76	–	–	9.07
20	13.68	–	–	9.73
25	17.96	–	–	12.77
30	21.26	–	–	15.11
35	23.15	–	–	16.46
40	23.53	–	–	16.66
45	22.53	–	–	16.02
50	20.52	–	–	14.59
51	20.03	–	–	14.24

[§] DBH denotes diameter at breast height. AP(Net) denotes average product measured in terms of net board feet (International 1/4) per tree per inch (bd.ft./tree/inch) for S = 66. Grade and stumpage price are defined in Table 4.2.

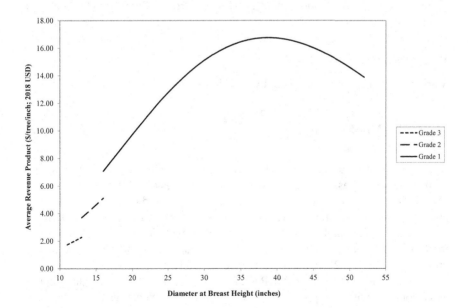

Figure 4.9 Average Revenue Product for Select Red Oak by Grade[§]

§2018 USD denotes 2018 US dollars; given S = 66 feet

net yield AP curve given in Figure 2.10. The ARP curve (as well as the AP curve) represents a technical efficiency frontier, must also satisfy the Law of Diminishing Returns, and again in this case stand dynamic and physiological changes.

While AR relates output to the revenue per unit of output it generates, ARP relates the average productivity of a variable input to the revenue it generates. The interpretation of ARP is tied directly to AP. According to Table 4.5b, the ARP for a 12-inch DBH select red oak is 2.01 $/tree/inch (= 0.32 $/bd.ft. × 6.35 bd.ft./tree/ inch). The AP is 6.35 bd.ft./tree/inch, but this does not imply that the productivity (measured as net volume) of each inch of DBH up to 12 inches is the same (see Table 4.5b).[10] Thus, ARP does not imply the revenue generated by each inch of DBH up to 12 inches is the same (see Table 4.5b).

Comparing the ARP of a 12-inch to a 14-inch DBH select red oak tree is instructive. The ARP of a 14-inch DBH select red oak tree according to Table 4.5b is 4.17 $/tree/inch. The two additional inches of DBH increase the ARP 2.07 times. This is due to the price change associated with the higher grades for red oak (Table 4.2), and at 14 inches of DBH AP is still increasing (Table 2.8 and Figure 2.10). As earlier, this does not imply that the productivity (measured as net volume) or the revenue generated by every inch of DBH is the same. However, what it does imply is that the same inches of DBH on a 14-inch red oak tree on average generates more revenue than those same inches of DBH on a 12-inch red oak tree. How would this discussion of the ARP that an input generates translate to the use of the same unit of labor used to provide a half vs. full day of lake trout or salmon fishing (see Table 4.1)? The use of the same unit of labor in the production of longer vs. shorter ISO beams? And the productivity of DBH in the Radiata Pine Plantation practical application?

Marginal Revenue Product (MRP)

Marginal revenue product is given by equation (4.9)

$$MRP = MR \cdot MP = \frac{\Delta[P \cdot Q(\bullet)]}{\Delta Q(\bullet)} \cdot \frac{\Delta Q(\bullet)}{\Delta x_j} = P \cdot MP \tag{4.9}$$

where the notation used is defined in equation (4.1) with MP denoting marginal product. Given the assumptions about the market (i.e., workable competition), P is constant and does not change if the amount of output sold changes. As with TRP and ARP, the focus is on measuring the productivity of a variable input in term the revenue generation. In this case the measure of productivity is MP. Table 4.5c gives the MRP for Select Red Oak based on the stumpage price and grade information contained in Table 4.2 and given a site index of 66 feet.

Figure 4.10 is the graph of MRP with respect to DBH. How does the graph of MRP compare with a graph of MR for the Select Red Oak application? If you had drawn the graph of MR as recommended, you would have discovered that it was similar to the graph of MR for the Radiata Pine Plantation practical application (Figure 4.7). While MR is a set of horizontal lines with respect to output, MRP is

Table 4.5c Select Red Oak Marginal Revenue Product[§]

DBH	MP(Net)	Marginal Revenue Product ($/tree/inch)		
(inches)	(bd.ft./tree/inch)	Grade 3	Grade 2	Grade 1
10	11.56	–	–	–
11	13.54	4.28	–	–
12	15.58	4.92	–	–
13	17.65	5.58	–	–
14	19.73	–	10.13	–
15	21.81	–	11.20	–
16	23.85	–	12.25	–
17	25.83	–	–	18.37
18	27.73	–	–	19.72
19	29.53	–	–	21.00
20	31.21	–	–	22.19
25	37.04	–	–	26.33
30	37.41	–	–	26.59
35	31.90	–	–	22.68
40	21.81	–	–	15.51
45	9.58	–	–	6.81
50	–2.12	–	–	–1.51
51	–4.22	–	–	–3.00

[§] DBH denotes diameter at breast height. MP(Net) denotes marginal product measured in terms of net board feet (International 1/4) per tree per inch (bd.ft./tree/inch) for S = 66 feet. Grade and stumpage price are defined in Table 4.2.

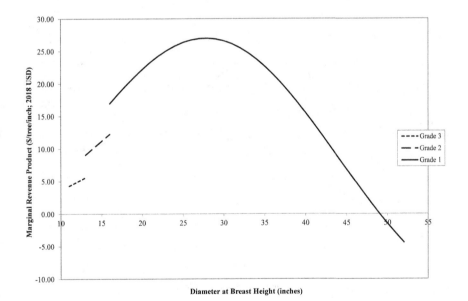

Figure 4.10 Marginal Revenue Product for Select Red Oak by Grade[§]

§2018 USD denotes 2018 US dollars; given S = 66 feet

not with respect to input. The shape of the MRP curve is similar to the net yield MP curve given in Figure 2.10. The MRP curve (as well as the MP curve) represents a technical efficiency frontier and must also satisfy the Law of Diminishing Returns and, as with TRP and ARP for select red oak, stand dynamic and physiological changes as well.

Table 4.5c shows that a 1-inch increment of DBH growth on an 18-inch DBH red oak generates more revenue than a 1-inch increment of DBH growth on either a 14-inch or a 12-inch DBH red oak. The value of an incremental inch is greater at higher grades. As with ARP this is due to the price change associated with the higher grades for red oak (Table 4.2), and MP is still increasing at 18 inches of DBH (Table 2.8 and Figure 2.10). MRP is noncontinuous even though MP is continuous. This is because of the price differences due to grade (Table 4.2). Thus, no MRP can be calculated for a 13-inch DBH Grade 2 or a 16-inch DBH Grade 1 red oak tree.

Reviewing the relationship between AP and MP shows that whenever MP > AP, AP is increasing; whenever MP < AP, AP is decreasing; and when MP = AP, AP is at its maximum value (Chapter 2 – Production Systems, Table 2.8 and Figure 2.10). The same relationship holds for ARP and MRP. Tables 4.5b and 4.5c and Figure 4.11 show that whenever MRP > ARP, ARP is increasing; whenever MRP < ARP, ARP is decreasing; and when MRP = ARP, ARP is at its maximum value.

The interpretation of MRP is different than ARP. While ARP determines the average revenue generated by the productivity of input for a range of inputs; for

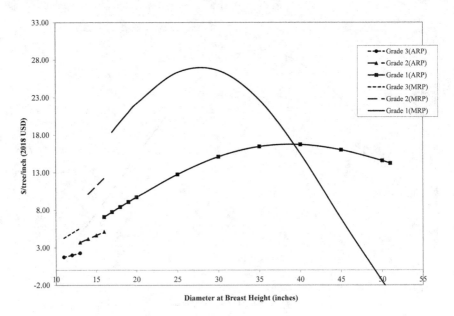

Figure 4.11 Average and Marginal Revenue Product for Select Red Oak by Grade[§]

[§]2018 USD denotes 2018 US dollars; given S = 66 feet

example, from 0 to 12 inches DBH or 0 to 14 inches DBH for a red oak tree, MRP is for an incremental change. For example, a 1-inch incremental change in DBH from a 12- to a 13-inch red oak tree generates an additional 5.58 $/tree, while a 1-inch incremental change in DBH from a 19- to 20-inch red oak generates an additional 22.19 $/tree.

Why does apparently the same 1-inch increment generate more revenue on going from a 19- to 20-inch DBH red oak than a 12- to 13-inch red oak? Answering this question requires your understanding of the underlying fundamental characteristics for systematically examining the production system – in short, reviewing the three fundamental questions asked in Chapter 2 – Production Systems concerning the production system. The functional form used in equation (2.4) is based on a Weibull model (Hahn and Hansen 1991); however, in simple geometric terms the volume of a cylinder or cone (e.g., a tree) is a function of diameter (DBH) and height (site index, S). Figure 4.12 illustrates how the same 1-inch increment, for a given height, will generate more volume (and revenue) on the 19- to 20-inch DBH red oak than on the 12- to 13-inch DBH red oak.

We know that as a tree grows in DBH they also grow in height, which will further increase the volume (and revenue) for the same 1-inch increment on the larger red oak. Can you do a similar type of analysis for labor in the ISO Beam, Micromill®, and Charter Boat Fishing applications? Or one of the other variable inputs under the direct control of you the manager? Is there enough information provided in the applications to answer the question? If not, what additional information would you need and how would you collect it?

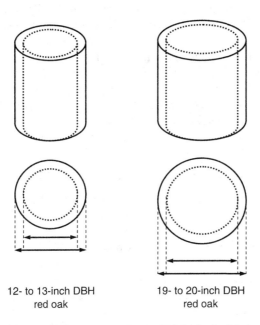

12- to 13-inch DBH
red oak

19- to 20-inch DBH
red oak

Figure 4.12 1-inch Increment to Diameter at Breast Height for Red Oak

Finally, think about how you might use this piece of economic information. If you know the revenue generated by using an additional increment of an input that you control directly, what is the most you would be willing to pay to use that input?

Revenue – Variability

Equation (4.2) can be used as a road map to discuss revenue variability:

$$TR = P \cdot Q(\bullet)$$

Revenue variability combines the variability associated with (i) the production system (foundation of the Architectural Plan for Profit), (ii) the market price (Pillar of Price), and (iii) the consumers' value (Pillar of Value). The variability associated with the production system was described in Chapter 2 – Production Systems. For example, Figures 2.17a and 2.17b illustrate the variability of energy conversion given the same dates but different years and also relative to a typical meteorological year.

In Chapter 3 – Costs, I examined the impact of changing the cost of small-diameter logs on the profit of the ISO Beam business example. A similar type of sensitivity analysis could be used with total revenue.[11] The data provided by Patterson et al. (2002) shows that the ISO Beam business is not profitable if 464 ISO beams are produced and sold per day, but it is profitable if 696 or 928 ISO beams are produced and sold per day. If the weighted average price per beam decreased by 0.46 $/beam to 7.30 $/beam, *ceteris paribus*, then revenue from producing and selling 696 ISO beams per day no longer covers the total production costs and a production level of 696 ISO beams per day is no longer profitable. If the weighted average price per beam increased by 2.16 $/beam to 9.92 $/beam, *ceteris paribus*, then revenue from producing and selling 464 ISO beams per day covers the total production costs and a production level of 464 ISO beams per day is profitable. For sensitivity analysis to be a useful tool, the entrepreneur would need to develop reasonable ranges of market prices per ISO beam based on their knowledge of the output market. Nonetheless, based on the earlier revenue sensitivity analysis, a production level of 464 beams per day is probably not going to be profitable.

Revenue Revisited – the Cautionary Tale of the Slab Mill

A slab is a broad, flat, thick piece of wood. Live or natural edge slabs still have the bark attached. Slabs are cut in various thicknesses from "1" to "3" or more. The thicker and longer the slab, the greater its value. Slabs are prized for counter tops, tables, and similar furniture. In addition, wood has to be dried before it can be made into furniture. On our college forest properties, we have large trees of the desired species readily available (e.g., black cherry – *Prunus serotina* Ehrh., northern red oak – *Quercus rubra* L., and sugar maple – *Acer saccharum* Marsh). In 2016 and 2017, I had my students conduct a business feasibility analysis of purchasing a slab mill and kiln to produce approximately 4,000 board feet of slabs per year.

Total annual costs (includes all fixed and variable costs) of producing 4,000 board feet (bf) of slabs annually was estimated at $16,234. The per unit average annual total costs are $4.00 per board foot or 4.00 $/bdft. An internet search of regional business selling slabs of similar species resulted in prices of approximately 36 $/bdft for black cherry, 22 $/bdft for sugar maple, and 22 $/bdft for red oak. You would think producing slabs would make amazing profits. If these possible profits are so amazing, why is not everyone in this market?

Producing saleable slabs is actually difficult – it is not the milling but the drying that can be problematic if done incorrectly. Selling slabs is a "small" niche market targeted to a certain socioeconomic and demographic customer. There were basically no markets in central New York for slabs. Revenue is the output quantity "sold" multiplied by the price you charge. Output produced but not sold does not generate revenue, only costs. Consequently, your analysis of "revenues" must also address why you are confident you can sell the output you produce. In the case of the slab mill, even though per unit production costs were low relative to a possible price, the probability of selling slabs consistently was very low based on market research. Thus, prices obtained from just an internet search without any justification are insufficient to analyze revenues completely.

How to Use Economic Information – Revenues – to Make Better Business Decisions

The following revenue concepts are important and bears repeating: Total revenue is the output quantity "sold" multiplied by the price you charge. Output produced but not sold generates no revenue *but does generate costs*. Consequently, your analysis of total revenue must also address why you are confident you can sell the output you produce – the value consumers place on the output (Pillar of Value) multiplied by the price you charge (Pillar of Price).

The concept of TR in the profit model is tied directly to the degree to which buyers think those goods and services make them better off than if they did without (Maital 1994) and market price. If your consumers do not value (Pillar of Value) the output(s) that you produce or provide, how much revenue are you going to generate by selling it? Probably none. As Maital (1994) points out, if this is the case, what are the benefits of cost cutting? Thus, how your business creates value, or new innovative outputs that create additional value, is an ongoing activity of managers (Maital 1994).

What is the economic information contained in TR? Based on equation (4.2), $TR = P \times Q(\bullet)$. TR is a function of price, P, and the amount of output produce or provided by the production system, $Q(\bullet)$. The economic information then seems to be price and the production system. A closer look at these two components is warranted, starting with price. The economic information summarized in price is (i) a measure of relative scarcity and a per unit measure of value; (ii) the intersection of supply and demand for the output; (iii) the market structure; and (iv) the assertions concerning human decision-making behavior given in Chapter 1 – Introduction. In short, price is economic information that consumers observe and use to make choices about whether to buy your output given their budget (Pillar of Price). Your ability to generate TR depends on the information you can obtain about your consumers' preferences and the market in which those preferences are expressed. The economic information summarized in the production system is technical efficiency and the Law of Diminishing Returns. This information is obtained from your answers to the three fundamental questions for systematically examining the production system given in Chapter 2 – Production Systems.

Total revenue is most commonly defined with respect to output. The general idea is, simply, how much revenue can I create by selling the output that I produce or provide? Given this idea, there are three descriptors of revenue: total revenue, average revenue, and marginal revenue. If you have limited ability to set the market price of your output, then $AR = MR = P$. In other words, the additional revenue you can generate by selling a single unit of output is the same as the per unit revenue generated by selling a given quantity of output. The usefulness of these revenue descriptors is the ability to compare them to the cost of producing the output to help you search for ways to increase profits.

Total revenue can also be defined with respect to inputs. These descriptors are total revenue product, average revenue product, and marginal revenue product. These descriptors of revenue rely on the precision that you answer the three fundamental questions to systematically examine the production system. They will allow you to relate the productivity of an input to the revenue it generates. The usefulness of these revenue descriptors is to compare what you pay for the inputs with the revenue that they generate to help you search for ways to increase profits.

In each case, a descriptor of revenue can be compared to costs to help you search for ways to increase profits. Alternative ways to think about these relationships are (i) given a market price, how many units of output must be produced *and sold* to cover some measures of costs; for example, average total cost, average variable cost, or average fixed costs, and is this production level feasible given the production system? Or, (ii) given various output levels, what would the price have to be to cover the same measures of cost and is this price feasible given the market structure? This will be discussed in the next chapter.

Finally, I began this chapter by talking about opportunity cost, which may have seemed a little odd given the focus is supposed to be on revenue generated by selling your output. Odd as it may seem, I am going to end this chapter talking about opportunity cost – the highest-valued alternative forgone. As a manager you must continually ask the following questions:

- What potential value am I forgoing based on my current production system, markets, and perceived consumer preferences?
- What potential value might I forgo based on changes in my production system, changes in the markets, and changes in consumer preferences?
- What economic information do I need to collect to help me answer these questions?

The economic information used to build the Pillars of Price and Value will help you answer these questions.

Notes

1 While this discussion focuses on output price, this discussion also holds with respect to the prices paid for inputs (i.e., wages).

2 As a hint, compare and contrast the profit model with the least cost/cost effective models to determine what economic information is contained in each.

3 For this particular production system, output could also be defined as taps or sap. In the case of taps, a lease of approximately 10 years is common. Pricing per tap ranges from a fixed price per tap to a base price with an adjustment based on syrup yield to a price dependent on the bulk price of syrup. In the case of sap, the price per gallon depends on the percent sugar content. The higher the percent sugar, the higher the price due to its higher quality (Wilmot 2011).

4 The USDA Forest Service's *Forest Inventory and Analysis National Core Field Guide* gives the grading factors for hardwood and softwood trees (USDA FS FIA 2006). The differences between hardwood grades are due to more than just diameter. Other factors include length of the section being graded, minimum diameter inside bark at top of section being graded, number of clear faces, and cull deductions due to crook and sweep (United States Department of Agriculture, Forest Service 2006).

5 Stumpage price denotes the output price for live standing trees (timber) on the stump.

6 What are the units on average cost? Review Chapter 3 – Costs to answer this question.

7 What are the units on marginal cost? Review Chapter 3 – Costs to answer this question.

8 Chapter 2 – Production Systems discussed TP in detail and I will not repeat that complete discussion here; however, you are encouraged to review that section of the chapter.

9 The focus of this discussion is commercial uses of the tree. Noncommercial uses such as bequest and option values will be discussed in Chapter 9 – Estimating Nonmarket Values.

10 Although it is mathematically possible for the average to be the same at each observation. This will not be the case for production systems following the Law of Diminishing Returns.

11 A more detailed discussion of sensitivity analysis and other techniques to analyze single and multi-period risk will be discussed in detail in Chapter 8 – Risk.

5 Profit

Individuals are motivated by profits and seek ways to improve their profits (Kant 2003). Entrepreneurs – in their search for economic profit – seek less costly ways of combining scarce resources into something valued more highly by consumers. They discover new cost structures and more efficient ways of producing and delivering scarce goods and services (Heyne et al. 2006: 174–175). Marginal analysis (MR relative to MC) will not prove if in fact you are maximizing profits or prove if the output level you are producing is "optimal." Marginal analysis allows for statements concerning a direction of change; for example, increasing or decreasing the amount of output you provide (Silberberg and Suen 2001).

Preamble

In Chapter 1 – Introduction, I discussed some assertions about individual decision-making behavior, one of which is that humans are maximizers. We seek to maximize our net benefits or profits. This is done by weighing the benefits and costs of a choice and illustrated in the Architectural Plan for Profit given in Figure 5.1.

The simple idea is to make the revenues (i.e., the Pillars of Price and Value given the outputs produced or provided by the production system) as large as possible relative to the costs (i.e., the Pillars of Cost and Value given the relevant inputs used by the production system). This is illustrated by Lichtkoppler and Kuehn (2003):

> Results of the 2002 Great Lakes charter captain surveys suggest that to continue profitability, charter captains should aggressively market their industry, increase revenues, and reduce expenses.
>
> (Lichtkoppler and Kuehn 2003: 4)

A similar argument is made by the authors of the Mobile Micromill® (Becker et al. 2004) and the Maple Syrup Operation (Graham et al. 2006; Huyler 2000; CFBMC 2000) practical applications. The purpose of these publications is to provide potential entrepreneurs with revenue and cost information concerning profits and how to increase profitability. This is consistent with the behavioral assertion described in Chapter 1 – Introduction.

DOI: 10.4324/9781315678719-5

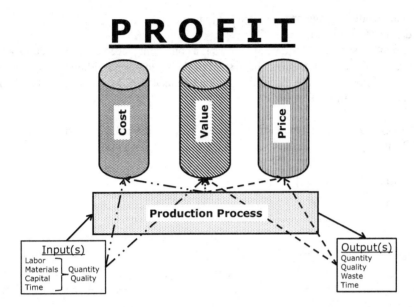

Figure 5.1 The Architectural Plan for Profit

In Chapter 1, the Managerial Analytical Method (Figure 1.4) and the Architectural Plan for Profit (Figure 1.7) were introduced. In Chapters 2 through 4, the Architectural Plan for Profit, as represented by the production systems, costs (Pillars of Cost and Value), and revenues (Pillars of Price and Value) were examined critically. The economic information contained in each component was described. In this chapter, I will put the parts back together to illustrate how the resulting economic information can be used by managers to help make better business decisions. As profits cannot be increased without first minimizing costs, I will start with a brief review of the least cost/cost effective models and then end with profit model.

Least Cost/Cost Effective Models

The decision-making behavior illustrated by the least cost model, equation (5.1), is to minimize the variable costs of producing or providing a given level of output:

$$\text{Min TVC} = \sum_j w_j \cdot x_j$$

s.t.   (5.1)

$$Q(x_1, x_2, ..., x_j) = Q^0$$

where
Min TVC denotes the objective of minimizing Total Variable Costs, $\text{TVC} = \sum_j w_j \cdot x_j$;
$\sum_j$ denotes the summation operator;

w_j denotes the jth wage or price paid for j^{th} input x_j;
x_j denotes the jth input;
s.t. denotes "subject to" and what follows is a constraint placed on the objective; and
$Q(x_1, x_2, \ldots, x_j) = Q^0$ denotes the system of producing or providing a good or service, Q, using inputs the manager has direct control over, $x_1, x_2, \ldots, x_j$, at a given quantity or quality, Q^0.

The decision-making behavior illustrated by the cost effective model, equation (5.2), is to produce or provide the most output for a given budget:

$$\text{Max } Q\left(x_1, x_2, \ldots, x_j\right)$$

$$\text{s.t.} \tag{5.2}$$

$$\sum_j w_j \cdot x_j = C^0$$

where
Max $Q(x_1, x_2, \ldots, x_j)$ denotes the system of providing or producing the maximizing quantity or quality of a good or service, Q, using inputs that the manager has direct control over, $x_1, x_2, \ldots, x_j$;
s.t. denotes "subject to";
$\sum_j w_j \cdot x_j = C^0$ denotes that the TVCs of using inputs $x_1, x_2, \ldots, x_j$ to produce or provide the good or service cannot exceed a given budget, C^0;
$\sum_j$ denotes the summation operator,
w_j denotes the jth wage or price paid for j^{th} input x_j; and
x_j denotes the jth input.

The least cost (equation (5.1)) and cost effective (equation 5.2)) model formulations show that production cost efficiency requires technical efficiency (Figure 1.4). If you are not technically efficient, you are wasting an input. If you are wasting an input, your costs cannot be minimized.

Profit Model

The profit model is given by equation (5.3):

$$\text{Max } \Pi = \text{TR - TC}$$
$$= P \cdot Q\left(x_1, x_2, \ldots, x_j\right) - \text{TVC - TFC} \tag{5.3}$$
$$= P \cdot Q(\bullet) - \sum_j w_j \cdot x_j - \text{TFC}$$

where
Max Π denotes maximization of profit (Π);
TR denotes Total Revenue, $\text{TR} = P \cdot Q(x_1, x_2, \ldots, x_j) = P \cdot Q(\bullet)$;
P denotes the market price of the good or service;
$Q(x_1, x_2, \ldots, x_j) = Q(\bullet)$ denotes the system of producing or providing a good or service, Q, using inputs that the manager has direct control over, $x_1, x_2, \ldots, x_j$;

TC denotes Total Cost, TC = TVC + TFC;
TVC denotes total variable costs, TVC = $\sum_j w_j \cdot x_j$;
$\sum_j$ denotes the summation operator;
w_j denotes the jth wage or price paid for j^{th} input x_j;
x_j denotes the jth input; for example, labor; and
TFC denotes Total Fixed Costs.

Equation (5.3) is the economic model of decision-making behavior that allows the explicit weighing of benefits relative to costs. Optimizing equation (5.3) requires managing and minimizing costs. Appendix 5A shows that the optimal input–output combination resulting from equation (5.3) must also satisfy equation (5.1) and must be production cost efficient and thus technically efficient. This chapter focuses on the profit model.

Practical Applications

The practical applications used in this chapter will include the Inside-Out (ISO) Beams (Patterson et al. 2002; Patterson and Xie 1998), Mobile Micromill® (Becker et al. 2004), Maple Syrup Operation (Huyler 2000; CFBMC 2000), and Great Lakes Charter Boat Fishing (Lichtkoppler and Kuehn 2003). Their summaries will not be repeated here because they were used in earlier chapters.

Profit Maximization

How do you know if a business has maximized profits – producing or providing the optimal amount of outputs using the optimal level of inputs – using equation (5.3)? The answer, while seemingly paradoxical, is that you do not know if they have *maximized* profits (Silberberg and Suen 2001). Then what is the purpose of the profit model? While at the outset it would seem that the greatest utility of equation (5.3) is defining the absolute level of outputs and inputs that maximize profits. This is not, however, the case. The greatest utility of equation (5.3) is developing a profit searching rule that can be used to compare the profitability of one production level relative to another systematically. Thus, equation (5.3) provides a profit searching rule to examine choices that are consistent with the assertion that your objective is to maximize profits.

The profit searching rule comes from marginal analysis. In Chapter 1 – Introduction, the concept of marginal analysis was introduced. I will summarize that discussion in the next section briefly. However, I would recommend that you review that discussion in Chapter 1.

Marginal Analysis

As a manager you will always search for ways to increase your profits, or as stated in the last section, to compare the profitability of one production level relative to another. Marginal analysis is a systematic examination of one choice relative to another given observable market conditions. Given the assertion of profit maximization, marginal analysis can determine if profits increase or decrease as production is increased or decreased by an incremental amount. The profit searching rule states that you should increase the amount of output you provide if it's incremental or marginal revenue is greater than its incremental or marginal cost. I will develop and examine the profit maximization searching rule with respect to output.[1]

Output Approach

Total Revenue

Total revenue is the first of two variables of profit as given in equation (5.3). In Chapter 4 – Revenue, I discussed the economic information in TR. Graphically, TR is illustrated by Figure 5.2.

Comparing Figure 5.2 with the TR for the Great Lakes Charter Boat Fishing (Figure 4.2) and ISO Beam (Figure 4.3) applications shows the same linear relationship between revenue and output. Comparing Figure 5.2 with the TR for select red oak by tree grade (Figure 4.4) and radiata pine by product class (Table 4.3 and Figure 4.5) shows that the relationship between revenue and output for any given tree grade or product class is linear. What this means is that selling double the output will double revenue.[2]

Total Cost

The second variable of profit as given by equation (5.3) is TC. In Chapter 3 – Costs, I discussed the economic information in TC. Graphically, TC is illustrated by Figure 5.3.

The shape of the TC curve is derived directly from the shape of the production system which is determined by the Law of Diminishing Returns. The TC curve depicts the technically efficient and the production cost efficient fixed and variable costs of producing any given level of output.[3] For example, Tables 3.3a and 3.3b illustrate the TCs of annual sap collection (Huyler 2000).

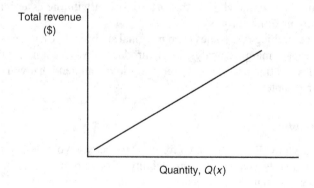

Figure 5.2 Total Revenue

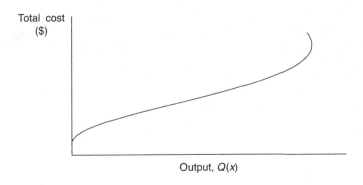

Figure 5.3 Total Cost

Profit

As defined by equation (5.3), profits are the residual after all opportunity costs (both explicit and implicit, see Chapter 1 – Introduction) have been taken into account. Graphically, profit can be depicted by overlaying the graph of TC on the graph of TR (Figure 5.4a).

Figure 5.4b illustrates that profit for any given level of output is the vertical distance between TR and TC. Moving from left to right on the output axis: (1) TR < TC and Π < 0 at low production levels the fixed and variable production costs outweigh the revenue received if they are sold. (2) TR = TC and Π = 0 at some output level profits switch from negative to positive. (3) TR > TC and Π > 0, the following output levels are of the most interest to entrepreneurs. (4) TR = TC and Π = 0 at some output level profits switch from positive to negative because the production system follows the Law of Diminishing Returns (i.e., the fixed factors of production constrain the ability to produce output in such a manner that using more variable input causes the amount of output produced per unit input (average product) to decline). (5) TR < TC and Π < 0 if the entrepreneur continues to produce output, the total costs will be greater than the revenue generated by their sales.

Analyzing the previous paragraph and Figure 5.4b shows that profits follow a reasonable path based on the economic information in TC and TR. This is illustrated in Figure 5.4c. Based on Figure 5.4c, the obvious output level where profits are the greatest is at the top of the curve. However, the intrinsic value of developing Figures 5.4a, 5.4b, and 5.4c is not to identify the top of the curve in Figure 5.4c but the profit searching rule that can be derived from its development.

Profit Searching Rule

Individuals are motivated by profits and seek ways to improve their profits (Kant 2003). If I produce or provide more (or less) output, what will happen to my profits? My managerial objective is for this output change to increase profits. Thus, I am looking for output changes that will lead to positive changes in profit. How can I use this

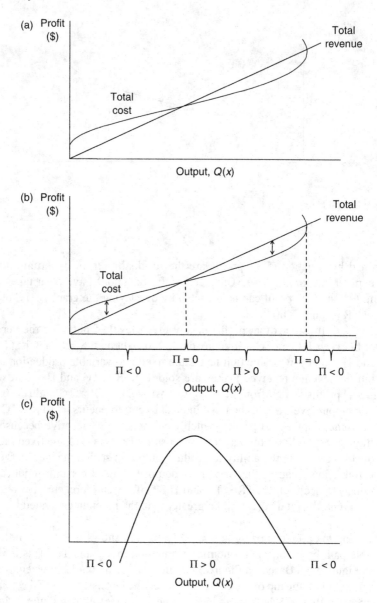

Figure 5.4 (a) Total Revenue and Total Cost; (b) Profit; (c) Profit

reasoning to develop a rule for searching if output changes will lead to positive profit changes?

This idea can be summarized by using algebra and Figure 5.5a. Let Q_1 denote the current output levels and $\Pi_1 = TR_1 - TC_1$ denotes the profit given Q_1. Let Q_2 denote alternative output levels produced or provided and $\Pi_2 = TR_2 - TC_2$ denotes

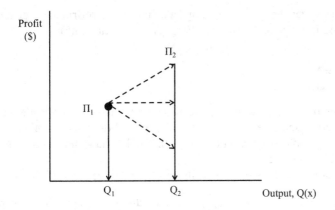

Figure 5.5a Profit Searching

the profit given Q_2. How profit changes by changing output can be represented algebraically by equation (5.4):

$$
\begin{aligned}
\frac{\Delta\Pi_{2,1}}{\Delta Q_{2,1}} &= \frac{\Pi_2 - \Pi_1}{Q_2 - Q_1} \\
&= \frac{TR_2 - TC_2 - [TR_1 - TC_1]}{Q_2 - Q_1} \\
&= \frac{TR_2 - TR_1 - TC_2 + TC_1}{Q_2 - Q_1} \\
&= \frac{TR_2 - TR_1}{Q_2 - Q_1} - \frac{TC_2 - TC_1}{Q_2 - Q_1} \\
&= \frac{\Delta TR_{2,1}}{\Delta Q_{2,1}} - \frac{\Delta TC_{2,1}}{\Delta Q_{2,1}}
\end{aligned}
\tag{5.4}
$$

What the last term in equation (5.4) shows is that I want to compare the change in TR resulting from the change in output to the change in TC resulting from the change in output. Examining the last term in equation (5.4) a little closer reveals two interesting relationships. First, $\Delta TR_{2,1} \big/ \Delta Q_{2,1}$ is exactly the same as equation (4.5) and defines marginal revenue (MR) or the change in TR ($TR_2 - TR_1$) from the production and sale of an additional unit of output ($Q_2 - Q_1$). In addition, equation (5.4) shows that, given the market assumption of workable competition, MR equals output price (i.e., MR = P). Second, $\Delta TC_{2,1} \big/ \Delta Q_{2,1}$ is exactly the same as equation (3.7) and defines marginal cost (MC) or the change in production costs ($TC_2 - TC_1$) from producing an additional unit of output ($Q_2 - Q_1$). The last term in equation

(5.4) summarizes the profit searching rule and can be rewritten, in general terms, as a comparison between MR and MC given in equation (5.5):

$$\frac{\Delta\Pi}{\Delta Q} = MR - MC \qquad\qquad (5.5)$$

According to the profit searching rule, for profit to increase the added revenue from the production and sale of the additional output (MR) must more than cover the additional variable production costs (MC). The left-hand side of equation (5.5) is illustrated by Figure 5.5b.

There are three possible paths illustrated in Figure 5.5b. If MR > MC, then $\Delta\Pi = \Pi_2 - \Pi_1 > 0$ and $\frac{\Delta\Pi}{\Delta Q} > 0$. This path shows an increase in profits. If MR = MC, then $\Delta\Pi = \Pi_2 - \Pi_1 = 0$ and $\frac{\Delta\Pi}{\Delta Q} = 0$. This path shows no increase in profits. If MR < MC, then $\Delta\Pi = \Pi_2 - \Pi_1 < 0$ and $\frac{\Delta\Pi}{\Delta Q} < 0$. This path shows a decrease in profits.

The profit searching rule is illustrated by using the Maple syrup operation practical application (CFBMC 2000). Table 5.1a defines the annual costs to produce maple syrup for a 2,550-gallon operation.

Table 5.1b defines the marginal production costs. I am currently producing 765 gallons of maple syrup per year. If I increase production to 1,530 gallons of maple syrup per year, this will add $11.26 per gallon of maple syrup per year to my costs (i.e., marginal costs). If I sell a gallon of maple syrup for more than $11.26 per gallon (i.e., marginal revenue), then my annual profits will increase.[4] If I sell a

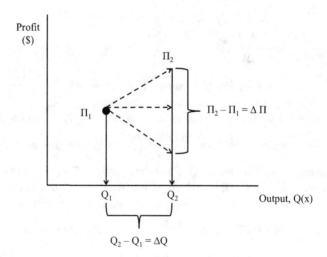

Figure 5.5b Profit Searching

Table 5.1a Annual Production Costs for 2,550-Gallon Maple Syrup Operation[‡]

Item	127.5 (gal/yr)	255 (gal/yr)	765 (gal/yr)	1,530 (gal/yr)	2,550 (gal/yr)
Total Variable Cost					
Labor	$1,601.79	$2,347.50	$4,641.17	$8,259.34	$13,083.57
Supplies	$1,208.08	$2,271.45	$5,068.54	$9,204.94	$14,812.56
Other	$471.12	$689.85	$1,261.92	$2,120.02	$3,667.98
Total	$3,280.99	$5,308.81	$10,971.62	$19,584.30	$31,564.11
Total Fixed Costs	$33,223.23	$33,223.23	$33,223.23	$33,223.23	$33,223.23
Total Cost	$36,504.22	$38,532.04	$44,194.85	$52,807.53	$64,787.34

[‡] Source of data CFBMC (2000). Costs are in 1999 US dollars using an exchange rate of 1.49 Canadian dollars per US dollar. (gal/yr) denotes gallons of maple syrup per year. These costs do not include the cost of establishing a sugarbush.

Table 5.1b Marginal Costs for 2,550-Gallon Maple Syrup Operation[‡]

Annual Production (gal/yr)	Total Variable Cost (USD/yr)	Marginal Cost (USD/gal)
127.5	$36,504.22	$15.90
255	$38,532.04	$11.10
765	$44,194.85	$11.26
1,530	$52,807.53	$11.74
2,550	$64,787.34	

[‡] Source of data CFBMC (2000). Costs are in 1999 US dollars (USD). (gal/yr) denotes gallons of maple syrup per year. (USD/gal) denotes 1999 US dollars per gallon of maple syrup.

gallon of maple syrup for less than $11.26 per gallon, then my annual profits will decrease.[5]

The profit searching rule in equation (5.5) can be used by entrepreneurs to increase their profits. Focusing on the MC term of the profit searching rule briefly, marginal cost has been defined as the change in total cost per unit change in output or as the change in variable production costs associated with changing the output level. Although both definitions are accurate, the difference highlights the fact that TFCs are not included in determining MC. This is illustrated in equations (3.7) and (3.8) from Chapter 3 – Costs. As is shown in equation (5.3), TFCs are an integral component in determining profit. Thus, while the profit searching rule can be used to determine if changing output will increase profits, equation (5.3) must be used to determine if the new output level will result in profits being positive. This requires including TFCs.

Profit Maximization Given a Noncontinuous Production Process, Costs, and Revenues

As has been discussed previously (e.g., Chapter 2 – Production Systems), not all production processes can be described in a continuous manner. Using the maple syrup operation practical application, Table 5.2a lists the total variable, total fixed, and total costs for three maple syrup operations.

Table 5.2a shows that if maple syrup entrepreneurs wants to increase the size of their operation from 1,530 to 2,550 or 5,100 gallons of maple syrup per year, not only would their variable production costs increase but the fixed costs would also increase.[6] Table 5.2b illustrates the average and incremental costs of increasing the operation size.[7] In contrast, Table 5.1a lists the costs for a 2,550-gallon maple syrup per year operation. Such an operation has the equipment and infrastructure to produce 127.5, 255, 765, 1,530, or 2,550 gallons of maple syrup per year. Thus, the fixed costs are the same no matter how much is produced. Note: I have changed the terminology from marginal cost to incremental cost when discussing the difference

Table 5.2a Total Annual Production Costs of Three Different Maple Syrup Operations[‡]

Cost Item	1,530 (gal/yr)	2,550 (gal/yr)	5,100 (gal/yr)
Variable Costs			
Labor	$8,259.34	$13,083.57	$25,144.14
Supplies	$9,204.94	$14,812.56	$28,748.85
Other	$2,120.02	$3,667.98	$6,528.32
Fixed Costs	$10,688.95	$15,048.79	$24,726.19
Total Cost	$30,273.25	$46,612.90	$85,147.50

[‡] Source of cost data CFBMC (2000). Costs are in 1999 US dollars using an exchange rate of 1.49 Canadian dollars per US dollar. (gal/yr) denotes gallons of maple syrup per year. These costs do not include the cost of establishing a larger sugarbush or the costs purchasing the additional equipment.

Table 5.2b Average and Incremental Annual Production Costs of Three Different Maple Syrup Operations[‡]

Annual Production (gal/yr)	Total Cost (USD/yr)	Average Cost (USD/gal)	Incremental Cost (USD/gal)
1,530	$30,273.25	$19.79	
			$16.02
2,550	$46,612.90	$18.28	
			$15.11
5,100	$85,147.50	$16.70	

$$\frac{\Delta TC}{\Delta Q} = \frac{\$85,147.50 - \$46,612.90\left(USD/yr\right)}{5,100 - 2,550\left(gal/yr\right)} = \$15.11\left(USD/gal\right)$$

[‡] Source of cost data CFBMC (2000). Annual production costs are in 1999 US dollars (USD/yr) using an exchange rate of 1.49 Canadian dollars per US dollar. (gal/yr) denotes gallons of maple syrup per year. (USD/gal) denotes 1999 US dollars per gallon of maple syrup. These costs do not include the cost of establishing a larger sugarbush or the costs purchasing the additional equipment.

between Tables 5.1a and 5.1b and Tables 5.2a and 5.2b. This illustrates the nature of the change required to adjust the size of an operation versus increasing/decreasing output from an operation of a given size. For example, increasing the size of the operation would require purchasing additional capital equipment (e.g., taps, vacuum lines, etc., see Table 3.1 in Chapter 3 – Costs) and land (e.g., obtaining a larger sugarbush), and so on. The annual costs of these purchases (e.g., payments to the bank for the loan to increase the size of your operation, which will be discussed in Chapter 6 – Capital Theory: Investment Analysis) must also be included. As the costs given in Tables 5.2a and 5.2b do not include these costs, they underestimate the total costs.

As was discussed in Chapter 4 – Revenue, differences in quality or other output attributes may cause differences in output price. For example, maple syrup is graded based primarily on color and taste. The grade that receives the highest consumer price is Grade A Golden with a delicate mild maple flavor followed in succession by Grade A Amber with a rich maple flavor, Grade A Dark with a robust full-bodied maple flavor, and Grade A Very Dark with a strong maple flavor (www.ams.usda.gov/sites/default/files/media/MapleSyrupStandards.pdf accessed 29 April 2018 and http://canadagazette.gc.ca/rp-pr/p2/2014/2014-12-31/html/sor-dors297-eng.html accessed 29 April 2018). A similar concept is illustrated in the Radiata Pine Plantation practical application in Tables 4.3, 4.4a, and 4.4b. The lowest-valued output is pulpwood and the highest-valued output is large pruned sawlogs as illustrated by Figure 4.5 in Chapter 4 – Revenue. Figure 4.7 in Chapter 4 – Revenue illustrates the MR associated with the different radiata pine product classes. However, unlike the incremental costs in Table 5.2b, Table 4.4 in Chapter 4 – Revenue illustrates the fact that no MR with any economic interpretation can be calculated between product classes. The same can be stated for any output that has differences in quality or other attributes that may cause differences in output price. In these cases, each profit position or investment must be estimated and compared. The choice would be that position giving you the greatest profit. In Chapter 6 – Capital Theory: Investment Analysis, I will discuss common tools that can be used to choose among different investments.

Breakeven Analysis

What if cost and revenue data are discrete, not continuous? What if collecting these "continuous" data are not reasonable or too costly? How does the Architectural Plan for Profit and its economic information help in management decisions?

Breakeven analysis provides different benchmarks in profit searching by an entrepreneur. Basically, its objective is to show how many units of output must be produced and sold to cover some measure of costs. I will examine three common breakeven points associated with average total costs, average variable cost, and marginal cost.

Average Total Cost

This breakeven point determines how many units of output must be produced and sold to cover total costs (variable plus fixed costs). This is illustrated in equation (5.6):

$$Q = \frac{TC}{P} \tag{5.6}$$

where TC are the total costs (total variable plus total fixed costs) for a given time period (e.g., monthly, quarterly, annually) and P is the expected market output price. There are four observations drawn from equation (5.6). First, the output level estimated by equation (5.6) can be compared to the production system, $Q(\cdot)$, to determine if it is feasible to produce that level of output for the defined time period. Second, the units on output price, P, are dollars per unit output. Rearranging equation (5.6) shows, the units on average total cost (ATC) are also dollars per unit output (see Chapter 3 – Costs).

$$Q = \frac{TC}{P}$$

$$P = \frac{TC}{Q} = ATC$$

Alternatively, for a given output production level and total costs, what is the price you must receive relative to the expected market price? Third, the condition expressed in equation (5.6) is equivalent to finding the point where total cost equals total revenue:

$$ATC = \frac{TC}{Q} = P$$

$$\left[\frac{TC}{Q} \right] \cdot Q = P \cdot Q$$

$$TC = TR$$

Fourth, the entrepreneur should conduct a sensitivity analysis, changing the total cost and market price within ranges of normal operations to determine operable ranges for Q.[8] Remember: (1) Product produced but not sold generates costs, not revenues. (2) Without a credible and defendable market price and the reason you are confident you can sell the output, your analysis will be inadequate.

Table 5.3 gives the annual average fixed, variable, and total costs for a maple syrup operation that produces 5,100-gallons of maple syrup annually.

In a 1998–1999 New Hampshire Forest Market Report published by the University of New Hampshire Cooperative Extension, the retail price was $33.10 per gallon of maple syrup (https://extension.unh.edu/resource/new-hampshire-forest-market-report-archive accessed 12 March 2021). Using linear interpolation given the information in Table 5.3 and illustrated in Figure 5.6, a maple syrup entrepreneur must produce and sell approximately 1,351 gallons of maple syrup annually at a price of $33.10 per gallon to cover the fixed and variable production costs.

Table 5.3 Annual Average and Marginal Costs for 5,100-gallon maple syrup operation[‡]

Annual Production (gal/yr)	Average Fixed Costs (USD/gal)	Average Variable Cost (USD/gal)	Average Total Cost (USD/gal)	Marginal Cost (USD/gal)
127.5	$193.93	$25.73	$219.66	
255	$96.97	$20.82	$117.78	$15.90
765	$32.32	$14.34	$46.66	$11.10
1,530	$16.16	$12.80	$28.96	$11.26
2,550	$9.70	$12.38	$22.07	$11.74
5,100	$4.85	$11.85	$16.70	$11.32

[‡] Source of cost data CFBMC (2000). Costs are in 1999 US dollars using an exchange rate of 1.49 Canadian dollars per US dollar. (gal/yr) denotes gallons of maple syrup produced per year. (USD/gal) denotes US dollars per gallons of maple syrup produced annually.

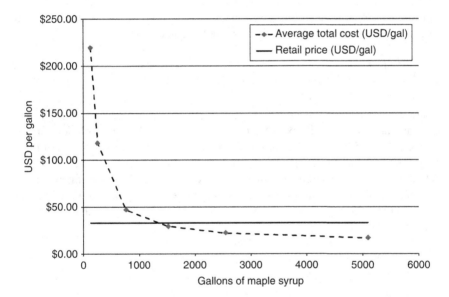

Figure 5.6 Average Annual Costs for 5,100-Gallon Maple Syrup Operation[‡]

‡Source of cost data CFBMC (2000). Costs are in 1999 US dollars using an exchange rate of 1.49 Canadian dollars per US dollar. (USD/gal) denotes US dollars per gallons of maple syrup produced annually. Retail Price is 33.10 (USD/gal) based on 1998–1999 New Hampshire Forest Market Report published by the University of New Hampshire Cooperative Extension (http://nhwoods.pbworks.com/w/page/44383953/NH%20Forest%20Market%20Reports accessed 11 July 2018).

As described in Chapter 3 – Costs and listed in Table 3.5, the cost data for the Charter Boat Fishing application provided by Lichtkoppler and Kuehn (2003) do not distinguish explicitly between fixed and variable operating expenses. The annual operating expenses for New York's Charter Boat Fishing Captains are $11,093 without boat payments. These operating expenses are total operating costs averaged over the responding Charter Boat Fishing Captains responding to a survey about operating expenses. Table 4.1 in Chapter 4 – Revenue lists the price per full-day or half-day trip by various fish species. Based on this information, New York's Charter Boat Fishing Captains' must sell 27 full-day or 36 half-day fishing trips for Lake Trout and Salmon to cover their annual operating costs given in Table 3.5. It is left to the reader to calculate the number of full- and half-day fishing trips for the rest of the listed species that Charter Boat Fishing Captains must sell to break even and cover operating expenses.

The ISO Beam and Mobile Micromill® applications can also be used to illustrate breakeven analyses. However, these analyses include payments to buy capital equipment. I will discuss these breakeven analyses in Chapter 6 – Capital Theory: Investment Analysis.

Average Variable Cost

This breakeven point determines how many units of output must be produced and sold to cover variable costs. This is illustrated in equation (5.7)

$$Q = \frac{TVC}{P} \tag{5.7}$$

where TVCs are the total variable costs for a given period (e.g., monthly, quarterly, annually) and P is the expected market output price. Four observations drawn from equation (5.7) are similar to those from equation (5.6). First, the output level estimated by equation (5.7) can be compared to the production system, $Q(\bullet)$, to determine if it is feasible to produce that level of output for the defined period. Second, the units on output price, P, are dollars per unit output, and rearranging equation (5.7) shows, the units on average variable cost (AVC) are also dollars per unit output (see Chapter 3 – Costs).

$$Q = \frac{TVC}{P}$$

$$P = \frac{TVC}{Q} = AVC$$

Alternatively, for a given output production level and variable costs what is the price you must receive relative to the expected market price. Third, the condition expressed in equation (5.7) is equivalent to finding the point where total variable cost first equals total revenue[9]

$$AVC = \frac{TVC}{Q} = P$$

$$\left[\frac{TVC}{Q} \right] \cdot Q = P \cdot Q$$

$$TVC = TR$$

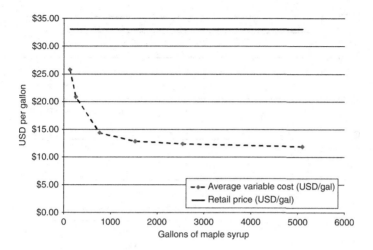

Figure 5.7 Average Annual Variable Costs for 5,100-Gallon Maple Syrup Operation‡

‡Source of cost data CFBMC (2000). Costs are in 1999 US dollars using an exchange rate of 1.49 Canadian dollars per US dollar. (USD/gal) denotes US dollars per gallons of maple syrup produced annually. Retail price is 33.10 (USD/gal) based on 1998–1999 New Hampshire Forest Market Report published by the University of New Hampshire Cooperative Extension (http://nhwoods.pbworks.com/w/page/44383953/NH%20Forest%20Market%20Reports accessed 11 July 2018).

Fourth, the entrepreneur should conduct a sensitivity analysis changing the total variable cost and market price within ranges of normal operations to determine operable ranges for Q.[10] Remember: (1) Product produced but not sold generates costs, not revenues. (2) Without a credible and defendable market price and the reason you are confident you can sell the output, your analysis will be inadequate.

Examining Table 5.3 shows that the average variable production costs are less than the retail price of $33.10 per gallon of maple syrup. This is illustrated in Figure 5.7.

As no cost information is given below producing and selling 127.5 gallons of maple syrup per year, this maple syrup entrepreneur must annually produce and sell about 127.5 gallons of maple syrup at a retail price of $33.10 per gallon to cover the variable production costs.

Marginal Cost

The final breakeven point compares MC with output price as illustrated in equation (5.8):

$$MC < P \tag{5.8}$$

There are four observations drawn from equation (5.8). First, as with the previous two breakeven points, the units on output price, P, are dollars per unit output and the units on marginal costs (MC) are also dollars per unit output (see Chapter 3 – Costs). Second, the condition $MC \leq P$ bounds profit between its minimum and

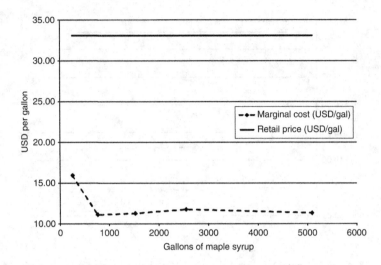

Figure 5.8 Marginal Costs for 5,100-Gallon Maple Syrup Operation‡

‡Source of cost data CFBMC (2000). Costs are in 1999 US dollars using an exchange rate of 1.49 Canadian dollars per US dollar. (USD/gal) denotes US dollars per gallons of maple syrup produced annually. Retail price is 33.10 (USD/gal) based on 1998–1999 New Hampshire Forest Market Report published by the University of New Hampshire Cooperative Extension (http://nhwoods.pbworks.com/w/page/44383953/NH%20Forest%20Market%20Reports accessed 11 July 2018).

maximum points.[11] Third, the reader will note the similarity of the breakeven point given in equation (5.8) with the profit searching rule given in equation (5.5) and illustrated in Figure 5.5. Combining the second and third observations show that if MC < P, then the additional production costs of increasing output by one unit (MC) will be less than the price that same unit could be sold for (P). As a result, profits are increasing. Finally, the entrepreneur should conduct a sensitivity analysis changing marginal cost and market price within ranges of normal operations to determine operable ranges for Q. Remember: (1) Product produced but not sold generates costs, not revenues. (2) Without a credible and defendable market price and the reason you are confident you can sell the output, your analysis will be inadequate.

Table 5.3 also gives the marginal costs for a maple syrup operation that produces 5,100-gallons of maple syrup annually. The marginal costs and a retail price of $33.10 per gallon are illustrated in Figure 5.8.

Based on these cost data, each additional gallon of maple can be sold for greater than its production costs.

To Produce or Not to Produce Decision

Analyzing the decision of whether to produce or not seems fairly simple: If profits are positive, then produce. If profits are negative, then stop producing. The analysis of the latter decision is not that simple. The key to thinking about this decision is to remember that total costs comprise variable and fixed production costs. If you stop producing, then variable costs would go to zero, but you would still have to cover the fixed costs in the short run. Thus, in the short run, if profits are negative do you lose less money by shutting down or producing?

Table 5.4 summarizes the three conditions relevant to analyzing the decision to produce or not.

Condition I is obvious, as revenue will cover variable and fixed production costs. Condition II, given in Table 5.4, states the loss associated with producing is less than by not producing. The complete analysis of Condition II is shown in Table 5.5.

The left-hand column of Table 5.5 shows that if output price or average revenue is greater than average variable costs, then total revenue is greater than the total variable costs of producing the output. The right-hand column shows that the total revenue does not cover the combined variable and fixed production costs. The conclusion is profits are negative, but the costs of producing are less than paying the

Table 5.4 To Produce or Not to Produce: Summary‡

Condition	Conclusion	Decision
I. $AR = P \geq ATC$ and $P \cdot Q \geq$ $TVC + TFC$	$\Pi > 0$	Produce
II. $AR = P > AVC$ and $AR = P < AVC + AFC = ATC$	$\Pi < 0$	Produce: Loss associated with producing is less than not producing
III. $AR = P \leq AVC$ and $AR = P \leq AVC + AFC = ATC$	$\Pi < 0$	Shutdown: Loss associated with producing is greater than just paying fixed costs

‡ P denotes the market output price given workable competition AR = P. AVC and TVC denote average and total variable costs, respectively. AFC and TFC denote average and total fixed costs, respectively. ATC denotes average total cost. Q denotes the output level when MC = MR = P. Mathematically, ATC and AVC are at their lowest value when MC = ATC and MC = AVC, respectively. Π denotes profit.

Table 5.5 To Produce or Not to Produce: Condition II‡

Condition II	
$AR = P > AVC$	$AR = P < ATC + AFC$
$P \cdot Q > TVC$ and $P \cdot Q - TVC > 0$	$P \cdot Q < TVC + TFC$
$P \cdot Q - TVC - TFC > - TFC$	$\Pi = P \cdot Q - TVC - TFC < 0$

Conclusion
$\Pi = P \cdot Q - TVC - TFC < 0$ with $P \cdot Q - TVC - TFC < TFC$
Decision
Produce: Loss associated with producing is less than not producing

‡ P denotes output price given workable competition AR = P. AVC and ATC denote average and total variable costs, respectively. TFC denotes total fixed cost. Q denotes the output level when MC = MR = P. Mathematically, ATC and AVC are at their lowest value when MC = ATC and MC = AVC, respectively. Π denotes profit.

Table 5.6 To Produce or Not to Produce: Condition III[‡]

Condition III	
$AR = P \leq AVC$	$AR = P \leq AVC + AFC$
$P \cdot Q \leq TVC$ and $P \cdot Q - TVC \leq 0$	$P \cdot Q \leq TFC + AFC$
$P \cdot Q - TVC - TFC \leq - TFC$	$\Pi = P \cdot Q - TVC - TFC < 0$
Conclusion	
$\Pi = P \cdot Q - TVC - TFC < 0$ with $P \cdot Q - TVC - TFC \geq TFC$	
Decision	
Shutdown: Loss associated with producing is greater than just paying fixed costs	

[‡] P denotes market output price given workable competition AR = P. AVC and ATC denote average and total variable costs, respectively. TFC denotes total fixed cost. Q denotes the output level when MC = MR = P. Mathematically, ATC and AVC are at their lowest value when MC = ATC and MC = AVC, respectively. Π denotes profit.

fixed costs of not producing. The entrepreneur should continue producing in the short run.

Condition III, given in Table 5.4, states that the loss associated with producing is greater than with not producing. The complete analysis of Condition III is shown in Tables 5.6. The left-hand column of Table 5.6 shows that if output price or average revenue is less than average variable costs, then total revenue is less than the total variable costs of producing the output. The right-hand column shows that the total revenue does not cover the combined variable and fixed production costs. The conclusion is profits are negative, but the costs of producing are greater than paying the fixed costs of not producing. The entrepreneur should stop producing.[12]

Profit – Variability

As with the production system, costs, and revenues, I will use sensitivity analysis to examine variability with respect to profits.[13] As given by equation (5.3),

$$\Pi = TR - TC \tag{5.3}$$
$$= TR - TVC - TFC$$
$$= P \cdot Q(\bullet) - \sum_j w_j \times x_j - TFC$$

a change in any one of the components on the right-hand side will affect profits. For example, how will profits vary if (i) output price, P, changes; (ii) sales volume, $Q(\cdot)$, changes; (iii) variable costs change; and (iv) fixed costs change, *ceteris paribus*. The data provided by Patterson et al. (2002) allow examining profit variability.

Table 5.7a summarizes the financial information provided by Patterson et al. (2002) for a 928 ISO beam daily production level. Table 5.7b summarizes how profits (and two metrics of profit) vary given: (i) output price, P, changes by 10%; (ii) sales volume, $Q(\cdot)$, decreases by 10%; (iii) per unit log costs (variable costs)

Table 5.7a Profit Description of 928 ISO Beam Daily Production Level[‡]

Production[†]		
ISO Beams Annual	232,000	
Chips (Tons per Year)	20,015	
Revenue		
ISO Beams Annual	$1,800,320	
Chips (Tons per Year)	$440,334	
Total Revenue		$2,240,654
Cost		
Annual Capital Cost (FC)	$441,092	
Salaries/Wages(VC & FC)	$611,620	
Utilities/Office (FC)	$32,350	
Residue to Boilers (FC)	$33,000	
Logs (VC)	$717,701	
Total Cost		$1,835,763
Profit		$404,891

[‡] Data taken from Patterson et al. (2002). FC denotes fixed cost. VC denotes variable costs.
[†] While a joint production process, ISO Beams and chips are produced in fixed proportions based on Patterson et al. (2002)

Table 5.7b Profit Sensitivity Analysis of 928 ISO Beam Daily Production Level

Component	Unit	Annual Profit	Profit Margin[‡]	Breakeven ISO Beams[†]
−10%	6.98	$224,859	0.11	206,684
Price	7.76	$404,891	0.18	190,077
($/Beam)				
10%	8.54	$584,923	0.24	175,941
−10%	208,800	$180,826	0.09	190,077
ISO Beams	232,000	$404,891	0.18	190,077
−10%	3.23	$476,392	0.21	182,674
Per Unit Log	3.59	$404,891	0.18	190,077
Costs				
($/Stem)				
10%	3.95	$332,792	0.15	197,542
−10%	396,982	$449,001	0.20	185,510
Capital Costs	441,092	$404,891	0.18	190,077
($/Year)				
10%	485,201	$360,782	0.16	194,644

[‡] Profit Margin is metric describing the per dollar amount of total revenue going to profits directly. This was described in Chapter III – Costs equation (3.9).
[†] Breakeven ISO Beams are the number of ISO Beams that must be produced and sold to cover total costs (variable plus fixed costs) as defined by equation (5.6).

change by 10%; and (iv) annual capital costs (fixed costs) change by 10%, *ceteris paribus*.

Within the ranges described in Table 5.7b, producing and selling 928 ISO beams per day is profitable. Holding all other components constant but selling 10% fewer

ISO beams had the greatest absolute impact on profits. This can be seen by the profit margin decreasing by half and the number of ISO beams that must be sold to cover total costs unchanged. The next greatest absolute impact on profits would be a 10% decrease in the market price, again holding all other components constant. Table 5.7b provides the entrepreneur useful information by (i) bounding variability, (ii) providing this information in a concise format, and (iii) facilitating making short-term business management decisions. *However*, for any sensitivity analysis to be a useful tool, the entrepreneur would need to develop reasonable ranges for the components of profit given in Table 5.7b based on their knowledge of the output and input markets.

How to Use Economic Information – Profits – to Make Better Business Decisions

I have described the entrepreneur's objective as maximizing profit. The description of profit is given in equation (5.3) and illustrated in the Architectural Plan for Profit (Figure 5.1). As can be seen by Figure 5.1, profits rests on the economic information within the Pillars of Price, Value, and Cost. Finally, these pillars rest on the foundation that is the production system. Chapters 2 through 4 examined each component of the profit model individually and its relationship to the Architectural Plan for Profit. This chapter looked at the profit model and the Architectural Plan. for Profit as a whole.

The economic information contained in profits is a union of the economic information contained in Chapter 2 – Production Systems, Chapter 3 – Costs, and Chapter 4 – Revenue. I will not repeat the information contained in each of these chapters, instead recommending that the reader review the ending section of each of these listed chapters.

The utility of the profit model is the profit searching rule derived from the assertion of profit maximization. This rule states that the profits of an activity increase if the marginal or incremental revenues are greater than the marginal or incremental opportunity costs. This simple rule provides entrepreneurs with a method to systematically analyze one production level with an alternative. The marginal or incremental costs are derived from the economic information in the Pillars of Cost and Value for the inputs and the production system. The marginal or incremental revenues are derived from the economic information in the Pillars of Price and Value for the outputs from the production system.

I have called the weighing of marginal or incremental revenues against marginal or incremental costs a "searching" rule for a reason. Profit maximizing is a dynamic not a static process. Input and output markets change, resulting in fluctuations in the prices you receive for your outputs and pay for your inputs. In addition, while there may be fixed components of a production system in the short run, you – as a manager – are continually searching for more technically efficient and production cost efficient input–output combinations. Finally, you are continually searching for ways to create additional value with respect to the outputs you produce or provide for your customers and for new outputs that are congruent with your current business. Revenue is only generated if you sell your outputs, and customers will only buy your outputs if they value them greater than if they did without them.

Appendix 5A – Profit and Least Cost Models

Profit Model

Let equation (A.1) define the profit model of a production system that uses only one input and produces only one output:

$$\Pi = P \cdot Q(x) - wx - TFC \tag{A.1}$$

where the notation used is defined by equation (5.3). The first order conditions for maximizing equation (A.1) with respect to input is given in equation (A.2a):

$$\frac{d\Pi}{dx} = P\frac{dQ(x)}{dx} - w = 0 \tag{A.2a}$$

given the production system is twice differentiable with $\frac{dQ(x)}{dx} > 0$ and $\frac{d^2Q(x)}{dx^2} < 0$. Equation (A.2a) can be rewritten as

$$P\frac{dQ(x)}{dx} = w \tag{A.2b}$$

The left-hand side of equation (A.2b) is P · MP or marginal revenue product (MRP; see Chapter 4 – Revenue) and the right-hand side is the marginal factor cost or wage paid for the input. The optimal amount of the input, x*, is such that the equalities of equations (A.2a) and (A.2b) hold and Q(x*) defines the optimal amount of output.

Least Cost Model

Equation (5.1) can be formulated and solved using a Lagrangian equation:[14]

$$\text{Min } L = wx - \lambda\left(Q(x) - Q(x^*)\right) \tag{A.3}$$

where λ is the Lagrangian multiplier and Q(x*) identifies the given level of production. The first order conditions require that:

$$\frac{\partial L}{\partial x} = w - \lambda\frac{\partial Q(x)}{\partial x} = 0 \tag{A.4}$$

$$\frac{\partial L}{\partial \lambda} = Q(x) - Q(x^*) = 0 \tag{A.5}$$

the production system is twice differentiable as earlier and the Karush (1939) and Kuhn and Tucker (1951) conditions are satisfied for optimal value of x. Equation (A.4) can be rewritten as:

$$\lambda \frac{\partial Q(x)}{\partial x} = w \tag{A.6a}$$

where λ is the shadow price for the value of the marginal product. Equation (A.5) requires that $Q(x) = Q(x^*)$. Inserting this requirement into equation (A.6a) gives

$$\lambda \frac{\partial Q(x^*)}{\partial x^*} = w \tag{A.6b}$$

In this case the value of the marginal product, λ, is what you could sell the additional product for in the market. Thus, the shadow price is the output price and equation (A.6b) is the same as equation (A.2b). Therefore, if profits are maximized, costs must be minimized. As equations (5.2) and (5.3) define a primal–dual relationship, the result described earlier also holds for equation (5.3).

With two or more inputs, equation (A.6b), resulting from the first order conditions, can be rewritten as

$$\lambda \frac{\partial Q(x_1^*)}{\partial x_1^*} = \lambda \cdot MP_1^* = w_1$$

$$\lambda \frac{\partial Q(x_2^*)}{\partial x_2^*} = \lambda \cdot MP_2^* = w_2 \tag{A.7}$$

$$\frac{w_1}{MP_1^*} = \frac{w_2}{MP_2^*}$$

The last expression of equation (A.7) is the equimarginal principle and the solution to the least cost problem. Thus, if all inputs are used in the production process such that the ratios of their wages to their marginal products are equal, then the production level will be production cost efficient and technically efficient.

Appendix 5B – Calculus of Profit Maximization

Output Approach

Let equation (B.1) define the profit model:

$$\Pi = P \cdot Q(\bullet) - \sum_j w_j x_j - TFC \tag{B.1}$$

where the notation used is defined by equation (5.3). In Chapter 3 – Costs, a relationship was developed between the total variable cost, $\sum_j w_j x_j$, and the various levels of output from the production system, $Q(\bullet)$. Based on this relationship, an implicit functional relationship defining total variable costs could be expressed as $\sum_j w_j x_j = C(Q(\bullet))$. The first order conditions for maximizing equation (B.1) with respect to output is given in equation (B.2a):

$$\frac{\partial \Pi}{\partial Q(\bullet)} = P\frac{\partial Q(\bullet)}{\partial Q(\bullet)} - \frac{\partial C(Q(\bullet))}{\partial Q(\bullet)} \tag{B.2a}$$

$$= P\frac{\partial Q(\bullet)}{\partial Q(\bullet)} - \frac{\partial\left(\sum_j w_j x_j\right)}{\partial Q(\bullet)} = 0$$

The second order condition for a maximum would require that $\frac{\partial^2 \Pi}{\partial Q(\bullet)^2} < 0$ or

the profit function is concave. Equation (B.2a) can be rewritten as

$$P = \frac{\partial\left(\sum_j w_j x_j\right)}{\partial Q(\bullet)} \tag{B.2b}$$

The left-hand side of equation (B.2b) is marginal revenue, MR, or Price, P (see Chapter 4 – Revenue), and the right-hand side is marginal cost (MC, see Chapter 3 – Costs). The optimal amount of the output, $Q^*(\bullet)$, is such that the equalities of equations (B.2a) and (B.2b) hold. Equations (B2a) and (B2b) also show the profit-maximizing searching rule is derived directly from the profit maximization.

Input Approach

Again, let equation (B.1) defines the profit model:

$$\Pi = P \cdot Q(\bullet) - \sum_j w_j x_j - TFC \tag{B.1}$$

The first order conditions for maximizing equation (B.1) with respect to the inputs are given in equation (B.3):

$$\frac{\partial \Pi}{\partial x_j} = P\frac{\partial Q(\bullet)}{\partial x_j} - \frac{\partial\left(w_j x_j\right)}{\partial x_j} = 0; \forall j \tag{B.3}$$

where $\forall j$ denotes for all j. The second order conditions for maximizing equation (B.1) are given in equations (B.4a) and (B.4b):

$$\frac{\partial^2 \Pi}{\partial x_j^2} < 0; \forall j \tag{B.4a}$$

$$\frac{\partial^2 \Pi}{\partial x_j^2} \cdot \frac{\partial^2 \Pi}{\partial x_k^2} - \frac{\partial^2 \Pi}{\partial x_j \partial x_k} > 0; \forall j \neq k \tag{B.4b}$$

Because $\partial^2 \Pi / \partial x_j^2 = P \cdot \partial^2 Q(\bullet) / \partial x_j^2$, Silberberg and Suen (2001) show that equations (B.4a) and (B.4b) can be written as

$$\frac{\partial^2 Q(\bullet)}{\partial x_j^2} < 0; \forall j \tag{B.4c}$$

$$\frac{\partial^2 Q(\bullet)}{\partial x_j^2} \cdot \frac{\partial^2 Q(\bullet)}{\partial x_k^2} - \frac{\partial^2 Q(\bullet)}{\partial x_j \partial x_k} > 0; \forall j \neq k \tag{B.4d}$$

Equations (B.4a) and (B.4c) define the Law of Diminishing Returns (see Chapter 2 – Production Systems). Equations (B.4b) and (B.4d) state that changing the amount used of the jth input will affect its own marginal product and the marginal products of all the other inputs. The overall impact must still be similar to the Law of Diminishing Returns (Silberberg and Suen 2001).

The term $P \partial Q(\bullet) / \partial x_j$ in equation (B.3) is $P \cdot MP$ or marginal revenue product (MRP; see Chapter 4 – Revenue) of the jth input. The second term in equation (B.3) defines the derivative of total factor cost of the jth input, $w_j x_j$, with respect to the jth input. This term, $\partial(w_j x_j) / \partial x_j$, defines the marginal factor cost (MFC) of the jth input or its wage, w_j. Equation (B.3) can be rewritten as

$$P \frac{\partial Q(\bullet)}{\partial x_j} = \frac{\partial(w_j x_j)}{\partial x_j} = w \frac{\partial x_j}{\partial x_j} = w_j; \forall j \tag{B.5}$$

The interpretation of equation (B.5) parallels equation (B2b). First, equation (B.5) states that the optimal amount of the jth input is defined when its $MRP_j = MFC_j = w_j$. This condition must hold for all inputs simultaneously. Thus, the profit searching rule with respect to input is similar to that of output: weighing some form of additional or incremental revenue with some form of additional or incremental cost. Second, marginal revenue equals price given the assumption of workable competition in the output market. If the same assumption is made with respect to the input market, the parallel would be that marginal factor cost of the jth input equals its wage or $MFC_j = w_j$. What the profit searching rule described in equation (B.5) tells me is that for profit to increase, the added revenue from the sale of the additional output produced using the jth input (MRP_j) must more than cover the jth input's marginal factor cost (MFC_j) or the price (wage) that I have to pay for the additional input, w_j. This is illustrated by Figures B.1a and B.1b.

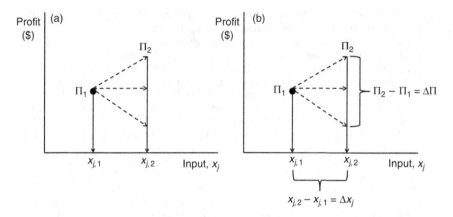

Figure 5B.1 (a and b) Profit Searching

The reader will notice the parallels between Figures B.1a and B.1b and Figures 5.5a and 5.5b.

With two inputs, B.5 can be rewritten as

$$P\frac{\partial Q(x_1,x_2)}{\partial x_1} = P \cdot MP_1 = MRP_1 = w_1$$

$$P\frac{\partial Q(x_1,x_2)}{\partial x_2} = P \cdot MP_2 = MRP_2 = w_2 \qquad \text{(B.6)}$$

$$\frac{P \times MP_1}{w_1} = \frac{P \times MP_2}{w_2} = \frac{MRP_1}{w_1} = \frac{MRP_2}{w_2}$$

$$P = \frac{w_1}{MP_1} = \frac{w_2}{MP_2}$$

The last expression of equation (B.6) adds output price to the equimarginal principle defined in equation (A.7). Reiterating the discussion of equation (B.5), the output level that satisfies this expression is economically efficient, production cost efficient, and technically efficient.

Notes

1 Appendix 5B uses calculus to develop the necessary and sufficient conditions for profit maximization using an output and input approach. This appendix also is used to derive the profit searching rule.
2 The assumption we have been using is that the market has been characterized by workable competition – no one buyer or group of buyers and no one seller or group of sellers can influence price. Output price is constant. In other words, the market sets the price and producers have almost no ability to manipulate the price of their output.

3 The definitions of technical efficiency and production cost efficiency are found in Chapter 2 – Production Systems and Chapter 3 – Costs, respectively.

4 A change in output from 765 gallons of maple syrup per year to 1,530 gallons of maple syrup per year would not really be considered a marginal change. I will describe it as a marginal change for the purposes of illustrating the profit searching rule.

5 In 2022, the average price of a gallon of maple syrup ranged from \$33.10 to \$52.20. The average price for the United States was \$34.70 down \$1.20 from 2021 (https://www.nass.usda.gov/Statistics_by_State/New_England_includes/Publications/Current_News_Release/2023/Northeast-2023-Maple-Syrup-Report.pdf accessed 1 September 2023). Average gallon price in United States dollars is a weighted average of retail, wholesale, and bulk sales.

6 In essence the fixed costs listed in Table 5.2a are variable costs when comparing among different-sized operations: Different levels of the fixed assets of capital and land are required for different-sized operations. This is analogous to the difference between short-run and long-run analysis (see Chapters 7 and 8 in Pindyck and Rubinfeld 1995).

7 Table 5.2b also illustrates economies of scale (or increasing returns to scale). As the size of the operation increases, the total production cost per unit of output decreases; namely, the average cost decreases as the size of the operation increases and the incremental costs are below the average costs. This was described in Chapter 3 – Costs.

8 Equation (5.6) estimated the breakeven production level, Q, given total cost, TC, and market price, P, are known. Alternatively, if TC and Q are known, then rearranging equation (5.6) gives ATC = P or a breakeven price. What would be the interpretation of comparing this breakeven price with the market price? This will be discussed in the section entitled "To produce or not to produce."

9 The relationship described by TVC = TR can also be used to define a contribution margin

Contribution Margin = TR – TVC

which defines the portion of revenue that offsets fixed costs (https://hbr.org/2017/10/contribution-margin-what-it-is-how-to-calculate-it-and-why-you-need-it accessed 12 July 2018).

10 Equation (5.7) estimated the breakeven production level, Q, given total variable cost, TVC, and market price, P, are known. Alternatively, if TVC and Q are known, then rearranging equation (5.6) givens AVC = P or a breakeven price. What would be the interpretation of comparing this breakeven price with the market price? This will be discussed in the section entitled "To Produce or Not to Produce Decision."

11 Students who are familiar with calculus are challenged to show that the condition MC ≤ P bounds profit between its minimum and maximum points.

12 The length of a shutdown could be temporary or permanent depending on the economic conditions leading to the shutdown and the entrepreneur's prognostication of future economic conditions. Basically, an entrepreneur can only lose money for so long.

13 A more detailed discussion of sensitivity analysis and other techniques to analyze single and multi-period risk will be discussed in detail in Chapter 8 – Risk.

14 Information concerning using Lagrangian multipliers to solve constrained optimization problems can be found in Lambert (1985) and Chiang (1984).

6 Capital Theory

Investment Analysis

Preamble

In the previous chapters we examined the economic information used to build the Architectural Plan for Profit and developed the single-period optimally efficient resource or profit searching rule. The purpose was to address the statement "How do I use economic information to make better business decisions" An assumption, although not stated explicitly, was that time – as a relevant input – was considered to have a zero-opportunity cost. Labor and materials were examined in terms of their opportunity costs with respect to profit (see Figure 5.1).[1] While I included time (i.e., plantation age) as an input in the production process for the Radiata Pine Plantation practical application, I did not examine its impact on the Architectural Plan for Profit directly.

To understand the purpose of this chapter better, a brief discussion of capital, wealth vs. profits, and capital theory would be helpful. Capital represents accumulated produced resources or assets used to generate wealth. Capital is often grouped into four (to six) broad categories:[2]

1. Human capital comprises abilities, knowledge, creativity, judgement, competence, and skills embodied in people and acquired through education, training, and experience to perform labor. Labor is often distinguished from human capital as it represents the measure of the physical or mental work done by people. Often separated out are social and intellectual capital.
2. Financial capital is money or money-like resources used by entrepreneurs for producing goods/services (e.g., purchasing long-lived assets such as machines, tools, equipment, facilities, etc.)[3] and by individuals for investment (e.g., retirement, college, etc.) and consumption (e.g., house or other durable consumer goods).
3. Natural capital is land, including renewable resources such as trees, water, solar, wind, and so forth and nonrenewable resources such as natural gas, oil, and coal.
4. Manufactured or physical capital is a long-lived asset produced by the economic system that is expected to generate value (i.e., producing other goods/services) over its useful or economic life.[4]

DOI: 10.4324/9781315678719-6

To illustrate the opportunity cost of time as a relevant input, I will concentrate on financial capital. As financial capital is a relatively scarce resource, there is an opportunity cost associated with its use. Borrowing financial capital requires paying for the privilege of using someone else's money over time. For example, buying a car most often requires borrowing money from a bank and paying the loan off over a number of specified years. Lending financial capital requires being paid by someone else for the privilege of using your money over time. For example, you might invest your money in Apple® stock to obtain an annual dividend.

Wealth is created by accumulating resources or assets – capital – used to generate multiple single-period profits and multi-period investment profits. Wealth is the capitalization of these profits. Capital theory expands the single-period optimally efficient resource allocation or profit searching rule, MR = MC developed in Chapter 5 – Profit, to determine multi-period optimal efficient resource allocations consistent with the wealth maximization assertion. The examples used to illustrate multi-period optimal resource allocations will be derived using primarily physical capital, as they are long-lived assets expected to have costs and revenues occurring over multiple periods rather than a single period.

Background

To examine how the opportunity cost of time affects the Architectural Plan for Profit, think about the following example: College students often obtain loans to help finance their college education. Table 6.1a contains an example set of loans obtained by a college student.

The student loans have the following conditions: (1) the annual interest rate is 7.43 percent, (2) no interest accrues while you are in school, (3) payment starts six months after graduation, and (4) you are permitted up to 10 years to repay the loan through monthly payments. Based on Table 6.1a, over a four-year college career the amount borrowed is $17,125 and based on a 7.43% interest rate, the monthly payments would be $202.65. Table 6.1b shows that at the end of the 10-year repayment period the amount paid in interest payments is $7,193.

According to Table 6.1b, the interest payment is 1.3 times the loan for the senior year. As a point for comparison, if no interest was charged the monthly payments would be $142.71 (= 17,125/120).

So, what is the economic interpretation of the interest rate in the preceding example and how does it relate to the opportunity cost of time? Why is it positive? How does a positive interest rate affect the Pillars of Cost, Value, and Price and ultimately Profit as illustrated in Figure 6.1?

To examine the effects of time on the Architectural Plan for Profit, I will have to first address these questions. I will then describe the mechanics of compounding and discounting or accounting for time. I will next examine six common tools that are used to analyze the profitability of investments and end with a discussion on capital budgeting.

Table 6.1a Example Student Loan Amounts

Year	Loan Amount[‡]
Freshman	$2,625
Sophomore	$3,500
Junior	$5,500
Senior	$5,500
Total	$17,125

[‡] Annual loan amounts are in 2018 US dollars

Table 6.1b Student Loan Interest Payments

Monthly payments[‡]	$202.65
Total payments[†]	$24,318.00
Principal borrowed	$17,125.00
Interest payments	$7,193.00

[‡] Monthly payments are calculated using the following formula:

$$a = V_0 \frac{\dfrac{r}{m}\left(1+\dfrac{r}{m}\right)^{t\cdot m}}{\left(1+\dfrac{r}{m}\right)^{t\cdot m}-1}$$

$$= V_0 \frac{\dfrac{r}{m}}{1-\left(1+\dfrac{r}{m}\right)^{-t\cdot m}}$$

where a = payment, r = the annual interest rate, t = length of the loan, m = number of payments per year, and V_0 = the principal borrowed. Based on the conditions on student loans, the monthly payment is

$$202.65 = 17{,}125 \frac{\dfrac{0.0743}{12}\left(1+\dfrac{0.0743}{12}\right)^{10\cdot12}}{\left(1+\dfrac{0.0743}{12}\right)^{10\cdot12}-1}$$

[†] $24,318 = 202.65 \times 120$

Practical Applications

The practical applications used in this chapter will include the Inside-Out (ISO) Beams (Patterson et al. 2002; Patterson and Xie 1998), Mobile Micromill® (Becker et al. 2004), Maple Syrup Operation (Huyler 2000; CFBMC 2000), Great Lakes

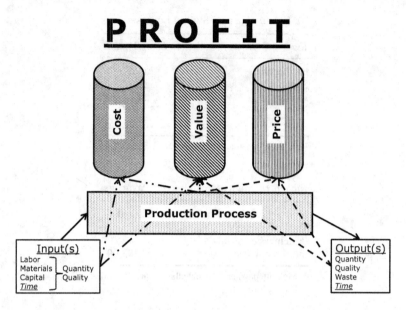

Figure 6.1 The Architectural Plan for Profit

Charter Boat Fishing (Lichtkoppler and Kuehn 2003), Select Red Oak (Hahn and Hansen 1991), and Radiata Pine Plantation. Their summaries will not be repeated here because they were used in earlier chapters.

The Interest Rate

Previous choices that were analyzed dealt with production and consumption holding time constant. Now the fundamental question is consumption today or consumption in the future. Using the definition of an opportunity cost – the highest valued alternative forgone – we can rephrase the question as What is the opportunity cost of consumption today? Answer: I am forgoing consumption in the future. Or, what is the opportunity cost of consumption in the future? Answer: I am forgoing consumption today. The opportunity cost described here is the opportunity cost of consumption at different points in time or the opportunity cost of time. The interest rate enumerates the opportunity cost of time. If production is the focal point of the discussion, the interest describes the opportunity cost of financial capital or the fact that you have alternative investment opportunities. As described by Hirshleifer (1970), the objective is to determine a preferred time-pattern of consumption or production. That is balancing consumption or production now versus sometime in the future. Irving Fisher (1930) postulated that people are impatient given the choice of consuming now versus the possibility of greater income sometime in the future from not consuming but investing today. It is this tension or time preference that gives rise to the opportunity cost of time and the interest rate being positive.

In addition to time preference, the interest rate is also defined as a function of risk and inflation (Brealey et al. 2008; Silberberg and Suen 2001). I will describe each of these factors and the difference between nominal and real interest rates.

Time Preference

As stated earlier, the concept of time preference was described by Irving Fisher (1930) as people being impatient given the choice of current versus future consumption. Based on this impatience, time preference is defined as the following:

> Time Preference – We value current consumption or income more highly than that accruing in the future. Therefore, we must be compensated if we are to put off current consumption.

This concept of time preference is not universally accepted as the principal factor of a positive interest rate. Silberberg and Suen (2001) summarize these arguments. They instead describe the concept of dynamic consistency of intertemporal utility functions; namely, they assume that the marginal value of consumption in period k in terms of forgone consumption in period $k + j$ is independent of the date but depends on the consumption levels in the two time periods. That is, the marginal value of consumption depends only on the level of consumption, not on which time periods are involved. These authors also argue that if production technology is increasing over time, then current consumption reduces future consumption by the rate of production technology change, or conversely if current consumption is forgone, then future consumption would increase by the rate of production technology change. Thus, the rate of production technology change would be sufficient to imply that the interest rate is positive.[5]

Hirshleifer (1970) defines that an individual's time preference depends on endowment, market opportunities, and productive opportunities. The endowment of most college students is low relative to their parents or Bill Gates, the founder of Microsoft®. For example, it would be tenable to postulate that $1,000 would constitute a large percent of a college student's endowment but a relatively smaller percent of their parent's endowment and would be inconsequential to Gates' endowment. Consequently, a college student's rate of time preference for that $1,000 would be positive and larger than that of their parents. While their parents would still probably have a positive rate of time preference for the $1,000, Gates' time preference for $1,000 would likely be relatively low, if not zero.[6]

In a 2011 study of the degraded Batulanteh watershed in Indonesia, Hidayati (2011) found that the local population preferred planting fruit rather than timber trees. Timber trees usually take a long time to mature but are used to build and maintain irrigation dams. The local poor, mainly "subsistence," population preferred fast-growing fruit trees yielding annual harvestable fruits to fulfill their daily needs for foods. Galor and Özak (2016) found that higher potential crop yield experienced during the pre-industrial era increased the long-term orientation; that is, a lower rate of time preference, of individuals in the modern period. As an additional point of comparison, how would you describe the time preference of a subsistence farmer for that same $1,000 compared to the typical college student?

Risk and Uncertainty

Not all future events are known with 100% certainty. The greater the gamble the greater the reward we would require for forgoing current consumption. This relationship is captured by the concept of risk and uncertainty.

> Risk and Uncertainty – Exposure to the chance of loss. If the chance can be described in statistical terms, this is commonly described as risk. If the chance cannot be described in statistical terms, this is commonly described as uncertainty.[7]

Risk and uncertainty can be categorized as market, biological, or political. While market risk is not unique to natural resources, they may have production processes that often take a long time. For example, in the Radiata Pine Plantation practical application, the process could take up to 30 years (Chapter 2 – Production Systems). The owners of this radiata pine plantation are gambling that there will be a market for radiata pine in the future and that the future value of the radiata pine will cover all production costs. The possibility that the owners are growing the radiata pines for 30 years subjects them to many different biological hazards such as losing the trees due to drought, fire, insects, or diseases. Assessing biological risk is important for more than just forestry. BlackRock is an investment management firm controlling approximately $159.6 billion in assets in 2019. Their traditional risk analysis has included only market risk. They have updated their risk analysis to include biological risk primarily associated with climate change (www.blackrock.com/corporate/investor-relations/larry-fink-ceo-letter accessed 15 January 2020).

Political risk can come in different forms. For example, many local, regional, and state regulations can limit or restrict the types of management activities that can be performed (e.g., Ellefson et al. 1995; Forman-Cook et al. 2015). At the national level, for example, the Endangered Species Act of 1973 (16 USC §§ 1531–1544) prohibits any person from "taking" a listed species (16 USC §§ 1538(a)(1) (B)). Takings are actions that "harass, harm, pursue, hunt, shoot, kill, trap, capture, collect, or to attempt to engage in such conduct" (16 USC §§ 1532(19)). Kennedy et al. (1996) describes such a case with the red-cockaded woodpecker.[8] Federal tax credits for wind energy have been allowed to expire three times since the 1970s and are extended for only one- to three-year terms at a time (Spengle 2011). Development of renewable energy is slow, in part, because there is a chance the federal tax credits will expire before projects are completed, changing the investment return for projects. Investors may be wary of taking that financial risk (Byrne 2012). Finally, national macroeconomic monetary and fiscal policies can effect uncertainty, as in the lowering of the US credit rating from AAA to AA+ by Standard & Poor's Rating Service on 18 April 2011 impacting the discount rate to reflect a perception of greater policy-making uncertainty (www.reuters. com/article/us-usa-sp-downgrade-text-idUSTRE7750D320110806 accessed 23 August 2018; www.concertedaction.com/wp-content/uploads/2012/05/Standard-Poors-Sovereign-Government-Rating-And-Methodology.pdf accessed 23 August 2018).

Inflation

Inflation is related directly to the sum of money required to purchase goods and services. If it takes more money to purchase the same goods and services this year than it did last year, then this describes inflation.

> Inflation (Deflation) – A fall (rise) in the *purchasing power of money*, often experienced as a rise (fall), on average, of the monetary value of goods, services, and assets. [Emphasis added]
>
> (Colander 2014; Heyne et al. 2006)

Simply, inflation means each dollar will buy fewer goods and services than before. For example, a 3 Musketeers candy bar cost $1.50 last month. This month, the same candy bar costs $1.60. Your income has not changed in that month, but it now takes more of your money to buy the same candy bar. Basically, the purchasing power of your money has fallen due to the price increase (or inflation).

The problems created by inflation are caused almost entirely by uncertainty of the future purchasing power of money. Thus, inflation distorts the signals that are provided through market prices observed by consumers and entrepreneurs. If the fall in the purchasing power of money was certain and constant over time, consumers and entrepreneurs would factor this constant into all economic decisions. If inflation affected all goods and services equally, then while the absolute price levels would increase the tradeoff relationships would not change and therefore economic decisions would remain the same. However, inflation affects goods, services, and assets differently; thus, it impacts the relative prices (Erdbrink and Gladstone 2012; Colander 2014).

Nominal, Real, and Risk-Free Interest Rates

Interest rates are most often defined as real and nominal. Fisher (1930) developed the relationship between the nominal and real interest rate given in equation (6.1):

$$i = (1+r) \cdot (1+\omega) - 1$$
$$= r + \omega + r \cdot \omega$$

(6.1)

where i denotes the nominal interest rate, r denotes the real interest rate, and ω denotes the anticipated inflation rate ($\omega \geq 0$). Basically, the difference between the nominal and real interest rates is accounting for inflation.[9]

In addition, Silberberg and Suen (2001) and Brealey et al. (2008) note that market interest rates have historically included a risk premium to account for external factors other than inflation. Let the risk-adjusted real interest rate, $\tilde{r}$, be given by equation (6.2a):[10]

$$\tilde{r} = r_f + \eta \tag{6.2a}$$

where r_f denotes a risk-free real interest rate (e.g., the return on 1-year US Treasury bills) and η denotes a risk premium ($\eta \geq 0$). If anticipated inflation is low, equation (6.2a) can be modified to include a risk premium:

$$\tilde{i} = \tilde{r} + \omega = r_f + \eta + \omega \tag{6.2b}$$

Equations (6.2a) and (6.2b) can be used as models for the real and nominal opportunity costs of capital as defined by the capital markets.[11] While it is not accurate to do so, for practical purposes I will drop the distinction between the risk-adjusted real interest rate and the real interest rate, and the risk-adjusted nominal interest rate and the nominal interest rate. In addition, for practical purposes, I will use the definitions and relationships given in equations (6.3a) and (6.3b) between the real and nominal interest rates in this and the next two chapters:

Real Interest Rate

$$\begin{aligned} r &= r_f + \eta \\ &\cong tp + \eta \end{aligned} \tag{6.3a}$$

Nominal Interest Rate

$$\begin{aligned} i &= (1+r) \cdot (1+\omega) - 1 \\ &= r + \omega + r \cdot \omega \\ &= r_f + \eta + \omega + (r_f + \eta) \cdot \omega \\ &\cong tp + \eta + \omega + (tp + \eta) \cdot \omega \end{aligned} \tag{6.3b}$$

where the risk-free interest rate is a proxy for time preference, tp.

As can be seen by equations (6.3a) and (6.3b), the difference between the nominal and real interest rate is accounting for inflation. It would be reasonable to ask: Should you choose the nominal or real interest rate? As stated previously, the problems created by inflation are caused almost entirely by uncertainty of the future purchasing power of money. Forecasting the rate of inflation tomorrow can probably be done with a high level of confidence. However, the further you predict into the future, the less confident you would be concerning your prediction about inflation; thus, my preference is for using the real interest rate.

The Interest Rate – Revisited

Just as there are markets for goods and services, there are also markets for consumers and entrepreneurs to exchange funds for current versus future consumption or production (i.e., borrowing and lending). In the market for goods and services, the intersection of supply and demand or market equilibrium will result in a market equilibrium price and quantity. The markets for borrowing and lending are called financial capital markets. Market equilibrium in the financial capital markets would result in equilibrium prices for borrowing and lending and the amount of funds available at that price. The price for borrowing and lending is the interest rate. The interest rate can be used to describe the opportunity cost of time, but it also can be used to describe the opportunity cost of financial capital or the fact that there are alternative investment opportunities. In general, borrowers of financial capital will try to obtain the lowest interest rate possible, so the amount paid in interest will be as small as possible (e.g., Table 6.1b). Conversely, if a person is lending financial capital, they will try to obtain the largest interest rate possible so the amount they receive in interest payments will be as large as possible, *ceteris paribus*. If financial capital markets function perfectly, the opportunity cost of time would be equal to the opportunity cost of financial capital (Price 1993). Unfortunately, this is not the case (Hirshleifer 1970; Johansson and Löfgren 1985; Price 1993; Klemperer 1996; Luenberger 1998; Silberberg and Suen 2001). That is, there is often a difference between an individual's borrowing and lending rates, with the rate charged for borrowing financial capital being usually greater than what they receive for lending or investing.[12] Nonetheless, if the price or opportunity of borrowing financial capital is less than what the individual would be willing to pay (the opportunity cost of time), the individual would borrow the financial capital. Moreover, if the price or opportunity cost of loaning financial capital is greater than what the individual would have been willing to accept (the opportunity cost of time), the individual would loan or invest their financial capital.

Fisher (1930), Henderson and Quandt (1980), Luenberger (1998), Silberberg and Suen (2001), Copeland et al. (2005), and Brealey et al. (2008) describe two broad categories of information financial capital markets use to define the opportunity cost. The first can be described as internal factors or the amount and timing of the cash flows associated with a specific investment. For example, the Inside-Out (ISO) Beam (Patterson et al. 2002; Patterson and Xie 1998), Mobile Micromill® (Becker et al. 2004), Maple Syrup Operation (Huyler 2000; CFBMC 2000), and Great Lakes Charter Boat Fishing (Lichtkoppler and Kuehn 2003) practical applications all describe in varying levels of detail the timing of specific revenues and costs associated with each activity.

The second information category can be described as external factors; for example, the purchasing power of the cash flows in the different periods, the risk, derived demand and supply concepts, and other relevant business information such as patents, research and development, and entrepreneurial history. I will examine each briefly. The purchasing power of the cash flow in different periods addresses whether revenues and costs are appreciating in real terms. As Klemperer (1996),

Davis et al. (2001), Silberberg and Suen (2001), and Brealey et al. (2008) point out, there is no universal or unique risk premium. Each investment reflects its own unique combination of market, biological, and political risk factors. Chapter 11 – Market Equilibrium and Structure discusses that the demand for any productive resource is derived from the demand for the commodities they produce (Figures 11.9a, 11.9b, and 11.9c). In addition, the linking of production processes (i.e., the output of one firm is the input into another until a final consumer product is manufactured) describes the concept of derived supply (Figures 11.10a and 11.10b). The relative strengths of these forward and backward linkages among the markets will impact the opportunity cost of financial capital for any investment. Finally, entrepreneurs engage in activities to develop new cost structures and more efficient ways to produce and deliver goods and services to consumers (Hayne et al. 2010). The financial capital markets consider these innovations, research and development progress, and patents in assessing the opportunity cost of financial capital. Thus, there is no unique real or nominal interest rate that could be used to examine all investments. The opportunity cost of financial capital is set by the capital markets using both internal and external factors of each investment (Brealey et al. 2008; Johnstone 2008).

What Is the Appropriate Interest Rate?

The conclusion from the previous discussion was that there is no unique interest rate (i.e., opportunity cost of time and the opportunity cost of capital) that can be used to examine all investments. So where does this leave us with respect to analyzing investments, especially in sustainably managing natural resources with production systems that may take 20 to 100-plus years? Or a solar array that might have a 20-, 40-, or 60-year economic or useful life?

The basic assumption from Chapter 1 – Introduction that individuals are maximizers and that they maximize their net benefits is still tenable even if accounting for time is included in the analysis. Consequently, for any given risk level, the investment chosen should increase an investor's net benefit no less than the next best alternative investment. The interest rate used to analyze investments would depend on a number of factors unique to each individual, including the their time preference, wealth, objectives, alternative uses of capital (e.g., mutual funds, stocks and bonds), degree of risk aversion, length of investment, and variability of returns associated with each investment.

A hurdle rate is often used to describe the minimum interest rate or the minimum acceptable rate of return on a project or investment required by a manager (Klemperer 1996; Brealey et al. 2008). A hurdle rate of return is a simple tool that can be used to sort investments. Investments that clear this "hurdle" indicate closer analysis is warranted by using net present value described later in this chapter. A hurdle rate is based on associated risks – riskier projects generally have higher hurdle rates than those with less risk, cost of capital, and the returns of other possible investments or projects. For example, Bullard et al. (2002) illustrates this by examining different hurdle interest rates required by nonindustrial private forest landowners in Mississippi. The nominal before tax interest rates were 8.0% for forestry investments lasting five years, 11.3% for forestry investments lasting 15 years, and 13.1% for forestry investments lasting 25 years. The real interest rates for the same investment horizons were 5.7%, 8.9%, and 10.7% respectively. According to a 2006 report by James W. Sewall Company, Institutional Investor, Timber Investment Management Organizations, and Real Estate Investment Trusts real interest rates range from 6% to 9% (Timberland Report 2006, Discount Rates and TimberLand Investments, Vol. 8, No. 2, https://forisk.com/wordpress/wp-content/assets/discountratesVol8No3.pdf accessed 1 September 2023). In a study by Manley (2010) of New Zealand Forest landowners, the nominal before tax interest rates ranged from 1.7% to 10.7%.

From a corporate finance perspective, businesses finance capital purchases with either debt or equity.[13] The weighted average cost of capital (WACC) accounts for these two sources of financing capital given in equation (6.4).

$$\text{WACC} = r_D\left(1-\tau_C\right)\frac{D}{D+E} + r_E\frac{E}{D+E} \qquad (6.4)$$

where r_D is the cost of debt (%), τ_C – corporate tax rate (%), r_E is the cost of equity (%), D is the firm's debt, E is the firm's equity, D/(D+E) percent financing that is debt, and E/(D+E) percent financing that is equity. A firm's WACC is the overall required return for a firm's capital investments with risk that is similar to that of the overall firm (Brealey et al. 2008). According to Copeland et al. (2005), the WACC will decline as debt financing increases relative to equity financing. Increasing equity financing causes the cost of equity to increase as shareholders positions become increasingly risky. Finally, the WACC should be interpreted as the marginal cost of financing new capital investments – not as an historic financing cost (Copeland et al. 2005).[14]

As described earlier, identifying an appropriate interest rate or cost of capital is not always straightforward. Again, from a corporate finance perspective, a company's WACC represents the cost of financial capital for investments of risk similar to business as usual; however, this may not always be the case. For investments of lesser or greater risk, other means of determining a cost of financial capital with an appropriate risk premium should be used (e.g., the capital asset pricing model).

Present Value and Future Value

Time is a relevant input, and people place different weights on cash flows that occur in different periods. In order for this economic information to be portrayed correctly and used accurately in decision making, various formulae have been developed to find the equivalence of these many revenues and costs at a common reference point. These formulae were developed when analysts did not have ready access to personal computers. The two most important ones are future value and present value. With these two formulae and spreadsheets, you should be able to handle most problems.[15]

Using future and present value formulae are based on the following definitions. The chronological date of the reference point is set by the analyst. All costs and revenues in the tth period occur at the end of the period. Periods are one year long. Thus, all cash flows occur on 31 December of any given year. Compounding is the process of carrying a revenue or cost forward in time at a defined interest rate. Discounting is the process of carrying a revenue or cost backward in time at a defined discount rate.[16] Capitalizing is the process of discounting a series of cash flows to one point in time.[17]

Analyses involving compounding and discounting can become intricate, and thus keeping track of revenues and costs can be problematic and capitalizing them frustrating. For this reason, I will present a simple tool that can assist in working with these problems before I talk about the future and present value formulae. This tool is called a cash flow diagram.

Cash Flow Diagrams

For all practical purposes, the interest rate entrepreneurs' face will be positive. This interest rate will be used to place weights on *any* revenue or cost. The mechanics of accounting for revenues and costs in different time periods start with drawing a representation of the cash flows associated with the investment. This representation is a cash flow diagram and is illustrated by Figure 6.2a.

The cash flow diagram starts with a horizontal line called the timeline that represents the duration of the investment and is divided into periods. For example, Figure 6.2a could represent a seven-year investment horizon with seven annual periods, or a 70-year investment horizon with 10-year periods. Costs and revenues are pictured with vertical arrows; revenues or cash flows generated by the investment are depicted by arrows pointing upward from the timeline where the transaction occurred; cost or cash flows paid out by the investors are depicted by arrows pointing down (Figure 6.2b).[18]

As can be seen by Figure 6.2b, there are costs at years 0, 3, and 6; and there are revenues at years 2, 4, and 7. The power of a cash diagram is that it can take a relatively complex situation and portray it in a concise format. For example, a management plan calls for $225 per acre to prepare the site for planting pine. Planting

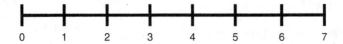

Figure 6.2a The Timeline of a Cash Flow Diagram

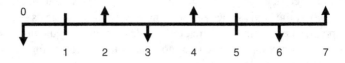

Figure 6.2b The Cash Flow Diagram

pine seedlings costs $100 per acre in year 1. A pulpwood thinning is planned at age 15. The expected cost of this thinning is $150 per acre and the expected pulpwood revenue is $350 per acre. You expect that yearly administrative expenses will be $20 per acre. The management plan calls for a clearcut at age 30 with an expected revenue of $15,000 per acre.[19] Figure 6.3 illustrates the cash flow diagram for this series of cash flows related to this management plan.

A direct relationship can also be drawn between a cash flow diagram and the production system. Figure 6.4a illustrates the total product curve for the Wisconsin

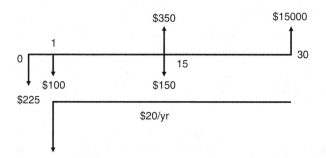

Figure 6.3 Example Cash Flow Diagram

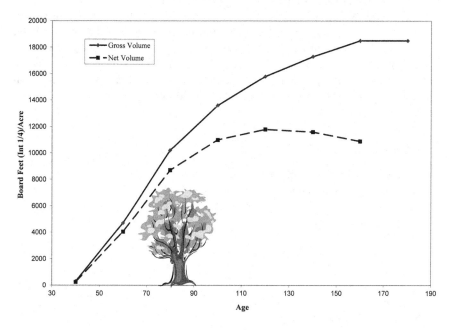

Figure 6.4a Unthinned Oak Stand in Southwestern Wisconsin (Medium Site) Production Curve[‡]

[‡] Volume is measured as board feet (International 1/4) per acre (bf/ac) given in Table 2.6 and Figure 2.7.

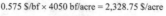

0.575 $/bf × 4050 bf/acre = 2,328.75 $/acre

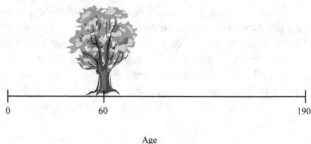

0	60	190

Age

Figure 6.4b Unthinned Oak Stand in Southwestern Wisconsin (Medium Site) Cash Flow
Diagram‡

‡ Volume is measured as net board feet (International 1/4) per acre (bf/ac) given in Table 2.6. Price is
measured as $/bf. An average 2017 western/central New York oak sawtimber price was $0.575 per
board foot (www.dec.ny.gov/docs/lands_forests_pdf/paststumpage.pdf accessed 29 August 2018).

Oak practical application. Figure 6.4b converts this total product curve into a cash
flow diagram. The horizontal axis on Figures 6.4a and 6.4b are identical. The volume in Figure 6.4a is converted into a revenue cash flow in Figure 6.4b by multiplying by stumpage price. I challenge the reader to draw a similar set of figures
using the Radiata Pine Plantation practical application.

The flexibility and utility of a cash flow drawing a cash flow diagram cannot
be overstated: The power of a cash diagram is that it can take a relatively complex
situation and portray it in a concise format. The cash flow diagram should be drawn
before any calculations are made. The cash diagram can be shown to a landowner
or client and agreed upon and will save you from most misunderstandings that
will cost you time and money later. A student in 2000 gave me the following poem
which summarizes all these ideas

It's So Simple

Investment solutions are hard to find
Miscalculations will put you in a bind
Keeping time and money together
Can prove to be rough
What do I do?
When the going gets tough
If you find yourself
Stuck in a jam
Don't lose your calm
Draw the Cash Flow Diagram

Sean Lyman
College of Environmental Science and Forestry
B.S. 2001, A.A.S. 1999

Future Value Formula

The basic concept of a future value is to find the equivalence of a revenue or cost in the future. This is illustrated by the cash flow diagram in Figure 6.5.

The future value formula is given by equation (6.5):

$$V_t = V_0 (1+r)^t \tag{6.5}$$

where V_t defines the equivalent value of a cash flow t one-year periods in the future, V_0 defines the value of a cost or revenue in time 0, r denotes the real interest rate from equation (6.3a), and t denotes the number of one-year periods that V_0 is compounded.[20]

Examining Figure 6.5 and equation (6.5) reveals the following three features. First, Figure 6.5 illustrates the finding of the equivalence of a cash flow, V_0, t one-year periods in the future, V_t. That is, an individual would be indifferent between the value V_0 now and the value V_t t one-year periods in the future. Second, the procedure for finding the equal values is given by equation (6.5). The economic information required to calculate V_t are the initial cash flow, V_0, the interest rate, r (in decimal form), and the number of one-year periods, t. For example, if I invest $20,000 at 6%, what is its value nine years from today? The solution is illustrated in Figure 6.6.

Figure 6.5 Future Value Cash Flow Diagram

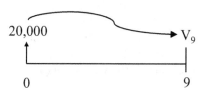

Figure 6.6 Future Value Example

$$V_9 = 20,000 \cdot (1+0.06)^9$$
$$= 20,000 \cdot (1.06)^9$$
$$= 33,789.58$$

The interpretation of Figure 6.6 is that given the economic information of an initial value of $20,000, a 6% interest rate that reflects both time preference and risk, and a period of nine years, an individual would be indifferent between $20,000 now and $33,789.58 nine years from today. Finally, Figure 6.6 and equation (6.5) represent the fundamental concept of compensation required to forgo current consumption. This will be illustrated using equations (6.6a) through (6.6c):

$$
\begin{aligned}
V_1 &= V_0 + V_0 \cdot r \\
&= V_0 (1+r)
\end{aligned}
\tag{6.6a}
$$

The right-hand side of equation (6.6a) shows that the difference between consumption now and in period 1 is the amount of compensation $V_0 \cdot r$. As the interest rate r is defined as a percent, the amount of compensation is a percent of what was forgone. Equation (6.6b) illustrates the compensation required to forgo consumption between periods 1 and 2:

$$
\begin{aligned}
V_2 &= V_1 + V_1 \cdot r \\
&= V_1 (1+r)
\end{aligned}
\tag{6.6b}
$$

Equation (6.6c) illustrates the compensation required to forgo consumption between now and in period 2 by using the definition of the compensation given in equation (6.6a):

$$
\begin{aligned}
V_2 &= V_1 (1+r) \\
&= V_0 (1+r) \cdot (1+r) \\
&= V_0 (1+r)^2
\end{aligned}
\tag{6.6c}
$$

If this process is repeated, the result is equation (6.5). The compensation is modeled using a geometric progression. The economic implications of this will be examined after a discussion of present value.

Present Value Formula

The basic concept of a present value is to find the equivalence of a future revenue or cost. This is illustrated by the cash flow diagram in Figure 6.7.

The present value formula is given by equation (6.7)

$$
\begin{aligned}
V_0 &= V_t (1+r)^{-t} \\
&= \frac{V_t}{(1+r)^t}
\end{aligned}
\tag{6.7}
$$

where V_0 defines the equivalent value of a cash flow in time 0, V_t defines the value of a cost or revenue t one-year periods in the future, r denotes the discount rate from equation (6.3a), and t denotes the number of one-year periods that V_t is discounted.

Figure 6.7 Present Value Cash Flow Diagram

Figure 6.8 Present Value Example

$$V_0 = 100,000 \cdot (1+0.06)^{-20}$$
$$= 100,000 \cdot (1.06)^{-20}$$
$$= \frac{100,000}{(1.06)^{20}}$$
$$= 31,180.47$$

Examining Figure 6.7 and equation (6.7) reveals the following three features. First, Figure 6.7 illustrates the finding of the equivalence now, V_0, of a cash flow, t one-year periods in the future, V_t. That is, an individual would be indifferent between the value V_t t one-year periods in the future or the value V_0 now. Second, the procedure for finding the equal values is given by equation (6.7). The economic information required to calculate V_0 are the initial cash flow, V_t, the discount rate, r (in decimal form), and the number of one-year periods, t. For example, what is the value today of receiving $100,000 20 years from now given a 6% discount rate? The solution is illustrated in Figure 6.8.

The interpretation of Figure 6.8 is that given the economic information of a future value 20 years from now of $100,000 and a 6% discount rate that reflects both time preference and risk, an individual would be indifferent between $100,000 20 years from now and $31,180.47 today.

Third, equation (6.7) describes two alternative mathematical forms for calculating present value. The top form $V_0 = V_t(1 + r)^{-t}$ is very similar to the future value formula given in equation (6.5). The difference is the minus sign in the exponent. Consequently, if the minus sign is forgotten, you will be calculating a future value and not a present value. Given the potential for a mistake, there is a simple procedure for checking if the calculation is correct. The V_0 numeric value should always be less than the V_t numeric value. Thus, if you are calculating a present value using equation (6.7) and its numeric value is greater than its equivalent future value, you have made a mistake. Conversely, if you are calculating a future value using equation (6.5) and its numeric value is less than its equivalent present value, you have made a mistake.

Future and Present Value Formulae Revisited

Equations (6.5) and (6.7) define the future and present respectively and are repeated here:

Future Value Formula

$$V_t = V_0 (1+r)^t$$

Present Value Formula

$$V_0 = V_t (1+r)^{-t}$$

$$= \frac{V_t}{(1+r)^t}$$

In both formulae the compensation is defined by the geometric progression $(1 + r)^t$ or $(1 + r)^{-t}$. Thus for any given interest rate $(1 + r)^t$ grows very quickly in magnitude as time increases. Conversely for any given discount rate, $(1 + r)^{-t}$ becomes small in magnitude very quickly as time increases. The choice of the interest or discount rate has a similar effect. The economic implications of these simple algebraic relationships are important when dealing with production systems that may take decades to result in a saleable good such as stumpage that can be sold to produce lumber or furniture. The entrepreneur or a consultant working for a landowner or stakeholders must be very thoughtful in determining the appropriate cash flow diagram that represents all the relevant costs and revenues and the appropriate interest or discount rate.[21]

Analytical Hazards

Nominal Versus Real Analysis

As described in a previous section, the interest rate can be defined as real – including time preference and risk – or nominal – including time preference, risk, and inflation. Cash flows to be analyzed can also be defined in terms of nominal – including inflation – and real – not including inflation. A nominal cash flow compares one "pile" of money relative to another "pile" of money used to purchase a good or service. Referring back to the 3 Musketeers candy bar example, the pile of money required to purchase the same candy bar increased, yet you are purchasing the same candy bar. Basically, the purchasing power of your money has fallen due to inflation. A real cash flow compares the ability to buy a good or service using "constant" dollars defined by specific point in time. Again, referring to the candy bar example, in constant dollars, one month later the $1.50 would only buy you 94% of the candy bar.[22]

As we have nominal and real interest rates and nominal and real cash flows, what combinations are analytically tenable? The general rule is that if you are using nominal cash flows, or cash flows that have not been adjusted for inflation, use the nominal interest rate. If you are using real cash flows, or cash flows that have been adjusted for inflation, use the real interest rate. My preference is to use real cash flows and real interest rates, as trying to predict future inflation can be extremely difficult at best. In addition, what you can buy with the pile of money is more important than just the pile of money.

Cash Flow Periodicity

From a business perspective, cash flows can occur daily, monthly, quarterly, or annually. For example, payments for financing capital purchases usually occur monthly. However, financial reporting is often done on an annual basis. As stated previously, nominal (real) cash flows must be paired with a nominal (real) interest or discount rate. So it is with mixing daily, monthly, quarterly, or annual cash flows in an analysis.

To illustrate this hazard, your business has decided to build a 1-megawatt (MG) ground-mounted solar panel system. A mid-range system will cost $1,052,800 (www.solarelectricsupply.com/commercial-solar-systems/ground-mount accessed 7 July 2021). The WACC used for financing this capital purchase was 6.0% with a 15-year financing period. Table 6.2 summarizes the financing costs, comparing annual versus monthly periods.

Table 6.2 1 Megawatt (MW) Ground Mount Solar Array Financing Costs

Solar Array[‡]	$	1,052,800.00		1,052,800.00
Loan Length	Year	15	Months	180
Interest Rate	Annual	6.0%	Monthly[†]	0.5%
Loan Payment[†]	$/Year	108,399.20	$/Month	8,884.12
Total Loan Payment[‡‡]	$	1,625,987.97	$	1,599,142.44
Total Interest Payment	$	573,187.97	$	546,342.44

‡ The wholesale solar array costs are obtained from www.solarelectricsupply.com/commercial-solar-systems/ground-mount accessed 2 July 2021 and reflect only materials costs

† The monthly interest rate is the annual interest rate divided by 12.

‡‡ The annual loan payments are calculated using the annual installment payment formula and the monthly loan payments are calculated using the periodic installment payment formula found in Appendix 6A

Examining Table 6.2 quickly shows that lower total interest costs are associated with the monthly payments. This is consistent as interest is only accruing on the remaining principal for a month rather than a year and the remaining principal is decreasing every month. This results in a $26,845.52 interest payment savings.

A monthly payment of $8,884.12 equals an annual loan payment of $106,609.50. However, if an annual loan payment is determined using the annual installment payment formula found in Appendix 6A, the result is $108,339.20. Thus, aggregating a monthly payment to determine an annual payment is different. Consequently, if other similar "cash flows" are determined on an annual basis, then aggregating monthly loan payments in effect lowers the cost of capital (or the discount rate) relative to these other expenditures, biasing the analysis.

The Mobile Micromill® Practical Application (Becker et al. 2004)

I would caution readers to exercise due diligence when reviewing published analyses. I will use the Mobile Micromill® practical application to illustrate the easy mistakes that can be made. Table 6.3a contains the cost data for purchasing the mill.

Table 6.3b contains the monthly and annual payments, the total amount paid, and the interest paid using a seven-year loan period and an annual interest rate of 7% as calculated incorrectly by Becker et al. (2004: 8). Table 6.3c contains the monthly and annual payments, total payment, and interest paid calculated correctly.

Comparing Tables 6.3b and 6.3c shows that the incorrect calculations for the mill alone resulted in a $1,307.53 higher monthly payment, a $15,690.35 higher annual payment, and a $109,832.43 higher interest payment. The same incorrect calculations were made for all of the supporting equipment: monthly overpayment of $215.92, yearly overpayment of $2,591.08, and interest overpayment of $13,955.42. These errors were then included in the summary of annual fixed and variable costs (Becker et al. 2004: Table 7 p. 27) resulting in annually overestimating fixed costs by $18,281.43. They were also carried over into the breakeven analysis (Becker et al. 2004: Table 8 p. 30). As the financing costs were a relatively small component of the total costs, these errors would not change the overall interpretation of their breakeven analysis. However, the methods used were not correct and misrepresented the financing costs.

Table 6.3a Mobile Micromill® Example[‡]

Item	Cost (2003 US$)
Micromill®	$426,185.00
Sales tax	$0.00
Mill delivery, setup, and training	$7,000.00
Total delivered price	$433,185.00
Down payment (30%)	$129,955.50
Amount financed	$303,229.50

[‡] Cost data are taken from Becker et al. (2004: 8). Costs are in terms of United States 2003 dollars (2003 US$).

Table 6.3b The Incorrect Financial Analysis as Provided by Becker et al. (2004: 8)

Total Payoff Amount[‡]	$494,262.28
Annual Payments[†]	$70,608.90
Monthly Payments[‡‡]	$5,884.07
Interest Paid[††]	$191,032.78

[‡] The Total Payoff Amount is a future value calculation using a monthly interest rate and compounding periods

$$494,262.28 = 303,229.50 \cdot \left(1 + \frac{0.07}{12}\right)^{7 \cdot 12}$$

[†] The Annual Payments are

$$70,608.90 = \frac{494,262.28}{7}$$

[‡‡] The Monthly Payments are

$$5,8840.07 = \frac{70,608.90}{12}$$

[††] The Interest Paid is

$$191,032.78 = 494,262.28 - 303,229.50$$

Table 6.3c The Correct Financial Analysis

Monthly Payments[‡]	$4,576.55
Annual Payments[†]	$54,918.55
Total Payment[‡‡]	$384,429.85
Interest Paid[††]	$81,200.35

[‡] Monthly Payments are

$$4,576.55 = 303,229.50 \frac{\frac{0.07}{12}}{1 - \left(1 + \frac{0.07}{12}\right)^{-7 \cdot 12}}$$

[†] The Annual Payments are

$$54,918.55 = 4,576.55 \cdot 12$$

[‡‡] The Total Payment is

$$384,429.85 = 4,576.55 \cdot 7 \cdot 12$$

[††] The Interest Paid is

$$81,200.95 = 384,429.85 - 303,229.50$$

Investment Analysis Tools

The concept of forgoing current consumption generally implies that you are investing financial capital in some opportunity such that at a future date you will be able to increase your consumption. A similar argument could be made with respect to production, in that you are investing in a technology that will allow you to produce more in the future. In any case, we need some way to reliably examine these alternative investments that is consistent with the assumption that individuals are maximizers. I will examine six common investment analysis tools: (1) net present value, (2) benefit-cost ratio, (3) profitability index, (4) internal rate of return, (5) return on investment, and (6) breakeven analysis.

Net Present Value

Net Present Value (NPV) is the sum of the present value of the revenues minus the sum of the present value of the costs, as shown in equation (6.8)

$$
\begin{aligned}
NPV_T &= \sum_{t=0}^{T} R_t \left(1+r\right)^{-t} - \sum_{t=0}^{T} C_t \left(1+r\right)^{-t} \\
&= \sum_{t=0}^{T} \left(R_t - C_t\right)\left(1+r\right)^{-t} \\
&= \sum_{t=0}^{T} \frac{R_t}{\left(1+r\right)^{t}} - \sum_{t=0}^{T} \frac{C_t}{\left(1+r\right)^{t}} \\
&= \sum_{t=0}^{T} \frac{R_t - C_t}{\left(1+r\right)^{t}}
\end{aligned}
\tag{6.8}
$$

where R_t denotes the revenue at time t, r denotes the discount rate, and C_t denotes the cost at time t.[23] The economic information required to use NPV are (1) the amount and timing of all cash flows and (2) an appropriate discount rate. The interpretation of NPV is tied directly to its general decision criterion.[24] If NPV > 0, this implies the investment is returning the desired discount rate *plus* a present value of additional net revenue. The implication is the wealth of an investor increases and the investment is acceptable. If NPV = 0, this implies the investment is returning the desired discount rate. The investment does not increase or decrease wealth. The investor is indifferent, as their wealth does not change. If NPV < 0, the investment is rejected as the investor's wealth decreases.[25]

   While the decision criterion seems straightforward – wealth increases, decreases, or remains unchanged, context does matter. From Chapter 1 – Introduction, wealth is the accumulation of whatever people value – monetary and nonmonetary. For example, in 2017 Ingersoll Rand completed an energy audit for the academic buildings on campus. The purpose of an energy audit is to analyze the energy flows in a building or home and understand its energy dynamics. During the energy audit, the auditor looks for opportunities to reduce the amount of energy input into a building or home. The owner can evaluate what identified measures they would like to invest in to make the building or home more energy efficient. Most of the laboratory fume hoods are standard type units that only use an exhaust duct. However, a few include an auxiliary air supply duct. These bring in nonconditioned outside air directly in front of the hood so that this was the air exhausted to the outside. This is problematic for two reasons. First, when the weather changes, the air supply pours frigid or hot and humid air over the user, making it very uncomfortable to work. Second, these weather changes may affect the procedure inside the hood. An energy conservation measure (ECM) suggested was to modify these fume hoods with variable exhaust and supply flow controls that would provide an energy savings as well as tempering outside air makeup. The sensors will detect contaminants and the controls will quickly ramp up airflows to mitigate exposure and dilute the air. When there are no contaminants, the airflow is reduced to the minimum setting to save energy. The NPV of this ECM was negative. So, on a purely financial analysis, the recommendation would be to not update the fume hood controllers. However, installing the new fume hood controls is consistent with the college's academic and research mission and provided a productive research and learning work environment for faculty and students.

Table 6.4 illustrates calculating the NPV of the management plan with a cash flow diagram given in Figure 6.3 given a discount rate of 9%. I would like to highlight three aspects of the information based in Table 6.4. First, based on the results of the NPV calculations, this management plan would increase the wealth of the landowner by 663.27 $/acre. That is, investing in this management plan returns the landowner the required 9% discount rate plus 663.27 $/acre of additional present value of net revenue. While calculating the NPV can be somewhat onerous and the result should be calculated correctly, interpreting the result accurately is paramount to providing useful economic information to make better business decisions. Second, the present value of the annual administrative costs can be calculated by summing the

Table 6.4 Net Present Value Example based on the Cash Flow Diagram given in Figure 6.3‡

Year	Revenue	Cost	Present Value Revenues	Present Value Costs
0		225.00		225.00
1		100.00		91.74
15	350.00	150.00	96.09	41.18
Annual Administrative Cost		20.00		205.47
30	15,000.00		1,130.57	
Total			1,226.66	563.39

‡ The units on all revenues and costs are dollars per acre ($/acre). The discount rate equal 9% or 0.09.

Annual Administrative Costs

$$205.47 = \sum_{t=1}^{30} 20 \cdot (1.09)^{-t} = 20 \cdot \frac{(1.09)^{30} - 1}{0.09 \cdot (1.09)^{30}}$$

Net Present Value = 1,226.66 − 563.39 = $663.27 per acre

present value of each individual yearly cost. Or they can be determined by using the present value of a terminating every-period series formula given in Appendix 6A. Finally, Table 6.4 shows the calculations are comprised of rows, columns, and cells. Each row represents a specific cash flow from the cash flow diagram (Figure 6.3). The column headings denote if the cash flow represents a revenue, cost, or present value. The cells under the present value column headings contain equation (6.7) with the appropriate cell references to the specific cash flow, timing, and discount rate. Basically, Table 6.4 is a spreadsheet.

As Luenberger (1998: 27) states: "It is widely agreed (by theorists, but not necessarily by practitioners) that, overall, the best [investment analysis] criterion is that based on net present value." NPV is the standard by which all other investment analysis tools are evaluated. NPV is consistent with the assumption that individuals maximize their wealth (Brealey et al. 2008; Copeland et al. 2005; Luenberger 1998). This does not imply that NPV is perfect as an investment analysis tool. As larger NPV values are preferred to smaller ones, NPV is biased towards projects with large numbers for revenues and costs; namely, as the scale of an investment increases, so does the NPV. NPV may also be biased toward projects with longer investment horizons with positive net cash flows. These criticisms can be ameliorated by calculating revenues and costs on a per unit basis; for example, per acre as in Table 6.4, an equal annual equivalent analysis, or a replacement chained NPV analysis. I will discuss more about these in the section titled Capital Budgeting. As described in equation (6.8), the amount and timing of all cash flows and the discount rate are all known with certainty. In Chapter 8 – Risk, I will examine approaches that can be used if the cash flows are not known with certainty.

Benefit-Cost Ratios

Benefit-cost ratio (BCR) calculates an investment's discounted benefits per dollar of discounted costs. This is shown in equation (6.9)

$$BCR_T = \frac{\sum_{t=0}^{T} R_t (1+r)^{-t}}{\sum_{t=0}^{T} C_T (1+r)^{-t}} = \frac{\sum_{t=0}^{T} \dfrac{R_t}{(1+r)^t}}{\sum_{t=0}^{T} \dfrac{C_t}{(1+r)^t}} \tag{6.9}$$

where the variables are defined as before. The economic information required to use BCR are the same as NPV: (1) the amount and timing of all cash flows and (2) an appropriate discount rate. Interpreting the BCR is tied directly to its general decision criterion. If BCR > 1, this implies the investment is returning greater per dollar revenues than per dollar costs in present value terms. The implication is the wealth of an investor increases; that is NPV > 0, and the investment is acceptable. If BCR = 1, this implies the investment's per dollar revenues are equal to its per dollar costs in present value terms. The investment does not increase or decrease wealth, that is NPV = 0. The investor is indifferent, as their wealth does not change. If BCR < 1, then the investment is rejected. The wealth of the investor decreases as the per dollar costs are greater than the per dollar revenues in present value terms, that is NPV < 0.

Using the cash flow diagram of the management plan given in Figure 6.4, the BCR is given by equation (6.10):

$$BCR = \frac{1,226.66\left(\frac{\$}{acres}\right)}{563.39\left(\frac{\$}{acres}\right)} = 2.18 \tag{6.10}$$

Three aspects of the economic information resulting from equation (6.10) should be noted. First, the BCR is a ratio 2.18:1, or for every $2.18 of present value of revenue, there is $1.00 of present value of cost. Second, the interpretation of BCR seems simpler than NPV and follows from the first aspect; a BCR greater than one and the project is acceptable. Third, the BCR provides information on how much the discounted costs (revenue) could increase (decrease) before NPV < 0. In this case, the discounted cost would have to increase by a factor of 2.18 before NPV $= 0$. Conversely, the discounted revenues would have to decrease by a factor of 0.459 (= 1 divided by the BCR or $1 \div 2.18$) before NPV $= 0$. This mathematical relationship allows the BCR to be used as a cardinal metric of sensitivity: Are these implied increases or decreases within normal ranges of operations for costs and revenues of the investment?

To illustrate this, I will use an example from a research project I led (Wagner et al. 2000). The project involved the economic feasibility of a local entrepreneur – who owned a number of businesses including logging, sawmill, blue stone, and several convenience stores – purchasing a Morbark ® model 2348 Flail Chiparvestor to supply the local particle board mill with a consistent supply of chips. The purchase price of the chipper was $575,000, and 20% of its purchase price was paid upon delivery of the chipper or $115,000 in year 0. The investment horizon was for five years, at which time the entrepreneur would sell it for 17% of its purchase price or $97,750. There were five annual loan payments of $117,000 and insurance payments of $5,750 (1% of the purchase price) per year starting in year 1. The estimated diesel fuel use was 33 gallons of diesel per hour. The cost of diesel was $1.15 per gallon and the chipper would be used on average 1,750 hours per year, giving an annual diesel cost of $66,413. The annual maintenance cost was estimated at $118,000. The estimated annual salary (including benefits) of the chip operator was $62,500. The estimated annual cost of the rest of the operation (e.g., felling, skidding, and hauling) was $1,150,000. The verbal agreement was delivering 57,000 tons of clean green chips per year starting in year 1 at the current price of delivered clean green chips of $27.00 per ton. The analysis was done in real terms using a real discount rate is 8.6%. The only cash flow in time 0 was the amount due upon delivery of the chipper. A summary of the financial analysis was

---

Summary of Financial Analysis

$\sum PV(C) = \$6,087,818.70$	Discount rate = 8.6%
NPV = $25,712.75	Output price = 27.00 $/ton
BCR = 1.004	Output quantity = 57,000 tons

---

where $\sum PV(R)$ and $\sum PV(C)$ denote the sum of the present value of the revenues and costs respectively. The NPV is $25,713, which seems okay, but the BCR is 1.004, which gives me pause and requires me to look more closely at the annual revenues and annual costs. Using the BCR of 1.004 to examine the change in either the sum of the present value of the revenues ($\Delta\sum PV(R)$) or the sum of the present value of the costs ($\Delta\sum PV(C)$) gives

$$\Delta\sum PV(R)) = 1.004 \cdot \sum PV(C) - \sum PV(C) = \$25,712.75$$

$$\Delta\sum PV(C) = \sum PV(R) - 0.996 \cdot \sum PV(R) = \$25,712.75$$

These changes are equal to the NPV. This makes perfect sense as decreasing the present value of the revenues by \$25,712.75 or increasing the present value of the costs by \$25,712.75 will cause NPV = 0. While this makes perfect sense, it does not provide great help in answering the question: Are these implied increases or decreases within normal ranges of operations for costs and revenues of the investment? An addition calculation is required; namely, the equal annual equivalent (EAE).[26] The EAE calculates the constant annual cash flow generated by a project over its lifespan as if it were an annuity.

$$EAE[\Delta\sum PV(R)] = EAE[\Delta\sum PV(C)] = 6,542.09 \text{ \$/year}$$

The initial analysis assumed a constant output price of 27.00 \$/ton. As output prices are rarely constant, assume that the output price drops to 26.75 \$/ton. This would be an annual decrease in revenues of \$14,250. This annual decrease in price by 0.25 \$/ton gives an annual decrease in revenue of \$14,250, which is a little more than twice the allowable change of \$6,542 resulting in an NPV of −\$30,294.86. This is due to the expected annual quantity being produced and "sold" of 57,000 tons annually. The importance of this analysis is that it requires knowledge of the production system and specifically the Pillars of Value and Price. Thus, the entrepreneur *must* know their output markets – in this case possible output price variability as change in output price by a quarter will cause NPV < 0. Based on the analysis, the entrepreneur would only buy the chipper if the particle board plant would write a five-year contract insuring purchasing 57,000 tons of clean chips at 27.00 \$/ton. The particle board plant would not agree to such a contract and the entrepreneur did not buy the chipper. This analysis was done using revenue, but the same type of analysis must be done with respect to the expected production level and the Pillars of Cost and Value for the inputs.

There are, however, three concerns with using BCRs. Examining equation (6.9) shows that BCR is a fraction; thus, as the denominator of a fraction increases (decreases) faster than the any changes in the numerator, the value of the fraction will decrease (increases). This mathematical relationship leads to the first concern: The magnitude of the BCR is related directly to how costs (and consequently revenues) are defined and treated; for example, the treatment of initial investment cost versus operating costs. In the cash flow diagram given in Figure 6.3 for the management plan, if the year 1 planting costs of \$100 per acre, the year 15 thinning costs of \$150 per acre, and the yearly administrative expenses of \$20 per acre are defined as normal operating expenses and included as part of the investment's net cash flow in the numerator in equation (6.9), while the initial investment cost of \$225 is defined as the denominator in equation (6.9), the BCR would be 3.95. If only positive net revenues (e.g., $R_t - C_t > 0$, for all t) are included in the numerator and only negative net revenues (e.g., $R_t - C_t < 0$, for all t) in the denominator, the BCR would be 2.29. However, the NPV does not change given these various cost definitions.

An additional ECM recommended by Ingersoll Rand's 2017 energy audit was to replace steam traps. Steam traps separate the steam system from the condensate system. Traditional steam traps can fail in the open or closed position. When a steam trap fails in the open or leaking-by position, some or all of the energy that was added at the boiler is lost into the condensate return system. Replacing or repairing failed traps will improve the efficiency of the steam distribution system and save energy. The cost to replace the steam traps is $45,461. There is a New York State Energy Research and Development Authority incentive of $13,927. The estimated energy cost savings are $13,473 per year: This cost savings can be interpreted as a revenue. The estimated useful life of a steam trap is 15 years. The discount rate is 4% given the size of the capital investment. In this example, an initial incentive is provided to purchase an asset. This incentive can be described as a cost savings; i.e., part of revenue, or as a reduction in cost. These two approaches are given mathematically as

$$BCR_T = \frac{\sum_{t=1}^{T} R_t (1+r)^{-t} + R_0}{\sum_{t=0}^{T} C_T (1+r)^{-t}} \neq \frac{\sum_{t=1}^{T} \frac{R_t}{(1+r)^t}}{\sum_{t=0}^{T} \frac{C_t}{(1+r)^t} - R_0} = BCR_T$$

with the cost savings given by the left-hand side of the inequality and the reduction in cost given by the right-hand side. The "cost savings" BCR = 3.60 while the "reduction in cost" BCR = 4.75 even though it is the same net cash flow. This mathematical reality leads to the second concern: The BCR is biased towards investments with small, discounted cost elements. Finally, BCR is not related directly to economic efficiency because wealth is not typically maximized when the BCR is maximized (Rideout 1986). Thus, the BCR is not consistent with the assumption that individuals maximize their wealth.

Profitability Index

Profitability index (PI) calculates the investment's present value of all future net cash flows per dollar of initial cost or the investment's NPV minus the initial cost per dollar of initial cost and is given by equation (6.11):

$$PI_T = \frac{NPV_T + C_0}{C_0} = 1 + \frac{NPV_T}{C_0}$$

$$= \frac{\sum_{t=0}^{T} \frac{R_t}{(1+r)^t} - \sum_{t=0}^{T} \frac{C_t}{(1+r)^t} + C_0}{C_0} \tag{6.11}$$

$$= \frac{\sum_{t=0}^{T} R_t (1+r)^{-t} - \sum_{t=0}^{T} C_t (1+r)^{-t} + C_0}{C_0}$$

This will calculate the investment's discounted cash flow per dollar of initial cost, C_0.[27] Investments with $1 + (NPV_T/C_0) > 1$ are acceptable as $NPV_T > 0$. Investments with $1 + (NPV_T/C_0) = 1$ are breakeven as $NPV_T = 0$. Investments with $1 + (NPV_T/C_0) < 1$ are unacceptable as $NPV_T < 0$.

Using the cash flow diagram of the management plan given in Figure 6.3, the PI calculated using equation (6.11) is 3.95. This means every $1.00 per acre of initial costs generates $3.95 per acre of NPV.

As can be seen, the PI is related directly to BCR. In fact, equation (6.11) is a variant of a BCR described in the previous section. The PI tries to address the problem of scale associated with NPV. However, there are better procedures to account for scale that will be discussed in the section entitled Capital Budgeting. Because the PI is a variant of the BCR, it suffers from the same criticisms and is not consistent with the assumption that individuals maximize their wealth.

Internal Rate of Return

The internal rate of return (*irr*) is generally attributed to Fisher (1930). However, Boulding (1935) and Keynes (1936) also published manuscripts discussing the *irr* at roughly the same time. I will use Boulding (1935) as my primary reference as he most clearly lays out the foundation of the *irr* as used in forestry. Based on Boulding (1935), the *irr* is defined incorrectly as the "interest rate" or "discount rate" that sets the NPV equal to zero, as illustrated by equation (6.12)

$$\sum_{t=0}^{T} \frac{R_t}{(1+irr)^t} - \sum_{t=0}^{T} \frac{C_t}{(1+irr)^t} = \sum_{t=0}^{T} \frac{(R_t - C_t)}{(1+irr)^t} = 0 \tag{6.12}$$

where R_t denotes revenues at time t with $R_t \geq 0$, C_t denotes costs at time t with $C_t \geq 0$, $(R_t - C_t)$ denotes the net cash flow at time t, with $(R_0 - C_0) < 0$ and at least one $(R_t - C_t) > 0$ for $t > 0$; and *irr* is the internal rate of return. The economic information required to determine the *irr* consists only of the amount and timing of all cash flows and the result is the "internal rate of return." The decision criteria, however, requires that an appropriate discount rate obtained from the financial capital markets be provided. If the *irr* is greater (less) than an appropriate discount rate, the investment is acceptable (not acceptable). The larger (smaller) the *irr* is relative to the appropriate discount rate, the greater (lesser) the likelihood that the investment's NPV, given the appropriate discount rate (time preference + risk), is greater than (less than) 0. Consequently, *irr* is best interpreted as a riskless rate of value growth or riskless ordinal metric of profitability. This interpretation is consistent with Boulding (1935). For example, using the cash flow diagram of the management plan given in Table 6.4 and Figure 6.3, the *irr* is approximately 0.1253. The required discount rate is 9%; the *irr* is 1.39 times larger than the discount rate indicating the greater the likelihood NPV > 0.

There are four main problems with the *irr*. First, mathematically the *irr* is a function of the "root" or "zero" of a polynomial equation. The degree of the polynomial defines the number of potential roots or zeros. As some of the roots may be

Table 6.5 The Cash Flow of Producing 464 Inside-Out Beams Annually

| | Revenue ($) | | Cost ($) | | Net Cash |
Year	Beams & Chips	Logs	Capital, G & A†		Flow
0			1,492,153		−1,492,153
1	1,120,328	358,851	637,970		123,507
2	1,120,328	358,851	637,970		123,507
3	1,120,328	358,851	637,970		123,507
4	1,120,328	358,851	637,970		123,507
5	1,120,328	358,851	637,970		123,507
6	1,120,328	358,851	637,970		123,507
7	1,120,328	358,851	637,970		123,507
8	1,120,328	358,851	637,970		123,507
9	1,120,328	358,851	637,970		123,507
10	1,120,328	358,851	637,970		123,507

Source: Patterson et al. (2002)
†G & A is general and administrative costs

positive, negative, or zero, the *irr*s may be positive, negative, or zero. Descartes' Rule of Signs is used to estimate the number of positive and negative zeros: The number of positive real zeroes in a polynomial function is the same or less than by an even number as the number of changes in the sign of the coefficients. Thus, if the net cash flow changes sign once or twice, you may (or may not) be able to calculate an *irr* that makes economic sense. For example, Table 6.5 gives the cash flows for producing 464 ISO beams annually. The net cash flow changes sign once and the *irr* is −3%.

Second, calculating *irr*(s) becomes exceedingly complicated when the project involves positive and negative net cash flows scattered though time. If the net cash flow changes signs more than twice, there may be multiple positive *irr*s according to Descartes' Rule of Signs. Given the complexity of the many different cash flows, *irr*(s) should only be determined iteratively. These are the steps that I would advise to iteratively estimate an *irr*: (1) Set up the spreadsheet just like you are going to calculate NPV. (2) Determine if the net cash flow changes signs at least once. (3) Starting with zero (0), change the *irr* until equation (6.12) is approximately equal to zero.[28] Repeat this process until you are satisfied that you have determined all of the potential *irr*s as defined by Descartes' Rule of Signs.[29]

Third is interpreting the *irr*.[30] Some people interpret the *irr* as a rate of return similar to the discount rate because equation (6.12) appears to be the NPV formula given in equation (6.8). This interpretation is incorrect. A classic example of this misinterpretation is given by the following set of articles: Webster et al. (2009), Wagner (2009), and Pickens et al. (2009). Unfortunately, the *irr* can only be interpreted as a discount rate under very strict circumstances (Wagner 2009; also see Appendix 6C). Interpreting the *irr* similar to a discount rate drawn from the financial capital market does not follow from estimating it mathematically. The *irr* depends solely on the amount and timing of a project's net cash flow and nothing else; thus, it is not a function of time preference, risk/uncertainty, or inflation (Boulding 1935). The discount rate is established in the financial capital markets, and is the expected rate of return offered by other investments of equivalent risk and investment horizon to the project being evaluated, and is based on the financial capital market's assessment of the internal and external factors of each investment (Brealey et al. 2008; Johnstone 2008).

Finally, the *irr* favors projects that have low capital costs and relatively early returns and uses a single "rate" over the life of the project. The internal rate of return is not consistent with the assumption that individuals maximize their wealth (e.g., Brealey et al. 2008; Copeland et al. 2005; Davis et al. 2001; Rideout and Hesseln 2001; Luenberger 1998; Klemperer 1996; Gregory 1987; Johansson and Löfgren 1985; Leuschner 1984; Clutter et al. 1983). As the *irr*'s decision criteria requires defining an appropriate market-derived discount rate, Why not use NPV?

Earlier in this chapter I described a hurdle rate of return or a minimal acceptable rate of return. This is often used to define the "appropriate discount rate" in the *irr* decision rule. While using a hurdle rate of return or minimal acceptable rate of return, if derived correctly, to define an appropriate discount rate is okay, the *irr* is still not a decision criterion consistent with our assertion of wealth maximization.

Return on Investment

Return on investment (ROI) is a non-discounted ratio of revenues to costs. There are many similar variations of ROI that use different measures of revenues to costs. Two of the common ones are return on assets and return on equity. The variations are given by equation (6.13a) through (6.13e):

Return on Investment

$$\frac{\text{Book Value}_{t+1} - \text{Book Value}_t}{\text{Book Value}_t} \tag{6.13a}$$

$$\frac{(\text{Net Income} + \text{Interest}) \cdot (1 - \text{tax rate})}{\text{Book Value}} \tag{6.13b}$$

$$\frac{\text{Income}}{\text{Total Assets}} \tag{6.13c}$$

$$\frac{\text{Net Income}}{\text{Book Value}} \tag{6.13d}$$

$$\frac{\text{Book Value}_T - \text{Book Value}_t}{\text{Book Value}_t} \tag{6.13e}$$

The ratio is commonly used as a measure of efficiency. The greater the ratio, the greater the measure of per dollar revenue or income is to per dollar asset value. The definition of ROI depends directly on the definitions of the terms in the numerator and the denominator. The problems with ROI are due to accounting measures of value versus economic cash flow (Chapter 1 – Introduction). The larger "T" is in equation (6.13e), the more the overstatement of efficiency due to the non-discounted analysis of Book Value at time T. In addition, examining the Book Value at time t versus time T ignores all the positive and negative cash flows in between these two observations. Different rules of accounting (e.g., depreciation) would cause different measurements of ROI. Neither the merits of an investment nor efficiency depend on how accountants classify cash flows. Interest payments are included in equation (6.13b), thus an argument might be made that ROI includes at the minimum time preference and risk. Unfortunately, there is nothing to tie the implied time preference and risk to any positive or negative cash flows before or after time t and t + 1 to the net income, nor is there an indication of whether the risk is appropriate for the cash flows before or after time t and t + 1 and the net income. Finally, ROI is a one-period view of the world (i.e., now and some period in the future: t + 1 or T). No reference can be made to any specific point in or length of the investment horizon. As a result, ROI is not necessarily consistent with the assumption that individuals maximize their wealth.

Breakeven Analysis

Breakeven analysis determines how many units must be produced and sold to cover some measure of costs: financing, fixed costs (operation and maintenance [O&M], or sales, general, and administrative [SG&A]), variable production costs. I have categorized breakeven analysis into two groups. The first group is the payback period and the discounted payback period. The second group is similar to the breakeven analysis from Chapter 5 – Profit: (a) estimating the total revenue that must be earned annually to cover the present value of the financing, operation, and maintenance costs for the investment horizon; (b) estimating how many units of output that must be produced and "sold" annually to cover the present value of the financing, operation, and maintenance costs for the investment horizon at an expected annual market price; and (c) estimating a price you would have to receive annually to cover the present value of the financing, operation, and maintenance costs for the investment horizon at an expected annual output or production level.

Payback Period

The payback period of an investment is found by counting the number of years it takes before the cumulative forecasted net cash flow equals the initial investment. This is a non-discounted summation. Using the cash flow diagram of the management plan given in Figure 6.4, the payback period is 30 years. The Mobile Micromill® practical application (Becker et al. 2004; Table 8 p. 30) is another example (albeit a problematic example) of a payback period. In this example, only under one of the three market scenarios examined does the Mobile Micromill® pay back within the five-year planning horizon.

The payback period's decision criterion is: The shorter the payback period the better. The logic is shorter payback periods are associated with smaller risk. Unfortunately, as a possible risk metric there is no specific definition of "shorter." For example, a piece of equipment may have a defined useful or economic life. A payback period shorter than the equipment's useful life is preferred to one close to or longer than its useful life. As equipment is used it wears out. A payback period shorter than the equipment's useful life illustrates a good chance that the equipment will cover its initial cost before incurring major repairs or having to be replaced. Alternatively, if an asset class is associated with rapid technological changes, then shorter payback periods may reduce the chances of a loss through obsolescence. A shorter payback period can also be associated with the possibility of greater liquidity. But again, the definition of shorter is purely arbitrary, and the possibility of greater liquidity comes at the cost of maximizing wealth. Payback periods are most often used for relatively small investments similar to considering the replacement of incandescent light bulbs with new LED light bulbs when it is not worth the time and effort to do a more sophisticated analysis. In these cases, the goal is to reduce operating costs. However, there is no specific or mathematical definition of what constitutes a "relatively small investment."

There are two problems with using the payback period. First, this is a non-discounted sum, therefore it does not account for the discount rate, risk, or any other measures of the opportunity cost of time. Second, it ignores all net cash flows after the payback period. As a result, the payback period is not consistent with the assumption that individuals maximize their wealth. The payback period is often used as an unsophisticated quick check on an investment before examining it further.

Discounted Payback Period

The discounted payback period of an investment is found by counting the number of years it takes before the sum of the present value of the revenues is greater than the sum of the present value of the costs or before the cumulative net present value is just greater than zero.

$$\sum_{t=0}^{?} \frac{R_t}{(1+r)^t} - \sum_{t=0}^{?} \frac{C_t}{(1+r)^t} = \sum_{t=0}^{?} \frac{(R_t - C_t)}{(1+r)^t} = 0$$

Referring to the energy audit conducted by Ingersoll Rand and the recommendation to replace steam traps described earlier, the discounted payback period is three years, and the estimated useful life of a steam trap is 15 years. Again, the logic is shorter discounted payback periods are associated with smaller risk. However, the definition of shorter is purely arbitrary. While it does include a discount rate or opportunity cost of time, it ignores all net cash flows after the payback period. As a result, the discounted payback period is not consistent with the assumption that individuals maximize their wealth.

Breakeven: Total Revenue

As defined previously, this technique determines the total revenue that must be earned annually to cover the present value of the financing, operation, and maintenance costs for the planning horizon. As costs will often vary over the planning horizon, converting a varying cost cash flow into an equivalent constant or consistent cost cash flow will make the analysis easier. This is accomplished by the following steps:

1. Calculating the sum of the present value of the cost cash flow [PV(Cost)] for the investment or planning horizon T using equation (6.14):

$$PV(Cost) = \sum_{t=0}^{T} C_t (1+r)^{-t} \tag{6.14}$$

2. Using an equal annual equivalent (EAE) formula to annuitize the present value of the costs or convert a varying cost cash flow into an equivalent constant or consistent cost cash flow using equation (6.15):[31]

$$EAE(Cost) = PV(Cost) \cdot \frac{r \cdot (1+r)^T}{(1+r)^T - 1} = PV(Cost) \cdot \frac{r}{1 - (1+r)^{-T}} \tag{6.15}$$

Steps 1 and 2 are illustrated graphically in Figures 6.9a and 6.9b.

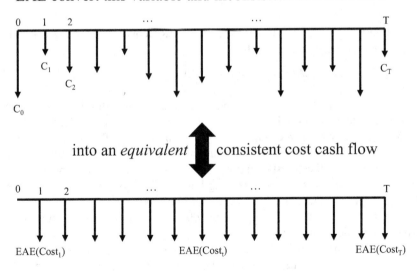

Figure 6.9a Equal Annual Equivalent Example

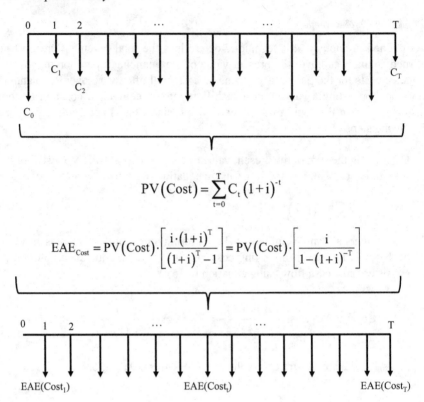

$$PV(Cost) = \sum_{t=0}^{T} C_t (1+i)^{-t}$$

$$EAE_{Cost} = PV(Cost) \cdot \left[\frac{i \cdot (1+i)^T}{(1+i)^T - 1}\right] = PV(Cost) \cdot \left[\frac{i}{1-(1+i)^{-T}}\right]$$

Figure 6.9b Equal Annual Equivalent Example

3. Setting the required annual revenue or EAE(Revenue) equal to the calculated EAE(Cost) using equation (6.16):

$$EAE(Revenue) = EAE(P \times Q) = EAE(Cost) \tag{6.16}$$

I will use the Radiata Pine Plantation practical application to illustrate calculating a breakeven total revenue. Tables 6.6a and 6.6b summarize the cost information used in Chapter 3 – Costs with columns 1 to 4 defining the cash flow diagrams for the unpruned and pruned Radiata Pine Plantation practical application, respectively.

As can be seen, these cost cash flows include fixed and variable inputs and vary over the 30-year investment or planning horizon. The last column is the present value of each management action using an 8% discount rate. The sum of the present value costs is 5,840.93 NZ$/ha and 7,007.86 NZ$/ha for the unpruned and pruned plantations, respectively.

Calculating the equal annual equivalent of these sums requires the unpruned and pruned plantations to generate an annual equivalent revenue of 518.83 and 622.49 NZ$/ha/year, respectively. Tables 6.7a and 6.7b show that the present value of the total revenues from the sale of sawtimber and pulp generated in year 30 using an

Table 6.6a Unpruned Radiata Pine Plantation Management Actions Present Value of Total Cost Using an 8% Discount Rate

Plantation Age	Management Action[†]	Fixed Cost (NZ$/ha)	Variable Cost (NZ$/ha)[‡]	Total Cost (NZ$/ha)	Present Value Total Cost (NZ$/ha)
0	Planting		691.39	691.39	691.39
0	Planting QC	40.00		40.00	40.00
1	Herbicide		249.90	249.90	231.39
2	Herbicide		249.90	249.90	214.25
5	DS	40.00		40.00	27.22
6	DS	40.00		40.00	25.21
8	PCT		500.00	500.00	270.13
	PCT QC	45.00		45.00	24.31
29	Road	1,000.00		1,000.00	107.33
30	Clearcut				
	Harvesting		29,844.50	29,844.50	2,965.81
	Equipment		426.35	426.35	42.37
	W&L		426.35	426.35	42.37
	HM		4,263.50	4,263.50	423.69
Annual	Admin	60.00		60.00	737.47
∑(Present Value of Costs)					5,840.93
Equal Annual Equivalent of Costs (NZ$/ha/year)					518.83

[†] Planting QC – planting quality control audit; DS – *Dothistroma septosporum* spray; PCT – precommercial thinning; PCT QC – precommercial thinning quality control audit; Road – upgrading/building harvest roads; Equipment – moving harvest machinery to the site; W&L – scaling the logs to determine product class (Weights) and yield tax (Levies) for research and development; HM – harvest management; Admin – administration
[‡] NZ$/ha – 2016 New Zealand dollars per hectare

Table 6.6b Pruned Radiata Pine Plantation Management Actions Present Value of Total Cost Using an 8% Discount Rate

Plantation Age	Management Action[†]	Unit[‡]	Quantity	Unit Cost	Fixed Cost (NZ$/ha)[‡]	Variable Cost (NZ$/ha)
0	Planting	Stem/ha	1,000	0.83		830.00
0	Planting QC	NZ$/ha		40.00	40.00	
1	Herbicide	Stem/ha	1,000	0.30		300.00
2	Herbicide	Stem/ha	1,000	0.30		300.00
5	DS	NZ$/ha		40.00		40.00
6	DS	NZ$/ha		40.00		40.00
6	Prune	Stem/ha	500	2.70		1,350.00
6	Prune QC	NZ$/ha		45.00	45.00	
8	Prune	Stem/ha	300	2.25		832.50
8	Prune QC	NZ$/ha		45.00	45.00	

(*Continued*)

Table 6.6b (Continued)

Plantation Age	Management Action[†]	Unit[‡]	Quantity	Unit Cost	Fixed Cost (NZ$/ha)[‡]	Variable Cost (NZ$/ha)
8	PCT	NZ$/ha		300.00		300.00
8	PCT QC	NZ$/ha		45.00	45.00	
29	Road	NZ$/ha		1,000.00	1,000.00	
30	Clearcut					
	Harvesting	m³/ha	765.1	35.00		26,778.50
	Equipment	m³/ha	765.1	0.50		382.55
	W&L	m³/ha	765.1	0.50		382.55
	HM	m³/ha	765.1	5.00		3,825.50
Annual	Admin	NZ$/ha		60.00	60.00	
∑(Present Value of Costs)						7,007.86
Equal Annual Equivalent of Costs (NZ$/ha/year)						622.49

[†] Planting QC – planting quality control audit; DS – *Dothistroma septosporum* spray; Prune QC – pruning quality control audit; PCT – precommercial thinning; PCT QC – precommercial thinning quality control audit; Road – upgrading/building harvest roads; Equipment – moving harvest machinery to the site; W&L – scaling the logs to determine product class (Weights) and yield tax (Levies) for research and development; HM – harvest management; Admin – administration

[‡] NZ$/ha – 2016 New Zealand dollars per hectare

Table 6.7a Present Value of Radiata Pine Unpruned Yield Revenue at Plantation Age 30 by Product Using an 8% Discount Rate[§]

Product Class[§]	Stumpage Price[‡] (NZ$/m³)	Product (m³/ha)	Revenue (NZ$/ha)	Present Value Revenue (NZ$/ha)
Pulpwood	36.00	241.5	8,694.00	863.92
L1	82.00	45.0	3,690.00	366.76
L2	68.00	49.5	3,366.00	334.84
S1	94.00	138.5	13,019.00	1,293.65
S2	78.00	367.6	28,672.80	2,849.32
	Total Revenue		57,441.80	
∑(Present Value of Revenues)				5,708.48
Equal Annual Equivalent of Revenues (NZ$/ha/year)				507.07

[‡] Stumpage prices are 2016 New Zealand dollars per cubic meters (NZ$/m³)

[§] Radiata pine output is defined in terms of quantity (cubic meters per hectare (m³/ha)) and quality (logs and log grades). User-defined log grades are characterized by product class (e.g., large vs. small sawlogs, pruned vs. unpruned sawlogs, or pulp logs, etc.), diameter and length of each product class, and sweep (as measured by the maximum deviation of the log's centerline) (West et al. 2013).

8% discount rate is 5,708.48 and 6,321.77 NZ$/ha giving an equal annual equivalent revenue of 507.07 and 561.55 NZ$/ha/year, respectively.

Just examining the sums of the present value of the revenues and costs shows the net present values are negative, so why go to the trouble of calculating this breakeven analysis using equal annual equivalent revenues and costs?

Table 6.7b Present Value of Radiata Pine Pruned Yield Revenue at Plantation Age 30 by Product Using an 8% Discount Rate[§]

Product Class[§]	Stumpage Price[‡] (NZ$/m³)	Product (m³/ha)	Revenue (NZ$/ha)	Present Value Revenue (NZ$/ha)
Pulpwood	36.00	192.2	6,919.20	687.78
L1	82.00	26.9	2,205.80	219.26
L2	68.00	62.7	4,263.60	423.57
P1	147.00	77.2	11,348.40	1,127.47
P2	141.00	105.8	14,917.80	1,482.52
S1	94.00	84.0	7,896.00	784.41
S2	78.00	206.0	16,068.00	1,596.75
	Total	Revenue	63,618.80	
Σ(Present Value of Revenues)				6,321.77
Equal Annual Equivalent of Revenues (NZ$/ha/year)				561.55

‡ Stumpage prices are 2016 New Zealand dollars per cubic meters (NZ$/m³)
§ Radiata pine output is defined in terms of quantity (cubic meters per hectare (m³/ha)) and quality (logs and log grades). User-defined log grades are characterized by product class (e.g., large vs. small sawlogs, pruned vs. unpruned sawlogs, or pulp logs, etc.), diameter and length of each product class, and sweep (as measured by the maximum deviation of the log's centerline) (West et al. 2013).

The answer is that the difference between the equal annual equivalent revenues and costs defines how much additional annual net revenue must be generated for net present value to equal 0 or the investment to break even. In this case, the difference is 11.77 and 60.94 NZ$/ha/year for the unpruned and pruned plantations, respectively. As an entrepreneur, you could search for additional sources of revenues, such as sale of recreational leases or the emerging carbon markets. The unpruned and pruned plantations generate 472.97 and 425.46 net ton of CO_2 equivalent per hectare (t CO_2e/ha) over the 30-year investment horizon.[32] At the time of this analysis, the contract rate was 20 NZ$/t CO_2e/ha. The equal annual equivalent of this net revenue flow from selling carbon is 755.24 and 672.31 NZ$/ha/year, which more than covers the required additional revenue for these investments to break even.

Breakeven: Output Production Level

This technique estimates how many units of output must be produced and "sold" annually to cover the present value of the financing, operation, and maintenance costs for the planning horizon at an expected annual market price. This requires using a similar procedure as that described earlier:

1. Calculating the present value of the cost cash flow [PV(Cost)] using equation (6.14)
2. Using an equal annual equivalent (EAE) formula to annuitize the present value of the costs or convert a varying cost cash flow into an equivalent constant or consistent cost cash flow using equation (6.15)

3. Setting the required annual revenue or EAE(Revenue) equal to the calculated EAE(Cost) and then dividing by EAE(Price)[33]

$$EAE(P \times Q) = EAE(Cost)$$

$$EAE(Q) = Q = \frac{EAE(Cost)}{EAE(P)}$$

where the EAE(P) is your estimate of the output's annual market price and EAE(Q) = Q is the resulting estimate of the annual output production level over the planning horizon. There are many ways of estimating your annual market price. For example,

- If you have historic price data, you could calculate a simple average and assume that the average price is constant over the planning horizon.
- If you have historic price data and some statistical acumen, you could forecast output prices over the planning horizon and, using the sum of the present value of the forecasted prices, calculate the equal annual equivalent of this price series.
- You could use the most recent price and assume this is constant over the planning horizon.
- You could use the most recent price, assume a constant annual price appreciation based on your knowledge of the market and using the sum of the present value of these prices, and calculate the equal annual equivalent of this price series.

For example, the 1 MW ground-mounted solar array financing costs are given in Table 6.2. The annual loan payments are $108,399.20. Simply, the 1 MW ground-mounted solar array must generate an equal annual equivalent of revenue for 15 years to break even. Using the US Energy Information Administration's (EIA) Energy Data Browser (www.eia.gov/electricity/data/browser/ accessed 2 July 2021), the residential electricity price in 2020 for New York State was 0.18 $/kWh. Using the same EIA data for New York State and a 20-year price series (2021 to 2020), the residential electricity prices increased at 1.5% annually during this period. Using this annual change, residential electricity prices can be estimated for the next 15 years. Using steps 1 to 3 and a discount rate of 6%, the EAE(P) was 0.20 $/kWh/year. This solar array must produce (108,399.20/0.20) = 541,996 kWh/year to break even over the 15-year period. In Syracuse, New York, based on data provided by the PVWatts Calculator, an annual conversion amount would be 1,166,675 kWh/year but may range from 1,118,958 to 1,181,608 kWh/year (https://pvwatts.nrel.gov/ accessed 2 July 2, 2021).[34]

Based on this uncomplicated example, the 1 MW ground-mounted solar array's production system would be able to produce the required breakeven annual output level to cover the annual financing costs. The purpose of the uncomplicated example was to illustrate how to determine a breakeven output level. However, it is also important to understand the caveats of this example on determining a breakeven output level. The estimated annual costs did not include any investment tax credit programs, local taxes (property, etc.), land rental costs, annual insurance costs, annual conversion degradation, labor, operation and maintenance costs, etc. as described by Feldman et al. (2021). Also, the price represents a simple retail residential price and does not reflect alternative electricity providers such as community solar projects that often offer residential consumers a discount on retail prices. In Chapter 7 – The Natural Resources Management Puzzle, I will address some of these caveats directly.

Breakeven: Price

This technique estimates a price you would have to receive annually to cover the present value of the financing, operation, and maintenance costs for the investment horizon at an expected output or production level. This requires using a similar procedure as that described above

1. Calculating the present value of the cost cash flow [PV(Cost)] using equation (6.14)
2. Using an equal annual equivalent (EAE) formula to annuitize the present value of the costs or convert a varying cost cash flow into an equivalent constant or consistent cost cash flow using equation (6.15)
3. Setting the required annual revenue or EAE(Revenue) equal to the calculated EAE(Cost) and then dividing by estimated annual production level[35]

$$EAE(P \times Q) = EAE(Cost)$$
$$EAE(P) = P = \frac{EAE(Cost)}{EAE(Q)}$$

where the EAE(Q) is your estimate of the annual output production level and EAE(P) = P is the resulting estimate of the annual market price over the planning horizon. As with estimating the EAE(P), there are various ways of estimating EAE(Q), all of which depend on your knowledge of the production system as outlined in Chapter 2 – Production Systems. For example,

- You could use the most recent output level and assume this is constant over the planning horizon.
- You could use the most recent output level, assume a constant annual change in production level based on your knowledge of the production system and, using the sum of the discounted values of the output levels, calculate the equal annual equivalent of this discounted output series.

To illustrate how to calculate a breakeven price, I will again use the 1 MW ground-mounted solar array with annual loan payments of $108,399.20 and an annual conversion rate of 1,166,675 kWh/year with a range of 1,118,958 to 1,181,608 kWh/year. Based on Feldman et al. (2021), photovoltaic modules degrade in their ability to convert insolation at 0.7% per year. Using this annual degradation rate, output levels can be estimated for the next 15 years. Using steps 1 to 3, a discount rate of 6%, and an initial output level of 1,166,675 kWh, the EAE(Q) was 1,119,601 kWh/year. This solar array must receive a price of (108,399.20/1,119,601) = 0.096 $/kWh/year to break even over the 15-year period.[36] As defined earlier, in 2020 the New York State residential electricity price was 0.18 $/kWh.

Based on this uncomplicated example, the 1 MW ground-mounted solar array's required breakeven annual price is below the market price. Again, the purpose of the uncomplicated example was to illustrate how to determine a breakeven price. The same caveats described earlier still hold for this analysis, and I will address them in Chapter 7 – The Natural Resources Management Puzzle.

Investment Analysis Tools – Revisited

As Brealey et al. (2008), Kierulff (2008), and Graham and Harvey (2001) describe NPV, BCR, payback periods, and *irr* are the most common investment analysis tools used in business. This result is consistent with the same conclusion reached by Luenberger in 1998. While none of the investment analysis tools examined for determining acceptable investments is infallible, NPV is the best criterion to use and is the standard by which all other investment analysis tools are compared (Brealey et al. 2008; Copeland et al. 2005; Luenberger 1998). Consequently, my recommendation is that NPV should always be used in addition to and regardless of other investment analysis tools requested.

Patterson et al. (2002) used NPV to examine the feasibility of producing inside-Out (ISO) beams using softwoods and hardwoods. What is interesting about Patterson et al.'s investment analysis is the use of three production levels and five discount rates; as the authors' note this was done to account for risk. This approach will be examined in more detail in Chapter 8 – Risk. The Maple Syrup Operation (Huyler 2000; CFBMC 2000) and Great Lakes Charter Boat Fishing (Lichtkoppler and Kuehn 2003) practical applications do not explicitly use an investment analysis tool like NPV or calculate annual loan payments. But these authors recognize the importance of these financial capital costs by including them in their analyses. The Radiata Pine Plantation practical application was mentioned at the beginning of this chapter to introduce time as a relevant input. The timing of cutting trees based on an appropriate silvicultural system is often the principal tool used in sustainably managing a forested ecosystem. The investment analysis of these silvicultural systems will be covered in Chapter 7 – The Natural Resources Management Puzzle. Finally, while the production system described in the Radiata Pine Plantation practical application included time as an input, Select Red Oak (Hahn and Hansen 1991) does not. Thus, the description of the production process for Select Red Oak does not facilitate any type of investment analysis. Additional research and information would be required to answer any questions concerning the opportunity cost of time in this practical application. I would encourage the reader to review the practical applications given the earlier discussion.

While NPV is the best criterion to use and is the standard by which all other investment analysis tools are compared, I often combine NPV with the BCR and an output production and/or price breakeven analysis. Each provides additional useful information at a relatively low cost. I use NPV as the decision criterion. The BCR is calculated using the same information as NPV and gives a quick cardinal assessment of sensitivity; namely, increases in discounted costs or decreases in discounted revenues before NPV = 0 and if these are within normal ranges of operations for costs and revenues of the investment. A breakeven analysis gives the feasibility of the production system to provide the output given the market conditions.

Capital Budgeting

In the previous section, I examined tools that can be used to determine if a single investment is acceptable and concluded NPV is the best criterion to use in making this decision. However, often an entrepreneur is faced with choosing among a number of alternative investments. In addition, the choice is made more difficult by having a fixed budget with which to make these investments. The purpose of this section is to determine how to choose among investments.

Investments can be classified by attributes, not unlike classifying a tree into family, genus, and species. I will use three attributes to classify investments. The primary attributes are:

Mutually exclusive – Only one investment can be chosen; e.g., using an area of land to plant radiata pine for timber or using the same land for a ground-mounted solar array; a sugar maple for a sugarbush or sugar maple for sawtimber.[37]

Independent – Investments are not dependent on one another with respect to adoption; e.g., a precommercial thinning on one stand does not preclude a commercial thinning on a different stand. Alternatively, a rooftop solar array on my house does not preclude a rooftop solar array on your house.

Interdependent – The feasibility of one investment is dependent on whether other investments are undertaken and the timing of those investments.

The secondary attributes are:

Divisible – If you can invest in part of a project; e.g., adding money to a savings account.

Indivisible (or lumpy) – If you cannot invest in part of the project, it is an all-or-nothing proposition; e.g., building a factory or infrastructure such as a bridge or tunnel – you cannot generally buy half a car or build half a bridge; you have to buy the whole car or build the whole bridge.

The tertiary attributes are:

> Repeating – If you can replicate the exact project; e.g., a management regime
> that calls for repeating patterns of regeneration and harvest of the same
> forested ecosystem or replacing a solar array at the end of its useful life.
> Nonrepeating – If you cannot replicate the exact project.

The majority of the capital budgeting problems you will deal with will be mutually
exclusive or independent investments. The secondary and tertiary attributes will
define the most appropriate tool to use to choose among investment alternatives.
I will describe three examples of common mutually exclusive investment first, then
one example of independent investments.

Mutually Exclusive, Indivisible, and Nonrepeating Investments

NPV is the preferred decision criteria for capital budgeting of two or more mutually exclusive projects that are nonrepeating. I will use the following two investments in this section.

Investment A

The investment's cash flow diagram and NPV analysis given a 5% discount rate
are given in Figure 6.10.

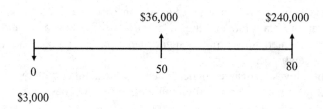

Year	Revenue	Cost	Net Cash Flow	PV(NCF)[‡]
0		3,000	-3.000	-3,000.00
50	36,000		36,000	2,475.59
80	240,000		240,000	3,311.42

[‡] PV(NCF) denotes present value of the cash flow calculated using equation (6.7)

Discount Rate = 5.5%

Net Present Value = $2,787.02

Figure 6.10 Investment A's Cash Flow Diagram and Spreadsheet

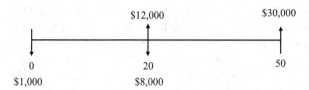

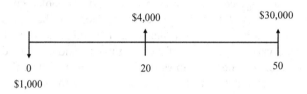

Year	Revenue	Cost	Net Cash Flow	PV(NCF)[‡]
0		1,000	-1.000	-1,000.00
20	12,000	8,000	4,000	1,507.56
50	30,000		30,000	2,616.11

[‡] PV(NCF) denotes present value of the cash flow calculated using equation (6.7)

Discount Rate = 5%

Net Present Value = $3,123.67

Figure 6.11 Investment B's Cash Flow Diagrams and Spreadsheet

Investment B

The investment's cash flow diagram and NPV analysis given a 5.5% discount rate are given in Figure 6.11.

As the entrepreneur has only $3,000 of initial capital, these two investments are mutually exclusive. These investments were defined as nonrepeatable: That is, they are "one-shot" investments. Given the defined investment horizons, NPV – as illustrated by equation (6.8) – is well suited to analyze mutually exclusive, inde-pendent, and nonrepeating investments. From Figures 6.9 and 6.10, the NPVs of investments A and B are $2,787.021 and $3,123.67, respectively. Investing in B would be preferred as it results in the highest NPV.

Examining Figures 6.10 and 6.11 reveals that they have different investment horizons; namely, 80 years for Investment A and 50 years for Investment B. In addition, Investment A has a positive net cash flow in year 50 while Investment B has a positive net cash flow in year 30. Finally, Investment A would use all of the $3,000 of the available capital while Investment B would use only $1,000; namely, the investments have different scales. A reasonable question could be raised about potential uses of any positive intermediate net cash flows or differences in scale when analyzing which investment is preferred. These positive net cash flows *could* be reinvested in short-term or long-term investments or used as cash. The operative work in this last sentence is "could"; as an analyst you have no idea how these positive net cash flows might be used. A best guess of an entrepreneur's opportunity cost of either choice would be their weighted average cost of capital for investments of risk similar to business as usual. As an analyst, you have no idea of any future weighted average costs of capital or the risk of any potential future investments. Various versions of this reinvestment discussion have been raging since the 1950s. Recent works by Magni and Martin (2017) and Arjunan and Kannapiran (2018) examined various iterations of these arguments and concluded empirically that any realized positive net cash flows resulting from an investment are independent of the investment and their further uses are irrelevant for accepting or rejecting these types of mutually exclusive investments.

Mutually Exclusive, Indivisible, Repeating Investments With Unequal Investment Horizons and Equal Risk

A common issue when choosing between mutually exclusive projects concerns investments with unequal investment horizons. These investments can be further classified as having equal or unequal risk. I will first examine those investments with equal risk. As described earlier, NPV can be biased towards projects with longer investment horizons that have positive net cash flows, especially if the investments can be repeated. Thus, NPV could provide inaccurate information for decision making. Investment C is a repeatable project with an initial cost of $20,000 and annual revenues lasting for 10 years. The revenues start at $3,400 and decrease by $50 annually for the 10-year investment horizon. This is illustrated in Figure 6.12.

Investment D is a repeatable project with an initial cost of $35,000 and annual revenues lasting for 15 years. The revenues start at $4,200 and decrease by $50 annually for the 15-year investment horizon. This is illustrated in Figure 6.13.

Comparing the NPVs of these two investments shows that Investment D would be preferred to Investment C. As Investment D has a longer investment horizon, the potential for unequal lives bias is present.

There are two accepted methods to address this potential bias: (1) the replacement chain or common life method and (2) equal annual equivalent method (Fehr 2017; Brigham and Huston 2019). The replacement chain method calculates the NPV of repeatable investments to a common year. For example, Investment C has a 10-year investment horizon and Investment D has a 15-year investment horizon; thus, the common year would be 30. This is illustrated in Table 6.8. Correcting for the investment horizon bias shows Investment C is now preferred to Investment D.

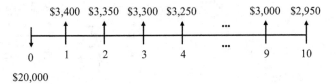

Year	Revenue	Cost	NCF[‡]	PV(NCF)[‡]
0		20,000	-20,000	-20,000.00
1	3,400		3,400	3,238.10
2	3,350		3,350	3,038.55
3	3,300		3,300	2,850.66
4	3,250		3,250	2,673.78
⋮	⋮	⋮	⋮	⋮
9	3,000		3,000	1,933.83
10	2,950		2,950	1,811.04

[‡] NCF denotes net cash flow. PV(NCF) denotes present value of the net cash flow given a 5% discount rate.

Net Present Value = $4,671.30
Equal Annual Equivalent = $604.95
Replacement Chain NPV = $9,299.63

Figure 6.12 Mutually Exclusive, Indivisible, Repeating Investments With Unequal Investment Horizons and Equal Risk – Investment C

The second is the equal annual equivalent (EAE) method. There are three steps to using the EAE in capital budgeting.

1. Determine each investment's NPV. For Investments C and D these are given in Figures 6.11 and 6.12 as $4,671.30 and $5,430.16, respectively.
2. Annuitize each investment's NPV using an EAE given in equation (6.17):[38]

$$\text{EAE}(\text{NPV}) = \text{NPV} \cdot \frac{r \cdot (1+r)^T}{(1+r)^T - 1} = \text{NPV} \cdot \frac{r}{1-(1+r)^{-T}} \tag{6.17}$$

The EAE for Investment C is

$$\text{EAE}_C = \$4,671.30 \cdot \frac{0.05}{1-(1.05)^{-10}} = \$604.95$$

The EAE for Investment D is

$$\text{EAE}_D = \$5,430.16 \cdot \frac{0.05}{1-(1.05)^{-15}} = \$523.15$$

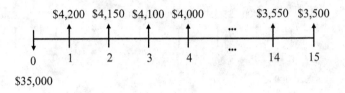

Year	Revenue	Cost	NCF[‡]	PV(NCF)[‡]
0		35,000	-35,000	-35,000.00
1	4,200		4,200	3,764.17
2	4,150		4,150	3,541.73
3	4,100		4,100	3,334.95
4	4,050		4,050	3,134.10
⋮	⋮	⋮	⋮	⋮
9	3,550		3,550	1,792.99
10	3,500		3,500	1,683.56

[‡] NCF denotes net cash flow. PV(NCF) denotes present value of the net cash flow given a 5% discount rate.

Net Present Value = $5,430.16
Equal Annual Equivalent = $523.15
Replacement Chain NPV = $8,042.16

Figure 6.13 Mutually Exclusive, Indivisible, Repeating Investments With Unequal Investment Horizons and Equal Risk – Investment D

3. Compare the EAEs for each investment and select the investment with the largest EAE. Investment C's EAE is larger than Investment D's, thus Investment C is preferred.

There are two observations from this analysis. First, the replacement chain NPV and the EAE methods will give you consistent results for these types of mutually exclusive investments. Second, as shown by Newman et al. (2014), the EAE calculated using the NPV or replacement chain NPV are equivalent. This can be shown by using the investments' replacement chain NPVs given in Table 6.8 and equation (6.17).

Mutually Exclusive, Indivisible, Repeating Investments With Unequal Investment Horizons and Unequal Risk

The last mutually exclusive problems I will examine are those with unequal investment horizons and unequal risk. Fehr (2017) examines this problem and concludes that the replacement chain method is preferred to EAE as, in addition to different

Table 6.8 Mutually Exclusive, Indivisible, Repeating Investments With Unequal Investment Horizons and Equal Risk: Replacement Chain Net Present Value (RCNPV) and Equal Annual Equivalent Analysis (EAE)[‡]

Investment C				Investment D			
Year	R	C	PV(NCF)	Year	R	Cost	PV(NCF)
0		20,000	−20,000.00	0		35,000	−35,000.00
1	3,400		3,238.10	1	4,200		4,000.00
2	3,350		3,038.55	2	4,150		3,764.17
3	3,300		2,850.66	3	4,100		3,541.73
4	3,250		2,673.78	4	4,050		3,331.95
5	3,200		2,507.28	5	4,000		3,134.10
6	3,150		2,350.58	6	3,950		2,947.55
7	3,100		2,203.11	7	3,900		2,771.66
8	3,050		2,064.36	8	3,850		2,605.83
9	3,000		1,933.83	9	3,800		2,449.51
10	2,950	20,000	−10,467.22	10	3,750		2,302.17
11	3,400		1,987.91	11	3,700		2,163.31
12	3,350		1,865.41	12	3,650		2,032.46
13	3,300		1,750.06	13	3,600		1,909.16
14	3,250		1,641.47	14	3,550		1,792.99
15	3,200		1,539.25	15	3,500		−15,152.04
16	3,150		1,443.05	16	4,200	35,000	1,924.07
17	3,100		1,352.52	17	4,150		1,810.63
18	3,050		1,267.34	18	4,100		1,703.63
19	3,000		1,187.20	19	4,050		1,602.72
20	2,950	20,000	−6,425.97	20	4,000		1,507.56
21	3,400		1,220.40	21	3,950		1,417.82
22	3,350		1,145.20	22	3,900		1,333.21
23	3,300		1,074.39	23	3,850		1,253.45
24	3,250		1,007.72	24	3,800		1,178.26
25	3,200		944.97	25	3,750		1,107.39
26	3,150		885.91	26	3,700		1,040.59
27	3,100		830.33	27	3,650		977.65
28	3,050		778.04	28	3,600		918.34
29	3,000		728.84	29	3,550		862.46
30	2,950		682.56	30	3,500		809.82

[‡] R denotes Revenue, C denotes Cost, PV(NCF) denotes Present Value of the Net Cash Flow (NFC) calculated using a 5% discount rate

Investment C	Investment D
RCNPV = $9,299.63	RCNPV = $8,042.16
EAE = $604.95	EAE = $523.15

investment horizons, they have different discount rates due to different risk characteristics. The EAE does not capture this value enhancement associated with an investment.

Investment E is a repeatable investment with an initial cost of $1,000 and annual revenues of $205 lasting for 10 years. The discount rate associated with this investment is 5%. This is illustrated in Figure 6.14.

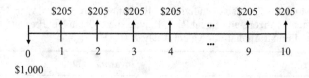

Year	Revenue	Cost	NCF[‡]	PV(NCF)[‡]
0		1,000	-1,000	-1,000.00
1	205		205	195.24
2	205		205	185.94
3	205		205	177.09
4	205		205	168.65
⋮	⋮	⋮	⋮	⋮
9	205		205	132.14
10	205		205	125.85

[‡] NCF denotes net cash flow. PV(NCF) denotes present value of the net cash flow given a 5% discount rate.

Net Present Value = $582.96
Equal Annual Equivalent = $75.50
Replacement Chain NPV = $1,160.55

Figure 6.14 Mutually Exclusive, Indivisible, Repeating Investments With Unequal Investment Horizons and Unequal Risk – Investment E

Investment F is a repeatable project with an initial cost of $2,000 and annual revenues of $285.00 lasting for 15 years. The discount rate associated with this investment is 6% due to additional risk. This is illustrated in Figure 6.15.

Examining the NPV and EAE of these investments shows that Investment F would be preferred to Investment E. However, examining the replacement chain NPV shows that when accounting for the additional risk and different investment horizons, Investment E is preferred. This is illustrated in Table 6.9 and is consistent with the conclusion reached by Fehr (2017).

Independent, Indivisible, and Nonrepeating

The rule for independent investments is to determine all projects whose NPV ≥ 0 and find the combination of projects with the largest total NPV within the given budget. Figure 6.16 gives a list of 10 different independent investments.

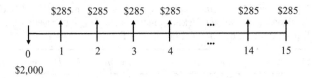

Year	Revenue	Cost	NCF[‡]	PV(NCF)[‡]
0		-2,000	-2,000	-2,000.00
1	285		285	268.87
2	285		285	253.65
3	285		285	239.29
4	285		285	225.75
⋮	⋮	⋮	⋮	⋮
14	285		285	126.06
15	285		285	118.92

[‡] NCF denotes net cash flow. PV(NCF) denotes present value of the net cash flow given a 6% discount rate.

Net Present Value = $767.99
Equal Annual Equivalent = $79.07
Replacement Chain NPV = $1,088.45

Figure 6.15 Mutually Exclusive, Indivisible, Repeating Investments With Unequal Investment Horizons and Unequal Risk – Investment F

If the entrepreneur has a budget of $40,000, $30,000, or $20,000, which investments would be acceptable? Deciding which investments are acceptable can be cumbersome as all feasible combinations must be determined, and from those that are feasible the one that generates the greatest wealth for the investor must be chosen. Luenberger (1998) illustrates how the use of linear programming with a binary decision variable – a variable that can only have a value of 0 (reject) and 1 (accept) – can solve these types of problems. However, a discussion of binary linear programming is beyond the scope of this book.

Capital Budgeting – Final Thoughts

I have focused on examining mutually exclusive and independent investments. The majority of the investments you encounter will be either of the two described earlier. However, when capital and other resources are limited, capital budgeting decisions can become tremendously complex. In these cases, get help.

Table 6.9 Mutually Exclusive, Indivisible, Repeating Investments With Unequal Investment Horizons and Unequal Risk: Replacement Chain Net Present Value (RCNPV) and Equal Annual Equivalent Analysis (EAE)[‡]

Investment E – Discount Rate = 5%				Investment F – Discount Rate = 6%			
Year	R	C	PV(NCF)	Year	R	Cost	PV(NCF)
0		1,000.00	−1,000.00	0		2,000.00	−2,000.00
1	205.00		195.24	1	285.00		268.87
2	205.00		185.94	2	285.00		253.65
3	205.00		177.09	3	285.00		239.29
4	205.00		168.65	4	285.00		225.75
5	205.00		160.62	5	285.00		212.97
6	205.00		152.97	6	285.00		200.91
7	205.00		145.69	7	285.00		189.54
8	205.00		138.75	8	285.00		178.81
9	205.00		132.14	9	285.00		168.69
10	205.00	1,000.00	−488.06	10	285.00		159.14
11	205.00		119.86	11	285.00		150.13
12	205.00		114.15	12	285.00		141.64
13	205.00		108.72	13	285.00		133.62
14	205.00		103.54	14	285.00		126.06
15	205.00		98.61	15	285.00	2,000.00	−715.61
16	205.00		93.91	16	285.00		112.19
17	205.00		89.44	17	285.00		105.84
18	205.00		85.18	18	285.00		99.85
19	205.00		81.13	19	285.00		94.20
20	205.00	1,000.00	−299.63	20	285.00		88.86
21	205.00		73.58	21	285.00		83.83
22	205.00		70.08	22	285.00		79.09
23	205.00		66.74	23	285.00		74.61
24	205.00		63.56	24	285.00		70.39
25	205.00		60.54	25	285.00		66.40
26	205.00		57.65	26	285.00		62.65
27	205.00		54.91	27	285.00		59.10
28	205.00		52.29	28	285.00		55.75
29	205.00		49.80	29	285.00		52.60
30	205.00		47.43	30	285.00		49.62

[‡] R denotes Revenue, C denotes Cost, PV(NCF) denotes Present Value of the Net Cash Flow (NFC)

Investment E – Discount Rate = 5%	Investment F – Discount Rate = 6%
RCNPV = $1,160.55	RCNPV = $1,088.45
EAE = $75.50	EAE = $79.07

Capital Theory: Investment Analysis – Variability

The time horizons of investment alternatives or projects in natural resource management may be very long. For example, in northern hardwood forests an uneven-age management plan may define 50 to 100 years between entries that generate revenue by harvesting trees. How certain are the estimates of product prices, costs,

Project	Initial Cost ($)	Horizon	Net Present Value ($)
1	763	9	456
2	4,687	20	273
3	5,995	11	−93
4	8,666	7	217
5	1,829	8	495
6	9,895	11	−82
7	790	9	157
8	6,112	17	81
9	1,227	14	−86
10	8,614	6	208

Figure 6.16 Independent, Indivisible, Nonrepeating Investments

and harvest volumes for 50 to 100 years in the future? Alternatively, a commercial solar array may have an initial 15- to 25-year investment horizon by a power purchase agreement, but output prices are variable. Using a single price over this investment horizon is problematic given its historic variability. One approach for dealing with potential variability is to evaluate tenable pessimistic, realistic, and optimistic scenarios for each alternative. This approach is called sensitivity analysis and will be described in more detail in Chapter 8 – Risk.

How to Use Economic Information – Capital Theory: Investment Analysis – to Make Better Business Decisions

There is an opportunity cost associated with time. As a student, the opportunity cost of going to an 8:00am class is time not spent sleeping. While there has been no money assigned to this opportunity cost, it is a cost nonetheless. In business decisions where time is a relevant input, the interest or discount rate can be used to describe the opportunity cost of time; but it also can be used to describe the opportunity cost of financial capital or the fact that there are alternative investment opportunities. The opportunity cost of financial capital represents the internal and external factors of investments as assessed by the financial capital markets. If the price of borrowing financial capital is less than what the individual would be willing to pay (the opportunity cost of time), the individual would borrow the financial capital. Alternatively, if the price of loaning financial capital is greater than what the individual would have been willing to accept (the opportunity cost of time), the individual would loan or invest their financial capital.

Many different formulae have been developed to find the equivalence, at a common reference point, of revenues and costs that may occur at different points in time. The two most important ones are future value and present value. With these two formulae and the flexibility of spreadsheets, you should be able to handle most of your problems. The key to analyzing investments that have a variety of revenues and costs throughout time is to draw a cash flow diagram of the potential investment.

As Luenberger (1998: 27) states: "It is widely agreed (by theorists, but not necessarily by practitioners) that, overall, the best [investment analysis] criterion is that based on net present value." My advice is to follow the recommendations of theorists and put theory into practice by using NPV. This tool provides the flexibility to analyze investments described as mutually exclusive, independent, and interdependent. In addition, it is consistent with the assumption that individuals maximize their wealth. NPV is also consistent with the Architectural Plan for Profit, and the same economic information used to build it are used in calculating NPV.

A point of clarification with respect to the Architectural Plan for Profit is needed now that time is an explicit relevant input and has a defined opportunity cost (i.e., the interest or discount rate) and that NPV is the most appropriate investment analysis tool: The correct term at the top of the Architectural Plan for Profit should be wealth. Consequently, when the discussion revolves around capital theory, the Architectural Plan for Profit graphic will use wealth.

Some concluding thoughts concerning cost–benefit analysis described in this chapter.[39] First, when reporting results of a cost–benefit analysis to a client, use appropriate and logical levels of precision. For example, reporting the net present value of an investment opportunity as $1,456.17 invites questions: Can future management actions be priced to the nearest one cent? Can you defend this level of precision? Can you defend this level of precision for costs and revenues that may occur 5, 10, 15, 20, 25, 30, ... years in the future? Rounding to the nearest $1 (or better yet $10 or $100) is usually more honest. Second, lowball your revenues and highball your costs or round your revenues down and your costs up. It is always easier to explain to your client why costs were under budget and revenues over budget (your wonderful management of the project) than the opposite situation; that is, plan for the worst, hope for the best. Finally, use common sense; use it early and often. For example, if two alternatives return $1,235 and $1,245 respectively, is the second one clearly superior to the first? Even if the level of certainty is the same between the two alternatives, the $10 difference is less than a 1% change. Which alternative provide returns you would be comfortable implementing if it were your own money or your grandmother's money? Professional honesty and integrity is always the best policy.

Appendix 6A – Financial Formulae

The following are common financial formulae. Table 6A1 gives the notations that are used in the formulae.

Future value of a terminating every-period series

$$V_t = a \cdot \frac{(1+r)^t - 1}{r} = a \cdot \frac{1 - (1+r)^{-t}}{r \cdot (1+r)^{-t}}$$

Table 6A.1 Financial Formulae Notation

Variable	Description
V_0	the value of a cost or revenue in time 0
V_t	the value of a cost or revenue in time t
r	the annual discount/interest rate expressed as a decimal
g	the annual increase in revenue or cost expressed as a decimal
t	the number of annual periods over which interest is charged
a	an equal periodic payment
w	the years between periodic payments
m	number of payments per year (e.g., m = 12 denotes monthly payments; m = 4 denotes quarterly payments)

Present value of a terminating every-period series

$$V_0 = a \cdot \frac{(1+r)^t - 1}{r \cdot (1+r)^t} = a \cdot \frac{1 - (1+r)^{-t}}{r}$$

Sinking fund formula, annual installment payments of a terminating every-period series, equal annual equivalent of a terminating every-period series

$$a = V_t \cdot \frac{r}{(1+r)^t - 1} = V_t \cdot \frac{r \cdot (1+r)^{-t}}{1 - (1+r)^{-t}} = V_0 \cdot \frac{r}{1 - (1+r)^{-t}} = V_0 \cdot \frac{r \cdot (1+r)^t}{(1+r)^t - 1}$$

Future value of a terminating periodic series

$$V_t = a \cdot \frac{(1+r)^t - 1}{(1+r)^w - 1}$$

Present value of a terminating periodic series

$$V_0 = a \cdot \frac{(1+r)^t - 1}{\left[(1+r)^w - 1\right] \cdot (1+r)^t}$$

Equal periodic equivalent of a terminating periodic series

$$a = V_0 \cdot \frac{\left[(1+r)^w - 1\right] \cdot (1+r)^t}{(1+r)^t - 1} = V_t \cdot \frac{(1+r)^w - 1}{(1+r)^t - 1}$$

Present value of a perpetual periodic series

$$V_0 = \frac{a}{(1+r)^w - 1} = \frac{a \cdot (1+r)^{-w}}{1 - (1+r)^{-w}}$$

Equal periodic equivalent of a perpetual periodic series

$$a = V_0 \cdot \left[(1+r)^w - 1 \right]$$

Present value of a perpetual every-period series

$$V_0 = \frac{a}{r}$$

Equal annual equivalent of a perpetual every-period series

$$a = V_0 \bullet r$$

Periodic installment or loan payment

$$a = V_0 \cdot \frac{\dfrac{r}{m} \cdot \left(1 + \dfrac{r}{m} \right)^{t \cdot m}}{\left(1 + \dfrac{r}{m} \right)^{t \cdot m} - 1} = V_0 \cdot \frac{\dfrac{r}{m}}{1 - \left(1 + \dfrac{r}{m} \right)^{-t \cdot m}}$$

Mills and Goforth (1975) – Present value of a perpetual periodic series with an annual increase

$$V_0 = \frac{a \cdot \left(1 + \dfrac{g}{r} \right)^{-w}}{1 - \left(1 + \dfrac{g}{r} \right)^{-w}}$$

Appendix 6B – Sustainability and the Interest Rate

The weight the discount rate places on determining the present value of any cash flow is illustrated by this simple example in Table 6B.1.

As can be seen in Figure 6B.1, the weight placed on any revenue or cost in the future decreases exponentially. One of the tenets of sustainability is that the use of resources should not have an impact on future generations. However, based on Table 6B.1, the weight placed on any future revenue or cost is very small. This is troublesome when the future is when most of the revenues may occur, which brings to mind the old saying that the future is worth nothing. The implication of Table 6B.1 is that the incentive is to use resources in the present going against the tenet of sustainability just described. This is what Chichilnisky (1997) termed the Dictatorship of the Present. Discussions surrounding the choice of the discount

Table 6B.1 Discount Rate Example, $r = 6\%$

Year	$(1 + r)^{-t}$
5	0.74726
10	0.55839
15	0.41727
20	0.31180
25	0.23300
30	0.17411

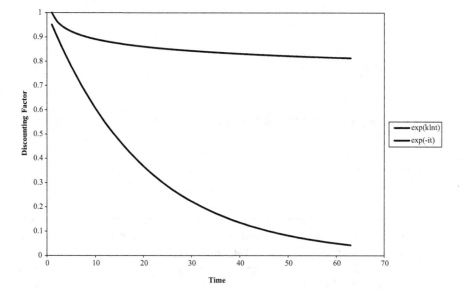

Figure 6B.1 Hyperbolic Discounting Factor and Continuous Time Discounting Factor[‡]

[‡] $\exp(\kappa \cdot \ln t) = e^{(\kappa \cdot \ln t)}$ denotes the hyperbolic discounting factor and $\exp(-it) = e^{(-it)}$ denotes the constant time discounting factor with $|\kappa| = i = 0.05$.

rate and its impact on sustainable forest management are not new and draw on the debate about social versus private interest rates (e.g., Mikesell 1977; Baumol 1968; Feldstein 1964a, 1964b). Harou (1985) discusses a method to develop a social discount rate that would be less than the private discount rate, reducing the Dictatorship of the Present. Kant (2003) continues this discussion arguing against using a discount rate obtained from the financial capital markets for valuing the flow of forest-based ecosystem goods and services that are not traditionally traded in markets.

An alternative proposed to the discounting factor $(1 + r)^{-t}$ is called hyperbolic discounting (Hepburn and Koundouri 2007; Gowdy and Erickson 2005;

Price 2004; Pearce et al. 2003; Casalmir 2000; Li and Löfgren 2000; Cropper and Laibson 1999; Chichilnisky 1997; Liabson 1997; Munasinghe 1993). This concept is drawn from the Weber-Fechner Law establishing that human responses to a change in a stimulus are nonlinear and are inversely proportional to the existing level of the stimulus. The notion of a hyperbolic discount rate is that a "higher value is placed on benefits delivered in the near term, followed by a sharp drop and flattening out in the medium term, so that the value of something stays fairly constant out into the distant future" (Gowdy and Erickson 2005: 214–215).

Equation (B1) defines r(t) as the non-constant discount rate at time t

$$r(t) = \frac{\frac{d\Delta(t)}{dt}}{\Delta(t)} = \frac{\dot{\Delta}(t)}{\Delta(t)} = \frac{\kappa}{t} \tag{B1}$$

where *k* is a negative constant. The hyperbolic discounting factor, $\Delta(t)$, is given by equation (B2)

$$\Delta(t) = e^{\kappa \ln t} = t^{\kappa} \tag{B2}$$

where e denotes the exponential function and ln denotes the natural log. The relationship between a hyperbolic discounting factor and a continuous time discounting factor e^{-it} are as follows:[40] The non-constant discount rate, r(t), and the non-hyperbolic discounting factor approach zero as $t \to \infty$. If $k < 0$ and constant, then r(t) < 0. Nevertheless, $k < 0$ implies that $0 < \Delta(t) = e^{k \ln t} \leq 1$, $\forall t \geq 1$. This is consistent with $0 < x(t) = e^{-it} \leq 1$, $\forall t \geq 0$ where i denotes a market interest rate (e.g., $0 < i < 1$). In addition, given the definition of r(t) and that $\left[\frac{dx(t)}{dt} \right] \cdot \left[\frac{1}{x(t)} \right] = -i$, $\left| \frac{\kappa}{t} \right|$ would imply a non-constant time preference concept, at the minimum. If $t \geq 1$, $\kappa < 0$, and $|\kappa| = i$, then $0 < e^{-it} < e^{k \ln t} \leq 1$.[41] This is illustrated by Figure 6B.1.

With a non-constant hyperbolic discount rate, $\left| \frac{\kappa}{t} \right|$, the preferences between periods (e.g., t and t+1) are dynamically inconsistent (Liabson 1997). With a financial capital market determined discount rate, i, the preferences between periods (e.g., t and t + 1) are dynamically consistent and equal to the discount rate. This is illustrated by Figure 6B.2.

As illustrated by Figures 6B.1 and 6B.2, hyperbolic discounting does address the problem of the future being worth nothing given the discounting factor $(1 + r)^{-t}$. However, hyperbolic discounting factors are not accepted as the rule in financial markets, so they can be described as an academic exercise.

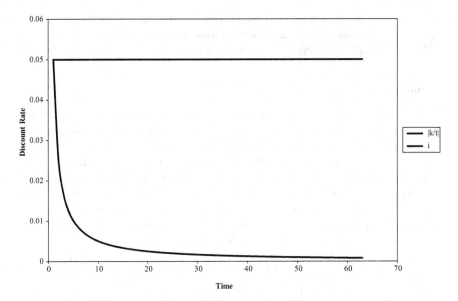

Figure 6B.2 Non-Constant Discount Rate and Interest Rate[‡]

[‡] $\left|\dfrac{\kappa}{t}\right|$ denotes the non-constant discount rate and i denotes the interest rate with $|\kappa| = i = 0.05$.

Appendix 6C – Misinterpreting the Internal Rate of Return in Forest Management Planning and Economic Analysis

Misinterpreting the Internal Rate of Return in Sustainable Forest Management Planning and Economic Analysis (Updated and Unabridged Version)

JOHN E. WAGNER

SUNY – College of Environmental Sciences and Forestry, Syracuse, NY

Sustainable forest management planning includes accounting for revenues and costs that accrue throughout time. While debate continues as to the how to account for these cash flows, the most used techniques are Net Present Value, Benefit Cost Ratios, and Internal Rate of Return (irr). Managing forests sustainably depends critically on interpreting the results and management implications of these techniques accurately. It is appealing to equate the irr with a market-derived rate of return given its definition and accept/reject criterion. Unfortunately, its mathematical derivation does not support this interpretation and past use of irr often illustrates this confusion and misinterpretation. The irr only reflects the amount and timing of the net cash flows for a given venture and does not include any social, economic, or other external factors found in market-derived discount rates. Therefore the irr does not reflect an appropriate rate of return or opportunity cost of capital for sustainable forest management. My purpose is to provide a theoretical

argument that can be used to help correct this misinterpretation and stimulate discussions on the economics of sustainable forest management.
    KEY WORDS: Internal Rate of Return, Sustainable Forest Management

Introduction

There is general agreement that sustainable forest management includes positive weights given to the concepts of ecological, social, and economic sustainability (Floyd 2002). Economic sustainability often deals with accounting for revenues and costs that accrue throughout time. While debate continues as to the appropriate methods to account for these cash flows, the Internal Rate of Return (*irr*) – as well as other economic analysis tools, e.g., Net Present Value (NPV) and Benefit-Cost Ratios (BCR) – has been used in forest products analyses and forest management planning for many years. The following is not meant to be an all-encompassing review of *irr* as used in forestry but to illustrate the history of its use: Bentley and Teeguarden (1965), Webster (1965), Gansner and Larsen (1969), Marty (1970), Samuelson (1976), Fortson and Field (1979), Schallau and Wirth (1980), Klemperer (1981), Kurtz et al. (1981), Mills and Dixon (1982), Clutter et al. (1983), Dennis (1983), Bengston (1984), Harpole (1984), Leuschner (1984), Harou (1985), Johansson and Löfgren (1985), Risbrudt and Pitcher (1986), Bailey (1986), Hansen (1986), Gregory (1987), Shaffer et al. (1987), Hu and Burns (1988), Pearce (1990), Uys (1990), Dangerfield and Edwards (1991), Fight et al. (1993), Hatcher et al. (1993), Buongiorno et al. (1995), Klemperer (1996), Hseu and Buongiorno (1997), Mehta and Leuschner (1997), Terreaux and Peyron (1997), Kadam et al. (2000), Brukas et al. (2001), Davis et al. (2001) [and earlier editions], Rideout and Hesseln (2001), Battaglia et al. (2002), Buongiorno and Gilles (2003), Duerr (2003), van Gardingen et al. (2003), Jagger and Pender (2003), Zinkhan and Cubbage (2003), Siry et al. (2004), Venn (2005), Fox et al. (2007), Legault et al. (2007), Heiligmann (2008), Bettinger et al. (2009), and Webster et al. (2009).
    The unique feature of the *irr* as compared to NPV or BCR is that while the inputs of NPV and BCR are: 1) the amount and timing of all cash flows and 2) an appropriate opportunity cost of capital given as a discount or interest rate, and the result is a number that represent the NPV or the BCR; the input of *irr* consists only of the amount and timing of all cash flows and the result is the "internal rate of return" that sets the present value of the net cash flow equal to zero. The *irr*, as with the NPV or BCR, is used in project evaluation (Hartman and Schafrick 2004; Copeland et al. 2005; Brealey et al. 2008). The general rule is if the *irr* is greater than (less than) an appropriate opportunity cost of capital the investment is acceptable (not acceptable).[42] As Hazen (2003) describes, and is evident by the literature review, the appeal of using the *irr* is interpreting it as a rate of return. Unfortunately, representing the *irr* as a rate of return similar to the interest rate used to calculate NPV or BCR is, as the title of the article states, misinterpreting the *irr*. The choice of a discount rate in sustainable forest management is important as capital is often invested for long periods of time (Bullard et al. 2002; Hepburn and Koundouri 2007). The level of sustainable forest management is tied to the discount rate; for example, the direct impacts on rotation age calculations (e.g.,

Johansson and Löfgren 1985). Indirect impacts could include the social-political implications of dramatic changes in harvest levels and resulting changes in forest structure (Brukas et al. 2001; Sandulescu et al. 2007). In addition, the indirect impacts on the provisions of forest-based ecosystem goods and services other than timber (Kant 2003). This misinterpretation appears to be common among practitioners (e.g., Heiligmann 2008; Webster et al. 2009; Wagner 2009; Pickens et al. 2009) and maybe inadvertently advanced by academicians.

The purpose of this article is to provide a theoretical basis that can be used in helping correct this enduring misinterpretation and stimulate discussions among all those involved in sustainable forest management (e.g., academics, practitioners, and stakeholders). Addressing the issues surrounding the use of the *irr* as an investment evaluation tool is *not* the purpose of this article. This has been done, is being done, and will continue being done in the literature; for example, Dudley (1972), Just et al. (2004), Copeland et al. (2005), Brealey et al. (2008), Fehr (2017), Arjunan and Kannapiran (2018), Brigham and Huston (2019) examine the consistency of *irr* as an investment evaluation tool relative to NPV. Nor is the purpose to address issues of optimal rotation age; for example, Samuelson (1976), Johansson and Löfgren (1985), and Terreaux and Peyron (1997) have shown that using *irr* to determine economically optimal rotation ages provides a different answer than using the "Faustmann" model (Faustmann 1849; Pressler 1860; Ohlin 1921). Thus, I will divide the article into four sections. First is a discussion of what an appropriately defined discount or interest rate represents. Second is a discussion of the mathematical derivation of the *irr* and the resulting feasible economic interpretation of the *irr* as a rate of return. Using these sections as a theoretical basis, the third is a discussion of interpreting the *irr* in the context of even-age to uneven age sustainable forest management. Finally, I will conclude with a few brief remarks.

What Is the Interest or Discount Rate?

The interest or discount rate describes the opportunity cost of capital or the fact that there are alternative investment opportunities. The opportunity cost of capital reflects not only the amount and timing of the net cash flows (internal factors), but also the purchasing power of the net cash flow in the different periods, risk, and other relevant business information such as patents, research and development, and entrepreneurial history, etc. (external factors) (Fisher 1930; Henderson and Quandt 1980; Luenberger 1998; Silberberg and Suen 2001; Copeland et al. 2005; Brealey et al. 2008). For any given risk level, the investment chosen should increase an investor's wealth no less than the next best alternative investment. Thus, the opportunity cost of capital is set by the capital markets (Brealey et al. 2008; Johnstone 2008).[43]

Interest rates are most often defined as real and nominal. Fisher (1930) developed the relationship between the nominal and real interest rate as:

$$i = (1+r)\cdot(1+\omega)-1 = r+\omega+r\cdot\omega \qquad \text{(C1a)}$$

where i denotes the nominal interest rate, r denotes the real interest rate, and ω denotes the anticipated inflation rate ($\omega \geq 0$). If the anticipated inflation rate is close to zero, equation (C1a) is often written as

$$i = r + \omega \tag{C1b}$$

In addition, Silberberg and Suen (2001) and Brealey et al. (2008) note that historically market interest rates have included a risk premium to account for external factors other than inflation. Taking some liberty so as to be brief, let the risk adjusted real interest rate be given by equation (C2a)

$$\tilde{r} = r_f + \eta \tag{C2a}$$

where r_f denotes a risk-free real interest rate (e.g., the return on 1-year U.S. Treasury bills) and η denotes a risk premium ($\eta \geq 0$). Thus equation (C1b) can be expanded to include a risk premium:

$$\tilde{i} = \tilde{r} + \omega = r_f + \eta + \omega \tag{C2b}$$

Equations (C2a) and (C2b) can be used as models for the real and nominal opportunity costs of capital as defined by the capital markets.[44] As Klemperer (1996), Davis et al. (2001), Silberberg and Suen (2001), and Brealey et al. (2008) point out there is no universal or unique risk premium. Thus, there is no unique real or nominal interest rate which could be used to examine all investments.

A market-derived appropriate opportunity cost of capital is often described as the hurdle rate of return, the guiding rate of return, or the minimum acceptable rate of return. Bullard et al. (2002) illustrates this by examining different interest rates required by nonindustrial private forest landowners in Mississippi. In business the weighted average cost of capital (see Copeland et al. 2005; Brealey et al. 2008) is used to approximate a market-derived opportunity cost of capital. Consequentially, an appropriate opportunity cost of capital reflects internal and external factors associated with alternative investment opportunities.

While my primary focus is on market-derived opportunity costs of capital, there are additional bodies of literature that discuss a market-derived versus socially-derived versus hyperbolic interest rates. I will briefly discuss if the *irr* is consistent with the concepts of social and hyperbolic discount rates in the conclusions.

The economic Interpretation of the Internal Rate of Return as a Rate of Return

The *irr* is generally attributed to Fisher (1930). However, Boulding (1935) and Keynes (1936) also published manuscripts discussing the *irr* at roughly the same time. I will use Boulding (1935) as my primary reference as he most clearly lays out the foundation of the *irr* as used in forestry. Based on Boulding (1935), the *irr* is commonly defined as the "interest rate" or "discount rate" that sets the NPV equal to zero as illustrated by equation (C3)

$$\sum_{t=0}^{T} \frac{R_t}{(1+irr)^t} - \sum_{t=0}^{T} \frac{C_t}{(1+irr)^t} = 0 \qquad (C3)$$

where R_t and C_t denote revenue and cost flows at time t, respectively, R_t and C_t a–e real numbers with R_t, $C_t \geq 0$, $(R_0 - C_0) < 0$, and $(R_t - C_t) > 0$ for at least one value of $1 \leq t \leq T$, T is a positive finite whole real number, and *irr* is the internal rate of return.

Interpreting the *irr* as a rate of return is tied directly to its appearance as a discount or interest rate in equation (C3). However, this interpretation does not follow from its mathematical derivation. While the issues surrounding determining the *irr* have been discussed in the literature, I will provide brief overview of calculating the *irr* to setup its interpretation as a rate of return and interpretation within the context of even-age to uneven-aged sustainable forest management.

Calculating the Internal Rate of Return

As Boulding (1935) and others (e.g., Lorie and Savage 1955; Gansner and Larsen 1969; Norstrøm 1972; Clutter et al. 1983; Klemperer 1996; Luenberger 1998; Bidard 1999; Hazen 2003; Hartman and Schafrick 2004; Copeland et al. 2005; Brealey et al. 2008; Johnstone 2008) have pointed out, calculating *irr* can be complicated and result in unique or multiple solutions. Equation (C3) can be rewritten as a polynomial equation of degree 'T'

$$P(N_T) = \sum_{t=0}^{T} N_t X^t = 0 \qquad (C4)$$

where $N_t = (R_t - C_t)$ and

$$X = \frac{1}{1+irr} \qquad (C5)$$

While the following mathematical statements may seem obvious they are important to restate as interpreting the *irr* as a rate of return and in the context of sustainable forest management depends on them directly. The X's are the zeros or roots of this polynomial which depend only on the magnitudes of N_t and t. In addition, N_t is a constant real number for all t. By definition there are 'T' possible roots or zeros for this polynomial which may be positive or negative real numbers or complex numbers. Equation (C5) shows that *irr* is a function of the root of the polynomial described in equation (C4).

Before a searching technique is used to determine the root(s) of equation (C4), one can determine the number of positive real roots. The general approach to determine the number of positive and negative roots (both real and complex numbers) is Descartes' Rule of Signs (Aufmann et al. 1993; Newnan 1983; Levin 2002) which states that the maximum number of positive real roots of $P(N_T)$ is equal to the number of sign changes between consecutive nonzero coefficients or less by an even number. Consequently, the net cash flow can change signs once or twice and you may (or may not) be able to calculate an *irr* that makes economic sense. If we assume that the roots of the polynomial in equation (C4) are positive, real, and rational, Descartes' Rule of Signs does not guarantee however, that *irr*(s) will be positive. Solving equation (C5) for *irr* gives

$$irr = \frac{1}{X} - 1 \tag{C6}$$

if $\frac{1}{X} < 1$ then *irr* is negative. Various other approaches have been employed to determine if a cash flow will provide a unique positive real root (e.g., Norstrøm 1972; de Faro 1973; Luenberger 1998).[45]

The *irr*(s) obtained from solving equations (C4), (C5), and (C6) can be expressed as either a decimal or percent and are a function of the roots of $P(N_T)$. The interest or discount rate can also be expressed as either a decimal or percent. They, however, reflect the market's assessment of the internal and external factors surrounding an investment.

Unique Internal Rate of Return

As illustrated above and defined by Hazen (2003: 32) interpreting *irr*s as rates of return is "not part of their mathematical definition". Thus, interpreting any *irr*, calculated using equation (C3), as a rate of return is based on two assumptions. First, all revenues and costs are known with certainty (Boulding 1935; Luenberger 1998; Hazen 2003). Second, *any* net cash flow invested and *any* net cash not withdrawn remain invested at the *irr* (Bentley and Teeguarden 1965; Marty 1970; Dudley 1972; Beaves 1988; Price 1993; Copeland et al. 2005; Johnstone 2008; Kierulff 2008). These assumptions imply that if the initial cost of the project (e.g., C_0 in equation (C3)) was deposited in a "bank" and compounded annually using the *irr* for T years, at the end of T years you would be able to withdraw the required amount (e.g., R_T in equation (C3)) zeroing out the account (Foster and Brooks 1983; Price 1993; Luenberger 1998; Copeland et al. 2005; Johnstone 2008).[46] In this bank, the capital markets do not define the rates of return, transactions costs are zero, all revenues and cost are known with certainty, and there is no risk (Luenberger 1998; Johnstone 2008). Interpreting the *irr* as a rate of return is illustrated by Example 1 (Table 6C.1 and Figure 6C.1) and Example 2 (Table 6C.2 and Figure 6C.2).

In both cases the projects last for 15-years. In Example 1 there is an initial cost and three unequal withdrawals in years 5, 10, and 15. The *irr* is 10.26%. As can be seen any net cash not withdrawn continues to be invested at the *irr*. At the end of 15 years the final withdrawal of $1,900.00 zero's out the account. In Example

Table 6C.1 Example 1 of a Unique Real Internal Rate of Return (*irr*)[‡]

Year	Revenue	Cost	N	PV(N)		Years	
					0 to 5	*6 to 10*	*11 to 15*	
0		2000.00	−2000.00	−2000.00 *irr* = 0.10258	2000.00	1758.90	1166.03 Beginning Balance
5	1500.00		1500.00	920.56	1258.90	1107.14	733.96 Interest Income
10	1700.00		1700.00	640.28	−1500.00	−1700.00	−1900.00 Withdraw
15	1900.00		1900.00	439.17	1758.90	1166.03	−0.01 Ending Balance
Sum			3100.00	0.00			

[‡] *N* denotes Net Cash flow and PV(*N*) denotes the present value of the net cash flow.

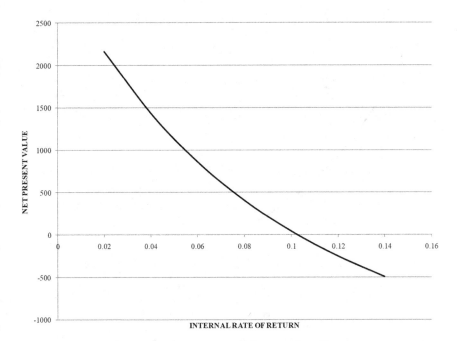

Figure 6C.1 Example 1 of a Unique Real Internal Rate of Return (*irr*)

2 there is an initial $2,000.00 cost and an additional $2,000.00 deposit in year 10. This cash flow has no negative roots as the coefficients of the polynomial are real and alternate in sign (Levin 2002). The *irr* is 6%. Again, any net cash flow not withdrawn or deposited is continues to be invested at the *irr*.

Examples 1 and 2 are defined as pure investments with $\dfrac{\partial P(N)}{\partial \hat{i}} < 0$ where $\hat{i}$ denotes rates of return with $-1 < \hat{i} < \infty$ (Hartman and Schafrick 2004). A unique

Table 6C.2 Example 2 of a Unique Real Internal Rate of Return (*irr*)‡

					Years			
Year	Revenue	Cost	N	PV(N)	0 to 5	6 to 10	11 to 15	
0		2000.00	−2000.00	−2000.00 *irr* = 0.0602	2000.00	178.94	2239.68	Beginning Balance
5	2500.00		2500.00	1866.41	678.94	60.74	760.30	Interest Income
10		2000.00	−2000.00	−1114.72	−2500.00	2000.00	−3000.00	Withdraw/ Deposit
15	3000.00		3000.00	1248.31	178.94	2239.68	−0.01	Ending Balance
Sum			1500.00	0.00				

‡ *N* denotes Net Cash flow and PV(*N*) denotes the present value of the net cash flow.

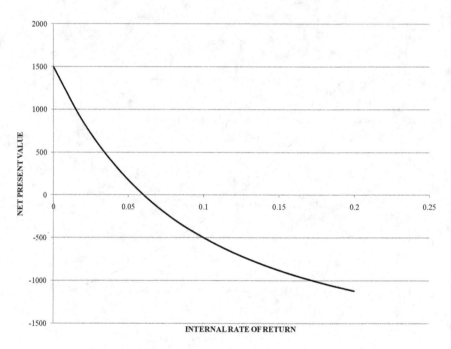

Figure 6C.2 Example 2 of a Unique Real Internal Rate of Return (*irr*)

real root does not however preclude the possibility of complex roots. I will use an example given by Hartman and Schafrick (2004) to illustrate this point. The net cash flow is given in Example 3 (Table 6C.3 and Figure 6C.3).

While there is a unique real *irr* of 219% there are two complex roots where $\frac{\partial P(N)}{\partial \hat{i}} = 0$. Consequently, the net cash flow cannot be defined as a pure investment. There is a portion of the graph were $\frac{\partial P(N)}{\partial \hat{i}} > 0$ defining a loan or money is withdrawn from the project (Hartman and Schafrick 2004). Examining Example 3 illustrates this point. At the end of year 1 there is an ending balance of −$2.81 as a

Table 6C.3 Example 3 of a Unique Real Internal Rate of Return (*irr*) with Complex Roots (Hartman and Schafrick 2004)‡

						Years		
Year	Revenues	Cost	N	PV(N)		0 to 1	1 to 2	2 to 3	
0		1.00	−1.00	−1.00		1.00	−2.81	2.04	Beginning Balance
1	6.00		6.00	1.88	*irr* = 2.19	2.19	−6.15	4.46	Interest Income
2		11.00	−11.00	−1.08		−6.00	11.00	−6.50	Withdraw/ Deposit
3	6.50		6.50	0.20		−2.81	2.04	0.00	Ending Balance
Sum				0.50	0.00				

‡ *N* denotes Net Cash flow and PV(*N*) denotes the present value of the net cash flow.

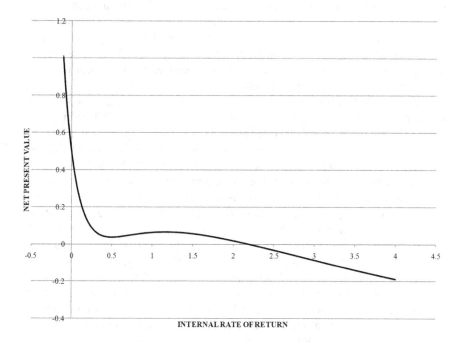

Figure 6C.3 Example 3 of a Unique Real Internal Rate of Return (*irr*) With Complex Roots (Hartman and Schafrick 2004)

result of withdrawing $6.00. There is a penalty in year 2 of −$6.15 for withdrawing more than the balance. In year 2 there is also a deposit of $11.00 this creates a positive ending balance of $2.04. Finally, in year 3 there is a withdrawal of $6.50 which is equal to year 2's ending balance plus interest zeroing out the account. In this case the bank continues to invests any positive ending balances and charges a penalty on negative ending balances at the *irr*. Again, the capital markets do not define the rates of return, transactions costs are zero, all revenues and cost are known with certainty, and there is no risk.

Consistent with its mathematical derivation, the *irr* defines an annual "rate of return" for a project that depends *exclusively* on the amount and timing of a given project's cash flow (Boulding 1935; Copeland et al. 2005; Brealey et al. 2008). As Boulding (1935: 482) states: "Thus, bound up in the very structure of any net revenue series there is a rate of return which pertains to it, and which can be calculated if we know all the terms of the net revenue series and *nothing else* [emphasis added]." The opportunity cost of capital represents both internal and external factors. There is no information provided in Examples 1, 2 or 3 to determine if any of these investments would increase an investor's wealth no less than an alternative investment of similar risk.

Multiple Internal Rates of Return

Consistent with Descartes' Rule of Signs, Lorie and Savage (1955: 237) describe the classic general net cash flow that will result in multiple roots and consequently, multiple *irr*s as one with "initial cash outlays, subsequent net cash inflows, and final cash outlays". Nonetheless, the assumptions used for interpreting multiple *irr*s, calculated using equation (C3), as rates of return are the same as defined above. Example 4 (Table 6C.4 and Figure 6C.4) defines an investment with three *irr*s; namely, 0%, 14.87%, and 24.58%.

The net cash flow is characterized by an initial investment of $100.00, an additional investment of $110.00 in year 10, and withdrawals of $60.00 in years 5 and 15. As shown by Table 6C.4, for all three *irr*s the ending balance in year 5 is negative requiring the payment of a penalty (for the *irr*s > 0) in year 10. In year 15 there is a withdrawal which is equal to year 10's ending balance plus interest zeroing out the account. Each *irr* defines an annual "rate of return" for the project that depends *exclusively* on the amount and timing of a given project's cash flow. As with Example 2 (Table 6C.2 and Figure 6C.2) the bank continues to invests any positive ending balances and charges a penalty on negative ending balances at the *irr*. As before, the capital markets do not define the rates of return, transactions costs are zero, all revenues and cost are known with certainty, and there is no risk. Finally, as Hazen (2003) and Johnstone (2008) describe, there is nothing in the calculation of the *irr*s that leads to determining which of the three is the "correct" rate of return as each provide sufficient funds to zero out the account at the end of 15-years given the net cash flow.[47] As Hazen (2003: 46) points out it is "not meaningful to compare [multiple] internal rates of return within a single project. . . . The magnitude of the internal rate by itself carries no further information."

Revisiting the Reinvestment Assumption: Interpreting the irr

As noted by Bentley and Teeguarden (1965), Marty (1970), Dudley (1972), Beaves (1988), Price (1993), Davis et al. (2001), Copeland et al. (2005), Brealey et al. (2008), Johnstone (2008), and Kierulff (2008), the assumption of any net cash flow invested and any net cash not withdrawn continue to be invested at the *irr*(s) is an implied component of using equation (C3).[48] An alternative approach is to calculate a Modified Internal Rate of Return (*mirr*).[49] Lin (1976) and Kierulff (2008) develop a *mirr* that requires defining an appropriate opportunity cost of capital for any net cash flows that continue to be invested or withdrawn (i.e., net cash flows that are

Table 6C.4 Example 4 of a Multiple Real Internal Rate of Returns (*irrs*)‡

						Years			
Year	Revenues	Cost	N	PV(N)		0 to 5	6 to 10	11 to 15	
0		10.00	−10.00	−10.00		10.00	−50.00	60.00	Beginning Balance
5	60.00		60.00	60.00	*irr* = 0	0.00	0.00	0.00	Interest Income
10		110.00	−110.00	−110.00		−60.00	110.00	−60.00	Withdraw/ Deposit
15	60.00		60.00	60.00		−50.00	60.00	0.00	Ending Balance
Sum			0.00	0.00					

						Years			
Year	Revenues	Cost	N	PV(N)		0 to 5	6 to 10	11 to 15	
0		10.00	−10.00	−10.00		10.00	−40.00	30.00	Beginning Balance
5	60.00		60.00	30.00	*irr* = 0.1487	10.00	−40.00	30.00	Interest Income
10		110.00	−110.00	−27.50		−60.00	110.00	−60.00	Withdraw/ Deposit
15	60.00		60.00	7.50		−40.00	30.00	0.00	Ending Balance
Sum			0.00	0.00					

						Years			
Year	Revenues	Cost	N	PV(N)		0 to 5	6 to 10	11 to 15	
0		10.00	−10.00	−10.00		10.00	−29.99	20.00	Beginning Balance
5	60.00		60.00	20.00	*irr* = 0.24578	20.01	−60.01	40.01	Interest Income
10		110.00	−110.00	−12.22		−60.00	110.00	−60.00	Withdraw/ Deposit
15	60.00		60.00	2.22		−29.99	20.00	0.01	Ending Balance
Sum			0.00	0.00					

‡ *N* denotes Net Cash flow and PV(*N*) denotes the present value of the net cash flow.

not used to finance any further investments into the project) and an appropriate opportunity cost of capital for any net cash flows that are financed. This formulation is given in equation (C7):

$$
mirr = \left(\frac{\sum_{t=0}^{T} R_t \left(1+r_{(R)}\right)^{T-t}}{\sum_{t=0}^{T} C_t \left(1+r_{(C)}\right)^{-t}} \right)^{\frac{1}{T}} - 1
$$

$$
= \left(\frac{FV(R)}{PV(C)} \right)^{\frac{1}{T}} - 1
$$

(C7)

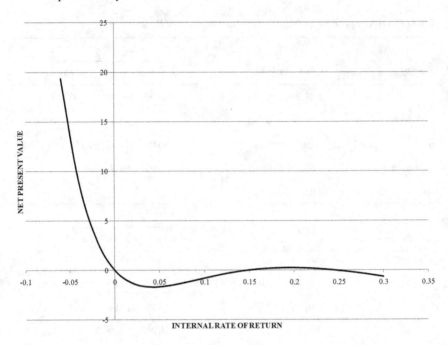

Figure 6C.4 Example 4 of a Multiple Real Internal Rate of Returns (*irrs*)

where $r_{(R)}$ and $r_{(C)}$ represent the appropriate opportunity costs of capital for rein-vesting and financing any net cash flows, respectively. The denominator defines the present value of the costs discounted using the appropriate opportunity cost of capital for any net cash flows that are financed, PV(C).[50] The numerator defines the future value of any net cash flows that are available to be reinvested or with-drawn using the appropriate opportunity cost of capital for reinvesting, FV(R). As described by Beaves (1988), the denominator and numerator convert a net cash flow with positive and negative components into an equivalent one with an indexed negative net cash flow in time zero and an indexed positive net cash flow in time T.

Table 6C5 gives *mirr* calculation for Example 4 assuming $r_{(R)}$ = 7% and 5% and $r_{(C)}$ = 7% and 5%.

As can be seen, equation (C7) converts the net cash flow from one with two negative and two positive net cash flows to an equivalent one with an indexed negative net cash flow at time 0 and an indexed positive net cash flow at time 15. By definition the new equivalent cash flow will have a unique real positive root that will result in a unique positive *mirr*. The *mirr* is an annual rate of return weighted by the appropriate opportunity costs of capital for financing and reinvest-ing.[51] Interpreting *mirr* as a rate of return given the equivalent cash flow is similar to that described in Examples 1, 2, or 3.

Table 6C.5 Calculation of a Modified Internal Rate of Return (*mirr*) Using Example 4‡

							Years	
Year	Revenues	Cost	N	PV(Cost)	FV(Revenue)		0 to 15	
0		10.00	−10.00	10.00			77.53	Beginning Balance
5	60.00		60.00		118.03	*mirr* = 0.05698	100.50	Interest Income
10		110.00	−110.00	67.53		$r(C)=0.05$	−178.03	Withdraw
15	60.00		60.00		60.00	$r(R)=0.07$	0.00	Ending Balance
Sum			0.00	77.53	178.03			

							Years	
Year	Revenues	Cost	N	PV(Cost)	FV(Revenue)		0 to 15	
0		10.00	−10.00	10.00			65.92	Beginning Balance
5	60.00		60.00		118.03	*mirr* = 0.06848	112.11	Interest Income
10		110.00	−110.00	55.92		$r(C)=0.07$	−178.03	Withdraw
15	60.00		60.00		60.00	$r(R)=0.07$	0.00	Ending Balance
Sum			0.00	65.92	178.03			

							Years	
Year	Revenues	Cost	N	PV(Cost)	FV(Revenue)		0 to 15	
0		10.00	−10.00	10.00			65.92	Beginning Balance
5	60.00		60.00		97.73	*mirr* = 0.05989	91.82	Interest Income
10		110.00	−110.00	55.92		$r(C)=0.07$	−157.73	Withdraw
15	60.00		60.00		60.00	$r(R)=0.050.05$	0.00	Ending Balance
Sum			0.00	65.92	157.73			

mirr denotes the modified internal rate of return
$r_{(R)}$ denotes the opportunity cost of capital for reinvesting any positive net cash flows
$r_{(C)}$ denotes the opportunity cost of capital for financing any negative net cash flows
PV(Cost) denotes present value of the costs
FV(Revenue) denotes future value of the revenues.

Interpretation of the Internal Rate of Return Within the Context of Sustainable Forest Management

Net cash flows of even-aged to uneven-aged forest management activities can be simple to complex. Although in general, these net cash flows often result in a unique *irr*; interpreting unique, or multiple, *irr*(s) resulting from even-aged to uneven-aged forest management as rates of return must still be consistent with those described in Examples 1 through 4. Is this interpretation consistent with the ideals of sustainably managing even-aged to uneven-aged forests? Unfortunately there is no single accepted definition of sustainable forest management, and I will not attempt to

address that issue here;[52] however, common themes do emerge from these definitions which include maintaining the forest-based ecosystem, use of forest-based
ecosystem goods and services that does not impact future generations, multiple
stakeholders, and scale. I will start by examining if the *irr*(s) calculated (i) for single and multiple rotation even-aged management systems, (ii) for a representative
individual tree or stand, and (iii) for a regulated uneven-aged management system
are consistent with the common themes of sustainable forest management. I will
end this section by examining the reinvestment assumption.

Equation (C3) has often been used to calculate the *irr* of a single harvest even-
aged management regime where R_t and C_t are defined as cash flows resulting from
using forest-based ecosystem goods and services. In addition, equation (C3) reveals
that flows of any forest-based ecosystem goods or services before t = 0 and after
t = T have a value of 0 and are not included in the calculation of the *irr*. In addition, Bentley and Teeguarden (1965), Johansson and Löfgren (1985), Uys (1990),
and Hseu and Buongiorno (1997) note that formulation of equation (C3) implies
land is so abundant that it is obtained at zero cost in time 0 and has no value after
the harvest in time T, its opportunity cost is zero.[53] The *irr* represents the annual
value growth of the net cash flow resulting from a single harvest management
regime and nothing else. Interpreting the resulting *irr* as a rate of return in this context must be consistent with Examples 1 through 4. In addition, this *irr* cannot be
compared with *irr*s derived from other mutually exclusive patterns of forest-based
ecosystem goods and services flows. There is nothing explicit in the formulation of
equation (C3) or in interpreting the resulting *irr* that states whether the use of the
forest-based ecosystem goods and services is consistent with – at the minimum –
maintaining the forest-based ecosystem or use of forest-based ecosystem goods
and services that does not impact future generations (i.e., socially, economically, or
ecologically sustainable). Consequently, no statement concerning the sustainability
of this single harvest even-aged management regime can be made.[54]

Assume the pattern of revenues, R_t, and costs, C_t, from using forest-based ecosystem goods and services defined for the period t = 0, . . . , T is repeatable. Equation (C8) derives the *irr* model given this pattern is repeated an infinite number of
times

$$\sum_{\theta=0}^{\infty}\left[\sum_{t=0}^{T}R_t\left(1+irr\right)^{-t}-\sum_{t=0}^{T}C_t\left(1+irr\right)^{-t}\right]\cdot\left(1+irr\right)^{-\theta T}=0$$

$$\frac{\sum_{t=0}^{T}R_t\left(1+irr\right)^{-t}-\sum_{t=0}^{T}C_t\left(1+irr\right)^{-t}}{1-\left(1+irr\right)^{-T}}=0$$

(C8)

Equation (C8) is analogous to the "Faustmann" model first defined by Faustmann
(1849), Pressler (1860), and Ohlin (1921) where the numerator defines the single
harvest even-aged management regime and the rotation age T is given. As shown
by Uys (1990) if one or more *irr*(s) can be found that sets the numerator of equation (C8) equal to zero, then the fraction is equal to zero implying that the *irr*(s)

of equation (C3) are identical to those of equation (C8). This is illustrated in equation (C9)

$$\sum_{t=0}^{T} R_t \left(1+irr\right)^{-t} - \sum_{t=0}^{T} C_t \left(1+irr\right)^{-t}$$

$$= \frac{\sum_{t=0}^{T} R_t \left(1+irr\right)^{-t} - \sum_{t=0}^{T} C_t \left(1+irr\right)^{-t}}{1-\left(1+irr\right)^{-T}} = 0 \tag{C9}$$

Interpreting the resulting *irr* must be consistent with Examples 1 through 4. The *irr* represents the net cash flow of this particular flow of forest-based ecosystem goods and services for the period t = 1, . . . , T and nothing else. This *irr* cannot be compared with *irr*s derived from other mutually exclusive patterns of forest-based ecosystem goods and services flows.

Analyzing equations (C8) and (C9) in terms of sustainable forest management, while the magnitudes of the *irr*(s) will change as T changes reflecting the different value growth of the net cash flows, *irr* completely ignores the opportunity cost of not harvesting the land at time T (i.e., stand rent and land rent – Johansson and Löfgren 1985). In addition, the *irr* would not reflect a rate of return on the capital asset land (i.e., the forest-based ecosystem). An argument could be made that the Faustmann model requires maintaining the forest-based ecosystem so that it can produce a flow of resources for current and future generations, *ceteris paribus*. While I am not advocating that a Faustmann type model satisfies all the tenets of sustainable forest management, it is a conceptual improvement compared to the single harvest model; however, as the *irr* cannot distinguish between a single and infinite harvest model there is nothing explicit in the formulation of equations (C8) and (C9) to state whether the use of the forest-based ecosystem goods and services is socially, economically, or ecologically sustainable.[55]

Grisez and Mendel (1972), Mendel et al. (1973), Godman and Mendel (1978), Herrick and Gansner (1985), Dennis (1987), Davies (1991), Klemperer (1996), Hseu and Buongiorno (1997), Heiligmann (2008), and Webster et al. (2009) have used the *irr* to describe the annual value growth rate of a representative individual tree or stand. This is illustrated by equation (C10)

$$irr = \left(\frac{R_T}{C_t}\right)^{\frac{1}{(T-t)}} - 1; \quad 0 \le t < T \tag{C10}$$

where C_t denotes the value of the trees at time t and R_T denotes the harvest value of the trees at time T.[56] Equation (C10) has also been used in developing regeneration marking guide's take or leave decision associated with a selection silvicultural harvesting system. Unfortunately, the common interpretation of the *irr* given by equation (C10) as a financial rate of return is not accurate in this case. The *irr* given in equation (C10) describes the expected annual value growth of the trees *ex-ante*.

In addition, the *irr* may only be interpreted as an annual growth in value if and only if reinvestment takes place (Price 1993). *Ex-post*, if C_t and R_T occur, then *irr* does describe the annual value growth of the trees. That said, the only accurate statement that can be made concerning the *irr* is that if it is greater than the appropriate opportunity cost of capital, there is a greater likelihood that a landowner's wealth will increase. Whether a landowner's wealth increases (or not) is tied directly to the opportunity cost of capital not the *irr*. Using equation (C10) to help develop a marking guide's take or leave decision does not include: i) the implications of one or more trees occupying the same growing space; and ii) the current tree occupying the site and not allowing the next tree to take its place (i.e., the opportunity cost of the land or land rent) (Johansson and Löfgren (1985) and Hseu and Buongiorno (1997)). Finally, as Chang (1981) and Chang and Gadow (2010) point out it is not the size of the tree but the tree's rate of value growth *of the whole stand* [emphasis added] that determines whether a tree should be kept, trees that cannot satisfy this requirement should be harvested. This is important given a selection system. Consequently, caution is advised when using equation (C10) to define when to cut a representative individual or single tree of a given diameter using a selection system.

Economic analysis of uneven-aged forest management is often more complex than even-aged management. An uneven-aged forest is comprised of uneven-aged stands. Uneven-aged stands are comprised of three or more distinct age classes. For a regulated uneven-aged stand each age class occupies an equivalent amount of area, as measured by basal area class per acre or number of trees per acre by diameter class, over the length of the cutting cycle. Diameter distributions are commonly used to regulate the uneven-aged stands and thus the forest. The structure of an uneven-aged forest is such that cutting in a diameter class will impact the growth in other diameter classes. This is in contrast to an even-age forest where age classes are spatially distinct such that cutting one age class does not impact the growth of any other age class. It is this particular interrelationship among the diameter classes of an uneven-aged forest that make it more interesting and difficult to analyze economically.

While Amacher et al. (2009) provide an excellent summary of current research in this area; for purposes of illustration I will use the economic models based on those developed by Chang (1981), Rideout (1985), Buongiorno et al. (1995), and Chang and Gadow (2010) to examine a single uneven-aged stand in a steady-state or regulated condition. If viewed as an economic asset, an uneven-aged stand can be modeled using two equivalent approaches. The value of the reserve growing stock at the beginning of each cutting cycle is the investment necessary to generate the value of the inventory at the end of the cutting cycle. Alternatively, the value of the initial reserve growing stock represents the opportunity cost of the investment necessary to obtain the periodic harvest net cash flow. These models are given in equation (C11), respectively:

$$\frac{P\cdot\left[Q(T,G)\cdot(1+irr)^{-T}-G\right]}{1-(1+irr)^{-T}} = \frac{P\cdot\left[Q(T,G)-G\right]\cdot(1+irr)^{-T}}{1-(1+irr)^{-T}}-P\cdot G = 0 \quad (C11)$$

where P denotes stumpage price; Q(T,G) denotes the volume growth of the uneven-aged stand as a function of the cutting cycle, T, and the structure of the reserve growing stock, G. The numerator of the left-hand side equation is the value associated with a single cutting cycle. The denominator of the left-hand side equation is used to show this cutting cycle will be repeated an infinite number of time. This form of equation (C11) is the same as that given in equations (C8) and (C9). Thus, if one or more *irr*(s) can be found that sets the numerator of the left-hand side equation equal to zero, then the fraction is equal to zero implying that the *irr*(s) of a single cutting cycle are identical to those of an infinite number of cutting cycles. The economic interpretation of the resulting *irr* must be consistent with Examples 1 through 4. The *irr* represents the net cash flow of this particular steady-state condition and nothing else. This *irr* cannot be compared with *irr*s derived from other mutually exclusive steady-state conditions. Again, as the *irr* cannot distinguish between a single and infinite cutting cycle model there is nothing explicit in the formulation of equation (C11) to state whether the uneven-aged stand is being managed socially, economically, or ecologically sustainably.[57]

In economies that are transitioning from central planning to a mixed or free market, such as those in many of the Eastern European countries that were under the influence of the old Soviet Union, the capital markets may not be well developed enough to assess investments in forest management (Brukas et al. 2001). In addition, the inclusion of economic analyses in forest management is improving but in some countries (e.g., Romania) central planning still can have a nontrivial influence (Sandulescu et al. 2007). Brukas et al. (2001) address the issue of what would be the appropriate discount rates to analyze forest management decisions given this context. The primary tool used by these authors to estimate discount rates is the *irr*. The net cash flows the authors used are based on the existing forest structures resulting from past central planning, the *irr*(s) were determined by optimizing a Faustmann model – similar to equation (C8) – that included intermediate stand treatments and given constant real prices (Brukas et al. 2001). The estimated *irr*s reflect only the internal factors related to timber growth resulting from past central planning, a single harvest regime, and a defined rotation age. They do not account for the opportunity cost of the land or stand properly nor any of the external market and socio-political factors affecting Lithuania. As these *irr*s are calculated based on a model similar to equation (C9), they are not consistent with the ideals of sustainable forest management. Given the lack of well-developed capital markets, using a discount rate that is a "little less than *irr*" (Brukas et al. 2001: 153) as an initial approximation of the opportunity cost of capital might seem reasonable in this circumstance; however, even in these circumstances I would council extreme caution as these *irr*s do not reflect the macro or micro socio-political-economic environment surrounding managing Lithuania's forests.

Conclusions

Portraying the *irr* as a rate of return or an interest or discount rate (i.e., an opportunity cost of capital set by the capital markets) is an inaccurate interpretation

(Hirshleifer 1970; Hagemann 1990; Luenberger 1998; Hazen 2003; Copeland et al. 2005; Brealey et al. 2008). Brealey et al. (2008: 123) provide an excellent summary of a potential cause of this misinterpretation that I will paraphrase: People may often confuse the *irr* and the opportunity cost of capital because both appear as discount rates in the NPV formula. The *irr* is a *profitability measure* which depends *solely* on the amount and timing of the project's cash flow. The opportunity cost of capital is a *standard of profitability* for the project which is used to calculate how much the project is worth in terms of wealth maximization. Misinterpreting the *irr* gives misleading information to decision makers whether they are private or public land managers or stakeholders. Boulding noted this in 1935:

> We will now assume that there is some rate of return, *i* (*irr*), which is characteristic of the investment as a whole. This is of course a rate of interest, or a rate of discount. But it must be emphasized that it is a rate of interest which the enterprise itself produces, and which, as we shall see later, is bound up with the very structure of the net revenues themselves. *That is to say, it is an internal rate, and while it may be equal to external rates of interest it must not be confused with them.* [Emphasis added]
>
> (Boulding 1935: 478)

Thus defined and interpreted accurately, the *irr* includes only those internal factors of any net cash flow. A market-derived opportunity cost of capital reflects not only the internal factors but also external factors associated with a project.

I would argue that the *irr* as defined traditionally using equations (C3), (C9), (C10), (C11), and (C12) reflect a single harvest regime which is inconsistent with concepts of ecological, social, and economic sustainability and therefore the ideals of sustainable forest management. This conclusion was reached assuming a market-derived opportunity cost of capital. I would also argue that the *irr* is not consistent with a social discount rate. The literature on the social discount rate is too vast to review here; however, Just et al. (2004) discusses that the social discount rate is a function of a social rate of time preference, changes in production technology, risk and uncertainty, and macro variables such as population growth, unemployment, and growth of per capita consumption. They point out that a social discount rate cannot be determined without referencing a specific economy. The *irr* does not include any of these external factors. Finally, Nocetti et al. (2008) and Hepburn and Koundouri (2007) note that conventional discounting factor, $(1 + i)^{-t}$, using a constant discount rate, *i*, is not consistent with intergenerational equity and sustainable development as net cash flows in the far future are virtually irrelevant to decisions made today. Thus, these authors argue that the appropriate social discount rate should decrease with time as this is consistent with human decision-making behavior. This has led to research examining the implications of hyperbolic discount rates on long term investments such as in sustainable forest management. A hyperbolic discount rate is a function of time such that it is high for current net cash flows and declines asymptotically for future net cash flows. Again the literature on hyperbolic discounting is too vast to review here succinctly;[58] however, the *irr* as defined by equations (C3), (C9), (C10), and (C12) is not consistent with these recent advancements.

Using a tool such as the *irr* to analyze forest management actions (e.g., Heiligmann 2008; Webster et al. 2009; Pickens et al. 2009) because it is commonly used by business (e.g., Graham and Harvey 2001; Kierulff 2008; Pickens et al. 2009; Cubbage et al. 2014) is problematic for three reasons. First, the ideals associated with sustainable forest management are not consistent with the use of *irr*. The *irr* only describes the potential net value growth of the defined net cash flow and nothing else; it cannot be compared with *irr*s derived from other mutually exclusive patterns of forest-based ecosystem goods and services flows; and it does not include any social, economic or ecological external factors generally associated with sustainability. Second, *irr* is often interpreted as a rate of return, which runs counter to Boulding's (1935) statements. This interpretation assumes that all revenues and costs are known with certainty (i.e., no risk) and any net cash flow invested and any net cash not withdrawn are continue to be invested at the *irr*. The implications of these assumptions restrict interpreting the *irr* as a rate of return and are unfortunately not well understood. Third, *irr* may provide a measurement of the absolute growth of a portfolio of financial instruments – including timberland instruments – and can be compared against a specific investment goal. However, as a portfolio's *irr* can be affected by factors beyond an investment manager's control, it is a short-term measurement (e.g., three months). This is too short a time for analyzing sustainable forest management actions. Thus, the *irr* conveys very limited short-term information as a profitability measure and nothing else.[59]

Sustainable forest management depends on interpreting the results and management implications of tools such as *irr*, NPV, and BCR accurately. While the focus of this discussion was on *irr*, omitting similar discussions with respect to NPV and BCR is not meant to imply they are not misinterpreted within in the context of sustainable forest management. Academic debates concerning how to account for these cash flows appropriately and defining the concept of optimality within the context of sustainability continues. Unfortunately, these discussions are often not mirrored elsewhere. My purpose is to inform and stimulate these discussions among all those involved in sustainable forest management.

Notes

1 In earlier chapters I described the primary factors of production as labor, land, and capital. The secondary factors of production were materials and energy as they were obtained from labor, land, and capital. This is consistent with the historic definition of the factors of production. More recently the concept of capital has increased to encompass more than the traditional physical capital; namely, land and the renewable and nonrenewable outputs from land are now included in capital as natural capital. Therefore, from now on I will define the factors of production as labor, materials, and capital.

2 Different authors provide different groupings. I have chosen this particular grouping as it best facilitates developing and discussing the concepts that I present in this chapter and Chapter 7 – The Natural Resources Management Puzzle. It is based on an article by Maack and Davidsdottir (2015). A fifth factor has sometimes been included: Entrepreneurship – an individual's ability to combine financial, human, natural, and physical

capital to earn single to multi-period profits. I have not included it in this discussion as I view this as part of human capital, and improving entrepreneurship is a goal of this book.

3 Long-lived assets are expected to have costs and revenues occurring over multiple periods rather than a single period.

4 The time period over which an asset is expected to contribute positively to an organization's operations assuming normal levels of capital recovery, operations, and maintenance (often described as the minimum of the annuitized ownership costs) and before repairing it becomes more expensive than replacing it.

5 Specifically, Silberberg and Suen (2001) qualify this statement by assuming that if a person's utility function is strictly increasing and quasi-concave, then the tradeoff between consumption in two time periods is the rate of production technology change if bound solutions are ruled out. The example they use is that of Robinson Crusoe and an edible bush. If the bush grows at a constant rate, the tradeoff between consumption in any two consecutive periods is 1 plus the growth rate.

6 Could you define an example in which a college student may exhibit a zero rate of time preference? What about loaning a fellow student the money for a 12-ounce can of Coke®?

7 The concepts of risk and uncertainty will be defined in more detail in Chapter 8 – Risk.

8 In addition, Kennedy et al. (1996) propose a novel approach to reduce this particular type of political risk based on the work by the Ronal Coase in his 1960 article entitled "The Problem of Social Cost" for which he received the Nobel Memorial Prize in Economic Sciences in 1991.

9 If the anticipated inflation rate is close to zero, equation (6.1) is often written as
$i = r + \omega$
However, I would counsel readers strongly *not* to use this simplified version.

10 Silberberg and Suen (2001) and Brealey et al. (2008) provide a more complete discussion on this topic.

11 If readers are interested, Brealey et al. (2008) provide a very detailed discussion of this topic.

12 While accounting for imperfect financial capital markets is beyond the scope of this book, interested readers may review the articles by Brazee (2003) and Wagner et al. (2003) as examples of analyzing a forestland owner's timber harvest behaviors given imperfect financial capital markets, assuming that landowner's maximize wealth.

13 Financing capital by debt is done by borrowing money from institutions or individuals. Financing capital by equity is done by selling shares in the business.

14 This discussion is not meant to be a complete review of the WACC. Interested readers should go to texts such as Brealey et al. (2009) and Copeland et al. (2005) for a more in-depth discussion.

15 Appendix 6A contains some of the more common formulae.

16 The material presented earlier on the interest rate also hold for the discount rate.

17 Profit (Architectural Plan for Profit) or income is a flow concept while wealth is a stock concept. Wealth is the capitalization of multiple single-period profits or multi-period investment profits or income.

18 In Chapter 3 – Costs, the DIRTI-5, overhead and maintenance, and sales, general, and administrative costs were introduced; specifically, depreciation. Depreciation is an annual noncash expense that would not be included in a cash flow diagram.

19 I am indebted to the many forest economists that I have drawn my examples from and must acknowledge their work: Buongiorno and Gilles (2003), Davis et al. (2001), Rideout and Hesseln (2001), Klemperer (1996), Pearce (1990), Gregory (1987), Johansson and Löfgren (1985), Leuschner (1984), and Clutter et al. (1983).

20 I will use the real interest rate in defining the future and present value formulae, which is consistent with my suggestion of using real cash flows and the real interest rate. However, nominal cash flows and the nominal interest rate can be used as well.

21 Appendix 6B revisits the concept of the interest rate a little more in depth.

22 This can also be described algebraically. Let $P \times Q$ define the market value. This market value can increase in three ways: (i) P constant and Q increases, (ii) P increases and Q is constant, and (iii) P increases and Q increases. A nominal market value increase is when P increases and Q is constant. A real market value increase is when P is constant and Q increases. If P increases and Q increases and if Q increases faster than P, then this describes a real market value increase. However if P increases faster than Q, then this describes a nominal market value increase.

23 A revenue at time 0 may seem odd. This could be described as an incentive payment.

24 I will discuss more on this topic for all seven investment analysis tools in the section entitled Capital Budgeting.

25 The decision to finance a capital investment should be separate from the decision to invest in the capital (i.e., NPV $\geq$ 0). This is because the financing cost of capital could be done with debt or with equity. There are tax advantages of using debt vs. equity financing. However, accumulating too much debt will increase a firm's risk and thus the financing cost of capital (Brealey et al. 2008). Choosing a discount rate to determine if NPV $\geq$ 0 is not always straightforward. The WACC is often used to determine the financing cost of capital as well as the discount rate for NPV analysis. The advantage of the WACC is taking into account a firm's debt and equity. A disadvantage is if the capital investment is more or less risky than the firm's average investment. Other methods such as the capital asset pricing model may be used to determine a discount rate (Brealey et al. 2008). If the financing cost of capital and discount rates are the same, then including their annual payment on capital in an NPV calculation is no problem. A more in-depth discussion of this topic can be found in Brealey et al. (2008).

26 I will discuss more about these in the section on Capital Budgeting, so I will only provide a very brief discussion of it here.

27 A discounted cash flow (DCF) finds the present value of expected future cash flows and is given mathematically as

$$DCF_T = \sum_{t=1}^{T}(R_t - C_t)(1+r)^{-t}$$

If $DCF_T \geq C_0$ $(< C_0)$, this defines an acceptable (unacceptable) investment. This is consistent with NPV, as $DCF_T > C_0$ implies $DCF_T - C_0 = NPV_T \geq 0$. Finally, PI = BCR if and only if $\sum PV(C) = C_0$ and $DCF = \sum PV(R)$ where $\sum PV(C)$ is the sum of the present value of the costs as given by the DCF and $\sum PV(R)$ is the sum of the present value of the revenues as given by the DCF.

28 I would advise to not use the IRR function contained in many spreadsheet programs or found on the internet, as they only work with very simple cash flows such as those with a single initial cost, C_0, and an annual cash flow. Regardless, these approaches are still subject to the Descartes' Rule of Signs. There are other spreadsheet functions such as MIRR, but again I would advise that you not use these unless you understand completely how these functions work, what they are calculating, and how to interpret the results.

29 Given the possibility of multiple *irr*s, which one do you choose? Some *irr* proponents have proposed the following ad hoc rules: (1) Negative and irrational results are ignored, as they are meaningless economically. (2) Choose the smallest positive *irr* as the most conservative economic estimate. The second rule is consistent with estimating the *irr* iteratively starting with zero.

30 Appendix 6C contains a paper that I wrote detailing the problem with misinterpreting the *irr*.

31 The equal annual equivalent has various names; e.g., equal annual annuity, equal annual worth, and equivalent uniform annual worth.

32 The net carbon is a sum of carbon gains and losses over the 30-year investment horizon.

33 This relationship can be simplified:

$$EAE(Q) = Q = \frac{EAE(Cost)}{EAE(P)} = \frac{PV(Cost) \cdot \dfrac{r \cdot (1+r)^T}{(1+r)^T - 1}}{PV(P) \cdot \dfrac{r \cdot (1+r)^T}{(1+r)^T - 1}}$$

$$= \frac{PV(Cost)}{PV(P)} = \frac{\displaystyle\sum_{t=0}^{T} C_t (1+r)^{-t}}{\displaystyle\sum_{t=0}^{T} P_t (1+r)^{-t}}$$

34

35 Again, this equation can be simplified:

$$EAE(P) = P = \frac{EAE(Cost)}{EAE(Q)} = \frac{PV(Cost) \cdot \dfrac{r \cdot (1+r)^T}{(1+r)^T - 1}}{PV(Q) \cdot \dfrac{r \cdot (1+r)^T}{(1+r)^T - 1}}$$

$$= \frac{PV(Cost)}{PV(Q)} = \frac{\displaystyle\sum_{t=0}^{T} C_t (1+r)^{-t}}{\displaystyle\sum_{t=0}^{T} Q_t (1+r)^{-t}}$$

36 Given this specific example using a solar array, the EAE(P) is also called a levelized cost of energy (LCOE) (Short et al. 1995). The LCOE allows alternative technologies to be compared using different scales of operation, different investment and operating time periods, or both. Thus, the LCOE could be used to compare the cost of energy generated by a renewable resource with that of a standard fossil fueled generating unit (Short et al. 1995).

37 Tapping a sugar maple for its sap damages the part of the tree containing the most saw-timber value. In addition, a long straight bole is optimal for a sawtimber tree but less optimal for a sugar bush tree. Thus for all practical purposes given this example, sugar maple are either grown for sawtimber or tapped for sap.

38 While equation (6.14) shows the EAE being estimated using NPV, an EAE can also be estimated using present value of costs (EAE_{Cost}) or present value of revenues ($EAE_{Revenues}$)

$$EAE(Cost) = \left[\sum_{t=0}^{T} C_t (1+r)^{-t} \right] \cdot \frac{r \cdot (1+r)^T}{(1+r)^T - 1} = \left[\sum_{t=0}^{T} C_n (1+r)^{-t} \right] \cdot \frac{r}{1 - (1+r)^{-T}}$$

$$EAE(Revenue) = \left[\sum_{T=0}^{T} R_t (1+r)^{-t} \right] \cdot \frac{r \cdot (1+r)^T}{(1+r)^T - 1} = \left[\sum_{t=0}^{T} R_t (1+r)^{-t} \right] \cdot \frac{r}{1 - (1+r)^{-T}}$$

39 The following discussion resulted from discussions with Dr. David Newman, Provost College of Environmental Science and Forestry, Syracuse, New York USA.

40 Chiang (1984) derives the continuous compounding factor from the discrete compounding factor

$$\lim_{m\to\infty}\left(1+\frac{i}{m}\right)^{t\cdot m}=e^{it}$$

Thus, the continuous discounting factor is e^{-it}.

41 However, if $-\kappa>\dfrac{i\cdot t}{\ln t}$, $\forall t>1$, then $0<e\kappa\ln t<e^{-it}<1$.

42 While no investment analysis criterion is criticism free, the following authors discuss the caveats of using *irr* as an investment criterion especially when choosing among mutually exclusive projects (e.g., Alchian 1955; Dudley 1972; Beaves 1988; Klemperer 1996; Cary and Dunn 1997; Hajdasinski 1996, 1997; Luenberger 1998; Hazen 2003; Hartman and Schafrick 2004; Copeland et al. 2005; Brealey et al. 2008; Johnstone 2008; Kierulff 2008).

43 It should be noted that not all investors face perfect capital markets (Johansson and Löfgren 1985; Price 1993; Klemperer 1996; Luenberger 1998; Silberberg and Suen 2001). Often there is a difference between their borrowing and lending rates, with the rate charged for borrowing capital being usually greater than they receive for lending or investing.

44 Brealey et al. (2008) provide a very detailed discussion of this topic that is much too long to be repeated here.

45 Lin (1976) and Hazen (2003) also provide a review of this literature.

46 It should be noted that NPV and BCR is often calculated assuming revenues and costs are known with certainty. They also have the same implied continuing investment assumption concerning *any* net cash flow invested and *any* net cash not withdrawn. This assumption is different than reinvesting any positive net cash flows thrown off by the investment into alternative investments when calculating NPV or BCR as part of capital budgeting (Magni and Martin 2017; Arjunan and Kannapiran 2018). With NPV and BCR, the continuing investment of net cash flows are analyzed using a market-derived discount or interest rate while with *irr* they are not (Copeland et al. 2005).

47 While this statement is technically accurate, there are various ad hoc rules that have been described to determine the "correct" *irr* if using it as a profitability measure; for example, (1) negative results (both real and complex numbers) are ignored as they are meaningless economically, and (2) choose the smallest positive *irr* as the most economically conservative estimate (Beaves 1988; Hazen 2003; Hartman and Schafrick 2004; Brealey et al. 2008; Kierulff 2008). The second rule is consistent with estimating the *irr* iteratively starting with zero.

48 The following discussion concerning the reinvestment assumption is in the context of interpreting the *irr* **not** the *irr* as an investment decision criterion. Various versions of this reinvestment discussion with respect to *irr* as an investment decision criterion have been raging since the 1950s. Recent works by Magni and Martin (2017) and Arjunan and Kannapiran (2018) examined various iterations of these arguments and concluded empirically that any realized positive net cash flows resulting from an investment are independent of the investment and their further uses are irrelevant for accepting or rejecting these types of mutually exclusive investments.

49 A Modified Internal Rate of Return is also used to convert a net cash flow with multiple *irr*s into an equivalent cash flow with a unique real positive *irr* (i.e., a *mirr*) that can then be used as a profitability measure. While there are various formulations of the *mirr* (e.g., Hirshleifer 1970; Marty 1970; Lin 1976; Schallau and Wirth 1980; Harpole 1984; Beaves 1988; Liu and Wu 1990; Hajdasinski 1996, 1997; Cary and Dunn 1997; Davis et al. 2001; Hazen 2003; Brealey et al. 2008; Kierulff 2008), I will highlight only one as the interpretation of the *mirr* as a rate of return is the same regardless of the formulation.

50 As described by Magni and Martin (2017) and Arjunan and Kannapiran (2018), reinvestment assumptions are irrelevant for accepting or rejecting investments. Thus $r_{(R)} = r_{(C)}$ and *mirr* reduces to *irr* as a decision criterion.
51 From a corporate finance perspective, businesses firms finance capital purchases with either debt or equity. The weighted average cost of capital (WACC) is the more widely accepted approach to determine a business opportunity cost of capital than the *mirr* (Copeland et al. 2005; Brealey et al. 2008).
52 For example, Kant (2003) discusses the limitations of a traditional discounting approach to analyze sustainable forest management based on evolutionary and institutional economic schools of thought.
53 A variable for the purchase and sale of land can be included in equation (C3)

$$\sum_{t=0}^{T} R_t \left(1 + irr\right)^{-t} + L_T \left(1 + irr\right)^{-T} - \sum_{t=0}^{T} C_t \left(1 + irr\right)^{-t} - L_0 = 0$$

where L_T denotes the market value of the land at time T and L_0 denotes the market value of the land a time 0. If R_t, C_0, L_T, $L_0 > 0$ and $irr > 0$, then including the purchase and sale of the land into the *irr* calculation will, almost assuredly, change the magnitude of the *irr*(s), but will not change whether the net cash flow has a unique or multiple *irr*s. The inclusion of the market value of land does not change the interpretation of the *irr* representing the annual value growth of the net cash flow resulting from a single harvest even-aged management regime.
54 The same argument could also be made with respect to calculating the NPV or BCR in this case.
55 Chang (1998) developed a version of the Faustmann model that allows for the discount rate and rotation ages to vary. If the opportunity of all future rotations is a constant –as defined by Chang (1998) – then the result described in equation (C9) and the interpretation of *irr* does not change.
56 Equation (C11) is derived from equation (C3) directly.
57 Chang and Gadow (2010) developed a version of the Faustmann model for an uneven-aged stand that allows for the discount rate and cutting cycles to vary. If the opportunity of all future cutting cycles is a constant – as defined by Chang and Gadow (2010) – then the result described in equation (C12) and the interpretation of *irr* does not change.
58 I would point readers to Hepburn and Koundouri (2007) for a recent examination of hyperbolic discounting with respect to forest management.
59 A potential caveat would be given some publically available data from privately held businesses; an *irr* is the only financial metric that can be calculated.

References

Alchian, A.A. (1955) The rate of interest, Fisher' rate of return over costs and Keynes' internal rate of return, *The American Economic Review*, 45(5):938–943.
Amacher, G.S., Olikaninen, M., and Koskela, E. (2009) *Economics of Forest Resources*, Cambridge, MA: Massachusetts Institute of Technology Press.
Arjunan, K.C., and Kannapiran, K. (2018) *The Controversial Reinvestment Assumption in IRR and NPV Estimates: New Evidence Against Reinves tment Assumption*, Economic Papers Australia, forthcoming (https://papers.ssrn.com/sol3/papers.cfm?abstract_id=2918744).
Aufmann, R.N., Barker, V.C., and Nation, R.D. (1993) *Precalculus*, 2nd ed., Boston, MA: Houghton Mifflin Company.
Bailey, R.L. (1986) Rotation age and establishment density for planted slash and loblolly pine, *Southern Journal of Applied Forestry*, 10:166–168.

Battaglia, M., Mummery, D., and Smith, A. (2002) Economic analysis of site survey and productivity modelling for the selection of plantation areas, *Forest Ecology and Management*, 162:185–195.

Beaves, R.B. (1988) Net present value and rate of return: Implicit and explicit reinvestment assumptions, *The Engineering Economist*, 33(4):275–302.

Bengston, D.N. (1984) Economic impacts of structural particleboard research, *Forest Science*, 10(3):685–697.

Bentley, W.R., and Teeguarden, D.E. (1965) Financial maturity: A theoretical review, *Forest Science*, 11(1):76–87.

Bettinger, P., Boston, K., Siry J.P., and Grebner, D.L. (2009) *Forest Management and Planning*, New York, NY: Elsevier Academic Press.

Bidard, C. (1999) Fixed capital and internal rate of return, *Journal of Mathematical Economics*, 31:523–541.

Boulding, K.E. (1935) The theory of a single investment, *The Quarterly Journal of Economics*, 49(3):475–494.

Brealey, R.A., Myers, S.C., and Allen, F. (2008) *Principles of Corporate Finance*, 9th ed., New York, NY: McGraw-Hill, Inc.

Brukas, V., Thorsen, B.J., Helles, F., and Tarp, P. (2001) Discount rate and harvest policy: Implications for Baltic forestry, *Forest Policy and Economics*, 2(2):143–156.

Bullard, S.H., Gunter, J.E., Doolittle, M.L., and Arano, K.G. (2002) Discount rates for nonindustrial private forest landowners in Mississippi: How high a hurdle? *Southern Journal of Applied Forestry*, 26(1):26–31.

Buongiorno, J., and Gilles, J.K. (2003) *Decision Methods for Forest Resource Management*, Boston, MA: Academic Press.

Buongiorno, J., Peyron, J.L., Houllier, F., and Bruciamacchie, M. (1995) Growth and management of mixed-species, uneven-aged forests in the French Jura: Implications for economic returns and tree diversity, *Forest Science*, 41(3):397–429.

Cary, D., and Dunn, M. (1997) Adjustment of modified internal rate of return for scale and time span differences, *Proceedings of the Academy of Accounting and Financial Studies*, 2(2):57–63.

Chang, S.J. (1981) Determination of the optimal growing stock and cutting cycle for an uneven-aged stand, *Forest Science*, 27(4):739–744.

Chang, S.J. (1998) A generalized Faustmann model for the determination of optimal harvest age, *Canadian Journal of Forest Research*, 28(5):652–659.

Chang, S.J., and Gadow, K.V. (2010) Application of the generalized Faustmann model to uneven-aged forest management, *Journal of Forestry Economics*, 16:313–325

Clutter, J.L., Fortson, J.C., Pienaar, L.V., Brister, G.H., and Bailey, R.L. (1983) *Timber Management: A Quantitative Approach*, New York, NY: John Wiley & Sons.

Copeland, T.E., Weston, J.F., and Shastri, K. (2005) *Financial Theory and Corporate Policy*, 4th ed., Reading, MA: Pearson Addison-Wesley Publishing Company.

Cubbage, F., Mac Donagh, P., Balmelli, G., Olmos, V.M., Bussoni, A., Rubilar, R., De La Torre, R., Lord, R., Huang, J., Hoeflich, V.A., Murara, M., Kanieski, B., Hall, P., Yao, R., Adams, P., Kotze, H., Monges, E., Pérez, C.H., Wikle, J., Abt, R., Gonzalez, R., and Carrero, O. (2014) Global timber investments and trends, 2005–2011, *New Zealand Journal of Forestry Science*, 44(suppl 1):S7.

Dangerfield, C.W., Jr., and Edwards, M.B. (1991) Economic comparison of natural and planted regeneration of loblolly pine, *Southern Journal of Applied Forestry*, 15(3):125–127.

Davies, K. (1991) Forest investment considerations for planning thinning and harvesting, *Northern Journal of Applied Forestry*, 8(3):129–131.

Davis, L.S., Johnson, K.N., Bettinger, P.S., and Howard, T.E. (2001) *Forest Management: To Sustain Ecological, Economic, and Social Values*, 4th ed., Long Grove, IL: Waveland Press.

de Faro, C. (1973) A sufficient condition for a unique nonnegative internal rate of return: A comment, *Journal of Financial and Quantitative Analysis*, 8(4):683–684.

Dennis, D.F. (1983) Tax incentives for reforestation in public law 96–451, *Journal of Forestry*, 293–295.

Dennis, D.F. (1987) Rates of value change on uncut forest stands in New Hampshire, *Northern Journal of Applied Forestry*, 4(2):64–66.

Dudley, C.L., Jr. (1972) A note on reinvestment assumptions in choosing between net present value and internal rate of return, *The Journal of Finance*, 27(4):907–915.

Duerr, W.A. (2003) *Introduction to Forest Resource Economics*, New York, NY: McGraw-Hill.

Faustmann, M. (1849) Berechnung des Wertes Welchen Waldboden sowie noch nitch haubare Holzbestände für die Waldwirtschaft besitzen, *Allgemeine Forst- und Jagd-Zeitung*, 15. Reprinted as Faustmann, M. (1995) Calculation of the value which forest land and immature stands possess for forestry, *Journal of Forest Economics*, 1(1):7–44.

Fight, R.D., Bolon, N.A., and Cahill, J.M. (1993) Financial analysis of pruning Douglas-Fir and ponderosa pine in the Pacific Northwest, *Western Journal of Applied Forestry*, 10(1):58–61.

Fisher, I. (1930) *The Theory of Interest*, New York, NY: Macmillan.

Floyd, D. (2002) *Forest Sustainability: The History, the Challenge, the Promise*, Durham: The Forest History Society.

Foster, B.B., and Brooks, G.N. (1983) Rates of return: Internal or composite, *Journal of Forestry*, 81(10):669–670.

Fortson, J.C., and Field, R.C. (1979) Capital budgeting techniques for forestry: A review, *Southern Journal of Applied Forestry*:141–143.

Fox, T.R., Allen, H.L., Albaugh, T.J., Rubilar, R., and Carlson, C.A. (2007) Tree nutrition and forest fertilization of pine plantations in the Southern United States, *Southern Journal of Applied Forestry*, 31(1):5–11.

Gansner, D.A., and Larsen, D.N. (1969) *Pitfalls of Using Internal Rate of Return to Rank Investments in Forestry*, United States Department of Agriculture Forest Service Research Northeast Research Station, Note NE-106 (https://www.fs.usda.gov/research/treesearch/19826).

Godman, R.M., and Mendel, J.J. (1978) *Economic Values for Growth and Grade Changes of Sugar Maple in the Lake States*, USDA Forest Serv ice North Central Research Station Research Paper NC-155 (https://www.fs.usda.gov/research/treesearch/10676).

Graham, J.R., and Harvey, C.R. (2001) The theory and practice of corporate finance: Evidence from the field, *Journal of Financial Economics*, 60:187–243.

Gregory, G.R. (1987) *Forest Resource Economics*, New York, NY: John Wiley & Sons.

Grisez, T.J., and Mendel, J.J. (1972) *The Rate of Value Increase for Black Cherry, Red Maple, and White Ash*, Research Paper NE-231, Upper Darby, PA: USDA Forest Service Northeastern Research Station.

Hagemann, H. (1990) Internal rate of return, in J. Eatwell, M. Migate, and P. Newman, eds. *The New Palgrave Capital Theory*, New York, NY: W.W. Norton & Company.

Hajdasinski, M.M. (1996) Adjusting the modified internal rate of return, *The Engineering Economist*, 41(4):173–186.

Hajdasinski, M.M. (1997) NPV-compatibility, project ranking, and related issues, *The Engineering Economist*, 42(4):325–339.

Hansen, B.G. (1986) Selecting a tax rate for use in analyzing forest industry capital investments, *Northern Journal of Applied Forestry*, 3:101–103.

Harou, P. (1985) On a social discount rate for forestry, *Canadian Journal of Forest Research*, 15:927–934.

Harpole, G.B. (1984) Internal rate of return may be used to define initial equity for composite rate-of –return analyses, *Forest Science*, 30(4):1096–1102.

Hartman, J.C., and Schafrick, I.C. (2004) The relevant internal rate of return, The *Engineering Economist*, 49(2):139–158.

Hatcher, R.L., Johnson, L.A., and Hopper, G.M. (1993) Economic potential of black walnut on small acreage tracts, *Southern Journal of Applied Forestry*, 17(2):64–68.

Hazen, G.B. (2003) A new perspective on multiple internal rates of return, *The Engineering Economist*, 48(1):31–51.

Heiligmann, R.B. (2008) Here's how to . . . increase financial returns from your woodland, *Forestry Source*, 13(7):13–14.

Henderson, J.M., and Quandt, R.E. (1980) *Microeconomic Theory: A Mathematical Approach*, 3rd ed., New York, NY: McGraw-Hill.

Hepburn, C.J., and Koundouri, P. (2007) Recent advances in discounting: Implications for forest economics, *Journal of Forest Economics*, 2–3(13):169–189.

Herrick, O.W., and Gansner, D.A. (1985) Forest-tree value growth rates, *Northern Journal Applied Forestry*, 2(1):11–13.

Hirshleifer, J. (1970) *Investment, Interest and Capital*, Upper Saddle River, NJ: Prentice-Hall, Inc.

Hseu, J., and Buongiorno, J. (1997) Financial performance of maple-birch stands in Wisconsin: value growth rate versus equivalent annual income, *Northern Journal of Applied Forestry*, 14(2):59–66.

Hu, S.-C., and Burns, P.Y. (1988) Profits from growing Virginia pine Christmas trees in Louisiana, *Southern Journal of Applied Forestry*, 12(2):122–124.

Jagger, P., and Pender, J. (2003) The role of trees for sustainable management of less-favored lands: The case of eucalyptus in Ethiopia, *Forest Policy and Economics*, 5:83–95.

Johansson, P.-O., and Löfgren, K.-G. (1985) *The Economics of Forestry and Natural Resources*, Oxford, UK: Basil Blackwell Ltd.

Johnstone, D. (2008) What does an IRR (or two) mean? *Journal of Economic Education*, 39(1):78–87.

Just, R.E., Hueth, D.L., and Schmitz, A. (2004) *The Welfare Economics of Public Policy: A Practical Approach to Project and Policy Evaluation*, Northampton, MA: Edward Elgar.

Kadam, K.L., Wooley, R.J., Aden, A., Nguyen, Q.A., Yancey, M.A., and Ferraro, F.M. (2000) Softwood forest thinnings as a biomass source for ethanol production: A feasibility study for California, *Biotechnological Progress*, 16:947–957.

Kant, S. (2003) Extending the boundaries of forest economics, *Forest Policy and Economics*, 5:39–56.

Kierulff, H. (2008) MIRR: A better measure, *Business Horizons*, 51:321–329.

Keynes, J.M. (1936) *The General Theory of Employment, Interest and Money*, London, UK: Macmillan (http://ebooks.adelaide.edu.au/k/keynes/john_maynard/k44g/ accessed 16 June 2009).

Klemperer, W.D. (1981) Interpreting the realizable rate of return, *Journal of Forestry*, 79(9):616–617.

Klemperer, W.D. (1996) *Forest Resource Economics and Finance*, New York, NY: McGraw-Hill, Inc.

Kurtz, W.B., Garrett, H.E., and Williams, R.A. (1981) Young stands of scarlet oak in Missouri can be thinned profitably, *Southern Journal of Applied Forestry*, 5(1):12–16.

Legault, I., Ruel, J.-C., Pouliot, J.-M., and Beauregard, R. (2007) Analyse Financière de Scénarios Sylvicoles Visant la Production de Bois D'œuvre de Bouleaux Jaune et à Papier, *The Forestry Chronicles*, 83(6):840–851.

Leuschner, W.A. (1984) *Introduction to Forest Resources Management*, New York, NY: John Wiley & Sons.

Levin, S.A. (2002) *Descartes' Rule of Signs – How HARD CAN IT Be?* (http://sepwww.stanford.edu/oldsep/stew/descartes.pdf accessed 8 July 2009)

Lin, S.A.Y. (1976) The modified internal rate of return and investment criterion, *The Engineering Economist*, 21(4):237–247.

Liu, J.P., and Wu, R.Y. (1990) Rate of return and optimal investment in an imperfect capital market, *American Economists*, 34(2):65–71.

Lorie, J.H., and Savage, L.J. (1955) Three problems in rationing capital, *The Journal of Business*, 28(4):229–239.

Luenberger, D.G. (1998) *Investment Science*, New York, NY: Oxford University Press.

Magni, C.A. and Martin, J.D. (2017) *The Reinvestment Rate Assumption Fallacy for IRR and NPV: A Pedagogical Note* (https://mpra.ub.uni-muenchen.de/83889/ accessed 20 September 2018).

Marty, R. (1970) The composite internal rate of return, *Forest Science*, 16(3):276–279.

Mehta, N.B., and Leuschner, W.A. (1997) Financial and economic analyses of agroforestry systems and a commercial timber plantation in the La Amistad biosphere reserve, Costa Rica, *Agroforestry Systems*, 37:175–185.

Mendel, J.J., Grisez, T.J., and Trimble, G.R., Jr. (1973) *The Rate of Value Increase for Sugar Maple*, USDA Forest Service Northeastern Research Station Research Paper NE-250, Upper Darby, PA: USDA.

Mills, T.J., and Dixon, G.E. (1982) *Ranking Independent Timber Investments by Alternative Investment Criteria*, US Department Agriculture, Pacific Southwest Forest and Range Experiment Station, Research Paper PSW-166, Berkeley, CA: Pacific Southwest.

Newnan, D.G. (1983) *Engineering Economic Analysis*, 2nd ed., San Jose, CA: Engineering Press, Inc.

Nocetti, D., Jouini, E., and Napp, C. (2008) Properties of the social discount rate in a Benthamite framework with heterogeneous degrees of impatience, *Management Science*, 54(10):1822–1826.

Norstrøm, C.J. (1972) A sufficient condition for a unique nonnegative internal rate of return, *Journal of Financial and Quantitative Analysis*, 7(3):1835–1839.

Ohlin, B. (1921) Till frågan om skogarnas omloppstid, *Ekonomisk Tidskrift*, 22. Reprinted as Ohlin, B. (1995) Concerning the question of the rotation period in forestry, *Journal of Forest Economics*, 1(1):89–114.

Pearce, P.H. (1990) *Introduction to Forestry Economics*, Vancouver, BC: University of British Columbia Press.

Pickens, J., Johnson, D.L., Orr, B.D., Reed, D.D., Webster, C.E., and Schmierer, J.M. (2009) Expected rates of value growth for individual sugar maple crop trees in the Great Lakes region: A reply, *Northern Journal of Applied Forestry*, 26(4):145–147.

Pressler, M.R. (1860) Aus der Holzzuwachlehre (zweiter Artikel), *Allgemeine Forst- und Jagd-Zeitung*, 36. Reprinted as Pressler, M.R. (1995) For the comprehension of net revenue silviculture and the management objectives derived thereof, *Journal of Forest Economics*, 1(1):45–88.

Price, C. (1993) *Time, Discounting and Value*, Oxford, UK: Blackwell Publisher.

Rideout, D.B. (1985) Managerial finance for silvicultural systems, *Canadian Journal of Forest Research*, 15:163–166.

Rideout, D.B., and Hesseln, H. (2001) *Principles of Forest & Environmental Economics*, 2nd ed., Fort Collins, CO: Resource & Environmental Management, LLC.

Risbrudt, C.D., and Pitcher, J.A. (1986) Financial returns from timber stand improvement investments, *Northern Journal of Applied Forestry*, 3(2):52–58.

Samuelson, P.A. (1976) Economics of forestry in an evolving society, *Economic Inquiry*, 14(4):466–492. Reprinted as Samuelson, P.A. (1995) Economic of forestry in an evolving society, *Journal of Forest Economics*, 1(1):115–149.

Sandulescu, E., Wagner, J.E., Pailler, S., Floyd, D.W., and Davis, C.J. (2007) Policy analysis of a government-sanctioned management plan for a community-owned forest in Romania, *Forest Policy and Economics*, 10(1–2):14–24.

Schallau, C.H., and Wirth, M.E. (1980) Reinvestment rate and the analysis of forestry enterprises, *Journal of Forestry*, 78(12):740–742.

Shaffer, R.M., McNeel, J.F., Overboe, P.D., and O'Rourke, J. (1987) On-board log truck scales: Application to Southern timber harvesting, *Southern Journal of Applied Forestry*, 11(2):112–116.

Silberberg, E., and Suen, W. (2001) *The Structure of Economics: A Mathematical Analysis*, 3rd ed., New York, NY: McGraw-Hill, Inc.

Siry, J.P., Robison, D.J., and Cubbage, F.W. (2004) Economic returns model for silvicultural investments in young hardwood stands, *Southern Journal of Applied Forestry*, 28(4):179–184.

Terreaux, J.P.H., and Peyron, J.L. (1997) A critical view of classical rotation optimization, in N.A. Moiseev, K. von Gadow, and M. Krott, eds. *Planning and Decision-Making for Forest Management in the Market Economy*, Pushkino: IUFRO International Conference, Moscow Region Russia, 25–29 September 1996.

van Gardingen, P.R., McLeish, M.J., Phillips, P.D., Fadilah, D., Tyrie, G., and Yasman, I. (2003) Financial and ecological analysis of management options for logged-over dipterocarp forests in Indonesian Borneo, *Forest Ecology and Management*, 183:1–29.

Venn, T.J. (2005) Financial and economic performance of long-rotation hardwood plantation investments in Queensland, Australia, *Forest Policy and Economic*, 7:437–454.

Wagner, J.E. (2009) Expected rates of value growth for individual sugar maple crop trees in the Great Lakes region: A comment, *Northern Journal of Applied Forestry*, 26(4):141–144.

Wagner, J.E., Nowak, C.A., and Casalmir, L.M. (2003) Financial analysis of diameter-limit cut stands in Northern Hardwoods, *Small-Scale Forest Economics, Management and Policy*, 2(3):357–376.

Webster, C., Reed, D., Orr, B., Schmierer, J., and Pickens, J. (2009) Expected rates of value growth for individual sugar maple crop trees in the Great Lakes region, *Northern Journal of Applied Forestry*, 26(4):133–140.

Webster, H.H. (1965) Profit criteria and timber management, *Journal of Forestry*, 63(4):260–266.

Uys, H.J.E. (1990) A new form of internal rate of return, *South African Forestry Journal*, 154:24–26.

Zinkhan, F.C., and Cubbage, F.W. (2003) Chapter 6, Financial analysis of timber investments, in E.O. Sills and K.L. Abt, eds, *Forest in a Market Economy*, Dordrecht, Netherlands: Kluwer Academic Publishers.

7 The Natural Resources Management Puzzle

Preamble

The natural resources management puzzle begins with recognizing that it is a multi-input, multi-period, multi-output joint production process as described in Chapter 2 – Production Systems. Solving this management puzzle is analogous to solving a Rubik's Cube®. Each solid color face represents a desired output/ outcome level. The resources management conundrum is to produce the desired outputs/outcomes given a management decision made about the levels of one output/outcome (a face) impacts the levels of the other outputs/outcomes (the other faces). Any management decision implies using inputs – labor, materials, capital, and time – to manipulate the system (the unsolved Rubik's Cube) to produce the desired outputs/outcomes (the solved Rubik's Cube).

The natural resources management puzzle can also be described as a really fascinating capital analysis problem. There are two caveats associated with this statement. First is defining what capital is in this context: financial, natural, and physical capital.[1] The primary focus of this chapter will be on natural and physical capital. Second, the underlying management question is when to replace capital; for example, replacing a physical capital asset like a machine or solar array or a natural capital asset like a stand of trees used for timber. These management decisions require using financial capital – usually someone else's financial capital. The methods discussed in this chapter will provide you with the means to justify your capital replacement decision to the owners of the financial capital you are using.

Introduction

In Chapter 6 – Capital Theory: Investment Analysis, time was identified as a relevant input and its opportunity cost was defined by the discount or interest rate. A result is that the Pillars of Cost, Value, and Price reflect decreasing weights placed on future costs and revenues (Figure 7.1).

Wealth is created by accumulating resources or assets – capital – used to generate multiple single-period profits and multi-period investment profits. Wealth is the capitalization of these profits.

DOI: 10.4324/9781315678719-7

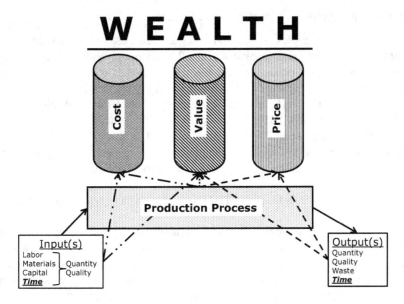

Figure 7.1 The Architectural Plan for Profit (Wealth)

An investment's impact on wealth is determined by its net present value (NPV). Combining NPV with the benefit–cost ratio (BCR) and an output production and/ or price breakeven analysis provides additional useful information at a relatively low cost. NPV is the decision criterion, BCR gives a quick cardinal assessment of sensitivity, and a breakeven analysis gives the feasibility of the production system to provide the output given the market conditions.

Physical and natural capital within the built-to-wildlands continuum can produce three (3) generic cash flow categories: (1) costs with no direct revenue stream, (2) costs with annual direct revenue stream, and (3) costs with periodic direct revenue stream. I will describe each separately as well as the analytical methods used to examine the cash flows and justify replacement decisions. I will also discuss some of the analytical hazards to watch out for with these analyses.

Practical Applications

The practical applications used in this chapter will include the following: (1) A capital asset associated with costs but no direct revenue stream. This will be illustrated by examining when to replace a car. (2) A capital asset associated with costs and a direct revenue stream. This will be illustrated by examining when to replace a solar array. (3) A capital asset associated with costs and a periodic revenue stream. This will be illustrated by determining when to cut a Loblolly Pine Plantation.

Capital: Costs With No Direct Revenue Stream

Physical capital examples of the first category are cars/trucks, machinery, and equipment. These physical capital assets often do not provide a direct revenue stream. Natural capital examples are the benefit streams of aesthetics, privacy, recreation, and protecting nature. These are the primary reasons family forest landowners own forestland (Butler and Leatherberry 2004; Belin et al. 2005; Hagan et al. 2005; Butler 2008, 2010; Majumdar et al. 2008; Hatcher et al. 2013; Butler et al. 2016; Creighton et al. 2016; Snyder et al. 2019; Wagner 2020). The analytical method in both cases is to minimize the present value of the ownership costs or to minimize the annuitized ownership costs relative to the perceived benefit stream. These are based on the least cost and cost effective models described in Chapter 1 – Introduction equations (1.1) and (1.2), respectively, and will be described and discussed later.

To illustrate the analytical methods used with this category, I will use a personal car, as most of you at some point in time will own a car and wonder when you should replace it. Newman et al. (2014) describes three reasons for this to occur with primarily physical capital: (i) obsolescence – occurs when the technology is surpassed by newer or a different technology; (ii) depletion – the loss of market value as the asset is depreciated; and (iii) deterioration – as the asset ages it wears out. As a result, the operations and maintenance cost of physical capital will generally increase over time while the salvage value will generally decrease over time. Consequently, your personal business management question to be analyzed is when to replace your physical capital – your car. This is illustrated by the cash flow diagram in Figure 7.2.

While I will focus on an asset most of you are familiar with, the flexibility of the analytical methods to be presented cannot be understated. The same analytical methods used to determine when to replace your car are also used to determine the cost-effective management activities for producing a landowner's desired state of nature within a forested ecosystem. Or the cost-effective vegetation management strategies for a power transmission line right-of-way to provide the same reduction

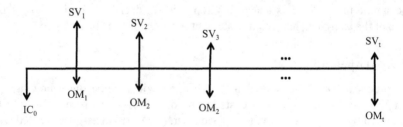

Figure 7.2 Cash Flow Diagram of a Personal Car

IC denotes the initial cost of the personal car; SV denotes salvage value at time t; OM denotes operation and maintenance costs at time t

in ground fault disruption probability for the minimum cost, as ground fault disruptions can cost utilities millions of dollars in fines and liability (Goodfellow et al. 2017; Ballard et al. 2003; Nowak et al. 1992).

Capital replacement is a variant of Chapter 6 – Capital Theory: Investment Analysis' discussion on capital budgeting. That analysis revolved around calculating net present values of all alternative investments to determine which investment(s) provided the greatest NPV. As alluded to earlier, this analysis revolves around comparing the cost effectiveness of various alternatives. Cost effectiveness in this context is defined as minimizing the present value of the annual costs of owning the asset. This is illustrated in Figure 7.3.

An interesting twist in the cost-effective analysis of capital replacement is that the lifespans of the various capital replacement alternatives may not be known prior to the analysis.

The costs of owning a car can be described as: (1) Financial capital recovery costs – the annual opportunity cost of the initial funds (minus present value of the salvage value) used to purchase the asset. (2) Operating (consumable) costs – the annual expenses of using the asset; for example, for a car these costs include fuel; filters, oil, and grease (FOG); and tires. (3) Maintenance costs – the annual expenses to restore an asset to a previous operating condition or to keep an asset in its current operation condition; for example, for a car these costs include regular scheduled maintenance and repairs.[2]

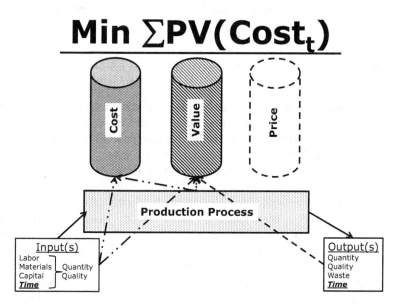

Figure 7.3 The Architectural Plan for Profit: Minimization of the Sum of the Present Value of the Costs

Financial Capital Recovery Costs

Capital recovery costs are the annual opportunity costs of the financial capital tied up in the asset at a point in time and thus unavailable for any alternative investments. The annual capital recovery costs are calculated using an equal annual equivalent (EAE) introduced in Chapter 6 – Capital Theory: Investment Analysis in equation (6.14). The capital recovery EAE is comprised of two parts. First is the EAE of the initial investment given by equation (7.1a)

$$EAE_{IC,t} = IC_0 \cdot \frac{r \cdot (1+r)^t}{(1+r)^t - 1} = IC_0 \cdot \frac{r}{1-(1+r)^{-t}} \tag{7.1a}$$

where IC_0 denotes the initial cost, r denotes the discount rate, and t denotes the time period. Equation (7.1a) is analogous to an annual loan payment (principal plus interest) given t time periods. As you would expect, as t increases the EAE will decrease but the interest payment will increase. Second is the salvage or market value EAE given by equation (7.1b)

$$EAE_{SV,t} = SV_t \cdot \frac{r}{(1+r)^t - 1} = SV_t \cdot \frac{r \cdot (1+r)^{-t}}{1-(1+r)^{-t}} \tag{7.1b}$$

where SV_t denotes the salvage or market value at time t, r denotes the discount rate, and t denotes the time period. Salvage value is a function of condition, total miles or production hours, and age of the asset. The annual capital recovery cost at time t, CR_t, is given by equation (7.1c):

$$CR_t = EAE_{IC,t} - EAE_{SV,t} = \left[IC_0 - SV_t (1+r)^{-t} \right] \cdot \frac{r}{1-(1+r)^{-t}} \tag{7.1c}$$

I will use my purchase of a new car in 2018 for approximately $27,000 to illustrate calculating capital recovery costs. These are illustrated in Table 7.1a.

The initial cost in equations (7.1a) and (7.1c) is equal to $27,000. A new car will lose 20% to 30% of its value in the first year, and then lose roughly 10% to 15% in value annually for the next five years assuming 15,000 miles per year (www.kbb.com/whats-my-car-worth/ accessed 5 July 2019; www.carfax.com/blog/car-depreciation accessed 5 July 2019). After approximately 75,000 miles, the salvage value decreases more rapidly due to scheduled major repairs; for example, timing belt, water pump, and so on. The salvage value of a similar car after 150,000 miles is approximately $2,000 (www.kbb.com/whats-my-car-worth/ accessed 5 July 2019). The salvage values used in equations (7.1b) and (7.1c) are given in Table 7.1a.

The capital recovery column of Table 7.1a is calculated using equation (7.1c). This column shows that the annual capital recovery costs decrease the longer you own the car. This makes sense as you are spreading out the capital cost over more years. If the decision to replace the car were based solely on the capital recovery column of Table 7.1a, this implies you would own the car until it dies.

Table 7.1a Estimated Capital Recovery Cost of My 2018 New Car Given a 5% Discount Rate

Year	Initial Cost	Expected Salvage Value	$IC_0\text{-}PV(SV_t)$	CR_t	Estimated Total Miles
	($)	($)	($)	($/year)	
0	27,000				
1		20,250	7,714	8,100	15,000
2		17,858	10,803	5,810	30,000
3		15,748	13,396	4,919	45,000
4		13,888	15,575	4,392	60,000
5		10,800	18,538	4,282	75,000
6		7,708	21,248	4,186	90,000
7		5,501	23,090	3,990	105,000
8		3,926	24,343	3,766	120,000
9		2,802	25,194	3,544	135,000
10		2,000	25,772	3,338	150,000

IC_0 denotes Initial Cost; $PV(SV_t)$ denotes the present value of Salvage Value at time t; CR_t denotes Capital Recovery Cost at time t

Operation and Maintenance Costs

While the capital recovery costs decrease the longer you own the asset, logic would imply operation and maintenance costs would increase the older the asset (Newman et al. 2014). Like salvage value, operation and maintenance costs are a function of the age, condition, and total miles or production hours of the asset. The accumulated present value of operation and maintenance costs at any time t are given by equation (7.2a)

$$\sum\nolimits_t PV(OM) = \sum_{k=0}^{t} OM_k (1+r)^{-k} \qquad (7.2a)$$

where $\sum_t PV(OM)$ denotes the sum of the present value of the operation and maintenance (OM) costs and r denotes the discount rate. The annuitized value of equation (7.2a) is calculated using an equal annual equivalent, $EAE_{OM,t}$, given in equation (7.2b):

$$EAE_{OM,t} = \sum\nolimits_t PV(OM) \cdot \frac{r}{1-(1+r)^{-t}} = \sum\nolimits_t PV(OM) \cdot \frac{r \cdot (1+r)^t}{(1+r)^t - 1} \qquad (7.2b)$$

Based on the car model, Edmunds® (www.edmunds.com/tco.html accessed 8 July 2019) will provide estimated operating and maintenance costs given the following assumptions: (i) 10% down payment, (ii) 60-month traditional car loan, and (iii) driving 15,000 miles per year. These costs are given in Table 7.1b.

Table 7.1b Estimated Five-Year Operation and Maintenance Costs of My 2018 New Car

	Year 1	Year 2	Year 3	Year 4	Year 5	Total
Tax Credit	$0	$0	$0	$0	$0	$0
Insurance	$824	$853	$883	$914	$946	$4,420
Maintenance	$417	$808	$525	$2,302	$987	$5,039
Repairs	$0	$0	$111	$262	$384	$757
Taxes & Fees	$1,909	$21	$64	$21	$64	$2,079
~~Financing~~	~~$1,311~~	~~$1,054~~	~~$781~~	~~$488~~	~~$176~~	~~$3,810~~
~~Depreciation~~	~~$2,797~~	~~$2,024~~	~~$1,915~~	~~$2,246~~	~~$2,127~~	~~$11,109~~
Fuel	$1,517	$1,562	$1,609	$1,658	$1,707	$8,053
					Total	$20,348

Source: www.edmunds.com/tco.html (accessed 8 July 2019)

Table 7.1c Equal Annual Equivalent Estimated Operation and Maintenance Costs, $EAE_{OM,t}$, of My 2018 New Car Given a 5% Discount Rate

Year	Estimated OM Cost	$\sum_t PV(OM)$	$EAE_{OM,t}$	Estimated Total Miles
	($)	($)	($/year)	
0				
1	4,070	3,876	4,070	15,000
2	4,070	7,567	4,070	30,000
3	4,070	11,083	4,070	45,000
4	4,070	14,431	4,070	60,000
5	4,070	17,619	4,070	75,000
6	4,151	20,717	4,082	90,000
7	4,234	23,726	4,100	105,000
8	4,319	26,649	4,123	120,000
9	4,405	29,488	4,149	135,000
10	4,493	32,247	4,176	150,000

$\sum_t PV(OM)$ denotes the Sum of the Present Value of the Operation and Maintenance (OM) Costs

Examining Table 7.1b shows that the financing and depreciation rows have been removed from the operating and maintenance costs due to these components being included in the capital recovery costs. The total non-discounted cost over five years is $20,348 or an average of 4,070 $/year based on the cost data provided by Edmunds®.

As Edmunds® only provides five years of data; I will assume these costs will increase at 2% per year after year 5. The estimated operating and maintenance costs over a 10-year period are given in Table 7.1c. The third and fourth columns of Table 7.1c are calculated using equations (7.2a) and (7.2b), respectively.

As expected, the annuitized operation and maintenance costs increase with time.

Ownership Costs

The expected annual ownership costs of an asset are given by equation (7.3):

$$EAE_{O,t} = CR_t + EAE_{OM,t} \qquad\qquad (7.3)$$

The expected annual ownership costs for my 2018 new car are given in Table 7.1d.

There are three observations based on the analysis presented and summarized in Table 7.1d. First, while the annuitized capital recovery costs decrease, the increase in the annuitized operation and maintenance costs is not sufficient for the annual ownership costs to have a minimum value. While typical of a car used as an example, this is not the case for all assets. In general, if operation and maintenance costs increase faster than capital recovery costs decrease, then a graph of the annual ownership costs will have a U-shape. This will give annual ownership costs a minimum. If ownership costs have a minimum, then replace the current asset when its annuitized ownership costs are greater than an alternative asset (Newman et al. 2014). Second, estimating future operation and maintenance costs are often difficult. In the car example, most of the major repair costs would start occurring around 75,000 miles.[3] The simple 2% annual increase in these costs may not capture this adequately. Sensitivity analysis should be used to include tenable ranges for these major repair costs in future operation and maintenance costs.[4] Finally, if the ownership decision were based solely on the expected annual ownership costs, the anticipated decision – given Table 7.1d – would be to keep the car until it dies. However, ownership decisions are typically not based exclusively on the analysis summarized in Table 7.1d. For example, while a car may not provide a direct annual revenue stream, it does provide the owner with an expected annual benefit

Table 7.1d Equal Annual Equivalent of Expected Ownership Costs ($EAE_{O,t}$) of My 2018 New Car Given a 5% Discount Rate

Year	CR_t	$EAE_{OM,t}$	$EAE_{O,t}$	Estimated Total Miles
	($/year)	($/year)	($/year)	
0				
1	8,100	4,070	12,170	15,000
2	5,810	4,070	9,879	30,000
3	4,919	4,070	8,989	45,000
4	4,392	4,070	8,462	60,000
5	4,282	4,070	8,351	75,000
6	4,186	4,082	8,268	90,000
7	3,990	4,100	8,091	105,000
8	3,766	4,123	7,889	120,000
9	3,544	4,149	7,693	135,000
10	3,338	4,176	7,514	150,000

CR_t denotes Capital Recovery Cost at time t; $EAE_{OM,t}$ denotes the Annuitized Operation and Maintenance Costs at time t

stream that includes basic transportation and driver comforts. Newer cars, on the other hand, have better driver amenities and safety and mechanical technologies; that is, obsolescence of the older car. So just like the laboratory fume hood example from Chapter 6 – Capital Theory: Investment Analysis, the decision to replace the old car could include factors not summarized explicitly in Table 7.1d.

Capital: Costs With Annual Direct Revenue Stream

Physical capital examples of the second category are solar arrays and wind turbines. An interesting example in this category is the energy audit described in Chapter 6 – Capital Theory: Investment Analysis. In an energy audit, the energy cost savings of any proposed energy conservation measure define the annual direct revenue stream. Natural capital examples are the potential annual revenue streams from outputs such as recreational leases, maple syrup, pine straw, mushrooms, and wetlands mitigation bank (https://www.nrcs.usda.gov/wetland-mitigation-bank ing-program accessed 3 September 2023). As most of these can be produced within forested ecosystems and with timber jointly, I will discuss them after the Capital: Costs With Periodic Direct Revenue Stream section.

The analytical methods revolve around calculating net present values of all alternative investments as described in Chapter 6 – Capital Theory: Investment Analysis and choosing the alternative that maximizes wealth. This is illustrated graphically by the Architectural Plan for Wealth given in Figure 7.1. To illustrate the analytical methods used with this category empirically, I will use a 1,000-kilowatt (kW) ground mount solar array.[5] The town in which I live has contracted with a solar array company to build a 1MW community solar array on cleared and unused land at the town's transfer station. This land has been cleared and unused since at least 1994. I will start with revenues and then move to costs. The analysis of the cost structure will be similar to that just described in the previous section; namely, (1) Financial Capital Recovery Costs and (2) Operation and Maintenance Costs.

Expected Annual Revenues

The expected annual revenues will be based on a power purchase agreement (PPA), which is a financial agreement where a developer arranges for the design, permitting, financing, and installing of the solar energy system on an identified property at little to no cost to the owner. The developer sells the power generated to identified customers at a fixed rate that is typically lower than the local utility's retail rate. PPAs range from as short as 15 years to as long as 30 years. At the end of the PPA there are several options. The PPA can be extended, modified, or terminated or the solar array can be purchased by the client at fair market value (Curtis et al. 2021). For this example, I will assume a 20-year PPA, and after 20 years the existing PPA will be extended on a yearly basis.

An output from a solar array is kilowatt-hours per year (kWh/year). A 1,000 kW ground mount solar array located near Syracuse, New York, USA, is expected to convert from 1,137,696 kWh/year (pessimistic estimate) to 1,201,395 kWh/year (realistic estimate) to 1,186,212 kWh/year (optimistic estimate) based on data obtained from https://pvwatts.nrel.gov/ (accessed 9 July 2021). Solar arrays are expected to suffer an insolation conversion efficiency loss of 0.5% to 1.0% per year (Feldman et al. 2021). For this example, I will use an annual 0.7% insolation conversion efficiency loss.

The discount offered by the solar array company is 10% off the retail price (a pay-as-you go model). The 2020 average retail price of residential electricity in New York State was 0.1834 $/kWh (www.eia.gov/electricity/data/browser/#/topic/7?agg=0,1&geo=g002&endsec=vg&linechart=ELEC.PRICE.US-ALL.A&columnchart=ELEC.PRICE.US-ALL.A&map=ELEC.PRICE.US-ALL.A&freq=A&ctype=linechart&ltype=pin&rtype=s&maptype=0&rse=0&pin= accessed 9 July 2021). Thus, the expected price received by the solar array company in 2020 was 0.1651 $/kWh. To be conservative, I will assume a constant price.[6]

The cash flow diagram illustrating these revenues is given in Figure 7.4a. The accumulated present value of the revenues at any point is given by equation (7.4a)

$$\sum_{t} PV(R) = \sum_{k=0}^{t} P \bullet Q(k) \bullet (1+r)^{-k} \tag{7.4a}$$

where $Q(k)$ denotes the amount of insolation converted in any given year taking into account an annual insolation conversion efficiency loss of 0.7% and r denotes the discount rate of 5%. The annuitized value of equation (7.4a) is calculated using an equal annual equivalent, $EAE_{R,t}$, given in equation (7.4b):

$$EAE_{R,t} = \sum_{t} PV(R) \cdot \frac{r}{1-(1+r)^{-t}} = \sum_{t} PV(R) \cdot \frac{r \cdot (1+r)^{t}}{(1+r)^{t}-1} \tag{7.4b}$$

The output and revenue information for the 1,000 kW ground mount solar array is given in Table 7.2a.

$PV(R)$ denotes the Present Value of the Revenue at time t; $\sum_{t} PV(R)$ denotes the Sum of the Present Value of the Revenue at time t; $EAE_{R,t}$ denotes Equal

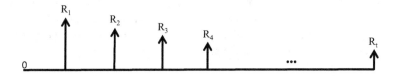

Figure 7.4a Revenue Cash Flow Diagram of a 1,000 kW Ground Mount Solar Array

R_t denotes the annual revenue at time t

Table 7.2a Estimated Revenue of a 1,000 kW Ground Mount Solar Array Located Near Syracuse, New York, USA, Given an Insolation Conversion Efficiency Loss of 0.7% per Year, a 5% Discount Rate, and a Constant Retail Price of 0.1651 $/kWh

Year	Output	Revenue	PV(R)	$\sum_t PV(R)$	$EAE_{R,t}$
	(kWh/yr)	($/yr)	($/yr)	($)	($/year)
1	1,186,212	195,844	186,518	186,518	195,844
5	1,153,345	190,417	149,197	836,685	193,253
10	1,113,539	183,845	112,865	1,469,624	190,323
15	1,075,107	177,500	85,381	1,948,432	187,716
20	1,038,002	170,174	64,589	2,371,726	184,985
25	1,002,177	165,459	48,861	2,584,649	183,387
30	967,588	159,749	36,962	2,791,931	181,619
35	934,193	154,235	27,961	2,948,736	180,084
40	901,951	148,912	21,152	3,067,357	178,760
45	870,822	143,773	16,001	3,157,091	177,623
50	840,767	138,811	12,105	3,224,974	176,654
52	829,037	136,874	10,826	3,247,248	176,308
55	811,749	134,020	9,157	3,276,327	175,830

Annual Equivalent of the Present Value of the Revenue at time t and illustrated in Figure 7.4b.

Given the annual loss in insolation conversion efficiency, as described earlier, and assuming a constant output price, revenues will decrease. This is illustrated in the second and third columns of Table 7.2a and the solid line in Figure 7.4b. The cumulative present value of the revenues, given in Equation (7.4a), is illustrated by the dashed line in Figure 7.4b. As the annual revenues are decreasing, the present value of the annual revenues are also decreasing. The cumulative present value of annual revenues is increasing but at a decreasing rate. The annuitized value of the cumulative present value of the annual revenues is given by equation (7.4b) and is illustrated by the dotted line in Figure 7.4b. The equal annual equivalent or the annuitized value of the cumulative present value of the revenues is more constant over time. True to its name and as illustrated in Chapter 6 – Capital Theory, it converts this decreasing cash flow to an equivalent and constant cash flow. So why is it decreasing? The answer to the why is to pick a year, say 40, and start with the revenues. At 40, revenues are decreasing, and the present value of the revenues are decreasing. This leads the cumulative value of the present value of the revenues to increase but at a decreasing rate. Consequently, less is being added to cumulative present value of the revenues every year and the EAE(Revenue) reflects this fact. Thus, the amount on the horizontal axis is the constant and equivalent amount over the 40-year period of the cumulative present value of the revenues.

Financial Capital Recovery Costs

The initial capital cost of the 1,000 kW ground mount community solar array is 1.59 $/W (Feldman et al. 2021). This cost includes engineering, procurement and construction/developer (EPC) net profit; contingency (4%); developer overhead;

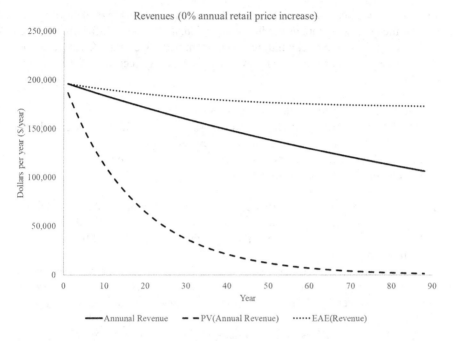

Figure 7.4b Estimated Revenue of a 1,000 kW Ground Mount Solar Array Located in Syracuse, New York, USA, Given an Insolation Conversion Efficiency Loss of 0.7% per Year, a 5% Discount Rate, and a Constant Retail Price of 0.1651 $/kWh

sales tax (if any); permitting, interconnection, and inspection; EPC overhead; install labor and equipment; electrical balance of system (BOS); structural BOS; inverter; and modules (Feldman et al. 2021). A 30% federal investment tax credit that was available through 2019 (The Energy Policy Act of 2005 Pub.L. 109–58) reduces the initial capital cost to $1,113,000.

At the estimated end of the solar array's economic life, there are four alternatives described by Curtis et al. (2021):

1. Extending the performance period – If a system is operational and has not suffered extensive damage, it might be possible to continue operations past the original planned performance period;
2. Refurbishing the solar array – Replacing solar panels and fixing any deficiencies in the electrical and structural BOS;
3. Repowering the solar array – Repowering a solar array results in an almost new system in all aspects and takes advantage of improved efficiencies; and
4. Decommissioning the solar array – Removing the solar array and electrical and structural BOS.

An objective of this analysis is estimating the end of this solar array's useful life, assuming it will be replaced or repowered. Repowering a solar array may have slightly lower costs than a new system in that it can take advantage of existing land use permits, site selection, utility interconnection, and physical infrastructure such as access road and grading, buildings, equipment pads, and foundations. However, there are several concerns when repowering a solar array according to Curtis et al. (2021):

- Regulations regarding solid and hazardous waste;
- Regulations regarding replaced and/or reused dated modules, inverters, electrical and structural BOS interfacing with new technology;
- Regulations regarding solar array system materials that are recycled; and
- Regulations regarding tax implications.

To make this analysis straightforward, I will assume that repowering the solar array will cost 1.59 \$/W and the advantage of using the existing site will reduce this cost to 1.113 \$/W. However, to remove the old array will cost \$212,000 based on the information provided by Curtis et al. (2021; Table 2 p. 11).

The annual capital recovery cost at time t, CR_t, is the same as was used for the capital asset with costs and no revenue stream given by equations (7.1a) to (7.1c). The capital recovery cost information for the 1,000 kW ground mount solar array is given in Table 7.2b.

IC_0 denotes Initial Cost; $PV(SV_t)$ denotes the present value of Salvage Value at time t; $EAE_{CR,t}$ denotes equal annual equivalent Capital Recovery Cost at time t and illustrated in Figure 7.4c. As with a capital asset that has costs and no direct

Table 7.2b Estimated Capital Recovery Cost of a 1,000 kW Ground Mount Solar Array Located Near Syracuse, New York, USA, Given a 5% Discount Rate

Year	Initial Cost	Expected Salvage Value	IC_0-$PV(SV_t)$	$EAE_{CR,t}$
	($)	($)	($)	($/year)
0	1,113,000			
1			1,113,000	1,168,650
5			1,113,000	257,075
10			1,113,000	144,139
15			1,113,000	107,229
20			1,113,000	89,310
21		−212,000	1,189,096	92,745
25		−212,000	1,175,604	83,412
30		−212,000	1,162,052	75,593
35		−212,000	1,151,434	70,320
40		−212,000	1,143,114	66,619
45		−212,000	1,136,595	63,947
50		−212,000	1,131,487	61,979
52		−212,000	1,129,768	61,340
55		−212,000	1,127,485	60,509

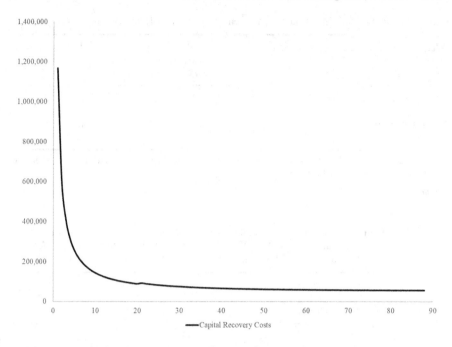

Figure 7.4c Estimated Capital Recovery Costs of a 1,000 kW Ground Mount Solar Array Located in Syracuse, New York, USA

revenue stream, the longer the asset is held the lower the capital recovery costs. In the case of the solar array, starting in year 21, the end of the initial PPA, the solar array can be repowered. This is illustrated by the salvage value cost and jump in the capital recovery costs in Figure 7.4c in year 21.

Operation and Maintenance Costs

As discussed in Chapter 2 – Production Systems, a solar array is described to have almost no variable inputs but only fixed inputs. This is illustrated by Table 7.2c.

For the purposes of the empirical example, I will use an initial operation and maintenance cost (O&M) of 19 $/kW-year. Based on information provided by Walker et al. (2020), warranties on all system components range from 10 to 20 years. I will assume that the warranty on this system is for 15 years. Again, based on Walker et al. (2020), the O&M costs will increase annually at 1.5% for the warranty period. To account for the increase in probability of a failure of any component from year 16 on, the O&M costs will increase at 2.5%. The accumulated operation and maintenance cost at any time t are given by equation (7.2a). The annuitized value of equation (7.2a) is calculated using an equal annual equivalent, $EAE_{OM,t}$, given in equation (7.2b). The operation and maintenance costs are given in Table 7.2d.

Table 7.2c Estimated Operation and Maintenance Costs of a 1,000 kW Solar Array

Technology Type (Photovoltaic)	Fixed O&M ($/kW-year)	Fixed O&M Std. Dev. ($/kW-year)	Variable O&M ($/kWh)
<10 kW	21	20	n/a
10–100 kW	19	18	n/a
100–1,000 kW	19	15	n/a
1–10 MW	16	9	n/a

$/kW-year denotes dollars per kilowatt-year, which is equivalent to 1 kilowatt of power used for 8,760 hours; n/a denotes not applicable

Source: Feldman et al. (2021)

Table 7.2d Estimated Operation and Maintenance of a 1,000 kW Ground Mount Solar Array Located Near Syracuse, New York, USA, Given a 5% Discount Rate and Annual Cost Increase of 1.5% for Years 1 to 15 and 2.5% for Years 16 and Beyond

Year	Estimated OM Cost	$\sum_t PV(OM)$	$EAE_{OM,t}$
	($)	($)	($/year)
0			
1	19,000	18,095	19,000
5	20,166	84,642	19,550
10	21,724	156,087	20,214
15	23,403	216,392	20,848
20	26,479	268,784	21,568
25	29,958	315,229	22,366
30	33,895	356,402	23,184
35	38,349	392,901	23,995
40	43,389	425,257	24,783
45	49,090	453,940	25,539
50	55,541	479,368	26,258
52	58,353	488,711	26,534
55	62,840	501,909	26,936

$\sum_t PV(OM)$ denotes the Sum of the Present Value of the Operation and Maintenance (OM) Costs at time t; $EAE_{OM,t}$, denotes the Equal Annual Equivalent Estimated Operation and Maintenance Costs at time t and illustrated in Figure 7.4d. As expected, the annuitized operation and maintenance costs increase the longer the solar array is held illustrated by the solid line in Figure 7.4d. This is like the 2018 new car example. The kink in the curve is at year 16 when the solar array is out of warranty. The present value of the annual O&M costs decreases due to the 5% discount rate and is illustrated in Figure 7.4d by the dashed line. However, the equal annual equivalent of the O&M costs is increasing as illustrated by the dotted line in Figure 7.4d

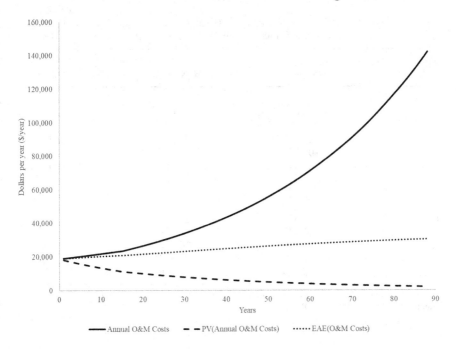

Figure 7.4d Estimated Operation and Maintenance Costs of a 1,000 kW Ground Mount Solar Array

The estimated annual ownership costs are the sum of the annual capital recovery and operation and maintenance costs and are given in Table 7.2e and the cash flow diagram is given in Figure 7.4e.

Ownership Analysis – Maximizing Wealth

The ownership cash flow diagram is given in Figure 7.4f. The NPV equation associated with this cash flow diagram is given in equation (7.5):

$$\begin{aligned}
NPV_t &= \sum_{k=0}^{t} (R_k - C_k) \cdot (1+r)^{-k} \\
&= \sum_{k=1}^{t} R_k (1+r)^{-k} + SV_t (1+r)^{-t} - \sum_{k=1}^{t} OM_k (1+r)^{-k} - IC_0
\end{aligned}$$

(7.5)

However, Figure 7.4f and equation (7.5) only examine the ownership analysis of keeping the solar array for t years. What if after the solar array's useful life, you would like to replace it with another array? Again, after that array replace it with another and so on? Figure 7.4g illustrates how Figure 7.4c and equation (7.5) can be extended to address this capital replacement problem.

Table 7.2e Annual Expected Ownership Costs ($EAE_{O,t}$) of a 1,000 kW Ground Mount Solar Array Located Near Syracuse, New York, USA, Given a 5% Discount Rate

Year	$EAE_{CR,t}$ ($/year)	$EAE_{OM,t}$ ($/year)	$EAE_{O,t}$ ($/year)
0			
1	1,168,650	19,000	1,187,650
5	257,075	19,550	276,625
10	144,139	20,214	164,353
15	107,229	20,848	128,077
20	89,310	21,568	110,878
25	83,412	22,366	105,778
30	75,593	23,184	98,778
35	70,320	23,995	94,315
40	66,619	24,783	91,402
45	63,947	25,539	89,486
50	61,979	26,258	88,237
52	61,340	26,534	87,875
55	60,509	26,936	87,444

CR_t denotes Capital Recovery Cost at time t (Table 7.2b); $EAE_{OM,t}$ denotes the Annuitized Operation and Maintenance Costs at time t (Table 7.2d)

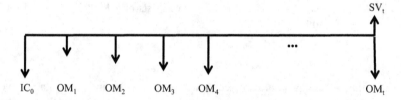

Figure 7.4e Cost Cash Flow Diagram of a 1,000 kW Ground Mount Solar Array

IC_0 denotes the initial cost of the array; OM_t denotes the annual operation and maintenance costs at time t; SV_t denotes the salvage value of the array at time t

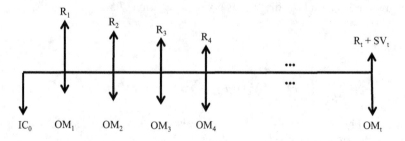

Figure 7.4f Ownership Cash Flow Diagram of a 1,000 kW Ground Mount Solar Array

R_t denotes the annual revenue at time t; SV_t denotes the salvage value of the array at time t; IC_0 denotes the initial cost of the array; OM_t denotes the annual operation and maintenance costs at time t

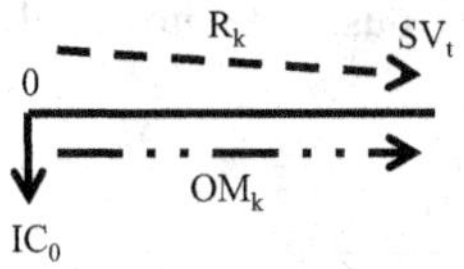

$$NPV_t = \sum_{k=1}^{t} R_k (1+r)^{-k} + SV_t (1+r)^{-t} - \sum_{k=1}^{t} OM_k (1+r)^{-k} - IC_0$$

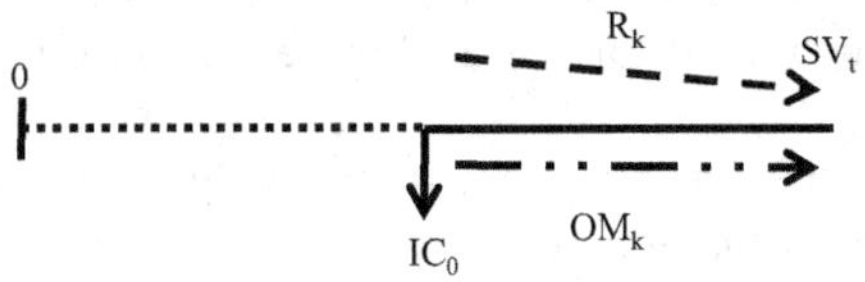

$$NPV_t (1+r)^{-t} = \left[\sum_{k=1}^{t} R_k (1+r)^{-k} + SV_t (1+r)^{-t} - \sum_{k=1}^{t} OM_k (1+r)^{-k} - IC_0 \right](1+r)^{-t}$$

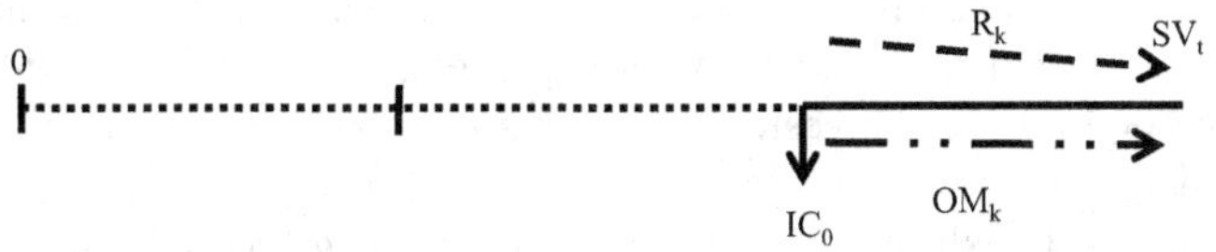

$$NPV_t (1+r)^{-2t} = \left[\sum_{k=1}^{t} R_k (1+r)^{-k} + SV_t (1+r)^{-t} - \sum_{k=1}^{t} OM_k (1+r)^{-k} - IC_0 \right](1+r)^{-2t}$$

Figure 7.4g Capital Replacement Ownership Cash Flow Diagram of a 1,000 kW Ground Mount Solar Array

R_t denotes the annual revenue at time t; SV_t denotes the salvage value of the array at time t; IC_0 denotes the initial cost of the array; OM_t denotes the annual operation and maintenance costs at time t; r denotes the discount rate

What the cash flow diagrams in Figure 7.4g show is that the next solar array cannot be put in place until the previous solar array is removed. In addition, the series of replacement arrays are represented by the NPV of each. This series of NPVs can be modeled using equation (7.6a):

$$NPV_t = \sum_{k=1}^{t} R_k (1+r)^{-k} + SV_t (1+r)^{-t} - \sum_{k=1}^{t} OM_k (1+r)^{-k} - IC_0$$

$$NPV_t (1+r)^{-t} = \left[\sum_{k=1}^{t} R_k (1+r)^{-k} + SV_t (1+r)^{-t} - \sum_{k=1}^{t} OM_k (1+r)^{-k} - IC_0 \right](1+r)^{-t}$$

$$NPV_t (1+r)^{-2t} = \left[\sum_{k=1}^{t} R_k (1+r)^{-k} + SV_t (1+r)^{-t} - \sum_{k=1}^{t} OM_k (1+r)^{-k} - IC_0 \right](1+r)^{-2t} \qquad (7.6a)$$

$$\vdots$$

$$(NPV_\infty)_t = NPV_t + NPV_t (1+r)^{-t} + NPV_t (1+r)^{-2t} + NPV_t (1+r)^{-3t} + \cdots$$

If each solar array is very similar to the previous, mathematically, this series of NPVs can be simplified to equation (7.6b):

$$\left(NPV_\infty\right)_t = \sum_{\theta=0}^{\infty} NPV_t\left[\left(1+r\right)^{-t}\right]^\theta = \frac{NPV_t}{1-\left(1+r\right)^{-t}} \tag{7.6b}$$

Maximizing equation (7.6b) requires determining the optimal time, T, to retain the current and all future solar arrays. Table 7.2f summarizes the analysis results analysis for the 1,000 kW ground mount solar array. Figure 7.4h describes the complete NPV analysis graphically.

While the NPV_t trend is increasing quickly in the early years, the growth slows in the later years reaching a maximum at year 81. The $(NPV_\infty)_t$ increases until reaching a maximum in year 52 then decreases. The optimal capital replacement decision is to retain the solar array for 52 years then replace it. At year 52, maximum $(NPV_\infty)_t$ equals $1,768,664 (Table 7.2f). This value is the net present value of the current and all future net revenue streams from the current and all future very similar solar arrays. As an entrepreneur, you would be indifferent between $1,768,664 now and investing in a series of solar arrays as described by the cash flow diagrams in Figure 7.4g.

Figure 7.4h exhibits a shape similar to a profit graph (refer to Figure 5.4c). The profit searching rule in that case examined the effects on profit by increasing or decreasing output; namely, is the incremental change in revenue, marginal revenue, greater or less than the incremental change in costs, marginal cost, of producing more or less output? While Figure 7.4h has a shape similar to a profit graph, this

Table 7.2f Ownership Wealth Analysis of a 1,000 kW Ground Mount Solar Array Located Near Syracuse, New York, USA, Given a 5% Discount Rate

Year	Output (kWh/yr)	NPV_t ($)	$NPV_{\infty,t}$ ($)	LCOE ($/kWh)
1	1,186,212	−944,578	−19,836,128	1.0012
5	1,153,345	−360,957	−1,667,440	0.2363
10	1,113,539	200,537	519,409	0.1426
15	1,075,107	619,040	1,192,795	0.1126
20	1,038,002	928,859	1,490,681	0.0987
25	1,002,177	1,093,816	1,552,179	0.0952
30	967,588	1,273,477	1,656,831	0.0898
35	934,193	1,404,402	1,715,384	0.0865
40	901,951	1,498,986	1,747,163	0.0844
45	870,822	1,566,556	1,762,744	0.0832
50	840,767	1,614,120	1,768,324	0.0825
52	829,037	1,628,769	1,768,664	0.0823
55	811,749	1,646,933	1,767,714	0.0821

NPV_t denotes the net present value at time t given by equation (7.5), NPV_∞ denotes the net present value of replacing the solar array at time t given by equation (7.6b), LCOE denotes the Levelized Cost of Electricity

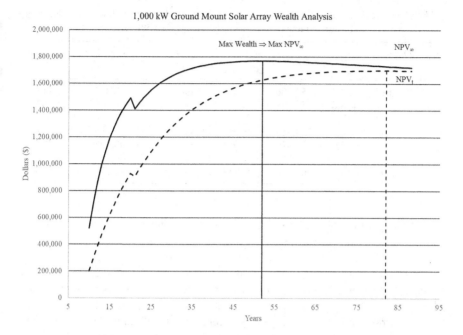

Figure 7.4h Net Present Value Analysis of 1,000 kW Ground Mount Solar Array

NPV$_t$ denotes the net present value at time t given by equation (7.5), NPV$_\infty$ denotes the net present value of replacing the solar array at time t given by equation (7.6b)

figure cannot be interpreted as profit, as equation (7.6a) is not a profit equation (Comolli 1981). Thus, the appropriate question to ask for the solar array is: Does *wealth* increase or decrease if I hold the solar array for an additional year? This requires defining the opportunity costs in terms of revenues, namely marginal revenue, and costs, namely marginal cost. The marginal revenue–marginal cost relationship wealth searching rule is given by equation (7.7)[7]

$$R_T - OM_T - rSV_T - EAE\left(NPV_\infty\right)_T = 0$$
$$MR_T = R_T = OM_T + rSV_T + EAE\left(NPV_\infty\right)_T = MC_T$$

(7.7)

with

$$EAE\left(NPV_\infty\right)_T = EAE_{R,T} - EAE_{CR,T} - EAE_{OM,T}$$

where T denotes the optimal time to retain the solar array and all other parameters have been defined previously. Table 7.2g summarizes the optimal capital replacement data for the 1,000 kW ground mount solar array.

The opportunity cost in terms of revenue, marginal revenue, is the incremental revenue of maintaining the array for an additional year. The marginal revenue at

Table 7.2g Optimal Capital Replacement Age of a 1,000 kW Ground Mount Solar Array
Located Near Syracuse, New York, USA, Given a 5% Discount Rate

Year	Output (kWh/yr)	R_t ($)	OM_t ($)	$r \cdot SV_t$ ($)	$EAE(NPV_\infty)_t$ ($/year)	$Max (NPV_\infty)_t$ ($)	$MR_t - MC_t$ ($)
49	846,694	139,789	54,186	−10,600	88,390	1,767,801	7,813
50	840,767	138,811	55,541	−10,600	88,416	1,768,324	5,453
51	834,881	137,839	56,929	−10,600	88,430	1,768,604	3,079
52	829,037	136,874	58,353	−10,600	88,433	1,768,664	688
53	823,234	135,916	59,812	−10,600	88,426	1,768,523	−1,722
54	817,471	134,965	61,307	−10,600	88,410	1,768,200	−4,152
55	811,749	134,020	62,840	−10,600	88,386	1,767,714	−6,605

year 52, R_{52}, is $136,874. If the solar array is retained for that year, it will generate $136,874 in revenues.

The opportunity cost in terms of costs are comprised of three terms: The operation and maintenance cost (OM_T), forgone interest income on the salvage value ($r SV_T$), and forgone current and future annuitized net revenue flows ($EAE(NPV_\infty)_T$). The operation and maintenance costs at year 52, OM_{52}, are $58,353. If you hold the solar array for an additional year, you forgo being able to use any cash generated by salvaging the array. Since salvaging the solar array will generate costs and not revenues, not salvaging the array in year 52, $r SV_{52}$, lowers the marginal cost by $10,600. As shown by Table 7.2g, this value is constant due to the assumption concerning the salvage value. Finally, retaining the current solar array implies that you cannot use the same location to establish a new solar array; that is, the natural and physical capital used to establish the site for the solar array. This is the amount of money the entrepreneur must receive to forgo the annuitized present value of net revenues from the current and future solar arrays. The forgone annuitized net revenue at year 52, $EAE(NPV_\infty)_{52}$, is $88,433.

Looking at Table 7.2g shows that equation (7.7) is not equal to zero. The reason is the analysis is done using annual data and not monthly, daily, or even hourly data. This level of precision is beyond what is necessary for this analysis, just like there are no "pennies" given in Table 7.2g. We are estimating output levels, prices, and costs over at least a 52-year period. I recommend highly that you as an analyst think very carefully about the appropriate level of precision. For example, I am not using pennies, but is providing the financial data to the nearest dollar also too great a level of precision?

This economic analysis of the 1,000 kW ground mount solar array asserted that economic information – parameters and variables that describe the market conditions and the production system – given in Tables 7.2a to 7.2g and Figures 7.4a to 7.4h remain the same for an infinite number of solar array replacements. This appears problematic and will be addressed directly in the section entitled Analytical Hazards – Forever Is a Long Time.

Finally, there is a unique breakeven calculation used in the energy sectors called the levelized cost of electricity or the levelized cost of energy (LCOE) that allows for parity across all generating technologies (Branker et al. 2011; Jenkin et al. 2019). LCOE is a single cost of energy (in $/MWh or $/kWh) at which NPV is zero for the specified discount rate over a specified period and is given by equation (7.8)

$$\text{LCOE} = \text{EAE}(P) = P = \frac{\text{EAE}(\text{Cost})}{\text{EAE}(Q)} = \frac{\sum_{t=0}^{T} C_t (1+r)^{-t}}{\sum_{t=0}^{T} Q_t (1+r)^{-t}} \tag{7.8}$$

where EAE(P) is the equal annual equivalent price and EAE(Cost) is the equal annual equivalent of the costs with EAE(Cost) = $\text{EAE}_{CR,T}$ + $\text{EAE}_{OM,T}$. The denominators of equation (7.8) appear awkward as it is either the equal annual equivalent of output, kWh, produced to a given time T or the cumulative present value of the quantity produced to a given time T. The key to making this less awkward is that this is a breakeven analysis no different from that discussed in Chapter 6 – Capital Theory: Investment Analysis – Breakeven: Price and Chapter 5 – Profit. It represents a price you would have to receive annually to cover the present value of the financing, operation, and maintenance costs for the investment horizon at an expected output or production level.

Calculating LCOE is very sensitive to the cost assumptions; for example, capital costs, utilization, discount rate (or cost of debt and equity for some analyses), fossil fuel prices, conversion efficiency, and project life (Branker et al. 2011; Jenkin et al. 2019). Comparing the LCOEs across different electricity-generating technologies can also be difficult due to electricity price variations; for example, electricity can be priced at five-minute intervals (http://mis.nyiso.com/public/ accessed 3 April 2022); summarized annually, quarterly, or monthly (www.eia.gov/outlooks/ steo/realprices/ accessed 3 April 2022), or summarized annually by state (www. eia.gov/electricity/state/newyork/ accessed 3 April 2022). Lastly, while LCOE is calculated using NPV, LCOE will be the same whether it is calculated using NPV or NPV_∞. I will leave it up to the reader to show that this statement is factual.

For the purposes of this example, I will use LCOE as a simple breakeven price as described in Chapter 6 – Capital Theory: Investment Analysis – Breakeven: Price and Chapter 5 – Profit to be compared to the expected market price received by the solar array company in 2020 of 0.1651 $/kWh ($ kWh^{-1}). Table 7.2f shows the LCOE in the last column to the right. At the wealth-maximizing time to replace the solar array, the LCOE is 0.0823 $/kWh ($ kWh^{-1}). The market price is twice this breakeven price or LCOE giving a high degree of confidence that you would be able to generate sufficient annual revenues to cover the present value of the financing, operation, and maintenance costs for the investment horizon at an expected output or production level.

Capital: Costs With Periodic Direct Revenue Stream

There are many examples of capital investments that produce periodic direct revenue streams: Wine Cellar (Goodhue et al. 2009), Cheese Cellar (Durham et al.

2015), Whisk(e)y Distillery (Page 2013), or Forest Ecosystem to produce stump-age[8] and biomass. The analytical methods used also revolved around calculating net present values of all alternative investments and choosing the alternative that maximizes wealth (Figure 7.1). To illustrate the analytical methods used with this category empirically, I will use producing stumpage. While the economic concern is still determining when to replace the capital that maximizes wealth, the out-puts from these investments' production systems are often described in terms of quantity and quality. For example, with wine, cheese, whiskey, and stumpage, the quality (grade or product class) of the output increases with time. With stumpage and biomass, the quantity of the output also increases with time.[9] Consequently, the capital replacement question can be rephrased as, What is the optimal quantity and quality of output to produce? I realize that forested ecosystems produce out-puts and outcomes more than just stumpage. I also realize forest landowners own forests for many different reasons other than just stumpage; for example, aesthet-ics, privacy, recreation, and protecting nature (Butler and Leatherberry 2004; Belin et al. 2005; Hagan et al. 2005; Butler 2008, 2010; Majumdar et al. 2008; Hatcher et al. 2013; Butler et al. 2016; Creighton et al. 2016; Snyder et al. 2019). One of the primary tools a landowner can use to manipulate forested ecosystems is to manage forest structure, species composition, and diversity by cutting trees sustainably.[10] To analyze a landowner's decision of when to cut their trees, I will start with a sim-ple case assuming the primary reason for forestland ownership is income from sell-ing stumpage. I will then relax this assumption to include other forest ecosystem outputs and outcomes and examine the impact on a landowner's cutting decision.

The two broad types of forest structures used to produce stumpage are even-aged and uneven-aged (Nyland 2016). I will discuss an even-aged structure first.

The Even-Aged Forest Problem

An even-aged forest contains a series of even-aged stands, and the spread of ages in an even-aged community does not differ by more than 20% of the intended rotation age (Nyland 2016). For example, loblolly pine (*Pinus taeda*) is native to the south-eastern United States. Its primary uses are for pulp, dimension lumber, and utility poles. Smaller loblolly pines are used for pulpwood, and as the trees increase in diameter and height, they can be used as chip-n-saw, sawtimber, plywood logs, or power poles. The lowest-valued output is pulpwood and the highest-valued output is power poles. Finally, like the solar array, I cannot age the next vintage of wine, cheese, or whiskey or start the next forest until I sell the current inventory. Alter-natively, the capital replacement question can be rephrased as, How long should I hold on to the current inventory? I will develop an economic analysis of a single and multiple rotation problems.

The Single Rotation Problem

Assume the forest landowner's sole objective is to maximize the net present value of the final harvest. To analyze this objective, I will use a management regime

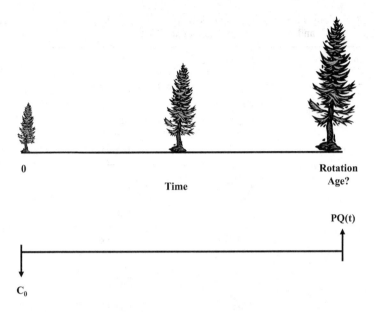

Figure 7.5 Single Rotation Problem With Cash Flow Diagram

defined by an initial cost for establishing a stand and then determining when to harvest the trees. This is illustrated in Figure 7.5.

Equation (7.9) is used to search for the largest NPV from all the potential rotation ages as illustrated in Figure 7.5

$$
NPV_t = \left. \begin{array}{l} P \cdot Q(t) \cdot (1+r)^{-t} - C_0 \\[2mm] \dfrac{P \cdot Q(t)}{(1+r)^{-t}} - C_0 \end{array} \right\} ; t = 0, 1, 2, \ldots \tag{7.9}
$$

where P denotes output price, Q(t) denotes the production process, P·Q(t) denotes the harvest revenue at time t, r denotes the real interest rate, and C_0 denotes the costs of establishing the stand.[11] Continuing with the Loblolly Pine Plantation practical application, Q(t) defines the cubic feet per acre yield given by equations defined in Amateis and Burkhart (1985) and Burkhart et al. (1985) and illustrated in Table 7.3 and Figure 7.6. The cost of establishing the stand includes shearing, raking, piling, chopping, burning, and herbicide. This removes whatever material may be on the site and killing any herbaceous plants that may hinder the growth of the loblolly pines. The site will then be planted with 1,210 seedlings per acre or a 6-foot by 6-foot spacing using 1+0 stock.[12] The establishment costs were estimated at $305.54 per acre (Forest Landowner 1996; https://www.forestlandowners.com/forest-landowner-magazine/ accessed 3 September 2023). The 1997 stumpage price for sawtimber or the output price was $1.81 per cubic foot (TimberMart

Table 7.3 Loblolly Pine Plantation Practical Application Yields, Mean Annual Increment (MAI), and Current Annual Increment (CAI)

Plantation Age	Site Index 65 Yield[†]	MAI[‡]	CAI[††]
10	1,285	116.84	
11	1,549	129.11	274.28
12	1,824	140.28	281.09
13	2,105	150.34	284.90
14	2,390	159.31	286.10
15	2,676	167.23	285.08
16	2,961	174.16	282.17
17	3,243	180.17	277.71
18	3,521	185.30	272.01
19	3,793	189.63	265.35
20	4,058	193.24	257.99
21	4,316	196.18	250.15
22	4,566	198.53	242.04
23	4,808	200.34	233.84
24	5,042	201.68	225.71
25	5,268	202.61	217.78
26	5,486	203.17	210.16
27	5,696	203.42	202.94
28	5,899	203.40	196.19
29	6,095	203.16	189.97
30	6,285	202.74	184.31

[†] Yield is measured as cubic feet per acre and is calculated given the following information: an index age of 25 and planting 1,210 one-year-old seedlings per acre
[‡] MAI or average product is measured as cubic feet per acre per year
[††] CAI or marginal product is measured as cubic feet per acre per year

South www.tmart-south.com/tmart/index.html accessed 12 April 2010). Finally, the real interest rate is 8%. Bullard et al. (2002) examined the hurdle rates of return for nonindustrial private forest landowners in Mississippi. They found for timberland investments ranging from 5 to 25 years, the real interest rates ranged from 6% to 11%.

The landowner must decide when to cut the trees to maximize the net present value of the final harvest. Table 7.4 illustrates calculating the NPV of various different potential rotation ages.

Focusing on the first three columns of Table 7.4 shows that the financially optimal single rotation age for the Loblolly Pine Plantation practical application is at a plantation age of 18, or T = 18.[13] This can also be illustrated by graphing the range of NPV values as shown in Figure 7.7.

Once the range of NPV values has been calculated, determining the financially optimal single rotation age for the Loblolly Pine Plantation practical application seems very straightforward. However, care must be taken with interpreting the results in Table 7.5 and Figure 7.7 economically. I will examine four observations

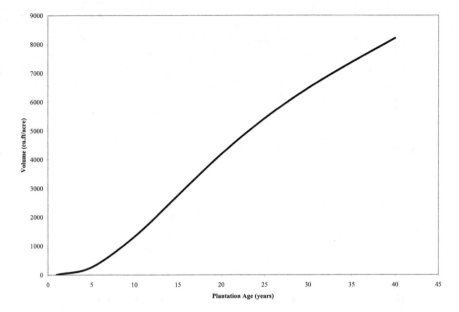

Figure 7.6 Yield of Loblolly Pine Plantation Practical Application

Volume is measured as cubic feet per acre (cuft/ac) given an index age of 25, a site index of 65, and planting 1,210 one-year-old seedlings per acre

Table 7.4 Single Rotation Problem for the Loblolly Pine Plantation Practical Application[‡]

Plantation Age	Yield (cuft/ac)	NPV ($/ac)	MRP ($/ac/yr)	r·PQ(t) ($/ac/yr)
15	2,675.73	1,221.20	515.99	387.45
16	2,960.80	1,258.72	510.73	428.72
17	3,242.97	1,280.88	502.66	469.58
18	3,520.69	*1,289.16*	492.34	509.80
19	3,792.70	1,285.11	480.29	549.18
20	4,058.05	1,270.33	466.96	587.61
21	4,316.04	1,246.36	452.77	624.96

[‡] Yield is measured as cubic feet per acre (cuft/ac). NPV denotes net present value and is measured as dollars per acre ($/ac). MRP denotes marginal revenue product and is measured as dollars per acre per year ($/ac/yr). r denotes the real interest rate. P denotes the output price. Q(t) denotes the yield at plantation age t. For example:

$$1289.16 \; \frac{\$}{acre} = 3520.69 \cdot 1.81 \cdot (1.08)^{-18} - 305.54$$

associated with interpreting the financially optimal single rotation age for the Loblolly Pine Plantation practical appliation at a plantation age of 18, or T = 18.

First, there is a difference between the age of the trees (i.e., stand age) and the time used to calculate the NPV (i.e., investment or plantation age). The site was

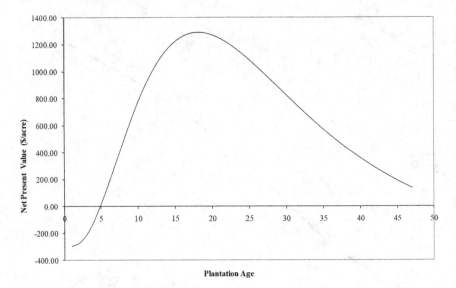

Figure 7.7 Net Present Value – Loblolly Pine Plantation Practical Application

Table 7.5 Optimality Conditions and Cash Flow Diagram for the Single Rotation Problem for the Loblolly Pine Plantation Practical Application[‡]

Plantation Age	Yield (ft³/Ac)	NPV ($/Ac)	MRP ($/Ac/PA)	rPQ(t) ($/Ac/PA)	
15	2,675.73	1,221.20	515.99	387.45	⎫
16	2,960.80	1,258.72	510.73	428.72	⎬ MRP > iPQ(t)
17	3,242.97	1,280.88	502.66	469.58	⎭
18	*3,520.69*	*1,289.16*	*492.34*	*509.80*	
19	3,792.70	1,285.11	480.29	549.18	⎫
20	4,058.05	1,270.33	466.96	587.61	⎬ MRP > iPQ(t)
21	4,316.04	1,246.36	452.77	624.96	⎭

MRP > *r*PQ(t)
MRP < *r*PQ(t)

[‡] Yield is measured as cubic feet per acre (cuft/ac). NPV denotes net present value and is measured as dollars per acre ($/ac). MRP denotes marginal revenue product and is measured as dollars per acre per year ($/ac/yr). *r* denotes the real interest rate. P denotes the output price. Q(t) denotes the yield at plantation age t.

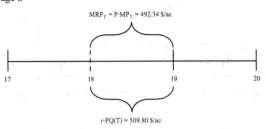

planted with 1+0 stock or seedlings that were one year old. Therefore, if the plantation is 18 years old the trees are actually 19 years old. Calculating the NPV is based on the length of the investment, not in this case the actual age of the trees as illustrated by the cash flow diagram in Figure 7.5.

Second, equation (7.9) defines a NPV calculation. Therefore, if NPV > 0, the investment is returning the desired discount rate *plus* a present value of additional net revenue (Chapter 6 – Capital Theory: Investment Analysis). In the Loblolly Pine Plantation practical application, the entrepreneur is earning the required 8% plus a present value of additional net revenue of $1,289.16 per acre.

Third, while this may seem like a trival question: How does the entrepreneur evaluate if they have maximized the NPV? Using Figure 7.7, the maximum NPV would occur at the top of the curve. Drawing on similarities from maximizing total product (Chapter 2 – Production Systems) and profit (Chapter 5 – Profit), a maximum was defined if a marginal condition, marginal product, or marginal profit were set equal to zero, respectively. The entrepreneur's management decision is whether to cut the plantation today or wait for next year. This requires defining the opportunity costs in terms of revenues and costs. If the entrepreneur decides to let the plantation grow for an additional year, there will be an increase in net revenue as the trees grow in quantity (volume per acre; e.g., cubic feet per acre or cubic meter per hectare) and quality (product class; e.g., pulpwood, chip-n-saw, sawtimber, plywood logs, and power poles); this describes the opportunity cost in terms of revenues. If the entrepreneur decides to let the plantation grow for an additional year, they will lose one years' worth of interest income on the net revenue from the sale of the timber; this describes the opportunity cost in terms of costs.

Fisher (1930) employed the same reasoning to derive the optimality conditions for equation (7.9) given in equation (7.10a)[14]

$$MRP_T = P \cdot MP_T = r \cdot \left[P \cdot Q(T) \right] = MC_T \tag{7.10a}$$

where MRP_T denotes the marginal revenue product (see equation (4.9)) at the optimal rotation age, T; P denotes output price; MP_T denotes marginal product (see equations (2.9) and (2.10)) at the optimal rotation age, T; r denotes the discount rate; Q(T) denotes the yield at the optimal rotation age T; and MC_T denotes the marginal cost at the optimal rotation age T (Chapter 3 – Costs). A closer examination of equation (7.10a) shows it is analogous to the profit searching rule described in Chapter 5 – Profit. However, as equation (7.9) is not a profit equation (Comolli 1981), from this point forward I will describe equation (7.10a) as the wealth searching rule. That is, the left-hand side of equation (7.10a) defines a marginal revenue concept and the right-hand side defines a marginal cost concept. If the entrepreneur decides to let the plantation grow for an additional year, there will be an increase in net revenue as the trees grow; MP_T describes current annual increment or how volume changes if the trees are allowed to grow for an additional year. Consequently $MRP_T = P \cdot MP_T$ defines the opportunity cost in terms of revenue. For the Loblolly Pine Plantation practical application, MRP is given by the fourth column

Table 7.6 Annual Value Growth of Loblolly Pine Plantation Practical Application[‡]

Plantation Age	Yield, Q(t) (cuft/ac)	P·Q(t) ($/ac)	MP, $\frac{\Delta Q(t)}{\Delta t}$ (cuft/ac/yr)	P·MP ($/ac/yr)	$P \cdot \frac{\frac{\Delta Q(t)}{\Delta t}}{P \cdot Q(t)} = \frac{\frac{\Delta Q(t)}{\Delta t}}{Q(t)}$
15	2,675.73	4,843.06	285.08	515.99	0.107
16	2,960.80	5,359.05	282.17	510.73	0.095
17	3,242.97	5,869.78	277.71	502.66	0.086
18	3,520.69	6,372.44	272.01	492.34	0.077
19	3,792.70	6,864.78	265.35	480.29	0.070
20	4,058.05	7,345.07	257.99	466.96	0.064
21	4,316.04	7,812.03	250.15	452.77	0.058

[‡] Yield is measured as cubic feet per acre (cuft/ac). P denotes 1.81 dollars per cubic foot ($/cuft). MP denotes marginal product and is measured as cubic feet per acre per year (cuft/ac/yr).

in Table 7.4. The MRP at the optimal single rotation age, T = 18, is given by equation (7.10b)

$$MRP_{18} = P \cdot MP_{18}$$

$$= 1.81 \left(\frac{\$}{\text{cuft}} \right) \cdot 272.01 \left(\frac{\text{cuft}}{\frac{\text{ac}}{\text{yr}}} \right) = 492.34 \left(\frac{\$}{\frac{\text{ac}}{\text{yr}}} \right) \qquad (7.10b)$$

$$= 1.81 \left(\$ \text{ cuft}^{-1} \right) \cdot 272.01 \left(\text{cuft ac}^{-1} \text{yr}^{-1} \right) = 492.34 \left(\$ \text{ ac}^{-1} \text{yr}^{-1} \right)$$

where price is 1.81 dollars per cubic foot ($/cuft or $ cuft⁻¹), marginal product is 272.01 cubic feet per acre per year (cuft/ac/yr or cuft⁻¹ac⁻¹yr⁻¹), and marginal revenue product is 492.34 dollars per acre per year ($/ac/yr or $ac⁻¹yr⁻¹) or the opportunity cost in terms of revenue.

If the entrepreneur decides to let the plantation grow for an additional year, they will lose one years' worth of interest income on the net revenue from the sale of the timber. The right-hand side term in equation (7.10a), $r \cdot [P \cdot Q(T)]$, is the discount rate times total revenue that would have been received had the timber been cut and is given in equation (7.10c)

$$MC_{18} = r \cdot \left[P \cdot Q(t) \right]$$

$$= 0.08 \cdot \left[1.81 \left(\frac{\$}{\text{cuft}} \right) \cdot 3,520 \left(\frac{\text{cuft}}{\text{ac}} \right) \right] = 509.80 \left(\frac{\$}{\frac{\text{ac}}{\text{yr}}} \right) \qquad (7.10c)$$

$$= 0.08 \cdot \left[1.81 \left(\$ \text{ cuft}^{-1} \right) \cdot 3,520 \left(\text{cuft}^{-1} \text{ac}^{-1} \right) \right] = 509.80 \left(\$ac^{-1}yr^{-1} \right)$$

where r denotes the 8% real discount rate; price is as defined in equation (7.10b); yield at plantation age, Q(18), is 3,520.09 cubic feet per acre (cuft/ac or cuft⁻¹ac⁻¹);

and the interest income lost if the trees are not harvested is 509.80 dollars per acre for a year ($/ac/yr or $ac^{-1}yr^{-1}) or the opportunity cost in terms of cost and marginal cost. In addition, $r \cdot [P \cdot Q(T)]$ is defined as stand rent or the opportunity cost of capital in the trees. This is the amount of money the trees' or stand's owner must receive to keep the trees or stand growing for an additional year (i.e., economic rent – the opportunity cost of capital in the trees or stand). Table 7.5 summarizes the optimality condition and the corresponding cash flow diagram given in equation (7.10a).

Before plantation age 18, MRP is greater than stand rent, $r \cdot [P \cdot Q(T)]$, and the entrepreneur's decision would be to let the plantation grow as their net value growth is greater than what could be made in an alternative investment. If the entrepreneur grows the plantation after plantation age 18, stand rent is greater than MRP and the entrepreneur's decision would be to cut the trees, as net value growth in the trees is less than the interest income that could have been earned at the defined discount rate. At plantation age 18 the opportunity cost in terms of revenue, MRP, is approximately balanced with the opportunity cost in terms of cost, stand rent. The reason that MRP does not equal stand rent exactly as described in equation (7.10a) is that the production system defines annual yields. If yields were defined in terms of days, weeks, or months, then we could pinpoint the precise date that would satisfy equation (7.10a). However, yield tables are generally not that precise and can often be defined using stand age increments of greater than one year; for example, the unthinned oak stand in southwestern Wisconsin yields are given every 20 years (see Table 2.6). Equation (7.10a) defines a wealth search rule to estimate the financially optimal single rotation age.

Equation (7.10a) can be rewritten to express the optimality condition as given in equation (7.11)

$$r = \frac{P \cdot MP_t}{P \cdot Q(t)} = \frac{MRP_t}{TR_t} = \frac{P \cdot \dfrac{\Delta Q(t)}{\Delta t}}{P \cdot Q(t)} = \frac{\dfrac{\Delta Q(t)}{\Delta t}}{Q(t)} \qquad (7.11)$$

which describes that the trees should be cut when the discount rate (the left-hand side of equation (7.11)) equals the percentage change in volume (the right-hand side of equation (7.11)) (Johansson and Löfgren 1985). Table 7.6 derives the right-hand side of equation (7.11). As the discount rate was defined as 8%, according to Table 7.6 and equation (7.11) the financially optimal single rotation age is 18.

As with Table 7.5, the reason equation (7.11) is not illustrated with the data provided in Table 7.6 is that the yields are not given in smaller time increments.

A close examination of equation (7.11) shows that output price would cancel out of the right-hand side term leaving $\dfrac{\dfrac{\Delta Q(t)}{\Delta t}}{Q(t)}$ or the percentage change in volume as shown in Table 7.6. In equation (7.9), I assumed a constant price; namely, the output was assumed to be sawtimber, thus the price reflected sawtimber. If the price is a function of product class and product class changes as the trees grow in height and diameter, then the price would not be constant. Nonetheless, the rule described in equation (7.11) seems reasonable. Allow the trees to grow if their annual net value growth is greater than the discount rate. If not, cut, as you could take the net revenue put it in a bank for one year at 8% and earn a greater net return than leaving the trees grow an additional year.

Fourth, how does the financially optimal single rotation age compare to the rotation age that defines the maximum sustained yield (Johansson and Löfgren 1985; Samuelson 1976b) or optimal biological rotation age?[15] This is determined when marginal product equals average product or when average product is maximized. In forestry terminology this is called the culmination of mean annual increment (CMAI). A rotation age defined by CMAI would give the maximum volume or biomass production per acre over multiple rotations. The not-so-simple answer is derived using equation (7.12), which starts with equation (7.10a).

$$P \cdot MP_T = r \cdot \left[P \cdot Q(T) \right]$$

$$\frac{\Delta Q(T)}{\Delta T} = r \cdot Q(T) \qquad\qquad (7.12)$$

$$\frac{\Delta Q(T)}{\Delta T} = r \cdot Q(T) \cdot \frac{T}{T}$$

$$CAI = \frac{\Delta Q(T)}{\Delta T} = rT \cdot \frac{Q(T)}{T} = rT \cdot MAI_T$$

$$CAI = rT \cdot MAI_T$$

where CAI denotes current annual increment (Chapter 2 – Production Systems) and MAI denotes mean annual increment (Chapter 2 – Production Systems). Interpreting the result of equation (7.12), CAI = $rT \cdot MAI_T$, depends on the relationship between CAI or marginal product and MAI or average product. This basic relationship is illustrated in Figure 7.8a.

Interpreting CAI = $rT \cdot MAI_T$ is divided into three arguments:

1. If $r > 0$, $T > 0$, and if $rT > 1$, then the financially optimal single rotation age is defined where CAI > MAI or a rotation age shorter than the CMAI.
2. If $rT < 1$, then the financially optimal single rotation age is defined where CAI < MAI or a rotation age longer than the CMAI.
3. If $rT = 1$, then the financially single optimal rotation age is defined where CAI = MAI or a rotation age equal to the CMAI.[16]

Comparing these arguments with the Loblolly Pine Plantation example, at the financially optimal single rotation age $rT = 0.08 \cdot 18 = 1.44 > 1$ and CAI and MAI at plantation age 18 or stand age 19 are 272.01 and 185.30 cubic feet per acre per year, respectively. Thus, the financially optimal single rotation age is less than the optimal biological rotation age as shown by Figure 7.8b.

The preceding four observations were made based on a very simple single rotation scenario; i.e., establishing the plantation and then harvesting. Examining the

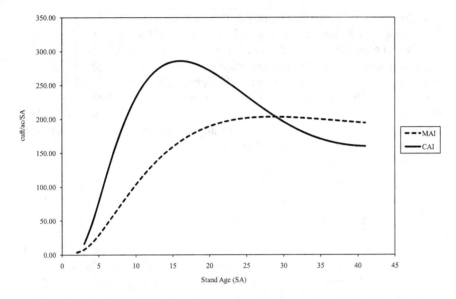

Figure 7.8a Average Product (Mean Annual Increment – MAI) and Marginal Product (Current Annual Increment – CAI) for the Loblolly Pine Plantation Practical Application

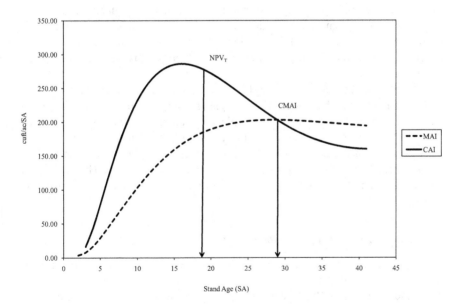

Figure 7.8b Optimal Financial Single Rotation Age Versus Biological Rotation Age for the Loblolly Pine Plantation Practical Application[‡]

[‡]MAI denotes mean annual increment. CAI denotes current annual increment. NPV_T denotes the financially optimal single rotation age. CMAI denotes the optimal biological rotation age.

cash flow diagram given in Figure 7.5, the NPV calculated using equation (7.9) determines the rotation age that maximizes the NPV of the final harvest and nothing else. The importance of this observation is that no value can be attributed to the land before or after the rotation. Johansson and Löfgren (1985) describe this implication as land is so abundant that its opportunity cost is zero. Bentley and Teeguarden (1965), Uys (1990), and Hseu and Buongiorno (1997) address this problem by modifying equation (7.9) to include the purchase and sale of the land. Equation (7.13) illustrates this as well as any other intermediate net cash flows (e.g., precommercial or commercial thinning).

$$NPV_t = P \cdot Q(t) \cdot (1+r)^{-t} + \sum_{k=1}^{K} \sum_{j=0}^{t} B_{kj} \cdot (1+r)^{-t} + L_t \cdot (1+r)^{-t}$$

$$-\sum_t C_t \cdot (1+r)^{-t} - L_0; \ t = 0,1,... \tag{7.13}$$

where B_{kj} denotes the net cash flow of the kth intermediate action and L_t and L_0 denote the sale and purchase price of the land at end and beginning of the rotation, respectively. The objective is to determine the optimal rotation age, T, that maximizes present value of net cash flow resulting from a single rotation scenario (e.g., establishment costs, any timber stand improvements such as herbicides, thinning, and a final harvest) including the purchase and sale of the land.[17] Equation (7.13) looks intimidating, and determining potential solutions is not as simple to display as those in equation (7.10a) and is beyond the scope of this book. However, the concepts of the opportunity cost in terms of revenue (i.e., marginal revenue) – What additional revenues may be gained by letting the plantation grow for an additional year? – and the opportunity cost in terms of costs (i.e., marginal cost) – What is being given up to keep the plantation in place? – are still useful in examining this more complex problem.

Finally, even as simple or complex as the problem given in equations (7.9) or (7.13) may describe, they still represent a single even-aged rotation problem. If the entrepreneur's goal is to replace the current plantation after it is cut with another plantation and so on, these formulations do not account for the extra cost of not cutting the plantation now, which is delaying the net revenue from all future rotations. The next section examines this issue. The reader will note the similarity of replacing a forest with replacing the solar array discussed previously.

The Even-Aged Multiple Rotation Problem

The issue of determining a financially optimal multiple rotation age is the focus of this section. To develop a model to examine the multiple rotation problem, I will again use the Loblolly Pine Plantation practical application and describe the management regime to include the cost of establishing the plantation and revenue generated from a harvest. As was discussed at the end of the previous section, the

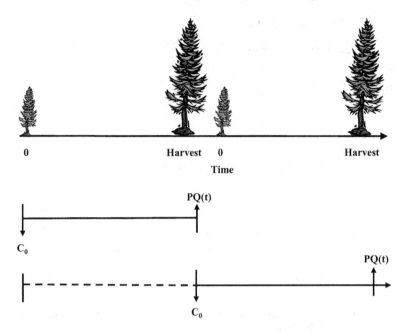

Figure 7.9 Multiple Rotation Problem With Cash Flow Diagram

harvest decision now must include the additional cost of delaying the net revenue from all future rotations. This is illustrated in Figure 7.9.

As illustrated by Figure 7.9, the timing of establishing future plantations depends on when the previous one is harvested. Calculating the present value of the two rotations illustrated in Figure 7.9 is shown in Figure 7.10.

Equation (7.14) extends this to an infinite number of rotations

$$
\begin{aligned}
\text{LEV}_t &= P \cdot Q(t) \cdot \left((1+r)^{-t} - C_0 + \left[P \cdot Q(t) \cdot \left((1+r)^{-t} - C_0\right] \cdot (1+r)^{-t}\right. \\
&\quad + \left[P \cdot Q(t) \cdot \left((1+r)^{-t} - C_0\right] \cdot (1+r)^{-2t} + \cdots \\
&= \text{NPV}_t + \text{NPV}_t (1+r)^{-t} + \text{NPV}_t (1+r)^{-2t} + \cdots
\end{aligned}
$$

(7.14)

There are three observations from examining equation (7.14). First, the left-hand term has the notation of LEV_t, which denotes Land Expectation Value at time t to distinguish the solution of equation (7.14) from equation (7.9).[18] Second, the parameters of equation (7.14) – P, Q(t), r, and C_0 – are held constant for an infinite number of rotations. I will revisit the implications of this observation later in this chapter. Third, solving for the optimal rotation age, T, that maximizes LEV is very problematic as there are an infinite number of rotation ages. Fortunately, this

$$NPV = PQ(1+r)^{-t} - C_0$$

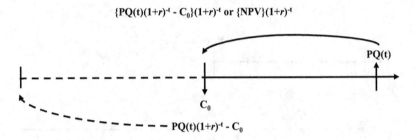

$$\{PQ(t)(1+r)^{-t} - C_0\}(1+r)^{-t} \text{ or } \{NPV\}(1+r)^{-t}$$

Figure 7.10 Present Value of the First Two Rotations for the Loblolly Pine Plantation Practical Application

problem formulation and its solution was described by Faustmann (1849), Pressler (1860), and Ohlin (1921) and is given in equation (7.15):

$$LEV_t = \left. \begin{array}{c} \sum_{\theta=0}^{\infty} \left(PQ(t) \cdot (1+r)^{-t} - C_0 \right) \cdot \left[(1+r)^{-t} \right]^{\theta} \\[2mm] \dfrac{PQ(t) \cdot (1+r)^{-t} - C_0}{1 - (1+r)^{-t}} \\[2mm] \dfrac{NPV_t}{1 - (1+r)^{-t}} \\[2mm] (NPV_\infty)_t \end{array} \right\} \quad ; \quad t = 0, 1, 2, \ldots \quad (7.15)$$

Equation (7.15) is often called the Faustmann formula or Faustmann model.[19]

The landowner must decide when to cut the trees to maximize the LEV.[20] Table 7.7 illustrates calculating the LEV of various different potential rotation ages.

$$1783.40 \, \$\!/_{acre} = \frac{2675.73 \cdot 1.81 \cdot (1.08)^{-15} - 305.54}{1 - (1.08)^{-15}}$$

$$= \frac{2675.73 \cdot 1.81 - 305.54 \cdot (1.08)^{15}}{(1.08)^{15} - 1}$$

Table 7.7 Multiple Rotation Problem for the Loblolly Pine Plantation Practical Application‡

Plantation Age	Yield (cuft/ac)	NPV ($/ac)	LEV ($/ac)
13	2,104.73	1,095.23	1,732.12
14	2,389.62	1,167.03	1,769.46
15	2,675.73	1,221.20	*1,783.40*
16	2,960.80	1,258.72	1,777.57
17	3,242.97	1,280.88	1,755.28
18	3,520.69	1,289.16	1,719.45
19	3,792.70	1,285.11	1,672.70
20	4,058.05	1,270.33	1,617.33

‡ Yield is measured as cubic feet per acre (cuft/ac). NPV denotes net present value and is measured as dollars per acre ($/ac). LEV denotes land expectation value and is measured as dollars per acre ($/ac).

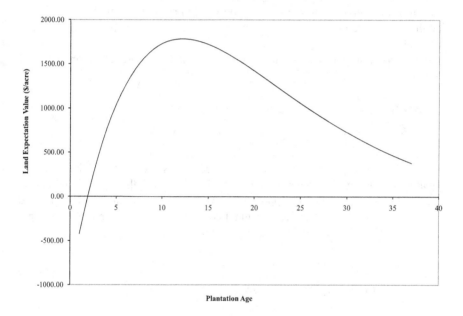

Figure 7.11 Land Expectation Value – Loblolly Pine Plantation Practical Application

Table 7.7 shows that the financially optimal multiple rotation age for the Loblolly Pine Plantation practical application is at a plantation age of 15, or T = 15.[21] This can also be illustrated by graphing the range of LEV values as shown in Figure 7.11.

What does an LEV of 1,783.40 dollars per acre ($/ac or $ac⁻¹) at plantation age 15 mean? LEV deals with more than just the current rotation; it takes into account *all* future rotations. An LEV of 1,783.40 $/ac ($ac⁻¹) at plantation age 15 is the present net value of the current and all future rotations. The assumption is that we started with bare land that is regenerated and then harvested. This exact management regime is going to be repeated forever. LEV calculates the value of that bare land to produce a periodic net revenue stream. Therefore, an LEV of 1,783.40 \$/ac is the value of the bare land given the Loblolly Pine Plantation practical application. You would not pay more than 1,783.40 \$/ac given you were going to follow the preceding management regime forever.

Examining Figure 7.11 reveals that it is very similar to Figure 7.7, which is logical because the numerator in equation (7.15) is the same as in equation (7.10). Thus, the analysis of equation (7.14) and Figure 7.11 can build on what has been already discussed. The maximum LEV would occur at the top of the curve in Figure 7.11. The entrepreneur's management decision is, "should the plantation be cut today or wait for next year?" This again requires defining the opportunity costs in terms of revenues and costs. If the entrepreneur decides to let the plantation grow for an additional year, net revenue will increase as the trees grow in quantity and quality. This describes the opportunity cost in terms of revenues. If the entrepreneur decides to let the plantation grow for an additional year, they will lose one year of interest income on the net revenue from the sale of the timber *plus* delaying the net revenue from all future rotations; this describes the opportunity cost in terms of costs.

The opportunity costs in terms of revenue and cost are given in equation (7.16a):[22]

$$MRP_T = P \cdot MP_T = r \cdot \left[P \cdot Q(T) \right] + r \cdot LEV_T = MC_T \tag{7.16a}$$

$$MRP_T = P \cdot MP_T = r \cdot \left[P \cdot Q(T) \right] + EAE \left(NPV_\infty \right)_T = MC_T$$

The left-hand side of equation (7.16a) is exactly the same as the left-hand side of equation (7.10a) and has the same interpretation; it defines the increase in net revenue as the trees grow and the opportunity cost in terms of revenue. The right-hand side of equation (7.16a) denotes marginal cost at the financially optimal multiple rotation age, T, and is given in equation (7.16b):

$$r \cdot \left[P \cdot Q(T) \right] + r \cdot LEV_T = MC_T \tag{7.16b}$$

$$r \cdot \left[P \cdot Q(T) \right] + EAE \left(NPV_\infty \right)_T = MC_T$$

The first term on the left-hand side of equation (7.16b) defines stand rent, $r \cdot [P \cdot Q(T)]$, and is the discount rate times total revenue that would have been received if the timber would have been cut or the opportunity cost of the capital in the stand. The concept of stand rent given in equation (7.16b) is the same as used in determining the financially optimal single rotation age and has the same interpretation. The second term on the left-hand side of equation (7.16b) defines land rent, $r \cdot LEV_T$, and is the cost – delaying the net revenue from all future rotations – due to lengthening the rotation age by one year (Johansson and Löfgren 1985). Land rent can also be defined as the equal annual equivalent (EAE) of the land as a natural capital asset. This is the amount of money the landowner must receive to keep the land growing the current trees for an additional year and forgo the present value of annualized net revenues from the current and future periodic timber harvests (i.e., economic rent). I would argue that land rent is the most important contribution of Faustmann as it requires the entrepeuner to think analytically about what comes after the current rotation.

The information contained in equation (7.16a) is illustrated in Table 7.8. The opportunity cost in terms of revenue at the financially optimal multiple rotation age, T = 15, is MRP_{15} = 515.99 dollars per acre per year ($/ac/yr or $ $ac^{-1}yr^{-1}$). If the plantation is not cut at plantation age 15 and allowed to grow, it will generate 515.99 dollars per acre of additional revenue. Stand rent, $r \cdot [P \cdot Q(T)]$, and land rent, $r \cdot LEV_T$, at the financially optimal multiple rotation age, T = 15, are 387.45 and 142.67 $/ac/yr respectively. The stand rent of 387.45 $/ac is the interest income that could be earned if the plantation is cut and the revenue is invested at 8% for one year. If the plantation is not cut and allowed to grow for an additional year, the entrepreneur would forgo 142.67 $/ac of potential income due to not establishing

Table 7.8 Optimality Conditions and Cash Flow Diagram for the Multiple Rotation Problem for the Loblolly Pine Plantation Practical Application‡

Plantation Age	Yield (cuft/ac)	LEV ($/ac)	MRP ($/ac/yr)	$r \cdot PQ(t)$ ($/ac/yr)	$r \cdot LEV$ ($/ac/yr)	MC ($/ac/yr)
13	2,104.73	1,732.12	515.66	304.76	138.57	443.33
14	2,389.62	1,769.46	517.85	346.02	141.56	487.57
15	2,675.73	*1,783.40*	515.99	387.45	142.67	530.12
16	2,960.80	1,777.57	510.73	428.72	142.21	570.93
17	3,242.97	1,755.28	502.66	469.58	140.42	610.00
18	3,520.69	1,719.45	492.34	509.80	137.56	647.35
19	3,792.70	1,672.70	480.29	549.18	133.82	683.00
20	4,058.05	1,617.33	466.96	587.61	129.39	716.99

‡ Yield is measured as cubic feet per acre (cuft/ac). LEV denotes land expectation value and is measured as dollars per acre ($/ac). MRP denotes marginal revenue product and is measured as dollars per acre per year ($/ac/yr). r denotes the real interest rate. P denotes the output price. Q(t) denotes the yield at plantation age t. MC denotes marginal cost and is the sum of $r \cdot PQ(t)$ plus $r \cdot LEV$ and is measured as dollars per acre per year ($/ac/yr). $r \cdot PQ(t)$ denotes stand rent and $r \cdot LEV$ denotes land rent.

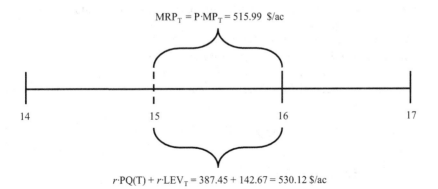

$MRP_T = P \cdot MP_T = 515.99$ $/ac

$r \cdot PQ(T) + r \cdot LEV_T = 387.45 + 142.67 = 530.12$ $/ac

Table 7.9 Comparison of the Financially Optimal Single and Multiple Rotation Ages for the Loblolly Pine Plantation Practical Application[‡]

Plantation Age	Yield (cuft/ac)	NPV ($/ac)	LEV ($/ac)	MRP ($/ac/yr)	r·PQ(t) ($/ac/yr)	r·LEV ($/ac/yr)
13	2104.73	1095.23	1732.12	515.66	304.76	138.57
14	2389.62	1167.03	1769.46	517.85	346.02	141.56
15	2675.73	1221.20	*1783.40*	515.99	387.45	142.67
16	2960.80	1258.72	1777.57	510.73	428.72	142.21
17	3242.97	1280.88	1755.28	502.66	469.58	140.42
18	3520.69	*1289.16*	1719.45	492.34	509.80	137.56
19	3792.70	1285.11	1672.70	480.29	549.18	133.82
20	4058.05	1270.33	1617.33	466.96	587.61	129.39

[‡] Yield is measured as cubic feet per acre (cuft/ac). NPV denotes net present value and is measured as dollars per acre ($/ac). LEV denotes land expectation value and is measured as dollars per acre ($/ac). MRP denotes marginal revenue product and is measured as dollars per acre per year ($/ac/yr). r denotes the real discount rate. P denotes the output price. Q(t) denotes the yield at plantation age t.

the next and all future rotations. Comparing Tables 7.5 and 7.8 or the financially optimal single and multiple rotation ages, respectively, show that the economic information contained in MRP and stand rent is the same.

Comparing equations (7.16a) and (7.10a) shows that the opportunity cost in terms of cost for LEV contains two components (stand rent and land rent) while for NPV the opportunity cost in terms of cost only contains stand rent. If land rent is positive, $r·LEV_T > 0$, then marginal revenue product must increase to cover this additional cost. Given that stumpage prices are constant at 1.81 dollars per cubic foot, this implies shortening the rotation age. In addition, Table 7.9 also shows that when LEV is maximized, the land rent component is also maximized. This is illustrated in Table 7.9 and Figure 7.12.

Figure 7.12 also compares the financially optimal multiple and single rotation ages with the optimal biological rotation age. As shown the optimal biological rotation age is the longest, followed by the financially optimal single rotation age with financially optimal multiple rotation age the shortest.[23] This also follows the fact that calculating the optimal biological rotation age uses almost no economic information, while calculating the financially optimal multiple rotation age uses the most economic information.[24]

Equation (7.14) and (7.15) describe the LEV of a very simple management regime. However, just as NPV can describe more complicated cash flows, so can LEV. Equation (7.17a) illustrates the net present value of a management regime with intermediate net cash flows (e.g., precommercial or commercial thinning, etc.)

$$NPV_t = P \cdot Q(t) \cdot (1+r)^{-t} + \sum_{k=1}^{K} \sum_{j=0}^{t} B_{kj} \cdot (1+r)^{-t}$$

$$-\sum_t C_t \cdot (1+r)^{-t}; \ t = 0,1,... \tag{7.17a}$$

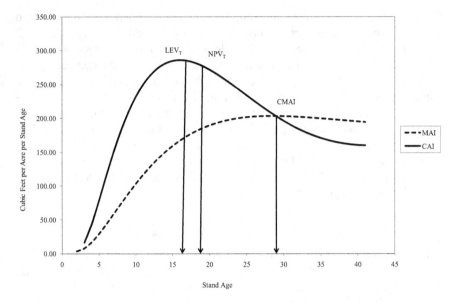

Figure 7.12 Comparison of Land Expectation Value, Net Present Value, and Optimal Biological Rotation Ages for the Loblolly Pine Plantation Practical Application‡

‡MAI denotes mean annual increment. CAI denotes current annual increment. LEV_T denotes the financially optimal multiple rotation age. NPV_T denotes the financially optimal single rotation age. CMAI
denotes the optimal biological rotation age.

where NPV_t denotes the net present value of a management regime with intermediate net cash flows; B_{kj} denotes the net cash flow of the kth intermediate action, and
the other variables are defined as before. The LEV of this management regime's
more complex cash flow is given in equation (7.17b):

$$LEV_t = \frac{NPV_t}{1-(1+r)^{-t}} = (NPV_\infty)_t \qquad (7.17b)$$

Examining equation (7.17b) reveals two observations. First, the objective is to
determine the optimal rotation age, T, that maximizes the value of the land asset.
Second, it is virtually identical to equation (7.15). Consequently, LEV can be used
to determine the financially optimal multiple rotation age of simple to complex
management regimes.[25]

In the Radiata Pine Plantation practical application, the outputs are defined in
terms of quantity; namely, cubic meters per hectare, m³/ha (m³ha⁻¹) in Table 2.7a.
As well as quality or user-defined product classes described by dimensions (i.e.,
minimum and maximum small end diameter, maximum large end diameter, and
length), shape (i.e., allowable sweep measured as the maximum deviation of
the log's centerline from a line joining the centers of the log's ends); branching
(i.e., maximum allowable size and branch angle), pruned vs. not pruned; and the

length of clear wood (i.e., the length of the log without knots). The New Zealand domestic product classes are Pulpwood, L1 – large, large-branched sawlogs, L2 – small sawlogs, P1 – large pruned sawlogs, P1 – small pruned sawlogs, S1 – large, small-branched sawlogs, and S2 – medium, small-branched sawlogs (West et al. 2013) in Table 2.7b. Tables 3.6a and 3.6b summarize the fixed and variable management costs for an unpruned and pruned Radiata Pine Plantation (the Pillars of Cost and Value). Table 4.3 provides a summary of the product classes and the 2016 New Zealand stumpage prices (NZ$m^{-3}) for radiata pine. According to Table 4.3, pulpwood has the lowest value and large pruned sawlogs have the highest value (the Pillars of Price and Value). Based on these data, I challenge the reader to calculate the land expectation value of the unpruned and pruned Radiata Pine Plantation at age 30.

The Uneven-Aged Cutting Cycle Problem (Selection System)

An uneven-aged forest contains one or more uneven-aged stands that are comprised of at least three distinct age classes or cohorts (as measured by some combination of age, diameter at breast height, and tree height) irregularly mixed within the area (Nyland 2016). Diameter distributions are commonly used to manage uneven-aged stands and thus the forest (Nyland 2016). This is characterized by using a reverse-J or the Arbogast-J (Arbogast 1957) to provide a balanced structure such that each diameter class occupies an equivalent area within the uneven-aged stand of a given basal area – as shown in Figure 7.13 (Nyland 2016). Periodic tree removal is used to bring the stand back to the balanced structure.

The structure of an uneven-aged forest is such that cutting in a diameter class will impact the growth in other diameter classes. This is in contrast to an even-age forest where age classes are spatially distinct such that cutting one age class does not impact the growth of any other age class. It is this particular interrelationship among the diameter classes of an uneven-aged forest that makes it more interesting and difficult to analyze economically.

Harvesting an uneven-aged stand never removes the growing stock completely. In contrast, regenerating an even-aged stand was based on harvest or removing the growing stock completely; that is, a clearcut.[26] The uneven-aged stand's ability to regenerate and produce volume is dependent on the diameter distribution of the tree species left in the reserve growing stock after a harvest. As there is not a distinct harvest that removes all the growing stock, the amount of time between the periodic harvests is defined as a cutting cycle. The earlier description of the production system of an uneven-aged stand is illustrated in Figure 7.14.

The long-termed sustained yield harvest from this balanced stand is defined as the periodic annual increment shown in Figure 7.14. Thus, the management decisions are to determine (1) the amount of reserve growing stock (usually measured as square feet of basal area per acre, BA/ac), (2) the appropriate diameter distribution and species composition for the reserve growing stock, and (3) the cutting cycle lengths that maximize the entrepreneur's wealth.

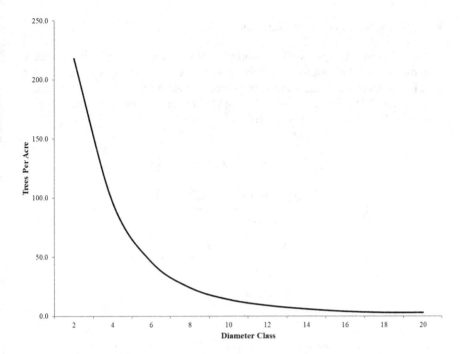

Figure 7.13 Arbogast-J of an Uneven-Aged Northeastern Hardwood Forest

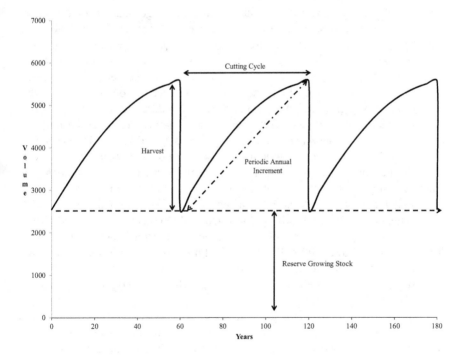

Figure 7.14 The Production System for an Uneven-Aged Stand

The economic analysis will be conducted at the individual uneven-aged stand level rather than at the uneven-aged forest level due to the complexities of uneven-aged forest-level problems.[27] The entrepreneur's wealth objective can be described by equation (7.18) as expressed by Chang (1981), Rideout (1985), Amacher et al. (2009), and Chang and Gadow (2010)

$$
\begin{aligned}
\text{USV}_{t,G} &= P \cdot \text{Vol} + \sum_{\theta=0}^{\infty} \left\{ P \cdot \left[Q(t,G) \cdot (1+r)^{-t} - G \right] \right\} \cdot \left[(1+r)^{-t} \right]^{\theta} \\
&= P \cdot \text{Vol} + \frac{P \cdot \left[Q(t,G) \cdot (1+r)^{-t} - G \right]}{1 - (1+r)^{-t}} \\
&= P \cdot \text{Vol} + \frac{P \cdot \left[Q(t,G) - G \right] \cdot (1+r)^{-t}}{1 - (1+r)^{-t}} - P \cdot G \qquad\qquad (7.18) \\
&= P \cdot (\text{Vol} - G) + \frac{P \cdot \left[Q(t,G) - G \right]}{(1+r)^{t} - 1} \\
&= P \cdot (\text{Vol} - G) + \sum_{\theta=0}^{\infty} \left\{ P \cdot \left[Q(t,G) - G \right] \cdot (1+r)^{-t} \right\} \cdot \left[(1+r)^{-t} \right]^{\theta}
\end{aligned}
$$

where $\text{USV}_{t,G}$ denotes the present value of the uneven-aged stand for a given cutting cycle t and reserve growing stock G; P denotes stumpage price; Vol denotes the initial volume; r denotes the real discount rate; and $Q(t,G)$ denotes the volume of the uneven-aged stand as a function of the cutting cycle, t, and the structure of the reserve growing stock, G.[28] The entrepreneur's management decision is to determine the optimal cutting cycle, t, and structure of reserve growing stock, G, that maximizes $\text{USV}_{t,G}$ given the initial stand condition as described by Vol.[29]

If viewed as an economic asset, then an uneven-aged stand can be modeled using two equivalent approaches illustrated graphically in Figures 7.15a and 7.15b. First, the value of the reserve growing stock at the beginning of each cutting cycle (P·G) is the investment necessary to generate the value of the inventory at the end of the cutting cycle P·[Q(t,G)]. The value of the initial reserve growing stock represents the opportunity cost of the investment necessary to obtain the periodic harvest net cash flow. Alternatively, the value of the reserve growing stock (P·G) represents the opportunity cost of the investment necessary to obtain the periodic harvest net cash flow, P·[Q(t,G) − G].[30] The timing of the harvest net cash flows (i.e., the cutting cycle length) will be determined by the value growth of the residual growing stock. The periodic harvest net cash flow is analogous to the interest income from the investment.

Changing the amount of reserve growing stock or the cutting cycle length changes the periodic harvest net cash flows and the economic asset's value. If the present value of the periodic net cash flows is greater than the initial reserve growing stock value, then investing in uneven-aged stand management provides a landowner with a greater net benefit than their alternative investment. However, if the

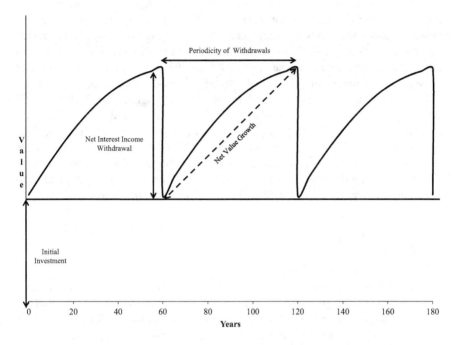

Figure 7.15a Economics of Uneven-Aged Management – Reserve Growing Stock as the Initial Investment Providing a Net Interest Income Withdrawal

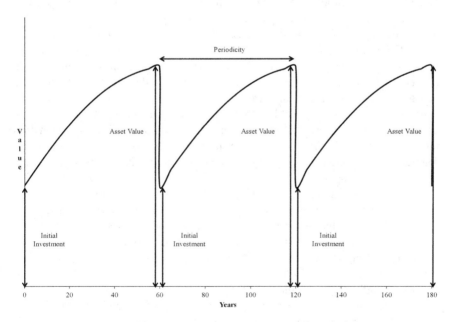

Figure 7.15b Economics of Uneven-Aged Management – Reserve Growing Stock as the Initial Investment to Obtain a Periodic Asset Value

present value of the periodic harvest net cash flows is less than the initial reserve growing stock value, then investing in an alternative investment would be better.

Marking guides to regenerate an uneven-aged stand are based on the concept of either a single-tree or a group selection (Nyland 2016). The silvicultural objective would be to maintain the classical Arbogast reverse-J structure across diameter classes within the uneven-aged stand as illustrated by Figure 7.14 (Nyland 2016). Grisez and Mendel (1972), Mendel et al. (1973), Godman and Mendel (1978), Herrick and Gansner (1985), Dennis (1987), Davies (1991), Klemperer (1996), Hseu and Buongiorno (1997), Heiligmann (2008), and Webster et al. (2009) have used an internal rate of return (*irr*) approach to describe the annual value growth rate of a representative individual or single tree of a given diameter to add a financial component to these regeneration marking guides.[31] This is illustrated by equation (7.19)

$$irr = \left(\frac{P \cdot q(T,g)}{P \cdot g} \right)^{\frac{1}{T}} - 1 \tag{7.19}$$

where P denotes the stumpage price, q(T,g) denotes the volume of the representative individual or single tree of a given diameter as a function of the length of the cutting cycle, T, and its volume at the beginning of the cutting cycle, g. The general rule is that if the tree's *irr* is greater (less) than an appropriate real discount rate, the tree is (is not) financially mature.[32] Using this general rule implies the annual value growth rate as given by the *irr* is equated with a real discount rate. Unfortunately, this common interpretation of the *irr* is not accurate. The *irr* given in equation (7.19) describes the expected annual value growth of the tree *ex ante*; that is, barring any fires, insect infestations, drought, or damage due to weather, and so on. *Ex post*, if P·q(T,g) does occur given P·g, then *irr* does describe the annual value growth of the tree. That said, the only accurate statement that can be made concerning the *irr* is that if it is greater than the appropriate real discount rate, there is a greater likelihood that an entrepreneur's wealth will increase. An entrepreneur's wealth increases is tied directly to the real discount rate, not the *irr*. Finally, using equation (7.19) to help develop a marking guide's take or leave decision does not include (i) the implications of one or more trees occupying the same growing space; (ii) the current tree occupying the site and not allowing the next tree to take its place (i.e., the opportunity cost of the land or land rent as described in equation (7.16b) (Johansson and Löfgren (1985) and Hseu and Buongiorno (1997)); or (iii) it is not the size of the tree, but rather the tree's effect on the rate of value growth *of the whole stand* that determines whether a tree should be kept – trees that cannot satisfy this requirement should be harvested (Chang 1981; Chang and Gadow 2010). This is important given a selection system. Consequently, caution is advised when using equation (7.19) to define the concept of financial maturity for a representative individual or single tree of a given diameter using a selection system.

This economic analysis of even-aged to uneven-aged systems asserted that the economic information – parameters and variables that describe the market conditions and the production system – given in Tables 7.3, 7.7, 7.8, 7.9, and 7.10 and

Figures 7.14, 7.15a, and 7.15b remain the same for an infinite number of rotations. This appears problematic and will be addressed directly in the section entitled Analytical Hazards – Forever Is a Long Time.

Analytical Hazards

The Production System – Revisited

The foundation of the Architectural Plan for Profit is the production system (Figure 7.1 and Chapter 2 – Production Systems). This still holds regardless of the three generic capital cash flows analyzed earlier. An entrepreneur can get lost in the mechanics of estimating a least cost or $(NPV_\infty)_T$ solution and assume the Pillars of Price, Value, and Cost are taken care of automatically. The Pillars of Price, Value, and Cost are built, in part, with the economic information generated from the production system (Figure 7.1). If inaccurate or incomplete production information is used to build the Pillars of Price, Value, and Cost, then Profits (or in this case Wealth) will not convey what the entrepreneur thinks it does. In this case make sure you are producing the output you believe you are by answering the three fundamental questions to systematically examine any production system sufficiently. Conclusion: Do not get so lost in or enamored by the mechanics of what you are doing that you forget if the economic interpretation of what you are doing makes sense. After all, the reason you do these calculations is to generate accurate economic information to help make better business decisions.

The financially optimal single and multiple rotation ages for the Loblolly Pine Plantation practical application were determined to be 1,289.16 $/ac at a plantation age of 18 and 1,783.40 $/ac at plantation age of 15, respectively (Table 7.7). These solutions were determined assuming a 1.81 $/cuft price for "sawtimber." According to Figure 7.6, the output is defined as volume measured in cubic feet per acre. Sawtimber is the output, so what is sawtimber? Sawtimber defines a specific quality, product class, or grade of output. Table 7.10 defines loblolly pine product classes by diameter at breast height (DBH).

Table 7.10 Loblolly Pine Product Class by Diameter at Breast Height (DBH) Range[‡]

Product Class	DBH Range
Pulpwood	4.6 inches ≤ DBH ≤ 9 inches
Chip-n-saw	9 inches ≤ DBH ≤ 12 inches
Sawtimber	12 inches ≤ DBH

[‡] Product class ranges are based on a paper entitled "Economics of growing slash and loblolly pine to a 33-year rotation – impact of thinning at various stumpage prices" by E. David Dickens, Coleman W. Dangerfield, Jr., and David J. Moorhead from the Warnell School of Forest Resources at the University of Georgia, Athens (https://bugwoodcloud.org/bugwood/productivity/pdfs/SeriesPaper6.pdf accessed 4 September 2023)

So, the question is: Are 19- or 16-year-old loblolly pine trees sawtimber? The answer is *NO*. A review of the loblolly pine production system – as given by Amateis and Burkhart (1985) and Burkhart et al. (1985) – shows that DBH is not one of the relevant inputs used in answering the question from Chapter 2 – Production Systems: What are the relevant inputs? While the description of the production system is complex, it is not sufficient for determining if in fact 19- or 16-year old loblolly pine trees are sawtimber and if the interpretations of the calculated NPV and LEV values make economic sense. This point needs to be re-emphasized: It is not the mathematical calculations or the wealth searching rule developed and described in equations (7.10a) and (7.16a) that are of concern; these mathematical calculations are done correctly. It is the economic interpretation of the results that is important. As the production system does not provide volume by DBH class, the financially optimal single and multiple rotation ages of 16 and 19 could be incorrect. Then using this information would not maximize wealth.

Tasissa et al. (1997) and Sharma and Oderwald (2001) provide mathematical relationships between volume, height, and DBH for loblolly pine. These relationships can be used to estimate DBH for the Loblolly Pine Plantation practical application. Based the information provided by these authors and the description of the management regime, it would take approximately 30 to 40 years to grow a 12-inch loblolly pine.[33] The land expectation value using a plantation age of 30 is 916 $/ac.

In contrast, the Select Red Oak practical application provides explicit information on the DBH of individual select red oak trees. However, the inputs are defined as DBH and site index. What is missing to determine a financially optimal rotation age is stand age. Thus, a secondary source of information would again be required to link DBH and site index to tree age. Then a financially optimal rotation age could be estimated for individual select red oak trees.

I purposefully developed and presented the Loblolly Pine Plantation practical application to highlight this particular analytical hazard. The conclusion from the initial paragraph bears repeating: Do not get so lost in or enamored by the mechanics of what you are doing that you forget if the economic interpretation of what you are doing makes sense. After all, the reason you do these calculations is to generate accurate economic information to help make better business decisions.

Forever Is a Long Time

The economic analysis of the 1,000 kW ground mount solar array asserted that economic information – parameters and variables that describe the market conditions and the production system – given in Tables 7.2a to 7.2g and Figures 7.4a to 7.4b remain the same for an infinite number of solar array replacements. Consequently, the efficient resource allocation rule of capital replacement that maximizes wealth given by equation (7.7) appears to be inflexible. On the surface, this appears problematic as forever is a very long time for the parameters and variables that describe the market conditions and the production system to be constant. However, I would again refer the reader to Tables 7.2a to 7.2g. These tables represent components of a spreadsheet, which is a useful tool to examine the impact of changing model parameters and variables (Conrad 2010).[34] Consequently, an entrepreneur should develop a strategy to revisit their analyses periodically given new information for the parameters and variables that describe market conditions and the production system.

Solar arrays can keep on converting insolation as long as physically and physically capable. However, solar array modules deteriorate, inverters wear out, and the electrical and structural BOS wears out. For example, the median installed price of a photovoltaic system has decreased by approximately $0.33 per year from 2010 to 2018 (www.nrel.gov/docs/fy19osti/73234.pdf accessed 19 September 2019). From 2010 to 2020, there was a 64%, 69%, and 82% reduction in the residential, commercial rooftop, and utility-scale (one-axis) PV system cost benchmark, respectively. A significant portion of that reduction can be attributed to total hardware costs (module, inverter, and hardware BOS), with module prices dropping 85% over that period (Feldman et al. 2021). Conversion efficiencies, under ideal conditions, have increased by approximately 0.3% to 0.4% per year (Feldman et al. 2021).

So, because future arrays will not be similar to this array, what use is all this analysis? Examining the Wealth Searching – Capital Replacement – Rule:

$$MR_T = R_T = OM_T + rSV_T + EAE(NPV_\infty)_T = MC_T$$

gives us the answer. A power of this replacement rule is that it forces you to think about what comes next and when – explicitly. As described by the replacement rule, this is captured by $EAE(NPV_\infty)_T$ directly. Namely, how sensitive is "T" to

- Changes in $EAE(NPV_\infty)_T$ due to future decrease in modular costs and electrical and structural BOS costs?
- Changes in $EAE(NPV_\infty)_T$ due increasing modular efficiencies?
- Changes in $EAE(NPV_\infty)_T$ due to variability in O&M costs and electric prices?

The relevant ranges for these "changes" is based on your knowledge gained by reviewing the relevant technical literature and knowledge of the markets.

To illustrate a simplified example, I will use an approach based on the work of Wagner and Holmes (1999). Assume that the NPV of future solar arrays will increase at the annual efficiency increases of solar panels of between 0.3% and 0.4 % per year. Thus, the opportunity cost of holding on to the current array for an additional year, t + 1, is a function of the possible increases of efficiencies available if the array is replaced at time t. Examining the Wealth Searching – Capital Replacement – Rule, the $EAE(NPV_\infty)_T$ is part of the marginal costs. Assuming the two other terms reflect costs associated with the existing solar array, increasing $EAE(NPV_\infty)_T$ will increase marginal costs. This can be model by

$$EAE\left(\overline{NPV_\infty}\right)_t = EAE\left(\left[NPV_t\,(1+\phi)^t\right]_\infty\right)_t$$

where $\mathrm{EAE}\left(\overline{\mathrm{NPV}}_\infty\right)_t$ is the equal annual equivalent of expected NPV_t at time t given increased efficiencies and $0.003 \leq \phi \leq 0.004$. To examine how this would work, let t = 21 and $\phi = 0.0035$; the estimated effects of increases in solar panel efficiencies on NPV_{21} are given by $(1 + \phi)^{21} = (1.0035)^{21}$

$$\mathrm{EAE}\left(\overline{\mathrm{NPV}}_\infty\right)_t = \mathrm{EAE}\left(\left[\mathrm{NPV}_t\,(1{+}\phi)^t\right]_\infty\right)_t$$

$$\mathrm{EAE}\left(\overline{\mathrm{NPV}}_\infty\right)_{21} = \mathrm{EAE}\left(\left[904{,}104(1.0035)^{21}\right]_\infty\right)_{21}$$

$$\mathrm{EAE}\left(\overline{\mathrm{NPV}}_\infty\right)_{21} = 75{,}885$$

Examining the result, the equal annual equivalent is now 75,885, which is an increase from 70,517. Consequently, the marginal cost of holding the array for an additional year is increasing.

Thus revenues, R_t, must increase to cover this additional opportunity cost. As the existing solar panels are losing efficiency annually, revenue decreases with time as is shown in the spreadsheet and in the graph of revenues given in an earlier slide. Thus, the only way to increase revenues is to replace the existing solar array earlier.

The modeling of the solar array increases in efficiency using $(1 + \phi)^t$ is unsophisticated due to the previously stated Shockley–Queisser limit defining the maximum solar conversion efficiencies is 33%. A more sophisticated model would have the increases in efficiencies become asymptotic at 33% given the existing efficiencies plus incorporating decreasing installation costs and so on. However, this type of sophisticated modeling is beyond the scope of this book and is discussed in various publications such as Jenkin et al. (2019), Walker et al. (2020), Feldman et al. (2020), Heeter et al. (2020), and Feldman et al. (2021). The purpose of this example is to illustrate the power of the Wealth Searching – Capital Replacement – Rule. A unique feature of capital assets is that they wear out. If you are given decision-making authority for managing these capital assets, I can virtually guarantee that you will also be asked at some point to justify or defend your

Table 7.11 Optimal Capital Replacement Age of a 1,000 kW Ground Mount Solar Array Located Near Syracuse, New York, USA, Given Solar Array Increases in Conversion Efficiency of $0.003 \leq \phi \leq 0.004$ Annually

ϕ	T
0	52
0.003	47
0.0035	46
0.004	45

As can be seen by Table 7.11, as the estimate of future solar array efficiency increases, the optimal time to replace the existing solar array will decrease.

management decisions concerning when to replace them, especially when you are using someone else's money. This wealth searching rule identifies explicitly what the economic information is that you will need to justify your decision. This wealth searching rule identifies explicitly how this economic information relates to each other in a meaningful that you will need to justify your decision.

An alternative approach to using equation (7.7) is the Obsolescence Replacement Rule of Thumb: A 20% loss in efficiency determines when to replace a solar array (www.nrel.gov/docs/fy12osti/51664.pdf accessed 22 December 2018). The reasoning behind the Obsolescence Replacement Rule of Thumb is to account for increasing solar conversion efficiencies given a maximum efficiency of approximately 33% and the annual insolation conversion efficiency loss. Based on this Obsolescence Replacement Rule of Thumb, the 1,000 kW ground mount solar array would be replaced after 20 to 40 years. According to Table 7.2g, the maximum wealth criteria would recommend replacing the solar array after 52 years. The Obsolescence Replacement Rule of Thumb appears reasonable and is a lot easier to calculate, so why not use it? Unfortunately, the answer to this question is to ask another: What is the economic information used in the Obsolescence Replacement Rule of Thumb? The simple answer is only the production system. It does not contain any information from the Pillars of Cost, Value, and Price. Production systems produce outputs. A purely physical measure of output ignores the fact that individuals assign values to outputs (as well as inputs). Production systems do not produce "values," rather they produce goods and services that individuals "assign value" to in a given context. Thus, this rule of thumb does not satisfy the assertion that individuals are wealth maximizers.

The economic analysis of the Loblolly Pine Plantation practical application asserted that the economic information – parameters and variables that describe the market conditions and the production system – given in Tables 7.3, 7.7, 7.8, 7.9, and 7.10 remain the same for an infinite number of rotations. Consequently, the wealth-maximizing efficient resource allocation rule of capital replacement given by equation (7.16a) appears to be inflexible. This financially optimal rotation age (capital replacement rule) was derived from the Faustmann formula given in equation (7.15). The Faustmann formula has a long and rich history – note the original article by Martin Faustmann was first published in 1849 – of addressing issues of variability associated with the parameters and variables. Hool (1966) and Lembersky and Johnson (1975) are two early papers examining the impacts of variability in the parameters and variables on the optimal rotation age. Amacher et al. (2009) continues this rich history. As forever is a long time and biological and market systems are dynamic, an entrepreneur should develop a strategy to revisit their analyses periodically given new information for the parameters and variables that describe market conditions, production system, and the management regime. As before, a spreadsheet is a useful tool to examine the impact of changing model parameters and variables (Conrad 2010).

Newman (1988, 2002) provides a review of the rich and historic literature associated with the Faustmann formula and its variations. Finally, many journals have had special issues devoted to research based on the Faustmann formula (e.g.,

Journal of Forest Economics 1995 1(1) and 2000 6(3), *Forest Science* 2001 47(4), *Forest Policy and Economics* 2001 2(2)). The number of articles and manuscripts using variations of the Faustmann formula with respect to sustainable forest management shows no signs of slowing down (Newman and Wagner 2012).

Figure 7.12 illustrates that the financially optimal single and multiple rotation ages and the optimal biological rotation age do not appear to be *all* that different. Thus, would it matter which one was chosen? This question is similar to the Obsolescence Replacement Rule of Thumb for a solar array. The answer is exactly the same: The optimal biological rotation age (or maximum sustained yield rotation age) only contains information on the production system; it does not contain any information on the Pillars of Price, Value, and Cost.[35] Hyytiäinen and Tahvonen (2003) examined this question and concluded that rotation ages based on the optimal biological criteria led to major losses in economic value. It is worth repeating: Production systems do not produce "values," rather they produce goods and services that individuals "assign value" to in a given context. They did not examine the financially optimal single rotation age as the landowners were managing their lands for multiple rotations. However, if the lands are managed for multiple rotations and the financially optimal single rotation age was chosen, this would also result in the loss in economic value.

The Faustmann formula describes the present value of a perpetual periodic generation of net revenues from forest management. For the forest to generate this periodic net revenue stream perpetually, an argument could be made that the Faustmann formula implies sustainably managing the forest – as an ecosystem – so it can produce this net revenue stream. Unfortunately, there is no single accepted definition of sustainable forest management, and I will not attempt to address that issue here; however, common themes emerge from these definitions that include maintaining the forest system, using forest-based ecosystem goods and services that do not impact future generations, multiple stakeholders, and scale. The Faustmann formula would seem to address one of the tenets of sustainable forest management. However, the determination of the financially optimal multiple rotation age requires that the exact same management regime be repeated forever and the land, as a biological and ecological production system, also remains constant forever. The latter condition is important to revisit briefly. The continual harvesting and regenerating a stand will probably impact the productive ability of the land (Erickson et al. 1999; Navarro 2003). In addition to making sure you are producing the output you expect, you need to be aware of how your management actions affect the production system – in this case the forested ecosystem. While the Faustmann formula is a conceptual improvement over the single rotation model because it includes a land rent component in the optimal financial rotation rule, entrepreneurs should be aware of all its economic as well as biological and ecological implications.

Finally, we know that landowners have a myriad of reasons for determining their optimal rotation age. In reality, they will use the rotation length that best meets their management objectives and time preferences, subject to market conditions. There may be social or cultural reasons for determining an optimal rotation age. For instance, if prices rise dramatically, would we expect landowners to harvest their timber sooner? Most assuredly we would, which pulls us away from CMAI. Likewise, if the government expands replanting subsidies, lowering the cost of management, would not we also expect an earlier harvest?

Advanced Topics

Optimal Financial Rotation Age Given an Existing Forest

The optimal single and multiple rotation ages described earlier assumed that the entrepreneur started with bare land, established, and then harvested the forest. What if the land had an existing forest? I will use the Loblolly Pine Plantation practical application to demonstrate the investment analysis of this scenario. Figure 7.16 illustrates this situation.

The existing forest is illustrated by the upper left-hand corner of Figure 7.16. Once this existing forest is harvested, a continuous regeneration–harvest pattern can be established, which is illustrated by the lower right-hand corner of Figure 7.16. This portion of Figure 7.16 is taken from Figure 7.9.

The investment analysis model to analyze this problem, based on that developed by Rideout (1985), is given by equation (7.20)

$$FV = P \cdot Q(N+t) \cdot (1+r)^{-t} + LEV_t \cdot (1+r)^{-t} \tag{7.20}$$

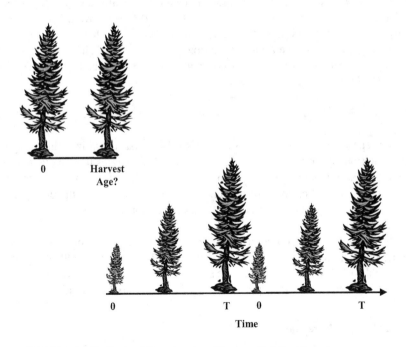

Figure 7.16 Financially Optimal Rotation Age Given an Existing Forest

Table 7.12 Investment Analysis of a 12-Year-Old Loblolly Pine Plantation Practical Application[‡]

Plantation Age	Yield (cuft/ac)	Total Revenue ($/ac)	FV ($/ac)
12	1,823.64	3,300.79	5,084.19
13	2,104.73	3,809.56	5,178.66
14	2,389.62	4,325.22	5,237.15
15	2,675.73	4,843.06	5,260.30
16	2,960.80	5,359.05	5,249.91
17	3,242.97	5,869.78	5,208.62
18	3,520.69	6,372.44	5,139.56

[‡] Yield is measured as cubic feet per acre (cuft/ac). Total revenue is measured as dollars per acre ($/ac). Forest value (FV) is measured as dollars per acre ($/ac). LEV_T is defined as 1,783.40 dollars per acre ($/ac) from Table 9.4.

$$5260.30 = 1.81 \cdot 2675.73 \cdot (1.08)^{-3} + 1783.40 \cdot (1.08)^{-3}$$

where FV denotes the forest value; $Q(N + t)$ denotes the per acre volume of the existing forest at plantation age N with $t = 0,1,2,3, \ldots$; and LEV_t denotes the land expectation value of the continuous regeneration–harvest management regime at a rotation age of t. The entrepreneur's objective is to maximize the FV. If equation (7.20) is to be maximized, each component must be maximized. As Rideout (1985) points out, this is problematic as the term $P \cdot Q(N + t) \cdot (1 + r)^{-t}$ would dominate the analysis. The term LEV_t denotes a steady-state condition; that is, for any given rotation age, t, the regeneration–harvest pattern is constant. The optimal steady-state condition is given by LEV_T from equation (7.16a). Substituting LEV_T into equation (7.20) gives equation (7.21):

$$FV_t = P \cdot Q(N+t) \cdot (1+r)^{-t} + LEV_T \cdot (1+r)^{-t} \; ; t = 0,1,2,3,\ldots \qquad (7.21)$$

The entrepreneur's objective is to determine the *t* that maximizes the FV given the plantation age of the existing stand. Table 7.12 illustrates this analysis for the Loblolly Pine Plantation practical application given that the existing plantation is 12 years old. Based on the information contained in Table 7.12, the entrepreneur should wait three years before cutting the existing plantation and regenerating the next rotation.[36]

The analysis presented here assumed the only revenue was from the sale of the timber without other costs or revenues. Equation (7.21) can be modified to include additional costs and revenues within the existing forest and the land expectation value terms. However, the analysis approach would be similar to that described earlier.

Forests Produce More Than Just Wood

The focus thus far has been on producing timber or biomass from the forest. Forests produce many other values besides timber or biomass; some may produce income directly and some may not. Familiar examples are maple syrup, mushrooms, pine straw, wildlife, and water flows. In some cases, they can be converted into outputs that can be sold in established markets easily; for example, maple syrup, mushrooms, or pine straw. Others can be marketed and sold as the right to participate in an experience; for example, recreation leases for hunting, fishing, hiking, or wildlife viewing. Or, instead of being sold they may be enjoyed directly by the entrepreneur/landowner as a component of the net benefit from owning forestland (e.g., Butler 2008, 2010; Butler et al. 2016). The economic analysis of producing these outputs has often been described as a joint production process of timber plus these non-timber outputs. This is illustrated by Figures 7.17a and 7.17b.

Figures 7.17a and 7.17b illustrate an "even-aged" conifer and "multi-aged" mixed hardwood-softwood forest respectively, and the joint production process of timber plus non-timber outputs as a function of structure, density, species diversity and composition, and time. Forest structure (e.g., trees per unit area by diameter distribution or a diameter distribution diagram (Nyland 2016)) can be used to identify timber and non-timber outputs at a given point in time (t) or for a given segment (t) to (t + j) with $j = 1,2,3, \ldots$. Or a desired suite of non-timber outputs can be used to describe a desired forest structure. Different wildlife species have different habitat requirements and different structural requirements. This is illustrated explicitly by the lines associated with different species corresponding to different habitat or forest structures on Figures 7.17a and 7.17b.

Forest structure changes can result from natural succession or from purposeful management actions that manipulate structure, density, and species diversity and composition to achieve or maintain a desired future condition given the

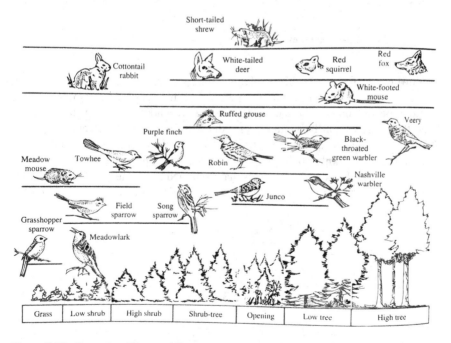

Figure 7.17a Even-Aged Forested Ecosystem

Sources: Smith (1959); Kimmins (1997)

Short-tailed shrew

White-tailed deer   Red squirrel   Red fox

White-footed mouse

Cotton-tail Rabbit

Ruffed Grouse

Veery

Meadow mouse   Purple Finch   Towhee

Nashville warbler

Grasshopper sparrow

Robin   Black-throated green warbler   Junco

Field sparrow   Song sparrow

Meadowlark

Grass   Low shrub   Shrub-tree   Low tree   High tree

Figure 7.17b Multi-Aged Forested System

landowner's goals and objectives. Manipulating structure is associated with cutting trees, preferably, via a silvicultural prescription. If the non-timber and final ecosystem outputs/outcomes value can be described as dependent on the age of the forest, then these values can be included into the Faustmann model given in equation (7.15). A reasonable question would be: How do these non-timber outputs/outcomes impact the timber only financially optimal multiple rotation age derived in equation (7.16a)? Two classic articles that examined this issue are Hartman (1976) and Calish et al. (1978).[37] The Hartman (1976) model is given in equation (7.22)

$$W_T = \frac{P \cdot Q(T) \cdot (1+r)^{-T} + \sum_{j=0}^{T} B_j \cdot (1+r)^{-t} - C_0}{1 - (1+r)^{-T}}$$

$$= \frac{P \cdot Q(T) \cdot (1+r)^{-T} - C_0}{1 - (1+r)^{-T}} + \frac{\sum_{j=0}^{T} B_j \cdot (1+r)^{-t}}{1 - (1+r)^{-T}} \qquad 7.22)$$

$$= LEV_T + E_T$$

where W_T denotes the entrepreneur's wealth, B_j denotes the non-timber or final ecosystem outputs/outcomes value as a function of a forest's age and accrues annually, and all other variables are defined as before. The first term on the right-hand side of equation (7.22) defines the land expectation value (LEV_T) given in equation (7.15). The second term defines the present value of the non-timber or final ecosystem outcomes/outputs value that accumulate until the wealth-maximizing optimal rotation age, T, given an infinite sequence of rotations, E_T.

The entrepreneur's decision is to determine the value for T that maximizes their wealth described in equation (7.22). The opportunity costs in terms of revenue and cost for determining the financially optimal multiple rotation age were given in equation (7.16a) without non-timber or ecosystem outputs/outcomes value. Amacher et al. (2009) defines an analogous wealth searching rule given in equations (7.23a) to (7.23c)

$$MB_T = P \cdot MP_T + B_T = r \cdot \left[P \cdot Q(T) \right] + r \cdot \left(LEV_T + E_T \right) = MC_T \qquad (7.23a)$$

$$MB_T = P \cdot MP_T + B_T \qquad (7.23b)$$

$$MC_T = r \cdot \left[P \cdot Q(T) \right] + r \cdot \left(LEV_T + E_T \right) \qquad (7.23c)$$

where B_T denotes the non-timber or ecosystem outcomes/outputs value at the wealth-maximizing optimal multiple rotation age, and all other variables are defined as before. Equation (7.23b) highlights the marginal benefit, MB_T, component. This includes the marginal revenue product from allowing the timber to grow an additional year, $P \cdot MP_T$, plus the benefit from the non-timber or ecosystem outputs/outcomes. Equation (7.23c) highlights the marginal cost, MC_T, component. This can still be divided into a stand rent term, $r \cdot [P \cdot Q(T)]$, and a land rent term, $r \cdot (LEV_T + E_T) = r \cdot LEV_T + r \cdot E_T$. As can be seen, stand rent is defined as before, but land rent now includes the present value of net benefits of the non-timber or ecosystem outputs/outcomes values for an infinite sequence of rotations, E_T. Specifically, $r \cdot LEV_T = EAE(NPV_\infty)_T$ denotes "timber" land rent or the opportunity cost of the land with respect to timber: The amount of money the land's owner must receive to keep the land growing the current trees and forgo the present value of net revenues from all future periodic timber harvests (i.e., economic rent). And $r \cdot E_T$ denotes the "non-timber" land rent or the opportunity cost of the land with respect to the non-timber values: The amount of money the land's owner must receive to keep the land growing the current forested ecosystem structure and forgo the present value of the net annual benefits from all future final ecosystem outputs/outcomes. These opportunity costs can be interpreted in the same manner as described for equations (7.16a) and (7.16b).

Amacher et al. (2009) describes the effects of the non-timber or final ecosystem outputs/outcomes values, B_j, on the financially optimal multiple rotation age (as given by equation (7.16a)) depends on the value of $B_T - r \cdot E_T$; namely, the final ecosystem output/outcome value at the wealth-maximizing optimal multiple rotation age and the opportunity cost of these values if the harvest is delayed. These authors showed that if the final ecosystem outputs/outcomes values increase as the forest grows older, $\dfrac{\Delta B_t}{\Delta t} > 0$ for all relevant values of t, including these values into

the rotation age decision will lengthen the financially optimal multiple rotation age. For example, Calish et al. (1978) illustrated this with Douglas fir and cutthroat trout, Roosevelt elk, aesthetics, or nongame wildlife in the United States' Pacific Northwest. If the final ecosystem outputs/outcomes values decrease as the forest

grows older, $\dfrac{\Delta B_t}{\Delta t} < 0$ for all relevant values of t, including these values into the

rotation age decision will shorten the financially optimal multiple rotation age. For example, Calish et al. (1978) illustrated this with Douglas fir and Columbian black-tailed deer and water yield in the United States' Pacific Northwest.[38] Finally, if the final ecosystem outputs/outcomes values do not change as the forest grows older,

$\dfrac{\Delta B_t}{\Delta t} = 0$ for all relevant values of t, including these values into the rotation age

decision will not change. For example, the short-tailed shrew in Figures 7.17a and 7.17b. Amacher et al. (2009) summarizes these implications:

> The landowner [entrepreneur] should harvest a stand of trees when the sum of the marginal harvest revenue and amenity benefit from delaying harvest for one period equals the opportunity cost of delay harvest, where the opportunity cost is defined as rent on the value of the stand plus the rent on the value of the land (timber plus amenities).
>
> Amacher et al. (2009: 51)

Implicit in the aforementioned analysis was that the stand was an independent entity. That is, nothing else within the landscape impacted the stand's timber and non-timber or amenity values. This implicit assumption can be relaxed to examine the effects of spatial and temporal interdependence among stands. Amacher et al. (2009) also provide an excellent review of the mathematical economic models and literature that examine this issue. The development of these models is beyond the scope of this book. However, I would encourage interested reader to examine the work of Amacher et al. (2009).

Recently, the focus has shifted from producing multiple outputs in a sustainable manner to sustaining the forest-based ecosystem that produces these outputs (e.g., Sexton et al. 1999; Patterson and Coelho 2009; Wunder and Wertz-Kanounnikoff 2009).[39] This evolutionary shift in focus has required rethinking and describing the production system with respect to forest-based ecosystem processes, goods, and services. The description of the production process begins with defining forest-based ecosystem processes. Brown et al. (2007: 332) defines ecosystem processes as "the complex physical and biological cycles and interactions that underlie what we observe as the natural world." Ecosystem processes are the cycles and interactions among the abiotic and biotic structures of the ecosystem that produce ecosystem goods and services (Brown et al. 2007). These ecosystem processes exist whether humans are present or not and whether humans have preferences for them or not and can be identified using various descriptors; for example nutrient cycling. Brown et al. (2007: 332) define ecosystem services as "the specific results of those [ecosystem] processes that either directly sustain or enhance human life (as does natural protection from the sun's harmful UV rays) or maintain the quality of ecosystem goods (as water purification maintains the quality of stream flow)." Brown et al. (2007: 330–331) define ecosystem goods as "the tangible, material products that result from ecosystem processes." So, while water and air purification are forest-based ecosystem services, water and air are ecosystem goods as is biomass in the form of timber and fiber (Brown et al. 2007). Boyd and Banzhaf (2005, 2007), Kroeger and Casey (2007) Escobedo et al. (2011), and Haines-Young and Potschin (2013) narrow the definition of ecosystem goods and services to end products of nature that are directly enjoyed, consumed, or used to produce human well-being. These contributions have been further classified as biotic and abiotic provisioning, regulating and maintenance/supporting, and cultural services (Common International Classification of Ecosystem Services https://cices.eu/ accessed 15 March 2021). For expositional ease, output to describe commodity goods such as wood fiber, biomass, forage, aquatic and terrestrial wildlife, water, recreation, and energy from primarily the provisioning ecosystem service classification and *outcomes* to describe final ecosystem services such as wildlife habitat, aesthetics, nutrient cycling, and the like from primarily the regulating and maintenance and cultural services. This definition is the most practical because it is well suited to measuring environmental quality and estimating values of ecosystem goods and services.[40] This end-product definition avoids the double counting that can result from adding the value of intermediate products to determine the value of a final good. As Boyd and Banzhaf (2007) describe, this does not mean that intermediate ecosystem goods and services are not valuable, rather their value is embodied in the value measurement of the end-product ecosystem outputs/outcomes. In addition, end-product ecosystem outputs/outcomes may not necessarily be the final product consumed. The final product consumed may include end-product ecosystem outputs/outcomes and conventional goods and services. For example, fish populations, surroundings, and water bodies are the end-product ecosystem services used by anglers directly to produce recreational benefits. In this case fish populations are both end-product ecosystem outputs as well as a final economic good (Boyd and Banzhaf 2005, 2007).

Some forest-based ecosystem outputs have markets that are well established, such as those for stumpage and timber (for example www.srs.fs.usda.gov/econ/timberprices/ accessed 2 October 2019). Other markets for forest-based ecosystem outputs are emerging; for example, the markets for carbon credits and offsets (https://ctxglobal.com/ accessed 22 September 2019, https://ww3.arb.ca.gov/cc/capandtrade/capandtrade.htm accessed 22 September 2019, and https://ec.europa.eu/clima/policies/ets_en accessed 22 September 2019) and wetlands mitigation banking (www.epa.gov/wetlandmitigation/ accessed 22 September 2019). Developing these markets was possible by creating a tradable good that has the following characteristics: (a) additional, (b) real, (c) quantifiable and verifiable, (d) permanent, and (e) exclusive with transferable ownership and legal title (e.g., Ruddell et al. 2007). This potentially allows entrepreneurs who own forestland, for example, to capture the benefits of producing carbon sequestration. Developing markets for other forest-based ecosystem outcomes will depend on (a) a perception that the provision of the forest-based ecosystem outcome is scarce, (b) developing tradable commodities with characteristics similar to those for carbon credits, (c) developing institutions (e.g., banks, brokers, etc.) to aid in transactions among consumers and producers, and (d) the ending market structures (e.g., Kemkes et al. 2009). Whether any of these forest-based ecosystem outputs/outcomes will have any impact on an entrepreneur's management activities will depend on whether the market value set by society is large enough for entrepreneurs to modify their management behavior. For example, Hancock Timberland Investor (2000) showed that when the alternative uses of timberland are commercial or residential development, very high carbon prices would be required to have any meaningful impact on land conversion as development values are just too high relative to forestland values. Time will tell if and how the development of markets for forest-based ecosystem goods and services will affect forestland management (Kline et al. 2009).

Capital Theory: Natural Resources Management Puzzle – Variability

This has been described as a natural or physical capital analysis problem. The optimal capital replacement rules included the opportunity cost of keeping the current asset in place and forgoing the net revenue of replacing it. This cost is defined as $EAE(NPV_\infty)_T$ or $r \cdot LEV_T$. Recognizing and thus including this cost was a theoretical breakthrough in analyzing these problems accurately. The practical implication is that the investment horizons are infinite. Forever is a long time for parameters and variables of these problems to remain constant. Natural and physical production systems are dynamic due to changes in production technology or in the ecosystem. Markets are also dynamic due to output price variability, macroeconomic events, and new outputs from the joint production processes. One approach to dealing with potential variability associated with parameters and variables is to evaluate tenable pessimistic, realistic, and optimistic scenarios for each alternative. This is approach is called sensitivity analysis and will be described in more detail in Chapter 8 – Risk.

How to Use Economic Information – the Natural Resources Management Puzzle – to Make Better Business Decisions

The natural resources management puzzle begins with recognizing that it is a multi-input, multi-period, multi-output joint production process. Any management decision implies using inputs – labor, materials, capital, and time – to manipulate the production system to produce the desired outputs/outcomes. As with previous chapters, the Architectural Plan for Profit or in this case Wealth (Figure 7.1) describes the required economic information. Also as defined in Chapter 6 – Capital Theory: Investment Analysis, the net present value (NPV) formula is the best criterion to use given these analyses (Luenberger 1998). To illustrate the economic information depicted graphically in Figure 7.1, I will tie the information directly to the NPV formula:

$$NPV_T = \sum_{t=0}^{T} P_t \cdot Q(L,M,K,t)(1+r)^{-t} - \sum_{t=0}^{T} C_t (1+r)^{-t}$$

$$= \sum_{t=0}^{T} \left(P_t \cdot Q(L,M,K,t) - C_t \right)(1+r)^{-t}$$

$$= \sum_{t=0}^{T} \frac{P_t \cdot Q(L,M,K,t)}{(1+r)^t} - \sum_{t=0}^{T} \frac{C_t}{(1+r)^t}$$

$$= \sum_{t=0}^{T} \frac{P_t \cdot Q(L,M,K,t) - C_t}{(1+r)^t}$$

where $Q(L,M,K,t)$ is the production system using the inputs labor (L), materials (M), capital (K), and time (t) to produce output(s)/outcomes(s). The Pillars of Cost and Value for the inputs – L, M, K, t – is represented by C_t. The Pillar of Price for the output(s)/outcome(s) is represented by P_t. The Pillar of Value for the output(s)/outcome(s) is represented by $P_t \cdot Q(L,M,K,t)$. The opportunity cost of time is given by $(1+r)^{-t}$ and is represented in the Pillars of Cost, Value, and Price. The Architectural Plan for Profit/Wealth and NPV identifies the specific economic information the entrepreneur must collect.

The natural resources management puzzle can also be described as a capital analysis problem. In this context, capital is defined as natural and physical capital. The generic cash flow categories associated with this capital were (1) costs with no direct revenue stream, (2) costs with annual direct revenue stream, and (3) costs with periodic direct revenue stream. A unique aspect of analyzing the puzzle given these capital assets and cash flows is their repeating characteristic; namely, replacing a piece of equipment or solar array or managing a forested ecosystem sustainably. This unique aspect is modeled economically using

$$\left(NPV_\infty \right)_T = \frac{NPV_T}{1-(1+r)^{-T}}$$

Given the analytical tools described earlier, addressing the statement how to use economic information to make better business and management decisions correctly given the first cash flow is to minimize the annuitized ownership costs relative to the annual benefits received from the natural or physical capital asset. The economic data and analysis required to make this decision are summarized in Table 7.1d. Addressing the statement correctly given the second cash flow is similar to the profit searching rule – marginal revenue relative to marginal cost – given in Chapter 5 – Profit with a few significant adjustments: In addition to the operation and maintenance costs, the marginal cost includes the forgone interest income on the salvage value and forgone future net revenues of not replacing the current asset. The economic data and analysis required to make this decision are summarized in Table 7.2g. Finally, addressing the statement correctly given the third cash flow is also similar to the profit searching rule found in Chapter 5 – Profit again with significant additions: The marginal cost includes the forgone interest income on the current asset sale's value and forgone future net revenues of not replacing the current asset. The economic data and analysis required to make this decision are summarized in Table 7.9.

Addressing the statement given the second and third cash flows was similar as the analytical tool, $(\text{NPV}_\infty)_T$, was the same. While the first cash flow did not have any direct revenues, the resulting marginal cost analysis was the same as in the second and third cash flows. This illustrates the robustness of the Architectural Plan for Profit/Wealth and NPV in identifying the economic information and how to use it in business and management given the three different empirical examples.

The mechanics of calculating and the economic implications of solving the natural resources management puzzle can be complex, and an entrepreneur could get lost in the mechanics and forget if the economic interpretation of what is being done makes sense. If inaccurate or incomplete economic information is used to describe the production system and this inaccurate information is used to build Pillars of Price, Value, and Cost, then Wealth will not convey what the entrepreneur believes. After all, the reason you do all these calculations is to generate accurate economic information to help make better business and management decisions. A unique feature of capital assets is that they wear out. If you are given decision-making authority for managing these capital assets, I can virtually guarantee that you will also be asked at some point to justify or defend your management decisions concerning when to replace them especially when you are using someone else's money. The wealth searching rule identifies explicitly what is the economic information you will need to justify your decision. The wealth searching rule identifies explicitly how this economic information relates to each other in a meaningful that you will need to justify your decision. This is the power of the Wealth Searching – Capital Replacement – Rule to aid in making better business and management decisions.

Appendix 7A – Calculus of the Capital Replacement Solar Array Problem

The financially optimal capital replacement problem was given in equation (7.6b) and repeated here:

$$\text{NPV}_{\infty,t} = \frac{\sum_{k=1}^{t} R_k \left(1+r\right)^{-k} + \text{SV}_t \left(1+r\right)^{-t} - \sum_{k=1}^{t} \text{OM}_k \left(1+r\right)^{-k} - \text{IC}_0}{1 - \left(1+r\right)^{-t}} \tag{7.6b}$$

For computation ease, I will make two modifications: First, using a continuous discount rate and compounding factor as compared to a discrete discount rate and compounding factor. Chiang (1984) derives the continuous compounding factor from the discrete compounding factor given in equation (A.1):

$$\lim_{m \to \infty} \left(1 + \frac{r}{m}\right)^{t \cdot m} = e^{\hat{r}t} \tag{A.1}$$

Based on equation (A.1), a relationship can be derived between a discrete and continuous interest rate and a discrete and continuous compounding factor. These are given in equations (A.2a) and (A.2b), respectively:

$$\hat{r} = \ln(1+r) \tag{A.2a}$$

$$(1+r)^t = e^{\hat{r}t} \tag{A.2b}$$

I will drop the distinction between a discrete and continuous interest rate and use the notation e^{rt}. Consequently, e^{rt} can be substituted into equation (7.6b) for $(1+r)^{-t}$. Second, I will use integral notation to define the sum of the present value of the revenues and operation and maintenance costs:

$$(NPV_\infty)_t = \frac{\int_0^t R_k e^{-rk} dk + SV_t e^{-rt} - \int_0^t OM_k e^{-rk} dk - IC_0}{1 - e^{-rt}} \tag{A.3}$$

The searching rule given in equation (7.7) is determined by taking the first derivative of $NPV_{\infty,t}$ with respect to time, t, and setting this derivative equal to zero. This is given in equation (A.4):

$$\frac{d(NPV_\infty)_t}{dt} = \frac{d\left[\dfrac{\int_0^t R_k e^{-rk} dk + SV_t e^{-rt} - \int_0^t OM_k e^{-rk} dk - IC_0}{1 - e^{-rt}}\right]}{dt} = 0 \tag{A.4}$$

Equation (A.4) can be simplified using the following steps given that T represents the optimal capital replacement time that sets this expression equal to zero

$$\frac{(1-e^{-rT}) \cdot (R_T e^{-rT} - rSV_T e^{-rT} - OM_T e^{-rT}) - (NPV_T) \cdot (re^{-rT})}{\left[(1-e^{-rT})\right]^2} = 0$$

$$(1-e^{-rT}) \cdot (R_T e^{-rT} - rSV_T e^{-rT} - OM_T e^{-rT}) - (NPV_T) \cdot (re^{-rT}) = 0$$

$$(e^{-rT}) \cdot (R_T - rSV_T - OM_T) - \frac{(NPV_T)}{(1-e^{-rT})} \cdot (re^{-rT}) = 0 \tag{A.5}$$

$$R_T - rSV_T - OM_T - r \cdot \frac{(NPV_T)}{(1-e^{-rT})} = 0$$

$$R_T - rSV_T - OM_T - EAE(NPV_\infty)_T = 0$$

$$R_T = rSV_T + OM_T + EAE(NPV_\infty)_T$$

$$MR_T = R_T = rSV_T + OM_T + EAE(NPV_\infty)_T = MC_T$$

where EAE(NPV$_\infty$)$_T$ denotes the equal annual equivalent of (NPV$_\infty$)$_T$ at the optimal time T. The last expression of equation (A.5) is equivalent to equation (7.7) and defines the wealth-maximizing optimal capital replacement searching rule. In mathematical terms, equations (A.5) and (7.7) describe the first order or necessary conditions for an optimum. As the first order conditions could describe the optimum for a maximum or a minimum, an additional set of requirements is needed to ensure a maximum. These are described as second order conditions. The mathematical development of the second order conditions is beyond the scope of this book. I would refer an interested reader to Chiang (1984) if they wish to explore this further.

Appendix 7B – Calculus of the Even-Aged Forest Rotation Problem

The financially optimal multiple rotation even-aged model developed by Faustmann (1849), Pressler (1860), and Ohlin (1921) is given by equation (B.1a):

$$LEV_t = \frac{PQ(t)\cdot(1+r)^{-t}-C_0}{1-(1+r)^{-t}}$$

$$= \frac{PQ(t)-C_0\cdot(1+r)^t}{(1+r)^t-1}$$

(B.1a)

As described in Appendix 7A, a continuous interest rate and compounding factor can be used for computational ease. Again, I will drop the distinction between a discrete and continuous interest rate and use the notation e^{rt}. Equation (B.1a) can be rewritten as:

$$LEV_t = \frac{PQ(t)\cdot e^{-rt}-C_0}{1-e^{-rt}}$$

$$= \frac{PQ(t)-C_0\cdot e^{rt}}{e^{rt}-1}$$

$$= \frac{PQ(t)-C_0}{e^{rt}-1}-C_0$$

(B.1b)

The wealth searching rule given in equation (7.16a) is determined by taking the first derivative of LEV$_t$ with respect to time, t, and setting this derivative equal to zero.[41] This is given in equation (B.4):

$$\frac{dLEV_t}{dt} = \frac{\left(1-e^{-rt}\right)\cdot\left(P\dfrac{dQ(t)}{dt}e^{-rt}-re^{-rt}PQ(t)\right)-\left(PQ(t)e^{-rt}-C_0\right)\cdot\left(re^{-rt}\right)}{\left[\left(1-e^{-rt}\right)\right]^2}=0$$

(B.4)

Equation (B.4) can be simplified using the following steps given that T represents the rotation age that sets this expression equal to zero:

$$
\frac{\left(1-e^{-rT}\right)\cdot\left(P\dfrac{dQ(T)}{dT}e^{-rT}-re^{-rT}PQ(T)\right)-\left(PQ(T)e^{-rT}-C_0\right)\cdot\left(re^{-rT}\right)}{\left[\left(1-e^{-rT}\right)\right]^2}=0
$$

$$
\left(1-e^{-rT}\right)\cdot\left(P\frac{dQ(T)}{dT}e^{-rT}-re^{-rT}PQ(T)\right)-\left(PQ(T)e^{-rT}-C_0\right)\cdot\left(re^{-rT}\right)=0
$$

$$
\left(e^{-rT}\right)\cdot\left(P\frac{dQ(T)}{dT}-rPQ(T)\right)-\frac{\left(PQ(T)e^{-rT}-C_0\right)}{\left(1-e^{-rT}\right)}\cdot\left(re^{-rT}\right)=0
$$

$$
P\frac{dQ(T)}{dT}-rPQ(T)-r\cdot\frac{\left(PQ(t)e^{-rT}-C_0\right)}{\left(1-e^{-rT}\right)}=0
$$

$$
P\frac{dQ(T)}{dT}=rPQ(T)+r\cdot\frac{\left(PQ(t)e^{-rT}-C_0\right)}{\left(1-e^{-rT}\right)}
$$

$$
MRP_T=P\frac{dQ(T)}{dT}=rPQ(T)-r\cdot\frac{\left(PQ(t)e^{-rT}-C_0\right)}{\left(1-e^{-rT}\right)}=rPQ(T)+rLEV_T=MC_T
$$

(B.5)

The last expression of equation (B.5) is the financially optimal multiple rotation even-aged searching rule described in equation (7.16a). In mathematical terms, equations (B.5) and (7.16a) describe the first order or necessary conditions for an optimum. As the first order conditions could describe the optimum for a maximum or a minimum, an additional set of requirements is needed to ensure a maximum. These are described as second order conditions. The mathematical development of the second order conditions is beyond the scope of this book. I would refer an interested reader to Johansson and Löfgren (1985) and Amacher et al. (2009) if they wish to explore this further.

A similar approach can be used to determine the financially optimal single rotation age searching rule given in equation (7.10a). The single rotation age problem can be written as

$$
NPV_t=PQ(t)\cdot e^{-rt}-C_0 \tag{B.6}
$$

The first order or necessary conditions for an optimum are

$$
\frac{dNPV_t}{dt}=P\frac{dQ(t)}{dt}e^{-rt}-rPQ(t)e^{-rt}=0 \tag{B.7}
$$

Equation (B.7) can be simplified using the following steps given that T represents the rotation age that sets this expression equal to zero:

$$P\frac{dQ(T)}{dT}e^{-rT} - rPQ(T)e^{-rT} = 0$$

$$P\frac{dQ(T)}{dT} - rPQ(T) = 0 \tag{B.8}$$

$$MRP_T = P\frac{dQ(T)}{dT} = rPQ(T) = MC_T$$

The last expression of equation (B.8) is the financially optimal single rotation even-aged searching rule described in equation (7.10a). As before, second order conditions are required to ensure a maximum. Again, I would refer an interested reader to Johansson and Löfgren (1985) and Amacher et al. (2009) if they wish to explore this further.

Appendix 7C –The Faustmann–Smith–Samuelson Model

The financially optimal multiple rotation age model for even-aged forests developed by Faustmann (1849), Pressler (1860), and Ohlin (1921) – equation (7.15) – describes the present value of a fixed asset to produce a perpetual period income flow. While it is probably the most familiar approach used to analyze an entrepreneur's investment in forest management, it should not be used *carte blanche*. For example, it is a stand-level model and cannot simply be aggregated to the forest-level (Wear and Newman 1991; Newman and Wear 1993; Yin 1997; Yin and Newman 1997; Yin et al. 1998). In addition, it does not allow for developing an aggregate supply curve using Hotelling's lemma (supply $= \dfrac{\partial\Pi(P)}{\partial P}$, see Varian 1992) as it does not conform to the mathematical conditions of a regular profit function (Wear and Newman 1991; Newman and Wear 1993; Yin 1997; Yin and Newman 1997). To address these concerns, Yin (1997) and Yin and Newman (1997) proposed an annual forest-level profit function based on the Faustmann–Smith–Samuelson model described by Smith (1968), Samuelson (1976b), and Comolli (1981)

$$\Pi(P_t, r_t, w_t, l_t) = \max\left\{P_t\left[Q(t) - r_t I(t)\right] - w_t K(t) - l_t L(t)\right\}; \quad t = 1, 2, 3, \dots \tag{C.1}$$

where
$\Pi(\bullet)$ = annual profits (\$)
P_t = stumpage price at time t (\$/volume);
$Q(t)$ = the production system as a function of time (volume);
r_t = the discount rate at time t;
$I(t)$ = the inventory at time t (volume);
w_t = wage for inputs at time t (\$/unit input);

K(t) = variable inputs used at time t;

l_t = the market rental rate for land (\$/unit land); and

L(t) = land area devoted to forest management at time t.

While a complete discussion comparing and contrasting equations (C.1) and (7.15) is beyond the scope of this book, I would counsel the reader to think critically when using any analytical model to help develop economic information used in the decision-making process.

Notes

1 These concepts were defined in Chapter 6 – Capital Theory: Investment Analysis.

2 As not all physical capital is created equal; the makeup of these costs change. For physical capital such as equipment, machinery, cars/trucks, etc., capital recovery costs decrease and operating and maintenance costs increase over time (www.publications. usace.army.mil/Portals/76/Publications/EngineerPamphlets/EP_1110-1-8_Vol_01. pdf?ver=2017-05-15-124253-820 accessed 6 November 2018). For physical capital such as solar arrays, capital recovery costs decrease over time and annual operating and maintenance costs are mostly constant. For natural capital such as forestland, ownership (operating) and management (maintenance) costs can vary over time.

3 For heavy equipment – large machines and vehicles used in construction, farming, and logging – time is measured in productive hours. For planning purposes companies will use about 10,000 productive hours before major repairs start. In addition, the resale value remains relatively high given these productive hours as heavy equipment lasts longer. I am indebted to Dr. Bruce Fox, Professor of Forestry, Northern Arizona University, for providing me with this information.

4 A formal discussion of sensitivity analysis can be found in Chapter 8 – Risk.

5 I would like to thank Mr. David Feldman of the National Renewable Energy Laboratory housed within the US Department of Energy and Mr. Michael Kelleher retired ESF Professor and retired National Grid executive for their assistance with this section.

6 The financial analyses of these projects often include annual price increases. For example, Heeter et al. (2020) uses a 1.5%, 2.5%, and 3.5% annual increase in utility prices. As utility prices are significantly lower than retail prices, these annual price increases are an important component in determining the financial feasibility of a utility project. Similar annual retail price increases can be estimated using the Energy Information Administration's Short-Term Energy Outlook Real and Nominal Prices (www.eia.gov/outlooks/steo/realprices/ accessed 28 February 2022) and the econometric models described by Wagner and Sendak (2005).

7 Appendix 7A derives equation (7.7) explicitly.

8 Stumpage is the merchantable volume – as measured by quantity (thousand board feet or cubic meters) and quality (log grade) – of a standing tree.

9 With the solar array, the quantity of output decreased with time due to increasing insolation conversion inefficiencies.

10 Forest structure is the horizontal and vertical distribution of layers or strata in a forest including the trees, shrubs, and ground cover including vegetation and dead and down woody material (Oliver and Larson 1990; McElhinny et al. 2005). A variety of attributes – tree diameter and height, trees per acre, basal area, live crown ratios, relative density, canopy cover – each contribute to overall structure but do not, individually, describe it completely. Species composition refers to the identity and variety of ecosystem components. Species diversity is composed to two factors: (i) species richness (number of species in a given area) and (ii) abundance (as described by evenness). A common metric of forest structure is trees per unit area by diameter class or distribution (Bettinger et al. 2017) or a diameter distribution diagram (Nyland 2016).

11　To be consistent with Chapter 6 – Capital Theory: Investment Analysis, I will use real interest rates, prices, and costs.

12　The two-number notation is used when defining seedlings for regeneration/afforestation planting, for example 1+0 or 2+1. The first number indicates how many years (growing seasons) seedlings grew in their original seedbed. The second number indicates how many years seedlings grew after being transplanted into a different nursery bed. Therefore a 1+0 seedling is one year old, and a 2+1 seedling is three years old when planted as part of a silvicultural prescription.

13　The reader may want to question if a 19-year-old loblolly pine tree does in fact describe a sawtimber tree.

14　I have taken some mathematical liberty in deriving the condition given in equation (7.10a). Appendix 7B develops these conditions more completely.

15　The interested reader may want to examine Binkley (1987) for a more in-depth discussion on this topic.

16　Newman (1988) using a different approach comes to the same conclusions that if $r > 1/T$ then financially optimal single rotation age is shorter than the CMAI; $r < 1/T$ then financially optimal single rotation age is longer than the CMAI; and if $r = 1/T$ then financially optimal single rotation age is equal to the CMAI.

17　Could the model described in equation (7.13) be used to examine sustainable forest management planning and sustainable forest management?

18　This left-hand term has also been called Soil Expectation Value (SEV) or Bare Land Value (BLV).

19　The problem formulation and its solution as presented by Faustmann in 1849 is

$$LEV_t = P \cdot Q(t) \cdot \left((1+r)^{-t} - C_0 + \left[P \cdot Q(t) \cdot \left((1+r)^{-t} - C\right]\right] \cdot (1+r)^{-t}$$

$$+ \left[P \cdot Q(t) \cdot \left((1+r)^{-t} - C\right)\right] \cdot (1+r)^{-2t} + \cdots$$

$$= \left[P \cdot Q(t) - C\right] \cdot \left((1+r)^{-t} + \left[P \cdot Q(t) - C\right] \cdot (1+r)^{-2t}\right.$$

$$+ \left[P \cdot Q(t) - C\right] \cdot (1+r)^{-3t} + \cdots + C_0$$

where the initial afforestation or establishment cost, C_0, is isolated from the reforestation cost, C. The assumption is that $C_0 = C$. This expression can be solved giving

$$LEV_t = \sum_{t=0}^{\infty} (PQ(t) - C) \cdot \left[(1+r)^{-t}\right] - C_0$$

$$= \frac{PQ(t) - C}{(1+r)^t - 1} - C_0$$

$$= \frac{NFV_t}{(1+r)^t - 1} - C_0$$

where NFV_t denotes a net future value at time t. Finally, it can be shown mathematically that

$$LEV_t = \frac{NFV_t}{(1+r)^t - 1} - C_0 = \frac{NPV_t}{1 - (1+r)^{-t}}$$

20　Navarro (2003) reviews two variations of the Faustmann formula given in equation (7.15).

21　The reader may want to question if a 15-year-old loblolly pine tree does in fact describe a sawtimber tree.

22　I have taken some mathematical liberty in deriving the condition given in equation (7.16a). Appendix 7B develops these conditions more completely.

23 This is the case generally. There are unique cases when results are ambiguous with respect to the CMAI or maximum sustained yield rotation and the financially optimal multiple rotation solution (Binkley 1987). Newman (1988) shows that the financially optimal multiple rotation age will never be larger than the financially optimal single multiple rotation age.

24 Amacher et al. (2009) show that if the market rental rate for bare land is included in the financially optimal single rotation formulation, equation (7.9), then the financially optimal single and multiple rotation ages calculated using equations (7.9) and (7.15) respectively will be the same. Samuelson (1976b) first discussed this in his seminal article.

25 While the Faustmann model is probably the most familiar approach used to analyze an entrepreneur's investment in forest management, it should not be used *carte blanche*. Appendix 7C provides a brief discussion of an alternative approach.

26 Even-aged stands can be regenerated also using a shelterwood or seed tree silvicultural system, for example. The end result is still an even-aged stand in which the overstory has been removed completely after sufficient regeneration.

27 The literature abounds with articles on this topic and it would be impossible to give a list here; however, I would recommend an interested reader start with the following: Adams and Ek (1974), Buongiorno and Michie (1980), Chang (1981), Hall (1983), Nautiyal (1983), Michie (1985), Rideout (1985), Buongiorno et al. (1995), Klemperer (1996), Kant (1999), Buongiorno (2001), Tarp et al. (2005), Tahvonen (2007), Zhou et al. (2008), and Amacher et al. (2009).

28 The entrepreneur's wealth objective presented in equation (7.18) was developed given an existing uneven-aged forest. Klemperer (1996) develops a cash flow diagram and corresponding economic model given the entrepreneur starts with bare land, regenerates an even-aged forest, and then converts it to an uneven-aged forest. Buongiorno (2001), Tarp et al. (2005), and Tahvonen (2007) provide an economic analysis of converting an even-aged to an uneven-aged forest.

29 If the uneven-aged stand is in a steady-state condition, equation (7.18) can be defined as

$$
\begin{aligned}
USV_{t,G} &= \sum_{t=0}^{\infty} \left\{ P \cdot \left[Q(t,G) \cdot (1+r)^{-t} - G \right] \right\} \cdot \left[(1+r)^{-t} \right] \\
&= \frac{P \cdot \left[Q(t,G) \cdot (1+r)^{-t} - G \right]}{1 - (1+r)^{-t}} \\
&= \frac{P \cdot \left[Q(t,G) - G \right] \cdot (1+r)^{-t}}{1 - (1+r)^{-t}} - P \cdot G
\end{aligned}
$$

30 In equation (7.18), if the uneven-aged stand is in a steady-state condition, $P \cdot V = 0$ and the opportunity cost of the reserve growing stock is $P \cdot G$. If not, $P \cdot [V - G]$ denotes the net revenue generated from an initial harvesting of the stand to the reserve growing stock level. Also, land costs are ignored for purposes of illustration. These could be included in the $P \cdot [V - G]$ term.

31 I would recommend highly that the reader review the discussion on the internal rate of return found in Chapter 6 – Capital Theory: Investment Analysis.

32 Klemperer (1996) does qualify his use of the *irr* rule by stating stand-level simulations should be used to develop marking guides, as equation (7.19) only gives a rough approximation of optimal stocking.

33 Of course, changing the management regime would also change the amount of time for a loblolly pine plantation to grow 12-inch trees. For example, multiple herbicide and fertilization treatments and one or more thinnings would allow growing 12-inch loblolly pines much faster than 30 to 40 years.

34 Chapter 8 – Risk will cover using sensitivity analysis to analyze the impact of parameter changes within the normal ranges of operations on the capital replacement decision. For

students interested in stochastic modeling based on equations (7.6a) and (7.6b), I would recommend starting with Chiang (1984, 1992), Johansson and Löfgren (1985), Getz and Haight (1989), Dixit and Pindyck (1994), Wagner and Holmes (1999), Amacher et al. (2009), and Conrad (2010).

35   A variation on the maximum sustained yield or optimal biological rotation is a concept termed forest rent. Gregory (1972) and later Johansson and Löfgren (1985) define forest rent as the maximum average net revenue or a net sustainable yield concept

$$FR_t = \frac{P \cdot Q(t) - C}{t}; t = 1, 2, 3, \ldots$$

where FR_t defines the forest rent at time t and all the other variables are defined as before. The entrepreneur's objective would be to determine the rotation age that maximizes forest rent. There are three problems with this calculation. First, the discount rate is set equal to zero. Second, the mathematical formulation of forest rent can tie a cost and revenue together that are not related; that is, tying current regeneration costs to current harvesting revenues. Finally, the rotation age that maximizes forest rent will, in general, be longer than the financially optimal single and multiple rotation ages (Johansson and Löfgren 1985; Hyytiäinen and Tahvonen 2003).

36   It is interesting to note for the Loblolly Pine Plantation practical application if the existing plantation is younger than a plantation age of 15, the optimal time to cut the existing plantation will always be at plantation age of 15. If the existing plantation is older than a plantation age of 15, the optimal time to cut the existing plantation will always be to harvest right away. You can verify this by calculating the first order condition of equation (7.21) or $\frac{dFV_t}{dt} = 0$.

37   Students who are interested in these types of production processes and analyses should start their review with the following literature: Hartman (1976), Calish et al. (1978), Nguyen (1979), Bowes and Krutilla (1985), Peters et al. (1989), Stednick (1996), Strange et al. (1999), Alexander et al. (2002), Haynes and Monserud (2002), and Amacher et al. (2009).

38   In addition, Amacher et al. (2009) described the case when the wealth-maximizing optimal multiple rotation age is infinite and the stand should never be harvested: If the ecosystem good or service values increase faster than the decrease in the harvest revenues due to diminishing returns in the timber production system. Finally, they also examine the case of wealth-maximizing optimal multiple rotation ages if there is an existing stand. A discussion of these topics is beyond the scope of this book, and I would point the reader to Amacher et al. (2009).

39   This topic was introduced in Chapter 1 – Introduction to distinguish between outputs and outcomes and will be developed in more detail here.

40   This will be the topic of Chapter 9 – Estimating Nonmarket Values.

41   Gaffney's (1957) classic paper is generally regarded as the beginning of using the first derivative in establishing the optimal rotation age and the superiority of the Faustmann formula over other methods of determining rotation age.

8   Risk

Preamble

Starting in Chapter 2 – Production Systems, the apparent deterministic description of the Architectural Plan for Wealth was questioned. In fact, the economic information that is used to build the Architectural Plan for Wealth, illustrated in Figure 8.1, and consequently in decision making is often stochastic.

In these chapters, the most referenced technique for dealing with the inherent variability of parameters and variables was sensitivity analysis. This was described as evaluating tenable pessimistic, realistic, and optimistic scenarios for each alternative. The unstated purpose was to identify those parameters or variables that had the most impact on the solution. This chapter will discuss this unstated purpose directly and provide a metric to determine which parameter or variables have the most impact on the solution. In addition, there are other techniques that can be used to address the variability associated with economic information. Analyzing the stochastic characteristics of the parameters and variables is often described using the terms risk and uncertainty interchangeably. These terms have very specific meanings and should not be used interchangeably; consequently, I will start with a short discussion of the concepts of risk and uncertainty.

Risk and Uncertainty

The concepts of risk and uncertainty were defined briefly in Chapter 6 – Capital Theory: Investment Analysis with respect to the interest or discount rate. I will now define them more formally based on the standard economic definitions as provided by Frank H. Knight (1921):

Risk is present when future events occur with measurable probability, frequency distributions, acceptable ranges, etc.
Uncertainty is present when the likelihood, frequency distribution, acceptable ranges, etc. of future events is indefinite or incalculable.

Risk can further be refined as objective risk – if the ranges are known and their probabilities measurable, and subjective risk – if the probabilities are based solely on

DOI: 10.4324/9781315678719-8

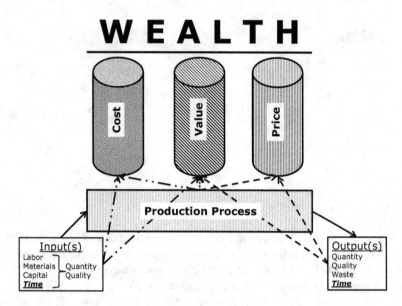

Figure 8.1 The Architectural Plan for Profit (Wealth)

human judgement (Loucks and Van Beek 2005). In addition, uncertainty has been disaggregated into reducible uncertainty and random uncertainty (Zio and Pedroni 2013). With reducible uncertainty, the more knowledge or information gained, over time previously unusable probabilities, frequency distributions, acceptable ranges, and so on will become practicable. However, random uncertainty cannot be reduced due to the inherent unpredictable changes or randomness of a physical or market phenomenon. For purposes of this chapter, I will include reducible uncertainties in risk, thus maintaining Knight's original risk and uncertainty definitions.

Techniques for Analyzing Risk

I will examine eight techniques for incorporating risk and uncertainty as economic information into the business decision-making process. The techniques are (1) the discount rate, (2) sensitivity analysis, (3) decision trees, (4) equally likely, (5) Bayes decision rule, (6) maximax, (7) maximin, and (8) minimax regret.

The Discount Rate

The nominal and real interest or discount rates include a risk component as illustrated in equations (6.3a) and (6.3b). There are two implications of including risk as part of the discount rate. First, as the perceived risk increases, so would the discount rate. Second, the degree of riskiness (the discounting factor $(1 + r)^{-t}$) then depends solely on when the event occurs. This is illustrated by Table 8.1.

Table 8.1 Discounting Factor $(1 + r)^{-t}$ Interest Rate Example, $r = 3\%, 6\%, 9\%$

Year	3%	6%	9%
5	0.86261	0.74726	0.64993
10	0.74409	0.55839	0.42241
15	0.64186	0.41727	0.27454
20	0.55368	0.31180	0.17843
25	0.47761	0.23300	0.11597
30	0.41199	0.17411	0.07537

As Table 8.1 illustrates, the weight $(1 + r)^{-t}$ placed on risk is only a function of time and decreases geometrically with time. Consequently, including risk as part of the discount rate does not allow for components of a project to have differing degrees of risk due to the presence or scale of costs and benefits unrelated to time. For example, managing a forested ecosystem's risk may be a function of stand age (time) but also of species, biological conditions, weather, and so on. Managing a solar array risk is a function of reduced conversion efficiencies due to time but also of weather and market price variability (Wagner et al. 2019; Knoke et al. 2001).

Including an uncertainty component in the discount rate would also increase it and would imply the effects of uncertainty also decrease with time (Table 8.1). This would only be appropriate if the uncertainty is indeed reducible by collecting more information. However, if the uncertainty is random due to the inherent randomness in the physical or market phenomenon, the uncertainty cannot be reduced. There is a significant amount of literature on the randomness of, for example, prices of financial assets. Consequently, an argument could be made that this market phenomenon is random and incorporating it as an uncertainty component in the discount rate is not tenable.[1]

Sensitivity Analysis

According to Hillier and Lieberman (1990) and Smith et al. (2008), sensitivity analysis is defined as a procedure of changing model parameters (e.g., output prices, input wages, discount rate, and production system) systematically to identify those that cause the most significant – not necessarily the largest – changes in the final result. The parameters that cause these changes should be determined with a greater level of accuracy than those that do not. In addition, sensitivity analysis will help with understanding the dynamics of the system being modeled. The procedure is simple to describe: To examine the impact of an individual parameter on the system, change one model parameter at a time. As defined by Smith et al. (2008), these impacts can be measured using the relative-sensitivity elasticity, $RSE_{t,v}$, given in equation (8.1)[2]

$$RSE_{t,v} = \frac{\dfrac{V_{t,v} - V_{t,0}}{V_{t,0}}}{\dfrac{v - v_0}{v_0}}; t = 1, 2, 3, \ldots \tag{8.1}$$

where

$V_{t,v}$ denotes the value of the final result at time t given the new parameter value v;

$V_{t,0}$ denote the value of the final result at time t given no parameter change;

v denotes the new parameter value; and

v_0 denotes the original parameter value.

The numerator and denominator denote percentage changes. The advantage of using equation (8.1) is that impacts can be compared regardless of units on the parameters; for example, stumpage price is measured as dollars per unit volume – United States dollars per cubic foot or New Zealand dollars per cubic meter – while regeneration costs are measured as dollars per acre or dollars per hectare and the real discount rate is a percentage. RSE is a fraction; once calculated it can be interpreted as a ratio of a 1% change in the denominator will cause an X% change in the numerator. Thus, those parameter values with relatively larger RSEs are more "critical."

To illustrate sensitivity analysis, I will use the Loblolly Pine Plantation practical application and the NPV and land expectation value (LEV; i.e., the Faustmann formula) models described in Chapter 7 – The Natural Resources Management Puzzle and given in equations (8.2) and (8.3) respectively[3]

$$NPV_t = P \cdot Q(t)^{-1} - C_0 \; ; t = 1,2,3,... \tag{8.2}$$

$$LEV_t = (NPV_\infty)_t = \frac{PQ(t) \cdot (1+r)^{-t} - C_0}{1 - (1+r)^{-t}} \; ; \quad t = 0, 1, 2, ... \tag{8.3}$$

where

P = stumpage price of $1.81 per cubic foot ($/cuft) for sawtimber;

Q(t) = the loblolly pine production system illustrated in Table 7.3 and defined by Amateis and Burkhart (1985) and Burkhart et al. (1985);

r = the 8% real interest rate; and

C_0 = $305.54 per acre regeneration costs.[4]

Tables 8.2a and 8.2b illustrate the impacts on NPV and LEV if the stumpage price increases or decreases by 25% to 2.72 $/cuft and 1.36 $/cuft, respectively. These sensitivity analyses are presented graphically in Figures 8.2a and 8.2b for NPV and LEV, respectively.

These tables and figures are to be read holding plantation age constant. For example, at a plantation age of 15 the magnitude of NPV and LEV are more sensitive to the 25% increase than decrease in stumpage price (Table 8.2b). In addition, the positive sign of the relative-sensitivity elasticity for stumpage price implies that an increase (decrease) in stumpage price will increase (decrease) the magnitude of NPV and LEV. At a plantation age of 15 the magnitude of NPV and LEV are more sensitive to the 25% decrease than increase in the real discount rate (Table 8.3b). The negative sign of the relative-sensitivity elasticity for real discount rate implies that an increase (decrease) in the real discount rate will decrease (increase) the

Table 8.2a Sensitivity Analysis of a 25% change in Stumpage Price on NPV and LEV[‡]

			Price = $2.72 per cu. ft.		Price = $1.36 per cuft	
Plantation	NPV	LEV	NPV	LEV	NPV	LEV
Age	($/acre)	($/acre)	($/acre)	($/acre)	($/acre)	($/acre)
10	772.00	1,438.13	1,043.56	1,944.02	503.92	938.74
11	897.19	1,570.94	1,200.31	2,101.69	597.97	1,047.02
12	1,005.25	1,667.39	1,335.60	2,215.34	679.14	1,126.49
13	1,095.23	1,732.12	1,448.25	2,290.44	746.73	1,180.98
14	1,167.03	1,769.46	1,538.15	2,332.16	800.67	1,213.99
15	1,221.20	**1,783.40**	1,605.97	**2,345.31**	841.37	**1,228.70**
16	1,258.72	1,777.57	1,652.95	2,334.31	869.55	1,227.99
17	1,280.88	1,755.28	1,680.69	2,303.17	886.20	1,214.42
18	**1,289.16**	1,719.45	**1,691.06**	2,255.49	**892.42**	1,190.29
19	1,285.11	1,672.70	1,686.00	2,194.48	889.38	1,157.61
20	1,270.33	1,617.33	1,667.49	2,122.97	878.28	1,118.18

[‡] NPV denotes net present value measured as dollars per acre ($/acre). LEV denotes land expectation value measured as dollars per acre ($/acre). Price is dollars per cubic foot ($/cuft).

Table 8.2b Relative Sensitivity Analysis of a 25% Change in Stumpage Price on NPV and LEV[‡]

	Price = $2.72 per cuft		Price = $1.36 per cuft	
Plantation	NPV	LEV	NPV	LEV
Age	Relative-Sensitivity Elasticities			
10	1.41	1.41	1.39	1.39
11	1.35	1.35	1.33	1.33
12	1.31	1.31	1.30	1.30
13	1.29	1.29	1.27	1.27
14	1.27	1.27	1.26	1.26
15	1.26	1.26	1.24	1.24
16	1.25	1.25	1.24	1.24
17	1.25	1.25	1.23	1.23
18	1.25	1.25	1.23	1.23
19	1.25	1.25	1.23	1.23
20	1.25	1.25	1.23	1.23

[‡] NPV denotes net present value. LEV denotes land expectation value. Price is dollars per cubic foot ($/cuft).

magnitude of NPV and LEV. Comparing a stumpage price to a real discount rate change, the relative-sensitivity elasticities show that NPV and LEV are more sensitive to the real discount rate changes, *ceteris paribus*. It is left to the reader to conduct a similar sensitivity analysis for a 25% increase and decrease in regeneration costs. McIntyre et al. (2010) provide an empirical example of using sensitivity analysis in a forest management context.

Table 8.3a Sensitivity Analysis of a 25% Change in the Real Discount Rate on NPV and LEV[‡]

Plantation Age	*r = 0.06*		*r = 0.06*		*r = 0.10*	
	NPV	*LEV*	*NPV*	*LEV*	*NPV*	*LEV*
	($/acre)	*($/acre)*	*($/acre)*	*($/acre)*	*($/acre)*	*($/acre)*
10	772.00	1,438.13	993.47	2,249.67	591.36	962.41
11	897.19	1,570.94	1,171.75	2,476.16	677.36	1,042.89
12	1,005.25	1,667.39	1,334.85	2,653.62	746.19	1,095.14
13	1,095.23	1,732.12	1,480.53	2,787.34	797.95	1,123.35
14	1,167.03	1,769.46	1,607.51	2,882.39	833.42	**1,131.34**
15	1,221.20	**1,783.40**	1,715.30	2,943.54	853.85	1,122.59
16	1,258.72	1,777.57	1,804.03	2,975.21	**860.75**	1,100.18
17	1,280.88	1,755.28	1,874.29	**2,981.52**	855.76	1,066.83
18	**1,289.16**	1,719.45	1,927.00	2,966.19	840.60	1,024.94
19	1,285.11	1,672.70	1,963.36	2,932.63	816.91	976.59
20	1,270.33	1,617.33	**1,984.69**	2,883.90	786.26	923.54

[‡] NPV denotes net present value measured as dollars per acre ($/acre). LEV denotes land expectation value measured as dollars per acre ($/acre).

Table 8.3b Relative Sensitivity Analysis of a 25% Change in the Real Discount Rate on NPV and LEV[‡]

Plantation Age	*r = 0.06*		*r = 0.10*	
	NPV	*LEV*	*NPV*	*LEV*
	Relativity-Sensitivity Elasticities			
10	−1.15	−2.26	−0.94	−1.32
11	−1.22	−2.30	−0.98	−1.34
12	−1.31	−2.37	−1.03	−1.37
13	−1.41	−2.44	−1.09	−1.41
14	−1.51	−2.52	−1.14	−1.44
15	−1.62	−2.60	−1.20	−1.48
16	−1.73	−2.69	−1.26	−1.52
17	−1.85	−2.79	−1.33	−1.57
18	−1.98	−2.90	−1.39	−1.62
19	−2.11	−3.01	−1.46	−1.66
20	−2.25	−3.13	−1.52	−1.72

[‡] NPV denotes net present value. LEV denotes land expectation value.

A similar sensitivity analysis can be conducted using the 1,000 kW ground mount solar array. A 25% increase and decrease in output price gives a relative-sensitivity elasticity of 1.70 for NPV_{29} and $(NPV_{\infty})_{29}$. This result is similar to the stumpage price relative-sensitivity elasticity for the Loblolly Pine Plantation practical application. A 25% increase in the discount rate gives relative-sensitivity elasticities of

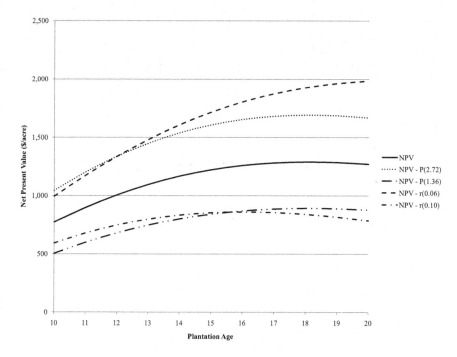

Figure 8.2a Sensitivity Analysis: Net Present Value (NPV)‡

‡P(2.72) denotes a stumpage price increase to 2.72 dollars per cubic foot. P(1.36) denotes a stumpage price decrease to 1.36 dollars per cubic foot. r(0.06) denotes a real interest rate decrease to 6%. r(0.10) denotes a real interest rate increase to 10%.

−0.70 and −0.98 for NPV_{29} and $(NPV_\infty)_{29}$, respectively. A 25% decrease in the discount rate gives relative-sensitivity elasticities of −0.88 and −1.62 for NPV_{29} and $(NPV_\infty)_{29}$, respectively. Comparing an output price to a real discount rate change, the relative-sensitivity elasticities show that NPV_{29} and $(NPV_\infty)_{29}$ are more sensitive to the output price changes, *ceteris paribus*. It is left to the reader to create tables similar to Tables 8.2a, 8.2b, 8.3a, and 8.3b for the solar array.

Sensitivity analysis is a very useful tool (Smith et al. 2008). However, there are five factors that require careful thought. First, sensitivity analysis requires changing model parameters systematically within the range of normal operations for a given business management problem. The entrepreneur would have to determine these ranges based on their knowledge of the Architectural Plan for Wealth given the problem. To illustrate sensitivity analysis, I chose a 25% change in output prices and real discount rates arbitrarily. For example, a more defendable approach to determining the range of normal operations for output prices would be to use historical real output price data to estimate standard deviations.[5] Figures 8.3a, 8.3b, and 8.3c illustrate nominal and real annual, quarterly, and monthly United States residential electricity prices, respectively.

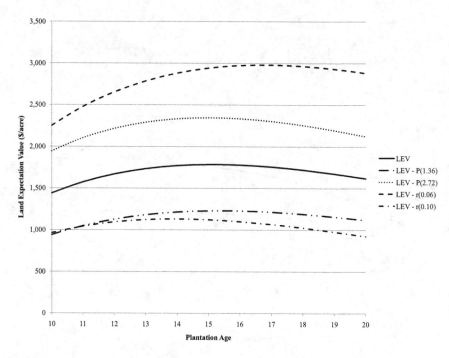

Figure 8.2b Sensitivity Analysis: Land Expectation Value (LEV)‡

‡P(2.72) denotes a stumpage price increase to 2.72 dollars per cubic foot. P(1.36) denotes a stumpage price decrease to 1.36 dollars per cubic foot. r(0.06) denotes a real interest rate decrease to 6%. r(0.10) denotes a real interest rate increase to 10%.

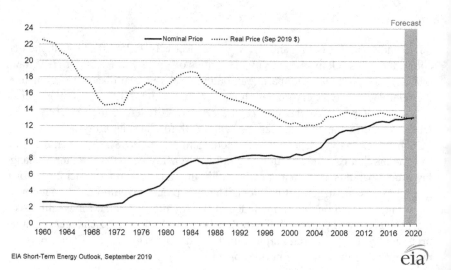

EIA Short-Term Energy Outlook, September 2019

Figure 8.3a Annual Residential Electricity Price

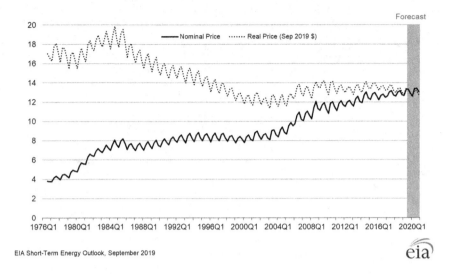

Figure 8.3b Quarterly Residential Electricity Price

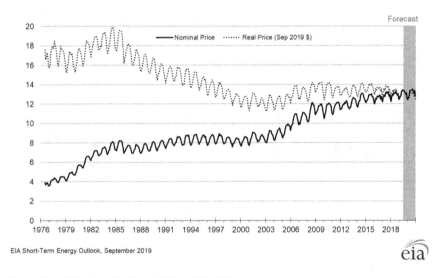

Figure 8.3c Monthly Residential Electricity Price

Figures 8.4a, 8.4b, and 8.4c illustrate nominal and real quarterly southern pine sawtimber, chip-n-saw, and pulpwood stumpage prices, respectively.[6]

More sophisticated statistical approaches use regression analysis to estimate prediction intervals (Wagner et al. 2019). Second, the relative-sensitivity

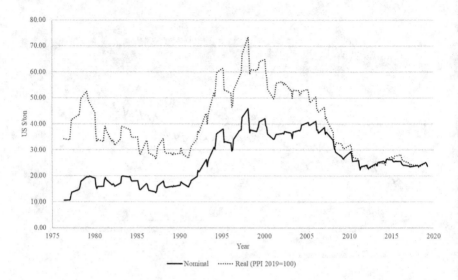

Figure 8.4a Southern Pine Sawtimber Stumpage Price

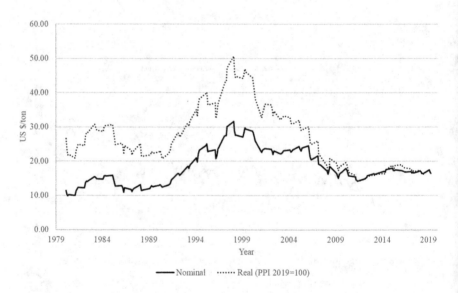

Figure 8.4b Southern Pine Chip-n-Saw Stumpage Price

elasticities change over the investment horizon. For output price, the relative-sensitivity elasticities decrease the longer the investment horizon, while for the real discount rate they increase the longer the investment horizon. This is due to time having a direct exponential impact on the real discount rate and discounting factor

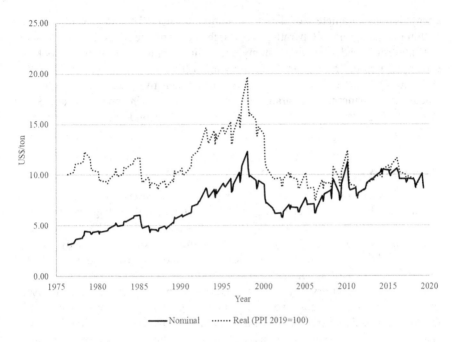

Figure 8.4c Southern Pine Pulpwood Stumpage Price

(i.e., $(1 + r)^{-t}$) but not on output price. Smith et al. (2008) noted this problem. Third, the loblolly pine and solar array examples were described as capital replacement problems. Changing parameters may not only have an effect on the magnitudes of NPV_t and LEV_t or $(NPV_\infty)_t$, but they may also change the optimal time to replace the capital. For example, changing stumpage price or regeneration costs in equation (8.2) will not change the financially optimal rotation age, but increasing (decreasing) the real interest rate will decrease (increase) the rotation age. Johansson and Löfgren (1985) using a methodology called comparative statics showed that for equation (8.3) there is an inverse relationship between changes in stumpage price and changes in the financially optimal multiple rotation age – this inverse relationship also holds for changes in the discount rate – and there is a direct relationship between changes in regeneration costs and changes in the financially optimal multiple rotation age.[7] A similar comparative static analysis for the solar array using equations (7.5) and (7.6b) is problematic given the discontinuities created in the discounted cash flow from the constant salvage value starting in year 20 as illustrated in Figure 7.4e. Fourth, the sensitivity analysis is for that given problem or context. If the context changes, then the entrepreneur would conduct a new sensitivity analysis. Finally, in my example I only changed one parameter at a time. To examine the impacts of interactions among parameters would require changing two parameters of the model simultaneously. This advanced technique within the discipline of Operations Research is beyond the scope of this textbook. For interested readers there are many excellent operations research textbooks on this topic. I would recommend starting with Hillier and Lieberman (1992), Winston (2004), and Levin et al. (1992). A relative-sensitivity elasticity can also be calculated if changing two parameters simultaneously. Winston (2004) and Smith et al. (2008) describe the procedure for estimating a second-degree relative-sensitivity elasticity.

Decision Trees

A cash flow diagram describes a set of sequential decisions. There is an implied assumption that the benefits and costs depicted in a cash flow diagram occur with 100% certainty. However, some of the benefits and costs may be dependent on circumstances that are out of your direct control. For example, cloudy weather will affect the conversion ability of a solar array, and tree growth may be affected by the probability of a wet or dry season, a fire, or an insect/disease infestation. The probability of a dry season may increase the probability of a fire or insect/disease infestation. Because we often want to consider more complex, sequential decisions, a decision tree provides a method to analyze decision making under risk. A decision tree shows the action, states of nature, and outcomes as nodes and branches of a dendritic or tree-like cash flow diagram. Figure 8.5 illustrates a decision tree.

A decision tree is composed of actions you as an entrepreneur can take, states of nature that are beyond your control, and a terminal branch that denotes the end of a branch. These are illustrated in Figure 8.5.

Actions/Decision fork (denoted by a square) – Represents a point in time where the entrepreneur takes an action or makes a decision.
State of Nature/Event fork (denoted by a circle) – When an outside force determines which of several random events will occur.
Terminal branch – If no fork (either an event or decision fork) emanates from the branch.

A unique feature of a decision tree is the probabilities that describe if a random event will occur. The probabilities of a specified state of nature must sum to 100%.

As illustrated in Figure 8.5, the entrepreneur can choose either action I or II. Given this decision an event will occur that is beyond their control. This state of nature, "A", will happen no matter which action (i.e., I or II) is chosen. The probabilities of all possible events occurring within any state of nature must be defined and described. In Figure 8.5 the state of nature, A, has two events that occur with the probabilities α_1 and α_2. These probabilities sum to 100%, thus defining the state of nature completely.

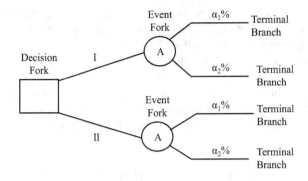

Where $\alpha_1 + \alpha_2 = 100\%$

Figure 8.5 Example Decision Tree

Once a decision tree has been determined, the entrepreneur can determine the expected value associated with each decision. This is done starting at the terminal branches and working backward toward the initial decision. Just like a cash flow diagram, the preferred investment analysis tool is net present value. However, in this case we will calculate an expected net present value due to the probabilities associated with each state of nature. To illustrate this, I will develop a decision tree for three possible management actions using a Loblolly Pine example:

Management Action I: The entrepreneur can precommercially thin the stand at plantation age 15 at a cost of $89.22 per acre and then clearcut the plantation at plantation age 25. An 8% real discount rate will be used on all cash flows.

Management Action II: The entrepreneur can use an herbicide spray release at plantation age 10 at a cost of $68.22 per acre and then clearcut the plantation at plantation age 25. An 8% real discount rate will be used on all cash flows.

Management Action III: The entrepreneur can use an herbicide spray release at plantation age 10 at a cost of $68.22 per acre plus the precommercial thin at plantation age 15 at a cost of $89.22 per acre and then clearcut the plantation at plantation age 25. An 8% real discount rate will be used on all cash flows.

No matter which management action is chosen, the growing season will be described as good, average, or poor. The probabilities associated with each type of growing season are based on historical observations by the entrepreneur and are given as the following: a good growing season occurs 20% of the time, an average growing season occurs 60% of the time, and a poor growing season occurs 20% of the time. Finally, no matter which management action is chosen, stumpage prices will remain the same, increase, or decrease. Again, the probabilities of changing stumpage prices are based on historical observations by the entrepreneur who has determined a 25% chance of stumpage price increasing, 50% change of stumpage prices remaining the same, and a 25% chance of stumpage prices decreasing. These data are given in Table 8.4 and the corresponding decision tree is given in Figure 8.6.

To describe how to read the decision tree, I will examine the branch I→A(1)→B(1). The management action is a precommercial thin, I; the growing season is good with a probability of 20% and will result in 6,367 cubic feet per acre

Table 8.4 Decision Tree Data for Loblolly Pine Plantation Practical Application

Action	Growing Season (A)			Stumpage Price (B)		
	Good (1)	Average (2)	Poor (3)	Increase (1)	No Change (2)	Decline (3)
	Percent			*Percent*		
	20	60	20	25	50	25
	Cubic feet per acre			*Dollars per acre*		
I	6,367	4,975	3,245	2.27	1.81	1.30
II	5,905	4,799	2,971	2.27	1.81	1.30
III	6,509	5,323	3,359	2.27	1.81	1.30

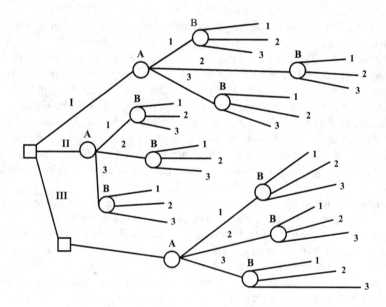

Figure 8.6 Decision Tree for the Loblolly Pine Plantation Practical Application

(cuft/ac) at plantation age 25, A(1); the stumpage price will be 2.27 $/cuft with a probability of 25%, B(1).

Examining Table 8.4, it might seem that management action III should be the preferred alternative as this has the largest volumes given the various growing seasons. However, this branch also has the largest cost relative to the other management choices. Is the difference between the present value of the costs and the present value of the expected revenues going to be greater than the other management options?

To determine the expected net present value of each management alternative, you start with the terminal branches and work backward. I will examine each management action separately.

Management Action I

Expected Stumpage Price ($/cuft), B

$$1.80 = 0.25 \times 2.27 + 0.50 \times 1.81 + 0.25 \times 1.30$$

Expected Revenue at Plantation Age 25 ($/ac), A

$$8,821.05 = 1.80 \times [0.20 \times 6,367 + 0.60 \times 4,975 + 0.20 \times 3,245]$$

Expected Net Present Value ($/ac)

$$1,259.91 = 8,821.05 \times (1.08)^{-25} - 89.22 \times (1.08)^{-15}$$

Management Action II

Expected Stumpage Price ($/cuft)

$$1.80 = 0.25 \times 2.27 + 0.50 \times 1.81 + 0.25 \times 1.30$$

Expected Revenue at Plantation Age 25 ($/ac)

$$8,366.64 = 1.80 \times [0.20 \times 5,905 + 0.60 \times 4,799 + 0.20 \times 2,971]$$

Expected Net Present Value ($/ac)

$$1,190.18 = 8,366.64 \times (1.08)^{-25} - 68.00 \times (1.08)^{-10}$$

Management Action III

Expected Stumpage Price ($/cuft)

$$1.80 = 0.25 \times 2.27 + 0.50 \times 1.81 + 0.25 \times 1.30$$

Expected Revenue at Plantation Age 25 ($/ac)

$$9,288.40 = 1.80 \times [0.20 \times 6,509 + 0.60 \times 5,323 + 0.20 \times 3,359]$$

Expected Net Present Value ($/ac)

$$1,296.65 = 9,288.40 \times (1.08)^{-25} - 89.22 \times (1.08)^{-15} - 68.00 \times (1.08)^{-10}$$

Based on the decision tree analysis, the entrepreneur should choose management action III.

As illustrated by the preceding example, decision trees allow the flexibility to assign probabilities to states of nature that are beyond your direct control. In addition, the probability of an event occurring is not solely a function of time. The entrepreneur can use this information to determine the expected net present value of alternative decisions. This flexibility comes at a cost. First, project evaluation contains many complexities and risks, so building a decision tree that reflects these aspects accurately is a complicated and time-consuming undertaking.

Second, determining the probabilities may be difficult. Probabilities may or may not be affected by management actions. For example, various management actions such as thinning and herbicide treatments do not affect the possible states of nature describing wet versus dry years, good or average, or poor growing seasons, and so on. However, various management decisions may affect the possible outcomes. For example, softwood tree growth and survival can be affected by various pathogens such as fusiform rust in slash pine (*Pinus elliotii*). The planting of rust-resistant trees can significantly affect growth, survival, and economic value of slash pine (Wagner and Holmes 1999) and thus, to reduce the probability of loss due to the rust pathogen, an entrepreneur could plant fusiform rust-resistant slash pine. Third, the decision tree described earlier does not have the probabilities tied to a time period explicitly. For example, it may be possible to determine the probability of a fire but more difficult to predict the year in which a damaging fire will occur.

Equally Likely

If we do not know how likely any of the states of nature are, there is no basis for presuming one state is more likely than any other. Therefore, we should consider all states equally likely and pick the decision with highest expected average net return. To develop this decision rule, I will first introduce a payoff or decision matrix using the three management actions described earlier as illustrated by Table 8.5.

The cells in the decision matrix represent the payoff of a given action with respect to a state of nature. In Table 8.5, the cells represent the net present value of a management action given a state of nature using a stumpage price of $1.81 $/cuft and a real interest rate of 8%. The expected net present values of each management action given equally likely probabilities are given in the last column and the calculations are given as the following:

Table 8.5 Decision Matrix for Equally Likely Decision Rule

Decision‡	Net Present Value ($/acre)			Equally
	Good	Average	Poor	Likely
PT	1,654.62	1,286.73	829.50	1,256.95
H	1,529.15	1,236.84	753.72	1,173.24
PT&H	1,660.66	1,347.21	828.14	**1,278.67**
Probability	1/3	1/3	1/3	

‡ PT denotes a precommercial thin at plantation age 15 at a cost of $89.22 per acre and then clearcut the plantation at plantation age 25. H denotes a herbicide spray release at plantation age 10 at a cost of $68.22 per acre and then clearcut the plantation at plantation age 25. PT&H denotes a herbicide spray release at plantation age 10 at a cost of $68.22 per acre plus the precommercial thin at plantation age 15 at a cost of $89.22 per acre and then clearcut the plantation at plantation age 25.

Management Action I

Expected Net Present Value ($/ac)

$$1,256.95 = (1,654.62 + 1,286.73 + 829.50) \times \frac{1}{3}$$

Management Action II

Expected Net Present Value ($/ac)

$$1,173.24 = (1,529.15 + 1,236.84 + 753.72) \times \frac{1}{3}$$

Management Action III

Expected Net Present Value ($/ac)

$$1,278.67 = (1,660.66 + 1,347.21 + 828.14) \times \frac{1}{3}$$

Based on the equally likely decision rule, management action III – an herbicide spray release at plantation age 10 at a cost of $68.22 per acre plus the precommercial thin at plantation age 15 at a cost of $89.22 per acre and then clearcut the plantation at plantation age 25 – should be chosen.

Bayes Decision Rule

The Bayes decision rule uses prior probability to determine the action with the maximum expected payoff. The decision matrix reflecting the Bayes decision rule is given in Table 8.6.

Table 8.6 Decision Matrix for the Bayes Decision Rule

Decision[‡]	Net Present Value ($/acre)			Bayes
	Good	Average	Poor	
PT	1,654.62	1,286.73	829.50	1,268.86
H	1,529.15	1,236.84	753.72	1,198.68
PT&H	1,660.66	1,347.21	828.14	**1,306.08**
Probability	0.2	0.6	0.2	

‡ PT denotes a precommercial thin at plantation age 15 at a cost of $89.22 per acre and then clearcut the plantation at plantation age 25. H denotes a herbicide spray release at plantation age 10 at a cost of $68.22 per acre and then clearcut the plantation at plantation age 25. PT&H denotes a herbicide spray release at plantation age 10 at a cost of $68.22 per acre plus the precommercial thin at plantation age 15 at a cost of $89.22 per acre and then clearcut the plantation at plantation age 25.

The probabilities in Table 8.6 are based on those in Table 8.4. The expected net present values of each management action given prior probabilities are given in the last column and the calculations are given as the following:

Management Action I

Expected Net Present Value ($/ac)

$1,268.86 = 0.2 \times 1,654.62 + 0.6 \times 1,286.73 + 0.2 \times 829.50$

Management Action II

Expected Net Present Value ($/ac)

$1,198.68 = 0.2 \times 1,529.15 + 0.6 \times 1,236.84 + 0.2 \times 753.72$

Management Action III

Expected Net Present Value ($/ac)

$1,278.67 = 0.2 \times 1,660.66 + 0.6 \times 1,347.21 + 0.2 \times 828.14$

Based on the Bayes decision rule, management action III – a herbicide spray release at plantation age 10 at a cost of $68.22 per acre plus the precommercial thin at plantation age 15 at a cost of $89.22 per acre and then clearcut the plantation at plantation age 25 – should be chosen.

Maximax

The maximax decision rule selects the action that contains the best of the best possible payoffs. This rule is described as the optimistic approach as it chooses the

Table 8.7 Decision Matrix for the Maximax Decision Rule

| Decision[‡] | Net Present Value ($/acre) | | | Maximum |
	Good	Average	Poor	Outcome
PT	1,654.62	1,286.73	829.50	1,654.62
H	1,529.15	1,236.84	753.72	1,529.15
PT&H	1,660.66	1,347.21	828.14	**1,660.66**

[‡] PT denotes a precommercial thin at plantation age 15 at a cost of $89.22 per acre and then clearcut the plantation at plantation age 25. H denotes a herbicide spray release at plantation age 10 at a cost of $68.22 per acre and then clearcut the plantation at plantation age 25. PT&H denotes an herbicide spray release at plantation age 10 at a cost of $68.22 per acre plus the precommercial thin at plantation age 15 at a cost of $89.22 per acre and then clearcut the plantation at plantation age 25.

best of the best. The decision matrix reflecting the maximax decision rule is given in Table 8.7.

The steps to determine the maximax are the following: (1) calculate the maximum possible payoff given each decision or action (this is illustrated by the last column in Table 8.7), and (2) determine the action associated with the maximum payoff from the preceding set. As illustrated by the last column in Table 8.7, management action III – a herbicide spray release at plantation age 10 at a cost of $68.22 per acre plus the precommercial thin at plantation age 15 at a cost of $89.22 per acre and then clearcut the plantation at plantation age 25 – should be chosen, as it gives the most optimistic outcome of $1,660.66 per acre.

Maximin

While the maximax decision rule is considered the optimistic approach, maximin is considered the pessimistic approach. The pessimistic decision maker wants to choose the action by considering the worst consequences of each possible action and picking the action with the least worst among them. The decision matrix reflecting the maximin decision rule is given in Table 8.8.

The steps to determine the maximin are the following: (1) calculate the minimum possible payoff given each decision or action (this is illustrated by the last column in Table 8.8), and (2) determine the action associated with the maximum payoff from the preceding set. As illustrated by the last column in Table 8.8, management action I – the precommercial thin at plantation age 15 at a cost of $89.22 per acre and then clearcut the plantation at plantation age 25 – should be chosen, as it gives the most conservative outcome of $829.50 per acre.

Minimax Regret

The minimax regret decision rule selects the action that minimizes the maximum regret. The decision maker may be worried most about recriminations or the "I told you so's" after an action has been chosen and nature reveals itself. The difference between the return from the best possible decision for a given state of nature and the return from the action taken is a measure of potential "regret" or the opportunity lost and is to be minimized.

Table 8.8 Decision Matrix for the Maximin Decision Rule

Decision[‡]	Net Present Value ($/acre)			Minimum Outcome
	Good	Average	Poor	
PT	1,654.62	1,286.73	829.50	**829.50**
H	1,529.15	1,236.84	753.72	753.72
PT&H	1,660.66	1,347.21	828.14	828.14

‡ PT denotes a precommercial thin at plantation age 15 at a cost of $89.22 per acre and then clearcut the plantation at plantation age 25. H denotes a herbicide spray release at plantation age 10 at a cost of $68.22 per acre and then clearcut the plantation at plantation age 25. PT&H denotes a herbicide spray release at plantation age 10 at a cost of $68.22 per acre plus the precommercial thin at plantation age 15 at a cost of $89.22 per acre and then clearcut the plantation at plantation age 25.

Table 8.9a Decision Matrix for Minimax Regret Decision Rule[‡]

Decision[‡]	Net Present Value ($/acre)		
	Good	Average	Poor
PT	1,654.62	1,286.73	829.50
H	1,529.15	1,236.84	753.72
PT&H	1,660.66	1,347.21	828.14
Maximum	1,660.66	1,347.21	829.50

‡ PT denotes a precommercial thin at plantation age 15 at a cost of $89.22 per acre and then clearcut the plantation at plantation age 25. H denotes a herbicide spray release at plantation age 10 at a cost of $68.22 per acre and then clearcut the plantation at plantation age 25. PT&H denotes a herbicide spray release at plantation age 10 at a cost of $68.22 per acre plus the precommercial thin at plantation age 15 at a cost of $89.22 per acre and then clearcut the plantation at plantation age 25.

The best possible outcome for each state of nature is calculated to determine the minimax regret. This is given by the last row of the decision matrix of Table 8.9a.

The regret matrix is calculated by differences between the best possible outcome for a given state of nature and all possible decisions given that state of nature. The regret matrix is illustrated by Table 8.9b.

The last column of Table 8.9b shows the maximum possible regret of each decision. It is this regret that is minimized. As illustrated by the last column in Table 8.9b, management action III – an herbicide spray release at plantation age 10 at a cost of $68.22 per acre plus the precommercial thin at plantation age 15 at a cost of $89.22 per acre and then clearcut the plantation at plantation age 25 – should be chosen because it minimizes the regret of the three management actions.

How to Use Economic Information –Risk – to Make Better Business Decisions

Because not all costs and revenues may be known with 100% certainty due to events beyond the control of an entrepreneur, I have introduced eight techniques that can be used to analyze decisions that include risk. The first two techniques

Table 8.9b Regret Matrix for Minimax Regret Decision Rule[‡]

Decision[‡]	Net Present Value ($/acre)			
	Good	Average	Poor	Maximum
PT	6.03	60.48	0.00	60.48
H	131.51	110.36	75.79	131.51
PT&H	0.00	0.00	1.37	**1.37**

6.03 = 1,660.66–1,654.62

‡ PT denotes a precommercial thin at plantation age 15 at a cost of $89.22 per acre and then clearcut the plantation at plantation age 25. H denotes a herbicide spray release at plantation age 10 at a cost of $68.22 per acre and then clearcut the plantation at plantation age 25. PT&H denotes a herbicide spray release at plantation age 10 at a cost of $68.22 per acre plus the precommercial thin at plantation age 15 at a cost of $89.22 per acre and then clearcut the plantation at plantation age 25.

examined (i.e., including risk in the interest or discount rate and sensitivity analysis) do not result in a decision rule per se but allow the entrepreneur to understand the dynamics of the system being modeled. Decision trees, equally likely, Bayes decision rule, maximax, maximin, and minimax regret all share the common traits of (i) defining a decision rule to identify the optimal course of action for mutually exclusive decisions and (ii) combining actions that are under the direct control of the entrepreneur with states of nature that are not. Decision trees, equally likely, and Bayes decision rule are described as decision problems under risk as probabilities associated with the various states of nature that are defined explicitly. Maximax, maximin, and minimax regret are described as decision problems under uncertainty as there are no probabilities associated with the various states of nature.

The techniques described are relatively straightforward to use by entrepreneurs. The analysis of these types of problems falls under the rubric of Decision Theory and Operations Research. If a reader is interested in further information on this topic, I would suggest starting your search with the following:

Winston, W. (2004) *Operations Research: Applications and Algorithms*, 4th ed., Boston, MA: Cengage Inc.

Hillier, F.S., and Lieberman, G.J. (2005) *Introduction to Operations Research*, 8th ed., New York, NY: McGraw-Hill.

Levin, R.I., Rubin, D.S., Stinson, J.P., and Gardner, Jr. E.S. (1992) *Quantitative Approaches to Management*, 8th ed., New York, NY: McGraw-Hill.

Risk and uncertainty can affect every component of the Architectural Plan for Wealth and are more often than not relevant to the decision-making process. Which technique is used depends on the questions that the entrepreneur asks and the level and detail of the information available. That said, I feel that the sensitivity analysis approach is often the most useful technique because it:

• Requires the entrepreneur to identify appropriate ranges for the production system, cost, value, and price of the Architectural Plan for Wealth given normal operating conditions;

- Results in a better understanding of the system being modeled by the Architectural Plan for Wealth;
- Identifies the parameters that are most likely to affect the model predictions; and
- Results in describing a decision analysis space of likely solution alternatives.

Notes

1 Gaspars-Wieloch (2019) discusses an interesting method for incorporating uncertainty into net present value calculations.
2 This relative-sensitivity index has the same mathematical form as elasticities described in Chapter 10 – Supply and Demand.
3 While I have focused on NPV and LEV or ($NPV_\infty)_t$, the same discussion would apply to the investment analysis tools described in Chapter 6 – Capital Theory: Investment Analysis.
4 A more complete description of these parameters is given in Chapter 7 – The Natural Resource Management Puzzle.
5 This statement is deceivingly simple, as the entrepreneur must decide the length of the price series to use, the most appropriate inflation deflator to use, and the most practicable base year to use for the sensitivity analysis.
6 The real residential electric prices are calculated using the consumer price index base year 2019. The real stumpage prices are calculated using the producer price index base year 2019.
7 Theory of comparative statics in economics refers to examining the direction of change in an outcome (e.g., quantity demanded) when an exogenous variable (e.g., own-price) changes. It is the direction of change (e.g., increase in own-price implies a decrease in the quantity demanded) and not the amount of the change that is predicted (Silberberg and Suen 2001).

9 Estimating Nonmarket Values

Preamble

The classic supply and demand graph of a market equilibrium defines the optimal price and quantity of the good or service being examined. What if there is no observable demand and consequently no market equilibrium? If there is no observable market equilibrium, there is no optimal quantity or optimal price. For example, without a market supply and demand curve for surfing, the assumption is that surfing is worth zero dollars and the alternative land use of development would provide greater economic benefit. In an article by Gregory Thomas, he profiled Dr. Chad Nelsen who showed that in 2012, 3.3 million surfers contributed at least $2 billion to the US economy annually (www.washingtonpost.com/surfonomics-quantifies-the-worth-of-waves/2012/08/23/86e335ca-ea2c-11e1-a80b-9f898562d010_story.html accessed 28 November 2019). In many cases, surfing provided greater economic benefit than development. As was noted by Costanza et al. (1998: 68), "to say that we should not do valuation of ecosystems is to deny the reality that we already do, always have and cannot avoid doing so in the future." Failure to quantify ecosystem values in commensurate terms with opportunity costs often results in an implicit value of zero being placed on ecosystem services (Dailey 1997). As illustrated, ecosystem services have values larger than zero. So as managers, how do we estimate these values with respect to the Architectural Plan for Profit?

Introduction

Ecosystem functions and processes provide a variety of ecosystem goods and services though passive and active management.[1] For example, tree biomass, an ecosystem good used to produce timber – a direct benefit – is derived from tree productivity, an ecosystem process. Carbon sequestration is also an ecosystem service derived from tree productivity (e.g., Hines et al. 2010). Fish populations, surroundings, and water body are ecosystem goods, and services, used by anglers directly to produce recreational benefits, are the result of ecosystem processes. Air quality is an ecosystem service that contributes to human health – a direct benefit – resulting from atmospheric deposition, an ecosystem process. Water quality is an ecosystem good – a direct benefit – resulting from nutrient and

DOI: 10.4324/9781315678719-9

hydrologic cycling, an ecosystem process. Many ecosystem outputs are traded in formal markets (e.g., timber, recreation leases, mushrooms, and maple syrup) and emerging markets (e.g., carbon sequestration). Many, however, are not traded in formal markets. Consequently, with these ecosystem goods and services there is no observable market equilibrium to determine the optimal level to produce (Chapter 11 – Market Equilibrium and Structure). There is no demand curve to help distribute them among various potential users (Chapter 10 – Supply and Demand). Finally, there is no pricing mechanism (a measure of relative scarcity) to help allocate the resources used in their production (Chapter 11 – Market Equilibrium and Structure).

That said, individuals value these nonmarket ecosystem services by observing their choices. Individuals are observed recreating (hiking, hunting, fishing, viewing wildlife, birding, etc.), and the primary reasons for families owning forestland are for aesthetics, privacy, recreation, and protection of nature (Butler 2008; Majumdar et al. 2008; Hatcher et al. 2013; Butler et al. 2016; Creighton et al. 2016; Snyder et al. 2019). At a state, regional, and national scale, people prefer clean water and air and wilderness. Consequently, given the lack of economic information generally available from a well-functioning market, the entrepreneur, landowner, or policy maker needs to develop economic information analogous to that obtained from markets to make informed decisions concerning how much of these ecosystem goods and services to provide.[2]

This can be illustrated by referring to the Architectural Plan for Profit in Figure 9.1.

The production system is describing the ecosystem processes and functions that provide the ecosystem services. In prior chapters, the boundaries of the Pillars

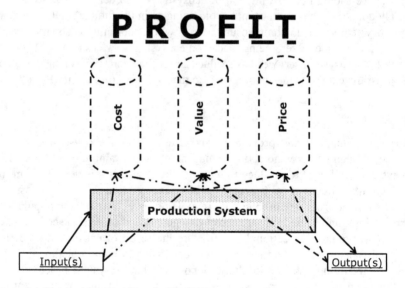

Figure 9.1 The Architectural Plan for Profit

of Cost, Value, and Price were all solid. The economic information used to build these pillars was available from the market. The methods discussed in this chapter will allow developing the Pillars of Cost, Value, and Price. Finally, the concept of profit should be revisited briefly. I have used the term profit in the Architectural Plan for Profit as a proxy for individuals comparing what they gave up to obtain a good or service (its opportunity cost) with the benefits received from obtaining it. Simply, individuals search to find the greatest positive difference between benefits and costs. With nonmarket ecosystem goods and services, the benefits, as measured by the Pillars of Price and Value, and net benefits or profit are inferred from observable choices individuals have made or choices individuals state they would make in a given context.

As the focus of estimating nonmarket benefits is measuring an economic value, the economic concept of value will be revisited. The two methods I will describe for estimating nonmarket benefits are revealed preference and stated preference.

Economic Value – Revisited

According to a seminal work on the economic concept of value by Brown (1984), an assigned value is the expressed relative importance or worth of an object to an individual in a given context. Therefore, an assigned value is observable based on the choices individuals make. Assigned values are relative; it is not the intrinsic nature of the object but the object relative to all other objects that gives rise to an assigned value (Brown 1984). Assigned values are relative, not absolute, and depend on the context surrounding an individual's choice. If the context changes, a value an individual assigns to an object relative to all other objects will also change. Price is related to assigned value and is defined as a per unit measure of assigned value and a measure of relative scarcity. As the price of a good or service increases relative to other goods and services, this particular good or service is scarcer relative to the other goods and services.

In well-functioning markets, measures of assigned value are derived from the intersection of the supply and demand curves for a particular good defining a market equilibrium (see Figure 11.3c). These assigned values are consumer surplus (the area under the demand curve bounded by a given quantity minus the relevant opportunity costs or the net benefit to the consumer for purchasing the good or service; see Figure 11.3c) and producer surplus (the net benefit to the producer for selling the good or service; see Figure 11.3c), respectively. When an observable exchange takes place between consumer and producer, the sum of these net benefits are maximized and are captured by the consumer and producer. If well-functioning markets do not exist for a particular ecosystem good or service, then these measures of economic value are not observable directly.

The objective of the Architectural Plan for Profit is maximizing profits or net benefits. As was described in Chapter 5 – Profit, the greatest utility of the Architectural Plan for Profit is not to estimate total profits or net benefits but to develop a systematic rule to compare the incremental (i.e., marginal) net benefits of one choice relative to another. As illustrated by Figures 10.16a and 10.16b, it is summing the incremental or marginal net benefits from individual choices that lead to estimates of total net benefit. These individual choices are represented by the various price–output combinations (Figures 10.16a and 10.16b). If well-functioning markets are absent, revealed and stated preference can be used to estimate these measures of economic value.

Assigned Measures of Value

Revealed and stated preference methods focus on estimating an assigned value for a nonmarket ecosystem good or service. There are two measures of assigned value that are relevant: Use and nonuse values.

Use Value

Individual's "use" environmental output(s)/outcome(s) *in situ* to enhance their welfare. Use values are composed of three types of assigned values. *Consumptive use values* include those observed through market exchanges (e.g., outputs such as stumpage, mushrooms, and maple syrup) and end products of nature (e.g., fuelwood for heating and cooking) that are consumed directly to produce human well-being. *Nonconsumptive use values* are end products of nature enjoyed or used directly and indirectly to produce human well-being. For example, catch and release fishing and the surroundings and water body are nonconsumptive direct use value used by anglers to produce recreational benefits. Nonconsumptive indirect use values are derived from ecosystem services such as water filtration, soil and water conservation, nutrient cycling, and a genetic library (Pagiola et al. 2004).[3] *Option values* describe the expressed relative importance to retain the opportunity to consume a resource in the future. That is, the preservation of the stock is valuable merely to keep our options open. For example, people may be willing to pay for preserving biodiversity or genetic materials to ensure the option of having these goods in the future. Option value may also reflect your willingness to pay to preserve the Alaska wilderness as you might want to visit it one day. There is an additional concept termed quasi-option, which is a value attached to the preservation of an option in order to stress the crucial role played by irreversibility and/or the expected value of more information and additional learning (Arrow and Fisher 1974; Conrad 1980; Perman et al. 2003; Basili and Fontini 2005; Freeman et al. 2014).

Nonuse Values

Nonuse values, often described as passive use values, are composed of two types of assigned values. First is existence value. That is the expressed relative importance to simply preserve the existence of some resource. Second is bequest value. That is the expressed relative importance to leave resources for future generations or their heirs. The difference between existence and bequest values is subtle and they are often combined.[4]

Total Economic Value

A market equilibrium is determined by maximizing the sum of producer and consumer surplus.[5] This is illustrated in Figure 11.3c. Market equilibrium price and quantity provide economic information used in consumption and production decisions by consumers and producers, respectively, and define a market value for a good or service. This market equilibrium also describes the total economic value (TEV) of a good or service and reflects the assigned value of a good or service. Figure 9.2 illustrates the decomposition of TEV.

Figure 9.2 shows TEV is comprised of use plus nonuse values. For a good like maple syrup, TEV reflects a consumptive use value. For an ecosystem good like a trout, the TEV would reflect a consumptive use value if the angler keeps it or a nonconsumptive direct use value if the angler practices catch and release or possibly a nonuse existence value for an individual. For a rooftop solar array, TEV would reflect a consumptive use value for the used converted energy and possibly a nonconsumptive direct use value associated with the bragging rights of having a rooftop solar array.

Many ecosystem goods and services are not traded in formal markets and, thus, there is no observable demand curve and no estimate of TEV. Consequently, the focus on estimating nonmarket values is deriving an individual's expressed willingness and ability to pay for a given quantity at a given place and time; namely, the demand curve.[6] The terminology "expressed relative importance or worth" was used deliberately as use and nonuse values being estimated are assigned values.

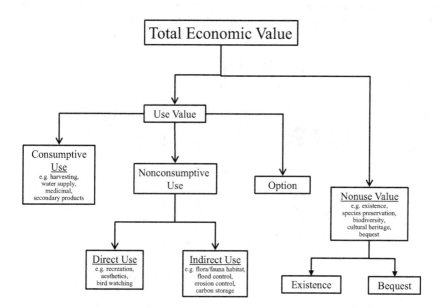

Figure 9.2 Total Economic Value

Adapted from National Research Council (2005) and Newman (2010)

It bears repeating, assigned values are relative, not absolute, and depend on the context surrounding an individual's choice. If the context changes, the value an individual assigns to an object relative to all other objects will also change.

Revealed Preference or Indirect Methods

The core of the revealed preference techniques is that the analyst observes choices people have made but does not ask them directly how much they value the ecosystem good or service. The logic of revealed preference is that because people are consuming these nonmarket goods and services, we can observe the choices they are making in consuming them. When producing any output (tennis shoes, clean air, reduction in noise pollution, purchase of a house, or recreational experiences, etc.), inputs must be used. Based on the behavioral assertion that people are maximizers (Chapter 1 – Introduction), if we observe the purchases of inputs, we can infer that an output's value must be at least as great as the cost of the inputs. Figure 9.3 illustrates this logic using the Architectural Plan for Profit.

Based on the description of the production system used to produce a defined set of nonmarket goods and services in a given context, the set of inputs are enumerated. Observing the expenditures individuals make on these inputs, the Pillar of Cost is estimated. As a result, a monetary value for the other components of the Architectural Plan for Profit can be inferred.

Revealed preference methods are used to estimate an individual's willingness to pay for nonmarket goods or services based on their existing choices.[7] In this respect the analysis is from the point of view of the consumer. In previous chapters the analysis has been from the point of view of the entrepreneur who produces or

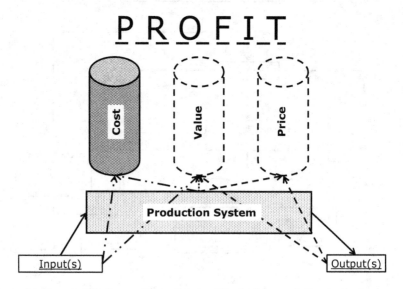

Figure 9.3 Revealed Preference Methodology – The Architectural Plan for Profit

provides a good or service. The student should keep in mind this change in perspective when studying this section.

An advantage of revealed preference methods is that they are based on observable individual choice behavior. That is, individuals "use" these environmental output(s) or outcome(s) *in situ* to enhance their welfare (Freeman et al. 2014). Observable choices are consistent with the definition of an assigned value as given by Brown (1984). Revealed preference methods are used to infer nonmarket "use" values (Freeman et al. 2014). If the questions being asked by an entrepreneur, landowner, or policy maker involve only use values, then any one of the following revealed preference methods discussed later is appropriate. In the case of "nonuse" values, there are no observable market interactions between the individual and the resource in question; consequently, revealed preference methods are inappropriate for measuring nonuse values (Freeman et al. 2014).[8]

I will describe three common revealed preference techniques: Cost-based approaches, hedonic model, and travel cost model.

Cost-Based Approaches

While the travel cost and hedonic models are probably the most recognized approaches used in the context described here, other approaches such as damage cost avoided and replacement or substitution cost and opportunity cost methods are also available.

Damage Cost Avoided and Replacement or Substitution Cost

These approaches are based on the premise that if an individual incurs costs to avoid damages caused by the loss of an ecosystem service or to replace the lost ecosystem services, then these ecosystem services must be worth at least what was paid to replace them. For example, the avoided damages are the likely costs with and without the ecosystem service, such as a wetland to protect against floods and storms, or the cost of a human-engineered water treatment plant to replace the loss of water quality services of the ecosystem. The water treatment plant would provide the equivalent service at least cost of all the alternatives examined.

In 2006, Kramer et al. examined the water quality of 25 lakes in the United States, focusing on eutrophication due to excess phosphorus loading. Agricultural and urban land uses are the leading contributors of phosphorus to surface waters. These nonpoint pollution sources include, but are not limited to, failing septic systems and fertilizers. Cost-effectiveness analysis can be used to determine which water quality mitigation strategies can achieve a water quality standard for the least cost. Their study examined the cost effectiveness of two different strategies in addressing lake water quality: septic system upgrades and riparian buffers along agricultural land in the watershed. Their results showed that riparian buffers were generally more cost effective in avoiding or replacing the lost ecosystem services of mitigating phosphorus.

Opportunity Cost Approach

The opportunity cost approach can be used to estimate nonconsumptive and nonuse values of a resource. This approach examines a resource's highest-valued alternative forgone when any choice is made. For example, determining the net present value of two mutually exclusive different land uses such as timber production and a nature reserve. If a public decision maker chooses the nature reserve with its smaller positive net present value, then the nonconsumptive and nonuse values are greater than that for timber production (Newman 2010).

In 1989, Newman and Healy examined the possible use of the Bladen Reserve located in a basin of the Bladen Branch, a major arm of the Monkey River, in southern Belize, Central America, as a nature reserve. Proposals were made throughout the 1980s to set approximately 35,000 ha of the Bladen aside for wildlife conservation and tourism. For poor countries, any decision to restrict the use of natural resources and thereby possibly forgo revenue must be made carefully. The forgone timber net revenues represent the opportunity cost of this nature reserve. The present value estimates of the net timber revenues ranged from 2.0 to 1.5 million US 1988 dollars due to the low stocking of the primary and secondary timber species and high harvesting (i.e., difficult terrain) and milling costs. The government of Belize, in the end, agreed with these results and declared a 44,000 ha portion of the Bladen Branch as an official Nature Reserve in 1990. The Belize government's choice to create a nature reserve implied they valued the nonconsumptive and non-use values of this land uses greater than the 2.0 million US dollars of using the land to generate net timber revenue.

Other examples of using the opportunity cost approach are Montgomery et al. (1994), Scapra et al. (2000), and Kniivilä and Saastamoinen (2002). Scapra et al. (2000) combines the opportunity cost approach with a hedonic model to determine how the biophysical characteristics of stands and the socioeconomic status of landowners influenced the non-timber forest values.

Hedonic Model

Rosen (1974) formalized the theory supporting hedonic models and laid the foundation on which they are built. Rosen's hedonic theory states that the market price of a good is a function of its characteristics or attributes. For example, what is a "use value" of a lake?[9] Or, what is a potential homeowner's willingness to pay for lakefront property? Figure 9.4a illustrates this problem.

The lake is an attribute or characteristic associated with one house but not the other. The houses are otherwise identical. A use value of the lake is not explicit; it is included in the price of the lake house. In the example shown in Figure 9.4a, a use value of the lake is $100,000. Unfortunately, not all comparisons are going to be as straightforward as that illustrated by Figure 9.4a. In Figure 9.4b, again the comparison is between two houses, one of which still has the lake attribute.

However, now the houses are not identical. The obvious difference is the lake house also has a garage. Now the price difference of $175,000 is for the combined net benefit of the lake, garage, and any other attribute differences plus any other

Market Price $300,000   Market Price $200,000

Figure 9.4a Hedonic Model: What Is the Value of the Lake?

Market Price $300,000   Market Price $125,000

Figure 9.4b Hedonic Model: What Is the Value of the Lake?

nonconsumptive use values. The hedonic model allows for estimating the combined use value or the implicit price of each attribute.

In a similar manner, a rooftop solar system is an attribute that could add value to a house price. In a 2011 study, Hoen et al. examined the sale premium associated with homes with photovoltaic (PV) systems in California using 21 different hedonic model formulations. Their research found strong evidence that homes with PV systems in California have sold for a premium over comparable homes without PV systems. More specifically, estimates for average PV premiums range from approximately $3.9 to $6.4 per installed watt (DC) among the 21 different hedonic model specifications, with most models coalescing near $5.5/watt.

Rosen's theory that the market price of a good is a function of observable and measurable attributes can be generalized using the hedonic price function illustrated by equation (9.1):

Market Price = f(positive attributes, negative attributes)   (9.1)

Using the hedonic model starts with creating a list of attributes that are proposed to be related to the good. Each of these attributes will affect the good's use value positively or negatively. Implicit price functions for these attributes can be quantified through statistical estimation techniques such as a regression model with the good's market price, the dependent variable, and its various attributes, the independent variables. Equation (9.2) illustrates a linear–linear hedonic price functional form of equation (9.1)

$$P_j = \beta_0 + \beta_1 X_{j1} + \beta_2 X_{j2} + \beta_3 X_{j3} + \cdots + \beta_K X_{jK} + \varepsilon_j$$
$$= \beta_0 + \sum_{k=1}^{K} \beta_k X_{jk} + \varepsilon_j \qquad (9.2)$$

where the βs are the coefficients to be estimated statistically and the Xs denote the attributes.[10] In addition, the βs denote the implicit price or value the consumer places on a specific attribute. When the hedonic model is linear–linear, as in equation (9.2), the implicit price function is a constant marginal implicit price, β_k. The implicit price is defined as dollars per unit of the attribute holding the level of all other attributes constant; for example, if the attribute is the number of feet or meters of lake frontage, then the units on the implicit price are dollars per foot or meter of lake frontage. If the sign of a coefficient for a given attribute is positive (negative), then an additional unit of that attribute will increase (decrease) the consumer's willingness to pay for the good. In this manner an implicit price function could be estimated for both the lake and garage shown in Figure 9.4b. Finally, workable competition is a key assumption to using a hedonic model as the resulting implicit price will represent a buyer's willingness to pay for that attribute accurately (Rosen 1974).

For the purpose of discussing hedonic models, I will rewrite equation (9.2) as equation (9.3)

$$P = f\left(\begin{matrix} X_1 & X_2 & X_3 & & X_k \\ [\pm]' & [\pm]' & [\pm]' & \cdots, & [\pm] \end{matrix} \right) \qquad (9.3)$$

where the signs in the brackets indicate whether the attribute has a positive or negative effect on market price. For example, in the lakefront property illustrated in Figure 9.4b, assuming the attributes (number of bedrooms, number of bathrooms, size, etc.) are the same, the hedonic model will be shown as

$$P = f\left(\begin{array}{cc} \text{Lake} & \text{Garage} \\ [+] & [+] \end{array}, S, N\right)$$

where the attributes of interest are the lake and garage and S represents other parcel and structural attributes for the property (e.g., finished square feet, home age, lot acreage, etc.), and N represents neighborhood attributes for the property (e.g., distance to shopping centers, school quality, etc.). In this example, a tenable proposition is that the implicit prices of the lake and garage attributes are positive. Thus, having both lake frontage and a garage would increase the market price of a house. The magnitudes of the implicit prices would indicate a per unit value the buyer places on each attribute (e.g., dollars per foot of lake frontage or dollars per garage square feet). Each attribute that is included in the hedonic model will have an estimated implicit price. Caution should be used with estimating hedonic pricing models. For example, the statistically estimated implicit prices are dependent on the market being in equilibrium and defined as workably competitive. In addition, if the hedonic model is underspecified (that is, important attributes are not included) or multicollinearity among attributes occurs, this will cause bias in the statistically estimated implicit prices. A more detailed discussion of the statistical analysis of hedonic models is beyond the scope of this book. If a reader is interested in these topics, I would recommend they review the topics of regression analysis and econometrics.

I will use two examples to illustrate the hedonic model: timber sale prices and amenity values.

Timber Sale Prices

From the point of view of a harvester (the buyer): What is their willingness to pay for standing trees (stumpage price)? Their willingness to pay would be affected by the various attributes associated with the trees from a timber sale; for example, species (Sp), quality or grade (G), hauling distance (HD), diameter at breast height (DBH), and volume (Vol). Using the market price of a timber sale, the hedonic price function is given in equation (9.4):

$$\text{Timber Sale Price} = f\left(\begin{array}{ccccc} \text{Sp} & \text{G} & \text{HD} & \text{DBH} & \text{Vol} \\ [?] & [+] & [-] & [+] & [+] \end{array}\right) \qquad (9.4)$$

The proposed impacts the various attributes have on the harvester's willingness to pay are given in the brackets below each attribute, holding the level of all other attributes constant (*ceteris paribus*). For example, as the volume (Vol) of the sale increases, holding the level of all other attributes constant, the tenable proposition is that the amount a harvester is willing to pay would also increase. As the DBH of the trees within a sale increases *ceteris paribus*, so should a harvester's willingness to pay for the sale. An increase in hauling distance (HD) would increase a harvester's cost of transporting the stumpage from where it is being harvested to a sawmill, *ceteris paribus*. A harvester would be expected to cover this increase in cost by lowering their willingness to pay for the sale. Tree grade (TG) is a measure of quality (Chapter 2 – Production Systems). As tree quality increases, higher-quality and more valuable products can be produced from the tree. A harvester would be willing to pay more for higher-grade trees, *ceteris paribus*. This was illustrated in Table 4.3 for the seven different product classes and their associated prices in the Radiata Pine Plantation practical application. Finally, it seems obvious that different tree species (SP) would have different market prices; for example, a black cherry (*Prunus serotina*) has a higher stumpage price per unit volume than a white pine (*Pinus strobes*). The reason for the question mark in equation (9.4) is that the relationship between species and stumpage price is dependent on the nature of the sale. For example, the species stumpage price relationship for black cherry (higher stumpage prices) would be positive if included in a sale with predominately white pine (with lower stumpage price). The species stumpage price relationship for white pine could be negative if included in a sale with predominately black cherry.

Puttock et al. (1990) examined 344 timber sales throughout southwestern Ontario from 1982 to 1987.[11] They developed a hedonic price function illustrated by equation (9.5)

$$P_j = f\left(\frac{TVol_j}{[+]}, \frac{PctSpVol_{1j}}{[+]}, \frac{PctSpVol_{2j}}{[+]}, \frac{AVol_j}{[+]}, \frac{G_j}{[-]}, \frac{HD_j}{[-]}, \frac{PI_j}{[+]} \right) \qquad (9.5)$$

where
P_j denotes the lump-sum sale price of the jth timber sale;[12]
$TVol_j$ denotes the total volume of the jth timber sale;
$PctSpVol_{1j}$ denotes the proportion of the total sales volume from highest value species group present in the jth timber sale (species are divided into three groups according to value and species);
$PctSpVol_{2j}$ denotes the proportion of the total sales volume from medium value species group present in the jth timber sale;
$AVol_j$ denotes the average volume per tree on the jth timber sale;
G_j denotes a quality index for the timber on the jth timber sale (This index is based on the percent of timber in grade 1, grade 2, and so on, with 1 denoting excellent quality and 4 denoting poor quality.);
HD_j denotes hauling distance from the jth timber sale to the purchasing mill; and
PI_j denotes an annual industry price index (This variable will account for inflation differences for the period 1982 to 1987.).

The terms in the brackets are the hypothesized signs for each attribute. I would advise the reader to take a moment and compare the hypothesized signs for each attribute given by Puttock et al. (1990) in equation (9.5) and the hypothetical hedonic model in equation (9.4). Are the hypothesized signs in equation (9.5) tenable?

Table 9.1 Results of the Hedonic Model of Southwestern Ontario Timber Sales From 1982 to 1987[‡]

Variable	Estimated Coefficient Value	Units
$TVol_j$	42.91	$\dfrac{CD}{m^3}$
$PctSpVol_{1j}$	4,528.8	$\dfrac{CD}{PctSpVol_{1j}}$
$PctSpVol_{2j}$	2,433.2	$\dfrac{CD}{PctSpVol_{2j}}$
$AVol_j$	2,699.5	$\dfrac{CD}{m^3}$
G_j	−1,170.7	$\dfrac{CD}{G_j}$
HD_j	−14.05	$\dfrac{CD}{km}$
PI_j	254.0	$\dfrac{CD}{CD}$

Source: Puttock et al. (1990)

[‡] CD denotes Canadian dollars, m^3 denotes cubic meters, km denotes kilometers, and all other variables defined as before where the first column lists the variables from equation (9.5), the second column defines the statistically estimated β coefficients for a linear–linear regression equation, and the third column define the units associated with the statistically estimated β coefficients.

Puttock et al. (1990) examined three different functional forms for the hedonic model. I will only examine the results of the linear–linear form, which are given in Table 9.1

The terms in the second column of Table 9.1 also define the implicit prices. For example, if the total volume of a timber sale increased by 1 m^3, this would add 42.91 Canadian dollars (CDs) to the timber sale value. A 1% increase in volume from the highest value species group would add 4,528.80 CDs to the timber sale value. A 1-kilometer increase in hauling distance would decrease the timber sales value by 14.05 CDs.

Amenity Values

Built-to-wildlands ecosystems provide amenity values. These amenity values can be provided by urban trees on a landowner's property or adjacent properties, street trees, parks, or a variety of land use/open space categories. I will describe briefly three different studies using hedonic models to estimate nonconsumptive indirect amenity use values.

Urban trees and open space provide many different types of benefits to citizens. These benefits include end-product ecosystem goods and services such as air quality improvement and shading by urban trees. Social benefits from urban trees and open space include improved quality of life. A study by Poudyal et al. (2009) examined the quality of open space and how it affects the property value in a neighborhood. The proposed linear–linear implicit hedonic price function is given in equation (9.6)

$$P = f(S,N,O) \tag{9.6}$$

where P represents the property's sale price, S represents parcel and structural attributes of the property (e.g., finished square feet, home age, lot acreage, number of bathrooms, age), N represents neighborhood attributes of the property (e.g., distance to shopping centers, school quality), and O represents land use amenities in the neighborhood.

A study by Sander et al. (2010) examined the values of urban trees to single family home property values as well as how values vary with different levels of tree cover. In addition, they examined whether tree cover affects home prices beyond the local parcel. The proposed log–linear implicit hedonic price function is given in equation (9.7)

$$\ln(P) = f(S,N,E) \tag{9.7}$$

where ln(P) represents natural log of the property's sale price, S represents parcel and structural attributes for the property, N represents neighborhood attributes for the property, and E represents environmental attributes of the property (e.g., proximity to lakes, percent tree cover).

Yoo (2012) expanded on the prior works by accounting for spatial variability among the environmental variables describing urban open space. She examined the four common hedonic pricing function forms and determined that the linear–linear best fit her data. The implicit hedonic price function is given in equation (9.8)

$$P = f(S,N,E) \tag{9.8}$$

where P represents the property's sale price, S represents parcel and structural attributes for the property, N represents neighborhood attributes for the property, and E represents eight land use categories, distance to each category, and four measures of spatial diversity given the land use categories within 100 meters (visual zone) and 1 kilometer of the house (walking distance).

While the hedonic pricing models presented in equations (9.6), (9.7), and (9.8) appear straightforward, the list of variables that define and describe each set of attributes is too extensive to provide here. In addition, a discussion of the methods used to estimate the hedonic prices statistically is beyond the scope of this book. However, I will discuss the implications of the resulting implicit prices for each study starting with Poudyal et al. (2009). Poudyal et al. (2009) examined how urban residents value variety, spatial configuration, and patterns of open space in their neighborhoods. They hypothesized that residents prefer heterogeneity (i.e., more diversity) within open space to homogeneity and fewer but larger plots of open space to many smaller plots. Again, the magnitudes and the signs associated with the statistically estimated implicit prices were used to test these hypotheses. Their results indicated that urban residents prefer a neighborhood with a variety of land uses within open spaces types (e.g., pine forest, hardwood forest, wetland, and pasture) to one with less diverse and homogenously composed open spaces (e.g., pine forest or hardwood alone), prefer open spaces that are more even and square/rectangular shape to those in crooked or convoluted shapes, and did not prefer neighborhoods with residential areas mixed with industrial or commercial land uses (Poudyal et al. 2009).

While past studies have shown that urban trees increase the sale price of homes, the study by Sander et al. (2010) is unique in adding a spatial component to the analysis. That is, to what extent do trees on adjacent and neighborhood properties affect property values? Referring to Figure 9.2, Sander et al. are using the statistically estimated implicit prices to provide economic information about use and indirect use values. Their results indicate that increasing tree cover increases home sale value up to a limit. For example, increasing tree cover to 44% within a 328-foot buffer increases home sale value, but increasing tree cover beyond this amount will decrease home sale value. Basically, homeowners value trees in their local neighborhoods, at distances that roughly correspond to the length of a city block. This value may reflect a preference for tree-lined streets and the shading and aesthetic environment they offer. Homeowners appear to place less value on tree cover beyond their immediate local neighborhood and on tree cover over 40% in their immediate local neighborhood. Urban trees provide positive externalities (Sander et al. 2010).

Yoo (2012) investigated how urban residents value the spatial configuration of their neighborhood. Her results found that house buyers positively value the environmental amenities from various types of open space and its configuration at the same time. In addition, within visual distance, property values were higher when land uses were more homogenous, but within walking distance, house buyers preferred more heterogeneous landscapes.

The values estimated by these studies are use values. The utility of these studies goes beyond determining housing prices. These studies provide urban planners, residents, and decision makers with economic information concerning broader issues of land use planning and urban tree planting goals.

Travel Cost Model

The travel cost model (TCM) begins with the realization that a major cost of outdoor recreation is the travel and time costs incurred to get to the recreation site (Clawson and Knetsch 1966). Because individuals reside at varying distances from the recreation site, the variation in distance, number of trips, and travel costs can be used to determine the willingness to pay for a recreation site (Whitehead et al. 2008). There are two general categories of TCMs: zonal travel cost model and individual travel cost model. After introducing the zonal and individual travel cost models, I describe a simple zonal travel cost model based on a study by Wagner and Choi (1999).

Zonal Travel Cost Model

Zonal travel cost models (ZTCM) are based on defining travel zones from an identified recreational site. For example, see Figure 9.5 for the High Peaks of Adirondack Park in New York State.

Within each travel zone, travels costs to the recreation site are assumed to be similar and individuals within the zones are assumed to have similar socioeconomic characteristics. Referring to Figure 9.5, within a 50-mile radius of the High Peaks travel costs are assumed to be zero, between 50 and 150 miles the travel costs are positive and constant for all people who live in that zone and travel to the High Peaks, and between 150 and 250 miles the travel costs are greater than the previous travel zone and constant for all people who live in that zone and travel to the High Peaks. This same pattern holds for all subsequent defined travel zones. The trips per capita from each zone are determined as well as the travel costs from each zone. The ZTCM is useful when using secondary data sources such as recreation permits or fee receipts that contain limited data (Loomis et al. 2009). These data can be used to develop a demand curve relating price to the number of visitors. If sufficient data are collected, a statistical relationship between price and number of visitors can be developed similar to the hedonic models presented earlier.[13] If not, numerical methods can be used to develop a demand curve. A discussion of the statistical analysis of ZTCMs is beyond the scope of this book. If a reader is

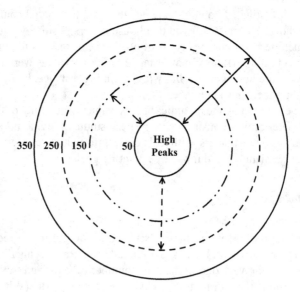

Figure 9.5 Zonal Travel Cost Model: What Is the Willingness to Pay to Recreate in the High Peaks of Adirondack Park in New York State?

interested in these topics, I would recommend they review the topics of regression analysis and econometrics.

There are five concerns with using a ZTCM. First, in ZTCMs average travel cost and zone average travel time cannot be separately included because they are nearly perfectly correlated (Randall 1994; Brown and Nawas 1973). That is, separating an individual's opportunity cost of time spent in transit and the cost of travel (e.g., the cost of gas) due to the potential co-relationship between these two variables: The longer the trip, the greater the cost of gas and the opportunity cost of time spent in transit. In addition, accounting for an individual's opportunity cost of time spent in transit is also problematic. For example, assuming the opportunity cost of time spent in transit is a function of the individual's wage or salary would require collecting socioeconomic information. If just in-transit time is collected, then the opportunity cost of time spent in transit is the same for all individuals within a given zone and each individual within a given zone has the same socioeconomic status. Second, the ZTCM does not address the problem of accounting for travel costs associated with visiting multiple sites in a single trip or substitute sites. Third, the ZTCM also does not account for users with zero travel costs as illustrated by Figure 9.5. Fourth, the ZTCM does not include the cost of equipment (e.g., tents, boots, fishing poles, and cameras, etc.) as they are not travel costs.[14] Finally, the ZTCM estimates a direct use value (see Figure 9.2).

Individual Travel Cost Model

The individual travel cost model (ITCM) requires collecting data directly from visitors to a recreation site using a survey. Data collected by the survey would include, for example, location of the visitor's home, how far they traveled to the site, how many times they have visited the site in a given time period, length of trip, travel expenses (gas, food, lodging, etc.), demographic information (income, age, education, etc.), how many different recreation sites or destinations were part of this trip, recreation site quality metrics, and so forth. Based on these data, an implicit ITCM can be defined by equation (9.9)

$$N_{ij} = f\left(C_{ij}, SED_{ij}, \theta_{ij}\right) \qquad (9.9)$$

where N_{ij} are the number of visits by the ith individual during a defined time period to site j, C_{ij} denotes travel costs of the ith individual to site j, SED_i denotes a set of social, economic, and demographic variables of the ith individual at site j, and θ_{ij} denotes a set of recreation site quality metrics of site j identified by the ith individual. As with hedonic models, the ITCM may take many different forms. Again, the most common are linear–linear, log–linear, linear–log, and log–log. Readers may note the similarities of the ITCM and the hedonic models presented earlier. The ITCM has been used to address the concerns raised by the ZTCM. In addition, Vaughan and Russell (1982) pioneered an extension of equation (9.9) called the varying parameters model that can be used to account for site quality differences (e.g., water quality). In addition, Bockstael et al. (1989) and Kaoru et al. (1995) illustrate the use of a random utility model that can account for site quality differences.[15] The ITCM can estimate direct and indirect use value (see Figure 9.2). However, a discussion of the statistical analysis of ITCMs is beyond the scope of this book. If a reader is interested in these topics, I would recommend they review the following articles: Bockstael et al. (1989), Willis and Garrod (1991), Dobbs (1993), Hesseln et al. (2003, 2004), Loomis et al. (2009), and Cavo (2018) and regression analysis and econometrics.

Zonal Travel Cost Model Example

A large landowner was interested in developing a stewardship plan to help manage the approximately 3,612 acres on and near the Moose River that flows through Fowlersville, New York. A study by Wagner and Choi (1999) examined the recreational use value for fishing access on the Moose River. The data used to develop the ZTCM were from the New York State Department of Environmental Conservation's 1996 Angler Survey (NYS DEC 1997). The five steps used were based on those described by Rideout and Hesseln (2001).

First, determine contiguous zones around the study area. The New York Department of Environmental Conservation's regional administrative structure was used to define the travel zones based on the data collected by the 1996 Angler Survey.[16] The estimated one-way driving distance from the most populated city from each region to Fowlersville, New York, rounded to the nearest 40-mile increment defined the radii for each zone. A travel distance of approximately 300 miles or less defined the limit of the ZTCM based on research by Loomis and Walsh (1997). Second, determine the population in each zone. The population of each region is obtained from the US Census Bureau. Third, determine the number of anglers visiting Region 6, containing the Moose River in Fowlersville, New York, from each DEC administrative regions, using the 1996 Angler Survey. These data are given in Table 9.2a.

The Region 6 Fisheries Unit in Watertown, New York, estimated that approximately 221 anglers visit the study area annually. Using the last column from Table 9.2a, the number of anglers visiting Fowlersville was determined. Fourth, estimate the per capita participation rates from each zone. These data are given in Table 9.2b.

Constructing the demand curve is the last step. Due to the limited data, a numerical rather than a statistical approach was used. The travel cost per angler was given by equation (9.10):

$$\text{Travel Cost} \left(\text{\$}\big/ \text{angler} \right) = \frac{0.31 \left(\text{\$}\big/ \text{mile} \right) \times \left[\text{Distance} \left(\text{mile} \big/ \text{vechile} \right) \times 2 \right]}{1.6 \left(\text{anglers} \big/ \text{vechile} \right)} \quad (9.10)$$

In 1999, the United States Internal Revenue Service used $0.31 per mile as a cost of traveling by car. In addition, the Region 6 Fisheries Unit in Watertown,

Table 9.2a Basic Zonal Travel Costs Data for Anglers Fishing in Region 6 Containing the Moose River in Fowlersville, New York[‡]

DEC Administrative Region	Center of the DEC Administrative Region	Number of Anglers	One-Way Travel (miles)	Percent Anglers Visiting Region 6[§] (%)
6	Utica	65,290	40	34.6
7	Syracuse	39,570	80	21.0
5	Saratoga Springs	4,700	120	2.5
4	Albany	5,880	120	3.1
8	Rochester	31,470	160	16.7
9	Buffalo	16,450	240	19.2
Other	New York City	5,220	280	2.8
Out of State		20,240	320	10.7
Total		18,8820		100

[‡] These data are based on New York State Department of Environmental Conservations (DEC) 1996 Angler Survey (NYS DEC 1997). The estimated driving distance from the most populated city from each region to Fowlersville, New York, were calculated by using Yahoo's travel map website (http://maps.yahoo.com) and rounded to the nearest 40-mile increment.

[§] The percent anglers visiting the ith region is determined as the number of anglers visiting the ith region divided by the total number of anglers visiting Region 6; for example, $\dfrac{65290}{188820} \times 100 = 34.6$ ·

Table 9.2b The Estimated Number of Anglers by Region of Residence for Anglers Fishing in the Moose River in Fowlersville, New York[‡]

DEC Region	Center of the DEC Administrative Region	Percent Anglers Visiting Region 6 (%)	Zone Population	Anglers Visiting the Study Site	Participation Rate per 100,000 Population
6	Utica	34.6	566,346	76.4	13.49
7	Syracuse	21.0	1,201,502	46.3	3.85
5	Saratoga Springs	2.5	528,946	5.5	1.04
4	Albany	3.1	895,611	6.9	0.77
8	Rochester	16.7	1,331,908	36.8	2.77
9	Buffalo	19.2	1,508,394	19.3	1.28
Other	New York City	2.8	11,957,748	6.1	0.05
Out of State		10.7	31,590,846[§]	23.7	0.07
Total		100		221.0	

[‡] The New York State Department of Environmental Conservation (DEC) Region 6 Fisheries Unit in Watertown New York, estimated that approximately 221 anglers visit the Moose River in Fowlersville, New York, annually

[§] Out-of-state population includes parts of Connecticut, Massachusetts, New Hampshire, New Jersey, Pennsylvania, Rhode Island, and Vermont

Table 9.3 Initial Travel Costs per Angler for Fishing on the Moose River in Fowlersville, New York

DEC Region	Center of the DEC Administrative Region	One-Way Travel (miles)	Travel Cost per Angler	Anglers Visiting the Study Site	Participation Rate per 100,000 Population
6	Utica	40	15.50	76.4	13.49
7	Syracuse	80	31.00	46.3	3.85
5	Saratoga Springs	120	46.50	5.5	1.04
4	Albany	120	46.50	6.9	0.77
8	Rochester	160	62.00	36.8	2.77
9	Buffalo	240	93.00	19.3	1.28
Other	New York City	280	108.00	6.1	0.05
Out of State		320	124.00	23.7	0.07
Total				221.0	

New York, estimated there are approximately 1.6 anglers per vehicle. Table 9.3 gives the travel cost per angler, assuming no change in travel costs.

The demand curve was developed using the information in Table 9.3 and four assumptions. First, the sole purpose of the travel was to go fishing. Fortunately for most anglers, single purpose and destination are the rule rather than the exception. Second, there were no benefits from the time spent traveling. Third, within each zone, anglers were assumed to face the same travel distance, prices, incomes, tastes, and substitute recreation opportunities. Therefore, within each zone anglers faced roughly the same travel cost, so that only travel costs by car would explain the difference in the decision of whether to visit the site. Consequently, per capita participation rates were assumed to be only a function of travel costs. Increasing the travel costs faced by each zone and multiplying the participation rate associated with the increased travel costs with total population in each zone, total number of visits to the site can be calculated. This is illustrated by Table 9.4.

Finally, the approach assumes the individuals respond in the same way to an entrance fee as they would to an increase in travel costs. The corresponding total quantities of visitors at varying travel costs (i.e., prices) define the demand curve and are given in Table 9.5 and shown graphically in Figure 9.6.

Given the zonal travel cost demand curve, the consumer surplus at each different price level can be estimated. This is given in the last column of Table 9.5 and shown graphically in Figure 9.7.

Stated Preference or Direct Method

As was stated earlier, the core of the revealed preference techniques is that the analyst observes choices people have made but does not ask directly how much they value the resource. The core of the stated preference techniques is simply to ask people directly how much they value the ecosystem good or service. There are two approaches that are used to elicit how much an individual values a resource directly based on a hypothetical situation: willingness to pay (WTP) and

Table 9.4 Travel Costs per Angler Assuming an Increase in Travel Costs of $15.50 for Anglers Fishing on the Moose River in Fowlersville, New York

DEC Region	Center of the DEC Administrative Region	One-Way Travel (miles)	Travel Cost per Angler	Anglers Visiting the Study Site	Participation Rate per 100,000 Population
6	Utica	40	31.00	21.8	3.85
7	Syracuse	80	46.50	10.9	0.90[‡]
5	Saratoga Springs	120	62.00	14.6	2.77
4	Albany	120	62.00	24.8	2.77
8	Rochester	160	77.50[§]	26.9	2.02[§]
9	Buffalo	240	108.50	0.8	0.05
Other	New York City	280	124.00	9.0	0.07
Out of State		320	139.50	0.0	0.00
Total				108.7	

[‡] Regions 4 and 5 were defined within the same travel cost zone. Their participation rates from Table 9.3 were averaged; thus, the participation rate for Syracuse, NY, given a $15.50 increase in travel costs was $0.90 = \dfrac{1.04 + 0.77}{2}$.

[§] A travel cost of $77.50 is not given in Table 9.3. However, $77.50 = \dfrac{62 + 93}{2}$ is the average of Regions 8 and 9's travel costs. The participation rate, $2.02 = \dfrac{2.77 + 1.28}{2}$, was calculated in a similar manner.

Table 9.5 Zonal Travel Cost Demand Schedule and Consumer Surplus for Anglers Fishing on the Moose River in Fowlersville, New York

Travel Cost Increase ($)	Number of Anglers	Consumer Surplus ($)
0.00	221.00	6,236.55
15.50	108.74	3,681.07
31.00	85.27	2,177.51
46.50	58.81	1,060.91
62.00	28.52	384.16
77.50	8.91	94.11
93.00	1.19	15.81
108.50	0.42	3.29
124.00	0.00	0.00

willingness to accept (WTA). I will first introduce the concepts of WTP and WTA and then describe contingent valuation – a common stated preference technique. I will conclude with a description of a contingent valuation study concerning deer management in an urban area.

Willingness to Pay Versus Willingness to Accept

The basic format for WTP is to ask the individual how much they would be willing to pay, for example, to enter a wilderness area, to canoe, to backpack, to fish,

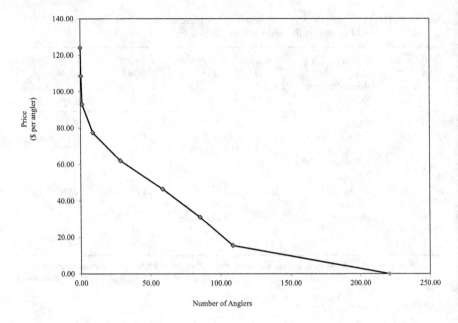

Figure 9.6 The Zonal Travel Cost Demand Curve for Anglers Fishing in Fowlersville, New York

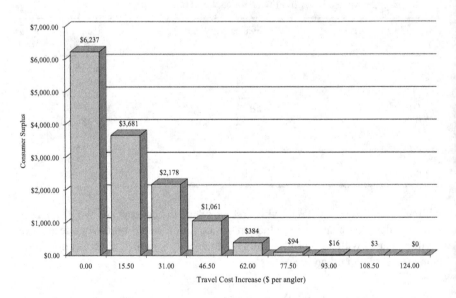

Figure 9.7 Consumer Surplus Estimated From the Zonal Travel Cost Demand Curve

to hike, or to have clean water or air. The WTP is the maximum amount that an individual would be willing to pay for the opportunity to consume a good or service is also described economically as compensating variation (Perman et al. 2003; Freeman et al. 2014). There are three provisos associated with WTP. First, the current level of utility or environmental quality defines the reference point. Second, in terms of compensating variation, there is a potential for a gain. If the buyer obtains the good or service from the seller, then the buyer's net benefit increases as a result of the transactions. Third, WTP is constrained by the individual's income; consequently, WTP as measured by compensating variation cannot be greater than an individual's income (Freeman et al. 2014). For example, the WTP for an environmental improvement contingent on the individual being entitled to the level of environmental quality prior any improvement; namely, the WTP to clean up an existing polluted river to an unpolluted state, achieving a gain.[17]

The basic format for WTA is to ask the individual how much they would be willing to accept in compensation for *not* being able, for example, to enter a wilderness area, to canoe, to backpack, to fish, to hike, or to have clean water or air. The WTA is the minimum amount that must be paid to individuals to make them indifferent to the loss of a good or service (Perman et al. 2003; Freeman et al. 2014). This amount is also described economically as compensating variation. There are two provisos associated with WTA. First, a changed level of utility or environmental quality defines the reference point. Basically, the individual is giving up something they have. Second, WTA is not constrained by the individual's income level: For example, the WTA compensation for a loss in environmental quality contingent on the individual being entitled to the level of environmental quality prior any deterioration; namely, the WTA compensation for the loss of river water quality due to pollution.[18] An interesting example of WTA compensating variation is a project lead by Dr. Chami from the International Monetary Fund. Dr. Chami examined the carbon dioxide (CO_2) storage services provided by whales such as blue whales and the phytoplankton they eat (www.imf.org/external/pubs/ft/fandd/2019/12/natures-solution-to-climate-change-chami.htm accessed 19 November 2019). There is a positive and synergistic relationship between these whales and the phytoplankton. On average these type of whales can sequester 33 tons of CO_2 over its life. When the whale dies and sinks to the ocean floor, this carbon is removed from the atmosphere for centuries. If whales are allowed to return to their pre-whaling numbers, approximately 4 to 5 million, this would also increase phytoplankton populations. This pre-whaling condition defines the reference point to estimating the minimum compensation required for any losses from it. Based on the work lead by Dr. Chami, a great whale is estimated to generate more than $2 million in present value *in situ* nonconsumptive use value over its lifetime, in terms of carbon storage, fishery enhancements, and tourism. The $2 million per great whale is then the minimum amount that must be paid to impacted individuals to make them indifferent to the loss of the services provided by these great whales.

Theoretically, WTA and WTP should converge; however, a review of WTA and WTP studies by Miceli and Minkler (1995), Loomis et al. (1998), Brown and

Gregory (1999), Morrison (2000), Horowitz and McConnell (2002), Perman et al. (2003), Venkatachalam (2004), Plott and Zeiler (2005), Tom et al. (2007), and Grutters et al. (2008), Isoni (2011), Kling et al. (2011), Carson (2012), Freeman et al. (2014), Brennan (2016) concluded that WTA is generally greater than WTP. The debate as to why this occurs is wide ranging and includes but is not limited to the following areas: (1) Income effect, as WTP is constrained by income while WTA is not. (2) Endowment effect, as what exists is seen as a reference point, and attitudes to surrendering some of what is already owned or experienced are quite different from those that come into play when there is the prospect of gain. Thus, the potential loss of something known or you have an existing property right to is greater than the potential gain of something unknown or you do not have an existing property right to. (3) Substitution effect, as a lack of substitutes would make it difficult to compensate individuals for the removal of a good leading to large WTA values. The less the good is like an ordinary market good (i.e., the dichotomy between a public versus private good), the greater the potential difference.[19] (4) Transaction costs, which describe the potential asymmetry between willingness to buy or not (WTP) and the willingness to sell or not (WTA) and the difficulty of delaying or reversing the decision in the future. (5) Experimental design effect, as surveys designed poorly will lead to bias in WTP versus WTA estimations. (6) Reflection of the experience with the good or service and the trading environment in which the values are elicited (Freeman et al. 2014). For example, most individuals are familiar with WTP as they use this concept when purchasing goods at the grocery store, an item of clothing, a movie ticket, tax accounting services, and so on. They are less familiar with the concept of WTA, especially in the context of environmental quality.

Given these concerns, a legitimate question is which approach, WTP or WTA, would elicit assigned values that would correspond closest to an individual's preferences. How individuals respond to gains versus losses is real. Enough is known about the disparities between WTA and WTP, described briefly earlier, to recognize that framing the questions will matter (Brown and Gregory 1999; Perman et al. 2003; Venkatachalam 2004; Carson 2012; Freeman et al. 2014). This includes defining the reference point: (i) a current level of environmental quality for WTP given a potential gain (or to avoid a loss) or (ii) a new, and possibly higher, level of environmental quality for WTA given a potential loss (or to not implement the improvement to reach the defined higher level of environmental quality).[20] For valuing losses in environmental quality WTA would be more appropriate as WTP may underestimate this value (Brown and Gregory 1999). However, Arrow et al. (1993) and Perman et al. (2003) concluded WTP should be used instead of WTA because the former is the conservative choice. Framing the questions also includes designing an appropriate WTP and/or WTA survey and sampling and statistical analysis procedures to address the concerns being examined (Brown and Gregory 1999; Venkatachalam 2004; Perman et al. 2003; Carson 2012; Freeman et al. 2014). Surveys and procedures designed poorly will give results that are not reliable or valid.[21] The intricacies of developing such surveys and procedures are beyond the scope of this book; however, the citations within this section provide an excellent place to start.[22] The next section will illustrate using the WTP and WTA question as part of a contingent valuation model.

Contingent Valuation Model

The contingent valuation model (CVM) is often attributed to Ciriacy-Wantrup (1947) and the earliest use is attributed to Davis (1963), who used it to estimate WTP for big game hunting in Maine. CVM as a tool for nonmarket evaluation came to prominence with the grounding of the oil tanker *Exxon Valdez* in Prince William Sound of the northern part of the Gulf of Alaska on 24 March 1989. At the time, this was the largest oil spill from a tanker in United States history, spilling over 11 million gallons of crude oil (www.epa.gov/emergency-response/exxon-valdez-spill-profile accessed 26 November 2019). As part of the damage settlement, Exxon was liable for not only the direct use values associated with Prince William Sound but also the nonuse values in the form of existence values (Figure 9.2). These nonuse values were estimated by using CVM. Carson et al. (2003) describes the CVM analysis that was used to estimate these values.

The focus of using CVM is to have individuals state their values or preferences for a nonmarket good and services such as environmental quality and similar indirect and nonuse values. Basically, the analyst is trying to get individuals to state their assigned value. An assigned value is the expressed relative importance or worth of an object to an individual in a given context (Brown 1984). Therefore, a CVM must define in terms understandable by the target audience the context in which they will make an observable choice (Carson 2012). The Architectural Plan for Profit in terms of the CVM model is given in Figure 9.8.

For example, the context will define a cause-and-effect relationship between different forest management actions and different levels of water quality (the production system). The individual will be given a range of choices that describe how much it will cost or how much compensation will be given for the different management actions associated with the different levels of water quality (the Pillars of Cost and Value). The choice made will define the Pillars of Price and Value and the Profit. The pillars' dashed lines are used to represent the contextual or situational nature in which individuals state their choices. That is, a CVM sets up a hypothetical market and an individual's assigned values are contingent upon the setup of this hypothetical market and the information provided. The tool used to elicit these choices is a survey.

The preceding paragraph provides a broad outline of the steps of implementing a CVM. The first step is to define the problem and context and identify the target audience. That is, what the cause-and-effect relationships are that individuals will be asked to state preferences about. Are these relationships described in an understandable manner and do they provide enough information so that respondents within the target audience can make reliable and valid choices? The second step is to develop a survey instrument and sampling and statistical procedures. As WTP is constrained by income, respondent's stated WTP in this hypothetical market would imply they have less income to spend on other goods. The survey instrument would

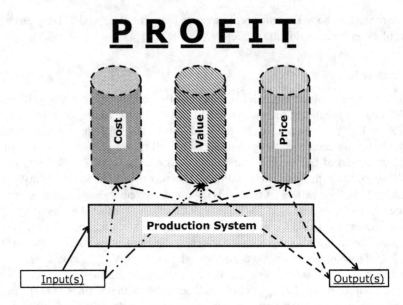

Figure 9.8 Contingent Valuation Model (Stated Preference Methodology) – The Architectural Plan for Profit

also include relevant social, demographic, and economic questions to help describe the target audience. Sampling and statistical procedures should recognize the possibility of non-response, zero bids, protest bids, and self-selection bias (i.e., the difference between a survey estimate and the actual population value due to a low response rate and a strong difference between respondents and non-respondents) and develop strategies to address this possibility. Developing an appropriate survey instrument and sampling and statistical procedures are not trivial exercises as value measurements derived depend directly on the soundness of the survey instrument and sampling and statistical procedures.[23] The third step is to administer the survey instrument based on the sampling procedure. The final step is to analyze the surveys using appropriate statistical techniques and report the results.

The CVM can provide measures of use and nonuse values (see Figure 9.2). This ability provides an advantage over revealed preference approaches if estimated values include nonuse components. However, care should be taken when implementing a contingent valuation study as a poor experimental design can introduce bias into the analysis. Perman et al. (2003), Venkatachalam (2004), Carson (2012), and Freeman et al. (2014) list some of these as the following: First, hypothetical bias – as stated previously, CVM sets up a hypothetical market and an individual's assigned values are contingent upon the setup, the information provided, and the bidding mechanism. In a real situation, if wrong choices are made, individuals suffer real consequences. Use and nonuse values estimated are based on what individuals say they would do in a given context, not what they actually do. Consequently, the hypothetical bias can lead to overestimates or underestimates of economic value (Arrow et al. 1993; Carson 2012). Second, embedding or scope bias – different values for the same good depending on whether the good is valued on its own or valued as a part of a more inclusive package. Third, sequencing bias – the value for a particular good differs depending on the order of the good in a sequence in multi-good valuation studies. Fourth, information bias – the estimated values depend directly on the level and nature of information provided to the respondents. Fifth, elicitation bias – the approach (bidding, auctions, payment cards, or take-it-or-leave-it choices, etc.) to get individuals to state their preferences. Sixth, perception bias – the WTP for a potential gain only makes sense if the individual can observe that a relevant change will take place. Finally, strategic bias – individuals may underestimate their WTP (i.e., free riding, individuals expect others would pay enough such that the good would be provided) or overestimate their WTP (i.e., individuals think that their stated WTP value would influence if the good is provided but that their stated WTP would not be used in any future pricing policy). A variation of perception bias is accounting for protest and zero bids (Halstead et al. 1992; Jorgensen and Syme 2000; Bowker et al. 2003; Meyerhoff and Liebe 2006). Protest could be positive bid outliers resulting from individuals who are opposed to the situation described in the survey for whatever reason. A zero bid could also be a protest bid or an individual who places no economic value on the good or service. These potential biases highlight the caution that should be used when developing an appropriate survey instrument and sampling and statistical analysis procedures.

Contingent Valuation Study Example – Deer Management (Bowker et al. 2003)

Wildlife/human interactions can produce positive and negative effects. Bird watching or viewing deer in an open field could be characterized as producing a positive net benefit. However, collisions between deer and cars, destruction created by deer browsing on gardens and other landscape plants, and tick-borne diseases could be characterized as a negative net benefit. A study conducted by Bowker et al. (2003) examined the willingness of residents of Sea Pines Plantation on Hilton Head Island, South Carolina, to pay to reduce the damage to landscaping by deer. The deer population was approximately one deer per hectare compared to an estimated carrying capacity of around one deer per 5 to 10 hectares. A CVM study was conducted to estimate the residents' WTP to reduce damage caused by the deer by 25% or 50% using lethal means versus nonlethal contraceptive. This approach was used because while there is a correlation between deer number and damage, determining an exact relationship is difficult due to environmental factors beyond the control of the researchers. The lethal means had a lower cost and an estimated greater degree of confidence in the outcome.

A mail survey was sent to 100% of the residents of this community. The survey contained questions about residents' perceptions of present and future damage to their landscape caused by deer; general social, economic, and demographic backgrounds; and WTP for either the lethal or the nonlethal means for decreasing damage caused by deer. Due to the emotions associated with the proposed control methods, accounting for a zero bid accurately was critical, and the survey design and sampling and statistical analysis procedures were devised to address this concern. Examples of the WTP question for the lethal and nonlethal means are the following.

Lethal Means

This program would involve the killing of deer by trained wildlife professionals. The program would be conducted during the winter months to maximize efficiency and safety and to minimize public conflict and inconvenience. All meat would be donated to food banks or other charitable organizations. Lethal removal is relatively cost efficient and is an option currently available for deer on Sea Pines. Assume it might be possible to implement a lethal removal program that would remove enough deer each year to reduce by 25% and/or 50% your economic losses resulting from deer damage to landscape plantings in your yard. How much would you be willing to pay each year for this benefit? _____ $/year

Nonlethal Means

Scientists are currently developing this form of nonlethal control. If successfully developed and approved, this program would involve the treatment of deer by trained wildlife professionals during late summer prior to the breeding season. Presently, contraception is experimental, relatively expensive to apply, and not currently available for management of deer on Sea Pines. However, assume that a contraceptive program could be done, and that this program would treat enough deer each year to reduce by 25% and/or 50% your economic losses resulting from deer damage to landscape plantings in your yard. How much would you be willing to pay each year for this benefit? _____ $/year

The results of the study are given in Table 9.6. Residents were willing to pay more for lethal versus nonlethal control means at both the 25% and 50% damage reduction levels. That is, residents were not willing to spend more for the nonlethal alternative. The lethal zero bidders were opposed to the lethal means and nonlethal zero bidders did not think the nonlethal alternative would be effective. Zero bidders comprised a large enough component that if put to a referendum either method would have been voted down.

Market Versus Nonmarket Evaluation

Care should be taken when comparing estimates of value derived from nonmarket methods with those observed from market. This caution was pointed out by Rosenthal and Brown (1985) and Canham (1986) and is illustrated in Figures 9.9a and 9.9b.

Figure 9.9a illustrates a demand curve estimated for a recreational activity using a nonmarket method (e.g., Figure 9.6) and the consumer surplus derived from the

Table 9.6 Results of the Willingness to Pay for Lethal Versus Nonlethal Control Methods for Deer in the Community of Sea Pines Plantation on Hilton Head Island in South Carolina

Without Zero Bids	Average Willingness to Pay	
	Lethal Control	Nonlethal Control
25% Damage reduction	$59.28	$39.05
50% Damage reduction	$88.23	$52.02

With Zero Bids	Average Willingness to Pay	
	Lethal Control	Nonlethal Control
25% Damage reduction	$43.64	$27.37
50% Damage reduction	$56.34	$45.75

Source: Bowker et al. (2003)

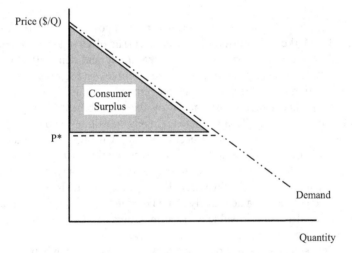

Figure 9.9a Estimated Value (Consumer Surplus) Based on a Nonmarket Valuation Method

demand curve (e.g., Figure 9.7).[24] Figure 9.9b illustrates the observed market transactions from a timber sale, for example. Comparing Figures 9.9a and 9.9b reveals two important observations.

First, the estimated market demand curve in Figure 9.9a has a negative slope and the demand curve faced by the entrepreneur of this recreational activity has a negative slope. The implication is that there are few substitutes for this recreational activity due to the possible uniqueness of the site and spatial monopoly due to distances between potential recreations sites (Rosenthal and Brown 1985; Canham

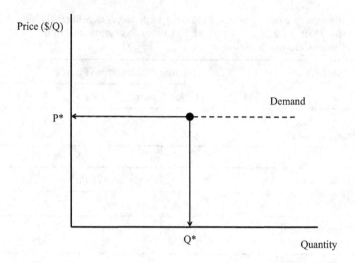

Figure 9.9b Observed Market Value

1986). The entrepreneur in this case has some market power with respect to pricing (Chapter 11 – Market Equilibrium and Structure). The observed market transaction from a timber sale (the intersection of market supply and demand) illustrated in Figure 9.9b is described by a point, not a line or curve. An incorrect interpretation of this observation would be that the market demand curve is identical to the price line and the market demand curve faced by the entrepreneur selling the timber would be perfectly elastic. That is, there are many substitutes, and the seller of the timber has no market power with respect to pricing (Chapter 11 – Market Equilibrium and Structure). This may not be the case, as the timber being sold may be a species that is relatively scarce and of high quality to create a spatial monopoly. If a market demand curve would have been developed, it would also have had a negative slope. Second, due to a negatively sloped demand curve shown in Figure 9.9a, estimates of total economic value include measures of consumer surplus. However, the measure of total economic value derived from Figure 9.9b includes no measure of consumer surplus. To make a reasonable comparison between the total economic value derived from a market versus nonmarket good or service, a consistent method should be used in both cases. Consequently, care should be taken when comparing measures of total economic value between market and nonmarket ecosystem goods and services.

The preceding example implies a choice of either timber or recreation. However, most often the decisions are not characterized as mutually exclusive or an all-or-nothing choice as Hayne et al. (2010) describe. Projects often produce multiple outputs in terms of market and nonmarket ecosystem goods and services. Decisions involve production levels for the different outputs. That is, should additional units of a market or nonmarket ecosystem good or service be produced or provided? This question describes an incremental or marginal analysis similar to the profit searching rule described in Chapter 5 – Profit; namely, weighing the additional, incremental, or marginal benefits against the additional, incremental, or marginal costs. Various approaches have been described to examine these tradeoffs. However, I will describe two approaches briefly. Both focus on estimating the costs, and if the decision is to add incremental units of the market or nonmarket ecosystem good or service, then the incremental benefits were expected to be greater than the incremental costs. These approaches have relied on simple to complex cost allocation procedures.

The first approach determines those costs that are specific to providing a given output and those that are common or joint with respect to the project. Specific or separable costs are attributed to a single output; for example, the cost of recreational docks around a multipurpose reservoir. Separable costs are costs resulting from an output being included in a multipurpose project and are often described as the incremental cost of adding the output as the last output in a multipurpose project. The output's cost allocation comprises its specific or separable costs and a share of the common or joint costs. A variety of procedures have been used to allocate the common or joint costs to each output. The classic example of this cost allocation approach is called separable cost–remaining benefits and was first described in 1958 by the Federal Inter-Agency River Basin Committee. The joint costs are allocated proportional to the benefits each output creates. In business management, Blocher et al. (2002) describes three common approaches to allocate the joint costs: (1) physical measures, (2) sales value at the split-off point, and (3) net realizable value measures. Blocher et al. (2002) describes the advantages and disadvantages of each approach. It should be noted that there is no nonarbitrary way of allocating truly joint costs (Carlson 1974; Blocher et al. 2002). Thus, the choice of which joint cost allocation approach to use must be an informed business management decision and once chosen used consistently. The outputs allocated costs is the sum of the separable costs plus the proportion of joint costs. However, for production decisions, the allocated joint costs are considered sunk as they occur before the split-off point (Blocher et al. 2002).[25] The incremental separable costs can then be weighed against the expected benefits. If the output benefit equals or exceeds (is less than) the smallest incremental cost, the output is included (not included) in the project at its current production level.

The second approach was described by Montgomery et al. (1994). These authors note explicitly that preserving an endangered species like the northern spotted owl is not an all-or-nothing decision. The appropriate unit of analysis for benefits and costs is the likelihood of survival and how certain society wants to be of species survival. Montgomery et al. develop a relationship between the probability of survival and the amount of habitat associated with that probability. As using this habitat–owl survival probability relationship, they develop a "marginal physical cost curve" relating estimated thousand board feet of timber from the potential habitat areas to a survival rate. While this marginal physical cost curve does not have the same dimensions as a traditional marginal cost curve, it allowed the authors to develop a marginal cost curve describing the opportunity cost of the lost timber harvest with respect to survival rate. This was done using the Timber Assessment

Market Model developed by Adams and Haynes (1980). The resulting marginal cost curve allows decision makers to examine the incremental costs in terms of increasing the probability of survival by 1% with estimated incremental benefits. A detailed discussion of the methods they used to develop this marginal cost curve is beyond the scope of this book. However, I would encourage interested students to read Montgomery et al. (1994) and subsequent articles using this approach.

Nonmarket Values – Variability

The approach to examine variability in previous chapters has been characterized as a sensitivity analysis approach, which is, basically, identifying which management variables have the most impact on a business or management decision. This sensitivity analysis approach was described in detail in Chapter 8 – Risk. This approach works well with cost-based approaches such as damage cost avoided, replacement or substitution cost methods, and the opportunity cost method. Examples of using sensitivity analysis in these contexts are given by Kramer et al. (2006) and Newman and Healy (1997) and were discussed in the section entitled "Cost-Based Approaches" in this chapter.

As future states of nature may be variable, an expected utility approach is the most appropriate method to estimate this option value. Specifically, Freeman et al. (2014) define the appropriate option value to estimate this variable state of nature as a dynamic willingness to pay (compensating variation) approach. This option value (Figure 9.2) is an *ex ante* concept, that is, the willingness to pay now for a future state which is "variable." This is a dynamic estimation, thus as more information becomes available the estimate of willingness to pay must be re-evaluated. A dynamic willingness to pay would already include considerations about delaying or waiting for more information, thus estimating a separate quasi-option value would be double counting this variability. Finally, a dynamic willingness to pay can be estimated using a contingent valuation approach. The survey must describe the context in which they will be making an observable choice in terms understandable by the target audience (Carson 2012; Freeman et al. 2014). If this is done incorrectly, the resulting estimate could underestimate the true dynamic willingness to pay (Freeman et al. 2014). A more detailed discussion of dynamic willingness to pay is beyond the scope of this book. I would recommend an interested reader start with Freeman et al. (2014).

How to Use Economic Information – Estimating Nonmarket Values – To Make Better Business Decisions

Markets provide economic information entrepreneurs can use to determine what to produce, how much to produce, and for whom to produce. However, not all of the ecosystem goods and services individuals use are exchanged in markets. Consequently, there is no observable market equilibrium to determine the optimal level to produce, no observable demand curve to help distribute them among various potential users, and no observable pricing mechanism to help allocate the resources used to produce them. That said, individuals value these nonmarket ecosystem goods and services, as can be seen by observing their choices. Given the lack of economic information generally available from a well-functioning market, the entrepreneur, landowner, or policy maker needs to develop economic information – the opportunity cost faced by an entrepreneur, landowner, or policy maker – analogous to that obtained from markets in order to make informed decisions concerning how much of these ecosystem goods and services to provide.

The two approaches to develop this economic information discussed were revealed and stated preference methods. What is the nature of the economic information generated from these methods? In a nutshell the economic information generated are the Pillars of Price and Value as illustrated by the estimated demand curve. If you are an entrepreneur, landowner, or policy maker, this basic economic information will help you make informed decisions concerning providing these ecosystem goods and services. The value concept estimated is different depending on which method is chosen. Revealed preference methods estimate an individual's value based on their existing choices. The individual is not asked directly a value for an ecosystem good or service. Consequently, revealed preference methods require observable choice behavior and are used to estimate use values but not nonuse values, as these are unobservable. The estimated value measures inferred from an individual's choices using a hedonic pricing model are direct and indirect use values, while the travel cost model can be used to estimate direct use values (Figure 9.10). The stated preference method examined

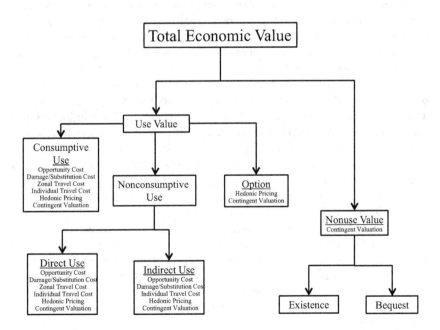

Figure 9.10 Total Economic Value – Revisited

was the contingent valuation model. This model is based on asking an individual directly their willingness to pay or willingness to accept compensation for an ecosystem good or service. Thus, it can be used to estimate use and nonuse values (Figure 9.10).

The nonmarket valuation methods discussed develop different measures of value. If the questions being asked by an entrepreneur, landowner, or policy maker involve consumptive use and nonconsumptive direct use values, then opportunity cost, damage/substitution cost, the travel cost, hedonic pricing, and contingent valuation methods are appropriate. If the questions being asked by an entrepreneur, landowner, or policy maker involve nonconsumptive indirect use values, then the opportunity cost, damage/substitution cost, individual travel cost, hedonic pricing, and contingent valuation methods are appropriate. All things being equal, willingness to pay estimated using the market-based approach values (e.g., opportunity cost, damage/substitute, travel cost, or hedonic) is generally preferred to survey approaches (e.g., contingent valuation). If the questions being asked involve nonuse values, then only a stated preference approach – such as the contingent valuation model – is appropriate. Finally, caution should be used when comparing value estimates from one of these methods to those observed from well-functioning markets. Using economic information inappropriately – whether it is derived using a nonmarket valuation method or observed from a market directly – will probably lead to poor business and management decisions.

Estimated nonmarket values are often used in cost-benefit analyses. There are three concerns about using nonmarket values as part of cost–benefit analysis. First, cost–benefit analysis is inherently an efficiency decision criterion, and an efficiency decision criterion may not be appropriate in all contexts, such as those associated with nonmarket values (Perman et al. 2003). Second, cost–benefit analysis uses market-based values. So if nonmarket values are used, using revealed preference market-based approaches is stronger even if stated preference hypothetical values are greater than market-based approach values, because inferred market-based approach values are derived from actual observable choices, *ceteris paribus*. Finally, as estimating nonmarket values can be expensive, it would be helpful if values from one study could be transferred to a different study. Transferring values, or benefits transfer, remains challenging due to (i) differences in the environmental features being valued among studies and sites and (ii) differences in the individuals evaluating the environmental features among studies and sites. Benefit transfer methods range from simple to sophisticated (Pearce et al. 2006; Atkinson and Mourato 2008; Freeman et al. 2014). The differences just described must be enumerated and appropriate adjustments made to reflect the differences. As a practical matter – that is, depending on the analytical context – some degree of imprecision may not be critical. However, what this level is is not well defined. In the case of non-timber forest benefits, Riera et al. (2012) examined this issue and has provided an eight-step set of guidelines. Nonetheless, I would follow the advice of these authors to use much caution when attempting to use benefits transfer as part of a cost–benefit analysis.

Appendix 9A – Hedonic Model

Rosen (1974) formalized the theory supporting the hedonic model and laid the foundation upon which current hedonic models are built. Rosen's hedonic theory states that the market price of a differentiated consumer good is a function of its utility-bearing characteristics. A hedonic model is essentially a regression model that links a good's price, the dependent variable, with its various attributes, the independent variables.

Historically, the focus has been to model housing prices in the real estate market. The basic concept is that a residential property is a heterogeneous good made up of a bundle of characteristics each of which has its own implicit price. That is, if a residential property contains different combinations of characteristics, it should be possible to estimate a characteristic's implicit price given a house's price is a function of the quantities of its various characteristics (Freeman et al. 2014). These characteristics include structural (i.e., the square footage a house and a yard, age of a house, number of bathrooms and bedrooms, and number of stories, etc.), neighborhood (i.e., school quality, population density, racial distribution, shopping centers, and school district, etc.), and environmental amenity variables (i.e., parks, forest reserves, lakes, and agricultural land, etc.). Based on this theoretical foundation, the general hedonic price function for housing can be written in the form of

$$P_j = f(S,N,E) \tag{A.1}$$
$$= f(X_j)$$

where P_j is the actual property sale price of the jth house, S is a vector of structural variables, N is a vector of neighborhood variables, and E is a vector of environmental amenity variables. For notational ease, X_j will be used to summarize the structural, neighborhood, and environmental amenity variables. The common functional forms for hedonic price function are given in Table 9A.1.

Table 9A.1 Common Hedonic Price Functional Forms

Linear–linear	Log–linear
$P_j = \beta_0 + \sum_{k=1}^{K}\beta_k X_{jk} + \varepsilon_j$	$\ln(P_j) = \beta_0 + \sum_{k=1}^{K}\beta_k X_{jk} + \varepsilon_j$
	$P_j = e^{\left(\beta_0 + \sum_{k=1}^{K}\beta_k X_{jk} + \varepsilon_j\right)}$
Linear–log	Log–log
$P_j = \ln(\beta_0) + \sum_{k=1}^{K}\beta_k \ln(X_{jk}) + \ln(\varepsilon_j)$	$\ln(P_j) = \ln(\beta_0) + \sum_{k=1}^{K}\beta_k \ln(X_{jk}) + \ln(\varepsilon_j)$

The partial derivative of the hedonic price function with respect to any characteristic in the model reveals that characteristic's implicit price function (Freeman et al. 2014).

$$\frac{\partial P_j}{\partial X_{jk}} = \frac{\partial f\left(X_{jk}\right)}{\partial X_{jk}} \Rightarrow \begin{cases} \dfrac{\partial P_j}{\partial S_i} = \dfrac{\partial f\left(S,N,E\right)}{\partial S_i} \\[2ex] \dfrac{\partial P_j}{\partial N_i} = \dfrac{\partial f\left(S,N,E\right)}{\partial N_i} \\[2ex] \dfrac{\partial P_j}{\partial E_i} = \dfrac{\partial f\left(S,N,E\right)}{\partial E_i} \end{cases} \tag{A.2}$$

That is, the resulting coefficients describe how a small change in one of the attributes affects the good's price, all else being equal. When equation (A.1) is linear, the marginal implicit price function given by equation (A.2) is a constant.

$$\frac{\partial P_j}{\partial X_{jk}} = \frac{\partial\left[\beta_0 + \sum\limits_{k=1}^{K}\beta_k X_{jk}\right]}{\partial X_{jk}} = \beta_k$$

If equation (A.1) is a log–log or double-log functional form, the marginal implicit price function given by equation (A.2) defines an elasticity.

$$\frac{\partial \ln\left(P_j\right)}{\partial \ln\left(X_{jk}\right)} = \frac{\partial\left[\ln\left(\beta_0\right) + \sum\limits_{k=1}^{K}\beta_k \ln\left(X_{jk}\right) + \ln\left(\varepsilon_j\right)\right]}{\partial \ln\left(X_{jk}\right)}$$

$$= \beta_k$$

$$\frac{\partial \ln\left(P_j\right)}{\partial \ln\left(X_{jk}\right)} = \frac{\left(\dfrac{\partial P_j}{P_j}\right)}{\left(\dfrac{\partial X_{jk}}{X_{jk}}\right)}$$

$$= \frac{\partial P_j}{\partial X_{jk}} \cdot \frac{X_{jk}}{P_j} = \beta_k$$

Semi-log functional forms of equation (A.1) describe percent changes of either the dependent or a characteristic. The marginal implicit price function given by equation (A.2) of the log–linear functional form defines the percentage change in P_j given a unit change in E_i, for example.

$$\frac{\partial\left[\ln\left(P_j\right)\right]}{\partial X_{jk}} = \frac{\partial\left[\beta_0 + \sum\limits_{k=1}^{K}\beta_k X_{jk}\right]}{\partial X_{jk}} = \beta_k$$

$$\frac{\partial\left[\ln\left(P_j\right)\right]}{\partial X_{jk}} = \frac{\left(\dfrac{\partial P_j}{P_j}\right)}{\partial X_{jk}} = \beta_k$$

The marginal implicit price function of the linear–log functional form defines the change in P_j given a percentage change in E_i, for example.

$$\frac{\partial P_j}{\partial \ln\left(X_{jk}\right)} = \frac{\partial\left[\ln\left(\beta_0\right) + \sum_{k=1}^{K}\beta_k\ln\left(X_{jk}\right) + \ln\left(\varepsilon_j\right)\right]}{\partial \ln\left(X_{jk}\right)}$$

$$= \beta_k$$

$$\frac{\partial P_j}{\partial \ln\left(X_{jk}\right)} = \frac{\partial P_j}{\left(\frac{\partial X_{jk}}{X_{jk}}\right)} = \beta_k$$

Equation (A.2) allows developing hypotheses concerning the effects of a variable on market price. If the environmental amenity variable is preferred by individuals, the hypothesized sign of equation (A.2) is positive. If not, the hypothesized sign of equation (A.2) is negative.

The hedonic price function is identical to the market price. As the title of Rosen's article suggests, pure competition is a key assumption. For only under the condition of pure competition will the model produce the desired results: The buyer's willingness to pay for the good's characteristics (Rosen 1974).

Pure competition leads to the following conditions. One, buyers are price takers, that is, they add zero weight to the market. Two, buyers and sellers make decisions that maximize their utility, and their perfect matching leads to equilibrium prices. Third, the distributions of buyer preferences and seller costs determine the market clearing price (Rosen 1974). In addition to these conditions, buyers are assumed to purchase only one unit of the consumer good. However, this assumption may be relaxed if multiple units are purchased to satisfy different needs (for example, a primary residence and vacation home) (Palmquist 2005).

Notes

1 In Chapter 7 – The Natural Resources Management Puzzle the concepts of ecosystem goods and services were defined.
2 For example, a 2009 special issue of the *Journal of Forest Economics* volume 15 numbers 1–2 is devoted to illustrating the use and limitations of estimating the nonmarket values of forest-based ecosystem goods and services in decision making related to the management of forest resources in Europe.
3 Indirect use values can also be described as positive externalities that ecosystems provide. A positive externality is defined as an activity by one agent that causes a gain of welfare to another agent and the affected agent is not indifferent to the change in welfare and the gain in welfare is uncompensated.
4 I have limited the discussion of nonuse values to existence and bequest values as these are probably the most recognizable and thus relevant. However, the discussion and identification of nonuse values is not limited to existence and bequest values. For example, intrinsic and cognitive values are oft times included as nonuse values, but the discussion of these concepts is beyond the scope of this book.
5 This topic will be discussed in detail in Chapter 11 – Market Equilibrium and Structure.

6 An alternative approach to determine an individual's expressed relative importance of an ecosystem good or services is to estimate their willingness to accept. A comparison of willingness to pay and willingness to accept will be discussed later in this chapter.

7 Willingness to pay is synonymous with the concept of demand and the demand curve (Chapter 10 – Supply and Demand).

8 Could contributions to organizations like Greenpeace be used as a proxy for nonuse existence value? While it is an observable choice that an individual could make, an individual could give to Greenpeace for many different reasons (e.g., a counterbalance to exploitive uses or a political statement). It would very hard to determine if this contribution was to save the whales (existence value) without asking individuals this question directly (Freeman et al. 2014). Asking an individual to value the existence of a species or ecosystem would be a stated preference approach.

9 I would recommend that the reader keep Figure 9.2 firmly in mind during this discussion.

10 There are many different functional forms that a hedonic price model may take. Appendix 9A – Hedonic Model provides a discussion of them.

11 Other examples are described in Holmes et al. (1990) and Bare and Smith (1999), who used a hedonic approach to examine the impact of various timber sale attributes on timber sale prices in Connecticut and the United States' Pacific Northwest, respectively.

12 A lump sum sale is the sale of standing timber for a fixed dollar amount agreed upon in advance by the landowner and the buyer. The dollar amount agreed upon is not a function of the volume of timber actually cut.

13 Klemperer (1996) noted this similarity by describing a statistically estimated ZTCM as a hedonic travel cost model.

14 If an item is purchased and used for the site in question and nowhere else, then perhaps the cost might be included; however, as most equipment is used at multiple sites and there is no good way to allocate the cost to the site being valued, the equipment costs are generally excluded.

15 Economists use the concept of utility to describe an individual's subjective evaluation of the satisfaction, or utility, derived from use and nonuse values. The most usual scale used to measure utility is ordinal.

16 A map of the DEC administrative regions can be found at www.dec.ny.gov/about/76070. html accessed 8 November 2019.

17 The concept of WTP can also be defined using equivalent variation: The maximum amount an individual would be willing to pay to avoid the loss of not being able to consume a good or service (Perman et al. 2003; Freeman et al. 2014). For example, the WTP for a deterioration in environmental quality contingent on the individual being entitled to the level of environmental quality prior any change; namely, the WTP to avoid the loss of not cleaning up a polluted river to an unpolluted state.

18 The concept of WTA can also be defined using equivalent variation: The minimum lump sum payment an individual would have to receive to induce that person to voluntarily forgo the opportunity to purchase a good or service (Perman et al. 2003; Freeman et al. 2014). For example, the WTA compensation for an improvement in environmental quality contingent on the individual being entitled to the improved level of environmental quality; namely, the WTA compensation for not restoring the polluted river to its pre-polluted state.

19 A public good is defined traditionally as a nonrival, nonexclusive, uncongested good. The example often given is national defense. A private good is defined traditionally as a rival, exclusive, congested good. Examples of private goods are bicycles, fly fishing rods, cars, and clothes. Public or private goods are distinguished by their definitions, *not* by the type of organization or institution making it available.

20 Kilgore et al. (2008) posed an interesting question with respect to forest stewardship or sustainably managing the forested ecosystem by family forest landowners. They examined the probability of these landowners' willingness to pay to be certified through

programs such as Sustainable Forestry Initiative or Forest Stewardship Council versus willingness to accept payments from a governmental organization to practice good forest stewardship. The results indicated that as the cost (willingness to pay) for certification increased, the probability that family forest landowners would become certified decreased. As the payments (willingness to accept) for enrolling in stewardship programs increased, so did the probability that family forest landowners would enroll. In this case markets existed, and the researchers examined participation probabilities based on the levels of willingness to pay and accept.

21 Reliability is a measure of accuracy that predicts how often one can repeat applications and obtain the same results. Validity is a measure of accuracy concerned with the extent to which the results really measure what they are supposed to measure; that is, that they are consistent with theory and identifying the presence of systematic error and eliminating it.

22 Probably the most cited reference with respect to survey methods is Dillman (1978). A newer version of the book is Dillman et al. (2009). In addition, Freeman et al. (2014) provide a literature review of survey methods. I would point the interested reader to these sources for developing a survey for either a stated or a revealed preference study.

23 For more detailed information, I would recommend Chapter 12 in Freeman et al. (2014) and Perman et al. (2003).

24 The willingness to pay estimates derived from revealed preference techniques result in Marshallian demand, as are the demand curves described in Chapters 10 – Supply and Demand and 11 – Market Equilibrium and Structure. Marshallian demand includes both income and substitution effects associated with changes in prices (Silberberg and Suen 2001). The consumer surplus resulting from revealed preference techniques reflects this economic information. A Marshallian demand is sometimes called a money demand. The willingness to pay estimates derived from contingent valuation result in Hicksian demand. Hicksian demand examines the pure substitution effects associated with changes in prices (Silberberg and Suen 2001). The consumer surplus resulting from contingent valuation (a stated preference technique) reflects this economic information. A Hicksian demand is sometimes called an income-compensated demand, as real income is held constant. As a result the Hicksian demand curve is everywhere below (above) the Marshallian demand curve given a decrease (increase) in price. If the percent of income spent on the good is small – and thus the income effect is small – and there are many substitutes – and thus the substitution effect is small and the Hicksian demand curve is more elastic – then the Hicksian and Marshallian demand curves will be similar. While it is not theoretically accurate to drop the distinction between Marshallian and Hicksian willingness to pay or demand, for purposes of illustration I will assume that revealed and stated preference methods provide comparable measures of demand.

25 A split-off point is the location in a production process where a main product or jointly manufactured products and by-products are hereafter manufactured separately.

10 Supply and Demand

Preamble

In the previous chapters the focus was primarily on the manager or entrepreneur and the assertion that they maximize profits. This assertion was used to develop the Architectural Plan for Profit given in Figure 10.1
The model describing maximizing profits is given in equation (10.1).

$$\text{Max } \Pi = \text{TR - TC}$$
$$= P \cdot Q(x_1, x_2, ..., x_j) - \text{TVC - TFC} \qquad (10.1)$$
$$= P \cdot Q(\bullet) - \sum_j w_j \cdot x_j - \text{TFC}$$

where the terms have been defined at the beginning of Chapters 2, 3, 4, and 5. The Architectural Plan for Profit identifies key pieces of economic information that the entrepreneur should obtain in their search for output levels that will increase their profits. The Architectural Plan for Profit (Figure 10.1) can be thought of as a graphical version of the mathematical equation for profit given in equation (10.1).

In this and the next chapter, I want to step back and take a broad look at the interactions among buyers and sellers. Following the same logic as I have used before, I want to start at the ending point and take that apart to reveal the economic information it contains. Figure 10.2 shows the familiar economic model of supply and demand or the interactions among buyers (demand) and sellers (supply).[1]

Figure 10.2 describes a market where an individual can choose to provide or produce a particular good or service and another individual can choose to purchase that particular good or service. Based on the assertion described in Chapter 1 – Introduction, each individual is a maximizer: Sellers maximize their profits ($\prod$) and buyers maximize their net benefits (NB). This is described by the paired expressions in equation (10.2)

$$\text{Max } \Pi = \left[P \cdot Q(\bullet) \right] - \text{TC} \qquad (10.2)$$
$$\text{Max NB} = \text{B-C} = \text{B-} \left[P \cdot Q(\bullet) \right]$$

DOI: 10.4324/9781315678719-10

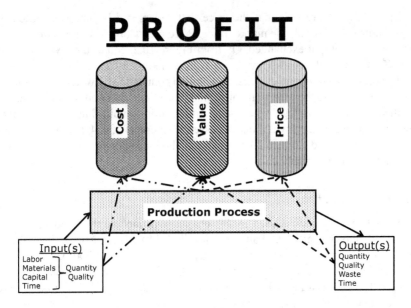

Figure 10.1 The Architectural Plan for Profit

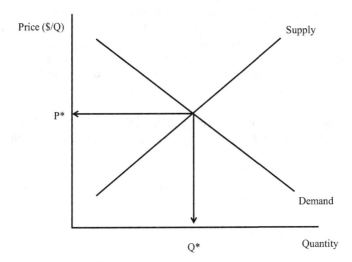

Figure 10.2 The Market – Supply and Demand

where B denotes the buyer's benefit from purchasing the good or service and C denotes the explicit portion of their opportunity cost. The paired expressions in equation (10.2) show that the seller's total revenue, $[P{\cdot}Q(\bullet)]$ (Chapter 4 – Revenue), is the same as the buyer's explicit cost, $[P{\cdot}Q(\bullet)]$. Comparing Figure 10.2

to equation (10.2) reveals that the price that sellers and buyers agree upon, P* from Figure 10.2, equals the market price, P, from equation (10.2). In addition, the amount of the output exchanged, Q* from Figure 10.2, equals the level of output, Q(•) (Chapter 2 – Production Systems), from equation (10.2).[2]

The previous paragraph establishes an initial connection between the supply and demand curves and the assertion concerning individual decision-making behavior. I will start with discussing the economic information contained in the supply curve and show how it reflects what was discussed in Chapters 2, 3, 4, and 5. Next, I will examine the demand curve to see if any parallels can be drawn between it and what we know about the supply curve.

Practical Applications

The practical applications used in this chapter will include the Inside-Out (ISO) Beams (Patterson et al. 2002; Patterson and Xie 1998), Mobile Micromill® (Becker et al. 2004), Maple Syrup Operation (Huyler 2000; CFBMC 2000), Great Lakes Charter Boat Fishing (Lichtkoppler and Kuehn 2003), Select Red Oak (Hahn and Hansen 1991), and Radiata Pine Plantation. Their summaries will not be repeated here as they have been used in earlier chapters.

Supply

A supply curve is traditionally drawn with a positive slope implying that there is a direct relationship between output price and the quantity of the output produced or provided; in other words, as the market price goes up, as a seller you would buy additional inputs to increase the quantity of output you produce or provide. This is illustrated in Figure 10.2 and seems like a reasonable response. In fact, this behavior is codified in the Law of Supply:

Ceteris paribus (other things being equal), as the price of a good or service increases (decreases) the supplier will increase (decrease) the quantity produced or provided.

The Law of Supply leads to defining the supply curve depicted in Figure 10.2:

The willingness and ability of entrepreneurs to make available a given quantity at a given place and time.

However, what is behind the Law of Supply and the definition of the supply curve that makes the relationship depicted in Figure 10.2 reasonable? Why is supply depicted as a positive relationship between market price and quantity produced or provided? How are the concept of supply and its graphic representation related to the Architectural Plan for Profit? I will answer these questions in the following sections.

Pillars of Price and Value and the Production System Foundation

An initial comparison of Figures 10.1 and 10.2 shows that both have a price ele-
ment; in Figure 10.1 it is the Pillar of Price and in Figure 10.2 it is the vertical
axis of Price and the price agreed upon by buyers and sellers, P*. In Figures 10.1
and 10.2, price represents a measure of relative scarcity and a per unit measure of
value or a marginal concept (see Chapter 1 – Introduction). Figures 10.1 and 10.2
also have output as a component; in Figure 10.1 it is the foundation described by
the production system (Chapter 2 – Production Systems) and in Figure 10.2 it is
the horizontal axis of Quantity and the output level of exchange agreed upon by
buyers and sellers, Q*. Again, it is worth noting that if the output produced does
not create value for the customer, they will not buy it (Q* of Figure 10.2) and you
will not generate any revenues (P*·Q* of Figure 10.2), only costs. For argument's
sake, let us assume that you produce an output like maple syrup. To produce or
make available a gallon of maple syrup, you would have to have knowledge of its
production system. Thus, you would have systematically answered the following
three questions discussed in Chapter 2 – Production Systems: (1) What are the
relevant fixed and variable inputs? (2) What are the outputs? and (3) How do you
describe the production process? Based on this line of reasoning, there would seem
to be a relationship between the supply curve given in Figure 10.2 and a production
system. This relationship is shown in Figure 10.3.

Examining Figure 10.3 reveals three observations. First, the horizontal axis
from the supply graph is the same as the vertical axis from the production system
graph; for example, from 127.5 to 2,550 gallons of maple syrup per year. Second, the output level of exchange agreed upon by buyers and sellers, Q*, from the

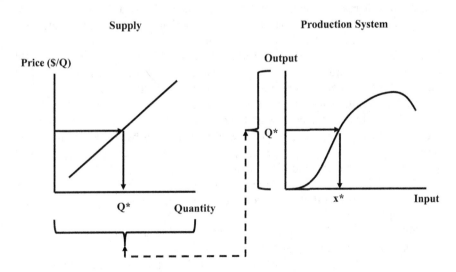

Figure 10.3 The Relationship Between Supply and the Production System

supply curve can be tied directly to the input level, x*, required to produce Q* as given by the production system; for example, Huyler (2000) and CFBMC (2000) describe the various input levels for various annual levels of maple sap and maple syrup respectively. A similar relationship could be developed between the supply of full- or half-day charter boat fishing trips and the input levels used to provide them. Finally, the economic information contained in the production system (Chapter 2 – Production Systems) and the foundation of the Architectural Plan for Profit should also be in the supply curve.

Pillars of Cost and Value

Building the Pillars of Cost and Value requires first identifying all the relevant fixed and variable inputs that depict the underlying fundamental characteristics of the production system and that you, as manager, have direct control over (Chapter 2 – Production Systems). Or answering the question: What are the relevant fixed and variable input(s)? Given the price or wage you must pay for each input, you can then develop descriptors of cost: Total cost; total variable and total fixed cost; average total, variable, and fixed cost; and marginal cost (Chapter 3 – Costs). Building the Pillar of Cost also allows the entrepreneur to develop a supply curve for the business. Supply (or the supply curve) fundamentally represents or models the entrepreneur's opportunity cost. Supply does depend on costs, but the cost of supplying is the opportunities forgone by the act of supplying (Heyne et al. 2006).

The definition of supply is the "willingness and ability to make available" a given level of output. From Chapter 5 – Profit, the profit searching rule describes comparing marginal revenue relative to marginal cost. A profit-maximizing entrepreneur will increase the level of output produced or provided if marginal revenue is greater than marginal cost. Thus, I would argue that your "willingness and ability" as a seller of an output is described by the marginal cost curve. Furthermore, I would contend that the minimum price that you would be willing to accept would be defined by the minimum of average variable cost. This contention is based on the "To Produce or Not to Produce" discussion and Tables 5.4, 5.5, and 5.6 from Chapter 5 – Profit. Thus, the supply curve is defined as the marginal cost curve above the minimum of average variable cost. To illustrate this, I will use a hypothetical softwood dimension lumber sawmill.[3] While it is hypothetical, it is based on a sawmill in New York State that produces between 5 and 10 million board feet of softwood dimension lumber annually or between 416.6 and 833.3 thousand board feet (MBF) of softwood dimension lumber per month. Table 10.1 describes the production system that uses two inputs: Labor and delivered logs to produce the output lumber.

Table 10.2 shows the total variable, average variable, and marginal costs associated with producing dimension lumber.[4]

Figure 10.4 is a graph of the average variable and marginal cost curves. This graph shows the shutdown point or the minimum point on the average variable cost curve as described in Tables 5.4, 5.5, and 5.6 from Chapter 5 – Profit.

Table 10.1 Production System of a Softwood Dimension Lumber Sawmill

Labor[§]	Logs[‡]	Lumber[†]
(Persons)	*(cuft/month)*	*(MBF/month)*
7.0	2,089,221.80	261.15
7.5	2,292,922.94	286.62
8.0	2,494,166.09	311.77
8.5	2,691,917.28	336.49
9.0	2,885,275.85	360.66
9.5	3,073,463.04	384.18
10.0	3,255,811.46	406.98
10.5	3,431,755.27	428.97
11.0	3,600,821.09	450.10
11.5	3,762,619.64	470.33
12.0	3,916,837.84	489.60
12.5	4,063,231.71	507.90
13.0	4,201,619.60	525.20
13.5	4,331,876.10	541.48
14.0	4,453,926.27	556.74
14.5	4,567,740.46	570.97
15.0	4,673,329.43	584.17
15.5	4,770,739.88	596.34
16.0	4,860,050.36	607.51
16.5	4,941,367.51	617.67
17.0	5,014,822.58	626.85
17.5	5,080,568.26	635.07
18.0	5,138,775.76	642.35
18.5	5,189,632.16	648.70
19.0	5,233,337.99	654.17
19.5	5,270,105.00	658.76
20.0	5,300,154.14	662.52
20.5	5,323,713.72	665.46
21.0	5,341,017.78	667.63
21.5	5,352,304.55	669.04
22.0	5,357,815.11	669.73

[§] The number of persons employed during a typical 10-hour shift
[‡] Denotes the cubic foot (cuft) volume of logs delivered to the sawmill per month
[†] The volume, measured as 1,000 board feet (MBF), of dimension lumber produced by the sawmill per month. This is calculated based on a lumber recovery factor of 8 board feet per log cubic foot (Spelter and Alderman 2005). A board foot is defined as board with the dimension of 1" × 1" × 12"; there are 12 board feet per 1 cu ft

Table 10.2 also shows the supply schedule derived from the average variable and marginal cost information. Figures 10.5a and 10.5b illustrate the supply curve for this softwood dimension lumber sawmill.[5]

Examining Table 10.2 and Figure 10.5b shows that this softwood dimension lumber sawmill is *not* willing and able to provide less than 450.10 thousand board feet (MBF) of lumber per month given the current production technology (Table 10.1) and the costs of labor and delivered logs (Table 10.2). If the market

Table 10.2 Variable and Marginal Costs and Supply of a Softwood Dimension Lumber Sawmill

Lumber	TVC§	AVC‡	MC†	Supply
(MBF/month)	(USD/month)	(USD/MBF)	(USD/MBF)	(USD/MBF)
261.15	91,975.50	352.19	315.74	–
286.62	100,030.66	349.01	316.35	–
311.77	108,018.80	346.47	317.55	–
336.49	115,911.70	344.47	319.31	–
360.66	123,684.81	342.94	321.60	–
384.18	131,316.89	341.81	324.45	–
406.98	138,789.75	341.03	327.85	–
428.97	146,087.94	340.56	331.84	–
450.10	153,198.56	340.36	336.47	340.36
470.33	160,110.99	340.42	341.78	341.78
489.60	166,816.70	340.72	347.86	347.86
507.90	173,309.03	341.22	354.79	354.79
525.20	179,583.03	341.93	362.69	362.69
541.48	185,635.27	342.83	371.71	371.71
556.74	191,463.72	343.90	382.04	382.04
570.97	197,067.57	345.15	393.89	393.89
584.17	202,447.10	346.56	407.58	407.58
596.34	207,603.60	348.13	423.49	423.49
607.51	212,539.20	349.86	442.11	442.11
617.67	217,256.81	351.74	464.12	464.12
626.85	221,760.01	353.77	490.44	490.44
635.07	226,052.98	355.95	522.37	522.37
642.35	230,140.36	358.28	561.77	561.77
648.70	234,027.27	360.76	611.43	611.43
654.17	237,719.18	363.39	675.77	675.77
658.76	241,221.86	366.17	762.14	762.14
662.52	244,541.34	369.11	883.75	883.75
665.46	247,683.83	372.20	1,067.08	1,067.08
667.63	250,655.74	375.44	1,373.97	1,373.97
669.04	253,463.54	378.85	1,990.16	1,990.16
669.73	256,113.82	382.42	3,847.57	3,847.57

§ Total variable cost (TVC) based on an average monthly salary for labor of 5,000 US dollars (USD) per month, a stumpage price of 0.02 US dollars (USD) per cubic foot (cu ft) (https://www.dec.ny.gov/lands/5259.html accessed 5 September 2023) for Adirondack eastern white pine (*Pinus strobus*), and an average transportation cost of 0.01 USD/cuft
‡ Average variable cost (AVC) is measured as US dollars (USD) per 1,000 board feet (MBF)
† Marginal cost (MC) is measured as US dollars (USD) per 1,000 board feet (MBF)

price is less than $340.36 per MBF of lumber, then it is cheaper for the sawmill to shut down than to produce any amount of lumber (Tables 5.4, 5.5, and 5.6).[6] Technically efficient and production cost efficient output levels are defined by the marginal cost curve (Chapter 3 – Costs). Thus, this sawmill's supply curve is defined as the marginal cost above the minimum average variable cost curve.

Following the logic used to develop a supply curve for the softwood dimension lumber sawmill, I can develop a supply curve based on the Maple Syrup case study

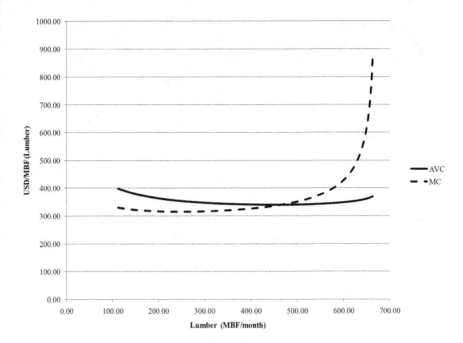

Figure 10.4 Average Variable and Marginal Cost of a Softwood Dimension Lumber Sawmill[§]

[§]AVC denotes average variable cost and MC denotes marginal cost

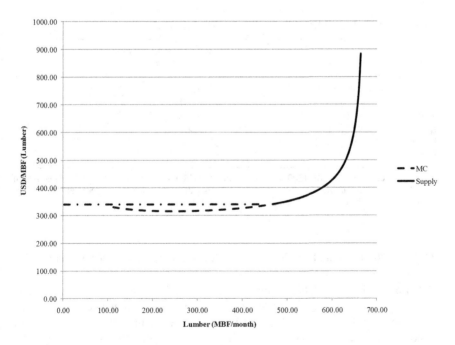

Figure 10.5a Marginal Cost and Supply Curves of a Softwood Dimension Lumber Sawmill[§]

[§]MC denotes marginal cost

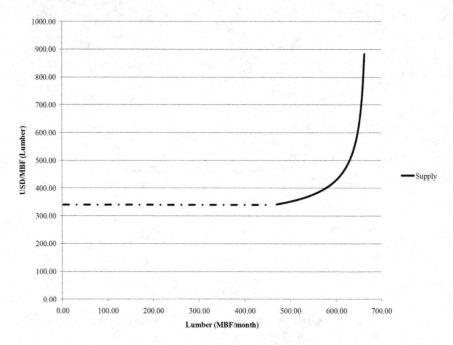

Figure 10.5b Supply Curve of a Softwood Dimension Lumber Sawmill

Table 10.3 Total Annual Variable Maple Syrup Production Costs[‡]

Maple Syrup (gal/yr)	Total Annual Variable Production Costs (USD)
127.5	$3,280.99
255	$5,308.81
765	$10,971.62
1,530	$19,584.30
2,550	$31,564.11
5,100	$60,421.31

[‡]   Source of cost data CFBMC (2000). Costs are in 1999 US dollars (USD) using an exchange rate of 1.49 Canadian dollars per US dollar. (gal/yr) denotes gallons of maple syrup per year. These costs do not include the cost of establishing a larger sugarbush or the costs of purchasing the additional equipment.

(CFBMC 2000). Annual maple syrup variable production cost information is given in Table 10.3.

If I extrapolate the data to a maple syrup operation that produces greater than 5,100 gallons of syrup annually, I can develop average variable and marginal cost curves given in Figure 10.6.[7] Figure 10.6 shows that the minimum average cost or shutdown price occurs at approximately $12.00 per gallon for maple syrup. Figures 10.7a and 10.7b show the supply curve for this maple syrup operation.

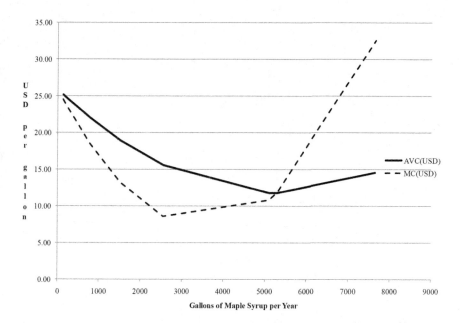

Figure 10.6 Average Variable and Marginal Cost Curves for Maple Syrup Production‡

‡Source of cost data CFBMC (2000). Costs are in 1999 US dollars (USD) per gallon using an exchange rate of 1.49 Canadian dollars per US dollar. AVC(USD) denotes average variable costs measured in 1999 US dollars. MC(USD) denotes marginal cost measured in 1999 US dollars.

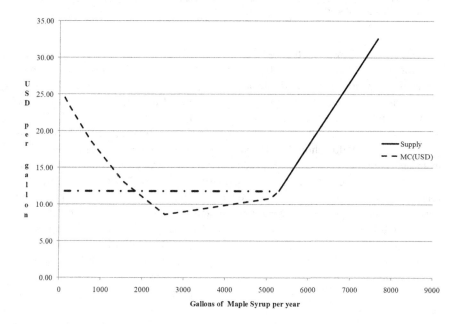

Figure 10.7a Marginal Cost and Supply Curves for Maple Syrup Production‡

‡Source of cost data CFBMC (2000). Costs are in 1999 US dollars (USD) per gallon using an exchange rate of 1.49 Canadian dollars per US dollar. MC(USD) denotes marginal cost measured in 1999 US dollars.

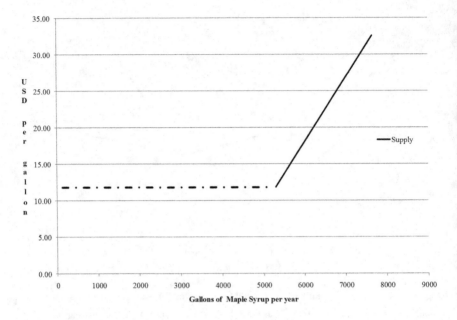

Figure 10.7b Supply Curve for Maple Syrup Production‡

‡Source of cost data CFBMC (2000). Costs are in 1999 US dollars (USD) per gallon using an exchange rate of 1.49 Canadian dollars per US dollar.

Figure 10.7b shows that the owners of this maple syrup operation are *not* willing and able to provide less than 5,100 gallons of maple syrup annually given current production technology and variable and fixed costs.

As stated previously, the supply curve is defined as the marginal cost curve above the minimum of average variable cost as illustrated by Figure 10.7b for maple syrup. Revisiting the solar array or wind turbine production system and Pillars of Cost and Value show that the vast majority of the costs are associated with installing the array or turbine plus the electrical and structural balance of the system (Hand 2010; Feldman et al. 2021; Ramasamy et al. 2022). Post these costs, the relevant inputs – operation and maintenance costs – are mostly constant, and the variable costs are essentially zero. Consequently, marginal costs associated with these production systems are small. For the purposes of the following discussion, I will assume they are essentially equal to zero. So, what does this imply about the supply curve or the opportunity cost of supply energy? While a similar argument can be developed for a solar array, I will use a wind turbine as it is easier to illustrate the analysis. Let Figure 10.8 describe a typical wind turbine power curve or production system curve.

Let equation (10.3a) define the profit equation given variable costs are equal to zero

$$\Pi = PQ(x)\text{-TFC} \tag{10.3a}$$

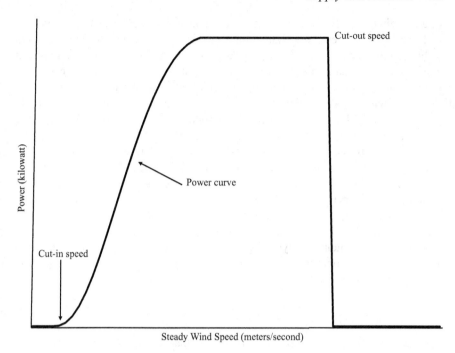

Figure 10.8 Typical Wind Turbine Power Curve

where Π denotes profit and Q(x) denotes power (kilowatts) as a function of input (wind speed; meters/second) for any given air density and blade length. Maximizing profit is given by equation (10.3b):[8]

$$\frac{\Delta\Pi}{\Delta x} = P \cdot \frac{\Delta Q(x)}{\Delta x} = 0 \Rightarrow \frac{\Delta Q(x)}{\Delta x} = 0 \qquad (10.3b)$$

Wind turbines are constructed to accept limited forces from the wind. The maximum "technical" efficiency is at the top of the curve shown in Figure 10.8. After that the turbine starts to "protect itself" by adjusting its blades to let more and wind slip past and thus harvests less and less wind energy as electricity. If wind speeds become too excessive, the turbine will shut down to protect its mechanical components from conditions beyond their normal ranges of operation. Thus, max profits are produced by the wind turbine at the top of its production function or when Marginal Product = ΔQ(x)/Δx = 0. For homeowner systems, the power is used by the homeowner and the price for electricity is positive (electric bill savings). However, the same may not be true for commercial wind farms/solar arrays. A unique feature of the energy (kWh) markets is that supply must equal demand. Without knowledge of output price ($/kWh or $kWh⁻¹), you have no idea if you should produce or not. For example, real-time location-based marginal pricing information (e.g., 5-minute interval prices given as US dollars per megawatt-hour, $/MWHr or $MWHr^{-1}) for New York State's Independent System Operators can be found at http://mis.nyiso.com/public/ (accessed 19 February 2020). In addition, as you cannot control or store the primary input, even at a zero-fuel cost, you cannot be assured of producing at Marginal Product = 0 even if output price is greater than 0.

This discussion shows that there is a positive relationship between the output price and your willingness and ability as a producer or provider of a given good or service. Simply put, the supply curve has a positive slope. What is also important and not explicitly visible is that the supply curve (e.g., Figures 10.5a, 10.5b, 10.7a, and 10.7b) is based on the production system as described in the previous section. There is a production system for producing a physical good such as maple syrup or dimension lumber (e.g., a 2 × 4 × 8); there are also production systems for producing nonphysical goods such as information provided by a consultant or a contract produced by a lawyer. Thus, the concept of supply and a supply curve is not dependent on producing a physical good. The supply curve is an economic model that represents the opportunity cost of producing or providing a good or service; namely, the act of supplying.

Profit and the Pillars of Price and Value

Based on the previous two sections, it appears that the supply curve is related to production costs directly. How is the supply curve related to profit and the Pillars of Price and Value? I will start with the definition of profit given in equation (10.4):

$$\Pi = TR - TC \qquad (10.4)$$
$$= P \cdot Q(\bullet) - TVC - TFC$$

where the terms have been defined previously. Figure 10.9 isolates the supply curve from Figure 10.2.

Examining Figure 10.9 also shows the concept of total revenue, $P^* \cdot Q^*$, can be derived from the supply curve. Total revenue is a value concept. Maital (1994: 6) describes value as the "degree to which buyers think those goods and services make them better off, than if they did without." As described in Chapter 1 – Introduction: If a person purchases a good, we know the minimum assigned value they place on that good, other things being equal. In addition, as was described by equation (10.2), your total revenue, a measure of value to you as an entrepreneur, is dependent directly on the value your consumer places on your good or service. Consequently, if you do not create value for the customer (the Pillar of Value), you will not generate any revenues, only costs (the Pillar of Cost).

Is total cost also a measure of value? I could make the algebraic argument that if the units on total revenue represent value, then the units on total cost would also represent value. When you are purchasing an input (e.g., labor) as part of producing or providing a good or service, Maital's (1994: 6) description of value is still applicable. As a buyer you will only purchase labor if it makes you better off (additional revenue from sales of the additional output produced by the labor relative to

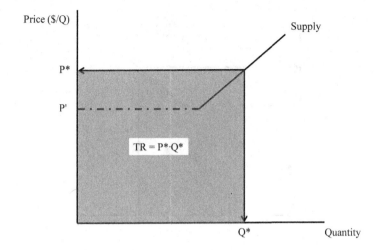

Price ($/Q)

Supply

P*

P'

TR = P*·Q*

Q* Quantity

Figure 10.9 The Supply Curve

its additional cost) than if you did without. Basically, if an input does not add value to your output, you will not buy it. In fact, total cost is the explicit component of opportunity cost or the highest-valued alternative forgone. Therefore, whether you are discussing total revenue or total cost, both concepts are important in building the Pillar of Value.

Returning to the profit equation given in equation (10.4), we have established that total revenue can be obtained from the supply curve as illustrated in Figure 10.9. Can the same be said about total cost? The simple answer is no; however, while total costs cannot be determined from the supply curve, total variable cost can. From Figures 10.5a, 10.5b, 10.7a, and 10.7b, I have shown that the supply curve is defined as the marginal cost curve above the minimum average variable cost. Mathematically, the area under the supply curve defines total variable costs.[9] This is illustrated in Figure 10.10.

Figures 10.9 and 10.10 define TR and TVC respectively. Subtracting TVC from TR or TR − TVC gives a measure of net benefit to the entrepreneur. This is illustrated in Figure 10.11.

This is obviously not profit as given by equations (10.1) or (10.4) and missing is total fixed costs (TFC). Figure 10.11 is a graphical representation of the definition of producer surplus that follows immediately.

> Producer surplus (PS) is the benefit to the entrepreneur from producing or providing a good or service for sale at a price defined by the market net of the opportunity costs of producing or providing it (e.g., the variable production costs).

As shown by Figure 10.11, PS is defined as the area below the market price line and above the supply curve. PS is the incentive for entrepreneurs to produce or provide

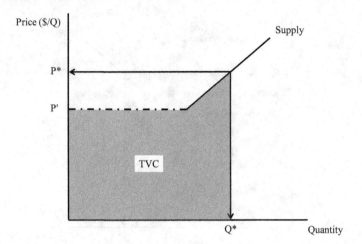

Figure 10.10 Total Variable Cost‡

‡TVC denotes total variable cost. P' denotes the minimum average variable cost. P* and Q* denote the market equilibrium price and quantity respectively.

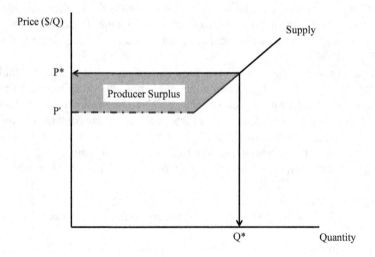

Figure 10.11 Producer Surplus

outputs. As described earlier, PS differs from profit in that it does not include TFC. Is the profit searching rule, developed in Chapter 5 – Profit of weighing incremental or marginal revenue relative to incremental or marginal cost, consistent with the definition of PS? Determining the point in Figure 10.2 that maximizes PS given P* will lead to the optimal output level of Q* (Figure 10.11). As the supply curve is defined as marginal cost, the optimal output level is given by equation (10.5a)

$$P = Supply = MC \tag{10.5a}$$

Assuming workable competition implies that output price, P, is equal to incremental or marginal revenue, MR (Chapter 4 – Revenue), equation (10.5b) is modified to reflect this:

$$MR = P = Supply = MC \qquad (10.5b)$$

Examining the far left-hand and the far right-hand terms give MR = MC, which is the profit searching rule given in Chapter 5 – Profit. Thus, using the profit searching rule to maximize profits implies maximizing PS and using the same rule to maximize PS implies maximizing profits.

As an entrepreneur, your willingness and ability to produce or provide a given amount of output is the result of the economic information you have collected based on the Architectural Plan for Profit. This is summarized in your supply curve. The amount and type of detailed economic information you collect will dictate the detail you can use in generating a supply curve for your business.

The Supply Curve

As described earlier, supply, the supply curve, or the supply schedule is an economic model describing the *opportunity cost* of producing or providing a good or service. As such it embodies the economic information contained within the Architectural Plan for Profit. The supply curve in Figure 10.2 is a representation of this economic model and can reflect responses an entrepreneur makes given changes in economic information. The change and response relationship modeled by the supply curve is then Change (changes in the economic information contained within the Architectural Plan for Profit) → Response (change in the quantity of the output produced or provided). The importance of modeling is in analyzing the change and response relationship; namely, to recognize and react to changes in economic information by modifying the quantity of output produced or provided, the types and amounts of inputs used, or production technology.

Modeling the change and response relationship is simplified by using the following implicit relationship between quantity supplied and a condensed set of variables reflecting the relevant economic information. This is given in Table 10.4 and equation (10.6):

$$Q_S = f(P; ProdSys, P_I, E_P) \qquad (10.6)$$

Equation (10.6) states that the quantity of any given good or service that an entrepreneur is willing and able to provide (Q_S) is a function of ($f(\cdot)$) the price of the good (P or own-price), the production system used to produce or provide the good or service (ProdSys), price of the inputs (P_I), and expected future prices for inputs and the output (E_P). I will analyze the effect of changing each variable on the quantity supplied and then reflect this in the supply curve model.

The supply curve given in Figure 10.2 is graphed with the price of the good or service (P) and the quantity supplied on the vertical and horizontal axes, respectively. Given the nature of the graph, the production system used, price of inputs,

Table 10.4 Factors That Affect Supply (Q_s)

Factor	Description	Supply Effect
P_Q	Own-price; market price of the output	Movement along the supply curve. As own-price increases (decreases) quantity supplied increases (decreases)
ProdSys	Technical efficiency of the production system	Increasing technical efficiency within the production system shifts the supply curve to the right and quantity supplied increases
P_I	Price of inputs	Price of input increases (decreases), variable production costs increase (decrease), supply curve shifts left (right) and quantity supplied decreases (increases)
E_P	Expected future prices for inputs and outputs	Expected increase (decrease) in future output price, supply curve shifts left (right) and quantity supplied today will decrease (increase)

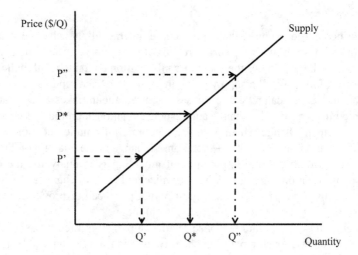

Figure 10.12 Modeling the Effect of Changes in Output Own-Price[‡]

[‡]Change: Output Own-Price → Response: changes in quantity supplied

and expected future price changes are held constant. Thus, I will start with changes in the price of the good or service (referred to as own-price in Table 10.4) and the entrepreneur's response. If an entrepreneur observes the output's own-price is increasing, then profit searching behavior would lead to increasing the quantity of output produced or provided. This change and response relationship is modeled by the supply curve given in Figure 10.12.

The entrepreneur after reviewing the production process and talking with any employees and managers determines that changes could be made to the production

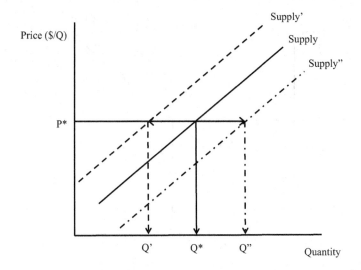

Figure 10.13 Modeling the Effect on Supply Given Changes in the Production System‡

$Q_S = f(P; \textbf{ProdSys}, P_I, E_P)$ all other variables held constant

‡Change: Production System → Response: changes in quantity supplied

process to make it more technically efficient (Chapter 2 – Production Systems) and production cost efficient (Chapter 3 – Costs). Thus, the profit-searching entrepreneur will change the production process so that more output could be produced using the same amount of inputs or producing the same amount of outputs using fewer inputs, reducing the per unit production costs. This change and response relationship is modeled by the supply curve given in Figure 10.13.

In Figure 10.13, increasing technical efficiency and production cost efficiency is modeled by a shift in the supply curve from "Supply to Supply" (all other variables held constant).

If the price of one or more inputs used in the production process increases, then this will cause the total variable production costs to increase (all other variables held constant). A profit-searching entrepreneur faced with increasing production costs will look for ways of reducing the use of the now higher priced inputs. Simply using fewer of these inputs will reduce production costs, but it will also result in a decrease in the quantity of output produced or provided. This change and response relationship is modeled by the supply curve given in Figure 10.14.

In Figure 10.14, the entrepreneur's response to increased input price from P_I to P_I'' will result in producing less output. This is modeled by shifting the supply curve to the left. One way an entrepreneur may attempt to deal with changing input prices is to search for substitutes for the inputs used currently. Finding lower-priced substitutes (i.e., changing input prices from P_I to P_I') will decrease the production costs and allow the profit-searching entrepreneur to increase the amount of output produced or provided.

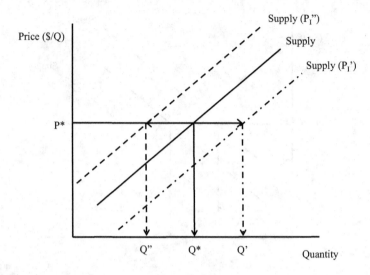

Figure 10.14 Modeling the Effect of Changes in the Price of Inputs‡

$Q_s = f(P; ProdSys, \mathbf{P_I}, E_p)$ all other variables held constant

‡Change: Price of Inputs → Response: changes in quantity supplied

If the entrepreneur expects the future price of the output to increase, they may decrease the quantity of output they are willing to sell today so that they would have them available for sale at the future date and price (all other variables held constant). This change and response relationship is modeled by the supply curve given in Figure 10.15.

In Figure 10.15, a profit-searching entrepreneur's reaction to an expected increase in the output price (E_p to E_p'') will be to make less output available for sale today. This is modeled by shifting the supply curve to the right. It is left to the reader to determine how the amount of output supplied would change if the entrepreneur expected future input prices to increase or decrease, then model these change and response relationships using the supply curve.

Demand

Re-examining Figure 10.2 shows that half of the market is described by supply and the other half is described by demand. Market equilibrium is defined by the intersection of supply and demand. Thus, equal attention must be given to demand. Reviewing equation (10.2) illustrates that a seller's profit is dependent upon the total revenue generated by consumers purchasing the outputs they produce or provide. Total revenue is only generated if consumers "think those goods and services make them better off, than if they did without" (Maital 1994: 6). Examining the Architectural Plan for Profit (Figure 10.1) illustrates the importance of the Pillar of

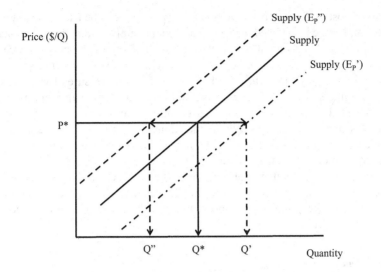

Figure 10.15 Modeling the Effect of Changes in the Expected Prices of Output‡

$Q_s = f(P; \text{ProdSys}, P_I, \mathbf{E_p})$ all other variables held constant

‡Change: Expected Price of Output→ Response: changes in quantity supplied

Value in describing demand. Basically, the Pillar of Value is built on your knowledge of the consumers that purchase your outputs.

A demand curve is drawn traditionally with a negative slope implying that there is an inverse relationship between output own-price and the quantity of the output purchased by consumers; in other words, as the market own-price decreases, consumers would buy more of the output. This is illustrated in Figure 10.2 and seems like a reasonable response. In fact, this behavior is codified in the Law of Demand:

Ceteris paribus (other things being equal), consumers purchase more (less) of a good during a given time interval the lower (higher) its relative price.

The Law of Demand leads to defining the demand curve depicted in Figure 10.2:

Willingness and ability of consumers to pay for a given quantity at a given place and time.

However, what is behind the Law of Demand and the definition of the demand curve that makes the relationship depicted in Figure 10.2 reasonable? Why is demand depicted as an inverse relationship between market price and quantity produced or provided?[10]

Opportunity Cost

Cost is not a concept that is often combined with demand. Cost is most often associated with the costs of producing or providing an output (e.g., Chapter 3 – Costs).

However, cost or more appropriately *opportunity cost* can be used to explain why the demand curve is depicted with a negative slope implying that there is an inverse relationship between output own-price and the quantity of the output purchased. An entrepreneur must remember that consumers are giving up purchasing other commodities if they buy yours. As the relative per unit measure of value or own-price consumers pay increases, the more consumers must give up or forgo in order to obtain your good or service. In this situation, consumers will choose to purchase less of your good or service, other things being equal. Conversely, if the relative per unit measure of value or own-price decreases, consumers will choose to purchase more of your good or service, other things being equal. Consumers will weigh the benefits that your good or service can provide them relative to the opportunity cost of obtaining it. Thus, the demand curve is depicted as an inverse relationship between market own-price and quantity and is a model of a consumer's opportunity cost.

Pillar of Value

Based on Chapter 2 – Production Systems and Chapter 3 – Costs, you should know all the economic information about producing or providing your outputs. Now, think about this, you sell a product (e.g., charter boat Fishing trips, maple syrup, energy from a solar array) and you don't know people's willingness and ability to pay (i.e., demand) for your product, how long will you stay in business? The Pillar of Value not only represents the value you receive from using various different inputs that you have direct control over, but it also represents economic information you must obtain about your consumers or customers. The statement by Maital bears repeating again: Consumers will only buy your products if they "think those goods and services make them better off, than if they did without" (Maital 1994: 6). Consequently, if your output does not create value for the consumer, they will not buy it. Thus, the importance of having this economic information seems obvious. What may be less obvious is where to obtain such information.

I will use an example taken from the forestry profession to illustrate obtaining the economic information on consumers for developing the Pillar of Value. The premise of the example is a consultant who works with private landowners to sustainably manage their forestlands. Creighton et al. (2002), Butler (2008), Majumdar et al. (2008), Hatcher et al. (2013), Butler et al. (2016), Creighton et al. (2016), and Snyder et al. (2019) summarize the socioeconomic, demographic, and land area owned statistics of privately owned forestland.[11] In the United States, families own 35% and other private entities own 21% of forestland giving a total of 56% of forestland owned by private landowners. Regionally, in the northern and southern United States, private forestland ownership is 75% and 86% of forestland, respectively. In the Rocky Mountain and Pacific Coast regions, private forestland ownership is 25% and 33%, respectively. Land holdings of less than 100 acres are 33% of total private forestland area. However, 94% of all private forest landowners hold lands of less than 100 acres and 61% hold only one acre. Private forest landowners have multiple reasons for owning forestland (Creighton et al. 2002;

Butler and Leatherberry 2004; Belin et al. 2005; Hagan et al. 2005; Butler 2008, 2010: Majumdar et al. 2008; Hatcher et al. 2013; Butler et al. 2016; Creighton et al. 2016; Snyder et al. 2019). The primary reasons are for aesthetics, privacy, recreation, and protection of nature. Near the bottom of reasons for forestland ownership is the generation of income (e.g., sale of timber). While these owners are not necessarily against selling timber, it is not the reason they own forestland and any sale of timber must be consistent with the primary reasons for owning forestland (Wagner 2020). Finally, they are older (55 years old plus), better educated, and have higher incomes than the general population (Butler 2008; Butler et al. 2016). Thus, the sustainable forest management services that you are trying to sell them should reflect their ownership preferences, relative size of the land holdings, and inheritance or family legacy concerns these owners will probably have in the near future. This point bears repeating: It is *their* preference set you are managing for, not yours. These are not your forests that you are trying to sustainably manage, it is *their* woods.[12] The last sentence is paraphrased from Dr. Brett Butler, United States Forest Service. The wording is important, as a "forest" is something someone else owns, woods are what the landowner owns and there is an emotional relationship with that ownership. That emotional relationship helps define their preference set for sustainably managing their woods. While this example deals with forestry explicitly, the main idea is of identifying your customer's preference set so that your output will match this preference set and they will purchase your output. And we are back to the Pillar of Value and your ability as an entrepreneur to generate revenue.

While very succinct, this example illustrates how you would now be better prepared to sell these landowners sustainable forest management plans that they would be willing and able to buy than if you did not have this economic information. All the sources used to develop the economic information in this example are publicly available (https://www.fia.fs.usda.gov/nwos/ accessed 5 September 2023). As an entrepreneur you should actively search out this type of information on your customers. This same type of information is available publicly for sustainable energy converted using solar or wind (Schelly and Letzelter 2020).

Finally, a value concept similar to producer surplus can be developed by combining the discussion from the previous sections with the Pillar of Value and Max NB = B − C from equation (10.2). Figure 10.16a illustrates a consumer's incremental choice for purchasing a good; for example, gallons of maple syrup.

At own-price P' the consumer would only purchase Q' gallons of maple syrup. The own-price P' represents the consumer's willingness and ability to pay for Q' gallons of maple syrup; but they only have to pay the market equilibrium price P*. Thus there is a surplus or net benefit of $[P^* \cdot Q' + \frac{1}{2} \cdot Q' \cdot (P - P')] - P^* \cdot Q' = \frac{1}{2} \cdot Q' \cdot (P - P')$ that the consumer captures from being able to purchase at the market equilibrium price of P*. At own-price P" the consumer would only purchase the Q" gallons of maple syrup. The own-price P" represents the consumer's willingness and ability to pay for Q" gallons of maple syrup, but they only have to pay the market equilibrium price P*. Thus, there is a surplus or net benefit of $[P^* \cdot Q" + \frac{1}{2} \cdot Q" \cdot (P - P")] - P^* \cdot Q" = \frac{1}{2} \cdot Q" \cdot (P - P")$ that the consumer captures from being

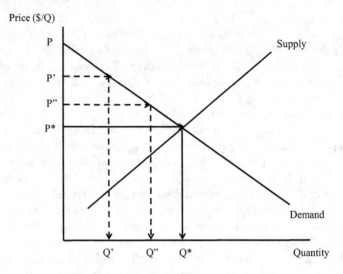

Figure 10.16a Deriving Consumer Surplus‡

‡ Price P denotes the own-price at which zero quantity is purchased by the consumer

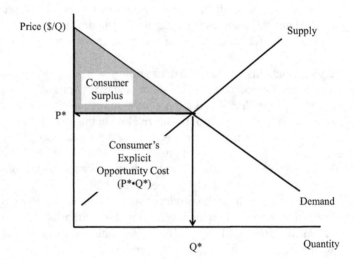

Figure 10.16b Consumer Surplus

able to purchase at the market equilibrium price of P^*. Finally at own-price P^* the consumer would purchase the Q^* gallons of maple syrup. The price P^* represents the consumer's willingness and ability to pay for Q^* gallons of maple syrup. Thus, there is a surplus or net benefit of $[P^* \cdot Q^* + \frac{1}{2} \cdot Q'' \cdot (P - P^*)] - P^* \cdot Q^* = \frac{1}{2} \cdot Q'' \cdot (P - P^*)$ that the consumer captures from being able to purchase at the market equilibrium price of P^*.[13] The surplus or net benefit to the consumer is illustrated in Figure 10.16b.

This leads to the definition of consumer surplus:

Consumer Surplus (CS) is the net benefit to the consumer from being able to buy a commodity at the market equilibrium price.

As shown by Figure 10.16b CS is the area above the market price line and below the demand curve. What Figure 10.16b also shows is that a consumer's surplus is maximized at the market equilibrium price, P*, and quantity, Q*. The reader should notice the parallels between the discussion of consumer and producer surplus.

Demand Curve

As described earlier, demand, the demand curve, or the demand schedule is an economic model describing the *opportunity cost* of consumers for the goods or services that you produce or provide. The demand curve in Figure 10.2 represents this economic model and can reflect reactions consumers have given changes in economic information they obtain from the markets and their preferences (Chapter 1 – Introduction). Based on your knowledge of the market and your customers' preferences, you are building the Pillar of Value contained within the Architectural Plan for Profit. As with supply curve, the demand curve is used to model change and response relationships. For example, External Change (your prototypical customer's annual income changes) → Consumer's Reaction (change in the quantity of the output they are willing and able to buy). How do you as an entrepreneur respond to this change? The importance of modeling is in analyzing the change and response relationship; namely, to recognize external changes affecting your consumers, their reaction to these external changes, and your response to this new economic information. In other words, how do you "shift" your supply in response to these external changes? Your response might be as simple as modifying the quantity of output produced or provided, or it might require modifying the attributes or characteristics of your output or creating new products and services in addition to the amount produced or provided of existing products.

Consumers view purchasing your products *not* as charitable giving, but in response to the perceived value they place on acquiring whatever it is that you produce or provide; namely, the Pillar of Value. Thus, as entrepreneurs, you will need to recognize external changes that affect consumers' socioeconomic and demographic environments, their reaction to these external changes, and how you might respond to these changes. Modeling this change and response relationship is developed by identifying the relevant economic information consumers obtain from the markets and socioeconomic and demographic factors that can be used to complete the description of their preferences. The economic variables and social and demographic factors are summarized in equation (10.7) and Table 10.5.

$$Q_D = f(P; P_S, P_C, Y, E_p, E_Y, SocDem) \quad (10.7)$$

Table 10.5 Demand's Economic Variables and Social and Demographic Factors[‡]

Economic Variables	
Variable	*Notation*
Own-Price	P
Price of Related Goods	P_S – Price of Substitutes
	P_C – Price of Complements
Income	Y
Expected Own-Price	E_P
Expected Income	E_Y
Elasticity (Price and Income Sensitivity)	
Social and Demographic Factors	
Demographics	
Exploit Openings	
Habit and Loyalty	
Trends and Exuberance	

[‡]I am indebted to Maital (1994) for the idea of presenting demand in this fashion

Table 10.5 and equation (10.7) state that the quantity of any given good or service that customers are willing and able to buy (Q_D) is a function of: the own-price of the good (P or own-price); price of related goods (i.e., substitutes (P_S) and complements (P_C)); expected prices of the good (E_P); income and expected income (Y and E_Y, respectively); and social and demographic factors (SocDem).

The traditional model of the demand curve is graphed with the own-price of the good or service (P) and the quantity demanded on the vertical and horizontal axes of Figure 10.2, respectively. Given the nature of this graph, all the other variables given in equation (10.7) and Table 10.5 are held constant. To analyze change and response relationships, I will start with the economic variables and in particular changes of the own-price of the good or service and consumers' reaction. If consumers observe the own-price of the output is increasing (decreasing), then maximizing net benefit searching behavior would lead to decreasing (increasing) the quantity of output purchased. This is modeled by the demand curve given in Figure 10.17.

In response to the external change in output own-price and consumers' reaction, the profit-seeking entrepreneur would modify the amount of output they produce or provide – that is, "shift" their supply – to match consumers' willingness and ability to pay. The change and response relationships associated with the other economic variables are summarized in Table 10.6 and illustrated in Figure 10.18.

I will discuss each very briefly. Substitutes are goods and services produced or provided by your competitors that consumers could use in place of your product. For example, Vermont, New Hampshire, or Canadian maple syrup or imitation maple syrup could be a substitute for New York maple syrup. If the price of these substitutes increases (decreases) relative to the price of New York maple syrup, consumers will be likely to increase (decrease) their purchases of New York maple

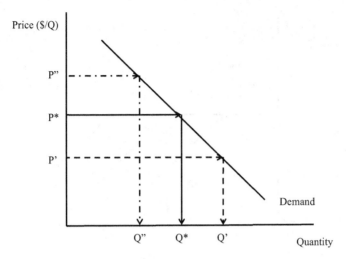

Price ($/Q)

P"

P*

P'

Demand

Q"   Q*   Q'   Quantity

Figure 10.17 Modeling the Effect of Changes in Output Price[‡]

[‡]External Change in market price of the output or Own-Price → Consumers' React by modifying their amount purchased → Entrepreneurial Response by modify the amount of output produced or provided to match consumer's willingness and ability to purchase. This change and response relationship is for what are termed "normal" goods. There is a unique class of goods called "Giffen" goods whereas the own-price of the good increases the amount purchased by the consumer also increases. While the discussion of this is beyond the scope of this book, I would encourage the interested reader to research this topic.

Table 10.6 Change and Response Relationships for the Economic Variables of Demand

Economic Variable	External Change	Consumers' Reaction $(Q_D)^{‡}$	Entrepreneur's Response $(Q_S)^{‡}$
Price of Substitutes (P_S)	Increase	Increase	Increase
	Decrease	Decrease	Decrease
Price of Complements (P_C)	Increase	Decrease	Decrease
	Decrease	Increase	Increase
Income (Y)[§]	Increase	Increase	Increase
	Decrease	Decrease	Decrease
Expected Future Prices (E_P)	Increase	Increase	Increase
	Decrease	Decrease	Decrease
Expected Future Income (E_Y)	Increase	Increase	Increase
	Decrease	Decrease	Decrease

[‡] Q_D denotes quantity demanded by consumer and Q_S denotes quantity produced or provided by the entrepreneur

[§] The consumers' reaction given changes in income is for what are termed "normal" goods. There is a unique class of goods called an "inferior" good in which as income increases the amount of the good consumers are willing and able to purchase decreases. The classic example is using the bus for transportation. As consumers' incomes increase the amount they use the bus decreases, all else held constant. While the discussion of this is beyond the scope of this book, I would encourage the interested reader to research this topic.

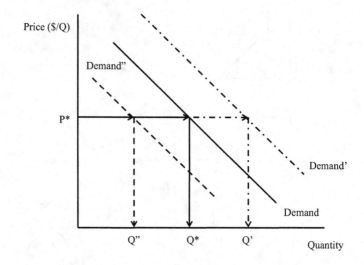

Figure 10.18 Modeling the Effect of Changes in Economic Variables Given in Table 10.6‡

‡External Change in prices or income → Consumers' React by modifying their amount purchased → Entrepreneurial Response by modify the amount of output produced or provided to match consumer's willingness and ability to purchase

syrup, all else held constant. Would you consider inside-out beams and solid wood beams as substitutes? Complements are goods and services that are used concurrently with your product. For example, hotels and restaurants are often complementary goods to the purchase of a charter boat fishing trip. If the price of these complements increases (decreases) relative to the price of a charter boat fishing trip, then consumers will be likely to decrease (increase) their purchases of charter boat fishing trips, all else held constant. Consumers' income must be allocated among various items. For example, if consumers' incomes decrease, they may switch from buying New York maple syrup to purchasing imitation maple syrup, all else held constant. If there is an expected increase in the price of New York maple syrup next year, then consumers will be more likely to purchase more (stock up) on New York maple syrup this year, all else held constant. Finally, if consumers' income is expected to increase next year, then consumers will be more likely to purchase more (stock up) on New York maple syrup this year, all else held constant.

While the actual change in the quantity demanded by consumers in Figures 10.17 and 10.18 cannot be estimated based on the aforementioned information, what the entrepreneur is observing critically are the reactions consumers have made to these external changes. Namely, the entrepreneur is concerned how their total revenue will be affected given consumers' reactions: Any movement along or shift in the demand curve (Figures 10.17 and 10.18) will affect the market equilibrium (Figure 10.2) and buyers' explicit cost, [P·Q(•)], transferred to the entrepreneur as their total revenue, [P·Q(•)], as described by equation (10.2). Knowing this economic information will allow entrepreneurs to fine tune their responses to consumers' reactions.

The responsiveness of consumers' reactions to external changes in prices and income is called elasticity. While the concept of responsiveness or elasticity seems simple enough, there still is a question of how it is measured. Total revenue is defined as $P \cdot Q(\cdot)$ where the units on price have been described as $/Q (e.g., in 2018 the average price per gallon of maple syrup was $33.80 (Chapter 5 – Profit)) and the units on $Q(\cdot)$ are generally described by some physical measurement (e.g., in the maple syrup example the physical measurement is gallons). However, neither price nor quantity are easily comparable even given similar products. For example, in the Select Red Oak example output is measured as the gross and net board foot volume measured in International 1/4 log rule per individual tree and own-price would then be dollars per gross or net board foot volume measured in International 1/4 log rule (Chapter 2 – Production Systems; Hahn and Hansen 1991). In contrast, output in the Radiata Pine example is measured as cubic meter per hectare or m^3ha^{-1} (Table 2.7a and 2.7b) and own-price would then be dollars per cubic meter NZ$ m^{-3} (Table 4.3). Thus, to account for the differences in price and output units, elasticity is defined as the following:

Elasticity – the percentage change in either price or income relative to the percentage change in quantity, holding all else constant.

The various types of demand elasticities and how to estimate them are given in Table 10.7. Elasticity describes a price or income and quantity effect on total revenue. As illustrated by Table 10.7, elasticity is a ratio of the relative price or income effects to the relative quantity effects (Nievergelt 1983). If the price or income effects are greater (less) than the quantity effects, the elasticity will be greater (less) than one.

I will analyze each briefly starting with own-price elasticity. A percentage increase in the own-price of the good or service will cause total revenue to increase (as P increases $P \cdot Q(\cdot)$ increases). However as there is also a negative relationship between own-price and quantity demanded: Consumers' reaction to an increase in own-price is to reduce their purchases resulting in a decrease in total revenue (as Q decreases $P \cdot Q(\cdot)$ decreases). If the own-price effects on total revenue are small relative to the quantity effects on total revenue, then own-price elasticity is less than one and the demand curve is defined as elastic. In this case a percentage increase in the own-price of a good would cause the total revenue to decrease. The opposite would occur with a percentage decrease in own-price. If the own-price effects on total revenue are large relative to the quantity effects on total revenue, then own-price elasticity is greater than one and the demand curve is defined as inelastic.[14] In this case a percentage increase in the price of a good would cause the total revenue to increase. The opposite would occur with a percentage decrease in price.

How can the entrepreneur use the information on own-price elasticity to their advantage? Whether the demand curve for your good or service is elastic or inelastic depends on three factors. First is the number of substitutes. If there are a large number of substitutes for your goods or services and if the own-price of your good or service increases, then consumers will shift to one of the many

Table 10.7 Demand Elasticities

Name	Definition[†]	Arc Elasticity[§]	Point Elasticity
Own-Price Elasticity (E_p)[‡]	$\dfrac{\%\Delta P}{\%\Delta Q_D}$	$\dfrac{\left(Q_D''-Q_D'\right)}{\left(P''-P'\right)} \cdot \dfrac{\dfrac{\left(P''+P'\right)}{2}}{\dfrac{\left(Q_D''+Q_D'\right)}{2}}$	$\dfrac{\partial Q_D(\bullet)}{\partial P}\cdot\dfrac{P}{Q_D}$
Cross-Price Elasticity (Substitute, E_{P_s})[††]	$\dfrac{\%\Delta P_S}{\%\Delta Q_D}$	$\dfrac{\left(Q_D''-Q_D'\right)}{\left(P_S''-P_S'\right)} \cdot \dfrac{\dfrac{\left(P_S''+P_S'\right)}{2}}{\dfrac{\left(Q_D''+Q_D'\right)}{2}}$	$\dfrac{\partial Q_D(\bullet)}{\partial P_S}\cdot\dfrac{P_S}{Q_D}$
Cross-Price Elasticity (Complement, E_{P_c})[††]	$\dfrac{\%\Delta P_C}{\%\Delta Q_D}$	$\dfrac{\left(Q_D''-Q_D'\right)}{\left(P_C''-P_C'\right)} \cdot \dfrac{\dfrac{\left(P_C''+P_C'\right)}{2}}{\dfrac{\left(Q_D''+Q_D'\right)}{2}}$	$\dfrac{\partial Q_D(\bullet)}{\partial P_C}\cdot\dfrac{P_C}{Q_D}$
Income (E_Y)	$\dfrac{\%\Delta Y}{\%\Delta Q_D}$	$\dfrac{\left(Q_D''-Q_D'\right)}{\left(Y''-Y'\right)} \cdot \dfrac{\dfrac{\left(Y''+Y'\right)}{2}}{\dfrac{\left(Q_D''+Q_D'\right)}{2}}$	$\dfrac{\partial Q_D(\bullet)}{\partial Y}\cdot\dfrac{Y}{Q_D}$

[†] %ΔP and %ΔY denotes the percentage change in price and income respectively. %ΔQ_D denotes the percentage change in quantity demanded.

[§] Arc elasticities and point elasticities are estimated assuming all else remains constant

[‡] Own-price elasticity is technically a negative number as the demand curve has a negative slope. However, it is often given as the absolute value. If $0 < |Ep| < 1$ then the demand is inelastic. If $|Ep| > 1$ then the demand curve is elastic. If $|Ep|$ = infinity then the demand curve is perfectly elastic. If $|Ep| = 0$ then the demand curve is perfectly inelastic.

[††] If the cross-price elasticity is negative, then the goods are complements, $E_{P_c} < 0$. If the cross-price elasticity is positive, then the goods are substitutes, $E_{P_s} > 0$.

substitutes and your total revenue would decrease. The demand for a good or service with many substitutes is defined to be relatively elastic. If there are a few substitutes for your goods or services and if the own-price of your good or service increases, then consumers will have limited ability to shift to a substitutes and your total revenue would increase. The demand for a good or service with few substitutes is defined to be relatively inelastic. As an entrepreneur you should be obtaining information about your market continually. In other words, how much market power do you have to set price? If you increase your price by a small percentage and observe a large percentage reduction in the amount of output you sell and total revenue, then you produce or provide a good or service with many substitutes. In this case you have little latitude to influence market price and the market is characterized by workable competition. I will discuss more about this topic in Chapter 11 – Market Equilibrium and Structure. Based on this discussion, would you think the demand for e-books is elastic or inelastic? According to information given by Amazon® in 2014 (https://www.forbes.com/

sites/ryanmac/2014/07/29/amazon-does-e-book-math-for-hachette-in-arguing-for-9-99-prices/?sh=428daa1e70d0 accessed 6 September 2023), for every e-book sold for \$14.99 it would sell 1.74 if priced at \$9.99. This would give an own-price elasticity of demand of is given in equation (10.8)

$$E_D = \frac{\%\Delta Q_D}{\%\Delta P_Q}$$

(10.8)

$$-2.22 = \frac{(1.74-1)\Big/1}{(7.99-14.99)\Big/14.99}$$

or a very elastic demand curve for e-book. What about the own-price elasticity of demand for cigarettes? For every 10% increase in the own-price of cigarettes, smoking goes down 4%, according to a 2014 report on smoking by the US Surgeon General (www.npr.org/sections/health-shots/2016/09/27/495439481/would-cali fornias-proposed-tobacco-tax-hike-reduce-smoking accessed 28 September 2016; The Health Consequences of Smoking – 50 Years of Progress: A Report of the Surgeon General, 2014 (https://www.ncbi.nlm.nih.gov/books/NBK179276/ accessed 6 September 2023). The own-price elasticity of demand is given in equation (10.9):

$$E_D = \frac{\%\Delta Q_D}{\%\Delta P_Q}$$

(10.9)

$$-0.4 = \frac{-0.04}{0.10}$$

As expected, this shows a very inelastic own-price elasticity of demand for cigarettes.

Second is the percent of consumers' income that is spent on your good or service. The larger the percent of consumers' budget spent on a good, the more sensitive they are to own-price changes and the more elastic the demand curve. For example, a home is one of the largest purchases consumers often make, and paying for the house requires a significant amount of their annual income. Thus, as the own-price of a home increases (including the interest rate on any mortgage), the more consumers will modify the type of home (e.g., square footage, urban vs. suburban, etc.) they will purchase. In 2008–2009 the housing market collapsed in the United States. While the cause-and-effect relationships surrounding this collapse are complex, before the collapse many consumers could get home loans with little to no down payments and relatively small initial interest rates on the large amounts borrowed. Based on this information, could you make the argument that consumers behaved as if the demand for housing was inelastic when it should have been elastic? What about the demand for the pen or pencil that you are using to take notes with, is the demand for that writing implement elastic or inelastic? Why?

Third, the more time consumers have to search for alternatives the more elastic the demand for the good or service. The internet has allowed most consumers to search for alternatives relatively quickly. In addition, with increasing access to smart phones and other handheld devices, consumers can often search immediately.

Cross-price elasticity describes the percentage change in the amount of a good or service that you sell to consumers given a percentage change in the price of either a substitute or a complement. Compare these two goods: sport utility vehicles (SUVs) and unleaded gas. Would you consider these two goods substitutes or complements? The US Department of Energy provides data on the historic nominal retail price of regular unleaded gas from January 1976 to November 2009 (www.eia.doe.gov/emeu/mer/prices.html accessed 28 December 2009). Based on these data, there were significant percent increases in the nominal price of regular unleaded gas starting in 2000 and peaking in 2008. These percentage changes in gas prices were followed by a significant percent decrease in the number of SUVs purchased as described by the *New York Times* 2 May 2008 article (www. nytimes.com/2008/05/02/business/02auto.html accessed 28 December 2009) and the *Wall Street Journal* Market Data Center (http://online.wsj.com/mdc/public/page/2_3022-autosales.html accessed 28 December 2009). Feng et al. (2005) showed that for consumers who own a single vehicle, a 1% increase in the price of gas would result in decreasing their probability of purchasing an SUV by 7%. If goods are substitutes, they will exhibit the opposite effect. For example, Feng et al. (2005) also showed that for consumers who own a single vehicle a 1% increase in the price of gas would result in increasing their probability of purchasing a car by 0.9%. Finally, Feng et al. (2005) showed that for consumers who own two vehicles as the price of gas increased the probability of owning a car plus an SUV decreased by 79.3% and the probability of owning a car plus an additional car increased by 69.5%. Based on the prior illustration using cars and SUVs, what do you think the cross-price elasticities for maple syrup made from New York sugar maple trees would be relative to that made from Vermont, New Hampshire, or Canadian sugar maple trees or imitation maple syrup?

As consumers' incomes change, they buy different goods and services. For example, as you go from a college student to a full-time job your income changes, as do your purchases. Income elasticity measures the responsiveness of consumers purchasing what you produce or provide to changes in income. If the income elasticity is positive, the good is described as a normal good. For example, maple syrup would be considered a normal good in that as your income increases your purchase of maple syrup would increase. The larger the income elasticity the greater the responsiveness to percent increases in income. If the income elasticity is negative the good is described as an inferior good. For example, imitation maple syrup may be considered as an inferior good in that as your income increases you would purchase less imitation maple syrup.

A related elasticity not given in Table 10.7 is called advertising elasticity. The purpose of advertising is to increase the sales of the goods or services that you produce or provide by showing a targeted group of consumers the superiority of your product relative to similar products. Advertising is a production expense; one way to measure the usefulness of advertising is to track for example how a 1% increase in your advertising expenditures will affect your total revenue. Advertising is more successful if it is targeted to those consumers that would be the most interested in your product (e.g., men versus women, old versus young, etc.) and reaching them using the appropriate media (e.g., print, radio, television, internet, etc.). Targeting consumers implies that their demand depends on economic, social, and demographic factors.

Table 10.5 lists a number of economic, social, and demographic factors that influence demand. This list is not meant to be all-encompassing. Its purpose is to get you to think past focusing only on the traditional economic variables. I have already given an example of some of the social and demographic factors that influence private forestland owners' demand for management services that you might sell. For example, the primary reason of owning forestland for these owners is aesthetics and not revenue from timber sales. While these landowners may not be opposed to generating a cash flow from selling timber or stumpage, they will be concerned about minimizing landownership costs relative to timber and non-timber outputs and outcomes from their forestland over time (Wagner 2020).[15] Thus, if you could exploit a potential opening that would generate a positive net revenue flow for the landowners (but not from timber sales), this would reduce their landownership costs. For example, the sale of carbon sequestration ecosystem services provided by forest management has received attention recently (Elliott 2011; Malmsheimer et al. 2011; Oliver and Fried 2013). A carbon offset is a reduction in emissions of carbon dioxide or other greenhouse gases made in order to compensate for emissions made elsewhere. Offsets are measured in metric tons of carbon dioxide-equivalent ($MTCO_2e$, $MtCO_2e$, MTCO2e, or MtCO2e); for example, 1,000 board feet of sugar maple (*Acer saccharum*) is approximately 2.36 $MtCO_2e$ or about 2.4 carbon credits (above and below ground). Markets for carbon offsets exist in the European Union (https://ec.europa.eu/clima/policies/ets_en accessed 3 February 2020), Australia (https://www.greeningaustralia.org.au/what-is-the-carbon-market/ accessed 6 September 2023), the over-the-counter markets in the United States (e.g., the Northeast Regional Greenhouse Gas Initiative – www.rggi. org/ accessed 3 February 2020 – and the Western Climate Initiative – www.wci-inc. org/ accessed 3 February 2020), and other locations. The sale of carbon offsets may not be a panacea for landowners, however, given the costs and requirements for creating, verifying, registering, and monitoring a carbon offset project for the long-term commitment period (Kerchner and Keeton 2015; White et al. 2018; https:// gatrees.org/wp-content/uploads/2020/02/GeneratingValuethroughForestCarbon-1. pdf accessed 6 September 2023; https://content.ces.ncsu.edu/an-introduction-to-forest-carbon-offset-markets accessed 3 February 2020; www.forestcarbonworks. org/ accessed 3 February 2020; https://americancarbonregistry.org/ accessed 19 February 2020).

Searching for new products and product information takes time that consumers could use to do something else with (opportunity cost); thus, consumers develop habits and loyalty to various products. For example, I will buy a certain make of car because my father always bought them. An entrepreneur should actively search for opportunities to develop that loyalty with their consumers. An entrepreneur should be aware (and cautious) of trends and exuberance. While large profits can be made if you are on the upswing of a trend, coming into this type of market late could be costly. An entrepreneur should be conscious of the relevant socioeconomic and demographic factors that describe their customers. The timber output from forests represents a unique situation with regards the socioeconomic and demographic factors. Producing a commercially viable tree may take from 20 to 30 years for southern yellow pines grown in the southern United States to 100 years for hardwoods grown in the northeastern United States. In the Radiata Pine Plantation practical application, the rotation ages described were 30 years. Forestland owners who derive revenue from the sale of stumpage (i.e., the value of standing timber) are in essence trying to predict consumers' preferences decades out in the future (Smith 1988). In addition, Smith (1988) speculated that species that were considered not very commercially viable today may become commercially viable in the future. For example, willows (genus *Salix*) are currently being viewed as a source of bioenergy and biofuels (Volk and Luzadis 2008).

Demand and Supply Variability

Fundamentally, the supply curve describes the entrepreneur's opportunity cost of producing or providing an output: Supply does depend on costs, but the cost of supplying is the opportunities forgone by the act of supplying. Supply, or the supply curve in Figure 10.2, is an economic model used to examine cause-and-effect relationships of an entrepreneur's opportunity cost. The cause would be an external change (i.e., changes in the economic information contained within the Architectural Plan for Profit) leading to an entrepreneur's response (e.g., change in the input use, production technology, and/or change in output produced or provided). This was summarized in Table 10.4.

Fundamentally, the demand curve describes the consumer's opportunity cost of obtaining your output. Demand, or the demand curve in Figure 10.2, is an economic model used to examine cause, effect, and response relationships of a consumer's opportunity cost. For example, a cause would be an external change in a consumer's annual income leading to a consumer's reaction, a change in the quantity of the output they are willing and able to buy, leading to an entrepreneur's response of modifying the quantity of output produced, modifying the attributes or characteristics of the output, or creating new products. This is illustrated in Tables 10.4, 10.5, 10.6, and 10.7.

This chapter is essentially building economic models to help an entrepreneur analyze variability in supply and demand systematically, recognizing an external change and the entrepreneur's possible response.

How to Use Economic Information – Supply and Demand – to Make Better Business Decisions

Successful entrepreneurs are actively searching for ways to increase their profits. This includes placing equal time and energy on understanding the concept of supply as well as demand. Fundamentally, supply represents the opportunity cost of the entrepreneur. The opportunity cost could be described by the physical production costs of manufacturing an inside-out beam or a gallon of maple syrup or converting a kilowatt-hour of energy. They also describe your time, labor, materials, and capital of producing or providing a good or service. These opportunity costs are modeled by a supply curve or supply schedule and embody the economic information contained within the Architectural Plan for Profit – the production system linked to the Pillars of Cost and Value. The economic model of supply provides an entrepreneur a systematic way of analyzing change and response relationships; namely, to recognize changes in economic information obtained from the market and then modifying the quantity of output produced or provided.

Fundamentally, demand, the demand curve, or a demand function represents the opportunity cost of consumers of the goods or services you produce or provide. The definition of demand is given as the willingness and ability to purchase the outputs that you produce or provide. Consumers must be willing; that is, placing value on your output. They also must be able: If a consumer is not able to purchase your output, you have no possibility of converting a consumer's expenditure into your total revenue. As just stated, your total revenue is dependent directly on your understanding of consumers' demand. The economic model of demand provides an entrepreneur a systematic way of analyzing change and response relationships; namely, to recognize external changes affecting your consumers, their reaction to these external changes, and your response to this new economic information. In other words, how do you "shift" your supply in response to these external changes? Your response might be as simple as modifying the quantity of output produced or provided, or it might require modifying the attributes or characteristics of your output or creating new products and services in addition to the amount produced or provided of existing products.

A brief examination of these last two paragraphs shows that they are almost identical in terms of wording. This was done on purpose and helps illustrate the important relationship between the concepts of supply and demand. Successful entrepreneurs realize this relationship and the equal importance of supply and demand in searching for ways to increase profits.

Notes

1 The reader should review the concept of an economic model as described in Chapter 1 – Introduction.

2 For the purposes of this chapter, the supply curve will describe a representative entrepreneur and the demand curve will describe a representative buyer or group of buyers. Various market structures and their implications for market equilibriums will be discussed briefly in Chapter 11 – Market Equilibrium and Structure.

3 Dimension lumber is lumber that is cut and finished to standardized width and depth usually measured in inches; for example, common sizes are 2×4, 2×6, 2×8, and 4×4. The actual finished width and depth are 1.5×3.5, 1.5×5.5, 1.5×7.5, and 3.5×3.5, respectively. This is due to the width of the saw and planning to square the lumber. Board lengths of dimension lumber can vary; however, standard lengths are 6, 8, 10, 12, 14, 16, 18, 20, 22, and 24 feet.

4 Chapter 3 – Costs shows the direct relationship between the definition of the production system and the determination of total and variable costs, average total and variable costs, and marginal cost. I would recommend that the reader review this information briefly.

5 For example, the retail price of a common grade 2 × 4 × 8 is 2.84 US dollars per piece (www.lowes.com/search?searchTerm=2x4x8 accessed 18 February 2020; www.home-depot.com/s/2x4x8%2520lumber?NCNI-5 accessed 18 February 2020). Given that the actual dimensions are 1.5" × 3.5" × 8' as described in endnote 3, there are 3.5 board feet per board

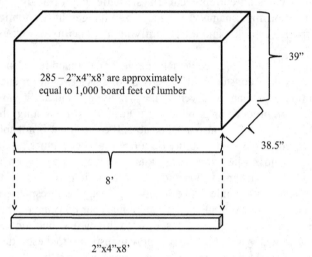

Illustration 10.1 Illustration of how many 2" × 4" × 8' are in 1,000 board feet of lumber

Thus, there are approximately 285 2 × 4 × 8 per 1,000 board feet of lumber. At the retail price given this equates to approximately 809 US dollars per 1,000 board feet of lumber. Illustration 10.1 shows approximately how many 2 × 4 × 8s are in 1,000 board feet of lumber

6 If a buyer is willing to pay more than $340.36 per MBF of lumber for less than 450.10 MBF of lumber per month and the market price is greater than $340.36 per MBF of lumber, then the sawmill's owners will produce at the technically efficient and production cost efficient output levels for the given market price and sell any excess lumber in the market.

7 The extrapolation was based on a second-degree polynomial of average total costs.

8 The mathematics of profit maximizing with respect to input is described in Appendix 5B – Calculus of Profit Maximization of Chapter 5 – Profit.

9 The area under the supply curve can be calculated using two mensuration formula provided in Illustration 10.2.
First is calculating the area of the rectangle: $P' \cdot Q'$. Second is using the trapezoid rule to calculate the area of the remaining component: $\Delta Q \cdot (1/2P' + 1/2P^*)$. The trapezoid rule is an algebraic approximation of the area under the marginal cost curve. For example, the TVC of producing 470.33 MBF of lumber per month is $160,110.99 (Table 10.2). The approximation of TVC based on the two mensuration formula is $160,096.67. It is left to the reader to check my calculations.

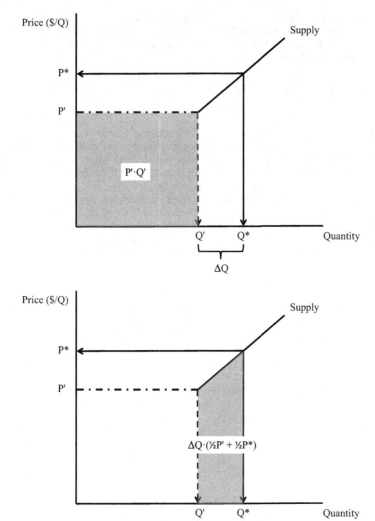

Illustration 10.2 Illustration of calculating the area under the supply curve

10 The reader will notice that this paragraph is almost identical to the first paragraph under the Supply section. This was done on purpose and helps illustrate the parallels between the concepts of supply and demand.

11 Forestland is defined as land that is at least 10% stocked by forest trees of any size, including land that formerly had such tree cover and that will be naturally or artificially regenerated. The minimum area for classification of forest land is one acre (Smith et al. 2009).

12   We will revisit this same issue in Chapter 11 – Market Equilibrium and Structure.
13   The calculation of consumer surplus used was based on a linear demand curve. If the demand curve is nonlinear, then readers familiar with calculus will be able to verify that consumer surplus is

$$
CS = \left[\int_{P}^{P*} Q(P)\, dP \right] - P* \cdot Q(P*)
$$

where Q(P) denotes output quantity is a function of own-price.
14   Own-price elasticity is technically a negative number as the demand curve has a negative slope. However, it is often given as the absolute value. If the demand curve is perfectly inelastic, own-price elasticity is equal to 0. If the demand curve is perfectly elastic, own-price elasticity is equal to infinity.
15   To underscore the importance of the economic, social, and demographic characteristics of your customers, or in this particular case family forest landowners, often the lower bound on the feasibility of any forest management recommendation you may propose is that the harvested timber must pay for the proposed management action.

11 Market Equilibrium and Structure

Preamble

In Chapter 10 – Supply and Demand, I was somewhat liberal with my use of the term market and market equilibrium with respect to describing Figure 10.2; namely, supply denoted a representative entrepreneur and demand denoted a representative consumer. This was done so that I could focus on the individual concepts of supply and demand as economic models that define the opportunity cost of the entrepreneur (supply) and the opportunity cost of a consumer (demand). In addition, I showed that the economic information in Figure 10.2 parallels what is in the Architectural Plan for Profit (Figure 11.1).

In this chapter I will look more broadly at supply and demand than in the last chapter; namely, a market for a particular good or service (e.g., energy, maple syrup, or inside-out beams) comprises all the producers and consumers of that product. Thus, a market supply curve is an aggregate of all the individual entrepreneurs' supply curves, and the market demand curve is an aggregate of all the individual consumers' demand curves. In this chapter I will focus on the role of the market, the various different market structures that an entrepreneur might face, and the various pricing strategies that an entrepreneur might use. Markets are interconnected, as outputs from one market are used as inputs into another to produce a final consumer good or service. This is illustrated with the concept of derived demand and its counterpart derived supply. The concept of derived demand is important especially for entrepreneurs whose focus is natural resource management and the goods and services that ecosystems produce.

Practical Applications

The practical applications used in this chapter will include the Inside-Out (ISO) Beams (Patterson et al. 2002; Patterson and Xie 1998), Mobile Micromill® (Becker et al. 2004), Maple Syrup Operation (Huyler 2000; CFBMC 2000), Great Lakes Charter Boat Fishing (Lichtkoppler and Kuehn 2003), Select Red Oak (Hahn and Hansen 1991), Radiata Pine Plantation, and Changing Timberland Ownership (Hagan et al. 2005).

DOI: 10.4324/9781315678719-11

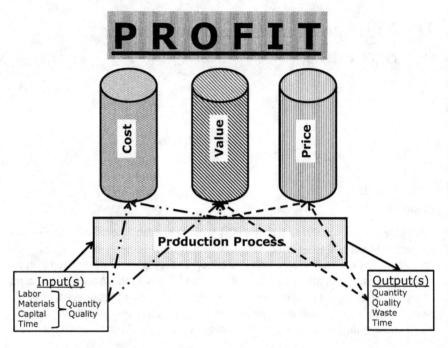

Figure 11.1 The Architectural Plan for Profit

The Market

A market supply curve is the horizontal sum of all entrepreneurs' supply curves (e.g., Chapter 10 – Supply and Demand; Figures 10.5b and 10.7b). Figure 11.2a illustrates deriving a market supply curve.

A market demand curve is the horizontal sum of all consumers' demand curves. Figure 11.2b illustrates deriving a market demand curve.

The market is the focus of economic activity and provides a place where economic information concerning the relative scarcity of a good or service is available and the choices individuals make are observed. An individual can choose to provide or produce a particular good or service and another individual can choose to purchase that particular good or service. A market can be a physical place, such as a grocery store or local farmers market, or it can be a place like eBay® where individuals offer to sell Les Paul Gibson guitars, bamboo flyrods, or one red paperclip (http://oneredpaperclip.blogspot.com/2005/07/about-one-red-paperclip.html, accessed 19 February 2020) and others can choose to purchase the item or make a counter offer. Finally, markets are where goods and services move between individuals (supply and demand) and also across geographic regions and time; for example, the sale of maple syrup produced in the Northeast to customers in the Pacific Northwest. Markets also reduce participants' transactions costs.[1]

The role markets play can be divided into four broad components.

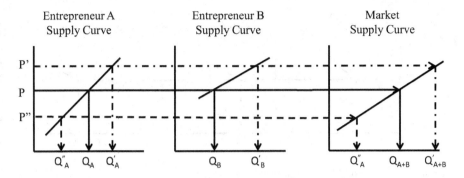

Figure 11.2a Market Supply Curve

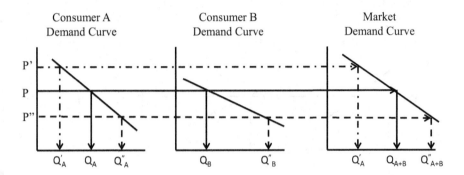

Figure 11.2b Market Demand Curve

Market Equilibrium

Market equilibrium is given by the intersection of the market supply curve (Figure 11.2a) and demand curve (Figure 11.2b).[2] In Chapter 10 – Supply and Demand I showed that the equilibrium also described the price and quantity combination that maximizes the sum of producer surplus (Figure 10.11) and consumer surplus (Figure 10.16b). Extrapolating this to the market, Figure 11.3a shows that the market producer surplus is the sum of each entrepreneur's maximized producer surplus.[3]

Again, extrapolating this to the market, Figure 11.3b shows that the market consumer surplus is the sum of each consumer's maximized consumer surplus.

Thus, if the market is described by workable competition, then market equilibrium can be found by maximizing the sum of producer and consumer surplus. This is depicted in Figure 11.3c.

Figure 11.3c describes interactions among buyers (market demand) and sellers (market supply) within a market. As I have asserted in earlier chapters and modeled by Figures 11.3a, 11.3b, and 11.3c, sellers' maximizing their profits and

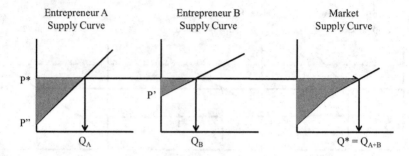

Figure 11.3a Market Producer Surplus‡

‡The shaded area below the P* price line and above the supply curve defines producer surplus (for example, see Figure 10.10). The area below the supply curve bounded by Q defines total variable cost (for example, see Figure 10.9).

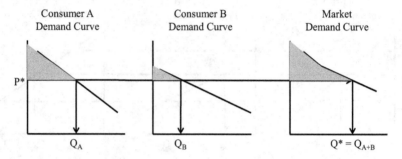

Figure 11.3b Market Consumer Surplus‡

‡The shaded area below the demand curve and above the P* price line defines consumer surplus (for example, see Figure 10.16b). The area below the P* price line bounded by Q defines consumers explicit costs (for example, see Figure 10.16b).

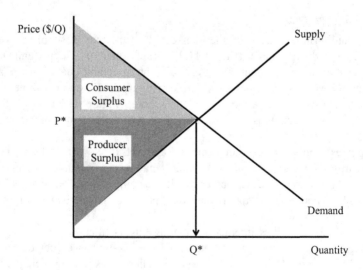

Figure 11.3c Market Equilibrium

buyers' maximizing their net benefits will result in the cooperative solution of market equilibrium price, P*, and quantity, Q*. As shown in Figure 11.3a, not every entrepreneur seeking to maximize profit produces or provides the same amount of output. Some entrepreneurs have higher production costs and could drop out if the market price fell (Table 5.4 and Figures 10.5b and 10.7b). Similarly, as shown by Figure 11.3b, not all net benefit maximizing consumers purchase the same amount of output. If the market price increases some will no longer purchase the output.

What and How Much to Produce or Provide?

Should maple syrup producers produce maple syrup? Should manufacturers of inside-out beams produce inside-out beams? Should charter boat fishing captains continue to provide fishing services? Should landowners continue to grow select red oak or radiata pine? How does Figure 11.3c help us answer these similar questions? Simply, Figure 11.3c models the situation that given the equilibrium market price, P*, entrepreneurs are willing and able to supply positive amounts of the output depending on their production system and cost structure. This is shown in Figure 11.3a.

How much output should each of these entrepreneurs produce or provide? Referring again to Figure 11.3a, entrepreneurs are willing and able to supply different amounts of the output depending on their production system and cost structure. This is summarized by the profit searching rule described in Chapter 5 – Profit and given in equation (11.1):

$$MR = P = Supply = MC \qquad (11.1)$$

As discussed in Chapter 10 – Supply and Demand, the decision of how much to produce is interesting given energy markets where supply must equal demand and the pricing information is given at five-minute intervals (http://mis.nyiso.com/public/ accessed 19 February 2020).

How to Produce?

Reviewing Chapters 2 – Production Systems and Chapter 3 – Costs, the answer to "How to Produce?" is straightforward. Entrepreneurs should produce in a technical efficiency (Chapter 2 – Production Systems) and production cost efficiency (Chapter 3 – Costs) manner. The relationship between technical efficiency, production cost efficiency, and the supply curve is given by Figure 11.4.

Each entrepreneur within a market is a profit maximizer (i.e., Architectural Plan for Profit Figure 11.1 and illustrated by Maximize $\Pi = TR - TC$). Profits are maximized by entrepreneurs simultaneously making total revenue (TR) as large as possible while simultaneously making total costs (TC) as small as possible for any given input(s)–output(s) combination. The producer surplus illustrated in Figure 11.4 shows this as the supply curve that is both technically efficient and production cost efficient. Thus, the producer surplus in Figures 11.3a and 11.3c is also technically efficient and production cost efficient.

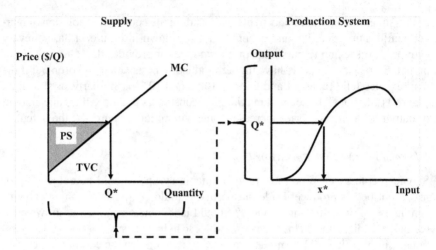

Figure 11.4 The Relationship Between Supply, Producer Surplus, and Production Cost Efficiency[‡]

[‡]PS denotes producer surplus and MC and TVC denote marginal cost and total variable cost, respectively (Chapter 10 – Supply and Demand).

For Whom to Produce or Provide?

Entrepreneurs produce or provide commodities for consumers. This statement seems obvious and simple. However, how do we model consumers' preferences for commodities? This is done using demand (equation (10.7) and Table 10.5 in Chapter 10 – Supply and Demand). Entrepreneurs produce or provide commodities for whoever is willing and able to pay for them. Consumers must be willing; that is, placing value on your output. They also must be able: If a consumer is not able, no transactions will take place. As shown by Figure 11.3b, not every consumer purchases the same amount of output, and some consumers will no longer purchase your output if the market price rises above a given level.

Market Structures

As defined previously, a market is the sum of all entrepreneurs and all consumers (Figures 11.3a, 11.3b, and 11.3c). However, market structures depend on a number of factors: (1) number and size of buyers, sellers, and potential entrants, (2) the degree of product differentiation, (3) amount and cost of information about product price and quality, and (4) conditions for entry and exit (Brickley et al. 2007). I will examine briefly six different market structures. The following discussion is not meant to be all-encompassing. I would encourage readers to research these topics further if they are interested. I will start with the market structure perfect competition and end with monopsony and oligopsony.

Perfect Competition

The conditions required for perfect competition are: (1) many buyers and many sellers, (2) no barriers to entry to or exit from the market, (3) perfect information with respect to price and products are available to all, (4) transaction costs are zero, and (5) homogenous products. The resulting market can be described by Figure 11.3c, and market price only reflects how scarce a good or service is relative to other goods and services. While the market demand curve has a negative slope (as does each consumer's demand curve), individual entrepreneurs face a demand curve that is perfectly elastic. That is the price line defined by the market equilibrium price – P* in Figures 11.3a, 11.3b, 11.3c –that defines an entrepreneur's demand curve. Thus, an entrepreneur's average revenue is identically equal to its marginal revenue, which is equal to market price (Chapter 4 – Revenue). Entrepreneurs are described as taking the price given by the market (i.e., price takers). In terms of the profit searching rule as given by equation (11.1), entrepreneurs' decisions are limited only to how much to produce or provide given the current market price.

As you can observe, the conditions required for perfect competition are extremely strict and one would probably be hard-pressed to point to a market that satisfies all these conditions. Thus, perfect competition is often viewed as one endpoint (a theoretical endpoint) on a continuum of potential different market structures.

Workable Competition

Workable competition is defined as the case where no one buyer or group of buyers and no one seller or group of sellers can influence price (Chapter 1 – Introduction).[4] This defines a competitive market and is the default market structure I have used for the book. The implication of this market structure is that there are many substitutes that are relatively easy to obtain. Thus, entrepreneurs and consumers have very little if any market power in terms of price setting. Entrepreneurs are described as taking the price given by the market (i.e., price takers). Therefore, the resulting market can be also described by Figure 11.3c and market price reflects how scarce a good or service is relative to other goods and services. While the market demand curve has a negative slope (as does each consumer's demand curve), individual entrepreneurs face a demand curve that is nearly elastic. That is the price line defined by the market equilibrium price – P* in Figures 11.3a, 11.3b, 11.3c – that for all practical purposes defines an entrepreneur's demand curve. While an entrepreneur may have a very limited ability to set price, with respect to the market as a whole their average revenue approximates marginal revenue, and both may be defined by market price (Chapter 4 – Revenue). In terms of the profit searching rule given by equation (11.1), an entrepreneur's decisions are basically limited to how much to produce or provide given the current market price.

Monopolistic Competition

Monopolistic competition is characterized by a structure in which there are many sellers of similar products that can be differentiated; for example, breakfast cereal, toothpaste, and laundry and dish detergent. What about maple syrup or dimension lumber sawn from radiata pine or other pine species? This differentiation can be the result of brand loyalty, advertising, and effective marketing. The more effective an entrepreneur differentiates their products from their competitors the more market power they have, allowing them to set their price. Because there is competition their price-setting behavior does not affect the market as a whole. No barriers keep entrepreneurs from entering or exiting the market.

The market an entrepreneur faces given monopolistic competition is given in Figures 11.5a and 11.5b. While Figures 11.5a and 11.5b look complicated I will examine each, paying close attention to the economic information these models provide. The entrepreneur's average and marginal cost curves in Figure 11.5a are the same as those discussed in Chapter 3 – Costs; namely, equations (3.5) and (3.7), respectively. Thus, the economic information contained in the cost components has already been examined.[5] The unique feature of Figure 11.5a is there is a consumer's demand curve that is different than the entrepreneur's marginal revenue curve. Instead of the entrepreneur facing a horizontal demand curve (as with perfect and workable competition), the demand curve has a negative slope. According to Chapter 10 – Supply and Demand, a consumer's demand curve has a negative slope or there is an inverse relationship between price and quantity due to their opportunity costs. From an entrepreneur's point of view, they want to turn a consumer's demand into revenue. Therefore, what is the relationship between a consumer's demand curve and an entrepreneur's revenue?

The consumer's demand curve defines an entrepreneur's average revenue curve.[6] Because a consumer's demand curve has a negative slope, the entrepreneur must lower price to get the consumer to buy additional units of output. Thus, there is a price effect (due to lowering the price) and an output effect (due to increasing

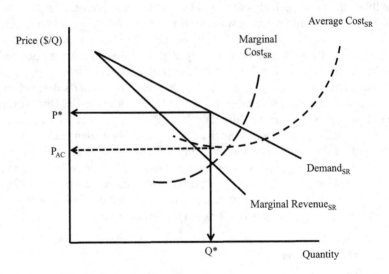

Figure 11.5a Market Equilibrium Given Monopolistic Competition in the Short Run as Viewed by an Entrepreneur‡

‡P* and Q* denote market equilibrium price and quantity; SR denotes short run; P_{AC} denotes the average total cost own-price.

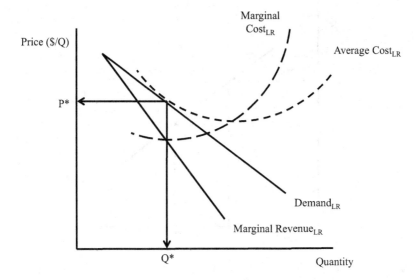

Figure 11.5b Market Equilibrium Given Monopolistic Competition in the Long Run‡

‡P* and Q* denote market equilibrium price and quantity; LR denotes long run

output). An entrepreneur's total revenue will decrease due to the price effect. But an entrepreneur's total revenue will increase due to the output effect. This is illustrated in Figure 11.5c.

$$\text{Price effect} = \Delta P \times Q_{old} = (P_{new} - P_{old}) \times Q_{old}$$
$$\text{Output effect} = \Delta Q \times P_{new} = (Q_{new} - Q_{old}) \times P_{new}$$

If the loss due to the price effect is less than the gain due to the output effect, the entrepreneur's total revenue will increase by lowering price.[7] Because of the ability to differentiate among similar outputs, the entrepreneur now has two decisions; namely, how much to produce and at what price. Entrepreneurs are still profit maximizers and the profit searching rule of MR = P = MC still holds. Thus, the most profitable level of output to produce or provide given Figure 11.5a would be Q*. The price the entrepreneur would charge would be what the customer is willing and able to pay; namely, P* given Figure 11.5a.

According to Figure 11.5a, P_{AC} defines the average "total" cost of producing the most profitable level of output, Q*. In addition, Figure 11.5a shows that P* is greater than P_{AC} or average total cost (ATC), which is illustrated by equation (11.2a):

$$P^* > P_{AC} = ATC = \frac{TC}{Q^*}$$

$$P^* > \frac{TC}{Q^*}$$

(11.2a)

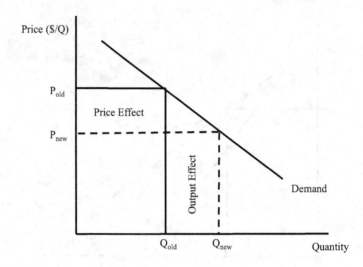

Figure 11.5c Price and Output Effects From a Negatively Sloped Market Demand Curve

Multiplying both sides of equation (11.2a) by Q* shows that profits are positive

$$P^* \cdot Q^* > \frac{TC}{Q^*} \cdot Q^*$$ (11.2b)

$$TR > TC$$

$$TR - TC = \Pi > 0$$

where TR denotes total revenue, TC denotes total cost, and Π denotes profit. Thus, in the short run, the entrepreneur would be making a positive economic profit.[8] Again, this is because entrepreneurs can differentiate their products.

One of the conditions of monopolistic competition is there are no barriers to entry or exit. As other entrepreneurs see that there are economic profits to be made, this will entice more entrepreneurs to enter this market, increasing competition and reducing the share of the market held by any one entrepreneur in the long run. Figure 11.5b illustrates the long-run market model. Due to the reduced market share, the demand curve faced by any entrepreneur will shift left as will the marginal revenue curve. The interpretation of the demand (average revenue) and marginal revenue curves do not change. The cost curves now represent the concept that there are no fixed inputs and no fixed costs. For example, in the long run you can build a new plant to produce additional ISO beams, purchase a larger sugarbush, or buy more hectares for your radiata pine plantation. In the long run economic profits are driven to zero as P* will equal P_{AC}. Entrepreneurs would still be making positive accounting profits, however.

How would you describe the market for maple syrup? If you produced New York maple syrup, would you be able to differentiate it from that produced in Vermont, New Hampshire, or Canada? How would you describe the market for dimension lumber sawn from a pine tree? If you produce dimension lumber from your radiata pine plantation, would you be able to differentiate your dimension lumber from that produced in the northeastern, midwestern, northwestern, or southern areas of the United States, Canada, or South America?

Oligopoly

An oligopoly is a market structure characterized by a few sellers who control most if not all of the market. Potential new entrepreneurs find there are significant barriers to entry (e.g., economies of scale, technology, patents). An oligopolist has two decisions to make: How much to produce and at what price. However, the oligopolist not only faces each consumer's negatively sloped demand curve, but they must also recognize that fellow oligopolists will react to any pricing and production decisions just as they would react to any pricing and production decisions made by their fellow oligopolists. It is the move–countermove strategic nature of the pricing and production decisions that makes modeling these markets interesting. The modeling approaches described by game theory have been used to analyze the interactions among oligopolists. While the technical nature of these models is beyond the scope of this book, I would point interested readers to Kreps (1990), Gibbons (1992), and Bierman and Fernandez (1993).

Monopoly

A monopoly is a market structure characterized by one seller and many buyers. There are significant barriers to entry for any potential new entrepreneurs (e.g., economies of scale, technology, patents, and regulation). A monopolist has two decisions to make; how much to produce and at what price. The market structure for a monopoly can be illustrated by Figure 11.6a.

As can be seen, Figure 11.6a is similar to Figure 11.5a. The interpretations of demand, marginal revenue, marginal cost, and average cost curves are the same as in Figure 11.5a. In a monopoly market, the entrepreneur does not have to worry about distinguishing themselves from other similar products or think strategically in terms of prices and production amounts as there are no similar products or sellers to contend with, respectively. That said, monopolists can still be characterized as a profit maximizer and will still employ the profit searching rule, MR = MC. Examining Figure 11.6a shows that the production decision follows the profit searching rule; namely, produce at the output level, Q^*, such that MR = MC. The pricing decision depends on the consumer's willingness and ability to pay. Even though there is a single seller in a monopoly market, the monopolistic entrepreneur may not charge as much as they want because the demand curve still has a negative slope or there is a negative relationship between own-price and quantity reflecting the consumer's opportunity costs (see Chapter 10 – Supply and Demand).[9] Given Figure 11.6a, the monopolists profit is given by

$$\Pi_{Monopoly} = TR - TC = P^*Q^* - P_{AC}Q^*$$

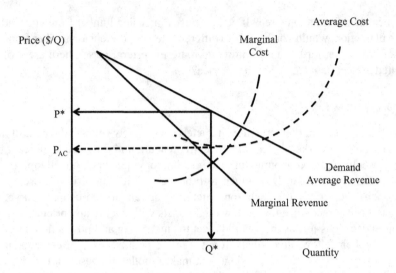

Figure 11.6a Market Equilibrium Given a Monopoly‡

‡P* and Q* denote market equilibrium price and quantity; P_{AC} denotes the average total cost own-price.

The key to analyzing a monopoly market is that a monopolist faces the same price effect and output effect discussed in Monopolistic Competition and shown in Figure 11.5c. The own-price elasticity or inelasticity of the demand curve will define if the price effect is less or greater than the output effect. The price plus output effects will define the monopolist's marginal revenue, which will then be set equal to marginal cost determining the monopoly market equilibrium price and quantity, total revenue, total cost, and profit.

Comparing the production and pricing decisions with those described in Monopolistic Competition, the reader will note that they are virtually the same. A further comparison of Figures 11.5a and 11.5b with Figure 11.6a is that there is no distinction between the long and short run for a monopolist. This is because there are barriers to entry that keep out any potential competitors. The classic example of a monopoly is the spatial monopolies for utilities (e.g., water and sewer) that are sanctioned by many municipal governments within urban areas. Electricity is a unique case in the United States with many states deregulating certain operations of utilities that sell to consumers. Thus, while consumers may choose from many different producers of electricity, the delivery structure (i.e., power lines and towers, etc.) are still monopolies sanctioned by governments.

The relationship between the market solutions given a monopoly versus a workable competition market are illustrated in Figure 11.6b. Figure 11.6b illustrates the market power that a monopolist has in terms of pricing and production decisions as compared to workable competition. In Figure 11.6b this is illustrated by the difference between P* and P_{WC}, with P* greater than P_{WC}. Again, the monopolist does not have unlimited market power with respect to pricing as the consumer's

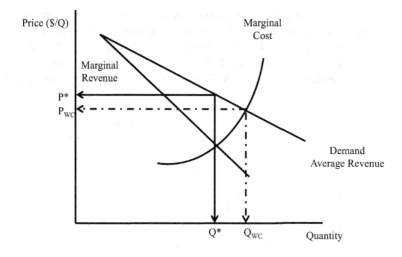

Figure 11.6b Market Equilibrium: Monopoly Versus Workable Competition‡

‡P* and Q* denote monopoly market equilibrium price and quantity; P_{wc} and Q_{wc} denote the workable competition market equilibrium price and quantity

demand curve has a negative slope.[10] The pricing decision depends on the monopolist's knowledge and modeling the consumer's demand and its own-price elasticity relative to the monopolist's marginal revenue. As illustrated by Figure 11.6b, the monopolist will produce or provide less output than given workable competition; namely, Q* is less than Q_{wc}. Production decisions are based on the marginal costs relative to the marginal revenues given that marginal revenue depends on pricing. Determining the degree of market power requires the entrepreneur to have a working knowledge of consumer's demand and demand elasticity (Chapter 10 – Supply and Demand) and their production process, costs, and revenues (Chapter 2 – Production System, Chapter 3 – Costs, and Chapter 4 – Revenue). Figure 11.6b shows a level of detail probably not available to entrepreneurs; however, it reflects the required economic information an entrepreneur must collect and the relationships that should be analyzed continuously. This is the value of Figure 11.6b.

Monopsony and Oligopsony

A monopsony is a market structure characterized by one buyer and many sellers. The classic example of a monopsony is a "One Mill Town." This mill is the only purchaser of labor and natural resource inputs that are available in a given region. An oligopsony is a market structure characterized by few buyers and many sellers. The presence of spatial constraints – for example, the high costs associated with transporting logs from where they are harvested to a pulp or paper mill – may allow these mills to exhibit monopsony or oligopsony power over the price they pay for these inputs (Murray 1995a, 1995b).

Like monopolistic competition, monopoly, and oligopoly market structures, a monopsony market structure gives the entrepreneur market power. In the case of a monopoly, the market power is reflected in output production and pricing decisions as illustrated in Figures 11.6a and 11.6b. In the case of a monopsony, the market power is reflected in the price or wage the monopsonist will pay for inputs – such as

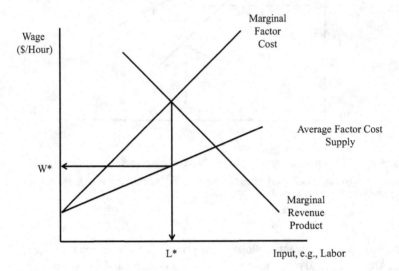

Figure 11.7a Market Equilibrium Given a Monopsony

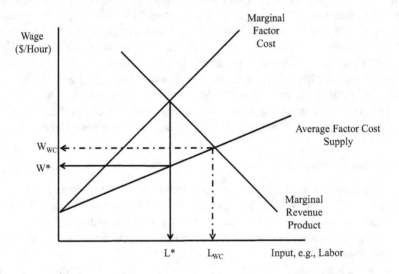

Figure 11.7b Market Equilibrium: Monopsony Versus Workable Competition‡

‡ W_{wc} and L_{wc} denote the market equilibrium wage and labor (e.g., hours) given workable competition

labor – and the amount they will purchase. Figure 11.7a models the monopsonist's decisions concerning input price and amount purchased.

At first glance Figure 11.7a may appear intimidating; however, we can actually build on the knowledge gained from Figures 11.5a, 11.5b, 11.6a, and 11.6b. Because monopolists are profit maximizers, it would be logical that the profit searching rule would still be a tenable guide to examining their decision-making behavior. However, the profit searching rule, as laid out in equation (5.5) and Figures 5.5a and 5.5b of Chapter 5 – Profit, is described with respect to output. There is an analogous profit searching rule that was developed in the Appendices 5A and 5B in Chapter 5 – Profit with respect to inputs and summarized in equation (11.3).

$$\frac{\Delta\Pi}{\Delta x_j} = MRP_j - MFC_j; \text{ for all inputs} \tag{11.3}$$

where MRP denotes Marginal Revenue Product or the additional revenue generated from selling the additional output produced using more of the jth input (e.g., labor); MFC denotes Marginal Factor Cost or the price or wage the entrepreneur must pay for the input.[11] Profits increase (decrease) if MRP is greater than (less than) MFC. This is modeled in Figure 11.7a by the monopsonist's choice of L*. To the left of L*, MFC is less than MRP so purchasing more L will increase profits. To the right of L*, MFC is greater than MRP so purchasing less L will increase profits.

Figure 11.7a shows that the marginal factor cost curve is above the average factor cost curve. That is, the amount the monopsonist is willing to pay for the input depends on the number of inputs that they purchase. The more they purchase the more they must pay for all of the inputs purchased, not just the additional unit. This is analogous to the marginal revenue being below the average revenue curve in Figure 11.6a.[12] In addition, the average factor cost describing the monopsonist's supply curve is analogous to average revenue describing the monopolist's demand curve.[13] Thus, the monopolist would only pay a wage of W* per hour for labor, as shown in Figure 11.7a, for the labor L* hours of labor.

An analogy can be drawn between an oligopsony and monopolistic competition in terms of price to pay for inputs and the number of inputs to purchase and the price to charge for outputs and the amount of outputs to produce, respectively. The oligopsonists' average factor cost curve defines their supply curve, but they must also recognize that their fellow oligopsonists will react to any pricing and input purchase decisions as they would react to pricing and production decisions made by their fellow oligopsonists. If oligopsonists compete against each other, the result will be to bid up the price paid for the input. However, if oligopsonists join together in input pricing decisions, each oligopsonist will benefit from a lower input price.

Figure 11.7b illustrates the market power that a monopsonist has in terms of input pricing and input purchasing decisions as compared to workable competition. The more inelastic the consumer's demand curve the greater the control the monopolist has over setting price. In Figure 11.7b this is illustrated by the difference between W* and W_{wc}, with W* less than W_{wc} and L* less than L_{wc}. The degree of market power – as illustrated by the difference between W* and W_{wc}

– depends on the elasticity of the supply curve. In the case of a single input buyer, the supply curve would be relatively inelastic and the difference between the marginal factor cost and the average factor cost curves would be large, as would the buyer's market power. If the supply curve is relatively elastic, there would be more buyers in the market and the power would be reduced for any one buyer to set input price.

A cartel can be formed if a few sellers come together to form a cartel. One of the most famous cartels is the Organization of Petroleum Exporting Countries (OPEC). Between 1973 and 1985 OPEC maintained a monopoly hold on the world oil market. However, any member of the cartel also knows that if they can sell just a little more, the quantity effect is greater than the price effect and their individual profits will increase. In the mid-1980s, member countries began arguing about production levels; in fact, some countries produced more than their defined quotas. The stronger control a cartel has over its members the more market power it can maintain. Why is this interesting? The Federation of Quebec Maple Syrup Producers (*Producteurs et productrices acéricoles du Québec*, PPAC) is a government-sanctioned private organization that sets quotas on how much a farm in Quebec can produce (http://ppaq.ca/en/category/production-en/ accessed 24 February 2020) and all Quebec farms must sell their syrup exclusively to PPAC (with the exception of small containers of less than 1.3 US gallons). In turn, PPAC stabilizes the bulk prices for syrup by maintaining an International Strategic Reserve of maple syrup. The PPAC amount paid per pound for the various grades of maple syrup is Golden $2.95, Amber $2.94, Dark $2.85, and Very Dark $2.55. Processing Grade is $1.80. The premium for certified organic maple syrup is $0.18/pound (https://ppaq.ca/en/communiques/bulk-maple-syrup-marketing-in-quebec/ accessed 6 September 2023). Given the maple syrup reserve, the PPAC is also a large exporter of maple syrup. The largest sales are to the United States, with Germany and United Kingdom as distant second and third (https://agriculture.canada.ca/en/sector/horticulture/reports/statistical-overview-canadian-maple-industry-2022#a2.1.4 accessed 6 September 2023). This market activity does impact global prices, to some degree US prices, and to varying degrees local markets (https://agriculture.vermont.gov/sites/agriculture/files/documents/AgDevReports/Maple%20Syrup%20Market%20Research%20Report.pdf accessed 24 February 2020). As a point of comparison, a barrel of maple syrup is approximately $1,383 (2019 Canadian dollars) and a barrel of US crude oil is approximately $51 (2020 US dollars).[14] Finally, between 2011 and 2012 approximately 3,000 tons of maple syrup were stolen from a PPAC warehouse. The theft was valued at approximately $18.7 million Canadian dollars.

Market Power

The essential part of the prior discussion on market structure is identifying if you as an entrepreneur have market power and what the implications are with respect to profit maximization. Successful entrepreneurs know the market structure for the outputs they produce or provide. As an entrepreneur your objective is to turn a consumer's willingness and ability to buy the commodities you produce into your revenue. Market structure defines the market power you have to capture this revenue given your ability to price your commodities relative to your competitors and the amount you produce relative to your competitors. If the market structure is described by few sellers, they are able to charge more and produce less than would result in a market with workable competition. This is the result of markets characterized by monopoly, oligopoly, or monopolistic competition. The elasticity of the demand curve, the number of sellers, and the interaction among the sellers defines the market power.

Successful entrepreneurs know the market structure for the inputs they purchase. As an entrepreneur your objective is to pay as little for inputs as possible. Market structure defines the market power you have to affect the price you pay for inputs. In a market characterized by few input buyers, these buyers have the market power to pay less and purchase fewer inputs than would result in a market described by workable competition. This is the result of markets characterized by monopsony and oligopsony. The elasticity of the supply curve, the number of buyers, and the interaction among the buyers defines the market power.

Additional Thoughts on Markets, Equilibrium, and Structure

The apparently simple model illustrated in Figure 11.3c is a culmination of all the economic information presented in the previous chapters. The Architectural Plan for Profit (Figure 11.1) presented at the beginning of these chapters summarizes the economic information that an entrepreneur should obtain to help them in their profit searching behavior. Markets are efficient mechanisms for entrepreneurs to respond to consumers' demand and for allocating commodities among consumers. The implication is that a market equilibrium is when entrepreneurs' profits and consumers' net benefits are as large as possible. What markets are not especially good at are equitable allocations of resources.[15] Furthermore, there are potential spillover or external effects that may affect individuals not involved in market transactions between entrepreneurs and consumers. The classic example of a negative externality is pollution created by entrepreneurs in the process of producing or providing outputs to consumers or consumers using an output. The pollution negatively impacts individuals (e.g., property damage, health, well-being, etc.) and this negative impact is not reflected in the market price (i.e., P* of Figure 11.3c) nor are these individuals compensated for the negative impacts. If pollution is tied to output production, entrepreneurs may be producing too much output. A classic example of a positive externality is my getting a flu shot every fall. My students benefit from the reduced probability of me passing on the flu. Again, market price will not reflect this positive externality nor do the students compensate me for the benefit they receive from my actions. In this case too few people will probably get flu shots. A more in-depth discussion of positive and negative externalities, their impacts on market equilibriums and potential solutions are beyond the scope of this book. If readers are interested there is a vast literature within the areas of resource and environmental economics on this topic.

Product Price Searching Strategies

Profit is equal to total revenue (P × Q) minus total cost. To make profits as large as possible you must make total revenue as large as possible and total costs as small as possible for any given input(s)–output(s) combination. Examining this relationship reveals that total revenue is half of profit and product price, P, is half of total revenue. Relatively small changes in product price may imply relatively large changes in total revenue, as price changes are magnified by the amount sold (Longenecker et al. 2006). Thus, a key to making total revenue as large as possible is to develop a sound pricing strategy. As an entrepreneur your pricing strategy depends on your knowledge of the market structure for your products. Your pricing strategy is to (1) set price to cover explicit and implicit measures of total costs; (2) reflect your consumers' willingness and ability to pay; and (3) recognize any competition.[16] Simply put, the goal of your pricing strategy is to charge as much as you can regardless of what it costs you to produce or provide the outputs.

Average Cost, Cost-Plus, or Full-Cost Pricing Strategies

According to Silberberg and Suen (2001: 181–182): "the cost of producing the last unit of output is the same as the cost of producing the first or any other unit of output and is, in fact, the average cost of the output." This defines the logic of average cost, cost-plus, or full-cost pricing strategies; namely, set output price to cover total accounting production costs plus an additional amount for markup or profit. Equations (11.4a) and (11.4b) illustrate this

$$P = \frac{TVC}{Q} + \frac{TFC}{Q} + m \cdot \left(\frac{TVC}{Q} + \frac{TFC}{Q} \right)$$

$$= ATC + m \cdot ATC = ATC \cdot (1 + m) \tag{11.4a}$$

$$P = \frac{TVC}{Q} + \frac{TFC}{Q} + \frac{\Pi_Q}{Q} \tag{11.4b}$$

where TVC denotes Total Variable Cost, TFC denotes Total Fixed Cost, ATC denotes Average Variable Cost, AFC denotes Average Fixed Costs, m in equation (11.4a) defines the entrepreneur's per unit markup above average total costs, and Π_Q in equation (11.4b) denotes the entrepreneur's target profit for producing a given output level, Q.[17] The target profit is often defined as a percentage of the assets; for example, buildings, equipment, and land.

Table 11.1 displays the annual and average production cost information for six maple syrup operations. Based on Table 11.1 for example, if the maple syrup entrepreneur of a 1,530-, 2,550-, or 5,100-gallon per year operation charged $19.79, $18.28, and $16.70 per gallon respectively, they would cover their fixed and variable annual production costs. Table 11.2 illustrates using these strategies for estimating an output price given the six different-sized maple syrup operations and given varying percentage of asset markup values.

Table 11.1 Total Annual and Average Production Costs of Six Different Maple Syrup Operations[‡]

Cost Item	127.5 (gal/yr)	255 (gal/yr)	765 (gal/yr)	1,530 (gal/yr)	2,550 (gal/yr)	5,100 (gal/yr)
Annual Production Costs						
Variable Costs						
Labor	$1,601.79	$2,347.50	$4,641.17	$8,259.34	$13,083.57	$25,144.14
Supplies	$1,208.08	$2,271.45	$5,068.54	$9,204.94	$14,812.56	$28,748.85
Other	$471.12	$689.85	$1,261.92	$2,120.02	$3,667.98	$6,528.32
Fixed Costs	$2,245.20	$3,449.24	$7,184.52	$10,688.95	$15,048.79	$24,726.19
Total Cost	$5,526.19	$8,758.05	$18,156.14	$30,273.25	$46,612.90	$85,147.50
Average Production Costs						
Average Variable Costs	$25.73	$20.82	$14.34	$12.80	$12.38	$11.85
Average Fixed Costs	$17.61	$13.53	$9.39	$6.99	$5.90	$4.85
Average Total Costs	$43.34	$34.35	$23.73	$19.79	$18.28	$16.70

[‡] Source of cost data CFBMC (2000). Costs are in 1999 US dollars using an exchange rate of 1.49 Canadian dollars per US dollar. (gal/yr) denotes gallons of maple syrup per year. These costs do not include the cost of establishing a larger sugarbush or the costs of purchasing the additional equipment.

Table 11.2 Average Cost, Cost-Plus-Markup, Full-Cost Pricing for Six Different Maple Syrup Operations[‡]

Cost Item	127.5 (gal/yr)	255 (gal/yr)	765 (gal/yr)	1,530 (gal/yr)	2,550 (gal/yr)	5,100 (gal/yr)
Total Variable Cost ($/gal)	$43.34	$34.35	$23.73	$19.79	$18.28	$16.70
Assets[†] ($/gal)	$248.84	$205.49	$157.12	$142.41	$114.97	$102.82
2%	$4.98	$4.11	$3.14	$2.85	$2.30	$2.06
4%	$9.95	$8.22	$6.28	$5.70	$4.60	$4.11
6%	$14.93	$12.33	$9.43	$8.54	$6.90	$6.17
8%	$19.91	$16.44	$12.57	$11.39	$9.20	$8.23
10%	$24.88	$20.55	$15.71	$14.24	$11.50	$10.28
Pricing ($/gal)						
2%	$48.32	$38.46	$26.88	$22.63	$20.58	$18.75
4%	$53.30	$42.56	$30.02	$25.48	$22.88	$20.81
6%	$58.27	$46.67	$33.16	$28.33	$25.18	$22.86
8%	$63.25	$50.78	$36.30	$31.18	$27.48	$24.92
10%	$68.23	$54.89	$39.45	$34.03	$29.78	$26.98

[‡] Source of cost data CFBMC (2000). Costs are in 1999 US dollars using an exchange rate of 1.49 Canadian dollars per US dollar. (gal/yr) denotes gallons of maple syrup per year. ($/gal) denotes 1999 US dollars per gallon.
[†] Assets include structures, equipment, and land. ($/gal) denotes 1999 US dollars per gallon using an exchange rate of 1.49 Canadian dollars per US dollar.

Table 11.2 shows that the owners of an operation producing 127.5 gallons of maple syrup per year would price between $48.32 and $68.23 per gallon of maple syrup. The owners of an operation producing 1,530 gallons of maple syrup per year would price between $22.63 and $34.03 per gallon of maple syrup. As a point of comparison, in a 1998–1999 New Hampshire Forest Market Report published by the University of New Hampshire Cooperative Extension, the retail price was $33.10 per gallon of maple syrup (https://extension.unh.edu/resource/new-hamp shire-forest-market-report-archive accessed 8 March 2021).

The advantage of these strategies is that they are relatively simple, and the entrepreneur should have all the necessary data to develop equivalent tables if they follow the Architectural Plan for Profit. There are, however, two concerns with using these methods. First, if actual sales are less than predicted sales or production, then average cost per unit sold will be higher than estimated and, thus, profit per unit will be smaller. Second, according to equations (11.4a) and (11.4b), fixed costs are simply allocated on a per unit basis to the product. For example, in Table 11.1 the fixed costs are allocated to the production of maple syrup. While the primary output of the maple syrup application was sap collection and production of maple syrup, these businesses often produce other maple sugar–related products (e.g., maple sugar, maple candies, etc.). In addition, they may also be tourist destinations. Thus, not all the variable and fixed costs are associated with just maple syrup production. As allocating these truly joint production costs among all the outputs is purely arbitrary (Carlson 1974; Blocher et al. 2002), caution should be taken when using average cost, cost-plus, or full-cost pricing strategies in the case of joint production.[18]

Marginal (Incremental) Cost Pricing

The concept of marginal cost price can be traced to the profit searching rule given in equation (11.1). The basic idea is that the price should cover the change in production cost of producing a change in output. The application of marginal cost pricing is illustrated by Figure 11.8.

As can be seen by Figure 11.8 the marginal cost – and consequently the price – of output Q_1 is different from the marginal cost (and price) of outputs Q_2 and Q_3. Based on this pricing strategy, each individual unit of output would be priced at its incremental production costs.[19] Thus, the price associated with Q_1 is $P_{Min\ AVC}$ or the price associated with the minimum point on the average variable cost curve. The prices associated with Q_2 and Q_3 are $P_{Min\ ATC}$ and P, respectively.

Using $P_{Min\ AVC}$ and $P_{Min\ ATC}$ as reference pricing points illustrates a potential problem with marginal cost pricing. Incremental production costs for output levels less than Q_1 would result in prices less than $P_{Min\ AVC}$ and will not be large enough to cover fixed production costs in the short run. Incremental production costs for output levels between Q_1 and Q_2 would result in prices greater than $P_{Min\ AVC}$ but less than $P_{Min\ ATC}$ and will by definition only be large enough to cover a portion of fixed production costs in the short run.[20] In addition, if the production process is described as non-continuous (e.g., need to add a new machine to increase production or a series of

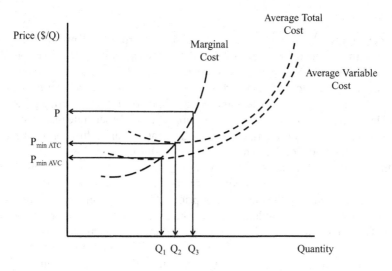

Figure 11.8 Marginal Cost Pricing

sequential steps must be completed before the input can move to the next step in the production process; Chapter 2 – Production Systems), the incremental costs will be enormous at the point of discontinuity but not elsewhere.

Price Searching Revisited

There are many other types of price searching strategies that an entrepreneur may use; for example, block pricing, peak-load pricing, price discrimination, commodity bundling, and price matching (Baye 2009). The strategies described earlier deal primarily with setting price to cover explicit and implicit measures of total costs. However, as described in Chapter 10 – Supply and Demand and the introduction to this chapter, market price is defined by supply and demand, where supply represents the entrepreneur's opportunity cost of producing or providing an output. What is missing from these strategies is an explicit examination of the demand (i.e., the opportunity cost of the consumer) and any possible market power that an entrepreneur may possess. Thus, your ability to set price depends on the own-price elasticity of demand (i.e., the price responsiveness of your consumers; Table 10.7, Chapter 10 – Supply and Demand); reflected by the appropriate market structure described earlier. As the market demand curve becomes relatively more elastic, $|E_p| \rightarrow \infty$, you have increasingly less market power to set price. As the market demand curve becomes relatively less elastic, $|E_p| \rightarrow 1$, you have increasingly more market power to set price. However, as the market demand curve becomes inelastic, $1 > |E_p| \rightarrow 0$, price searching to maximize profits would move you towards the elastic portion of the market demand curve.[21]

Derived Demand

The demand for any productive resource is derived from the demand for the commodities they produce. For example, students have a demand for paper for taking notes. Their demand for paper gives rise to a demand for trees to make the paper. The market for car loans is derived from the market for cars and that most people need a loan to buy a car. The same can be said for a house mortgage. Rideout and Hesseln (2001) illustrate this relationship using three separate markets: A natural resource market, an intermediate product market, and a final product market. A two-market model of derived demand can be illustrated by Figure 11.9a.

In addition, for productive resources (e.g., natural resources) to flow through intermediate markets to a final consumer good market, there must be a sufficient price difference among the market. The price difference illustrates the value added by each market. For example, there must be a sufficient price difference between the softwood stumpage market and pulp market for pulp mills to make a profit producing pulp. There must be a sufficient price difference between the pulp market and the market for notebook paper for paper mills to make a profit producing notebook paper. This is illustrated in Figure 11.9b.

As illustrated, the demand for natural resources, for the most part, is derived from the commodities they produce. As described by McGuigan and Moyer (1993) two sets of factors must be examined for these types of resources. First, we must identify the criteria or specifications used by firms purchasing the resources as inputs into their production process. For example, in the Radiata Pine Plantation practical application, Tables 2.7b and 4.3 describe the quantity and quality by product class. These product classes are defined by the sawmills that use this pine to manufacture dimension lumber. For the maple syrup application, the quality of sap is measured primarily by its sugar content using the Brix scale. For a renewable energy application, a solar array or wind turbine provides nondispatchable energy to a power grid. Thus, it could be part of an energy portfolio providing baseload energy. Referring to the Architectural Plan for Profit (Figure 11.1), if an input does not provide value for a production process, the entrepreneur will not purchase it.

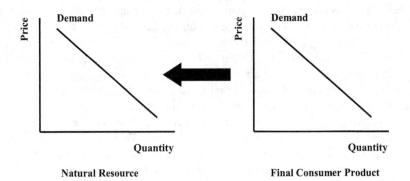

Natural Resource   Final Consumer Product

Figure 11.9a Derived Demand

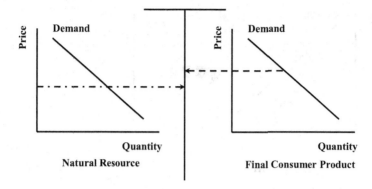

Figure 11.9b Derived Demand

Second, and perhaps the most important, we must identify the significant factors affecting the demand for the ultimate consumer good. For example, the Hancock Timber Resource Group, a Timber Investment Management Organization, examined the US softwood lumber market and found that housing is the

> largest end-use for softwood lumber, a change in housing starts translates fairly directly into a change in lumber usage and . . . that over the past thirty years, 86 percent of the variation in the volume of lumber produced in the U.S. can be explained by changes in the demand for housing as measured by single family housing starts.
>
> (Hancock Timberland Investor 2006)

They have updated the work done in 2006 to show the relationship of changing demographics (millennials ages 27 to 28 make up the largest age cohort of the US population), smaller, more affordable start homes, and increase in the repair and remodel market on the softwood lumber markets (Hancock Timberland Investor 2019). The Forest Research Group (www.forestresearchgroup.com/ accessed 27 February 2020) and F&W Forestry (https://fwforestry.net/forest-market-insights/ accessed 27 February 2020) publish reports describing the relationship of stumpage prices and timberland values given changes in regional, national, and international economic factors.

The impacts of the final consumer products market on the derived demand of the natural resource can be illustrated by Figure 11.9c. Figure 11.9c shows that demand shifts originate in the final consumer product market, filter through any intermediate markets, and finally impact the market for the natural resource. The magnitudes of the demand shifts moving from final consumer product to the market for the natural resource depend on the market structure associated with each of the markets, the economic variables and sociodemographic factors of demand given in equation (11.5), and the elasticities of supply and demand

$$Q_D = f(P; P_S, P_C, Y, E_p, E_Y, SocDem, N) \quad (11.5)$$

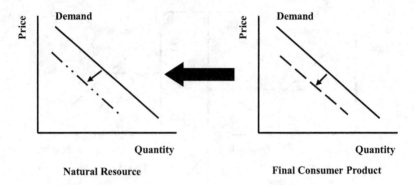

Natural Resource   Final Consumer Product

Figure 11.9c Derived Demand: Shifts Move From Final Consumer Product to Natural Resource

where the economic variables and sociodemographic factors of demand are defined in Chapter 10 – Supply and Demand, and N denotes the number of consumers in the market. When analyzing derived demand, it is helpful to focus on the production system inputs described as labor, materials, capital, and energy (Chapter 2 – Production Systems).

It is worth repeating the caution described by McGuigan and Moyer (1993): Entrepreneurs dealing with natural resources need to be keenly aware of the criteria or specifications used by firms purchasing these resources as inputs into their production process and the significant factors affecting the demand for the ultimate consumer good.

Derived Supply

Analogous to the concept of derived demand is derived supply. For example, softwood and hardwood stumpage are used as inputs in the production process for pulp, and pulp is an input into producing various different types and grades of paper. The paper is then packaged and sold to students who demand it for taking notes. This linking of production processes (i.e., the output of one firm is the input into another until a final consumer product is manufactured) describes the concept of derived supply and is illustrated by Figure 11.10a.

With derived demand, demand shifts started in the final consumer product market and filtered down through any intermediate markets to the market for natural resources. In the case of derived supply, the shifts start in the market for natural resources, filter through any intermediate markets, and end in the final consumer product market. For example, Prestemon et al. (2008), examining the response of trading partners for the United States given an invasive defoliator such as the Asian Lymantria moth, illustrates the concept of derived supply:

A ban on the importation of United States logs by our trading partners would have a much larger effect on the forest sector than the loss of affected tree

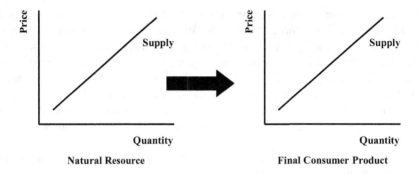

Figure 11.10a Derived Supply

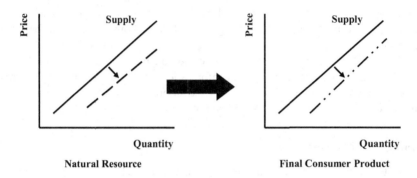

Figure 11.10b Derived Supply: Shifts Move From Natural Resource to Final Consumer
         Product

species directly caused by the [Asian Lymantria] moth invasion. Such a ban
would lower the price of industrial roundwood in the United States, and
simultaneously induce drops in processed wood product prices. The most
affected industries would be plywood where the average price would be
2.3 percent lower, chemical wood pulp (3.2 percent lower) and printing paper
(2.3 percent lower).

(Prestemon et al. 2008: 413)

The impacts of the changes in the market for natural resources on final consumer
products market can be illustrated by Figure 11.10b.

Figure 11.10b shows that a supply shift originating in the natural resources
market filters through any intermediate markets and impacts the final consumer
products market. The magnitudes of the supply shifts as they move from natural
resources market to final consumer product to the market depend on the market
structure associated with each of the markets, the economic variables of supply
given in equation (11.6), and the elasticities of supply and demand

$$Q_s = f(P; ProdSys, P_I, E_P, N) \quad (11.6)$$

where the economic variables of supply are defined in Chapter 10 – Supply and Demand and N denotes the number of suppliers in the market. The connection between the natural resources and intermediate production markets are that the output of the natural resource market is the input into an intermediate production market. Thus, the market equilibrium price in the natural resources market plus any transportation and transactions costs would describe the price of an input in the intermediate production market. The same can be argued for the connection between intermediate production and final consumer product market.

While McGuigan and Moyer (1993) described derived demand, a similar caution could be made for derived supply: Entrepreneurs dealing with natural resources need to be keenly aware of the criteria or specifications used by firms purchasing these resources as inputs into their production process and the significant factors affecting the supply of these inputs. Finally, overlaying the concept of derived demand on derived supply, you will get a picture of how economic information is transmitted from final consumer product market to the natural resources market through derived demand, then back to the consumer product market through derived supply. This constant flow of information back and forth among the markets makes McGuigan and Moyers' (1993) cautionary statements to entrepreneurs involved in any of these markets critical not to forget.

Know Your Markets

Markets are not static but dynamic over time due to changes in economic and sociodemographic factors. Successful entrepreneurs are not blind to these changes. Again, borrowing from McGuigan and Moyer (1993), entrepreneurs should be keenly aware of the significant factors affecting final product and input markets. This was illustrated in the examples given in the sections entitled Derived Demand and Derived Supply.

Understanding market price is key to knowing your markets. For example, many state agencies publish stumpage prices by some measure of tree quality (e.g., grade, defect, length, available quantity of a defined quality, etc.). Links to this information have been compiled by the United States Forest Service and can be found at www.srs.fs.usda.gov/econ/timberprices/ (accessed 26 February 2020). In the northeastern United States, similar publications are the *Sawlog Bulletin* and the *Sawlog Bulletin Magazine*, commonly called the *Log Street Journal* (https:// thelogstreet.com/ accessed 26 February 2020). Forestland owners who derive revenue from timber sale are in essence trying to predict stumpage prices decades out in the future (Smith 1988). Finally, Smith (1988) speculated that species considered not very commercially viable today may become commercially viable in the future.

The United States Energy Information Administration (www.eia.gov/ accessed 2 March 2020) provides time series information on energy prices. For example, Figure 11.11a shows the nominal and real annual residential electricity prices 1960 to 2018 with forecasted prices for 2019 to 2021.

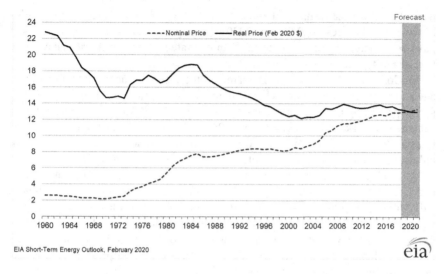

Figure 11.11a United States Annual Residential Electricity Price

Source: www.eia.gov/outlooks/steo/realprices/ (accessed 2 March 2020)

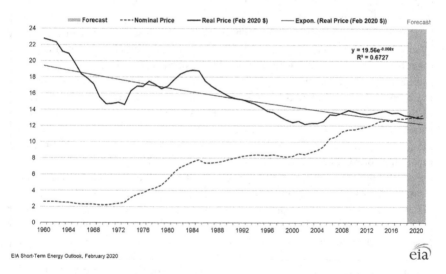

Figure 11.11b United States Annual Residential Electricity Price With Trend Line

Source: www.eia.gov/outlooks/steo/realprices/ (accessed 2 March 2020)

The real price of residential electricity has been decreasing since 1960. Using a simple log–linear or exponential trend line shown in Figure 11.11b, the real price of residential electricity has been decreasing by 0.8% per year from 1960 to 2019.

In the northeastern United States, heating oil and natural gas are the primary substitutes for heating homes. Using price data downloaded for heating oil and natural gas market from the United States Energy Information Administration (www.eia.gov/ accessed 2 March 2020), heating oil and natural gas real prices have been increasing at about the same annual rate that electrical prices have been decreasing for the years 1960 to 2019.

McConnell and Grahm (2016) examined the historical nominal and real average annual percentage rates of change in maple syrup prices for the primary maple syrup–producing northeastern states from 1916 to 2012. The nominal annual percentage rates of change ranged from 3.42% to 4.13%. The real annual percentage rates of change ranged from 0.84% to 1.12%. The United States Department of Agriculture's National Agricultural Statistics Service provides information on maple syrup production; namely, (i) Maple Syrup Taps, Yield, and Production – States and United States; (ii) Maple Syrup Price and Value – States and United States; (iii) Maple Syrup Season – States and United States; (iv) Maple Syrup Average Open and Close Season Dates – States and United States; (v) Maple Syrup Price by Type of Sale and Size of Container – States; (vi) Maple Syrup Bulk Price – States; and (vii) Maple Syrup Percent of Sales by Type – States (https://www.nass.usda. gov/Statistics_by_State/New_England_includes/Publications/Current_News_ Release/2023/Northeast-2023-Maple-Syrup-Report.pdf accessed 31 August 2023; https://www.nass.usda.gov/Statistics_by_State/New_England_includes/Publica- tions/Annual_Statistical_Bulletin/2021/2021_NewEngland_Annual_Bulletin.pdf accessed 31 August 2023).

Continuing the example taken from the forestry profession started in Chapter 10 – Supply and Demand, Hagan et al. (2005) examines the changes in timberland ownership during the 1980s and 1990s in the northeastern United States and the implications for management regimes. They determined a significant decrease in the number of acres owned by the forest industry and a corresponding increase in the number of acres owned by other types of landowners. As the number of forestland owners increased, the parcel size owned decreased. The implications for management are moving from managing commodity outputs, primarily timber, to managing forested ecosystems to produce a suite of ecosystem goods (e.g., renewable – timber – and nonrenewable – minerals) and services (e.g., water and air purification, carbon sequestration). Arano and Munn (2006) examined the management behavior of various ownership categories. They found that in Mississippi, Timber Investment Management Organizations and industrial landowners generally invest three times as much in management activities related directly to timber production as compared to family forest landowners. But these landowners control approximately 43% of the forestland in the United States (Butler et al. 2016). Belin et al. (2005) examined the attitudes of nonindustrial private forest landowners of Vermont, New Hampshire, and western Massachusetts toward an ecosystem approach to managing their forestlands. Even though the concept of an ecosystem-based management approach is not yet well defined, this concept seemed more consistent with their stated goals for owning forestland (Butler and Leatherberry 2004; Hagan et al. 2005; Butler 2008, 2010).

The question is where to obtain information on these economic, social, and demographic factors and how they may impact your business. For the examples used here, the information was available through various sources such as professional organization or society publications, extension publications, applied research publications, newsletters, and government websites. As an entrepreneur you must actively search out and read these types of publications.

How to Use Economic Information – Market Equilibrium and Structure – to Make Better Business Decisions

Markets are the primary means through which our economy determines what and how much of each product to produce, how to produce, and for whom to produce. Answering these questions also depends on the structures of any market. Successful entrepreneurs know the market structure for the commodities they produce or provide and for the inputs they purchase. As an entrepreneur your objective is to turn a consumer's willingness and ability to buy your commodities into revenues and to pay as little for inputs as possible. Market structure defines the market power you have to capture this revenue given your ability to price your commodities relative to your competitors and to affect the price you pay for inputs. The Architectural Plan for Profit provides an outline for you to collect economic information to analyze market structure and price searching.

Markets are dynamic. Profit searching behavior includes being aware of the economic and sociodemographic factors that affect your input and output markets. If you focus only on what is in front of you, you will potentially miss changes in downstream input and upstream output markets that might affect your business. The goal of obtaining economic information about your markets and their structure is to increase the percentage of proactive decision making relative to reactive decision making.

Appendix 11A – Price Searching Given Market Power

Price Searching Given Market Power

Reiterating, the goal of your pricing strategy is to (1) set price to cover explicit and implicit measures of total costs; (2) reflect your consumers' willingness and ability to pay; and (3) recognize any competition. Examining the discussed pricing strategies relative to these three goals shows that they basically met the first but not the second and third goals. In Chapter 10 – Supply and Demand, the concept of elasticity was introduced to examine the sensitivity of consumers' reactions to changes in prices and income. Focusing on own-price elasticity of demand will allow developing a pricing strategy that will include all three goals but require additional economic information; namely, estimating own-price demand elasticity (Table 10.7).

The general marginal cost pricing rule is derived from the definition of marginal revenue (MR) developed in Chapter 11 – Market Equilibrium and Structure Endnote 7, the definition of own-price elasticity of demand (Table 10.7), and the profit searching rule of MC = MR. This is summarized in equation (A.1a):

$$MR = P(Q) \cdot \left[\frac{1}{E_P} + 1 \right] = MC \qquad (A.1a)$$

Solving for own-price gives the general marginal cost pricing rule (equation (A.1b))

$$P = MC \cdot \left[\frac{1}{1 + \left(\dfrac{1}{E_P} \right)} \right] \qquad (A.1b)$$

where P denotes own-price, MC denotes marginal cost, and E_p denotes own-price elasticity of demand. Demand curves have a negative or zero slope, thus own-price elasticity is non-positive or $E_p \leq 0$. However, convention is to define own-price elasticity using its absolute value, |Ep|. By definition: (1) if |Ep| = 0 then the demand curve is perfectly inelastic; (2) if 0 < |Ep| < 1 then MR < 0 and the demand curve is inelastic and any price increase (decrease) will increase (decrease) an entrepreneur's total revenue; (3) if |Ep| = 1 the demand curve has unitary elasticity and MR = 0; (4) if |Ep| > 1 then MR > 0 and the demand curve is elastic and any price increase (decrease) will decrease (increase) an entrepreneur's total revenue; and (5) if |Ep| = infinity then the demand curve is perfectly elastic and the market structure is defined as workable competition.

If the entrepreneur has some market power in their commodity market, then the market demand curve they face has a negative slope and E_p < 0. An entrepreneur can change own-price and observe the amounts their consumers purchase. This would allow them to, at the minimum, calculate an arc own-price elasticity of demand from Table 10.7. If the entrepreneur determines that the arc own-price elasticity of demand is 0 < |Ep| < 1, this implies that the portion of the market demand curve they face is inelastic. The entrepreneur would be able to increase total revenue by decreasing the amount of the commodity sold by increasing price. Interestingly, decreasing the amount of commodity sold would also decrease total costs (less would have to be produced) and increase profits. If the entrepreneur determines that the arc own-price elasticity of demand is |Ep| > 1, this implies that the portion of the market demand curve they face is elastic. The entrepreneur would be able to increase total revenue by increasing the amount of the commodity sold by decreasing price. In any case, an entrepreneur with market power in the commodity market would search for the market price given by equation (A.1b) that satisfies the profit searching rule MR = MC. As the relevant portion of the MC is positive from Figures 10.5a and 10.7a, this implies the entrepreneur would search the portion of the demand curve associated with MR > 0 or the elastic portion. The resulting economic information is illustrated by the market solution described in

Figure 11.6a and summarized as: (1) an entrepreneur's profit-maximizing search is focused on the portion of demand curve that is elastic, and (2) the demand curve is the economic model of the opportunity cost of the consumer and their sensitivity to own-price changes. A caveat: An elasticity estimate is for a given product and given point in time. Consequently, given the market, these estimates would have to be updated frequently to be of any use.

Profit Margins

Although profit margins are not considered a pricing strategy, per se, they can be used as an indicator of pricing policy and a firm's ability to control costs. A profit margin is defined as the after-tax profits per dollar of revenue. They are measured as a percentage (i.e., $0 <$ profit margin < 1). Equation (A.2) defines a profit margin mathematically

$$\text{Profit Margin} = \frac{\text{After-tax Profit}}{\text{Total Revenue}} = \frac{\text{After-tax Profit}}{P \cdot Q} \qquad (A.2)$$

where P denotes price and Q denotes the amount of output sold. For example, a profit margin of 30% means that for every $1.00 of total revenue, $0.30 of after-tax profits are generated. Consequently, a low profit margin indicates a low margin of safety in terms of controlling cost and a higher risk that a decline in sales will erase profits and result in a loss.

Notes

1 Transactions costs can be described as searching and information costs (e.g., both consumers and producers search for each other, for information about products, etc.), bargaining costs (e.g., agreeing upon a price and quantity and quality), and enforcement costs (e.g., redress for any failure to complete agreed-upon actions by buyer and seller).
2 The default market structure is defined as workable competition (Chapter 1 – Introduction). I will expand upon this in the section entitled "Market Structures."
3 Entrepreneur A
   Marginal Cost = Supply = $1 + Q$
   Entrepreneur B
   Marginal Cost = Supply = $6 + 0.25 \cdot Q$
   Let market price be 10 $/Q. Given this information it is left to the reader to show that market producer surplus of $72.5 is equal to the sum of the individual producer surplus of each entrepreneur.
4 The concept of workable competition was first described by J.M. Clark in 1940 (Clark 1940). As the conditions required for perfect competition are rarely satisfied, he argued that the goal of governmental policy should be to make competition "workable," not necessarily perfect. His proposal sparked much discussion at the time. My use of the term implies that neither entrepreneurs nor consumers have sufficient market power to significantly alter the price searching rule of MR = P = Supply = MC even though the conditions required for perfect competition are not met.
5 Under purely competitive conditions, marginal cost (MC) curves are equated with supply and the marginal revenue (MR) curves are horizontal, and each MR curve can be represented by a specific, exogenously determined own-price, P_0. Give the MC curve, we can therefore express the optimal output as $Q^* = Q^*(P_0)$, or the optimal output is a

function of price, P_0. The expression $Q^* = Q^*(P_0)$ is a function mapping a real number (price) into a real number (optimal output). However, when the MR curves are downward sloping under imperfect competition (such as monopoly or monopolistic competition), the optimal output of the entrepreneur with a given MC curve will depend on the specific position of the MR curve; namely, an entrepreneur's MR is a function of the amount produced. In such a case, since the output decision involves a mapping from *curves* to real numbers, this is described as a *functional*: $Q^* = Q^*[MR]$. It is, of course, precisely because of this inability to express the optimal output as a *function* of price that makes it impossible to draw a supply curve for a firm under imperfect competition, as can be for its competitive counterpart (Chiang 1992).

6 As shown by Figure 10.16b, it is not the demand curve but the area $P \cdot Q$ that defines an entrepreneur's total revenue. Using the definition of average revenue (AR) from equation (4.3) (Chapter 4 – Revenue)

$$AR = \frac{TR}{Q} = \frac{P \cdot Q}{Q} = P$$

where TR denotes total revenue. AR is interpreted as total revenue per unit output, P. Consequently, TR can be defined mathematically as

$$TR = P \cdot Q = \left(\frac{P \cdot Q}{Q}\right) \cdot Q = AR \cdot Q$$

or AR multiplied by output (Q) gives total revenue. If the demand curve represents AR and $AR = P$, then the output level a consumer is willing and able to buy, Q, multiplied by AR would give $TR = AR^*Q = P^*Q$. Thus, I would argue that a consumer's demand curve represents an entrepreneur's average revenue curve. Consequently, the entrepreneur's interpretation of market price is as the revenue per unit sold or average revenue.

7 In Chapter 2 – Production Systems and Chapter 3 – Costs, I have developed a relationship between marginal and average product and marginal and average variable cost, respectively. Namely, if the average curve was decreasing (increasing), the margin curve was below (above) the average curve. This holds for average revenue and marginal revenue. Let total revenue (TR) be defined as

$$TR = P(Q) \cdot Q$$

where $P(Q)$ denotes that output price is a function of quantity; that is, demand has a negative slope. The first derivative of total revenue with respect to output defines marginal revenue (MR) (equation (4.5)):

$$MR = \frac{dTR}{dQ} = \frac{dP(Q) \cdot Q}{dQ}$$

$$= \frac{dP(Q)}{dQ} \cdot Q + P(Q)$$

The first term on the right-hand side is the price effect and the second term is the output effect. The price effect is negative because the demand curve has a negative slope, $\frac{dP(Q)}{dQ} < 0$. Consequently, the revenue received for all units of the output sold, not just the incremental one, $\frac{dP(Q)}{dQ} \cdot Q$, decreases as price increases. With a decrease in price, more output is sold. The output effect is positive but decreasing as the marginal revenue is less than the average revenue, P(Q), for any given Q. If $\frac{dP(Q)}{dQ} = 0$ then MR = P and P is not a function of the amount of output sold. Finally, marginal revenue can also be defined in terms of own-price elasticity (Table 10.7):

$$MR = \frac{dTR}{dQ} = \frac{dP(Q)}{dQ} \cdot Q + P(Q)$$

$$= P(Q) \cdot \left[\frac{Q}{P(Q)} \cdot \frac{dP(Q)}{dQ} + 1 \right]$$

$$= P(Q) \cdot \left[\frac{1}{E_P} + 1 \right]$$

Thus, when own-price elasticity of demand is inelastic, $1/E_P$ has a small negative number or has a high absolute value, and the marginal revenue decreases more steeply and vice versa.

8   I would recommend the reader review the discussion in Chapter 1 – Introduction on accounting versus economic profit as illustrated by Table 1.1.

9   Based on Figure 11.6a, is there a price below which a monopolist would stop producing?

10 While Figure 11.6a illustrates that monopolists cannot charge as much as they want, is a negatively sloped demand curve (the opportunity cost of the consumer) a sufficient check on monopoly pricing and profit? The simple answer is often *no*. There are many federal and state policies providing checks on monopoly pricing and profits.

11 The terms marginal factor cost as well as average factor cost in Figures 11.7a and 11.7b are used to denote that we are examining the cost of a factor of production such as labor. For example, the marginal factor cost of labor would be the hourly wage rate paid (\$/hour). In the case of workable competition in the input market, marginal factor cost would equal average factor cost.

12 Another analogy that can be used is that of marginal and average product (Chapter 2 – Production Systems). Figures 2.13 and 2.15 show that whenever average product is increasing (decreasing) marginal product is greater (less) than average product. This relationship between margins and averages holds for production systems, costs, and revenues.

13 As the monopsonist is the only buyer of the input, their expenditures bring forth the "supply" of the input (Pindyck and Rubinfeld 1995). The monopsonist's average expenditure per unit of input, or average factor cost, would then define the market supply curve for the input. Given the definition of average factor cost

$$AFC \cdot x_j = \frac{w_j \cdot x_j}{x_j} \cdot x_j = w_j \cdot x_j = TFC_j$$

The monopsonist's total factor cost of labor is illustrated in Figure 11.7a as the area of the rectangle defined by

$$AFC \cdot L^* = W^* \cdot L^*$$

14 A barrel of crude oil and a barrel of maple syrup contain roughly the same number of gallons. However, bulk maple syrup is sold by the pound and the weight is a function of the syrup's specific gravity or sugar content and grade. There are approximately 620 pounds of syrup per stainless steel barrel, and an average 2019 price was 2.23 \$/pound (https://www.statista.com/statistics/372430/farm-value-per-liter-of-maple-syrup-in-ontario/ accessed 6 September 2023).

15 I would recommend that readers review the section entitled Efficiency Versus Equity in Chapter 1 – Introduction.
16 Keat and Young (2000) describe this as the three C's of pricing: cost, customers, and competition.
17 The curious reader may want to compare and contrast equations (11.4a) and (11.4b) with equation (5.6).
18 A brief discussion of issues associated with joint costs can be found in the section entitled "Market Versus Nonmarket Evaluation" in Chapter 9 – Estimating Nonmarket Values.
19 The use of the term marginal cost in marginal cost pricing is not accurate. As Silberberg and Suen (2001: 182) have pointed out, "Marginal cost (in the finite sense) is the increase (or decrease) in cost resulting from the production of an extra increment of output, which is not the same thing as the 'cost of the last unit.'" Thus, a more accurate description of this should be incremental cost pricing.
20 The reader is referred to Tables 5.4, 5.5, and 5.6 from the section entitled To Produce or Not to Produce in Chapter 5 – Profit.
21 Appendix 11A gives a description of price searching given an entrepreneur has market power in their output market.

12 Taxes

Preamble

Benjamin Franklin's (1706–1790) famous quote in his letter to Jean Baptiste Le Roy in 1789 – "But in this world nothing can be said to be certain, except death and taxes" – seems just as relevant today as then. What are taxes and why do governments collect taxes? Simply, taxes are compulsory levies on private individual and organizations by governments for two general purposes to (i) raise revenue to finance expenditures on maintaining a satisfactory economic growth rate, promoting economic stability (e.g., legal, infrastructure, education, defense, etc.), and distributing income to conform to society's currently held standards of equity; and (ii) discourage the consumption of goods and services with high social costs (e.g., alcohol, soda, tobacco, and pollution). Taxes can be levied on many aspects of economic activity; for example, income, wage, property, value added, sales, and inheritance. Focusing on the Architectural Plan for Profit, taxes can affect all of its pillars in one way or another.

For example, a tax on the use of a specific input in the production system may cause the entrepreneur to search for a lower cost substitute. A tax on the waste generated as the result of a production system may cause the entrepreneur to modify the product system to abate the waste. A tax on profit may cause the entrepreneur to change the amount of output produced.

There are many different types of taxes at the local, state, and national level that may affect an entrepreneur's management decisions. The primary focus will be on three common state taxes that impact managing forest and natural resources. These are property, productivity, and yield taxes. I will, however, briefly introduce three federal taxes – income, capital gains, and inheritance tax. To provide readers with a general context in which to think about taxes, I will introduce six principles of taxation: neutrality, certainty and understandability, equity, efficiency, adequacy, and time bias. To analyze the potential impacts on an entrepreneur's management decisions, I will only focus on two of them: neutrality and time bias.

Practical Applications

The practical applications used in this chapter will be the Loblolly Pine Plantation (Amateis and Burkhart 1985; Burkhart et al. 1985) and the Solar Array from Chapter 7 – The Natural Resources Management Puzzle.

DOI: 10.4324/9781315678719-12

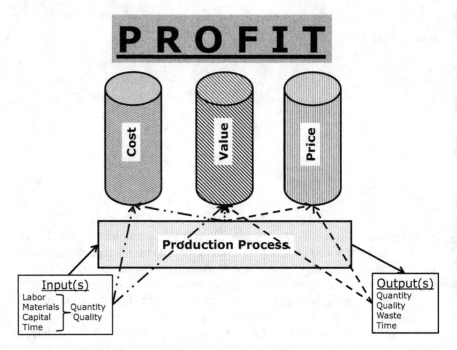

Figure 12.1 The Architectural Plan for Profit

Economic Principles of Taxation

Neutrality

A tax should interfere as little as possible with attaining the pre-tax optimum allocation and use of resources. A caveat to this principle is when a government's policy goal is to modify individual decision-making behavior away from consuming goods and services with high social costs (e.g., alcohol, soda, tobacco, and pollution).

The principle references the optimal resource allocation or profit searching rule of

Marginal Revenue = Marginal Cost

As taxes are a cost, this allows two general statements concerning the impacts of a tax on the profit searching rule. First, if taxes are perceived as a fixed cost, this can be modeled using equation (12.1a)

$$\text{Max } \Pi = TR - TVC - (TFC + TFC_\tau) \tag{12.1a}$$

where terms have been defined previously except TFC_τ, which denotes a tax as a fixed cost. Comparing profit searching with and without a fixed cost tax is

Profit Searching Rule

Without taxes $\rightarrow$ MR = MC
With Fixed Cost Taxes $\rightarrow$ MR = MC

Conclusion: Fixed cost taxes, generally, have no effect on profit searching, thus they are described as neutral with respect to profits. However, fixed costs do affect if profits are positive or negative and thus the decision to produce or not.

Second, if taxes are perceived as a variable cost, this can be modeled using equation (12.1b)

$$\text{Max } \Pi = \text{TR} - (\text{TVC} + \text{TVC}_\tau) - \text{TFC} \tag{12.1b}$$

where terms have been defined previously except TVC_τ, which denotes a tax as a variable cost. Comparing profit searching with and without a variable cost tax is

Profit Searching Rule

Without taxes $\rightarrow$ MR = MC
With Variable Cost Taxes $\rightarrow$ MR = MC + MC_τ

As illustrated, the marginal cost associated with a variable cost tax includes an additional component, MC_τ. Conclusion, a tax perceived as a variable cost will impact the profit searching rule.

Certainty and Understandability

The tax payment should be certain and nonarbitrary. The assessment methodology should be agreed upon and used by all. The time of payment, the manner of payment, and the quantity to be paid should be clear and plain to all.

Equity

Equity, as described in Chapter 1 – Introduction, denotes the concept of a just or fair (not necessarily equal) distribution of goods, services, output, income, and so on among all consumers. The classical descriptions of equity are horizontal and vertical.

Horizontal Equity – Fairness of justice in the treatment of individuals in similar circumstances.
Vertical Equity (Ability to Pay) – Fairness or justice in the treatment of individuals in different circumstances. Vertical equity is further divided into three categories:

Progressive: The net benefits represent a higher proportion of the lower-income person's income than of the rich person's income. Or the tax burden – the tax rate or tax payment as a proportion of income – increases as the level of income increases, the higher an individual's income, the larger the tax burden. In the United States, the income tax is a progressive tax.

Regressive: The net benefits represent a higher proportional net benefit to high-income people than to low-income people. Or the tax burden – the tax rate or tax payment as a proportion of income – increases as the level of income decreases; the lower an individual's income, the larger the tax burden. An example of a regressive tax is a sales tax on some goods and services.

Proportional: The net benefits affect individuals of each income level in the same proportion – the tax rate or tax payment as a proportion of income. This means the average tax rate equals the marginal tax rate. This is also called a flat tax. An example of a flat tax is the Tax Cut and Jobs Act – 2017 (Pub.L. 115–97), which eliminated the numerous tax brackets for corporations and instead imposed a tax rate of 21% on taxable income.

There are three additional concepts of equity when considering taxes based on a property's value:

Assessment equity – Comparable properties are assessed comparably within an assessment jurisdiction.

Tax equity – Comparable properties pay comparable taxes within a taxing jurisdiction or across jurisdictions.

Everybody pays – There is 100% compliance, and everyone bears their share of the burden.

Efficiency

Tax collection costs should not be an inordinately high percentage of tax revenues. The real costs of collecting the tax should be a minimum inconvenience to taxpayers.

Adequacy

Taxes should raise enough net revenue such that government projects can be funded adequately without burdening taxpayers too much.

Time Bias

Taxes based on a property's value are an annual expense; for example, state property and productivity taxes. However, forestlands often do not produce annual revenues that can be used to cover these annual taxes; revenues occur only periodically. Thus, there is a disconnect between the annual taxes paid on the value of the property and the cash generated by the property that can be used to pay the tax. For example, an entrepreneur cannot harvest the annual growth of the forest to pay the annual tax without harvesting the trees that generate the growth.

Income, Capital Gains, and Inheritance Taxes[1]

Income Tax

An income tax is a tax on the flow of ordinary income an individual earns or taxable income that a business generates in a given year. An individual's ordinary income includes, but is not limited to, the following categories:

1. Employee Compensation, Fringe Benefits, Bonuses, Commissions, Tips, etc.
2. Business and Investment Income, Partnership Income, S Corporation Income, etc.
3. Royalties, Rents, etc.
4. Virtual Currencies, Bartering, etc.

An individual's taxable income is given by equation (12.2a):

Taxable Income = Ordinary Income − (Deductions + Exemptions)   (12.2a)

Currently, individual ordinary income is taxed using a progressive taxing structure shown in Table 12.1.

An individual's tax payment is given by equation (12.2b):

Tax Payment = $\sum$[(Tax Rate) × (Taxable Income)] − Tax Credits   (12.2b)

To illustrate the progressive tax structure, Table 12.2 shows the 2020 tax payment, given a married couple filing jointly with an ordinary income of $175,000.

This table also illustrates the concept of an average tax and marginal tax rate. The average tax rate is given by equation (12.3):

Average Tax Rate = (Tax Payment ÷ Taxable Income)*100   (12.3)

Table 12.1 2020 Federal Income Tax Brackets and Rates for Single Filers, Married Couples Filing Jointly, and Heads of Households

Rate	For Single Individuals	For Married Individuals Filing Joint Returns	For Heads of Households
10%	Up to $9,875	Up to $19,750	Up to $14,100
12%	$9,876 to $40,125	$19,751 to $80,250	$14,101 to $53,700
22%	$40,126 to $85,525	$80,251 to $171,050	$53,701 to $85,500
24%	$85,526 to $163,300	$171,051 to $326,600	$85,501 to $163,300
32%	$163,301 to $207,350	$326,601 to $414,700	$163,301 to $207,350
35%	$207,351 to $518,400	$414,701 to $622,050	$207,351 to $518,400
37%	$518,401 or more	$622,051 or more	$518,401 or more

Source: www.irs.gov/newsroom/irs-provides-tax-inflation-adjustments-for-tax-year-2020#:~:text=35%25%2C%20for%20incomes%20over%20%24207%2C350,married%20couples%20filing%20jointly)%3B (accessed 16 March 2021)

According to Table 12.2, the average tax rate is 16.4%; thus, $0.164 of every $1.00 of taxable income is paid in taxes. The marginal tax rate of the third tax bracket in Table 12.2 is 22%; thus, $0.22 of every additional $1.00 of taxable income within this tax bracket is paid in taxes.

A business's taxable income is given by Table 12.3. The Tax Cut and Jobs Act of 2017 (Public Law 115–97) changed the corporate tax rate on all C corporation taxable income as of 2018 from a tiered tax rate ranging from 15% to as high as 39% depending on taxable income to a 21% tax rate on all taxable income, while some related business deductions and credits were reduced or eliminated.[2] This defines a flat tax. Tables 12.4a and 12.4b illustrate the implications of a flat tax on changing corporate taxable income.

With a flat tax as illustrated in Tables 12.4a and 12.4b, the average tax rate equals the marginal tax rate. According to Tables 12.4a and 12.4b, the average tax rate is 21%; thus, $0.21 of every $1.00 of taxable corporate income is paid in taxes. The marginal tax rate shown in Table 12.4a and 12.4b is also 21%; thus, $0.21 of

Table 12.2 Example 2020 Individual Ordinary Income Tax

Ordinary Income (Married Filing Jointly)	$175,000
2020 Married Filing Jointly – Deduction	−$24,800
Taxable Income	$150,200
Tax – 2020 Married Federal Tax Rates	
$0 to $19,750 (10%)	$1,975
$19,751 to $80,250 (12%)	$7,260
$80,251 to $171,050 (22%)	$15,389
$171,051 to $326,600 (24%)	
$326,601 to $414,700 (32%)	
$414,701 to $622,050 (35%)	
$622,051 or more (37%)	
Total Tax Payment	$24,624
Income After Taxes	$150,376
Average Tax Rate	16.4%

Table 12.3 Business Annual Taxable and Net or After-Tax Income[†]

Sales or Revenues
  − Sale Returns
  − Cost of Goods Sold (Production System Costs – Variable Costs)
Gross Profit
  − Operating Expenses (O&M, SG&A, Dirti-5 – Fixed Costs)
Income from Operations
  −/+ Other Operating Income & Expenses
  − Interest Expenses
Taxable Income
  − Tax Payment [= (Taxable Income) × (Tax Rate)]
Net Income

[†]This is analogous to an accounting income statement

Table 12.4a Corporate Income Tax Example

Sales/Revenues	$600,000
Sales Returns	−$5,000
Cost of Goods Sold (Variable Costs)	−$200,000
Gross Profit	$395,000
Operating Expenses (Fixed Costs)	−$75,000
Income from Operations	$320,000
Other Income & Expenses	$0
Interest Expense	−$5,000
Taxable Income	$315,000
US Corporate Income Tax − 21% on all C-corp taxable income as of 2018 (Tax Cut and Jobs Act 2017)	
Tax Payment	$66,150
Net Income	$248,850
Average Tax Rate = Marginal Tax Rate	21%

Table 12.4b Corporate Income Tax Example Given an Increase in "Other Income"

Sales/Revenues	$600,000
Sales Returns	−$5,000
Cost of Goods Sold (Variable Costs)	−$200,000
Gross Profit	$395,000
Operating Expenses (Fixed Costs)	−$75,000
Income from Operations	$320,000
Other Income & Expenses	*$10,000*
Interest Expense	−$5,000
Taxable Income	$325,000
US Corporate Income Tax − 21% on all C-corp taxable income as of 2018 (Tax Cut and Jobs Act 2017)	
Tax Payment	$68,250
Net Income	$256,750
Average Tax Rate = Marginal Tax Rate	21%

every additional $1.00 of taxable corporate income is paid in taxes. This flat tax illustrates the proportional concept within vertical equity.

To illustrate the impact of a flat tax on an entrepreneur's wealth searching decisions, I will use the solar array example from Chapter 7 – The Natural Resources Management Puzzle. Based on that analysis, the 1 MW solar array's economic life was 52 years and the wealth generated by the array was \$1,768,664. The taxable income for the solar array at any time t, as described in Table 12.3, is

$$TI_t = TR_t - OM_t - CR_t$$

where TI_t is the taxable income at time t, TR_t is the total revenue at time t, OM_t are the operation and maintenance costs at time t, and CR_t are the capital recovery costs at time t.[3] The after-tax or net income, NI_t, is the taxable income minus the tax payment and is given by

$$NI_t = TR_t - OM_t - CR_t - (TR_t - OM_t - CR_t) \cdot \tau$$
$$NI_t = TR_t \cdot (1 - \tau) - OM_t \cdot (1 - \tau) - CR_t \cdot (1 - \tau)$$

where τ is the flat tax rate of 21%. Consequently, the after-tax or net income is the after-tax total revenue minus the after-tax operation and maintenance costs minus the after-tax capital recovery costs. Using the same approach described in Chapter 7 – The Natural Resources Management Puzzle, the after-tax equal annual equivalences of each component can be determined.

I will start with the pre- and after-tax revenue as given in Table 12.5a. The output and annual pre-tax revenues were taken from Table 7.2a. The after-tax revenues at any time t is given by $TR_t \cdot (1 - \tau)$. The after-tax equal annual equivalent converts the cumulative after-tax total revenue present value to an equivalent consistent revenue stream.

Table 12.5b defines the pre- and after-tax capital recovery costs.

Table 12.5a Estimated After-Tax Revenue (ATR) of a 1,000 kW Ground Mount Solar Array Located Near Syracuse, New York, USA, Given an Insolation Conversion Efficiency Loss of 0.7% per Year, a 5% Discount Rate, a Constant Retail Price of 0.1651 \$/kWh, and a Flat Tax Rate of 21%

Year	Output	Revenue	ATR	$\sum_t PV(ATR)$	$EAE_{ATR,t}$
	(kWh/year)	(\$/year)	(\$/year)	(\$)	(\$/year)
1	1,186,212	195,844	154,716	147,349	154,716
5	1,153,345	190,417	150,430	667,949	154,279
10	1,113,539	183,845	145,238	1,167,970	151,258
15	1,075,107	177,500	140,225	1,546,229	148,967
20	1,038,002	170,174	135,386	1,832,375	147,035
25	1,002,177	165,459	130,713	2,048,841	145,370
30	967,588	159,749	126,202	2,212,593	143,932
35	934,193	154,235	121,846	2,336,469	142,692
40	901,951	148,912	117,641	2,430,179	141,626
45	870,822	143,773	113,580	2,501,070	140,715
50	840,767	138,811	109,660	2,554,697	139,938
52	829,037	136,874	108,130	2,572,294	139,661
55	811,749	134,020	105,876	2,595,265	139,280

$\sum_t PV(ATR)$ denotes the sum of the present value of the after-tax revenue at time t; $EAE_{ATR,t}$ denotes the after-tax equal annual equivalent of the present value of the revenue at time t

Table 12.5b Estimated After-Tax Capital Recovery Cost of a 1,000 kW Ground Mount Solar Array Located Near Syracuse, New York, USA, Given a 5% Discount Rate and a Flat Tax Rate of 21%

Year	Initial Cost	Expected Salvage Value	IC_0-$PV(SV_t)$	$EAE_{ACR,t}$
	($)	($)	($)	($/year)
0	1,113,000			
1			1,113,000	923,233
5			1,113,000	203,089
10			1,113,000	113,869
15			1,113,000	84,711
20			1,113,000	70,555
21		-212,000	1,189,096	73,268
25		-212,000	1,175,604	65,895
30		-212,000	1,162,052	59,719
35		-212,000	1,151,434	55,553
40		-212,000	1,143,114	52,629
45		-212,000	1,136,595	50,518
50		-212,000	1,131,487	48,964
52		-212,000	1,129,768	48,459
55		-212,000	1,127,485	47,802

IC_0 denotes initial cost; $PV(SV_t)$ denotes the present value of salvage value at time t; $EAE_{ACR,t}$ denotes the after-tax equal annual equivalent capital recovery cost at time t

The initial costs and expected salvage value were taken from Table 7.2b. The after-tax capital recovery costs at any time t is given by $CR_t \cdot (1 - \tau)$. Given the original purchase power agreement was for 20 years, as shown in 12.5b, the solar array can be repowered and replaced starting in year 21. The cost of salvageing the array is $212,000. The after-tax equal annual equivalent converts the cumulative after-tax capital recovery cost present value to an equivalent consistent capital recovery cost stream.

Table 12.5c defines the pre- and after-tax capital operation and maintenance costs. The pre-tax operation and maintenance costs were taken from Table 7.2c. The after-tax operation and maintenance costs at any time t is given by $OM_t \cdot (1 - \tau)$. The after-tax equal annual equivalent converts the cumulative after-tax operation and maintenance costs present value to an equivalent consistent operation and maintenance cost stream. The equal annual equivalent after-tax ownership costs are given in Table 12.5d.

I can now examine the per-tax vs. after-tax wealth decision of when to replace the solar array. The wealth decision to replace the solar array was given by equation (7.6b):

$$\left(NPV_\infty \right)_t = \sum_{\theta=0}^{\infty} NPV_t \left[\left(1+r\right)^{-t} \right]^\theta = \frac{NPV_t}{1-\left(1+r\right)^{-t}} \tag{7.6b}$$

Table 12.5c After-Tax Estimated Operation and Maintenance (AOM) of a 1,000 kW Ground Mount Solar Array Located Near Syracuse, New York, USA, Given a 5% Discount Rate, an Annual Cost Increase of 1.5% for the Years 1 to 15 and 2.5% for the Years 16 and Beyond, and a Flat Tax Rate of 21%

Year	Estimated OM Cost	AOM	$\sum_t PV(AOM)$	$EAE_{AOM,t}$
	($/year)	($/year)	($)	($/year)
0				
1	19,000	15,010	14,295	15,010
5	20,166	15,931	66,867	15,445
10	21,724	17,162	123,309	15,969
15	23,403	18,489	170,950	16,470
20	26,479	20,918	212,339	17,039
25	29,958	23,667	249,031	17,669
30	33,895	26,777	281,557	18,316
35	38,349	30,296	310,392	18,956
40	43,389	34,277	335,953	19,579
45	49,090	38,781	358,613	20,176
50	55,541	43,877	378,700	20,744
52	58,353	46,099	386,082	20,962
55	62,840	49,643	396,508	21,279

$\sum_t PV(AOM)$ denotes the sum of the present value of the after-tax operation and maintenance (AOM) costs at time t; $EAE_{AOM,t}$, denotes the after-tax equal annual equivalent estimated operation and maintenance costs at time t

Table 12.5d Annual Expected After-Tax Ownership Costs ($EAE_{AO,t}$) of a 1,000 kW Ground Mount Solar Array Located Near Syracuse, New York, USA, Given a 5% Discount Rate and a Flat Tax Rate of 21%

Year	$EAE_{ACR,t}$	$EAE_{AOM,t}$	$EAE_{AO,t}$
	($/year)	($/year)	($/year)
0			
1	923,233	15,010	938,243
5	203,089	15,445	218,534
10	113,869	15,969	129,839
15	84,711	16,470	101,181
20	70,555	17,039	87,594
25	73,268	17,669	83,565
30	65,895	18,316	78,034
35	59,719	18,956	74,509
40	55,553	19,579	72,207
45	52,629	20,176	70,694
50	50,518	20,744	69,708
52	48,964	20,962	69,421
55	48,459	21,279	69,081

ACR_t denotes the after-tax capital recovery cost at time t (Table 12.5b); $EAE_{AOM,t}$ denotes the annuitized after-tax operation and maintenance costs at time t (Table 12.5c).

Table 12.5e Pre-Tax and After-Tax Wealth Analysis of a 1,000 kW Ground Mount Solar Array Located Near Syracuse, New York, USA, Given a 5% Discount Rate and a Flat Tax Rate of 21%

Year	Output	$NPV_{\infty,t}$	$EAE_{NPV\infty,t}$	$ANPV_{\infty,t}$	$EAE_{ANPV\infty,t}$
	(kWh)	($)	($/year)	($)	($/year)
1	1,186,212	−19,836,128	−991,806	−15,670,541	−783,527
5	1,153,345	−1,667,440	−83,372	−1,285,091	−64,255
10	1,113,539	519,409	25,970	428,380	21,419
15	1,075,107	1,192,795	59,640	955,733	47,787
20	1,038,002	1,490,681	74,534	1,188,820	59,441
25	1,002,177	1,552,179	77,609	1,236,109	61,805
30	967,588	1,656,831	82,842	1,317,961	65,898
35	934,193	1,715,384	85,769	1,363,664	68,183
40	901,951	1,747,163	87,358	1,388,380	69,419
45	870,822	1,762,744	88,137	1,400,408	70,020
50	840,767	1,768,324	88,416	1,404,609	70,230
52	829,037	1,768,664	88,433	1,404,810	70,241
55	811,749	1,767,714	88,386	1,403,973	70,199

NPV_{∞} denotes the pre-tax net present value wealth of replacing the solar array at time t given by equation (7.6b); $EAE_{NPV\infty,t}$ denotes the pre-tax annuitized wealth at time t; $ANPV_{\infty}$ denotes the after-tax net present value wealth of replacing the solar array at time t; $EAE_{ANPV\infty,t}$ denotes the after-tax annuitized wealth at time t

Maximizing equation (7.6b) determines the optimal time, T, to replace the solar array. Table 7.2g shows that the maximizing wealth optimal time to replace the solar array was at 52 years. Interestingly, the maximizing wealth optimal time to replace the solar array is also given by the maximum of $EAE(NPV_{\infty})_t$. The pre-tax and after-tax wealth analysis is given in Table 12.5e.

Table 12.5e shows that the pre-tax wealth decision to replace the solar array at 52 years is the same as the after-tax wealth decision. This is also illustrated using Figure 12.2. The curves representing pre-tax and after-tax wealth, NPV_{∞} and $ANPV_{\infty}$ respectively, of this straightforward flat example show the original wealth line is reduced by 21% at each time t. Both curves are concave after year 21. Thus, the point describing maximizing $NPV_{\infty,t}$ is the same as maximizing $ANPV_{\infty,t}$.

Capital Gains Tax

To encourage long-term investing, the government may charge a lower tax rate for income generated from capital assets. For example, in the US the capital gains tax rate is tied to the ordinary income brackets. The tax rate on most capital gain is no higher than 15% for most taxpayers (www.irs.gov/taxtopics/tc409 accessed 26 December 2019). Examples of capital assets are home, personal-use items like household furnishings, and stocks or bonds. A key in defining a capital asset and its

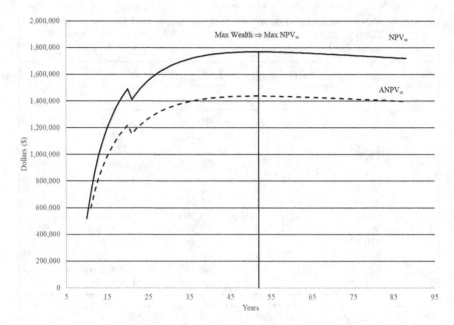

Figure 12.2 Pre-Tax and After-Tax Wealth Analysis of a 1,000 kW Ground Mount Solar Array Located Near Syracuse, New York, USA, Given a 5% Discount Rate and a Flat Tax Rate of 21% With NPV_{∞} and $ANPV_{\infty}$ Denoting the Pre-Tax and After-Tax Net Present Value Wealth, Respectively

gains is that the asset must have been held for longer than one year. Given such an asset, its capital gains are calculated using equation (12.4):

$$\text{Capital Gain} = \text{Sales Revenue} - \text{Purchase Price} \qquad (12.4)$$

For example, revenue from a commercial timber harvest may be classified as a capital gain depending on the context (Hayne et al. 2001). In addition to holding the stumpage for more than one year, qualifying for capital gains also depends on how the timber is sold or disposed. The four strategies to dispose of timber are: (1) outright or lump sum sale of stumpage – generally capital gains; (2) pay as cut stumpage – generally capital gains; (3) you cut and sell logs roadside – generally ordinary income; and (4) percentage sale – generally ordinary income (https:// smallfarms.cornell.edu/2015/07/financial-timber/ accessed 19 March 2021; www. timbertax.org/getstarted/sales/capitalgains/ accessed 19 March 2021).

Inheritance Tax

An inheritance tax serves to prevent the perpetuation of wealth and is seen as an important leveler of society. Inheritance (death) tax is imposed on the transfer of the "taxable estate" of a deceased person. The taxable estate consists of an accounting of everything you own or have certain interests in at the date of death: Cash and securities, real estate, insurance, trusts, annuities, business interests, and other assets valued at "current" fair market value (www.irs.gov/businesses/small-businesses-self-employed/estate-tax accessed 26 December 2019). While some of these items owned may be easy to value at current fair market value, others may not. Estate taxes or the inheritance tax is of concern to most family farm landowners as one of every five acres of family forest land is owned by someone who is at least 75 years old (Butler 2008). These owners will be looking to pass their land to their heirs. A concern of the inheritance tax is if the estate is primarily real estate; for example, for forestland, the heirs may not have the cash flow to pay the inheritance tax. Consequently, improper estate planning, which includes management of their forest proprieties, may force the heirs to liquidate the timber or land assets to pay inheritance taxes.

More information about estate taxes can be found in Estate Planning for Forest Landowners: What Will Become of Your Timberland? 2009 United States Forest Service Southern Research Station General Technical Report SRS-112 (Siegel et al. 2009; https://www.fs.usda.gov/research/treesearch/31987 accessed 6 September 2023).

Property Tax

Property tax is an *ad valorem* or "according to value" tax based on the assessed value of the real property. Real property is defined as land, buildings (warehouses, offices factories, and mills), and anything affixed to the land. In the case of forestland, real property may include standing timber as is the case in New York State (NY RPTL Section 102 (12) www.nysenate.gov/legislation/laws/RPT/102 accessed 11 December 2019). Assessed value is generally based on the highest and best use of the property, which may or may not be its current use. Highest and best use valuation is based on four conditions: What is (i) physically possible, (ii) financially feasible, (iii) legally permissible, and (iv) most productive from a financial perspective. Often, market transactions of comparable properties are used to determine highest and best use. States have different requirements for how frequently reassessments are conducted. Nine states do not have state provisions for when reassessments take place – this includes New York. Most states follow an annual to five- to ten-year schedule (https://taxfoundation.org/state-provisions-property-reassessment/ accessed 19 March 2021).

In the case of forestland, while standing timber is often part of real property, it may not be included as part of the assessed value for a variety of reasons. A principal one is that many states combine a modified property tax with a yield or severance tax as part of tax incentive programs to promote forest management (www.timbertax.org/statetaxes/quickreference/ accessed 19 March 2021).[4] However, to examine the potential impacts of a property tax on an entrepreneur's management decisions (i.e., the financially optimal multiple rotation age), I will examine two general cases: (1) the assessment includes both land and timber[5] and (2) the assessment includes only land.

The annual property tax payment is based on the assessed value of the real property multiplied by the property tax rate. This tax rate is often called the millage rate (or mill rate) and represents the amount per $1,000 of assessed value. Thus, a property tax rate of 1 mill is $1.00 per $1,000.00 of assessed value. The amount of tax paid is then 0.001 × (assessed value). The millage rate, τ, for a taxing district (e.g., town or county) is based on the district's projected budget, B, over the assessed property values in the district, V, as shown in equation (12.5):

$$\tau = \frac{\left(B \middle/ V\right)}{1000} \tag{12.5}$$

I will assume a tax rate of 8 mills or $\tau = 0.008$ to illustrate calculating a property tax.

Table 12.6 illustrates the annual property tax payment for the Loblolly Pine Plantation practical application assuming the assessed value of the land is the land expectation value of $1,783.40 per acre at a plantation age of 15 and the assessed value of the timber is the liquidation value of the timber which will be reassessed annually.

Volume at plantation age 12 = 1,823.64 cu ft/acre
Liquidation value = 1823.64 × 1.81 = $3,300.79 per acre
Tax payment on inventory = 3,300.79 × 0.008 = $26.41 per acre per year
Tax payment on land = 1783.40 × 0.008 = $14.27 per acre per year
Total property tax payment = 26.41 + 14.27 = $40.67 per acre per year

Table 12.6 shows that the land component is constant while the timber component increases with time. Consequently, the annual tax payment increases with time and can be described as a variable cost. If the timber is only reassessed periodically, then the property tax will still be a variable cost if the periodicity of reassessment is less than the rotation age. If the periodicity of the reassessment is greater than or equal to the rotation age, then the annually property tax will be a fixed cost.

Table 12.6 Property Tax Payments Given the Loblolly Pine Plantation Practical Application[‡]

Plantation Age	Yield (cu ft/acre)	Tax on Inventory ($/acre/year)	Tax on Land ($/acre/year)	Total Tax Payment ($/acre/year)
8	803.11	11.63	14.27	25.90
9	1,035.13	14.99	14.27	29.26
10	1,285.26	18.61	14.27	32.88
11	1,549.36	22.43	14.27	36.70
12	1,823.64	26.41	14.27	40.67
13	2,104.73	30.48	14.27	44.74
14	2,389.62	34.60	14.27	48.87
15	2,675.73	38.74	14.27	53.01

[‡] The stumpage price is equal to $1.81 per cubic foot (cu ft) and the tax rate is 8 mills

Equation (12.6) will be used to illustrate the impact of a property tax on the financially optimal multiple rotation age if described as a variable cost. The after-tax land expectation value for the financially optimal rotation age T, $LEV_T(\tau)$, is given by equation (12.6) and based on work by Amacher et al. (2009)

$$LEV_T(\tau) = LEV_T - \frac{\sum_{t=1}^{T} \tau \cdot (PQ(t) + LEV_T) \cdot (1+r)^{-t}}{1-(1+r)^{-T}}$$

$$= LEV_T - \frac{\sum_{t=1}^{T} \tau \cdot PQ(t) \cdot (1+r)^{-t}}{1-(1+r)^{-T}} - \frac{\tau \cdot LEV_T}{r}$$

(12.6)

where
LEV_T denotes the pre-tax land expectation value calculated using equation (7.13) at plantation T;
τ denotes the property tax rate;
r denotes real interest rate;
P denotes a stumpage price;
Q(t) denotes the production system; and
PQ(t) denotes the liquidation value of the inventory.

The right-hand side of equation (12.6) contains three components. The first is defined as the pre-tax land expectation value at rotation age T, LEV_T. The second is the present value of annual tax payment on the reassessed timber inventory. The third is the present value of the annual tax payment on the land. Table 12.7 illustrates the management implications if the annual property tax is a variable cost, equation (12.6), for the Loblolly Pine Plantation practical application using a mill rate of 0.008, a real interest rate of 8%, a stumpage price of $1.81 per cubic foot,

Table 12.7 After-Tax Land Expectation Value Given the Loblolly Pine Plantation Practical Application – Variable Cost

Plantation Age	Yield (cu ft/acre)	Present Value of the Tax on Inventory ($/acre)	Present Value of the Tax on Land ($/acre)	Pre-Tax Land Expectation Value ($/acre)	After-Tax Land Expectation Value ($/acre)
8	803.11	44.19	104.37	1,043.68	895.12
9	1,035.13	55.66	126.41	1,264.07	1,082.00
10	1,285.26	67.87	143.81	1,438.13	1,226.44
11	1,549.36	80.64	157.09	1,570.94	1,333.20
12	1,823.64	93.79	166.74	1,667.39	1,406.87
13	2,104.73	107.15	173.21	1,732.12	1,451.76
14	2,389.62	120.58	176.95	1,769.46	**1,471.93**
15	2,675.73	133.98	178.34	**1,783.40**	1,471.08

and the production system given by Amateis and Burkhart (1985) and Burkhart et al. (1985).

Table 12.7 shows that if the property tax is described as a variable cost it is non-neutral, which is consistent with the general conclusion derived from equation (12.1b). That is, the financially optimal multiple rotation age decreases as a result of the annual property tax on land and timber.[6] In addition, Klemperer (1996) showed that if the property tax is defined as a variable cost, it is also biased against high establishment costs.

If reassessment occurs only once during any potential rotation, then the annual property tax is a fixed cost. Equation (12.7a) illustrates the after-tax land expectation value $LEV_T(\tau)$, assuming the assessed value of the timber inventory and land is based on a defined rotation age T:

$$LEV_T(\tau) = LEV_T - \frac{\tau \cdot (LEV_T + PQ(T))}{r} \tag{12.7a}$$

Equation (12.7b) illustrates the after-tax land expectation value $LEV_T(\tau)$, assuming the assessment is based only on the land value defined rotation age T:[7]

$$LEV_T(\tau) = LEV_T - \frac{\tau \cdot LEV_T}{r} \tag{12.7b}$$

Table 12.8 illustrates the management implications if the annual property tax is a fixed cost, equations (12.7a) and (12.7b), for the Loblolly Pine Plantation practical application using a plantation age of 15 to define the land and timber inventory's assessed values.

As shown by Table 12.8, the after-tax financially optimal multiple rotation age is the same as the pre-tax rotation age. In this case the annual property tax is neutral

Table 12.8 After-Tax Land Expectation Value Given the Loblolly Pine Plantation Practical Application – Fixed Cost

Plantation Age	Present Value of the Tax on Inventory Plus Land ($/acre)	Pre-Tax Land Expectation Value ($/acre)	After-Tax Land Expectation Value Inventory Plus Land ($/acre)	After-Tax Land Expectation Value Land Only ($/acre)
9	662.65	1,264.07	601.42	1,085.73
10	662.65	1,438.13	775.48	1,259.79
11	662.65	1,570.94	908.30	1,392.60
12	662.65	1,667.39	1,004.75	1,489.06
13	662.65	1,732.12	1,069.48	1,553.78
14	662.65	1,769.46	1,106.81	1,591.12
15	662.65	**1,783.40**	**1,120.75**	**1,605.06**
16	662.65	1,777.57	1,114.93	1,599.23

with respect to management.[8] A property tax can cause you to stop management if the annual property tax payment is larger than the annualized pre-tax land expectation value. A property tax can also cause land use to change if the tax payment is larger than the opportunity cost of alternative land uses. For example, the fixed cost annual property tax payment is $53.01 or $14.27 per acre per year based on the assessed value of land and timber or land only, respectively (Table 12.6). The pre-tax land value can be annualized using equation (12.8):

$$LEV_A = LEV_T \times r \tag{12.8}$$

For the Loblolly Pine Plantation practical application, the annualized pre-tax land expectation value, LEV_A, is $142.67 (=1,783.40 × 0.08) per acre per year. This is consistent with the general conclusion derived from equation (12.1a).

The property tax can be neutral or non-neutral depending on if it is realized as a fixed or variable cost, respectively, by the entrepreneur. For example, in New York State property tax rates for class 1 residential properties in 1981/82 were 8.95% and in 2019/2020 were 21.167% giving a ~2.23% annual increase (https://www1.nyc. gov/site/finance/taxes/property-tax-rates.page accessed 11 December 2019). Property tax rate increases for 2019–2020 were capped at 2% per year (www.osc.state. ny.us/press/releases/july19/071119.htm accessed 11 December 2019). Finally, the 2019–2020 budget bill made the annual 2% increase cap permanent. So, are New York State property taxes neutral? The 2% annual cap decreases uncertainty. However, if the increases are perceived as not significant, then yes, the property tax is neutral. If the increases are perceived as significant, then no, the property tax is not neutral.

Property taxes are also considered to have a time bias. Forest properties generally do not provide annual positive net revenues to pay the tax. As a result, the burden of the property tax increases as the income from the property is moved into the future or the periodic incomes from the property become less frequent.

Productivity tax

A productivity tax is an annual tax based on the "ability" of the land to grow timber.[9] Forest productivity, FP_t, is defined as monetary value of the annual net yield minus average costs (Klemperer 1996) and is given by equation (12.9)

$$
\begin{aligned}
FP_t &= \frac{\dfrac{P \cdot Q(t) - C}{t}}{r} \\
&= \frac{P \cdot \dfrac{Q(t)}{t} - \dfrac{C}{t}}{r} \\
&= \frac{P \cdot MAI_t - AC}{r}
\end{aligned}
\tag{12.9}
$$

where

Q(t) denotes the estimated volume per acre for a given site quality or index at time t;

P denotes stumpage price;

C denotes the per acre costs;

r denotes the real interest rate;

MAI_t denotes the mean annual increment at stand age t or the average annual growth, equations (2.9) and (2.10); and

AC denotes the annual average costs or the annual per acre costs.[10]

The numerator gives the average annual net revenue for that stand based on the yield potential of a given site quality or index irrespective of the actual harvest or standing timber (Klemperer 1996; Koskela and Ollikainen 2003; Mutanen and Toppinen 2005).[11] The denominator is used to capitalize the expected ability of the stand to produce annual net revenues. The annual per acre tax payment is given by equation (12.10)

$$FP_t(\tau) = \tau \times FP_t \qquad (12.10)$$

where the tax rate, τ, is given by equation (12.5). Using the Loblolly Pine Plantation practical application, the annual forest productivity tax is \$28.23 per acre per year.

Forest Productivity at Plantation Age 15

$$FP_{15} = \frac{P \cdot \dfrac{Q(t)}{t} - \dfrac{C}{t}}{r} = \frac{1.81 \times 167.23 - \dfrac{305.54}{15}}{0.08} = 3,529.03 \, \$\big/ \text{acre}$$

Annual Forest Productivity Tax Payment

$$FT_{15}(\tau) = FT_{15} \times \tau = 3,529.03 \times 0.008 = 28.23 \, \$\big/ \text{acre} \big/ \text{year}$$

The capitalization of forest productivity as given in equation (12.9) assumes that a net revenue of $(P \times MAI_t - AC)$ is received every year. In the case of an even-aged forest, this would require a fully regulated forest structure.[12] In the case of an uneven-aged forest, this would require sufficient stocking such that an annual harvest could take place (Klemperer 1996). If the landowner does not have either of these forest structures, the forest would not produce the annual net revenue needed to cover the productivity tax. Thus, the productivity tax is generally considered to have a time bias.

As defined, the productivity tax is an annual fixed cost. As illustrated in Chapter 5 – Profit, fixed costs do not change the profit searching rule. Thus, the productivity tax is considered neutral. A productivity tax can cause you to stop management if the annual tax payment is larger than the annualized pre-tax land expectation value. A productivity tax can also cause land use to change if the tax payment is larger than the opportunity cost of alternative land uses. This is consistent with the general conclusion derived from equation (12.1a). For the Loblolly Pine Plantation practical application the annualized pre-tax land expectation value, LEV_A, is \$142.67 (= 1,783.40 × 0.08) per acre per year.

Yield Tax

A yield tax is normally levied at the time of harvest – every time there is a *positive revenue* or merchantable timber is removed – and is a percent of the value of the forest yield or harvest.[13] A yield tax payment, $Y_t(\tau)$, is given by equation (12.11)

$$Y_t(\tau) = P \times Q(t) \times \tau \tag{12.11}$$

Where τ denotes the yield tax rate and all other variables are defined as before. Using the Loblolly Pine Plantation practical application as an example, the yield tax is \$290.58 per acre using a yield tax rate of 6%.

Yield tax payment

$$Y_{15}(\tau = 6\%) = P \times Q(15) \times \tau = 1.81 \times 2675.73 \times 0.06 = 290.58 \, \$/\text{acre}$$

This tax eliminates the time bias of the property and productivity taxes; the entrepreneur only pays the tax when they have the revenue from a merchantable harvest.

A yield tax effectively reduces the stumpage price, and the revenue, the entrepreneur receives for any harvest. This is illustrated in equation (12.12):

$$\begin{aligned} \text{Revenue} &= P \times Q(t) - \left(P \times Q(t) \times \tau\right) \\ &= (P - P \times \tau) \times Q(t) \\ &= P \times (1 - \tau) \times Q(t) \end{aligned} \tag{12.12}$$

The pre-yield tax revenue for the Loblolly Pine Plantation practical application is \$4,843.07 (= 2,675.73 × 1.81) per acre and the post-yield tax revenue is \$4,552.49 (= 2,675.73 × 1.70). Chang (1982) and Johansson and Löfgren (1985) show that the impact of a reduction in stumpage price is to lengthen the financially optimal multiple rotation age. If the entrepreneur does not harvest, then they do not have to pay the yield tax. The yield tax is considered non-neutral. This is consistent with the general conclusion derived from equation (12.1b).

A yield tax is often used to replace the general property tax and is generally applied to renewable resources. A yield tax would seem to offer a logical means for eliminating some of the difficulties imposed on timber production by the property and productivity tax. However, a yield tax by its nature cannot provide a predictable, dependable source of income to the taxing entity (e.g., town, municipality, or state).

Forestry Tax Incentive Programs

Many states in the United States have a policy of promoting forestry and forest products by private landowners. Unfortunately, neither the annual property nor productivity tax helps meet this policy goal. These programs take two general forms: (1) a modified annual property or productivity tax, or (2) a modified annual property or productivity taxed coupled with a yield tax. A modified property or productivity tax is often developed using a reduced tax rate. The land is assessed in its current use rather than highest and best use, or a simple flat per acre rate is charged. Landowners must meet certain restrictions, and there are penalties for withdrawing from the program. The National Timber Tax website provides a summary of the forest tax structures of all 50 states (www.timbertax.org/statetaxes/quickreference/ accessed 19 March 2021).

In New York State, for example, Real Property Tax Law 480a provides forest landowners with a lower annual property tax coupled with a 6% yield tax on any commercial harvest (www.dec.ny.gov/lands/5236.html accessed 19 March 2021; www.tax.ny.gov/research/property/assess/manuals/vol4/pt2/sec4_08/sec480_a. htm accessed 19 March 2021; and www.tax.ny.gov/research/property/reports/forest/index.htm accessed 19 March 2021). To be eligible for this program, the following conditions must be met:

- A management plan prepared by a qualified forester *must be approved* by New York State's Department of Environmental Conservation listing all harvests, stocking levels, etc.
- Ten-year commitment and annual recommitment.
- Sufficient stocking of trees to allow a merchantable timber harvest within 30 years from original certification (§199.1 p Definitions). An owner *must* harvest a merchantable forest crop as specified in their management plan. Flexibility is allowed, however, in that an owner may request alterations in the work schedule for economic or biological reasons.
- The forest land cannot have been cut within the previous three years (with some exceptions).
- At least 50 contiguous acres are used exclusively for forest crops.
- The owner can use 10 standard cords (4-foot × 4-foot × 8-foot) or equivalent without paying a yield tax. Any noncommercial cutting as defined by the approved management plan is not subject to the yield tax.

How to Use Economic Information – Taxes – to Make Better Business Decisions

Paraphrasing Benjamin Franklin, two things in life are certain – death and taxes. This chapter's purpose is *not* to make you a tax expert, but to make you aware that taxes could impose a burden on a business or individual. Taxes are a cost that the entrepreneur must take into account. The cash flows that you analyze for your clients will probably have tax implications at the local, state, or federal level. Taxes can be described as a loss in revenue, as with a yield tax, that affects the Pillar of Revenue. Or a cost, as with the property and productivity tax, that affects the Pillar of Cost. Thus the rule of thumb concerning taxes is: There will always be tax implications from any business management action – maybe not today but sometime in the future. If it turns out there are not, you look like a genius for having thought of everything. If it turns out there are, you look like a genius for having thought of everything. Ignoring the tax implications of any management actions could add unexpected costs and penalties that you must cover, plus any legal actions brought by the taxing entity against you.

From the entrepreneur's point of view, the concern is the impact taxes will have on management decisions given financial parameters (e.g., prices, costs, and discount rates) and planning horizon within the context of their ownership goals and objectives. If dealing with a forest-related business, taxes may impact the existing forest condition (e.g., forest structure, density, species composition, and age). As Johansson and Löfgren have stated, "All kinds of taxes will decrease the value of the land" (Johansson and Löfgren 1985: 100). Besides the effect on land values, to what extent are management decisions such as rotation age, thinning timing and intensity, and regeneration method affected by taxes? Klemperer (1996) proposed using a spreadsheet to simulate the degree to which a given tax will affect management actions. This approach is similar in nature to sensitivity analysis I discussed in Chapter 8 – Risk and illustrated in Tables 8.2a, 8.2b, 8.3a, and 8.3b. The argument presented in Chapter 8 – Risk for using sensitivity analysis also holds in this case.

Notes

1 I will use the United States federal tax systems as the basis of this discussion.
2 A C corporation is a legal structure for a corporation in which the owners, or shareholders, are taxed separately from the entity.
3 As illustrated by Table 12.3, depreciation and interest expenses are part of taxable income. The 2017 Tax Act still allows businesses take depreciation. However, the rules for deducting depreciation are a little complicated; for example, due the Investment Tax Credit, the solar array's owner can only deduct 85% of the cost over a five-year period. In addition, a Modified Accelerated Cost Recovery System (MACRS) allows for an accelerated depreciation. In addition, there are differences between what the federal government vs. state governments will allow for the annual depreciation expense. Finally, the Internal Revenue Service rules regarding deducting interest expenses are also somewhat complicated (www.irs.gov/newsroom/basic-questions-and-answers-about-the-limitation-on-the-deduction-for-business-interest-expense accessed 9 March 2023). So, to keep the example as straightforward as possible, I will avoid these complications.
4 I will discuss these tax incentive programs later in this chapter.
5 This also called an unmodified property tax (Chang 1982).
6 Chang (1982) showed a similar result when both timber and land were reassessed annually.
7 A property tax that only includes the value of the forestland is called a land value or site value tax and in some cases a current use tax.

8 This result is consistent with how total fixed costs impact the development of the profit searching rule discussed in Chapter 5 – Profit.

9 There is a tax called a site productivity tax that is also based on the ability of the land to grow timber. The concept of site is based on a site index or land expectation value concept. This is generally an annual tax.

10 Equation (12.9) has the form of the present value of a perpetual every-period series described in Appendix A of Chapter 6 – Capital Theory: Investment Analysis.

11 An interested reader may want to compare and contrast equation (12.9) with the calculating forest rent given in Chapter 7 – The Natural Resources Management Puzzle.

12 A fully regulated or normal even-aged forest has equal acres in each age class up to and including the rotation age (Helms 1998).

13 A yield tax is often called a severance tax.

13 Developing Business Plans

Acknowledgements

The information provided in this chapter would not have been possible without the continued help and support of the State University of New York's College of Environmental Science and Forestry's (ESF's) Forest Properties Department. The professional staff deserve special mention:

Mr. Robert MacGregor – Director
Mr. Mark Appleby – Forest Property Manager I
Mr. Ryan Ash – Forest Property Manager II
Ms. Jill Rahn – Forest Resource Analyst
Mr. Ray Bartholomew – Forest Worker III
Mr. Norris Shute – Forest Worker III

Abstract

In this chapter I develop 10-year business plans for two existing for-profit businesses that are managed by ESF's Forest Properties Department: A maple syrup operation and a log yard and firewood operation. To illustrate the components of business planning, I will develop a 10-year business plan for a proposed for-profit business: A slab mill. These practical applications are used to illustrate how a business plan is derived from the economic information contained within the Architectural Plan for Profit and can be used to make business decisions about continuing to operate a business, in the case of the maple syrup operation and the log yard and firewood operation, or to start a new business, in the case of the slab mill. The financial analyses used draw on those presented earlier in this textbook and describe three fundamental financial accounting statements used in businesses.

Preamble

In Chapter 3 – Costs, I examined the statement: If you do not control costs, you will lose control of profits. In Chapter 4 – Revenue, I examined the statements: Revenue

DOI: 10.4324/9781315678719-13

is the output quantity "sold" multiplied by the price you charge. Thus, output produced but not sold generates no revenue but does generate costs. In Chapter 5 – Profit, I examined the statements: If your output does not provide the customer with value, they will not buy it, consequently generating no revenue to cover production costs and no profits. These still hold when writing a business plan. A business plan is derived from the economic information contained within the Architectural Plan for Profit as shown in Figures 13.1a and 13.b.

Wealth is created by accumulating resources or assets – capital – used to generate multiple single-period profits and multi-period investment profits. Wealth is the capitalization of these profits.

After a brief description of the standard financial statements used in business, I will use a proposed slab mill as a practical application to introduce, develop, and illustrate the components of a business plan. This will be followed by business plans for two existing ESF operations: a for-profit maple syrup operation and a log yard and firewood operation.[1] These are actual existing for-profit businesses located on the Svend O. Heiberg Memorial Forest located 25 miles south of Syracuse, New York, in the towns of Tully, Pompey, Truxton, and Fabius. The initial 1,650-acre forest was established in June 1948 and named after ESF professor Svend O. Heiberg. The current forest is 3,900 acres and serves as an outdoor classroom and laboratory for teaching, research, and outreach. It is composed of 1,395 acres of Allegheny hardwoods; 1,640 acres of conifer plantations; 590 acres of

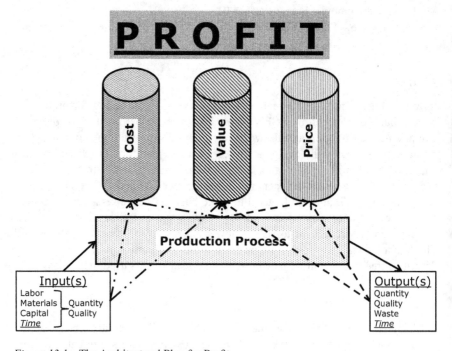

Figure 13.1a The Architectural Plan for Profit

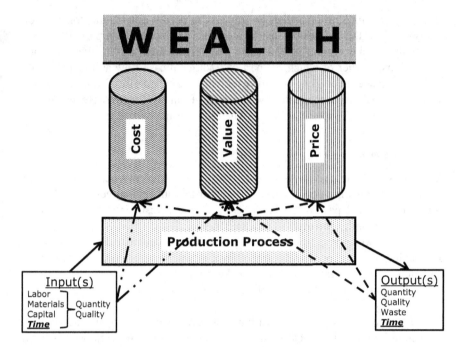

Figure 13.1b The Architectural Plan for Wealth

open and brushy areas; 245 acres containing the sugarbush, sap house, sugar house, administrative buildings, and classrooms, and so on; and 30 acres of water. The data used in these business plans are the actual business data provided to me by ESF's Forest Properties Department.

Business Plan Financial Information[2]

There are four fundamental financial accounting statements: (1) cash flow statement, (2) income statement, (3) balance statement, and (4) statement of changes in equity.[3] I will focus only on the first three. The cash flow statement shows the exchange of money between a company and the outside world for a defined time period. The income statement shows how much money a company made and spent for a defined time period. The balance statement shows what you own (assets), what you owe (liabilities), and what's left over (net value, net worth, or equity in the business).

The focus will be on using the economic information provided in these three statements, and derived from the Architectural Plan for Profit, as part of developing business plans and helping manage a business. Thus, I will be combining the two concepts of accounting: financial and managerial. The key difference between managerial and financial accounting is that managerial accounting information is aimed at helping managers within the organization make decisions: It is not based on past performance but on current and future trends. In contrast, financial accounting is aimed at providing information to parties outside the organization: Analyzing how the business has performed during a specific time period.

Finally, breakeven and net present value (NPV) analyses are two additional components, neither of which are part of traditional cash flow and income statements or balance sheet. They are, however, valuable economic information that can be derived easily from the cash flow statement. Both NPV and breakeven analysis were discussed in Chapter 6 – Capital Theory: Investment Analysis.

Cash Flow Statement

A cash flow statement provides data regarding all *cash* inflows a company receives from both its ongoing operations and external investment sources, as well as all *cash* outflows that pay for business activities and investments during a defined period (e.g., monthly, quarterly, and annually).

There are two approaches to creating the cash flow statement: The direct method and the indirect method. I will use the direct method as it is more straightforward for calculating net present value and breakeven analysis.

A cash flow statement includes the following cost categories:[4]

Cash balances are the amount of cash available at the beginning and ending of the accounting period. The cash balances could be positive or negative. Cash balance at the beginning of an accounting period is the cash balance from the end of the last accounting period. For net present value and breakeven analysis, the beginning and ending cash balances are ignored.

Financial activities include cash inflows from owners or cash outflows to owners. Financial activities include borrowing cash (inflow) from creditors and repaying the principal (cash outflow) to creditors. Interest payments to creditors (cash outflow) are reported in the operating activities section of the cash flow statement.

Investing activities involve cash outflows to purchase long-term assets such as plants, property, and equipment or cash inflows from selling long-term assets.

Operating activities involve cash inflow revenues from selling a product or service and cash outflows for expenses related to the company's core business activities; namely, fixed and variable costs such as wages and salaries, manufacturing, distributing, marketing, and tax payments.

I will include an amortization schedule for loans on purchasing capital assets as part of the cash flow statement. An amortization schedule shows how loan payments are split between interest and principal payments. As will be illustrated, the balance between principal and interest payments reverses over time as early payments consist primarily of interest and later payments consist primarily of principal. Because of the inverse relationship between principal and interest paid, the rate at which you *gain equity in a capital asset* is much slower in the initial years of a loan than in later years. Interest payments are deducted from annual income while principal payments reduce liabilities and increase equity in capital assets. This demonstrates the value of making extra principal payments, as each extra payment results in a larger repaid portion of the principal (i.e., building equity) and reduces the interest due on each future payment.

Income Statement

The income statement summarizes a company's revenues (sales) and operating expenses quarterly and annually for a company's fiscal year.[5] Examples of a company's revenues include sales of all the products it produces, service revenues, and fees earned.

Operating expenses are the expenses incurred in earning operating revenues.[6] Examples of a company's operating expenses include advertising; costs of goods sold (COGS); salaries and fringe benefits; the Dirti-5 (*d*epreciation, *i*nterest, *r*ent/ repairs, *t*axes, *i*nsurance); sales, general and administrative; and maintenance and overhead costs. COGS is the direct costs of producing the good or service and includes material cost, direct labor production costs, and any fixed costs associated with producing the good or service directly. COGS does not include administrative costs. If revenue increases, more resources are required to produce the goods or services; thus, COGS must also increase.

As with the cash flow statement, the income statement is developed using nondiscounted dollars. The income statement is different from the cash flow statement in at least three aspects. First, only the interest payments are included. The principal payment is a reduction of a liability and is reported on the balance sheet and cash flow statement. Second, depreciation is included in an income statement but not a cash flow statement. Depreciation is a noncash expense and thus would not appear in a cash flow statement. However, depreciation does impact income.[7] According to generally accepted accounting principles, there are four methods for calculating depreciation: (1) straight-line, (2) declining balance or accelerated depreciation, (3) sum-of-the-years' digits, and (4) units of production. I will calculate depreciation using a straight-line method. The steps to determine straight-line depreciation are

1. Subtract the estimated salvage value from the asset's purchase price.
2. Determine the estimated useful life of the asset. It is easiest if you use a standard useful life for each asset class.

Finally, the cash flow statement includes a cash balance that accumulates over the analysis time horizon. The income statement does not include this directly. This is included in the balance statement as part of the retained earnings calculation.

Net income, found at the bottom of the income statement, is the renowned bottom line of a business. Net income or net profit is an all-inclusive metric for a business's profitability that reflects how effectively a business is managing its revenues and costs.

Balance Statement

This statement shows what you own (assets), what you owe (liabilities), and what's left over (net value or equity in the business). A basic tenet of double-entry book-keeping is that total assets (what a business owns) must equal liabilities plus equity (how the assets are financed). In other words, the balance sheet must balance. Subtracting liabilities from assets shows the net worth of the business. As with the cash flow statement and the income statement, the balance sheet is developed using non-discounted dollars.

Slab Mill

I will use the slab mill as a practical application to illustrate the three financial accounting statements and the components of a business plan. In 2016 and 2017, I had my students conduct a business feasibility analysis of purchasing a slab mill and kiln to produce approximately 4,000 board feet of slabs per year. A slab is a broad, flat, thick piece of wood. Live or natural edge slabs still have the bark attached. Slabs are cut in various thicknesses from 1 inch to 3 inches or more. The thicker and longer the slab, the greater its value. Slabs are prized for counter tops, tables, and similar furniture. In addition, a slab must be kiln dried before it can be made into furniture. On our college forest properties, we have large trees of the desired species available (e.g., black cherry – *Prunus serotina* Ehrh., and sugar maple – *Acer saccharum* Marsh.). This analysis will be used to develop and illustrate the financial information and the components of a business plan empirically.

Business Plan Components

The number of components to include in a business plan range from 3 to 11 depending on sources ranging from business management textbooks to the internet. I will use the following, which correlate closely to the Architectural Plan for Profit.

Executive Summary

While an executive summary should be informative in nature, it should also capture the audience's attention immediately so that they are motivated to read the remainder of the document. A tightly informative introduction, body, and conclusion should allow someone with no prior knowledge of your business or industry to read your executive summary and understand the key findings from your research and the primary elements of your business plan. Your executive summary should highlight the best features of your business plan. An executive summary provides readers a brief report containing background information and a concise and succinct analysis of the topic being discussed or presented. It is intended as an aid to decision making by managers and has been described as the most important part of a business plan or feasibility analysis.

The following executive summary is derived from the students' business plans from 2016 and 2017:

Over a 10-year period, the Heiberg Slab Mill will aim to provide high-quality live-edge hardwood slabs (≥1 inches) by sustainably harvesting large diameter hardwood trees (≥12-inch diameter at breast height) from the College of Environmental Science and Forestry's (ESF's) Heiberg Forest. Creating a slab mill from the ground up requires many costs, both fixed and variable. Fixed costs include capital equipment loan payments for the mill, kiln, and storage facilities as well as spare parts, maintenance, electricity, and a small stipend for an ESF summer intern. Variable costs include forestry personal, forklift rentals for loading and unloading slabs, and logging costs. Revenue is a function of price and value; without proper knowledge of the market and your production system the business will fail. The first step for determining revenue was establishing a set price for the output based on the market. The price of 5.51 dollars per board foot ($/bdft) for sugar maple (*Acer saccharum* Marsh.) and 5.97 $/bdft for black cherry (*Prunus serotina* Ehrh.) was determined. After running through the analysis, at these price points the cumulative net present value was not positive until year six. Even then, we must sell 4,000 board feet per year, which is not feasible given the current slab market in central New York. For the reasons stated above, this business venture will not succeed.

Mission, Goals, and Objectives

The mission statement is a concise and succinct summary of what the business is or its reason for being (David and David 2003; David et al. 2014). A mission statement addresses:

- What the business produces and what distinguishes it from competitor's products;
- Who your customers are and how the unique characteristics of your product(s), e.g., quantity, quality, and so on, add value to the customer's experience;
- What your business philosophy (e.g., sustainable profits) and social responsibility are (e.g., to employees, stakeholders, environment, etc.).

A mission statement involves all levels of the organization and is customer focused.

Goals describe what you want your business to achieve. Thus, as a group, they describe the desired performance(s), the desired timeframe, and the necessary resources to reach the goals. Goals must support the mission.

Objectives describe actions that are intended to be accomplished over the 10-year planning horizon. Objectives are specific, measurable, achievable, relevant, and time-bound (SMART). Objectives must support the goals.

The relationship among mission, goals, and objectives is given graphically in Figure 13.2.

The following mission, goals, and objectives were derived from the students' business plans from 2016 and 2017:

Mission Statement: To sustainably harvest and provide high quality live-edge Sugar Maple and Black Cherry hardwood slabs for local artisans, woodworkers, and

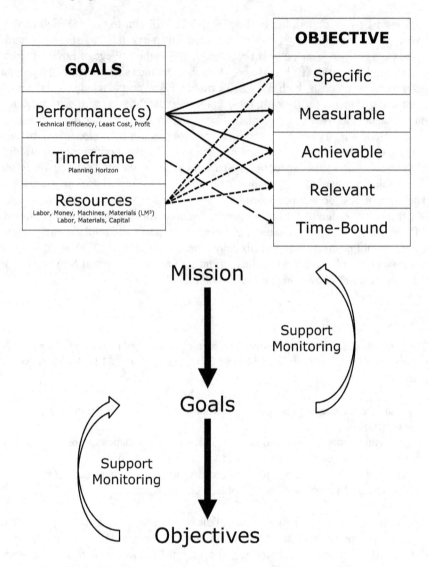

Figure 13.2 The Relationship Among Mission, Goals, and Objectives

craftspersons. The profits from our sales will be used to provide scholarships
for ESF's students and support the sustainable management of Heiberg's Forest
resources and training for its employees. We strive to treat our employees and
customers in a fair and ethical manner.

Goals: A goal of this 10-year business plan is to produce outputs in a technically
efficient and production cost effective manner, by sustainably harvesting large
diameter hardwood trees within Heiberg Forest, NY, for production of ≥1"-thick

live-edge slabs. Additionally, our plan is to manage and maintain Heiberg's forest structure and complexity for educational and research uses by ESF faculty and students and for recreational opportunities for ESF faculty and students and surrounding communities. Finally, these large diameter trees will be processed and kiln dried onsite for sale to regional artisans, woodworkers, and craftspersons within NY and surrounding areas.

Objectives: (1) By year 3, manage the business in a technically efficient and production efficient manner as measured by minimizing total variable costs and purchasing rightsized capital. (2) During the first five years, build strong relationships with working professionals, local artisans, woodworkers, and craftspersons in the area by selling live-edge slabs at fair market prices. (3) Throughout the 10 years, manage Heiberg Forest for educational, research, and recreational values by sustainably harvesting large diameter trees and following appropriate silvicultural prescriptions to facilitate healthy forest processes.

Production System

What Are the Inputs?

The fixed capital inputs are a Lucas 23 Dedicated Slab Mill, a kiln which includes the building and the dehumidification system (a Nyle L200 with a 4,000 board foot hardwood capacity), and an inventory/storage shed. The variable inputs are utilities, fuel, maintenance, a rented Sky Trak 6036 forklift, and labor. All the labor for this operation is provided by ESF's professional forest properties staff and a summer intern. Finally, a key variable input is the large diameter sugar maple and black cherry trees available within Heiberg Forest.

What Are the Output(s)?

The outputs are high-quality live-edge slabs of varying thickness, width, and length, which are differentiated products, each with their own unique characteristics, quality, and value. The primary waste outputs will be logging debris, and sawdust and scrap wood from the milling operation. These waste outputs are disposed of in the woods.

How Do You Describe the Production Process?

Large diameter sugar maple and black cherry will be marked, felled, and skidded to the road. The Lucas 23 dedicated slab mill will be transported to the location of the cut trees and the green slabs will be cut roadside. The green slabs will be transported to a staging area where they will be offloaded and inspected for potential defects prior to loading into a Nyle L200 4 thousand board foot (MBF) capacity kiln. Any defective green slabs will be set aside as potential rough lumber or firewood. It takes approximately two months to kiln dry the slabs. The drying process must be monitored to ensure the slabs dry properly and are not damaged.

If damaged during the drying process, instead of producing slabs one produces firewood of significantly lesser value. The kiln-dried slabs will be measured and photographed for marketing and inventory purposes. Available slabs will be posted on ESF's Forest Properties website. Finished slabs will then be put into a storage shed until they are sold.

Costs

The Pillars of Cost and Value reflect the slab mill's fixed and variable costs given in Tables 13.1a and 13.1b. Fixed costs remain constant throughout the production process no matter how much output is produced. In this business, the majority of these costs represent the loan payments for purchasing capital equipment. For the slab mill, the fixed costs (Table 13.1b) include the loans for the capital equipment: slab mill, kiln, and storage shed. The interest rate on the capital equipment loan is 6% for five years.[8] Other fixed costs include electricity and maintenance at 1,100.00 $/year. Variable costs flucuate throughout the production process and are related to the variable inputs. The variable costs are given in Table 13.1a and include hourly labor rate for two professional staff and one supervisor, renting a forklift for two days for loading and unloading slabs, and the logging costs. The variable costs provided in Table 13.1a reflect producing 4,000 board feet of live-edge slabs per year comprised of sugar maple and black cherry.

Revenues

As described in Chapter 4 – Revenue, revenue is price × quantity; however, revenue more importantly is a function of the Pillars of Price and Value. Price is a per

Table 13.1a Annual Operating Costs – Slab Mill

Annual Operating Costs – 2017		
Average logging costs (cutting, bucking, scaling and grading, skidding, hauling, labor)	$/MBF	350.00
Assume cut 5 MBF to mill 4 MBF Slabs	$/year	1,750.00
Forklift (2 days)	$/day	250.00
Assume 16 hours to move slabs to kiln and kiln to storage shed.	$/year	500.00
Labor rate per hour (includes benefits)	$/hr	27.00
2 professional staff @ 8 hours per day (cut logs into 4 MBF of slabs, move to kiln and then storage shed)	$/day	432.00
Labor – Assume 32 hours (4 days) to cut slabs, move to kiln and then storage shed	$/year	1,728.00
Supervisor rate per hour (includes benefits)	$/hr	37.50
1 person @ 8 hours per day (monitoring operation and kiln)	$/day	300.00
Supervisor – Assume 16 hours to monitor operations and kiln	$/year	600.00
Annual Electrical and Maintenance	$/year	1,100.00

Table 13.1b Capital Expenditures – Slab Mill

Capital Cost		
Purchase of Lucas Mill Slab Mill DSM 23 (60" Maximum Cut)	$	8,999.00
Shipping	$	1,000.00
Nyle L200 Kiln (4 MBF capacity)	$	5,000.00
Miscellaneous Kiln Parts	$	1,000.00
Build Kiln	$	12,000.00
Storage Shed	$	12,000.00
Capital Equipment Buffer	$	10,000.00
Amount Financed	$	49,999.00
Loan Length (years)	years	5
Annual Interest Rate on Loan		6%
Annual Loan Payment	$/year	11,869.58

$$a = V_0 \cdot \frac{r}{1-(1+r)^{-t}}$$

$$11,869.58 = 49,000 \cdot \left[\frac{0.06}{1-(1+0.06)^{-5}} \right]$$

unit measure of assigned value and a measure of relative scarcity. Output price is what the consumer pays for the product. But if the product does not provide the consumer value, they will not purchase it. Value can be described as the relative importance or worth a consumer places on a good or service that makes them better off than without that good or service. Output produced but not sold generates no revenue but does generate costs.

The market for large live-edge hardwood slabs is not very well known. Hardwood slabs are a niche product appealing to a specific subset of consumers. These consumers are usually hired or contracted artisans, woodworkers, and carpenters, who purchase slabs as as an input for their business. The price they pay for this input is driven by the potential value they see in it as an final product. However, in this particular market, finding reliable consumers who buy measurable amounts of live-edge slabs is an issue. For the proposed slab mill, the variable and fixed costs are relatively straightforward, unfortunately, this cannot be said for revenue. Determining a potential market for large live-edge slabs is easier said than done. Establishing a price based on the market was done initially by visiting multiple websites to query the price of live-edge slabs. For example, Berkshire Products prices (www.berkshireproducts.com/inventory.php accessed 5 May 2017) for sugar maple and black cherry are given in Tables 13.2a and 13.2b.

However, after making multiple phone calls to local slab retailers and reaching out to several woodworkers in Rochester, NY, and western Massachusetts, the market prices given in Tables 13.2a and 13.2b were far too high for the local market. Based off the input received from these individuals, they were willing to pay an average of 5.47 $/bdft for black cherry and 4.35 $/bdft for sugar maple.

Table 13.2a Sugar Maple – Data From Berkshire Products

Thickness(in)	Length(in)	Width(in)	bdft[‡]	Value($)	$/bdft
1.25	90	32	25.00	608.00	24.32
1.25	90	33	25.78	668.00	25.91
1.25	91	44	34.76	1,308.00	37.63
1.25	91	44	34.76	1,308.00	37.63
1.25	91	30	23.70	404.00	17.05
1.25	91	32	25.28	632.00	25.00
				Average Price ($/bdft)	27.92

Thickness(in)	Length(in)	Width(in)	bdft	Value($)	$/bdft
1.5	64	32	21.33	595.00	27.89
1.5	64	34	22.67	648.75	28.62
1.5	86	35	31.35	823.00	26.25
1.5	86	31	27.77	842.00	30.32
1.5	85	23	20.36	688.00	33.78
1.5	85	26	23.02	796.00	34.58
				Average Price ($/bdft)	30.24

Thickness(in)	Length(in)	Width(in)	bdft	Value($)	$/bdft
2	83	20	23.06	568.00	24.64
2	83	24	27.67	620.00	22.41
2	86	29	34.64	1,353.00	39.06
2	86	35	41.81	1,282.00	30.67
2	68	31	29.28	613.00	20.94
2	68	34	32.11	1,012.00	31.52
2	62	38	32.72	873.00	26.68
				Average Price ($/bdft)	27.99

Thickness(in)	Length(in)	Width(in)	bdft	Value($)	$/bdft
2.5	73	30	38.02	1,375.00	36.16
2.5	53	60	55.21	1,525.00	27.62
2.5	55	60	57.29	1,350.00	23.56
2.5	55	65	62.07	1,700.00	27.39
2.5	40	60	41.67	1,300.00	31.20
2.5	90	50	78.13	2,020.00	25.86
2.5	89	35	54.08	1,324.00	24.48
				Average Price ($/bdft)	28.04

Thickness(in)	Length(in)	Width(in)	bdft	Value($)	$/bdft
3	78	47	76.38	1,957.00	25.62
3	106	26	57.42	1,368.00	23.83
3	151	50	157.29	5,795.00	36.84
3	154	36	115.50	3,780.00	32.73
3	48	55	55.00	1,212.00	22.04
3	117	29	70.69	1,210.00	17.12
				Average Price ($/bdft)	26.36

[‡]bdft denotes board feet
Source: www.berkshireproducts.com/inventory.php (accessed 5 May 2017)

Table 13.2b Black Cherry – Data From Berkshire Products

Thickness(in)	Length(in)	Width(in)	bdft‡	Value($)	$/bdft
1.25	91	27	21.33	910.00	42.67
1.25	223	19	36.78	1,150.00	31.27
1.25	223	27	52.27	2,050.00	39.22
1.25	89	29	22.40	1,146.00	51.15
1.25	90	29	22.66	1,207.00	53.27
			Average Price ($/bdft)		43.52

Thickness(in)	Length(in)	Width(in)	bdft	Value($)	$/bdft
1.5	90	22	20.63	628.00	30.45
1.5	87	24	21.75	667.50	30.69
1.5	86	27	24.19	835.00	34.52
1.5	87	29	26.28	932.50	35.48
1.5	88	29	26.58	955.00	35.92
1.5	88	30	27.50	983.00	35.75
			Average Price ($/bdft)		33.80

Thickness(in)	Length(in)	Width(in)	bdft	Value($)	$/bdft
2	96	30	40.00	1,808.00	45.20
2	127	40	70.56	3,762.00	53.32
2	85	32	37.78	1,558.00	41.24
2	124	40	68.89	3,112.00	45.17
2	146	26	52.72	2,040.00	38.69
			Average Price ($/bdft)		44.73

Thickness(in)	Length(in)	Width(in)	bdft	Value($)	$/bdft
3	108	16	36.00	1,136.00	31.56
			Average Price ($/bdft)		31.56

‡bdft denotes board feet
Source: www.berkshireproducts.com/inventory.php (accessed 5 May 2017)

Profits

Profit is basically the amount of revenue that remains after accounting for all expenses. As defined previously, I will use the following financial accounting statements: (1) cash flow statement, (2) income statement, and (3) balance statement to illustrate this analysis, starting with the cash flow statement.

Cash Flow Statement

The cash flow statement shows the exchange of money between a company and the outside world for a defined time. The cash flow statement for the slab mill is given in Table 13.3. The estimated costs are based on the information contained in Tables 13.1a and 13.1b. The estimated revenues are based on selling 4 MBF of sugar maple for 4.35 $/bdft.

Table 13.3 Cash Flow Statement for the Slab Mill

		2017					Year						2027
	Units	0	1	2	3	4	5	6	7	8	9	10
Operating Activities:													
Cash Inflow (Revenue)													
Slab Sales‡	$/year	0.00	17,400.00	17,400.00	17,400.00	17,400.00	17,400.00	17,400.00	17,400.00	17,400.00	17,400.00	17,400.00

		2017					Year						2027
		0	1	2	3	4	5	6	7	8	9	10
Estimated Costs													
Operating Activities:													
Cash Outflow (Costs)													
Logging Costs – Harvesting	$/year	0.00	1,750.00	1,750.00	1,750.00	1,750.00	1,750.00	1,750.00	1,750.00	1,750.00	1,750.00	1,750.00
Forklift	$/year	0.00	500.00	500.00	500.00	500.00	500.00	500.00	500.00	500.00	500.00	500.00
Labor	$/year	0.00	1,728.00	1,728.00	1,728.00	1,728.00	1,728.00	1,728.00	1,728.00	1,728.00	1,728.00	1,728.00
Supervisor	$/year	0.00	600.00	600.00	600.00	600.00	600.00	600.00	600.00	600.00	600.00	600.00
Annual Electrical & Maintenance	$/year	0.00	1,100.00	1,100.00	1,100.00	1,100.00	1,100.00	1,100.00	1,100.00	1,100.00	1,100.00	1,100.00
Annual Interest payment – Capital	$/year	0.00	2,999.94	2,467.76	1,903.65	1,305.70	671.86	0.00	0.00	0.00	0.00	0.00
Financing Activities:													
Cash Outflow													
Annual Principal payment– Capital	$/year	0.00	8,869.64	9,401.82	9,965.93	10,563.89	11,197.72	0.00	0.00	0.00	0.00	0.00
Total Cost	$/year	0.00	17,547.58	17,547.58	17,547.58	17,547.58	17,547.58	5,678.00	5,678.00	5,678.00	5,678.00	5,678.00
Cash Balance		0.00	−147.58	−295.17	−442.75	−590.33	−737.91	10,984.09	22,706.09	34,428.09	46,150.09	57,872.09

‡ The estimated revenues are based on selling 4 MBF sugar maple slabs per year at a price of 4.35 $/bdft

The sugar maple price was used for three reasons. First, there is an abundance of sugar maple trees of slab size at Heiberg. Second is the advice given in Chapter 6 – Capital Theory: Investment Analysis – lowball your revenues and highball your costs or round your revenues down and your costs up. Sugar maples have the lowest estimated price at 4.35 $/bdft. Finally, the estimated costs are the same to produce sugar maple slabs as black cherry slabs.

There are two items in the cash flow statement in Table 13.3 that I would like to point out. First is how I incorporate the cash balance in the cash flow statement. I do not incorporate the cash balance as part of the cash flow statement as is done traditionally. The rationale for this is to facilitate using the cash flow statement in calculating the net present value of investing in the slab mill. Examining the cash balance shows that there is a negative balance until year 6, which is when the capital loan is paid off. Second, while principal and interest payments were defined explicitly in the cash flow statement, how these payments were determined is part of the amortization schedule, which I will describe next.

Amortization Schedule

As all revenues and costs are listed in annual terms, the loan payments used will be annual. The loan payment was determined in Table 13.1b. The estimated annual loan payments are split between interest and principal payments using the annual amortization schedule shown in Table 13.4.

Equation (13.1) determines how much of the annual payment is interest:

$$IP_k = Bal_{k-1} \times i; \ \ k = 1,...,n \tag{13.1}$$

Equation (13.2) determines how much of the annual payment is used to pay down principal:

$$PP_k = Pmt - IP_k; \ \ k = 1,...,n \tag{13.2}$$

Table 13.4 The Amortization Schedule Capital for Slab Mill

	Payment Number	Payment	Interest Portion	Principal Portion	Principal Balance
2017	0				49,999.00
2018	1	11,869.58	2,999.94	8,869.64	41,129.36
2019	2	11,869.58	2,467.76	9,401.82	31,727.54
2020	3	11,869.58	1,903.65	9,965.93	21,761.61
2021	4	11,869.58	1,305.70	10,563.89	11,197.72
2022	5	11,869.58	671.86	11,197.72	0.00
	Sum	59,347.91	9,348.91	49,999.00	

Equation (13.3) determines the annual principal balance (Bal_k) for the kth payment period:

$$Bal_k = Bal_{k-1} - PP_k; \quad k = 1,...,n \tag{13.3}$$

where
IP_k denotes the interest payment for the kth annual payment;
Bal_{k-1} denotes the principal balance (or the amount of the loan left to pay) of the $k-1$ annual payment period;
i denotes the annual discount rate;
PP_k denotes the principal payment for the kth annual payment;
Pmt denotes the annual payment (equation (13.1));
Bal_k denotes the principal balance (or the amount of the loan left to pay) of the kth annual payment period;
n denotes the total number of annual payments; and
k denotes the annual payment period.

In addition, this annual amortization schedule also includes a number of internal checks to make sure the calculations are accurate; for example, the total principal payments plus the total interest payments equals the total loan payments and the total principal payments is the amount that was borrowed.

The balance between principal and interest payments reverses over time. Because of this inverse relationship, the gain in equity in a capital asset is much slower in the initial years of a loan. As will be illustrated in the income statement and balance sheet, interest payments are deducted from annual income while principal payments reduce liabilities and increase equity in capital assets. This demonstrates the value of making extra principal payments, as each extra payment results in a larger repaid portion of the principal (i.e., building equity) and reduces the interest due on each future payment.

Income Statement

The income statement summarizes a company's revenues (sales) and operating expenses for a company's fiscal year. The slab mill's income statement is given in Table 13.5. As seen in Table 13.5, the income statement only includes interest payments. Because depreciation is a noncash expense, it is included in an income statement but not a cash flow statement. Depreciation is important as it does impact income. This can be seen in the net income row showing a change from negative to positive in year 3 as interest payment declines. Starting in year 6 the annual net income is $11,722 as the capital assets are depreciated fully. For this analysis I used a simple straight-line depreciation even though other depreciation methods are available.

Balance Statement

This statement shows your assets versus your liabilities and equity in the business. As the name implies, what a business owns (assets) must equal liabilities plus equity. The slab mill's balance statement is given in Table 13.6.

Table 13.5 Income Statement for the Slab Mill

Income Statement	Units	2017	2018	2019	2020	2021	Year	2023	2024	2025	2026	2027
		0	1	2	3	4	5	6	7	8	9	10
Revenues – Slab Sales	$/year	0.00	17,400.00	17,400.00	17,400.00	17,400.00	17,400.00	17,400.00	17,400.00	17,400.00	17,400.00	17,400.00
Expenses												
Logging Costs – Harvesting	$/year	0.00	1,750.00	1,750.00	1,750.00	1,750.00	1,750.00	1,750.00	1,750.00	1,750.00	1,750.00	1,750.00
Forklift	$/year	0.00	500.00	500.00	500.00	500.00	500.00	500.00	500.00	500.00	500.00	500.00
Labor	$/year	0.00	1,728.00	1,728.00	1,728.00	1,728.00	1,728.00	1,728.00	1,728.00	1,728.00	1,728.00	1,728.00
Supervisor	$/year	0.00	600.00	600.00	600.00	600.00	600.00	600.00	600.00	600.00	600.00	600.00
Annual Electrical & Maintenance	$/year	0.00	1,100.00	1,100.00	1,100.00	1,100.00	1,100.00	1,100.00	1,100.00	1,100.00	1,100.00	1,100.00
Annual Interest payment – Capital	$/year	0.00	2,999.94	2,467.76	1,903.65	1,305.70	671.86	0.00	0.00	0.00	0.00	0.00
5-Year Straight-Line Depreciation – Capital	$/year	0.00	9,999.80	9,999.80	9,999.80	9,999.80	9,999.80	0.00	0.00	0.00	0.00	0.00
Total	$/year	0.00	18,677.74	18,145.56	17,581.45	16,983.50	16,349.66	5,678.00	5,678.00	5,678.00	5,678.00	5,678.00
Net Income (+) or Loss (−)		0.00	−1,277.74	−745.56	−181.45	416.50	1,050.34	11,722.00	11,722.00	11,722.00	11,722.00	11,722.00

Table 13.6 Balance Statement for the Slab Mill

	Units	2017 0	2018 1	2019 2	2020 3	2021 4	Year 5	2023 6	2024 7	2025 8	2026 9	2027 10
Cash	$/year	0.00	−147.58	−295.17	−442.75	−590.33	−737.91	10,984.09	22,706.09	34,428.09	46,150.09	57,872.09
Capital Equipment	$/year	0.00	49,999.00	49,999.00	49,999.00	49,999.00	49,999.00	0.00	0.00	0.00	0.00	0.00
Less: Accumulated Depreciation	$/year	0.00	−9,999.80	−19,999.60	−29,999.40	−39,999.20	−49,999.00	0.00	0.00	0.00	0.00	0.00
Total Assets	$/year	0.00	39,851.62	29,704.23	19,556.85	9,409.47	−737.91	10,984.09	22,706.09	34,428.09	46,150.09	57,872.09
Loan – Capital Equipment	$/year	0.00	41,129.36	31,727.54	21,761.61	11,197.72	0.00	0.00	0.00	0.00	0.00	0.00
Retained Earnings	$/year	0.00	−1,277.74	−2,023.30	−2,204.75	−1,788.25	−737.91	10,984.09	22,706.09	34,428.09	46,150.09	57,872.09
Total Liabilities & Equity	$/year	0.00	39,851.62	29,704.23	19,556.85	9,409.47	−737.91	10,984.09	22,706.09	34,428.09	46,150.09	57,872.09

The balance statement shows explicitly what is reflected in the amortization schedule: The balance between principal and interest payments reverses over time. Because of this inverse relationship, the gain in equity in the capital increases over time as shown in the loan row. Also, the balance statement shows how the capital asset's depreciation reduces the business's total asset value. Given the simple example with only a single capital expenditure, in year 5 when the capital asset is depreciated completely, the total assets equal the cash balance, which is the same as the total liabilities. By year 10 the total asset and equity value of this business is $57,872.

Breakeven Analysis

I will estimate two separate breakeven analyses. These are based on the data provided in the cash flow statement (Table 13.3). The first is based on each separate column of the cash flow statement and provides three breakeven elements:

1. Breakeven Revenue – Estimates the total revenue that must be earned each year to cover the financing, operation, and maintenance costs for the investment horizon.
2. Breakeven Production Level – Estimates how many units of output that must be produced and "sold" each year to cover the financing, operation, and maintenance costs for the investment horizon at an expected market price.
3. Breakeven Output Price – Estimates a price you would have to receive each year to cover the financing, operation, and maintenance costs for the investment horizon at an expected output or production level.

These are given in Table 13.7a. The annual breakeven revenues are equal to the annual total costs from the cash flow statement given in Table 13.3. As shown in the cash flow statement, once the capital equipment loan is paid, the costs decrease significantly. The annual breakeven production level is based on an expected price of 4.35 $/bdft. The annual breakeven price was based on producing 4 MBF sugar maple slabs per year. This breakeven analysis shows expected results. In the first five years, the expected production and sales of 4 MBF of sugar maple slabs is insufficient to cover the financing, operation, and maintenance costs for the investment horizon. However, in the last five years the required production and sales levels fall as well as the required selling price due to paying off the capital equipment loan.

The second is based on an equal annual equivalent (EAE) analysis of the cash flow statement data.[9] The equal annual equivalent analysis summarizes the 10-year cash flow statement into three breakeven metrics:

1. EAE Breakeven Revenue – Estimates the total revenue that must be earned annually to cover the present value of the financing, operation, and maintenance costs for the investment horizon.

Table 13.7a Annual Breakeven Analysis for the Slab Mill‡

		2017					Year					2027
	Units	0	1	2	3	4	5	6	7	8	9	10
Annual Breakeven Revenue	$/year	0.00	17,547.58	17,547.58	17,547.58	17,547.58	17,547.58	5,678.00	5,678.00	5,678.00	5,678.00	5,678.00
Annual Breakeven Production	bdft/year	0.00	4,033.93	4,033.93	4,033.93	4,033.93	4,033.93	1,305.29	1,305.29	1,305.29	1,305.29	1,305.29
Annual Breakeven Price	$/bdft	0.00	4.39	4.39	4.39	4.39	4.39	1.42	1.42	1.42	1.42	1.42

‡ The annual breakeven revenue is equal to the annual total costs. The annual breakeven production level is based on an expected price of 4.35 $/bdft. The annual breakeven price is based on producing 4 MBF sugar maple slabs per year. MBF denotes thousand board feet and bdft denotes board feet.

Table 13.7b Equal Annual Equivalent (EAE) Breakeven Analysis for the Slab Mill[‡]

	Units	
EAE Breakeven Revenue	$/year	12,471.26
EAE Breakeven Production	bdft/year	2,866.96
EAE Breakeven Price	$/bdft	2.94

[‡] The EAE breakeven revenue was based on the cost of producing 4 MBF sugar maple slabs per year. The EAE breakeven production was based on an expected price of 4.35 $/bdft. The EAE breakeven price was based on producing 4 MBF sugar maple slabs per year. MBF denotes thousand board feet and bdft denotes board feet.

2. EAE Breakeven Production Level – Estimates how many units of output that must be produced and "sold" annually to cover the present value of the financing, operation, and maintenance costs for the investment horizon at an expected market price.
3. EAE Breakeven Output Price – Estimates a price you would have to receive annually to cover the present value of the financing, operation, and maintenance costs for the investment horizon at an expected output or production level.

These are given in Table 13.7b. Examining these three breakeven metrics shows the expected production and sales of 4 MBF of sugar maple slabs is sufficient to cover the financing, operation, and maintenance costs, and the required selling price is less than the expected market price for the investment horizon. These two breakeven analyses appear to support this being a viable business opportunity for the college.

Net Present Value

The slab mill's present values of the expected revenues and costs are given in Tables 13.8a and 13.8b. The annual and cumulative net present values (NPV) are given in Table 13.8c. For the first five years, the annual NPVs are negative, resulting in a negative cumulative NPV. This is consistent with paying off the capital equipment loan and is consistent with the cash flow and income statements. The cumulative NPV in year 10 is $36,275.94. This implies that the investment in the slab mill is returning the required 6% discount rate plus an addition net present value of net cash flow. This analysis appears to support this being a viable business opportunity for the college.

Based on the information provided in Tables 13.8a and 13.8b, the benefit–cost ratio (BCR) is 1.40. Using this as a cardinal metric of sensitivity, this implies that the discounted costs could increase by a factor of 1.4 and NPV would just be equal to zero. Or, the discounted revenues could decrease by a factor of 0.716 and NPV would just be equal to zero. This analysis also appears to support this being a viable business opportunity for the college. However, as described in Chapter 6 – Capital Theory: Investment Analysis, a critical question must be asked and answered: Are

Table 13.8a Present Value of the Expected Revenues for the Slab Mill[‡]

| Estimated Revenue | Units | 2017 | Year | | | | | | | | 2027 |
		0	1	2	3	4	5	6	7	8	9	10
Expected Revenue from Slab Sales	$/year	0.00	17,400.00	17,400.00	17,400.00	17,400.00	17,400.00	17,400.00	17,400.00	17,400.00	17,400.00	17,400.00
Present Value of Expected Revenues	$/year	0.00	16,415.09	15,485.94	14,609.38	13,782.43	13,002.29	12,266.31	11,571.99	10,916.98	10,299.03	9,716.07

‡ The expected revenue is based on producing and selling 4 MBF sugar maple slabs per year at an expected price of 4.35 $/bdft. The present value of the expected revenues is calculated based on a 6% discount rate.

		2017					Year					2027
		0	1	2	3	4	5	6	7	8	9	10
Operating Activities: *Cash Outflow (Costs)*												
Logging Costs – Harvesting	$/year	0.00	1,750.00	1,750.00	1,750.00	1,750.00	1,750.00	1,750.00	1,750.00	1,750.00	1,750.00	1,750.00
Forklift	$/year	0.00	500.00	500.00	500.00	500.00	500.00	500.00	500.00	500.00	500.00	500.00
Labor	$/year	0.00	1,728.00	1,728.00	1,728.00	1,728.00	1,728.00	1,728.00	1,728.00	1,728.00	1,728.00	1,728.00
Supervisor	$/year	0.00	600.00	600.00	600.00	600.00	600.00	600.00	600.00	600.00	600.00	600.00
Annual Electrical & Maintenance	$/year	0.00	1,100.00	1,100.00	1,100.00	1,100.00	1,100.00	1,100.00	1,100.00	1,100.00	1,100.00	1,100.00
Annual Interest payment – Capital Equipment	$/year	0.00	2,999.94	2,467.76	1,903.65	1,305.70	671.86	0.00	0.00	0.00	0.00	0.00
Financing Activities: *Cash Outflow*												
Annual Principal payment – Capital Equipment	$/year	0.00	8,869.64	9,401.82	9,965.93	10,563.89	11,197.72	0.00	0.00	0.00	0.00	0.00
Total	$/year	0.00	17,547.58	17,547.58	17,547.58	17,547.58	17,547.58	5,678.00	5,678.00	5,678.00	5,678.00	5,678.00
Present Value of Expected Costs		0.00	16,554.32	15,617.29	14,733.29	13,899.33	13,112.57	4,002.77	3,776.19	3,562.45	3,360.80	3,170.57

‡ The expected cost is based on producing and selling 4 MBF sugar maple slabs per year. The present value of the expected costs is calculated based on a 6% discount rate.

Table 13.8c Net Present Value of the Slab Mill‡

		2017					Year					2027
Net Present Value	Units	0	1	2	3	4	5	6	7	8	9	10
Annual	$/year	0.00	−139.23	−131.35	−123.91	−116.90	−110.28	8,263.55	7,795.80	7,354.53	6,938.23	6,545.50
Cumulative	$	0.00	−139.23	−270.58	−394.49	−511.39	−621.67	7,641.88	15,437.68	22,792.20	29,730.44	36,275.94

‡ The expected costs and revenues are based on producing and selling 4 MBF sugar maple slabs per year at an expected price of 4.35 $/bdft. The net present value is calculated based on a 6% discount rate.

these implied increases or decreases within normal ranges of operations for costs and revenues of the investment? This will be examined in the next section.

Analysis and Recommendation

The three financial accounting statements and the breakeven and NPV analyses appear to support this being a viable business opportunity for ESF. However, this potential business deals in a niche market and finding potential consumers for this product has proven to be the main issue with this business venture: There does not seem to be sustainable demand for live-edge slabs regionally. This conclusion was reached after making multiple phone calls to local slab retailers and reaching out to several woodworkers in Rochester, New York, and western Massachusetts. Consequently selling the required 4 MBF of live-edge slabs per year is highly unlikely even given the market at prices of 5.47 \$/bdft for black cherry and 4.35 \$/bdft for sugar maple. Although the total costs are relatively low overall and the input (large diameter trees) are highly accessible, the expected revenues appear to be more uncertain than the spreadsheet data and analyses seem to imply. Thus, an investment in the slab mill business would not be wise economically for ESF.

When doing these types of analyses: "Context Matters." While the various spreadsheets containing the cost and revenue data seem to point to this being a viable business opportunity for ESF, there is uncertainty surrounding the ability to sell the required 4 MBF of slabs given this niche product. Slabs produced but not sold generate no revenues but do generate costs. For example, if 4 MBF are produced annually but only 2 MBF are sold annually, the NPV = −\$27,756.82, and if only 3 MBF are sold annually the NPV = \$4,259.56.[10] Consequently, an investment in the slab mill business would not be wise economically for ESF.

Maple Syrup Business Plan

This is an ongoing business operation, unfortunately only partial cost and revenue records are available from 2001 to 2016. The cost and revenue information from 2017 to 2021 will be included in the financial statements. The investment analysis horizon for the business plan is 2021 to 2031. This allows for using historic and current capital and operations costs and revenues to develop a comprehensive business plan.

Background

The history of maple syrup production where the current Svend O. Heiberg Forest is located probably predates the white settlements of the early 1800s.[11] Maple syrup was likely as much a necessity as a luxury as it and honey may have been the only sweeteners readily available. Sap was collected via buckets hung on spiles in the early years and were replaced in the mid-60s by a tubing system that directed sap to a sap house for transportation to the sugar house. There have been three sugar houses built at different locations in Heiberg Forest. The latest built in 2001 is located near the classrooms and the maintenance garage. Maple syrup is produced by boiling sap in an evaporator to remove the excess water and concentrate the natural sugars. The first evaporator was purchased in the 1940s. The second was purchased in 2009 but did not have a steam hood, making working in the sugar house difficult and dangerous. The third was purchased in 2015 and included a steam hood that used the steam from boiling the sap to help preheat the sap before reaching the evaporating and finishing pans. All the evaporators used firewood as Heiberg as a virtually limitless supply of this renewable resource and a firewood processor. The latest wood burning arch has an airtight fire box with an attached blower for efficient firewood use.

The sugarbush at Heiberg has increased from 600 taps in the late 2000s to 2,000 taps in 2016. A sap collection house was built in 2001 as the sugarbush is 0.5 miles from the sugar house. As sap is approximately 97% water, reverse osmosis machines were purchased in 2009 and 2017 that use differentially permeable membranes to remove approximately 80% of the water to concentrate the sap from approximately 2% sugar into an 8% to 12% sugar solution. Removing this much water saves on the amount of firewood used to remove the remaining water by the evaporator.

Finally, ESF's maple syrup operation is in a unique situation. As the business is part of ESF and ESF is a state-run institution, any maple products produced cannot be seen to compete with the local private maple syrup producers. Thus, our only current retail outlets are at the campus bookstore, its website, and sales at Heiberg.

Executive Summary

The maple syrup business is a profitable business opportunity and should be continued. This recommendation is based on analyzing the data collected and provided by Forest Properties personnel. To maintain viability the costs and revenues must be managed actively. For example, reducing the amount of maple syrup wholesaled and increasing the amount sold to ESF's bookstore or to other organizations such as the Boy Scouts will diversify the revenue stream and increase profitability. Given the Forest Properties professional staff must manage other businesses and activities besides the maple syrup operation, they have invested in capital to maintain business standards and help reduce relying on labor. For example, replacing the lines in the sugarbush in a timely manner helps maintain the business. The current arch and evaporator have the capacity to handle a larger sugarbush to allow for a future sugarbush expansion without increasing the amount of labor required in the sugar shack. The maple syrup operation provides additional benefit to the college and local communities in terms of teaching and outreach.

Mission, Goals, and Objectives

The mission, goals, and objectives are given in Table 13.9. The mission, goals, and objectives reflect the fact that the maple syrup operation is a for-profit business. As this is a for-profit business, managing costs is critical for generating the largest

Table 13.9 Mission, Goals, and Objectives for the Maple Syrup Business

Mission Statement	

To provide the highest quality maple syrup and maple products to ESF students, staff, alumni, faculty, and the local communities by managing the forest resources sustainably. All profits fund ESFs mission of teaching, research, and outreach by supporting scholarships, paid student work opportunities at Heiberg, and continuing education for the forest properties staff. We strive to treat everyone in a fair and ethical manner.

Goal: To provide educational field trips on the process of maple syrup production.	Objective: At least one (1) field trip per year involving ESF students.
	Objective: At least one (1) field trip per year involving public school students.
Goal: Build lasting customer loyalty	Objective: Host an annual maple fest weekend for the college and local communities to demonstrate the maple syruping process from the sugarbush to the sugar house.
	Objective: Host an annual pancake breakfast to allow the college and local communities to taste our maple syrup and talk to the staff about the sustainability of the operation and purchase maple syrup from the staff directly.
Goal: Ensure long-term profitability by monitoring costs and revenues annually	Objective: Develop the three fundamental financial accounting statements annually
	Objective: Use these data to assess the cost effectiveness of the operation annually
Goal: Diversify the revenue stream	Objective: Within 2 years, develop an operational plan to diversify the revenue stream given the revenue generating constraints.
	Objective: Within 3 years, implement the operation plan.

profits regardless of the revenue stream. All the profits are used to support students and faculty.

While this is a for-profit business, given its unique nature not all the benefits generated by this business are measured in dollars. This is described in the mission statement and tied to the first goal and its corresponding two objectives directly. It is important to remember that context matters when analyzing data and developing a recommendation based on this analysis.

Production System

Tapping trees begins in January or February, depending on when the temperature is above 32 degrees Fahrenheit (0 degrees Celsius) during the day, and below 32 degrees Fahrenheit during the night. It takes two 4-hour days for four professional staff members to install 2,000 taps. Tapping requires drilling a horizontal hole (about 1½" deep) into the tree (Photo 13.1), keeping the hole 6 inches above or below, and 2 inches left or right of previous holes and defects.

Once the hole is cleaned out, the tap is inserted into a tree gently using a hammer (Photo 13.2).

Photo 13.1 Drilling Tap Hole

Photo 13.2 Inserting Tap and Dropline

The tap should not go too deep into the tree because it can obstruct the flow of sap. Sugar maple trees larger than 10 inches in diameter receive one tap. Taps are connected to drop lines, which are connected to lateral and main lines (Photo 13.3).

A vacuum system is housed in the sap house and pressurizes the main lines to an ideal range of 24–25 pounds per square inch pumping the sap into two 1,200-gallon tanks (Photos 13.4 and 13.5).

Photo 13.3 Lateral and Main Lines

Photo 13.4 Sugarbush to Sap House

Photo 13.5 Sap House Collection Tanks

Given ideal temperature conditions, the tanks collect around 1,500–2,000 gallons of sap per day. At the beginning of the day, sap is transported to the sugar house in a truck with a 500-gallon tank. The main, lateral, and drop lines were replaced completely in 2022. Best business practices recommend replacing the drop lines every three years. Given the complete replacement in 2022, the drop lines will be replaced again in 2025.

The sap is pumped into the sugar house into a 3,000-gallon sap holding tank (Photo 13.6). The sap holding tank is connected to a reverse osmosis (RO) unit that can filter 3,000 gallons of sap in four to five hours (Photo 13.7).

The excess water from the RO unit is stored in four 550-gallon tanks until the end of the RO cycle. The excess water is used to rinse and wash the RO unit at the end of the day. The RO increases technical efficiency by reducing the amount of firewood required. The concentrated sap is then gravity fed into the evaporator and is preheated using steam, collected in a steam-away hood from the boiling process, to 190 degrees Fahrenheit.

After the preheating process is complete, the boiling process to remove the remaining excess water begins. In order to be considered maple syrup, the sap must be boiled until it reaches 66 brix, or 66% sugar content. When the syrup has reached 66 brix, it is drained from the finishing pan into an open tank where diatomaceous earth is added to help aid in the filtering of the syrup. Once the syrup

Photo 13.6 Sugar House

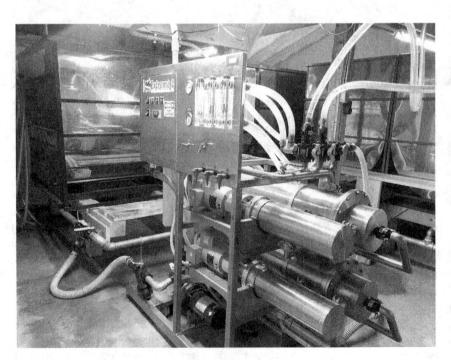

Photo 13.7 Reverse Osmosis Unit in Sugar House

Photo 13.8 Evaporator With Steam-Away Hood

is sent through the filter press, it goes into stainless steel barrels for storage or is canned in containers of varying sizes for specific orders. The steam from the boiling process is condensed in a 300-gallon poly tank and used to rinse the top of the steam-away hood and wash all the floors in the sugar house.

Given the time constraints of the professional staff, the current evaporator can produce approximately 30 gallons of syrup per four hours of boiling and uses 12 cords of hardwood firewood annually. Between 2016 and 2021, the annual gallons of syrup produced has ranged from 650 to 834 with an average of 730 gallons. The maple syrup season at Heiberg ranges from 24 to 30 days with the average being 26 days. As the maple syrup operation is not the only business the professional staff must work on, a day is defined as four to six hours. There are five professional staff involved with the business. On average it takes three professional staff per day to run the business during the maple syrup season. The jobs performed include tapping, moving sap to sugar house, boiling and packaging, repairs and maintenance, cleaning, removing taps, and communications and marketing.

The types of syrup produced are amber, dark, and golden delicate. If there is an order for containers of varying sizes, the syrup is pumped directly into the canning machine contained in the sugar house's kitchen. The canning machine can hold up to 40 gallons of syrup and it takes about four to five hours to bottle the 40 gallons (Photo 13.9).

Photo 13.9 Maple Syrup

The kitchen also contains the equipment to make the value-added products maple cream and maple candy from maple syrup (www.nnyagdev.org/maplefactsheets/CMB%20201%20Making%20Maple%20Cream1.pdf and www.massmaple.org/about-maple-syrup/make-maple-syrup/making-candy-and-cream/ accessed 8 July 2022). It takes 1 gallon of syrup and five hours to produce approximately 8 pounds of maple cream or candies (Photo 13.10).

The quality of the maple cream produced depends on the sugar content of the syrup and the daily changes in humidity and boiling point of water (www.

Photo 13.10 Maple Candy

nnyagdev.org/maplefactsheets/CMB%20201%20Making%20Maple%20Cream1. pdf accessed 8 July 2022).

The relevant inputs based on the preceding production function description are given in Table 13.10.

Costs

Cost data on capital expenditures has been collected since 2001. These are summarized as follows:

- Initial construction of current sap and sugar houses at a cost of $50,326 in 2001;
- Purchasing a new evaporator/arch, reverse osmosis unit, tubing, and vacuum pump for sugarbush, tapping equipment, and storage tanks at a cost of $62,600 in 2009;

Table 13.10 Relevant Inputs for the Maple Syrup Operation

Category	Description
Labor	
Sugarbush/Sap House	Two 4-hour days and four professional staff members install 2,000 taps.
Maple Syrup Season	The maple syrup season ranges from 24 to 30 four- to six-hour days with the average being 26 days.
	On average it takes three professional staff per day to run the business during the maple syrup season. The jobs performed include moving sap to sugar house, boiling and packaging, repairs and maintenance, cleaning, removing taps, and communications and marketing.
Capital	
Sugarbush/Sap House	Land; sugar maple trees; sap house; two 1,200-gallon storage tanks; vacuum pump.
Sugar House	Land; sugar house and kitchen; 3,000-gallon storage tank; reverse osmosis units; steam-away hood/evaporator/arch; lines and fittings.
Materials + Energy	
Sugarbush/Sap House	Drills and bits; hammers, taps, drop, lateral, and main lines; check valves and fittings; fuel; electricity; miscellaneous materials and supplies.
Sugar House	Firewood; electricity; miscellaneous materials and supplies.

- Upgrading the maple syrup canning machine at a cost of $6,000 in 2014;
- Purchasing two new sap tanks for sap house, new evaporator/arch/steam hood, building materials for a kitchen to attach to the sugar house, and insulating the sugar house at a cost of $63,683 in 2015;
- Purchasing a reverse osmosis (RO) unit, steel tank to hold sap in sugar house, and upgrading the kitchen at a cost of $34,713 in 2017;
- Trading in an old RO unit and purchasing a new vacuum pump for $3,773 in 2019; and
- Replacing the main, lateral, and drop lines in the sugarbush at a cost of $25,000 in 2022.

The interest rate on all capital equipment expenditures is 6% for five years. The amortization schedules for the 2014, 2015, 2017, and 2022 capital expenditures are given in Table 13.11.

The opearting costs from 2017 to 2021 are given in Table 13.12. When examining the operating cost data from 2017 to 2021, I look for anomalies. In 2017, 2018, and 2020 the operating costs were over $9,000. Examining the cost data more closely, in 2017 and 2018 the electric bill was over $3,000. The primary cause was the electric heater used to keep the RO unit from freezing running continuously. In 2019 the electric bill dropped to around $600. This was due to three factors. First, due to the professional staff analyzing past electrical costs, they were better able to

Table 13.11 Amortization Schedules for the 2014, 2015, 2017, and 2022 Capital Expenditures for the Maple Syrup Business

Upgrading the Canning Machine 2014

Year	Payment Number	Payment	Interest Portion	Principal Portion	Principal Balance
2014	0				6,000.00
2015	1	1,424.38	360.00	1,064.38	4,935.62
2016	2	1,424.38	296.14	1,128.24	3,807.38
2017	3	1,424.38	228.44	1,195.94	2,611.44
2018	4	1,424.38	156.69	1,267.69	1,343.75
2019	5	1,424.38	80.63	1,343.75	0.00
	Sum	7,121.89	1,121.89	6,000.00	

Sugar House Expansion 2015

Year	Payment Number	Payment	Interest Portion	Principal Portion	Principal Balance
2015	0				63,683.25
2016	1	15,118.17	3,821.00	11,297.18	52,386.07
2017	2	15,118.17	3,143.16	11,975.01	40,411.06
2018	3	15,118.17	2,424.66	12,693.51	27,717.55
2019	4	15,118.17	1,663.05	13,455.12	14,262.43
2020	5	15,118.17	855.75	14,262.43	0.00
	Sum	75,590.87	11,907.62	63,683.25	

Sugar House Expansion 2017

Year	Payment Number	Payment	Interest Portion	Principal Portion	Principal Balance
2017	0				34,713.00
2018	1	8,240.74	2,082.78	6,157.96	28,555.04
2019	2	8,240.74	1,713.30	6,527.44	22,027.60
2020	3	8,240.74	1,321.66	6,919.09	15,108.51
2021	4	8,240.74	906.51	7,334.23	7,774.28
2022	5	8,240.74	466.46	7,774.28	0.00
	Sum	41,203.71	6,490.71	34,713.00	

Sugarbush 2022

Year	Payment Number	Payment	Interest Portion	Principal Portion	Principal Balance
2022	0				25,000.00
2023	1	5,934.91	1,500.00	4,434.91	20,565.09
2024	2	5,934.91	1,233.91	4,701.00	15,864.09
2025	3	5,934.91	951.85	4,983.06	10,881.02
2026	4	5,934.91	652.86	5,282.05	5,598.97
2027	5	5,934.91	335.94	5,598.97	0.00
	Sum	29,674.55	4,674.55	25,000.00	

Table 13.12 Maple Business Operating Expenses Covering the Sugarbush, Sap House, and Sugar House

Operating Expenses – 2017

Firewood	$750.00
Gas & Diesel	$193.50
Electricity	$3,457.51
Repairs & Maintenance	$2,727.08
Supplies	$1,262.31
Summer Intern	$1,600.00
TOTAL	$9,990.40

Operating Expenses – 2018

Firewood	$750.00
Gas & Diesel	$193.50
Electricity	$3,457.51
Repairs & Maintenance	$1,954.40
Supplies	$1,267.31
Summer Intern	$1,600.00
TOTAL	$9,222.72

Dump Truck Maintenance – 2018

Maintenance	$7,870.44

Sugarbush Vacuum Pump – 2019

Vacuum Pump	$3,773.00

Operating Expenses – 2019

Equipment	$1,530.00
Supplies	$2,161.76
Repairs and Maintenance	$479.03
Gas & Diesel	$75.44
Firewood	$720.00
Electricity	$609.73
Summer Intern	$1,600.00
TOTAL	$7,175.96

Operating Expenses – 2020

Equipment	$585.66
Supplies	$4,514.24
Repairs and Maintenance	$1,552.86
Gas & Diesel	$57.50
Firewood	$720.00
Electricity	$571.91
Summer Intern	$1,600.00
TOTAL	$9,602.17

Operating Expenses – 2021

Supplies	$2,000.54
Gas & Diesel	$119.89
Firewood	$720.00
Electricity	$609.73
Summer Intern	$1,600.00
TOTAL	$5,050.16

Replacing Lines in Sugarbush 2025 and 2028

Lines	$2,000.00

Estimated Operating Expenses – 2022 to 2031‡

Total	$7,472.61

‡ The estimated operating expenses are based on an average of the average costs for years 2020 and 2021 multiplied by the expected syrup production

manage the electric heater. Second, the new vacuum pump in the sap house idles down when it reaches pressure, which saves electricity and the life of the pump. Third, from 2019 on the electric bill was not easily disaggregated to isolate the sugar house from other electricity uses at Heiberg; consequently, the electricity charges reflect primarily the sap house and underestimate the total electricity costs. In 2020, the supplies were $4,514, which was approximately $2,000 greater than in other years. This was due to replacing some of the vacuum lines in the sugarbush. A component of the mission statement is to provide paid student work opportunities at Heiberg. This intern will be employed by Forest Properties to help manage the existing for-profit businesses. The cost of the intern will be $12.00 per hour for 40 hours per week for 10 weeks during each summer of the planning horizon. In 2018 there were extensive repairs on the dump truck, which is used by all the businesses at Heiberg, and for rental equipment again due to the dump truck's extensive repairs.[12] The maple business operating budgets include 1/3 the cost of the summer intern. Finally, wages paid to the professional staff are conspicuously missing from the annual operating costs. This obvious omission will be addressed when I discuss "Analysis and Recommendations."

Revenues

There are three sources of revenue from selling maple syrup: (1) Sales from the sugar house during the pancake breakfast, annual maple fest, and people just stopping by Heiberg. (2) Sales to bulk, which are to ESF's bookstore and organizations such as the Boy Scouts. (3) Sales to wholesale, which go to Canada to become part of their maple syrup reserve.

Table 13.13a provides the total production of maple syrup for the complete investment horizon. Total production ranged from 650 to 834 gallons with an average of 730 gallons. The total production in 2019 stands out as different from the rest of the historic data. This is the result of two factors. First, a new vacuum pump was installed in 2019. Second, the weather conditions cooperated, resulting in a longer season. Wholesale sales have trended upward, and bulk sales have trended downward while sales from Heiberg have also trended downward. The large drop in sales from Heiberg in 2020 was due to cancelling the pancake breakfast and maple fest weekend due to COVID.

The prices received per gallon from the three categories are given in Table 13.13b.

Table 13.13a Maple Syrup Production

Year	Units	2017	2018	2019	2020	2021	Expected[‡] 2022–2031
Average number of taps	Taps	2,000	2,000	2,000	2,000	2,000	2,000
Total syrup production	Gallons	739	661	834	755	650	730
Heiberg syrup sales	Gallons	182	107	211	43	100	112
Bulk syrup sales	Gallons	418	297	359	359	246	276
Wholesale syrup sales	Gallons	139	249	496	340	305	342
Inventory	Gallons	89	37	49	13	0	0

‡ The expected total production for 2022–2031 is an average of the prior years. The expected sales quantity in each category is weighted based on the 2021 sales.

Table 13.13b Maple Syrup Pricing[‡]

Year	Units	2017	2018	2019	2020	2021	Expected 2022–2031
Expected Weighted Ave. Syrup Price	$/Gallon	32.69	36.12	32.69	37.89	46.12	46.12
Heiberg Syrup Price	$/Gallon	25.20	25.20	24.00	50.00	71.95	71.95
Bulk Syrup Price	$/Gallon	42.00	44.00	44.00	44.00	44.00	44.00
Wholesale Syrup Price	$/Gallon	24.00	24.00	24.00	21.00	23.53	23.53
Inventory	$/Gallon	32.69	36.12	32.69	37.89	46.12	46.12

‡ The expected weighted average syrup price is weighted based on the revenue from each sales category. Inventory is valued at the expected weighted average syrup price for that year. The expected pricing for 2022–2031 is equal to the pricing in 2021.

Table 13.13c Maple Syrup Revenue

Year	Units	2017	2018	2019	2020	2021	Expected 2022–2031
Total Revenue	$	27,745	22,918	31,619	25,708	25,161	28,224
Heiberg	$	1,881	2,700	5,059	2,150	7,168	8,041
Bulk	$	11,877	12,926	13,048	15,809	10,815	12,132
Wholesale	$	11,093	5,974	11,910	7,268	7,178	8,051
Inventory	$	2,894	1,318	1,602	481	0	0

Wholesaling the syrup earns the lowest price, followed by bulk pricing. The price at Heiberg has increased significantly since 2019. However, due to the unique nature of this being a for-profit business within a state institution, the price increases are such that they will not compete with local private maple syrup producers.

The revenue earned from maple syrup sales is given in Table 13.13c. Earning revenue from wholesale is very easy – the syrup is stored in stainless steel drums and transported to a local collection center. The collection center will purchase all the syrup ESF is willing to provide. The marginal revenue for sales at Heiberg is the greatest, but expanding these sales must be done carefully as ESF's maple syrup operation cannot be seen to be competing with local private maple syrup producers. This is related directly to the second goal of building lasting customer loyalty. The marginal revenue for bulk sales is almost twice that generated by wholesale. Expanding the bulk market again must be done carefully; however, one potential market would be bulk sales to other State University of New York Institutions' bookstores using containers with the specific institution's logo. This is related directly to the final goal of diversifying the revenue stream. However, this is moving forward slowly due to bureaucracy.

Profits

Financial Analysis

The cash flow statement is given in Table 13.14. The cash balance is negative from 2018 to 2022, which is due to paying off three (3) capital equipment loans. The cash balance by the end of the investment analysis horizon is $143,775.

The income statement is given in Table 13.15. Net income describes a business's profitability. Given the historic and expected costs and revenues, the income statement shows that this business is profitable starting in 2021. Based on these dates the profitability is relatively constant with a jump in profitability starting in 2028 after paying off the 2022 capital investment in the sugarbush.

The balance statement is given in Table 13.16. The driving factor of determining the assets is the cash balance from the cash flow statement. The driving factor of creating equity, after the capital loans are paid off, are the retained earnings which are equal to the prior years' retained earnings plus the current year's net income.

Table 13.14 Cash Flow Statement for the Maple Syrup Operation

Sugarbush & Sugar House	Units	2017	2018	2019	2020	2021	2022	2023	2024	2025	2026	2027	2028	2029	2030	2031
Revenues	Units					0	1	2	3	4	5	6	7	8	9	10
Operating Activities: Cash Inflow (Revenue)																
Retail Sales – Heiberg	$/year		2,700.00	5,059.00	2,150.00	7,168.00										
Bulk Sales – Boy Scouts, ESF Bookstore, etc.	$/year		12,925.50	13,048.00	15,809.20	10,814.67										
Wholesale – Canada	$/year		5,974.00	11,910.00	7,267.50	7,177.90										
Maple Cream, Candies, etc.	$/year															
Inventory	$/year		1,318.32	1,601.99	481.14	0.00										
Total Revenue	$/year		22,917.82	31,618.99	25,707.84	25,160.57	28,224.28	28,224.28	28,224.28	28,224.28	28,224.28	28,224.28	28,224.28	28,224.28	28,224.28	28,224.28

Sugarbush & Sugar House	Units	2017	2018	2019	2020	2021	2022	2023	2024	2025	2026	2027	2028	2029	2030	2031
Costs	Units					0	1	2	3	4	5	6	7	8	9	10
Operating Activities: Cash Outflow (Costs)																
Annual Operating Expenses 2018	$/year		9,420.10													
Dump Truck Maintenance – 2018	$/year		11,747.34													
New Sap Vacuum Pump – 2019	$/year			3,773.00												
Annual Operating Expenses 2019	$/year			5,937.31												
Annual Operating Expenses 2020	$/year				9,602.17											
Annual Operating Expenses 2021	$/year					5,050.16										
Replace vacuum lines	$/year									2,000.00			2,000.00			2,000.00
Annual Operating Expenses 2022–2032	$/year						7,326.17	7,326.17	7,326.17	7,326.17	7,326.17	7,326.17	7,326.17	7,326.17	7,326.17	7,326.17

Upgrade Canning Machine 2014																
Annual Interest Payment	$/year	156.69	80.63													
Annual Principal Payment	$/year	1,267.69	1,343.75													
Capital Assets (Sugar House) 2015																
Annual Interest Payment	$/year	2,424.66	1,663.05	855.75												
Annual Principal Payment	$/year	12,693.51	13,455.12	14,262.43												
Capital Assets (Sugar House) 2017																
Annual Interest Payment	$/year	2,082.78	1,713.30	1,321.66	906.51	466.46										
Annual Principal Payment	$/year	6,157.96	6,527.44	6,919.09	7,334.23	7,774.28										
Capital Asset (Sugarbush) 2022																
Annual Interest Payment	$/year						1,500.00	1,233.91	951.85	652.86	335.94					
Annual Principal Payment	$/year						4,434.91	4,701.00	4,983.06	5,282.05	5,598.97					
Total Cost		45,951	34,494	32,961	13,291	15,567	13,261	13,261	15,261	13,261	13,261	13,261	9,326	7,326	7,326	9,326
Cash Flow		−23,032.92	−2,874.61	−7,253.24	11,869.67	12,657.38	14,963.21	14,963.21	12,963.21	14,963.21	14,963.21	14,963.21	18,898.12	20,898.12	20,898.12	18,898.12
Cash Balance		−23,032.92	−25,907.53	−33,160.77	−21,291.10	−8,633.72	6,329.49	21,292.69	34,255.90	49,219.11	64,182.32	83,080.44	103,978.56	124,876.68	143,774.80	

Table 13.15 Income Statement for the Maple Syrup Operation‡

Sugarbush & Sugar House Income Statement	Units	2017 2018	2019	2020	2021	2022	2023	2024	2025	2026	2027	2028	2029	2030	2031
					0	1	2	3	4	5	6	7	8	9	10
Revenues (Maple Syrup)	$/year	22,917.82	31,618.99	25,707.84	25,160.57	28,224.28	28,224.28	28,224.28	28,224.28	28,224.28	28,224.28	28,224.28	28,224.28	28,224.28	28,224.28
Expenses															
Annual Operating Expenses 2018	$/year	9,420.10													
Dump Truck Maintenance – 2018	$/year	11,747.34													
New Sap Vacuum Pump – 2019	$/year		3,773.00												
Annual Operating Expenses 2019	$/year		5,937.31												
Annual Operating Expenses 2020	$/year			9,602.17											
Annual Operating Expenses 2021	$/year				5,050.16										
Replace vacuum lines	$/year								2,000.00			2,000.00			2,000.00
Annual Operating Expenses 2022–2032	$/year					7,326.17	7,326.17	7,326.17	7,326.17	7,326.17	7,326.17	7,326.17	7,326.17	7,326.17	7,326.17
Annual interest payment – 2014 Investment	$/year	156.69	80.63												
Annual interest payment – 2015 Investment	$/year	2,424.66	1,663.05	855.75											
Annual interest payment – 2017	$/year	2,082.78	1,713.30	1,321.66	906.51	466.46									

Annual interest payment – 2022 Investment	$/year	1,500.00	1,233.91	951.85	652.86	335.94								
5-Year Straight-Line Depreciation – 2014	$/year	1,200.00	1,200.00											
5-Year Straight-Line Depreciation – 2015	$/year	12,736.65	12,736.65	12,736.65										
5-Year Straight-Line Depreciation – 2017	$/year	6,942.60	6,942.60	6,942.60	6,942.60									
5-Year Straight-Line Depreciation – 2022	$/year	5,000.00	5,000.00	5,000.00	5,000.00									
Total	$/year	46,710.82	34,046.54	31,458.82	12,899.27	14,735.22	13,826.17	13,560.07	15,278.01	12,979.03	12,662.10	9,326.17	7,326.17	9,326.17
Net Income (+) or Loss (−)		−23,793.00	−2,427.55	−5,750.98	12,261.30	13,489.06	14,398.12	14,664.21	12,946.27	15,245.26	15,562.18	18,898.12	20,898.12	18,898.12

‡ Depreciation is calculated using a five-year straight line formula. $/yr denotes dollars per year.

Table 13.16 Balance Statement for the Maple Syrup Operation‡

Sugarbush & Sugar House	Units	2017	2018	2019	2020	2021	2022	2023	2024	2025	2026	2027	2028	2029	2030	2031
Balance Sheet (Maple Syrup, Candies, Cream, etc.)						0	1	2	3	4	5	6	7	8	9	10
Cash	$/year		-23,032.92	-25,907.53	-33,160.77	-21,291.10	-8,633.72	6,329.49	21,292.69	34,255.90	49,219.11	64,182.32	83,080.44	103,978.56	124,876.68	143,774.80
Capital Equipment – 2014	$		6,000.00	6,000.00												
Capital Equipment – 2015	$		63,683.25	63,683.25	63,683.25											
Capital Equipment – 2017	$		34,713.00	34,713.00	34,713.00	34,713.00	34,713.00									
Capital Equipment – 2022	$							25,000.00	25,000.00	25,000.00	25,000.00	25,000.00				
Less: Accumulated Depreciation – 2009	$/year															
Less: Accumulated Depreciation – 2014	$/year		-4,800.00	-6,000.00												
Less: Accumulated Depreciation – 2015	$/year		-38,209.95	-50,946.60	-63,683.25											
Less: Accumulated Depreciation – 2017	$/year		-6,942.60	-13,885.20	-20,827.80	-27,770.40	-34,713.00									
Less: Accumulated Depreciation – 2022	$/year							-5,000.00	-10,000.00	-15,000.00	-20,000.00	-25,000.00				
Total Assets	$		31,410.78	7,656.92	-19,275.57	-14,348.50	-8,633.72	26,329.49	36,292.69	44,255.90	54,219.11	64,182.32	83,080.44	103,978.56	124,876.68	143,774.80
Loan – 2014	$/year		1,343.75	0.00												
Loan – 2015	$/year		27,717.55	14,262.43	0.00											
Loan – 2017	$/year		28,555.04	22,027.60	15,108.51	7,774.28	0.00									
Loan – 2022	$/year							20,565.09	15,864.09	10,881.02	5,598.97	0.00				
Retained Earnings	$/year	-2,412.56	-26,205.56	-28,633.11	-34,384.08	-22,122.79	-8,633.72	5,764.40	20,428.61	33,374.88	48,620.14	64,182.32	83,080.44	103,978.56	124,876.68	143,774.80
Total Liabilities & Equity	$		31,410.78	7,656.92	-19,275.57	-14,348.50	-8,633.72	26,329.49	36,292.69	44,255.90	54,219.11	64,182.32	83,080.44	103,978.56	124,876.68	143,774.80

‡ Depreciation is calculated using a five-year straight line formula. $/yr denotes dollars per year.

As there are no shareholder payments, equity is equal to the cash balance after year 2027.

Breakeven Analysis

The annual breakeven metrics are given in Table 13.17a. The annual breakeven metrics for the Maple Syrup Operation shows: (1) The production system is capable of producing enough gallons of maple syrup per year given an expected price of 46.12 dollars per gallon. The expected production level of 730 gallons of maple syrup per year is well above the required breakeven production levels. (2) The required annual breakeven prices during the investment horizon are well below the expected price of 46.12 dollars per gallon as well as the expected wholesale price.

The equal annual equivalent (EAE) breakeven metrics for the maple syrup operation are given in Table 13.17b. The EAE breakeven metrics show: (1) The required EAE breakeven revenue to cover the present value of the financing, operation, and maintenance costs for the investment horizon are less than half the expected

Table 13.17a Annual Breakeven Analysis for the Maple Syrup Operation[‡]

| | | 2021 | | | | Year | | | | | 2031 |
	Units	0	1	2	3	4	5	6	7	8	9	10
Annual Breakeven Revenue	$/year	13,291	15,567	13,261	13,261	15,261	13,261	13,261	9,326	7,326	7,326	9,326
Annual Breakeven Production	gal/ year	368	431	368	368	423	368	368	259	203	203	259
Annual Breakeven Price	$/gal	20	21	18	18	21	18	18	13	10	10	13

‡ The annual breakeven revenue is equal to the annual total costs. The annual breakeven production level is based on an expected price of 46.12 dollars per gallon ($/gal). The annual breakeven price is based on producing 730 gallons of maple syrup per year starting in 2022.

Table 13.17b Equal Annual Equivalent (EAE) Breakeven Analysis for the Maple Syrup Operation[‡]

	Units	
EAE Breakeven Revenue	$/year	12,281
EAE Breakeven Production	gal/year	263
EAE Breakeven Price	$/gal	17

‡ The EAE breakeven revenue was based on the cost of producing 730 gallons of syrup per year starting in 2022. The EAE breakeven production was based on an expected price of 46.12 dollars per gallon ($/gal). The EAE breakeven price was based on producing 730 gallons of syrup per year starting in 2022.

revenues. (2) The required EAE breakeven production level of 266 gallons of syrup per year that must be produced and "sold" annually to cover the present value of the financing, operation, and maintenance costs for the investment horizon at an expected market price is again well below the expected production level of 730 gallons per year. Based on the data provided by ESF Forest Properties, every gallon of syrup produced in a given year is basically sold in that year. (3) The required EAE breakeven price of 16.83 dollars per gallon that must be received annually to cover the present value of the financing, operation, and maintenance costs for the investment horizon at an expected output or production level is well below the expected market price of 46.12 dollars per gallon. It is also below the expected wholesale price of 23.53 dollars per gallon.

These breakeven metrics provide a degree of confidence that the production system can produce the required levels of output and that output can be sold to cover annual and present value production costs. This analysis appears to support this being a viable business opportunity.

Net Present Value

The present value of the maple syrup's expected revenues and costs are given in Tables 13.18a and 13.18b. The annual and cumulative net present values (NPV) are given in Table 13.18c. The annual and cumulative NPVs are positive. This is consistent with the cash balance in cash flow statement and the net income in the income statement being positive. The cumulative NPV in year 10 is $130,291. This implies that the investment in the maple syrup operation is returning the required 6% discount rate plus an addition net present value of cash flow. This analysis appears to support this being a viable business opportunity for the college.

Based on the information provided in Tables 13.18a and 13.18b, the benefit–cost ratio (BCR) is 2.27. Using this as a cardinal metric of sensitivity, this implies that the discounted costs could increase by a factor of 2.27 and NPV would just be equal to zero. The discounted revenues could decrease by a factor of 0.44 and NPV

Table 13.18a Present Value of the Expected Revenues for the Maple Syrup Operation[‡]

		2021				Year					2031
Estimated Revenue	Units	0	1	2	3	4	5	6	7	8	9	10
Expected Revenue from Maple Syrup Sales	$/year		28,224	28,224	28,224	28,224	28,224	28,224	28,224	28,224	28,224	28,224
Present Value of Expected Revenues	$/year		26,627	25,120	23,698	22,356	21,091	19,897	18,771	17,708	16,706	15,760

‡ The expected revenues are based on producing and selling 730 gallons of maple syrup per year at an expected price of 46.12 dollars per gallon. The present values of the expected revenues are calculated based on a 6% discount rate.

Table 13.18b Present Value of the Expected Costs for the Maple Syrup Operation[‡]

		2021					Year					2031
		0	1	2	3	4	5	6	7	8	9	10
Total Expected Operating and Financing Activity Costs	$/year		15,567	13,261	13,261	15,261	13,261	13,261	9,326	7,326	7,326	9,326
Present Value of Expected Costs	$/year		14,686	11,802	11,134	12,088	9,909	9,349	6,202	4,597	4,336	5,208

[‡] The expected cost is based on producing and selling 730 gallons of maple syrup per year at an expected price of 46.12 dollars per gallon. The present values of the expected costs are calculated based on a 6% discount rate.

Table 13.18c Net Present Value of the Maple Syrup Operation[‡]

		2021					Year				2031
		0	1	2	3	4	5	6	7	8	9	10
Net Present Value	Units	0	1	2	3	4	5	6	7	8	9	10
Annual	$/year		11,941	13,317	12,563	10,268	11,181	10,548	12,568	13,112	12,370	10,553
Cumulative	$			23,811	37,128	49,691	59,959	71,141	81,689	94,257	107,369	119,739	130,291

[‡] The expected costs and revenues are based on producing and selling 730 gallons of maple syrup per year at an expected price of 46.12 dollars per gallon. The net present values are calculated based on a 6% discount rate.

would just be equal to zero. This analysis also appears to support this being a viable business opportunity for the college. However, as described in Chapter 6 – Capital Theory: Investment Analysis, a critical question must be asked and answered: Are these implied increases or decreases within normal ranges of operations for costs and revenues of the investment? This will be examined in the next section.

Analysis and Recommendation

The breakeven and NPV analyses appear to support this being a viable business opportunity for ESF. It is now time to revisit the obvious omission of paying the professional staff. To do this I must revisit the production system with respect to professional staff labor briefly:

• Installing 2,000 taps takes two 4-hour days and four professional staff members.
• As the maple syrup operation is not the only business the professional staff must work on, a day is defined as four to six hours. There are five professional staff involved with the business. On average it takes three professional staff per day to run the business during the maple syrup season. The jobs performed include tapping, moving sap to sugar house, boiling and packaging, repairs and maintenance, cleaning, removing taps, and communications and marketing.

In 2021 a total of 650 gallons of syrup were produced. Given two 4-hour days for tapping and a production rate of 30 gallons per four hours and one hour for the remaining tasks, this implies 362 hours worked for the 2021 maple syrup season. At an average wage of 32.25 dollars per hour, the labor cost would be $11,675. The net income in 2021 was $12,261, which is sufficient to cover the professional staff's salaries. The net income for 2022 to 2031 is also sufficient to cover the professional staff's salaries. Obviously, each year's annual net income will be decreased significantly by including professional staff salaries, but it is still positive starting in the year 2021. The balance sheet will show total assets and total liability and equity in year 2031 equals −$35,781. The important questions are why and what does this mean. The Why: The negative balance sheet is due primarily to the negative cash balances resulting from the paying off the three capital loans between 2018 to 2022 and the share of the 2018 maintenance and repair joint costs. Adding the professional staff salaries exacerbated the problem. For example, in 2019, 834 gallons of syrup were produced, which increased professional staff salaries. The negative cash balances started to decrease after 2020, but not fast enough to have a positive cash balance by the end of the investment horizon. The What: A business with a negative balance sheet is at risk. A negative balance sheet means that there are more liabilities than assets so there is no value in the business available for the shareholders. Consequently, if all its liabilities came due at once, the business would not be able to pay them, even if it liquidated assets, and would fail. Still, the cash flow is positive after year 2020, so this operation can keep up with its annual bills. Including professional staff's salaries in the profit analysis reduces the NPV to $25,571, but it is still positive and reflects the cash flow and net income. The BCR is now 1.12. So, increasing the costs due to professional staff's salaries is within the 2.30 multiplier or factor increase in discounted costs. *However*, just relying on the NPV and BCR would miss the economic information provided by the cash flow statement, income statement, and balance sheet.

The breakeven analyses show the required annual and EAE production levels are less than the least amount of syrup produced between 2017 and 2021. In addition, the required annual and EAE price is less than the expected price of 46.12 dollars per gallon for 2022 to 2031. But these margins are now reduced considerably. The NPV, BCR, and breakeven metrics still provide a degree of confidence to support this being a viable business opportunity.

These analyses also show that cost and revenues need to be managed carefully. This speaks directly to Goals #3 and #4 given in Table 13.9. For example, wholesaling maple syrup earns the lowest price, but generating revenue by wholesaling is very easy as the local collection center will purchase all the maple syrup ESF is willing to provide. If all wholesaling revenue could be switched to bulk sales, the cash balance and the balance sheet would be positive, the NPV would increase to $77,121, BCR would increase to 1.37, and the breakeven metrics still provide a degree of confidence to support this being a viable business opportunity. Again, this shows the importance of a complete set of economic information to help manage revenues and costs. Simply put, altering a revenue stream would change this operation from being at risk to *not* being at risk.

The analysis and recommendations must also include a discussion of "Context." The context is defined by the mission statement, goals, and objectives given in Table 13.9. Based on the data provided by Forest Properties, the maple syrup operation is a viable business opportunity and provides a positive net cash flow to the college; the mission statement also speaks to ESF's mission of teaching, research, and outreach. The maple syrup operation also provides benefit to the college as well as the surrounding communities. These are identified directly in Goals #1 and #2 and their corresponding objectives.

The conclusions of this analysis are (1) the maple syrup operation is a viable business opportunity; (2) to maintain viability the costs and revenues must be managed actively; (3) the maple syrup operation provides additional benefit to the college and local communities in terms of teaching and outreach. The recommendation is to continue the maple syrup operation as a business.

Log Yard and Firewood Business Plan

This is an ongoing business operation. While revenue information is available starting in 2006, detailed cost information is only available starting in 2018. The cost and revenue information from 2018 to 2021 will be included in the financial statements. The investment analysis horizon for the business plan is 2021 to 2031. This allows for using historic and current capital and operations costs and revenues to develop a comprehensive business plan.

Background

In addition to the maple syrup business, ESF's Forest Properties Department also manages a log yard and firewood business at Heiberg Forest. Sustainably managing Heiberg's forests has been ongoing since 1948. The purpose of this business is to generate a profit by sustainably managing Heiberg's hardwood and conifer forests to produce primarily high-quality hardwood logs and hardwood firewood, as there are basically no local markets for the conifers. The hardwood logs are sold to local mills. The firewood is sold to local households and used internally in the sugar house and to heat the maintenance garage.

Executive Summary

The log yard and firewood operations are workable business opportunities for ESF. These business opportunities are capable of providing ESF with a positive net income. The challenge posed by these opportunities is managing the periodically high maintenance, repair, and equipment rental costs due to aging equipment that can lead to periodic negative net income. They do provide benefits to the college in terms of teaching and research opportunities, provide benefits to the local communities in terms of recreational opportunities, and provide a sustainable source of logs to local businesses and firewood to local communities. The recommendation is to continue the log yard and firewood as ongoing operations with close attention paid to managing costs.

Mission, Goals, and Objectives

The mission, goals, and objectives are given in Table 13.19. The mission, goals, and objectives reflect the fact that the log yard and firewood are for-profit businesses. Again, managing costs is critical for generating the largest profits regardless of the revenue stream as all the profits are used to support students and faculty.

While this is a for-profit business, given its unique nature not all the benefits generated by this business are measured in dollars. This is described in the mission statement and tied to the first goal and its corresponding two objectives directly. It is important to remember that context matters when analyzing data and developing a recommendation based on this analysis.

Table 13.19 Mission, Goals, and Objectives for the Log Yard and Firewood Business

Mission Statement

To provide sustainably harvested, high quality hardwood logs to regional log buyers and hardwood firewood to local residents and internal use. Promote sustainable forest management strategies to ensure current and future forest productivity, public recreational values, and profits to support ESFs mission of teaching, research, and outreach by supporting scholarships, paid student work opportunities at Heiberg, and continuing education for the forest properties staff. We strive to treat everyone in a fair and ethical manner.

Goal: To provide educational field trips on sustainable forest management practices.	Objective: At least one (1) field trip per year involving ESF students.
	Objective: At least one (1) field trip per year involving public school students.
	Objective: Develop prescriptions for timber harvests and stand improvements that are consistent with teaching and research objectives.
Goal: Build lasting customer loyalty	Objective: Sustainably harvest 10,000 to 40,000 board feet of hardwoods logs annually.
	Objective: Process 140 to 160 tons of sustainably harvested logs annually.
Goal: Ensure long-term profitability by monitoring costs and revenues annually	Objective: Develop the three fundamental financial accounting statements annually.
	Objective: Use these data to assess the cost effectiveness of the operation annually.
Goal: Maintain a sustainable forest that continuously produces forest ecosystem values	Objective: Ensure annually that all water quality needs are met according to the New York State Best Management Practices Manual.
	Objective: Perform annual maintenance on 1/3 of established trails.
	Objective: Monitor post-harvest sites for regeneration and forest health to ensure desired outcomes of prescriptions are achieved.

Production System

In the context of ESF sustainable forest management harvesting activities, the connection between the log yard and firewood businesses are described as main product–by-product relationship, respectively. The main products of ESF's sustainable forest management harvesting are hardwood logs. Logs used in the firewood operation are a by-product in that they are of significantly lower per unit value, and they are the residual after the merchandisable logs have been sold. This relationship will be described in more detail later, and the distinction will become important in the discussion of costs.

The professional staff mark the trees in a defined area being managed following a vetted silvicultural prescription. The marked trees are felled by ESF's sawyer and skidded by another staff member to a forest road landing. This team can harvest between 10 and 20 thousand board feet (MBF) per week. The log buyer comes to the landing and ESF's technical staff will merchandise the logs at a log buyer's direction to obtain a higher valued log. The logs are tagged by the log buyer and then transported via ESF's log truck to a log yard near the maintenance building.

The relevant inputs based on the preceding production function description are given in Tables 13.20a and 13.20b.

Table 13.20a Relevant Fixed Inputs of the Log Yard Production System

Input	Description
Skidder	Owned and maintained by ESF and is used to transport logs from cutting locations to roadside landings.
Chainsaws	Chainsaws are owned and maintained by ESF and are used to fell trees, improve timber stands, and buck logs to length.
Log Truck	Owned and maintained by ESF and is used to move logs to the log yard, sort logs, and move unsold logs to the firewood concentration yard.
Maintenance	The log truck, skidder, and chainsaw all require annual routine maintenance to remain operational. The maintenance needed is fixed to how much the machine is used. This is handled by ESF.
Land	3,900 acres and serves as an outdoor classroom and laboratory for teaching, research, and outreach. It is composed of 1,395 acres of Allegheny hardwoods and 640 acres of conifer plantations.

Table 13.20b Relevant Variable Inputs of the Log Yard Production System

Input	Description
Labor	There are four professionals and two technical staff members that oversee and run the operation from the woods to the log yard, advertise the logs, and supervise the log buyers. In addition, a student intern works with the professional and technical staff during the summer.
Fuel, Filters, Oil, and Grease	A gas-oil mix is used in the chainsaw. Diesel fuel is used in the log truck and skidder. The amount used each year depends on the volume of logs harvested and transported.

A description of the outputs is given in Tables 13.20c. The annual log harvest data since 2012 are given in Table 13.21a. The quantity harvested varies from year to year for various reasons. For example, a significant portion of the ash (*Fraxinus* sp.) that was infected with the emerald ash borer (*Agrilus planipennis*) was

Table 13.20c Outputs of the Log Yard Production System

Outputs	Description
Grade 1 Sawlog	Logs in this category are deemed the most valuable based on their size, limited defects, and amount of clear wood.
Grade 2 Sawlog	Logs in this category are deemed of a lower quality based on their size, defects, and amount of clear wood.
Grade 3 Sawlog	Logs in this category are deemed the least valuable based on their size or defects.
Below Grade	Logs in this category are deemed not viable commercially for sawmill and are processed into firewood.
Sawdust Waste	Sawdust is created from the chainsaw when bucking logs. This waste is typically negligible and left on the ground. If a significant amount can be collected, it is used to clean up spills in the shop or as local animal bedding per request.

Table 13.21a Annual Harvest and Revenue Data From Log Sale

	Total	Hardwood
Revenue Data – Hardwood Logs	($)	(BdFt/Year)[†]
2006	2,340	
2007	7,559	
2008	16,821	
2009	17,729	
2010	7,415	
2011	13,096	
2012	31,374	42,971
2013	70,181	115,557
2014	66,372	96,162
2015	94,829	119,006
2016	37,782	58,783
2017	36,340	28,875
2018	12,787	17,315
2019	32,164	40,880
2020	52,923	54,185
2021	19,822	20,536
Expected Hardwood Log Volume 2022–2032		20,000 to 40,000
2020 Revenue Data – Logging Softwood	1,121	7,559
2020 Revenue Data – Contract Logging Softwood	7,526	

† BdFt/Year denotes board foot log volume sold per year.

removed between 2013 and 2015. In addition to 1,395 acres of Allegheny hardwoods, Heiberg has 1,640 acres of conifer plantations. In 2017, 282 tons of softwood were sold. In 2020, ESF contracted the logging of some of the softwood plantations. ESF's logging crew harvested a small proportion as they are better equipped to log hardwoods. Based on discussion with the Forest Properties professional staff, an annual harvest of 20,000 to 40,000 board feet of hardwood logs is expected for 2022 to 2032. For purposes of the financial analyses to follow, I will assume an annual harvest of 30,000 board feet of hardwood logs.

Log volume is described not only by quantity as measured by board feet, but also by quality or grade. Table 13.21b contains volume by log grade. Based on the data given in Tables 13.21a and 13.21b, ESF provides high-quality sustainably harvested hardwoods to local log buyers, which is consistent with the mission statement.

Logs not merchandised and sold are transported to the firewood concentration yard for further processing into firewood. This defines the split-off point between the log yard and firewood businesses.[13] The previous year's nonmarketable logs are taken from storage and loaded onto the firewood processor's log deck using a loader. The log deck feeds individual logs into a conveyor where they are cut into 16-inch (40.64-centimeter) sections and a hydraulic press splits the wood into four pieces. If a piece is particularly large, sometimes the split pieces will need to be split again. The split wood then drops onto an elevator and then into a truck or trailer.

Table 13.21b Price and Volume by Log Grade

2019 Log Price & Log Volume Harvest Data	Log Price[†]	Log Volume[‡]
Grade 1	936	28,228
Grade 2	475	11,315
Grade 3	275	1,337
2020 Log Price & Log Volume Harvest Data	Log Price[†]	Log Volume[‡]
Select, Prime, Veneer, and Grade 1	1,261	34,907
Grade 2	498	15,019
Grade 3	333	4,259
2021 Log Price & Log Volume Harvest Data	Log Price[†]	Log Volume[‡]
Select, Prime, and Veneer	1,309	8,394
Grade 1	973	3,941
Grade 2	685	6,488
Grade 3	326	1,713

[†] Log price denotes dollars per thousand board feet ($/MBF)
[‡] Log volume is measured in board feet

The relevant inputs based on the preceding production function description are given in Tables 13.22a and 13.22b. A description of the outputs is given in Tables 13.22c. Firewood is processed to satisfy internal and external demand. The annual firewood production data since 2018 are given in Table 13.23.

The internal demand is comprised of heating the maintenance garage and to fire the evaporator in the sugar house. Internal use totals 39 face cords, 12 to fire the evaporator and 27 to heat the maintenance garage, annually. External demand is comprised of local households using firewood as a heating source. Since 2018, the average annual external demand is 165 tons with a range of 104 to 241 tons. The last two columns in Table 13.23 are total tons and processed tons. The difference is that block wood sold to customers is not processed by the firewood

Table 13.22a Relevant Fixed Inputs of the Firewood Production System

Inputs	Description
Firewood Processor and Elevator	Blockbuster Model 18–20 which cuts logs to length and splits them into firewood. The processor can produce 2.5 tons of firewood per hour.
Loader	This loader lift logs onto the processor's log deck.
Maintenance	Firewood process, elevator, and loader all require annual routine maintenance to remain operational.

Table 13.22b Relevant Variable Inputs of the Firewood Production System

Inputs	Description
Logs	Below grade logs are stored for one year in the firewood concentration yard.
Fuel, Filters, Oil, and Grease	The amount used each year depends on the tons of firewood processed.
Labor	Processing firewood takes one to two technical staff.

Table 13.22c Outputs of the Firewood Production System

Outputs	Description
Firewood	Measured as tons or face cords for internal and external demand. Internal demand constitutes firewood to heat the maintenance garage and fire the evaporator. External demand is comprised of local household using firewood as a heating source. ESF prefers to sell firewood by the ton to avoid disputes over face cord size.
Block Wood	Block wood is unprocessed firewood logs. This is sold by the ton to local households or firewood processors.
Sawdust	Unfortunately, not enough sawdust is produced by the firewood processor to sell as a by-product primarily for animal bedding. The sawdust is collected and dispersed on the forest roads.

Table 13.23 Firewood Production for External Sales and Internal Use and Revenue

	Total ($)	Total Tons	Processed Tons
2018			154
External Sales: 100.5 ton split; 24 face cords; 63 tons block wood	8,409	184	
Internal Use: 27 face cords maintenance heat; 12 face cord sugar house	1,950	33	
2019			196
External Sales: 150.5 tons split; 15 face cord; 77.5 tons block wood	11,183	241	
Internal Use: 27 face cords maintenance heat; 12 face cord sugar house	1,950	33	
2020			68
External Sales: 25 ton split; 12 face cord; 69 tons block wood	5,213	104	
Internal Use: 27 face cords maintenance heat; 12 face cord sugar house	1,950	33	
2021			157
External Sales: 94.71 ton split; 35 face cord; 0 tons block wood	7,433	124	
Internal Use: 27 face cords maintenance heat; 12 face cord sugar house	1,950	33	
2022–2032			148
Expected External Sales: 95 ton split; 25 face cord; 60 tons block wood	8,030	175	
Expected Internal Use: 27 face cords maintenance heat; 12 face cord sugar house	1,950	33	

processor. Processing firewood is done on an on-demand basis, and due to liability reasons ESF is unable to deliver firewood. Customers must come to Heiberg to pick up their firewood order. When a customer picks up an order, the wood is split at approximately 2.5 tons per hour given the log size. ESF prefers to sell firewood by the ton to avoid disputes over face cord size. The expected external sales and internal uses for 2022 to 2032 were based on conversations with the Forest Properties professional staff. Finally, the firewood processor does produce sawdust as a waste product. Unfortunately, not enough sawdust is produced by the firewood processor to sell as a by-product primarily for animal bedding. The sawdust is collected and dispersed on the forest roads.

Costs

As described in the previous section, the log yard and the firewood businesses describe a main product–by-product relationship. This impacts how costs are defined and allocated in primarily the cash flow statement. In practice, costs incurred prior to the split-off point in a main product–by-product production process are allocated to the main product. The separable costs after the split-off point are allocated to each individual product. However, based on the cost data provided by the Forest Properties staff, costs are (i) associated with a specific business, (ii) joint or non-separable among all the businesses, or (iii) joint or non-separable between the log yard and firewood businesses. Thus, there are joint costs that must be allocated to each business. Unfortunately, as was discussed in Chapter 9 – Estimating Nonmarket Values, there is no nonarbitrary way of allocating joint costs (Carlson 1974; Blocher et al. 2002). The choice of which joint cost allocation approach to use must be an informed business management decision and once chosen used consistently. Those costs identified as joint will be allocated to each business based on the percent of revenue generated by each business annually.[14] The allocated joint costs are included as part of the three financial statements according to the generally accepted accounting principles as they impact each annually.

Cost data on capital expenditures has been collected since 2014. These are summarized as follows:

- The Blockbuster Model 18–20 with elevator was purchased in 2013 for $45,400;
- A surplus New York State Department of Transportation snowplow truck was purchased in 2015 for $43,500;
- The snowplow truck was converted into a log truck in 2015 for $13,000;
- A used 1997 Timberjack 360 skidder was purchased and refurbished in 2015 for $45,000; and
- The old log truck was surplused and a used 2007 Sterling log truck with a Serco 8500 log loader was purchased from a local railroad repair company in 2022 for $75,800.

The interest rate on all capital equipment expenditures is 6% for five years. The amortization schedules for the 2014, 2015, and 2022 capital expenditures are given in Table 13.24.

Table 13.24 Amortization Schedules for the 2014, 2015, and 2022 Capital Expenditures for the Log Yard and Firewood Businesses

Blockbuster Model 18–20 With Elevator

Year	Payment Number	Payment	Interest Portion	Principal Portion	Principal Balance
2013	0				45,400.00
2014	1	10,777.80	2,724.00	8,053.80	37,346.20
2015	2	10,777.80	2,240.77	8,537.02	28,809.18
2016	3	10,777.80	1,728.55	9,049.25	19,759.93
2017	4	10,777.80	1,185.60	9,592.20	10,167.73
2018	5	10,777.80	610.06	10,167.73	0.00
	Sum	53,888.98	8,488.98	45,400.00	

Surplus New York State Department of Transportation Snowplow Truck

Year	Payment Number	Payment	Interest Portion	Principal Portion	Principal Balance
2015	0				43,500.00
2016	1	10,326.74	2,610.00	7,716.74	35,783.26
2017	2	10,326.74	2,147.00	8,179.75	27,603.51
2018	3	10,326.74	1,656.21	8,670.53	18,932.98
2019	4	10,326.74	1,135.98	9,190.76	9,742.21
2020	5	10,326.74	584.53	9,742.21	0.00
	Sum	51,633.72	8,133.72	43,500.00	

Convert Snowplow Truck to Log Truck

Year	Payment Number	Payment	Interest Portion	Principal Portion	Principal Balance
2015	0				13,000.00
2016	1	3,086.15	780.00	2,306.15	10,693.85
2017	2	3,086.15	641.63	2,444.52	8,249.32
2018	3	3,086.15	494.96	2,591.19	5,658.13
2019	4	3,086.15	339.49	2,746.67	2,911.47
2020	5	3,086.15	174.69	2,911.47	0.00
	Sum	15,430.77	2,430.77	13,000.00	

Used Timberjack 360 Skidder

Year	Payment Number	Payment	Interest Portion	Principal Portion	Principal Balance
2015	0				45,000.00
2016	1	10,682.84	2,700.00	7,982.84	37,017.16
2017	2	10,682.84	2,221.03	8,461.81	28,555.35
2018	3	10,682.84	1,713.32	8,969.52	19,585.84
2019	4	10,682.84	1,175.15	9,507.69	10,078.15
2020	5	10,682.84	604.69	10,078.15	0.00
	Sum	53,414.19	8,414.19	45,000.00	

Purchase a Used 2007 Sterling Log Truck With a Serco 8500 Log Loader

Year	Payment Number	Payment	Interest Portion	Principal Portion	Principal Balance
2022	0				75,800.00
2023	1	17,994.65	4,548.00	13,446.65	62,353.35
2024	2	17,994.65	3,741.20	14,253.45	48,099.91
2025	3	17,994.65	2,885.99	15,108.65	32,991.25
2026	4	17,994.65	1,979.48	16,015.17	16,976.08
2027	5	17,994.65	1,018.56	16,976.08	0.00
	Sum	89,973.24	14,173.24	75,800.00	

With the exception of the Blockbuster with the elevator, the principal and interest payments from these capital expenditures are defined as costs associated with the log yard operation before the split-off point. The principal and interest payments for the Blockbuster with the elevator are capital costs associated with the firewood business.

In 2018 there was a large maintenance and repair expense due to extensive repairs on the aging dump truck, which is used by all the businesses at Heiberg. There was also a large expense for rental equipment again due to the dump truck's extensive repairs. In 2019 and 2020 there were again large maintenance and repair expenses, this time for the log truck and skidder. The skidder was 23 years old and the log truck was more than five years old in 2020. This illustrates the costs associated with aging heavy equipment. Finally, the cost of an intern will be $12.00 per hour for 40 hours per week for 10 weeks during each summer of the planning horizon. This intern is shared by both of these businesses. These costs were defined as joint in the cost data provided and were allocated to each business based on the percent of revenue generated by each business annually.

The log yard's operating costs from 2018 to 2021 are given in Table 13.25a.

Table 13.25a The Log Yard Operating Costs From 2018 to 2021

Cost – Logging (2018)	Non-Separable Joint Costs[‡]	Separable Costs
Fuel	$	421
Maintenance & Repair	$9,712	
Supplies	$621	555
Misc., Equipment Rental, etc.	$3,755	
Labor – Worker	$	5,400
Labor – Supervisor	$	3,750
Cost – Logging (2019)		
Fuel	$	1,202
Maintenance & Repair	$1,462	2,285
Supplies	$	1,518
Misc., Equipment Rental, etc.	$	605
Labor – Worker	$	8,100
Labor – Supervisor	$	5,625
Cost – Logging (2020)		
Fuel	$	525
Maintenance & Repair	$	6,257
Supplies	$	364
Misc., Equipment Rental, etc.	$	
Labor – Worker	$	10,800
Labor – Supervisor	$	7,500
Cost – Logging (2021)		
Fuel	$	1,175
Maintenance & Repair	$	1,174
Supplies	$	1,086
Misc., Equipment Rental, etc.	$	
Labor – Worker	$	5,400
Labor – Supervisor	$	3,750

‡ The non-separable joint costs were allocated to the log yard and firewood businesses based on the percent of revenue generated each year

Table 13.25b The Log Yard Average Operating Costs From 2018 to 2032

Average Operating Costs – Logging (2018–2032)		Joint + Separable Costs	Separable Costs
2018 Average logging costs (cutting, bucking, skidding, hauling, labor)	$/MBF†	400	167
2019 Average logging costs (cutting, bucking, skidding, hauling, labor)	$/MBF	218	202
2020 Average logging costs (cutting, bucking, skidding, hauling, labor)	$/MBF	294	294
2021 Average logging costs (cutting, bucking, skidding, hauling, labor)	$/MBF	243	243
2022–2032 Expected average logging costs (cutting, bucking, skidding, hauling, labor)	$/MBF	289	227

† $/MBF denotes dollars per thousand board feet

As seen in Table 13.25a, the costs are defined as the allocated non-separable joint costs and the separable costs. With the exception of 2018, the largest operating expense was labor. The total annual volume cut is the volume of logs sold given in Table 13.21a plus the dry thousand board feet equivalent of the annual tons of firewood sold in Table 13.23. Based these annual volumes, the average separable plus joint and separable operating costs are given in Table 13.25b.

Table 13.25b also illustrates the impact of allocating joint or non-separable costs on the average operating costs. The average joint plus separable operating costs were the highest in 2018 and 2020. The 2018 cost was due to a joint cost allocation from large maintenance and repair and equipment rental costs plus a relatively low harvest volume. In 2020, a large non-separable maintenance and repair cost due to aging equipment combined with the largest total labor costs overcame a small increase in harvested volumes resulting in an increase in average logging costs in 2020. In 2021 there were also no non-separable maintenance and repair and supply costs. Thus the expected logging costs per 1,000 board feet for 2022 to 2032 is an average of the separable logging costs from 2018 to 2021.

The firewood's operating costs from 2018 to 2021 are given in Table 13.26a. The largest operating costs occurred in 2018, which is consistent with the large joint cost allocation. In addition, 2018 had the largest labor costs. Based on the tons of firewood processed data given in Table 13.23, the average separable plus joint and separable operating costs are given in Table 13.26b.

Table 13.26b again illustrates the impact of allocating joint costs on the average operating costs. The joint plus separable average cost in 2018 is more than 30 $/ton compared to the next highest cost. The high average cost in 2020 was due to the low external sales of firewood. For the reasons given earlier, the expected firewood processing costs per ton for 2022 to 2032 is an average of the separable processing costs from 2018 to 2021.

Table 13.26a The Firewood Operating Costs From 2018 to 2021

Cost – Firewood (2018)	Non-Separable Joint Costs[‡]	Separable Costs
Fuel	$	427
Maintenance & Repair	$7,893	355
Supplies	$588	
Misc., Equipment Rental, etc.	$1,690	
Labor – Worker	$	4,267
Labor – Supervisor	$	2,750
Cost – Firewood (2019)		
Fuel	$	513
Maintenance & Repair	$151	440
Supplies	$	
Misc., Equipment Rental, etc.	$	
Labor – Worker	$	3,780
Labor – Supervisor	$	2,625
Cost – Firewood (2020)		
Fuel	$	198
Maintenance & Repair	$	
Supplies	$	
Misc., Equipment Rental, etc.	$	
Labor – Worker	$	3,240
Labor – Supervisor	$	2,250
Cost – Firewood (2021)		
Fuel	$	198
Maintenance & Repair	$	
Supplies	$	
Misc., Equipment Rental, etc.	$	
Labor – Worker	$	3,240
Labor – Supervisor	$	2,250

[‡] The non-separable joint costs were allocated to the log yard and firewood businesses based on the percent of revenue generated each year

Table 13.26b The Average Firewood Operating Costs From 2018 to 2021

Average Cost – Firewood (2018–2021)		Joint + Separable Costs	Separable Costs
2018 Average firewood processing costs	$/ton	117	51
2019 Average firewood processing costs	$/ton	38	35
2020 Average firewood processing costs	$/ton	84	84
2021 Average firewood processing costs	$/ton	36	36
2022–2032 Average firewood processing costs	$/ton	69	52

Revenues

There are two sources of revenue: Selling logs or firewood. The annual revenue from log sales since 2006 is given in Table 13.21a. The quantity harvested varies from year to year for many reasons. For example, significant ash (*Fraxinus* sp.) harvests due to the emerald ash borer (*Agrilus planipennis*) and 282 tons of softwood were harvested in 2017. Based on discussion with the Forest Properties professional staff, an annual harvest of 20,000 to 40,000 board feet of hardwoods is expected for 2022 to 2032. For purposes of the financial analyses to follow, I will assume an annual harvest of 30,000 board feet.

The price received for the hardwoods varies by species and quality or grade. Table 13.21b contains price and volume by log grade. Based on the data given in Table 13.21b, ESF provides high-quality sustainably harvested hardwoods to local log buyers, which is consistent with the mission statement. The expected price from 2022 to 2032 is the 2021 weighted log price with the weights based on the volume harvested in each grade. This equates to 965 dollars per thousand board feet ($/MBF). Log sales are similar to wholesaling maple syrup in that the prices are set by the purchaser, not by ESF's Forest Properties professional Staff. Each buyer has their mill's pricing sheet outlining prices paid by species and log grade. These mill pricing sheets are subject to frequent changes based on the mill's matching the demand for their output with the log supply input. Thus, revenues generated depend significantly on the quality of the logs provided by the sustainable forest management practices conducted by ESF's Forest Properties professional staff.

The second source of revenue is from the sale of firewood. The prices for firewood sold by tons, face cord, or block wood has been constant since 2018:[15]

- $60 per ton for split firewood
- $50 per face cord for split firewood
- $18 per ton for block wood

The revenue generated from processing firewood is given in Table 13.23. To account for internal uses, the same pricing schedule was used. This revenue represents the value of not having to buy firewood to heat the maintenance garage and to fire the evaporator, which is consistent with standard cost management operating procedures to account for not having to purchase an input from outside sources (Blocher et al. 2002). There have been discussions among the Forest Properties professional staff about updating the 2018 pricing. These discussions are very deliberate as this business is within a state institution, i.e., SUNY-ESF, which receives state funding and thus cannot be seen to compete with local private firewood businesses and, due to liability concerns, ESF cannot deliver firewood to customers.

Profits

Financial Analysis

The cash flow statement is given in Table 13.27. The cash balance is negative from 2018 to 2032. The early negative cash balance is due to paying off the early capital equipment loans and the 2018, 2019, and 2022 maintenance and repair costs. The negative cash balance decreases until 2023 when the principal and interest payments for 2022 log truck purchase begin. The loan payments for this investment

Table 13.27 Cash Flow Statement for the Log Yard and Firewood Operations

	Units	2017	2018	2019	Year	2021	2022	2023	2024	2025	2026	2027	2028	2029	2030	2031	2032
							0	1	2	3	4	5	6	7	8	9	10
Estimated Revenue																	
Operating Activities: Cash Inflow (Revenue)																	
Log Sales	$/year		12,786.56	32,163.57	61,570.29	19,822.00	28,956.95	28,956.95	28,956.95	28,956.95	28,956.95	28,956.95	28,956.95	28,956.95	28,956.95	28,956.95	28,956.95
Select, Prime, Veneer, and Grade 1	$/year		26,421.27	44,027.99		0.00											
Grade 2	$/year			5,374.63	7,479.08	4,444.28											
Grade 3	$/year			367.68	1,416.31	558.44											
Firewood	$/year		10,358.80	13,132.99	7,162.80	9,382.60	9,980.00	9,980.00	9,980.00	9,980.00	9,980.00	9,980.00	9,980.00	9,980.00	9,980.00	9,980.00	9,980.00
Revenue Log + Firewood Sales	$/year		23,145.36	45,296.56	68,733.09	29,204.60	38,936.95	38,936.95	38,936.95	38,936.95	38,936.95	38,936.95	38,936.95	38,936.95	38,936.95	38,936.95	38,936.95
% Firewood				0.45	0.10	0.32	0.26	0.26	0.26	0.26	0.26	0.26	0.26	0.26	0.26	0.26	0.26
% Log Sales				0.55	0.90	0.68	0.74	0.74	0.74	0.74	0.74	0.74	0.74	0.74	0.74	0.74	0.74
PV(Log + Firewood Sales)	$/year		23,145.36	45,296.56	68,733.09	29,204.60	38,936.95	36,732.98	34,653.75	32,692.22	30,841.71	29,095.96	27,449.02	25,895.30	24,429.53	23,046.72	21,742.19
Revenue Log			12,786.56	32,163.57	61,570.29	19,822.00	28,956.95	28,956.95	28,956.95	28,956.95	28,956.95	28,956.95	28,956.95	28,956.95	28,956.95	28,956.95	28,956.95
PV(Revenue Log)			12,786.56	32,163.57	61,570.29	19,822.00	28,956.95	27,317.88	25,771.59	24,312.82	22,936.62	21,638.32	20,413.51	19,258.03	18,167.95	17,139.58	16,169.41
Firewood			10,358.80	13,132.99	7,162.80	9,382.60	9,980.00	9,980.00	9,980.00	9,980.00	9,980.00	9,980.00	9,980.00	9,980.00	9,980.00	9,980.00	9,980.00
PV(Firewood)			10,358.80	13,132.99	7,162.80	9,382.60	9,980.00	9,415.09	8,882.16	8,379.40	7,905.09	7,457.64	7,035.51	6,637.27	6,261.58	5,907.15	5,572.78
Revenue Log + Firewood Sales			23,145.36	45,296.56	68,733.09	29,204.60	38,936.95	38,936.95	38,936.95	38,936.95	38,936.95	38,936.95	38,936.95	38,936.95	38,936.95	38,936.95	38,936.95
PV(Log + Firewood Sales)			23,145.36	45,296.56	68,733.09	29,204.60	38,936.95	36,732.98	34,653.75	32,692.22	30,841.71	29,095.96	27,449.02	25,895.30	24,429.53	23,046.72	21,742.19

		2017	2018	2019	Year	2021	2022	2023	2024	2025	2026	2027	2028	2029	2030	2031	2032
							0	1	2	3	4	5	6	7	8	9	10
Costs																	
Operating Activities: Cash Outflow (Costs)																	
Labor			3,200.00	3,200.00	3,200.00	3,200.00	3,200.00	3,200.00	3,200.00	3,200.00	3,200.00	3,200.00	3,200.00	3,200.00	3,200.00	3,200.00	3,200.00

		C1	C2	C3	C4	C5	C6	C7	C8	C9	C10	C11	C12	C13	C14	C15
Firewood	$/year	7,016.99	6,405.00	5,490.00	0.00	0.00	0.00	0.00	0.00	0.00	0.00	0.00	0.00	0.00	0.00	0.00
Labor Total	$/year	19,366.99	23,330.00	26,990.00	17,840.00	16,199.37	16,199.37	16,199.37	16,199.37	16,199.37	16,199.37	16,199.37	16,199.37	16,199.37	16,199.37	16,199.37
Estimated Logging Costs – Harvesting 2022–2032	$/year	0.00	0.00	0.00	3,200.00	3,200.00	3,200.00	3,200.00	3,200.00	3,200.00	3,200.00	3,200.00	3,200.00	3,200.00	3,200.00	3,200.00
Logging Costs – Fuel	$/year	421.14	1,202.13	524.63	1,174.86	0.00	0.00	0.00	0.00	0.00	0.00	0.00	0.00	0.00	0.00	0.00
Logging Costs – Maintenance & Repair	$/year	9,711.94	3,747.00	6,951.65	1,174.00	0.00	0.00	0.00	0.00	0.00	0.00	0.00	0.00	0.00	0.00	0.00
Logging Costs – Supplies	$/year	1,176.00	1,518.19	364.30	1,085.93	0.00	0.00	0.00	0.00	0.00	0.00	0.00	0.00	0.00	0.00	0.00
Logging Cost – Misc., Equip Rental, etc.	$/year	3,755.00	605.00	0.00	0.00	0.00	0.00	0.00	0.00	0.00	0.00	0.00	0.00	0.00	0.00	0.00
Estimated Firewood Processing Costs – 2022–2032	$/year					7,759.21	7,759.21	7,759.21	7,759.21	7,759.21	7,759.21	7,759.21	7,759.21	7,759.21	7,759.21	7,759.21
Firewood Processing Costs – Fuel	$/year	426.51	512.67	197.57	197.57											
Firewood Costs – Maintenance & Repair	$/year	8,248.02	591.00	0.00	0.00											
Firewood Costs – Supplies	$/year	587.91														
Firewood Cost – Misc., Equip Rental, etc.	$/year															
Annual Interest payment – Log Truck Loader/ Picker Upgrade	$/year	494.96	339.49	174.69	0.00	0.00	0.00	0.00	0.00	0.00	0.00	0.00	0.00	0.00	0.00	0.00
Annual Interest payment – Skidder	$/year	1,713.32	1,175.15	604.69	0.00	0.00	0.00	0.00	0.00	0.00	0.00	0.00	0.00	0.00	0.00	0.00

(Continued)

Table 13.27 (Continued)

		2017	2018	2019	Year	2021	2022	2023	2024	2025	2026	2027	2028	2029	2030	2031	2032
Annual Interest payment – Log Truck 2015	$/year		1,656.21	1,135.98	584.53	0.00	0.00	0.00	0.00	0.00	0.00	0.00	0.00	0.00	0.00	0.00	0.00
Annual Interest payment – Processor	$/year		610.06	0.00	0.00	0.00	0.00	0.00	0.00	0.00	0.00	0.00	0.00	0.00	0.00	0.00	0.00
Annual Interest payment – Log Truck 2020	$/year							4,548.00	3,741.20	2,885.99	1,979.48	1,018.56	0.00	0.00	0.00	0.00	0.00
Financing Activities: Cash Outflow																	
Annual Principal payment – Log Truck Loader/Picker Upgrade	$/year		2,591.19	2,746.67	2,911.47	0.00	0.00	0.00	0.00	0.00	0.00	0.00	0.00	0.00	0.00	0.00	0.00
Annual Principal payment – Skidder	$/year		8,969.52	9,507.69	10,078.15	0.00	0.00	0.00	0.00	0.00	0.00	0.00	0.00	0.00	0.00	0.00	0.00
Annual Principal payment – Log Truck 2015	$/year		8,670.53	9,190.76	9,742.21	0.00	0.00	0.00	0.00	0.00	0.00	0.00	0.00	0.00	0.00	0.00	0.00
Annual Principal payment – Processor	$/year		10,167.73	0.00	0.00	0.00	0.00	0.00	0.00	0.00	0.00	0.00	0.00	0.00	0.00	0.00	0.00
Annual Principal payment – Log Truck 2020	$/year							13,446.65	14,253.45	15,108.65	16,015.17	16,976.08	0.00	0.00	0.00	0.00	0.00
Total Cost	$/year		78,567.04	55,601.72	59,123.88	21,472.36	27,158.58	45,153.23	45,153.23	45,153.23	45,153.23	45,153.23	27,158.58	27,158.58	27,158.58	27,158.58	27,158.58
Current Cash Flow			−55,421.68	−10,305.16	9,609.21	7,732.24	11,778.37	−6,216.27	−6,216.27	−6,216.27	−6,216.27	−6,216.27	11,778.37	11,778.37	11,778.37	11,778.37	11,778.37
Cash Balance			−55,421.68	−65,726.84	−56,117.64	−48,385.40	−36,607.02	−42,823.30	−49,039.57	−55,255.85	−61,472.12	−67,688.39	−55,910.02	−44,131.65	−32,353.27	−20,574.90	−8,796.52

started in 2023 and ended in 2027. The cash balance by the end of the investment analysis horizon is −$8,797.

The income statement is given in Table 13.28. Net income describes a business's profitability. Given the historic and expected costs and revenues, the income statement shows that these businesses were profitable the year the initial set of capital loans were paid off in 2020. With the purchase of the newer but used log truck, the net income was negative starting in 2023. As the interest payment for the 2020 log truck capital expense decreased, these businesses are expected to be profitable starting in 2028 with the expected net income being constant.

The balance statement is given in Table 13.29. The driving factors of determining total assets are: (1) The cash balance from the cash flow statement reflecting maintenance and repair costs associated with old logging equipment. (2) The capital assets until they are depreciated completely at the end of their loan periods. The driving factor of creating equity, after the capital loans are paid off, are the retained earnings which are equal to the prior year's retained earnings plus the current year's net income. As there are no shareholder payments, assets are equal to equity, which are equal to the cash balances starting in 2027.

A negative balance sheet means that there are more liabilities than assets, so there is no value in the business available for the shareholders. Consequently, if all its liabilities came due at once, the business would not be able to pay them, even if it liquidated assets, and would fail. A business with a negative balance sheet is at risk. However, if it can keep up with its annual bills, it can survive. Extending the investment horizon to 2033 will show that cash balance, the balance sheet, and the income statement are all positive and these businesses are expected to generate sufficient revenue. In a private business the entrepreneur would have to determine how best to cover the shortfalls of the negative cash flow, negative net income between 2023 and 2027, and the negative balance sheet. In the context of the maple syrup, log yard, and firewood businesses, the loans are self-financed and the sole shareholder is ESF. These shortfalls are covered by ESF.

Breakeven Analysis

The annual breakeven metrics for 2022 to 2032 are given in Table 13.30a. The annual breakeven metrics for the log yard and firewood operations show: (1) Given the expected log yard operational costs during the loan period for the newer but used log truck, the harvests of logs sold to mills will have to increase to 38 MBF with an expected price of 965 $/MBF. (2) The breakeven price required for log sales is below the expected price given an anticipated annual harvest 30 MBF of logs plus 42 MBF of firewood logs. (3) The firewood operation would require a production level just less than the expected production of 148 tons per year. (4) The firewood operation would have to sell firewood for just less than the expected price of 60 $/ton.

Table 13.28 Income Statement for the Log Yard and Firewood Operations‡

Income Statement (Log Yard)	Unit	2017	2018	2019	Year	2021	2022	2023	2024	2025	2026	2027	2028	2029	2030	2031	2032
							0	1	2	3	4	5	6	7	8	9	10
Revenues (Log Yard)	$/year		23,145.36	45,296.56	68,733.09	29,204.60	38,936.95	38,936.95	38,936.95	38,936.95	38,936.95	38,936.95	38,936.95	38,936.95	38,936.95	38,936.95	38,936.95
Expenses																	
Labor	$/year		19,366.99	23,330.00	26,990.00	17,840.00	3,200.00	3,200.00	3,200.00	3,200.00	3,200.00	3,200.00	3,200.00	3,200.00	3,200.00	3,200.00	3,200.00
Logging Costs – Harvesting 2022–2032	$/year		0.00	0.00	0.00	0.00	16,199.37	16,199.37	16,199.37	16,199.37	16,199.37	16,199.37	16,199.37	16,199.37	16,199.37	16,199.37	16,199.37
Logging Costs – Fuel	$/year		421.14	1,202.13	524.63	1,174.86	0.00	0.00	0.00	0.00	0.00	0.00	0.00	0.00	0.00	0.00	0.00
Logging Costs – Maintenance & Repair	$/year		9,711.94	3,747.00	6,951.65	1,174.00	0.00	0.00	0.00	0.00	0.00	0.00	0.00	0.00	0.00	0.00	0.00
Logging Costs – Supplies	$/year		1,176.00	1,518.19	364.30	1,085.93	0.00	0.00	0.00	0.00	0.00	0.00	0.00	0.00	0.00	0.00	0.00
Logging Cost – Misc., Equip Rental, etc.	$/year		3,755.00	605.00	0.00	0.00	0.00	0.00	0.00	0.00	0.00	0.00	0.00	0.00	0.00	0.00	0.00
Estimated Firewood Processing Costs – 2022–2032	$/year		0.00	0.00	0.00	0.00	7,759.21	7,759.21	7,759.21	7,759.21	7,759.21	7,759.21	7,759.21	7,759.21	7,759.21	7,759.21	7,759.21
Firewood Costs – Fuel	$/year		426.51	512.67	197.57	197.57	0.00	0.00	0.00	0.00	0.00	0.00	0.00	0.00	0.00	0.00	0.00
Firewood Costs – Maintenance & Repair	$/year		8,248.02	591.00	0.00	0.00	0.00	0.00	0.00	0.00	0.00	0.00	0.00	0.00	0.00	0.00	0.00
Firewood Costs – Supplies	$/year		587.91	0.00	0.00	0.00	0.00	0.00	0.00	0.00	0.00	0.00	0.00	0.00	0.00	0.00	0.00
Firewood Cost – Misc., Equip Rental, etc.	$/year		0.00	0.00	0.00	0.00	0.00	0.00	0.00	0.00	0.00	0.00	0.00	0.00	0.00	0.00	0.00
Annual Interest payment – Log...	$/year		494.96	339.49	174.69	0.00	0.00	0.00	0.00	0.00	0.00	0.00	0.00	0.00	0.00	0.00	0.00

Item	Unit													
Annual Interest payment – Skidder	$/year	1,713.32	1,175.15	604.69	0.00	0.00	0.00	0.00	0.00	0.00	0.00	0.00	0.00	0.00
Annual Interest payment – Log Truck 2015	$/year	1,656.21	1,135.98	584.53	0.00	0.00	0.00	0.00	0.00	0.00	0.00	0.00	0.00	0.00
Annual Interest payment – Processor	$/year	610.06	0.00	0.00	0.00	0.00	0.00	0.00	0.00	0.00	0.00	0.00	0.00	0.00
Annual Interest payment – Log Truck 2022	$/year						4,548.00	3,741.20	2,885.99	1,979.48	1,018.56	0.00	0.00	0.00
5-Year Straight-Line Depreciation – Log Truck & Loader	$/year	11,300.00	11,300.00	11,300.00	0.00	0.00	0.00	0.00	0.00	0.00	0.00	0.00	0.00	0.00
5-Year Straight-Line Depreciation – Skidder	$/year	9,000.00	9,000.00	9,000.00	0.00	0.00	0.00	0.00	0.00	0.00	0.00	0.00	0.00	0.00
5-Year Straight-Line Depreciation – Processor	$/year	0.00	0.00	0.00	0.00	0.00	0.00	0.00	0.00	0.00	0.00	0.00	0.00	0.00
5-Year Straight-Line Depreciation – Log Truck 2022	$/year						15,160.00	15,160.00	15,160.00	15,160.00	15,160.00			
Total	$/year	68,468.07	54,456.60	56,692.06	21,472.36	27,158.58	46,866.58	46,059.78	45,204.57	44,298.06	43,337.14	27,158.58	27,158.58	27,158.58
Net Income (+) or Loss (−)	$/year	−45,322.71	−9,160.04	12,041.03	7,732.24	11,778.37	−7,929.63	−7,122.83	−6,267.62	−5,361.10	−4,400.19	11,778.37	11,778.37	11,778.37

‡Depreciation is calculated using a five-year straight line formula. $/yr denotes dollars per year.

Table 13.29 Balance Statement for the Log Yard and Firewood Operations[‡]

Balance Sheet	Units	2017	2018	2019	2020	2021	2022	2023	2024	2025	2026	2027	2028	2029	2030	2031	2032
Year							0	1	2	3	4	5	6	7	8	9	10
Cash	$/year		−55,421.68	−65,726.84	−56,117.64	−48,385.40	−36,607.02	−42,823.30	−49,039.57	−55,255.85	−61,472.12	−67,688.39	−55,910.02	−44,131.65	−32,353.27	−20,574.90	−8,796.52
Equipment – Log Truck/Loader/Picker Upgrade	$		56,500.00	56,500.00	0.00	0.00	0.00	0.00	0.00	0.00	0.00	0.00	0.00	0.00	0.00	0.00	0.00
Equipment – Skidder	$		45,000.00	45,000.00	45,000.00	0.00	0.00	0.00	0.00	0.00	0.00	0.00	0.00	0.00	0.00	0.00	0.00
Equipment – Processor	$		45,400.00	0.00		0.00	0.00	0.00	0.00	0.00	0.00	0.00	0.00	0.00	0.00	0.00	0.00
Equipment – Log Truck 2022	$							75,800.00	75,800.00	75,800.00	75,800.00	75,800.00	0.00	0.00	0.00	0.00	0.00
Less: Accumulated Depreciation – Log Truck/Loader/Picker Upgrade	$/year		−33,900.00	−45,200.00	−56,500.00	0.00	0.00	0.00	0.00	0.00	0.00	0.00	0.00	0.00	0.00	0.00	0.00
Less: Accumulated Depreciation – Skidder	$/year		−27,000.00	−36,000.00	−45,000.00	0.00	0.00	0.00	0.00	0.00	0.00	0.00	0.00	0.00	0.00	0.00	0.00
Less: Accumulated Depreciation – Processor	$/year		−45,400.00	0.00		0.00	0.00	0.00	0.00	0.00	0.00	0.00	0.00	0.00	0.00	0.00	0.00
Less: Accumulated Depreciation – Log Truck 2022	$/year							−15,160.00	−30,320.00	−45,480.00	−60,640.00	−75,800.00	0.00	0.00	0.00	0.00	0.00
													−55,910.02	−44,131.65	−32,353.27	−20,574.90	−8,796.52

Loan – Log Truck/Loader/Picker Upgrade	$/year	24,591.11	12,653.68	0.00	0.00	0.00	0.00	0.00	0.00	0.00	0.00	0.00	0.00	0.00	0.00	0.00	0.00
Loan – Skidder	$/year	19,585.84	10,078.15	0.00	0.00	0.00	0.00	0.00	0.00	0.00	0.00	0.00	0.00	0.00	0.00	0.00	0.00
Loan – Firewood Processor	$/year	0.00	0.00	0.00	0.00	0.00	0.00	0.00	0.00	0.00	0.00	0.00	0.00	0.00	0.00		
Loan – Log Truck 2022	$/year			62,353.35	48,099.91	32,991.25	16,976.08	0.00									
Retained Earnings	$/year	-13,675.92	-58,998.63	-68,158.67	-56,117.64	-48,385.40	-36,607.02	-44,536.65	-51,659.48	-57,927.10	-63,288.20	-67,688.39	-55,910.02	-44,131.65	-32,353.27	-20,574.90	-8,796.52
Total Liabilities & Equity	$/year	-14,821.68	-45,426.84	-56,117.64	-48,385.40	-36,607.02	17,816.70	-3,559.57	-24,935.85	-46,312.12	-67,688.39	-55,910.02	-44,131.65	-32,353.27	-20,574.90	-8,796.52	

*Depreciation is calculated using a five-year straight line formula. $/year denotes dollars per year.

Table 13.30a Annual Breakeven Analysis for the Log Yard and Firewood Operations[‡]

	Units	2022	2023	2024	2025	2026	Year	2028	2029	2030	2031	2032
		0	1	2	3	4	5	6	7	8	9	10
Annual Breakeven Total Revenue	$/year	27,159	45,153	45,153	45,153	45,153	45,153	27,159	27,159	27,159	27,159	27,159
Annual Breakeven Production – Logs	MBF/year	19	38	38	38	38	38	19	19	19	19	19
Annual Breakeven Production – Firewood	tons/year	143	143	143	143	143	143	143	143	143	143	143
Annual Breakeven Price – Logs	$/MBF	260	512	512	512	512	512	260	260	260	260	260
Annual Breakeven Price – Firewood	$/ton	58	58	58	58	58	58	58	58	58	58	58

[‡] The annual breakeven revenue is equal to the annual total costs. The annual breakeven log production level is based on an expected price of 965 dollars per thousand board feet ($/MBF). The annual breakeven firewood production level is based on an expected price of 60 dollars per ton ($/ton). The annual breakeven log price is based on an expected production of 30 thousand board feet of logs plus 42 thousand board feet of firewood logs annually starting in 2022. The annual breakeven firewood price is based on an expected production of 148 tons per year starting in 2022.

Table 13.30b Equal Annual Equivalent (EAE) Breakeven Analysis for the Log Yard and Firewood Operations[‡]

	Units	
EAE Breakeven Revenue – Log Yard	$/year	28,878
EAE Breakeven Revenue – Firewood	$/year	8,579
EAE Breakeven Production – Logs	MBF/year	30
EAE Breakeven Production – Firewood	tons/year	143
EAE Breakeven Price – Logs	$/MBF	404
EAE Breakeven Price – Firewood	$/ton	58

[‡] The EAE breakeven log revenue was based on the cost of producing 30 thousand board feet of logs plus 42 thousand board feet of firewood logs annually starting in 2022. The EAE breakeven firewood revenue was based on the cost of producing 148 tons of firewood annually starting in 2022. The EAE breakeven log production was based on an expected price of 965 dollars per thousand board feet ($/MBF). The EAE breakeven firewood production was based on an expected price of 60 dollars per ton ($/ton). The EAE breakeven log price was based on the cost of producing 30 thousand board feet of logs annually starting in 2022. The EAE breakeven firewood price was based on the cost of producing 148 tons of firewood annually starting in 2022.

The equal annual equivalent (EAE) breakeven metrics for the log yard and firewood operations are given in Table 13.30b. The EAE breakeven metrics show: (1) The required EAE breakeven log yard revenues to cover the present value of the financing, operation, and maintenance costs for the investment horizon are $79 less than the expected revenues. (2) The required EAE breakeven log production level of 30 MBF of logs per year that must be harvested and "sold" annually to cover the present value of the financing, operation, and maintenance costs for the investment horizon at an expected market price is equal to expected production level of 30 MBF per year. (3) The required EAE breakeven log price of 404 $/MBF that must be received annually to cover the present value of the financing, operation, and maintenance costs for the investment horizon at the expected annual production level of 30 MBF of logs plus 42 MBF of firewood logs is also lower than the expected price of 965 $/MBF. (4) The required EAE breakeven firewood revenues to cover the present value of the financing, operation, and maintenance costs for the investment horizon are $1,400 less than the expected revenues. (5) The required EAE breakeven annual firewood production level of 143 tons that must be processed and "sold" annually to cover the present value of the financing, operation, and maintenance costs for the investment horizon at an expected market price is just less than the expected annual production level of 148 tons. (6) The required EAE breakeven firewood price of 58 $/ton that must be received annually to cover the present value of the financing, operation, and maintenance costs for the investment horizon at the expected production level of 148 tons/year is again just lower than the expected price of 60 $/ton.

These breakeven metrics provide a qualified degree of confidence that the log yard and firewood production systems can provide the required output levels and the outputs can be sold to cover annual and present value production costs. The breakeven analyses appear to support these being workable business opportunities.

Net Present Value

The present value of the log yard and firewood expected revenues and costs are given in Tables 13.31a and 13.31b. The annual and cumulative net present values (NPV) are given in Table 13.31c.

The annual log yard NPVs are negative during the loan period for the newer but used log truck. However, the present values of the revenues are large enough such that the cumulative NPV is $10,959 by the end of the investment horizon. The annual firewood NPVs are all positive but relatively small. These small but positive annual firewood NPVs sum to a cumulative NPV that is slightly larger than the cumulative NPV for the log yard. The total NPV follows a pattern similar to the log yard's NPV. The ending NPV for the log yard and firewood businesses is positive and $22,668. The annual and cumulative total NPV are consistent with the annual cash flows and the breakeven analyses. This analysis appears to support these being workable business opportunities for the college.

Based on the information provided in Tables 13.31a and 13.31b, the benefit–cost ratio (BCR) of the combined log yard firewood operation is 1.04. Using this as a cardinal metric of sensitivity, this implies that the combined discounted costs could increase by a factor of 1.04 and NPV would just be equal to zero. The combined discounted revenues could decrease by a factor of 0.96 and NPV would just be equal to zero. In addition, I calculated the BCR for each operation based on the separable costs.

Table 13.31a Present Value of the Expected Revenues for the Log Yard and Firewood Operations‡

	Units	2022	2023	2024	2025	2026	Year	2028	2029	2030	2031	2032
		0	1	2	3	4	5	6	7	8	9	10
Expected Revenue from Log Sales	$/year	28,957	28,957	28,957	28,957	28,957	28,957	28,957	28,957	28,957	28,957	28,957
Present Value of Expected Revenues from Log Sales	$/year	28,957	27,318	25,772	24,313	22,937	21,638	20,414	19,258	18,168	17,140	16,169
Expected Revenue from Firewood Sales	$/year	9,980	9,980	9,980	9,980	9,980	9,980	9,980	9,980	9,980	9,980	9,980
Present Value of Expected Revenues from Firewood Sales	$/year	9,980	9,415	8,882	8,379	7,905	7,458	7,036	6,637	6,262	5,907	5,573
Expected Revenue from Log and Firewood Sales	$/year	38,937	38,937	38,937	38,937	38,937	38,937	38,937	38,937	38,937	38,937	38,937
Present Value of Expected Revenues from Log and Firewood Sales	$/year	38,937	36,733	34,654	32,692	30,842	29,096	27,449	25,895	24,430	23,047	21,742

‡ The expected log revenues are based on producing and selling 30 thousand board feet (MBF) annually at expected price of 965 $/MBF. The expected firewood revenues are based on producing and selling 148 tons annually at expected price of 60 $/ton. The present values of the expected revenues are calculated based on a 6% discount rate.

Table 13.31b Present Value of the Expected Costs for the Log Yard and Firewood Operations‡

	Units	2022	2023	2024	2025	2026	Year	2028	2029	2030	2031	2032
		0	1	2	3	4	5	6	7	8	9	10
Log Yard												
Expected Operating and Financing Activity Costs	$/year	18,579	36,574	36,574	36,574	36,574	36,574	18,579	18,579	18,579	18,579	18,579
Present Value of Expected Costs	$/year	18,579	34,504	32,551	30,708	28,970	27,330	13,098	12,356	11,657	10,997	10,375
Firewood												
Expected Operating and Financing Activity Costs	$/year	8,579	8,579	8,579	8,579	8,579	8,579	8,579	8,579	8,579	8,579	8,579

Total

	Units	2022	2023	2024	2025	2026	Year	2028	2029	2030	2031	2032
Expected Operating and Financing Activity Costs	$/year	27,159	27,159	45,153	45,153	45,153	45,153	45,153	27,159	27,159	27,159	27,159
Present Value of Expected Costs	$/year	27,159	27,159	42,597	40,186	37,912	35,766	33,741	19,146	18,062	17,040	16,075	15,165

‡ The expected log costs are based on producing and selling 30 thousand board feet (MBF) annually at expected price of 965 $/MBF. The expected firewood costs are based on producing and selling 148 tons annually at expected price of 60 $/ton. The present value of the expected costs is calculated based on a 6% discount rate.

Table 13.31c Net Present Value (NPV) of the Log Yard and Firewood Operations‡

		2022	2023	2024	2025	2026	Year	2028	2029	2030	2031	2032
	Units	0	1	2	3	4	5	6	7	8	9	10
Log Yard												
NPV Annual	$/year	10,378	-7,186	-6,779	-6,395	-6,033	-5,692	7,316	6,902	6,511	6,143	5,795
NPV Cumulative	$	10,378	3,192	-3,587	-9,982	-16,015	-21,707	-14,391	-7,489	-978	5,164	10,959
Firewood												
NPV Annual	$/year	1,401	1,321	1,247	1,176	1,109	1,047	987	931	879	829	782
NPV Cumulative	$	1,401	2,722	3,968	5,144	6,254	7,300	8,288	9,219	10,098	10,927	11,709
Total												
NPV Annual	$/year	11,778	-5,864	-5,532	-5,219	-4,924	-4,645	8,303	7,833	7,390	6,972	6,577
NPV Cumulative	$	11,778	5,914	382	-4,838	-9,762	-14,407	-6,104	1,730	9,120	16,091	22,668

‡ The expected log revenues and costs are based on producing and selling 30 thousand board feet (MBF) annually at expected price of 965 $/MBF. The expected firewood revenues and costs are based on producing and selling 148 tons annually at expected price of 60 $/ton. The net present values are calculated based on a 6% discount rate.

The BCR for the log yard was 1.003, implying a present value of the costs could increase by a factor of 1.003 and a present value of the revenues could decrease by a factor of 0.997 and NPV would just be equal to zero. This BCR should cause the reader to pause and think about the log yard operation financially. The logging operation is using aging equipment that has been associated with significant past maintenance, repair, and equipment rental costs. Between 2018 and 2021, annual maintenance, repair, and equipment rental costs ranged from $13,466.94 to $1,174 (Tables 13.25a and 13.27). Using the same logic developed in Chapter 6 – Capital Theory: Investment Analysis

$$\Delta\sum PV(R) = 1.003 \cdot \sum PV(C) - \sum PV(C) = \$10,959.16$$
$$\Delta\sum PV(C) = \sum PV(R) - 0.997 \cdot \sum PV(R) = \$10,959.16$$

where $\Delta\sum PV(R))$ and $\Delta\sum PV(C)$ denote the change in either the sum of the present value of the revenues or the sum of the present value of the costs, respectively, and $10,959.16 denotes the log yard's cumulative NPV. Thus, decreasing the present value of the revenues by $10,959.16 or increasing the present value of the costs by $10,959.16 will cause the log yard's cumulative NPV to equal 0. The equal annual equivalent (EAE) of this change in either the sum of the present value of the revenues or costs is 1,489 $/year.

$$EAE[\Delta\sum PV(R)] = EAE[\Delta\sum PV(C)] = 1,489 \ \$/year$$

The variability associated with the maintenance, repair, and equipment rental costs between 2019 and 2021 is $5,219. The EAE is well within the maintenance, repair, and equipment rental cost variability. The BCR analysis shows that maintenance, repair, and equipment rental costs associated with aging logging equipment need to be managed carefully.

The BCR for the firewood was 1.16, implying a present value of the costs could increase by a factor of 1.16 and a present value of the revenues could decrease by a factor of 0.0.86 and NPV would just be equal to zero. The log yard operation is more sensitive to changes in costs given these data than the firewood operation. This is consistent with the breakeven analyses and all the financial statements. Underlying these is the split-off point demarcation in defining joint or non-separable costs versus separable costs and the technique used to allocate those costs identified as joint or non-separable.

Analysis and Recommendation

The required EAE log production level is equal to the expected production level. But the required annual log production level is greater than the expected production level during the loan period associated with the newer but used log truck. The required annual and EAE log prices are less than the expected of 965 $/MBF. The breakeven analyses show the required annual and EAE firewood production levels are less than the expected production levels. However, the required annual and EAE firewood price of 58 $/ton is just less than the expected price of 60 $/ton. The breakeven analyses appear to support the log yard and firewood operations as being a workable business opportunity for ESF. The NPV analysis combined with the BCR analysis also support these being a workable business opportunity.

I have used the term "workable" with the log yard and firewood operations and viable for the maple syrup operation for a reason. These analyses show that cost and revenues need to be managed carefully. Specifically, the aging equipment associated with primarily the logging operation have caused significant past maintenance, repair, and equipment rental costs. These costs resulted in negative net income until 2028, a negative cash balance, and negative balance sheet. These financial outcomes were exacerbated by the 2022 necessary purchase of a newer but used log truck. The log yard's BCR calculated using separable costs was 1.003, implying if the present value of the costs increased by a factor of 1.003, which equates to a $583 increase in the present value of the costs, then the log yard's NPV would equal 0. Firewood being a by-product of the log yard operation fared better. The biggest separable costs have been associated with labor. Given the sale price of split firewood is 60 $/ton, it is critical to keep average production costs below this amount. The breakeven required price is 58 $/ton, which is below the market price of 60 $/ton and below the average production costs of 52 $/ton. All these financial metrics support the conclusion and recommendation that the log yard and firewood are workable business opportunities if costs are managed carefully.

These analyses and recommendations must also include a discussion of "Context." The context is defined by the mission statement, goals, and objectives given in Table 13.19. Based on the data provided by Forest Properties, these business opportunities provide teaching, research, and outreach prospects supporting the mission statement given in Table 13.19 as well as ESF's mission. The log yard and firewood operations also provide benefit to the college as well as the surrounding communities. These are identified directly in Goals #1, #2, and #4 and their corresponding objectives. These business opportunities do provide a positive net income to the college after year 2027. This supports Goal #3 and its corresponding objectives.

The conclusions of this analysis are (1) the log yard and firewood operations are workable business opportunities; (2) to maintain the financial viability of these opportunities the costs and revenues must be managed actively; (3) the log yard and firewood operations provide additional benefit to the college and local communities in terms of teaching and outreach. The recommendation is to continue these operations as a business.

How to Use Economic Information to Make Better Business Decisions

This chapter developed three practical applications of: "How to use economic information to make better business decisions." An observation from this chapter is that using actual data in analyses is messy. Data may not be in a convenient frequency. For example, the frequency of the data provided is annual, but the units of production are gallons of maple syrup, thousand board feet of logs, and tons of firewood. Thus, production decisions about producing an additional gallon of maple syrup, thousand board feet of logs, or ton of firewood are problematic. However, decisions if the business should continue or shut down can be recommended. These recommendations rely on average costs relative to output price and were described in Table 5.4 and reflected in Tables 13.30a and 13.30b.

In prior chapters, I have had a section discussing the impacts of variability. While I do not have a dedicated section this time, I have discussed the impact of variability by using the BCR as a cardinal metric of sensitivity by estimating the factor increases and decreases in the present value of the costs and revenues, respectively, to cause NPV to equal to 0. Neither the slab mill nor the maple syrup showed a great degree of sensitivity. In fact, even when adding in the professional staff salaries in the maple syrup operation, the changes in NPV were within the 2.30 factor increase in discounted costs. However, in the log yard business, the challenge of managing the periodically high maintenance, repair, and equipment rental costs due to aging heavy equipment can lead to periodic negative net income. These periodic costs implied an allowable increase in the present value of the costs by a factor of only 1.003 or $583 increase. Combining this with financial analyses stored in a spreadsheet allowed me to determine that if the average logging cost increased from 227 to 245 $/MBF then the NPV, based on logging's separable costs, would equal 0. The 245 $/MBF is within the range of average logging costs from 2018 to 2021. Moreover, 245 $/MBF is approximately equal to the average logging costs in 2021.

Throughout the book I have used the following statements, and I think it is appropriate to end the book with the same statements as a summary. If you want to make profits as large as possible you have to do two things simultaneously: First, make revenues as large as possible (the Pillars of Price and Value) while making costs as small as possible (the Pillars of Cost and Value) for any given input(s)–output(s) combination (the production system). If you do not control costs, you will lose control of profits. Entrepreneurs have more managerial control over costs than revenues by make decisions directly about inputs and costs (the Pillars of Cost and Value for inputs). Revenue depends on customers purchasing your output. If your output does not provide the customer value, they will not buy it. Consequently, revenue is the output quantity "sold" multiplied by the price you charge (the Pillars of Price and Value for outputs). Furthermore, output produced but not sold generates no revenue but does generate costs (the Pillar of Cost). Finally, profit is what is left over after you have paid *all* your costs. Profit is not a destination but a journey. Entrepreneurs – in their search for economic profit – seek least costly ways of combining scarce resources into something valued more highly by consumers. They discover new, more efficient cost structures for producing and delivering scarce goods and services.

Notes

1   Since 2013 I have required my students to develop 10-year business plans based on an existing for-profit business managed by ESF's Forest Properties Department and on a proposed for-profit businesses to be managed by ESF. The business plans presented will draw from these reports.

2 This is not meant to be a substitute for an accounting course. The structure of the three statements may not be as described by accounting textbooks. While they contain the same information, they were modified to best facilitate the analyses.

3 In addition to these accounting statements, there are also the notes to financial statements, statement of changes in equity, and statement of comprehensive income.

4 These descriptions are taken from Edmonds et al. (2015) and www.sec.gov/reportspubs/investor-publications/investorpubsbegfinstmtguidehtm.html#:~:text=There%20are%20four%20main%20financial,a%20fixed%20point%20in%20time (accessed 28 June 2022).

5 Under the accrual method of accounting, revenues are reported as of the date the goods are sold or the services have been performed. If a service is provided on December 27 but the customer is allowed to pay in February, the revenues are reported on the income statement that includes December 27.

6 Under the accrual method of accounting, these expenses should be reported in the same accounting period as the related revenues.

7 This depends on whether the cash flow statement starts with gross income or net income. If starting with net income, then depreciation, amortization, and any other noncash expense would be added to net income.

8 As described in Chapter 6 – Capital Theory: Investment Analysis, the decision to finance a capital investment should be separate from the decision to invest in the capital (i.e., $NPV \geq 0$). However, as the interest rate used to finance capital and the discount rate used for the decision to invest in capital will be defined as 6%, mathematically the present value of any capital expenditure loan payments will be equal to the capital's initial cost in a net present value analysis.

9 This is an application of the equal annual equivalent breakeven analysis that was discussed in Chapter 6 – Capital Theory: Investment Analysis.

10 Note these NPVs assume the cost of storing the non-sold slabs is zero. If an additional shed needs to be built to store these slabs, this will increase the capital costs as well as the cost of moving inventory.

11 The majority of this history was taken from "History of Maple Syrup Production at Heiberg Forest" written by Jim Crevelling in 2001. At the time this was written Mr. Crevelling was ESF's Southern Property Manager.

12 These joint costs were allocated to each business based on the revenue generated by each business. A more detailed discussion of joint costs will be provided later in the chapter.

13 A split-off point is the location in a production process where a main product or jointly manufactured products and by-products are hereafter manufactured separately.

14 Based on Blocher et al. (2002), the most appropriate joint cost allocation technique would seem to be the net realizable value method, as selling firewood by the ton or face cord requires additional processing after the split-off point. However, selling block wood does not require additional process. In addition, some of the joint costs must be allocated to the maple syrup operation and a split-off designation does not make sense. Consequently, the net realizable value method would not work. Thus, I will use a modification of the sales value at split-off and simply use sales value or revenue. Joint costs will be allocated to each business based on the percent of revenue generated by each business annually. The advantages of using this approach in this context is it is simple and allocates the joint costs relative to a product's revenue.

15 The per ton price and the per face cord price are the same assuming three face cords per standard cord and a standard cord of mixed hardwoods weights approximately 2.5 tons.

Bibliography

Acharya, B., Dutta, A., and Minaret, J. (2015) Review on comparative study of dry and wet torrefaction, *Sustainable Energy Technologies and Assessment*, 12:26–37.

Adams, D.M. and Ek, A.R. (1974) Optimizing the Management of Uneven-aged Forest Stands. *Can. J. For. Res.* 4(3):274–287.

Adams, D.M., and Haynes, R. (1980) The 1980 softwood timber assessment market model: Structure, projections and policy simulations, *Forest Science Monograph*, 26.

Alexander, S.J., Pliz, D., Weber, N.S., Brown, E., and Rockwell, V.A. (2002) Mushrooms, trees, and money: Value estimates of commercial mushrooms and timber in the pacific Northwest, *Environmental Management*, 30(1):129–141.

Amacher, G.S., Olikaninen, M., and Koskela, E. (2009) *Economics of Forest Resources*, Cambridge, MA: Massachusetts Institute of Technology Press.

Amateis, R.L., and Burkhart, H.E. (1985) Site index curves for loblolly pine plantations on cutover, site-prepared lands, *Southern Journal of Applied Forestry*, 9(3):166–169.

Andersch, A., Buehlmann, U., Wiedenbeck, J., and Lawser, S. (2013) Status and opportunities associated with product costing strategies in wood component manufacturing, *Forest Science*, 56(6):623–636.

Arano, K.G., and Munn, I. (2006) Evaluating forest management intensity: A comparison among major forest landowner types, *Forest Policy and Economics*, 9(3):237–248.

Arbogast, C., Jr. (1957) *Marking Guides for Northern Hardwoods Under the Selection System*, Station Paper LS-56, St. Paul, MN: U.S. Department of Agriculture, Forest Service, Lake States Forest Experiment Station, p. 20.

Arjunan, K.C., and Kannapiran, K. (2018) *The Controversial Reinvestment Assumption in IRR and NPV Estimates: New Evidence Against Reinvestment Assumption*, Economic Papers Australia, forthcoming (https://papers.ssrn.com/sol3/papers.cfm?abstract_id=2918744).

Arrow, K.J., Croppery, M.L., Gollierz, C., Groom, B., Healô, G.M., Newellk, R.G., Nordhaus, W.D., Pindyck, R.S., Pizeryy, W.A., Portneyzz, P.R., Sterner, T., Tolôô, R.S.J., and Weitzmank, M.L. (2014) Should governments use a declining discount rate in project analysis? *Review of Environmental Economics and Policy*, 8(2):143–333.

Arrow, K.J., and Fisher, A.C. (1974) Environmental preservation, uncertainty, and irreversibility, *The Quarterly Journal of Economics*, 88(2):312–319.

Arrow, K.J., Solow, R., Portney, P.R., Leamer, E.E., Radner, R., and Schuman, H. (1993) Report of the NOAA panel on contingent valuation, *Federal Register*, 58(10):4602–4614.

Atkinson, G., and Mourato, S. (2008) Environmental cost-benefit analysis, *Annual Review of Environment and Resources*, 33:317–344.

Ballard, B.D., and Nowak, C.A. (2003) *Cost-Effectiveness of Herbicide and Non-Herbicide Treatment Methods on a Powerline Corridor in New York State*, Final Report for Niagara Mohawk Power Corporation, Syracuse, NY and Albany: The Research Foundation of SUNY.

Bare, B.B., and Smith, R.L. (1999) Estimating stumpage values from transaction evidence using multiple regression, *Journal of Forestry*, 97(7):32–39.

Basili, M., and Fontini, F. (2005) Quasi-option value under ambiguity, *Economics Bulletin*, 4(3):1–10.

Baumol, W.J. (1968) On the social rate of discount, *The American Economic Review*, 58(4):788–802.

Baye, M.R. (2009) *Managerial Economics and Business Strategy*, 6th ed., New York, NY: McGraw-Hill Irwin.

Becker, D.R., Hjerpe, E.E., and Lowell, E.C. (2004) *Economic Assessment of Using a Mobile Micromill® for Processing Small-Diameter Ponderosa Pine*, General Technical Reports, PNW-GTR-623, Portland, OR: US Department of Agriculture, Forest Service, Pacific Northwest Research Station.

Belin, D.L., Kittredge, D.B., Stevens, T.H., Dennis, D.C., Schweik, C.M., and Morzuch, B.J. (2005) Assessing private forest owner attitudes toward ecosystem-based management, *Journal of Forestry*, 103(1):28–35.

Bentley, W.R., and Teeguarden, D.E. (1965) Financial maturity: A theoretical review, *Forest Science*, 11(1):76–87.

Bettinger, P., Boston, K., Siry, J.P., and Grebner, D.L. (2017) *Forest Management and Planning*, 2nd ed., New York, NY: Elsevier Academic Press.

Bierman, H.S., and Fernandez, L. (1993) Game *Theory with Economic Applications*, Reading MA: Addison-Wesley Publishing Company Inc.

Binkley, C.S. (1987) When is the optimal economic rotation longer than the rotation of maximum sustained yield? *Journal of Environmental Economics and Management*, 14(2):152–158.

Blocher, E.J., Chen, K.H., and Lin, T.W. (2002) *Cost Management: A Strategic Emphasis*, 2nd ed., New York, NY: McGraw-Hill Irwin.

Bockstael, N.E., McConnell, K.E., and Strand, I.E. (1989) A random utility model for sport-fishing: Some preliminary results for Florida, *Marine Resource Economics*, 6:245–260.

Boone, R.S., Kozlik, C.J., Bois, B.J., and Wengert, E.M. (1988) *Dry Kiln Schedules for Commercial Woods – Temperate and Tropical*, General Technical Reports FPL-GTR-57 Madison, WI: US Department of Agriculture, Forest Service, Forest Products Laboratory.

Boulding, K.E. (1935) The theory of a single investment, *The Quarterly Journal of Economics*, 49(3):475–494.

Bowes, M., and Krutilla, J. (1985) Multiple-use management of public forest lands, in A.V. Kneese and L.L. Sweeney, eds. *Handbook of Natural Resource and Energy Economics*, vol. II, Amsterdam: North Holland.

Bowker, J.M., Newman, D.H., Warren, R.J., and Henderson, D.W. (2003) Estimating the economic value of lethal versus nonlethal deer control in suburban communities, *Society and Natural Resources*, 16(2):143–158.

Boyd, J.W., and Banzhaf, H.S. (2005) Ecosystem services and government: The need for a new way of judging nature's value, *Resources*, 158:16–19.

Boyd, J.W., and Banzhaf, H.S. (2007) What are the ecosystem services? The need for standardized environmental accounting units, *Ecological Economics*, 63:616–626.

Boyd, J.W., and Krupnick, A. (2009) *The Definition and Choice of Environmental Commodities for Nonmarket Valuation*, RFF Discussion paper DP 09-35, p. 57, September (https://media.rff.org/documents/RFF-DP-09-35.pdf).

Branker, K., Pathak, M.J.M., and Pearce, J.M. (2011) A review of solar photovoltaic levelized cost of electricity, *Renewable and Sustainable Energy Reviews*, 15:4470–4482.

Brazee, R.J. (2003) The Volvo theorem: From myth to behavior model, in F. Helles, N. Strange, and L. Wichmann, eds. *Recent Accomplishments in Applied Forest Economics Research*. New York, NY: Kluwer Academic Publishers, A Division of Springer.

Brazee, R.J., and Amacher, G.S. (2000) Duality and faustmann: Implications for the evaluation of landowner behavior, *Forest Science*, 46(1):132–138.

Brealey, R.A., Myers, S.C., and Allen, F. (2008) *Principles of Corporate Finance*, 9th ed., New York, NY: McGraw-Hill, Inc.

Brennan, T.J. (2016) *How Much Relevance Does Reality Imply? (Re)Considering the Endowment Effect*, Resources for the Future Discussion Paper RFF DP 16-31 (https://media.rff.org/documents/RFF-DP-16-31.pdf).

Brickley, J., Smith, C.W., Jr., and Zimmerman, J.L. (2007) *Managerial Economics and Organizational Architecture*, 4th ed., Boston, MA: Irwin McGraw-Hill, Inc.

Brigham, E.F., and Huston, J.F. (2019) *Fundamentals of Financial Management*, 15th ed., Boston, MA: Cengage Learning.

Bromley, D.W. (1991) *Environmental Economy: Property Rights and Public Policy*, Cambridge, MA: Basil Blackwell.

Bromley, D.W. (1992) Property rights as authority systems: The role of rules in resource management, in P.N. Nemetz, ed. *Emerging Issues in Forest Policy*, Vancouver, BC: UBC Press, pp. 471–496.

Bromley, D.W. (1998) Rousseau's revenge: The demise of the freehold estate, in Harvey M. Jacobs, ed. *Who Owns America? Social Conflict Over Property Rights*, Madison, WI: The University of Wisconsin Press.

Brown, T.C. (1984) The concept of value in resource allocation, *Land Economics*, 60(3):231–246.

Brown, T.C., Bergstrom, J.C., and Loomis, J.B. (2007) Defining, valuing and providing ecosystem goods and services, *Natural Resources Journal*, 47(2):329–376.

Brown, T.C., and Gregory, R. (1999) Why the WTA-WTP disparity matters, *Ecological Economics*, 28:323–335.

Brown, W.G., and Nawas, F. (1973) Impact of aggregation on the estimation of outdoor recreation demand functions, *American Journal of Agricultural Economics*, 55(2):246–249.

Bullard, S.H., Gunter, J.E., Doolittle, M.L., and Arano, K.G. (2002) Discount rates for nonindustrial private forest landowners in Mississippi: How high a hurdle? *Southern Journal of Applied Forestry*, 26(1):26–31.

Bullard, S.H., and Straka, T.J. (2000) *Basic Concepts in Forest Valuation and Investment Analysis*, 2nd ed., Clemson, SC: Department of Forestry, Clemson University.

Buongiorno, J. (2001) Quantifying the implications of transformation from even to uneven-aged forest stands, *Forest Ecology and Management*, 151:121–132.

Buongiorno, J., and Gilles, J.K. (2003) *Decision Methods for Forest Resource Management*, Cambridge, MA: Academic Press.

Buongiorno, J. and Michie, B. (1980) A matrix model for uneven-aged forest management. *Forest Science*, 26:609–625.

Burdurlu, E., Ciritcioğlu, H.H., Bakir, K., and Özdemir, M. (2006) Analysis of the most suitable fitting type for the assembly of knockdown panel furniture, *Forest Products Journal*, 56(1):46–52.

Bureau of Land Resources (2018) *Stumpage Price Report No. 73, Division of Lands and Forests*, Albany, NY: New York State Department of Environmental Conservation, Winter (www.dec.ny.gov/lands/5259.html accessed 29 June 2018).

Burkhart, H.E., Cloeren, D.C., and Amateis, R.L. (1985) Yield relationships in unthinned loblolly pine plantations on cutover, site-prepared lands, *Southern Journal of Applied Forestry*, 9(2):84–91.

Burns, R.M., and Honkala, B.H., eds. (1990) *Silvics of North America Volume 2, Hardwoods*, Agriculture Handbook 654, Washington, DC: United States Department of Agriculture – Forest Service.

Butler, B.J. (2008) *Family Forest Owners of the United States, 2006*, General Technical Report NRS-27, Newtown Square, PA: U.S. Department of Agriculture – Forest Service, Northern Research Station.

Butler, B.J. (2010) *The Average American Family Forest Owner, the Consultant – the Annual Journal of the Association of Consulting Foresters* (www.acf-foresters.org/Content/NavigationMenu/Media/ConsultantMagazine/default.htm accessed 8 December 2009).

Butler, B.J., Hewes, J.H., Dickinson, B.J., Andrejczyk, K., Butler, S.M., and Markowski-Lindsay, M. (2016) *USDA Forest Service National Woodland Owner Survey A Technical Document Supporting the Forest Service Update of the 2010 RPA Assessment*, USDA FS Resource Bulletin NRS-99 (https://www.fs.usda.gov/nrs/pubs/rb/rb_nrs99.pdf accessed 3 October 2023).

Butler, B.J., and Leatherberry, E.C. (2004) American's family forest owners, *Journal of Forestry*, 102(7):4–9.

Butler, B.J., Tyrrell, M., Feinberg, G., VanManen, S., Wiseman, L., and Wallinger, S. (2007) Understanding and researching family forest owners: Lessons from social marketing research, *Journal of Forestry*, 105(7):348–357.

Byrne, E.E. (2012) *The Role of Politics in the Allocation of Funds from the American Recovery and Reinvestment Act for Renewable Energy*, MS Thesis SUNY – College of Environmental Science and Forestry, Syracuse, NY.

Calish, S., Flight, R.D., and Teeguarden, D.E. (1978) How do nontimber values affect Douglas-fir rotations? *Journal of Forestry*, 76:217–221.

Canadian Farm Business Management Council (CFBMC). (2000) *Report on the Economics of Maple Syrup Production, 75*, Albert St, Suite 903, Ottawa, ON: CFBMC.

Canham, H.O. (1986) Comparable valuation of timber and recreation for forest planning, *Journal of Environmental Management*, 23:335–339.

Carlson, S. (1974) *A Study on the Pure Theory of Production*, Clifton, NJ: Augustus M. Kelley Publishers.

Carson, R.T. (2012) Contingent valuation: A practical alternative when prices aren't available, *Journal of Economic Perspectives*, 26(4):27–42.

Carson, R.T., Mitchell, R.C., Hanemann, M., Kopp, R.J., Presser, S., and Ruud, P.A. (2003) Contingent valuation and lost passive use: Damages from the Exxon Valdez oil spill, *Environmental and Resource Economics*, 25:257–286.

Casalmir, L.M.P. (2000) *Economic Optimal Rotation Age Determination Under Sustainable Forestry*, MS Thesis State University of New York, College of Environmental Science and Forestry, Syracuse, NY.

Cavo, M. (2018) *Valuing Recreational Services at Fort Drum Military Installation Using an Individual Travel Cost Model Given Multi-Year Survey Data*, MS Thesis State University of New York, College of Environmental Science and Forestry, Syracuse, NY.

Chang, S.J. (1981) Determination of the optimal growing stock and cutting cycle for an uneven-aged stand, *Forest Science*, 27(4):739–744.

Chang, S.J. (1982) An economic analysis of forest taxation's impact on optimal rotation age, *Land Economics*, 58(3):310–323.

Chang, S.J. (1998) A generalized Faustmann model for the determination of optimal harvest age, *Canadian Journal of Forest Research*, 28(5):652–659.

Chang, S.J., Cooper, C., and Guddanti, S. (2005) Effects of the log's rotational orientation and the depth of the opening cut on the value of lumber produced in sawing hardwood logs, *Forest Products Journal*, 55(10):49–55.

Chang, S.J., and Gadow, K.V. (2010) Application of the generalized Faustmann model to uneven-aged forest management, *Journal of Forestry Economics*, 16:313–325.

Chapeskie, D., and Koelling, M.R. (2006) Chapter 11, Economics of Maple syrup production, in R.B. Heiligmann, M.R. Koelling, and T.D. Perkins, eds. *North American Maple Syrup Producers Manual*, 2nd ed., Wooster, OH: Ohio State University Extension, The University of Ohio.

Chiang, A.C. (1984) *Fundamental Methods of Mathematical Economics*, 3rd ed., New York, NY: McGraw-Hill, Inc.

Chiang, A.C. (1992) *Elements of Dynamic Optimization*, New York, NY: McGraw-Hill, Inc.

Chichilnisky, G. (1997) What is sustainable development? *Land Economics*, 73(4):467–491.

Ciriacy-Wantrup, S.V. (1947) Capital returns from soil conservation practices, *Journal of Farms Economics*, 29(4):1181–1196.

Clark, J.M. (1940) Toward a concept of workable competition, *The American Economic Review*, 39(2):241–256.

Clawson, M., and Knetsch, J.L. (1966) *Economics of Outdoor Recreation*, Resources for the Future, Baltimore, ME: Johns Hopkins Press.

Clutter, J.L., Fortson, J.C., Pienaar, L.V., Brister, G.H., and Bailey, R.L. (1983) *Timber Management: A Quantitative Approach*, Hoboken, NJ: John Wiley & Sons.

Coase, R.H. (1960) The problem of social cost, *Journal of Law and Economics*, 3:1–44.

Colander, D. (1992) The lost art of economics, *Journal of Economic Perspectives*, 6(3):191–198.

Colander, D. (2014) Economists do a lousy job teaching students about inflation, *Eastern Economic Journal*, 40:285–288.

Cole, D.H., and Grossman, P.Z. (2002) The meaning of property rights: Law versus economics? *Land Economics*, 78(3):317–330.

Comolli, P.M. (1981) Principles and policies in forestry economics, *The Bell Journal of Economics*, 12(1):300–309.

Conrad, J.M. (1980) Quasi-option value and the expected value of information, *The Quarterly Journal of Economics*, 94(4):813–820.

Conrad, J.M. (2010) *Resource Economics*, 2nd ed., Cambridge: Cambridge University Press.

Copeland, T.E., Weston, J.F., and Shastri, K. (2005) *Financial Theory and Corporate Policy*, 4th ed., Reading, MA: Pearson Addison-Wesley Publishing Company.

Copi, I.M., and Cohen, C. (1998) *Introduction to Logic*, 10th ed., Englewood Cliffs, NY: Prentice-Hall, Inc.

Costanza, R., d'Arge, R., de-Groot, R., Farber, S., Grasso, M., Hannon, B., Limburg, K., Naeem, S., O'Neil, R., Paruelo, J., Raskin, R., Sutton, P., and van den Belt, J. (1998) The value of ecosystem services: Putting the issues in perspective, *Ecological Economics*, 25(1):67–72.

Creighton, J.H., Baumgartner, D.M., and Blatner, K.A. (2002) Ecosystem Management and nonindustrial private forest landowners in Washington State, USA, *Small-Scale Forest Economics, Management and Policy*, 1(1):55–69.

Creighton, J.H., Blatner, K.A., and Carrol, M.S. (2016) For the love of the land: Generational land transfer and the future of family forests in Western Washington State, USA, *Small-Scale Forestry*, 15:1–15.

Cropper, M., and Laibson, D. (1999) The implications of hyperbolic discounting for project evaluation, in P.R. Portney and J.P. Weyant, eds. *Discounting and Intergenerational Equity*, Washington, DC: Resources for the Future.

Curtis, T., Heath, G., Walker, A., Desai, J., Settle, E., and Barbosa, C. (2021) *Best Practices at the End of the Photovoltaic System Performance Period*, NREL/TP-5D00-78678, Golden, CO: National Renewable Energy Laboratory (www.nrel.gov/docs/fy21osti/78678.pdf accessed 15 July 2021).

Cutshall, J.B., Grace, L.A., and Munn, I.A. (2000) *An Analysis of Inflation in Timber Harvesting Costs*, Forest and Wildlife Research Center Article No. FO126, Starkville: Mississippi State University.

Dailey, G. (1997) *Nature's Services: Societal Dependence on Natural Ecosystems*, Covelo, CA: Island Press.

David, F.R., and David, F.R. (2003) It's time to redraft your mission statement, *Journal of Business Strategy*, 24(1):11–14.

David, M.E., David, F.R., and David, F.R. (2014) Mission statement theory and practice: A Content Analysis and New Direction, *International Journal of Business, Marketing, and Decision Science*, 7(1):95–110.

Davies, K. (1991) Forest investment considerations for planning thinning and harvesting, *Northern Journal of Applied Forestry*, 8(3):129–131.

Davis, L.S., Johnson, K.N., Bettinger, P.S., and Howard, P.S. (2001) *Forest Management: To Sustain Ecological, Economic, and Social Values*, 4th ed., Long Grove, IL: Waveland Press.

Davis, R.K. (1963) *The Value of Outdoor Recreation: An Economic Study of the Maine Woods*, Ph.D. Dissertation, Harvard University, Cambridge, MA.

Dennis, D.F. (1987) Rates of value change on uncut forest stands in New Hampshire, *Northern Journal of Applied Forestry*, 4(2):64–66.

de Soto, H. (2003) *The Mystery of Capital: Why Capitalism Triumphs in the West and Fails Everywhere Else*. New York, NY: Basic Books.

Dillman, D.A. (1978) *Mail and Telephone Surveys – The Total Design Method*, New York, NY: John Wiley and Sons.

Dillman, D.A., Smyth, J.D., and Christian, L.M. (2009) *Internet, Mail, and Mixed-Mode Surveys: The Tailored Design Method*, 3rd ed., New York, NY: John Wiley and Sons.

Dixit, A.K., and Pindyck, R.S. (1994) *Investment Under Uncertainty*. Princeton, NJ: Princeton University Press.

Dobbs, I.M. (1993) Individual travel cost method: Estimation and benefit assessment with discrete and possibly grouped dependent variable, *American Journal of Agricultural Economics*, 75(1):84–94.

Dodson, E., Hayes, S., Meeka, J., and Keyesa, C.R. (2015) Montana logging machine rates, *International Journal of Forest Engineering*, 26(2):1–10.

Dudley, C.L., Jr. (1972) A note on reinvesment assumptions in choosing between net present value and internal rate of return, *The Journal of Finance*, 27(4):907–915.

Duerr, W.A. (1960) *Fundamentals of Forestry Economics*, New York, NY: McGraw-Hill, Inc.

Durham, C.A., Bouma, A., and Meunier-Goddik, L. (2015) A decision-making tool to determine economic feasibility and break-even prices for artisan cheese operations, *Journal of Dairy Science*, 98(12):8319–8332.

Edmonds, T.P., Edmonds, C.T., Olds, P.R., McNair, F.M., and Tsay, B.-Y. (2015) *Survey of Accounting*, 4th ed., New York, NY: McGraw-Hill, Inc.

Ellefson, P.V., Cheng, A.S., and Moulton, R.J. (1995) *Regulation of Private Forestry Practices by State Governments, Bulletin SB-605-1995*, St. Paul, MN: University of Minnesota, Agricultural Experiment Station.

Elliott, K.G. (2011) *The Brave New Work of Ecosystem Service Markets: The Consultant – Annual Journal of the Association of Consulting Foresters* (www.acf-foresters.org/ACFWeb/Membership/The_Consultant_Magazine/ACFWeb/Membership_Nav_Item/Consultant_Magazine.aspx?hkey=23f2c016-8346-4211-9eef-3d8105edacee accessed 3 February 2020).

Erdbrink, T., and Gladstone, R. (2012) Violence and Protest in Iran as Currency Drops in Value, *The New York Times*, 3 October 2012 (http://www.nytimes.com/2012/10/04/world/middleeast/clashes-reported-in-tehran-as-riot-police-target-money-changers.html?nl=tod aysheadlines&emc=edit_th_20121004&_r=0 accessed 1 September 2023).

Erickson, J.D., Chapman, D., Fahey, T.J., and Christ, M.J. (1999) Non-renewability in forest rotations: Implications for economic and ecosystem sustainability, *Ecological Economics*, 31:91–106.

Escobedo, F., Kroeger, T., and Wagner, J.E. (2011) Urban forests and pollution mitigation: Analyzing ecosystem services and disservices, *Environmental Pollution*, 159: 2078–2087.

Escobedo, F., Nowak, D.J., Wagner, J.E., De la Maza, C.L., Rodgiguez, M., Crane, D.E., and Hernández, J. (2006) The socioeconomics and management of Santiago de Chile's public urban forest, *Urban Forestry and Urban Greening*, 4(3–4):104–114.

Escobedo, F., Varela, S., Zhao, M., Wagner, J.E., and Zipperer, W. (2010) Analyzing the efficacy of subtropical urban forests in offsetting carbon emissions from cities, *Environmental Science & Policy*, 13:362–372.

Escobedo, F, Wagner, J.E., Nowak, D.J., De la Maza, C.L., Rodgiguez, M., and Crane, D.E. (2008) Analyzing the cost-effectiveness of Santiago, Chile's policy of using urban forests to improve air quality, *Journal of Environmental Management*, 86:148–157.

Faustmann, M. (1849) Berechnung des Wertes Welchen Waldboden sowie noch nicht haubare Holzbestände für die Waldwirtschaft besitzen, *Allgemeine Forst- und Jagd-Zeitung*, 15. Reprinted as Faustmann, M. (1995) Calculation of the value which forest land and immature stands possess for forestry, *Journal of Forest Economics*, 1(1):7–44.

Federal Inter-Agency River Basin Committee (FIRBC). (1958) *Proposed Practices for Economic Analysis of River Basin Projects* [known as the "GreenBook"], Federal Inter-Agency River Basin Committee, Washington, DC: Subcommittee on Benefits and Costs.

Fehr, D. (2017) Equivalent annual annuity vs. replacement chain approach for mutually exclusive investment projects, *Journal of Finance and Accountancy*, 22:1–5.

Feldman, D., Bolinger, M., and Schwabe, P. (2020) *Current and Future Costs of Renewable Energy Project Finance Across Technologies*, NREL/TP-6A20-76881, Golden, CO: National Renewable Energy Laboratory (www.nrel.gov/docs/fy20osti/76881.pdf).

Feldman, D., Ramasamy, V., Fu, R., Ramdas, A., Desai, J., and Margolis, R. (2021) *U.S. Solar Photovoltaic System Cost Benchmark: Q1 2020*, NREL/TP-6A20-77324, Golden, CO: National Renewable Energy Laboratory (www.nrel.gov/docs/fy21osti/77324.pdf).

Feldstein, M.S. (1964a) The social time preference discount rate in cost benefit analysis, *The Economic Journal*, 74(294):360–379.

Feldstein, M.S. (1964b) Net social benefit calculation and the public investment decision, *Oxford Economic Papers*, 16(1):114–131.

Feng, Y., Fullerton, D., and Gan, L. (2005) *Vehicle Choice, Miles Driven and Pollution Policies*, Working Paper #11553, Cambridge, MA: National Bureau of Economic Research (www.nber.org/papers/w11553 accessed 29 December 2009).

Ferraro, P.J., and Taylor, L.O. (2005) Do economists recognize an opportunity cost when they see one? A dismal performance from the dismal science, *The B.E. Journals in Economic Analysis & Policy*, 4(1):Article 7.

Field, B.C., and Field, M.K. (2002) *Environmental Economics: An Introduction*, 3rd ed., New York, NY: McGraw-Hill, Inc.

Fisher, I. (1930) *The Theory of Interest*, New York, NY: Macmillan.

Foerde, K., Knowlton, B.J., and Poldrack, R.A. (2006) Modulation of competing memory systems by distraction, *Proceedings of the National Academy of Sciences*, 103(31):11778–11783.

Forman-Cook, W.C., Malmsheimer, R.W., and Germain, R.H. (2015) Local regulation of timber harvesting in New York state, *Forest Science*, 61(6):1079–1087.

Freeman, A.M., Herriges, J.A., and Kling, C.L. (2014) *The Measurement of Environmental and Resource Values: Theory and Methods*, 3rd ed., Washington, DC: RFF Press.

Friedman, M. (1953) *Essays in Positive Economics*, Chicago, IL: The University of Chicago Press.

Fullerton, D., and Stavins, R.N. (1998) *How Do Economists Really Think About the Environment?*, Resources for the Future Discussion Paper 98–29, Washington, DC.

Gaffney, M.M. (1957) *Concepts of Financial Maturity of Timber and Other Assets*, A.E. Information Series No. 62, College Raleigh, NC: Department of Agricultural Economics North Carolina State.

Galor, O., and Özak, O. (2016) The agricultural origins of time preference, *American Economic Review*, 106(10):3064–3103.

Gaspars-Wieloch, H. (2019) Project net present value estimation under uncertainty, *Central European Journal of Operations Research*, 27(1):179–197.

Getz, W.M., and Haight, R.G. (1989) *Population Harvesting: Demographic Models of Fish, Forest, and Animal Resources*, Princeton, NJ: Princeton University Press.

Germain, R., Bick, S., Kelly, M., Benjamin, J., and Farrand, W. (2016) Case study of three high-performing contract loggers with distinct harvest systems: Are they thriving, striving, or just surviving? *Forest Products Journal*, 66(1–2):97–105.

Gevorkiantz, S.R., and Scholz, H.F. (1948) *Timber Yields and Possible Returns from the Mixed-Oak Farmwoods of Southwestern Wisconsin*, Publication No. 521, Madison, WI: US Department of Agriculture, Forest Service Lake States Forest Experiment Station, In Cooperation with Wisconsin Department of Conservation and University of Wisconsin.

Gibbons, R. (1992) *Game Theory for Applied Economists*, Princeton, NJ: Princeton University Press.

Godman, R.M., and Mendel, J.J. (1978) *Economic Values for Growth and Grade Changes of Sugar Maple in the Lake States*, USDA Forest Service North Central Research Station Research Paper NC-155 (https://www.fs.usda.gov/research/treesearch/10676).

Goodfellow, J., Nowak, C., and Wagner, J.E. (2017) *The Business Case for Herbicide Use in Integrated Vegetation Management Programs*, Final Research Report, Montreal, Quebec, Canada: Center for Energy Advancement Through Technological Innovation, VMTF 4101, CEATI International Inc.

Goodhue, R.E., LaFrance, J.T., and Simon, L.K. (2009) Wine taxes, production, aging and quality, *Journal of Wine Economics*, 4(1):65–83.

Gowdy, J., and Erickson, J.D. (2005) The approach of ecological economics, *Cambridge Journal of Economics*, 29:207–222.

Graham, J.R., and Harvey, C.R. (2001) The theory and practice of finance: Evidence from the field, *Journal of Financial Economics*, 60:187–243.

Graham, W.G., Goebel, P.C., Heiligmann, R.B., and Bumgardner, M.S. (2006) Maple syrup in Ohio and the impact of Ohio State University (OSU) extension program, *Journal of Forestry*, 104(7):94–100.

Gregory, G.R. (1972) *Forest Resource Economics*, New York, NY: John Wiley and Sons.

Gregory, G.R. (1987) *Forest Resource Economics*, Hoboken, NJ: John Wiley & Sons.

Grisez, T.J., and Mendel, J.J. (1972) *The Rate of Value Increase for Black Cherry, Red Maple, and White Ash*, Research Paper NE-231, Upper Darby, PA: USDA Forest Service Northeastern Research Station.

Grutters, J.P.C., Kessels, A.G.H., Dirksen, C.D., van Helvoort-Postulart, D., Anteunis, L.J.C., and Joore, M.A. (2008) Willingness to accept versus willingness to pay in a discrete choice experiment, *Value in Health*, 11(7):1110–1119.

Hagan, J.M., Irland, L.C., and Whitman, A.A. (2005) *Changing Timberland Ownership in the Northern Forest and Implications for Biodiversity*, Report # MCCS-FCP-2005-1, Brunswick, ME: Manomet Center for Conservation Science.

Hahn, J.T., and Hansen, M.H. (1991) Cubic and board foot volume models for the Central States, *Northern Journal of Applied Forestry*, 8(2):47–57.

Haines-Young, R., and Potschin, M. (2013) *Common International Classification of Ecosystem Services (CICES): Consultation on Version 4, August–December 2012*. EEA Framework Contract No EEA/IEA/09/003 (https://unstats.un.org/unsd/envaccounting/seearev/GCComments/CICES_Report.pdf).

Hall, D.O. (1983) Financial Maturity for Even-aged and All-aged Stands. *Forest Science*, 29(4):833–836.

Halstead, J.M., Luloff, A.E., and Stevens, T.H. (1992) Protest bidders in contingent valuation, *Northeast Journal of Agricultural and Resource Economics*, 21(2):160–169.

Hancock Timberland Investor. (2019) *U.S. Housing Picks Up, 3rd Quarter*. Hancock Timber Resource Group A Manulife Investment Management Company, Boston, MA.

Hancock Timberland Investor, Q3. (2006) *Housing Starts, Lumber Prices, and Timberland Investment Performance*, Hancock Timber Resource Group 3rd Quarter 2006, Group A Manulife Investment Management Company, Boston, MA (www.htrg.com/research_archives_2006.htm accessed 21 February 2010).

Hancock Timberland Investor, Q4. (2000) *Impact of Carbon Credits on Forestland Values*, Hancock Timber Resource Group 4th Quarter 2000 (www.htrg.com/research_archives_2000.htm accessed 21 May 2010).

Hand, M. (2010) *Wind Generation Technology Cost Modeling*. Wind Energy Systems Engineering Workshop (https://www.nrel.gov/wind/assets/pdfs/se_workshop_hand.pdf accessed 5 September 2023).

Hanna, S., Folke, C., and Mäler, K.-G. (1995) Property rights and environmental resources, in S. Hanna and M. Munasinghem, eds. *Property Rights and the Environment: Social and Ecological Issues*, The Beijer International Institute of Ecological Economics and The World Bank, Washington, DC: The International Bank for Reconstruction and Development.

Hardin, G. (1968) The tragedy of the commons, *Science*, 162(3859):1243–1248.

Harou, P. (1985) On a social discount rate for forestry, *Canadian Journal of Forest Research*, 15:927–934.

Hartman, R. (1976) The harvesting decision when a standing forest has value, *Economic Inquiry*, 14:52–55.

Hatcher, J.E., Jr., Straka, T.J., and Greene, J.L. (2013) The size of forest holding/parcelization problem in forestry: A literature review, *Resources*, 2:39–57.

Hayne, H.L., Hoover, W.L., Siegel, W.C., and Green, J.L. (2001) *Forest Landowners' Guide to Federal Income Taxes*, United States Forest Service Agricultural Handbook No. 718 (www.fs.fed.us/publications/2001/01jun19-Forest_Tax_Guide31201.pdf accessed 5 August 2010).

Haynes, R.W., tech. coord. (2003) *An Analysis of the Timber Situation in the United States: 1952–2050. Gen. Tech. Rep. PNW-GTR-560*, 254 p, Portland, OR: U.S. Department of Agriculture, Forest Service, Pacific Northwest Research Station.

Haynes, R.W., and Monserud, R.A. (2002) *A Basis for Understanding Compatibility Among Wood Production and Other Forest Values*, United States Department of Agriculture Forest Service Pacific Northwest Research Station, PNW-GTR-529 (https://www.fs.usda.gov/pnw/pubs/pnw_gtr529.pdf).

Heeter, J., O'Shaughnessy, E., and Chan, G. (2020) *Sharing the Sun: Understanding Community Solar Development and Subscriptions* (www.nrel.gov/docs/fy20osti/75438.pdf accessed 11 July 2021).

Heiligmann, R.B. (2008) Here's how to . . . increase financial returns from your Woodland, *Forestry Source*, 13(7):13–14.

Heiligmann, R.B., Koelling, M.R., and Perkins, T.D., eds. (2006) *North American Maple Syrup Producers Manual*, 2nd ed., Wooster, OH: Ohio State University Extension, The University of Ohio.

Helms, J.A., ed. (1998) *The Dictionary of Forestry*, Bethesda, MD: The Society of American Foresters.

Henderson, J.M., and Quandt, R.E. (1980) *Microeconomic Theory: A Mathematical Approach*, 3rd ed., New York, NY: McGraw-Hill, Inc.

Hepburn, C.J., and Koundouri, P. (2007) Recent advances in discounting: Implications for forest economics, *Journal of Forest Economics*, 2–3(13):169–189.

Herrick, O.W., and Gansner, D.A. (1985) Forest-tree value growth rates, *Northern Journal Applied Forestry*, 2(1):11–13.

Hesseln, H., Loomis, J.B., and González-Cabán, A. (2004) Comparing the economic effects of fire on hiking demand in Montana and Colorado, *Journal of Forest Economics*, 10:21–35.

Hesseln, H., Loomis, J.B., González-Cabán, A., and Alexander, S. (2003) Wildfire effects on hiking and biking demand in New Mexico: A travel cost study, *Journal of Environmental Management*, 69:359–368.

Heyne, P., Boettke, P., and Prychitko, D. (2006) *The Economic Way of Thinking*, 11th ed., Upper Saddle River, NJ: Pearson Prentice-Hall.

Hidayati, E. (2011) *Farmers' Perception of Environmental Problems: A Case Study in Batulanteh Watershed, Indonesia*, Master's Thesis, SUNY-ESF, Syracuse, NY.

Hillier, F., and Lieberman, G. (1990) *Introduction to Operations Research*, 5th ed., New York, NY: McGraw Hill, Inc.

Hines, S.J., Heath, S.L., and Birdsey, R.A. (2010) *Annotated Bibliography of Scientific Literature on Managing Forest for Carbon Benefits*, General Technical Report GTR-NRS-57, Newtown Square, PA: US Department of Agriculture, Forest Service, Northeastern Research Station.

Hirshleifer, J. (1970) *Investment, Interest and Capital*, Englewood Cliff, NJ: Prentice-Hall, Inc.

Hoen, B., Wiser, R., Cappers, P., and Thayer, M. (2011) *An Analysis of the Effects of Residential Photovoltaic Energy Systems on Home Sales Prices in California*, Ernest Orlando Lawrence Berkeley Laboratory, Manuscript # LBNL-4476E (https://eetd.lbl.gov/sites/all/files/publications/lbnl-4476e.pdf accessed 6 November 2019).

Holmes, T.P., Bentley, W.R., Broderick, S.H., and Hobson, T. (1990) Hardwood stumpage price trends and characteristics in Connecticut, *Northern Journal of Applied Forestry*, 7(1):13–16.

Hool, J.N. (1966) A dynamic programming-Markov chain approach to forest production control, *Forest Science Monograph*, 12:1–26.

Horowitz, J.K., and McConnell, K.E. (2002) A review of WTA/WTP studies, *Journal of Environmental Economics and Management*, 44:426–447.

Howard, T.E., and Chase, W.E. (1995) Maine stumpage prices: Characteristics and trends from 1963 to 1990, *Forest Products Journal*, 45(1):31–36.

Hseu, J., and Buongiorno, J. (1997) Financial performance of Maple-Birch stands in Wisconsin: Value growth rate versus equivalent annual income, *Northern Journal of Applied Forestry*, 14(2):59–66.

Huyler, N.K. (1982) Economics of maple sap and syrup production, in M.C. Clayton, Jr., J.R. Donnelly, W.J. Gabreil, L.D. Garrett, R.A. Gregory, N.K. Huyler, W.L. Jenkins, P.E. Sendak, R.S. Walters, and H.W. Yawney, eds. *Sugar Maple Research: Sap Production, Processing and Marketing of Maple Syrup*, General Technical Report NE-72, Broomall, PA: US Department of Agriculture, Forest Service, Northeastern Forest Experiment Station.

Huyler, N.K. (2000) *Cost of Maple Sap Production for Various Size Tubing Operations*, Research Paper NE-RP-712, Newtown Square, PA: US Department of Agriculture, Forest Service, Northeastern Research Station.

Hyytiäinen, K., and Tahvonen, O. (2003) Maximum sustained yield, forest rent or Faustmann, does it really matter, *Scandinavian Journal of Forest Research*, 18(5):457–469.

Isoni, A. (2011) The willingness-to-accept/willingness-to-pay disparity in repeated markets: Loss aversion or "bad-deal" aversion? *Theory and Decisions*, 71(3):409–430.

Jenkin, T., Feldman, D., Kwan, A., and Walker, B.J. (2019) *Estimating the Impact of Residual Value for Electricity Generation Plants on Capital Recovery, Levelized Cost of Energy, and Cost to Consumers*, NREL/TP-6A20-72217, Golden, CO: National Renewable Energy Laboratory (www.nrel.gov/docs/fy19osti/72217.pdf).

Jensen, O.W. (1982) Opportunity costs: Their place in the theory and practice of production, *Managerial and Decision Economics*, 3(1):48–51.

Johansson, P.-O., and Löfgren, K.-G. (1985) *The Economics of Forestry and Natural Resources*, Oxford: Basil Blackwell Ltd.

Johnstone, D. (2008) What does an IRR (or two) mean? *Journal of Economic Education*, 39(1):78–87.

Jorgensen, B.S., and Syme, G.J. (2000) Protest responses and willingness to pay: Attitude toward paying for stormwater pollution abatement, *Ecological Economics*, 33:251–265.

Just, R.E., Hueth, D.L., and Schmitz, A. (1982) *Applied Welfare Economics and Public Policy*, Englewood Cliff, NJ: Prentice-Hall, Inc.

Kant, S. (1999) Sustainable management of uneven-aged private forests: a case study from Ontario, Canada. *Ecological Economics*, 30:131–146.

Kant, S. (2003) Extending the boundaries of forest economics, *Forest Policy and Economics*, 5:39–56.

Kaoru, Y., Smith, V.K., and Liu, J.L. (1995) Using random utility models to estimate the recreational value of estuarine resources, *American Journal of Agricultural Economics*, 77(1):141–151.

Karush, W. (1939) *Minima of Functions of Several Variables with Inequalities as Side Conditions*, M.S. Thesis, Department of Mathematics, University of Chicago, Chicago.

Kay, J. (1996) *The Business of Economics*, Oxford: Oxford University Press Inc.

Keat, P.G., and Young, P.K.Y. (2000) *Managerial Economics: Economic Tools for Today's Decision Makers*, 3rd ed., Upper Saddle River, NJ: Prentice Hall.

Kemkes, R.J., Farley, J., and Koliba, C.J. (2009) Determining when payments are an effective policy approach to ecosystem service provisions, *Ecological Economics*, In Press (https://doi.org/10.1016/j.ecolecon.2009.11.032)

Kennedy, E.T., Costa, R., and Smathers, W.M., Jr. (1996) Economic incentives: New directions for red-cockaded woodpecker habitat conservation, *Journal of Forestry*, 94(4):22–26.

Kerchner, C.D., and Keeton, W.S. (2015) California's regulatory forest carbon market: Viability for northeast landowners, *Forest Policy and Economics, Elsevier*, 50(C):70–81.

Keynes, J.M. (1936) *The General Theory of Employment, Interest and Money*, London: Macmillan (http://ebooks.adelaide.edu.au/k/keynes/john_maynard/k44g/ accessed 16 June 2009).

Kierulff, H. (2008) MIRR: A better measure, *Business Horizons*, 51:321–329.

Kilgore, M.A., Stephanie Snyder, S., Taff, S., and Schertz, J. (2008) Family forest stewardship: Do owners need a financial incentive, *Journal of Forestry*, 106(7):357–362.

Kimmins, J.P. (1997) *Forest Ecology: A Foundation for Sustainable Management*, 2nd ed., Upper Saddle River, NJ: Prentice Hall.

Klemperer, W.D. (1996) *Forest Resource Economics and Finance*, New York, NY: McGraw-Hill, Inc.

Kline, J.D., Mazzotta, M.J., and Patterson, T.M. (2009) Toward a rational exuberance for ecosystem services markets, *Journal of Forestry*, 107(4):204–212.

Kling, C.L., List, J.L., and Zhao, J. (2011) A dynamic explanation of the willingness to pay and willingness to accept disparity, *Economic Inquiry*, 51(1):909–921.

Knight, F.H. (1921) *Risk, Uncertainty, and Profit*, New York, NY: Houghton Mifflin Company.

Kniivilä, M., and Saastamoinen, O. (2002) The opportunity cost of forest conservation in a local economy, *Silva Fennica*, 36(4):853–865.

Knoke, T., Moog, M., and Plusczyk, N. (2001) On the effect of volatile stumpage prices on the economic attractiveness of a silvicultural transformation strategy, *Forest Policy and Economics*, 2(3–4):229–240.

Konow, J., Saijo, T., and Akai, K. (2016) *Equity Versus Equality*, Munich Personal RePEc Archive, MPRA Paper No. 75376, posted 5 December, 10:16 UTC (https://mpra.ub.uni-muenchen.de/75376/).

Koskela, E., and Ollikainen, M. (2003) Optimal forest taxation under private and social amenity valuation, *Forest Science*, 49(4):596–607.

Kramer, D.G., Polasky, S., Starfield, A., Palik, B., Westphal, L., Snyder, S., Jakes, P., Hudson, R., and Gustafson, E. (2006) A comparison of alternative strategies for cost-effective water quality management in lakes, *Environmental Management*, 38(3):411–425.

Kreps, D.M. (1990) *Game Theory and Economic Modeling*, Oxford, UK: Clarendon Press.

Kroeger, T., and Casey, F. (2007) An assessment of market-based approaches to providing ecosystem services on agricultural lands, *Ecological Economics*, 64:321–332.

Kuhn, H.W., and Tucker, A.W. (1951) Nonlinear programming, in J. Neyman, ed. *Proceedings of the Second Berkeley Symposium*, Berkeley: University of California Press, pp. 481–492.

Lackey, R.T. (2004) Normative science, *Fisheries*, 29(7):38–39.

Lackey, R.T. (2007) Science, scientists, and policy advocacy, *Conservation Biology*, 21(1):12–17.

Lambert, P.J. (1985) *Advanced Mathematics for Economists: Static and Dynamic Optimization*, Oxford, UK: Basil Blackwell Ltd.

Ledec, G., and Goodland, R. (1988) *Wildlands: Their Protection and Management in Economic Development*, Washington, DC: The International Bank for Reconstruction and Development, The World Bank.

Lembersky, M.R., and Johnson, K.N. (1975) Optimal policies for managed stands: An infinite horizon Markov decision process approach, *Forest Science*, 21(2):109–122.

Leuschner, W.A. (1984) *Introduction to Forest Resources Management*, New York, NY: John Wiley & Sons.

Levin, R.I., Rubin, D.S., Stinson, J.P., and Gardner, F.S. (1992) *Quantitative Approaches to Management*, New York, NY: McGrawHill, International.

Li, C.Z., and Löfgren, K.G. (2000) Renewable resources and economic sustainability: A dynamic analysis with heterogenous time preferences, *Journal of Environmental Economics and Management*, 40:236–250.

Liabson, D. (1997) Golden eggs and hyperbolic discounting, *The Quarterly Journal of Economics*, 112(2):443–447.

Lichtkoppler, F.R., and Kuehn, D. (2003) *New York's Great Lakes Charter Fishing Industry in 2002*, Ohio Sea Grant College Program OHSU-TS-039, Columbus, OH: Sea Grant Great Lakes Network, The Ohio State University.

Longenecker, J.G., Moore, C.W., Petty, J.W., and Palich, L.E. (2006) *Small Business Management: An Entrepreneurial Emphasis*, 3rd ed., Mason, OH: Thomson South-Western.

Loomis, J.B., Peterson, G., Champ, P., Brown, T., and Lucero, B. (1998) Paired comparison estimates of willingness to accept versus contingent valuation estimates of willingness to pay, *Journal of Economic Behavior and Organization*, 35:501–515.

Loomis, J.B., Tadjion, O., Watson, P., Wilson, J., Davies, S., and Thilmany, D. (2009) A hybrid individual-zonal travel cost model for estimating the consumer surplus of golfing in Colorado, *Journal of Sports Economics*, 10(2):155–167.

Loomis, J.B., and Walsh, R.G. (1997) *Recreation Economic Decisions: Comparing Benefits and Costs*, State College, PA: Venture Publishing, Inc.

Loucks, D.P., and Van Beek, E. (2005) *Water Resources Systems Planning and Management: An Introduction to Methods, Models, and Applications*, United Nations Educational, Scientific and Cultural Organization (https://unesdoc.unesco.org/ark:/48223/pf0000143430 accessed 9 October 2019).

Luenberger, D.G. (1998) *Investment Science*, Oxford, UK: Oxford University Press.

Maack, M., and Davidsdottir, B. (2015) Five capital impact assessment: Appraisal framework based on theory of sustainable well-being, *Renewable and Sustainable Energy Reviews*, 50:1338–1351.

Magni, C.A., and Martin, J.D. (2017) *The Reinvestment Rate Assumption Fallacy for IRR and NPV: A Pedagogical Note* (https://mpra.ub.uni-muenchen.de/83889/ accessed 20 September 2018).

Maital, S. (1994) *Executive Economics: Ten Essential Tools for Managers*, New York, NY: The Free Press.

Majumdar, I., Teeter, L., and Butler, B. (2008) Characterizing family forest owners: A cluster analysis approach, *Forest Science*, 54(2):176–184.

Malmsheimer, R.W., Bowyer, J.L., Fried, J.S., Gee, E., Izlar, R.L., Miner, R.A., Munn, I.A., Oneil, E., and Stewart, W.C. (2011) Managing forests because carbon matters: Integrating energy, products, and land management policy, *Journal of Forestry*, 109(7S):S7–S50 (www.safnet.org/documents/JOFSupplement.pdf).

Mankiw, N.G. (2018) *Principles of Economics*, 8th ed., Independence, KY: South Western Cengage.

Manley, B. (2010) Discount rates used for forest valuation – results of 2009 survey, *New Zealand Journal of Forestry*, 54(4):19–23.

Marckers, H., Heiligmann, R.B., and Koelling, M.R. (2006) Chapter 8, Syrup filtration, grading, packaging, and storage, in R.B. Heiligmann, M.R. Koelling, and T.D. Perkins, eds. *North American Maple Syrup Producers Manual*, 2nd ed., Wooster, OH: Ohio State University Extension, The University of Ohio.

McConnell, C.R., and Brue, S.L. (2005) *Economics*, 16th ed., New York, NY: McGraw-Hill, Inc. Irwin.

McConnell, T.E., and Grahm, G.W. (2016) History of Northeastern US maple syrup price trends, *Forest Products Journal*, 66(1–2):106–112.

McElhinny, C., Gibbons, P., Brack, C., and Bauhaus, J. (2005) Forest and woodland stand structural complexity: Its definition and measurement, *Forest Ecology and Management*, 218(1–3):1–24.

McGuigan, J.R., and Moyer, R.C. (1993) *Managerial Economics*, 6th ed., Minneapolis, MN: West Publishing Company.

McIntyre, R.K., Jack, S.B., McCall, B.B., and Mitchell, R.J. (2010) Financial feasibility of selection-based multiple-value management on private lands in the South: A heuristic case study approach, *Journal of Forestry*, 108(3):230–237.

McKenzie, R.B., and Lee, D.R. (2006) *Microeconomics for MBAs: The Economic Way of Thinking for Managers*, Cambridge, UK: Cambridge University Press.

Mead, D.J. (2013) *Sustainable Management of Pinus radiata Plantations*, FAO Forestry Paper No. 170, Rome: FAO.

Mendel, J.J., Grisez, T.J., and Trimble, G.R., Jr. (1973) *The Rate of Value Increase for Sugar Maple*, USDA Forest Service Northeastern Research Station Research Paper NE-250, Upper Darby, PA: USDA.

Mentzer, J.T., DeWitt, W., Keebler, J.S., Min, S., Nix, N.W., Smith, C.D., and Zacharia, Z.G. (2001) Defining supply chain management, *Journal of Business Logistics*, 22(2):1–25.

Meyerhoff, J., and Liebe, U. (2006) Protest beliefs in contingent valuation: Explaining their motivation, *Ecological Economics*, 57:583–594.

Miceli, T.J., and Minkler, A.P. (1995) Willingness-to-accept versus willingness-to-pay measures of value: Implications for rent control, eminent domain, and zoning, *Public Finance Review*, 23(2):255–270.

Michie, B.R. (1985) Uneven-Aged Stand Management and the Value of Forest Land. *Forest Science*, 31(1):116–121.

Mikesell, R.F. (1977) *The Rate of Discount for Evaluating Public Projects*, Washington, DC: American Enterprise Institute for Public Policy Research.

Mills, T.J. (2000) Position advocacy by scientists risks scientific credibility and may be unethical, *Northwest Science*, 74(2):165–167.

Möhring, B. (2001) The German struggle between the 'Bodenreinertragslehre' (land rent theory) and 'Waldreinertragslehre' (theory of the highest revenue) belongs to the past – but what is left? *Forest Policy and Economics*, 2:195–201.

Montgomery, C.A., Brown, G.M., Jr., and Adams, D.M. (1994) The marginal cost of species preservation: The Northern spotted owl, *Journal of Environmental Economics and Management*, 26:111–128.

Morrison, G.C. (2000) WTP and WTA in repeated trial experiments: Learning or leading? *Journal of Economic Psychology*, 21:57–72.

Munasinghe, M. (1993) *Environmental Economics and Sustainable Development*, World Bank Environment Paper No. 3, Washington, DC: The World Bank.

Murray, B.C. (1995a) Measuring oligopsony power with shadow prices: U.S. market for pulpwood and sawlogs, *The Review of Economics and Statistics*, 77(3):486–498.

Murray, B.C. (1995b) Oligopsony, vertical integration, and output substitution: Welfare effects in U.S. pulpwood markets, *Land Economics*, 71(2):193–206.

Mutanen, A., and Toppinen, A. (2005) Finnish Sawlog market under forest taxation reform, *Silva Fennica*, 39(1):117–130.

National Research Council. (2005) *Valuing Ecosystem Services: Toward Better Environmental Decision-Making*, Washington, DC: The National Academies Press (https://doi.org/10.17226/11139).

Nautiyal, J.C. (1983) Towards a method of uneven-aged forest management based on the theory of financial maturity. *Forest Science*, 29(1):47–58.

Navarro, G.A. (2003) Re-examining the theories supporting the so-called Faustmann formula, in F. Helles, N. Strange, and L. Wichmann, eds. *Recent Accomplishments in Applied Forest Economics Research*, Dordrecht, The Netherlands: Kluwer Academic Publishers.

Newman, D.G., Lavelle, J.P., and Eschenbach, T.G. (2014) *Engineering Economic Analysis*, 12th ed., Oxford, UK: Oxford University Press.

Newman, D.H. (1988) *The Optimal Forest Rotation: A Discussion and Annotated Bibliography*, General Technical Report SE-48, Ashville, NC: U.S.D.A. Forest Service Southeastern Forest Experiment Station.

Newman, D.H. (2002) Forestry's golden rule and the development of the optimal forest rotation literature, *Journal of Forest Economics*, 8:5–27.

Newman, D.H. (2010) Forestry foundations – total economic value, *The New York Forester*, 66(3):5–7.

Newman, D.H., and Healy, R.G. (1997) Evaluating the opportunity cost of establishing a nature reserve, in G.K. Meffe and C.R. Carroll, eds., *Principles of Conservation Biology*, 2nd ed., pp. 529–531, Sunderland, MA: Sinauer Associates, Inc.

Newman, D.H., and Wagner, J.E. (2012) Putting Samuelson's economics of forestry into context: The limits of forest economics in policy debates, *Journal of Natural Resources Policy Research*, 4(3):214–218.

Newman, D.H., and Wear, D.N. (1993) Production economics of private forestry: A comparison of industrial and nonindustrial forest owners, *American Journal of Agricultural Economics*, 75(3):674–684.

New York Department of Environmental Conservation – NYS DEC. (1997) *New York Statewide Angler Survey 1996 Report 1: Angler Effort and Expenditures*, Albany, NY: New York State Department of Environmental Conservation, Division of Fish and Wildlife.

Nguyen, D. (1979) Environmental services and the optimal rotation problem in forest management, *Journal of Environmental Management*, 8:127–236.

Nhuchhen, D.R., Basu, P., and Acharya, B. (2014) A comprehensive review on biomass torrefaction, *International Journal of Renewable Energy & Biofuels*, 2014:56.

Nievergelt, J. (1983) The concept of elasticity in economics, *Society for industrial and Applied Mathematics*, 25(2):261–265.

Nowak, C.A., Abrahamson, L.P., Neuhauser, E.F., Foreback, C.G., Freed, H.D., Shaheen, S.B., and Stevens, C.H. (1992) Cost-effective vegetation management on a recently cleared electric transmission line right-of-way, *Weed Technology*, 6:828–837.

Nyland, R. (2016) *Silviculture: Concepts and Applications*, 3rd ed., Long Grove, IL: Waveland Press, Inc.

O'Hara, K.L. and Gersonde, R.F. (2004) Stocking control concepts in uneven-aged silviculture, *Forestry*, 77(2):131–143.

Ohlin, B. (1921) Till frågan om skogarnas omloppstid, *Ekonomisk Tidskrift*, 22. Reprinted as Ohlin, B. (1995) Concerning the question of the rotation period in forestry, *Journal of Forest Economics*, 1(1):89–114.

Oliver, C.D., and Larson, B.C. (1990) *Forest Stand Dynamics*, New York NY: McGraw-Hill, Inc.

Oliver, M., and Fried, J. (2013) *Do Carbon Offsets Work? The Role of Forest Management in Greenhouse Gas Mitigation*, USDA Forest Service, Science Findings, Issue 155 (www. fs.usda.gov/treesearch/pubs/43931 accessed 3 February 2020).

Page, I.B. (2013) *Why Do Distilleries Produce Multiple Ages of Whisky?* Selected Paper prepared for presentation at the Agricultural & Applied Economics Association's 2013 AAEA & CAES Joint Annual Meeting, Washington, DC, 4–6 August (https://tind-customer-agecon.

s3.amazonaws.com/b90d95fe-805b-46e6-9e17-f4d027b61046?response-con
tent-disposition=inline%3B%20filename%2A%3DUTF-8%27%272013AAEA_ibpage.
pdf&response-content-type=application%2Fpdf&AWSAccessKeyId=AKIAXL7W7Q3
XHXDVDQYS&Expires=1564500708&Signature=R0Pr95WU622JTglBYAEJwpoBcU
E%3D accessed 30 July 2019).

Pagiola, S., von Ritter, K., and Bishop, J. (2004) *How Much Is an Ecosystem Worth? Assessing the Economic Value of Conservation*, Washington, DC: The International Bank for Reconstruction and Development, World Bank (http://www-wds.worldbank.org/external/default/main?pagePK=64193027&piPK=64187937&theSitePK=523679&menuPK=64187510&searchMenuPK=64187283&siteName=WDS&entityID=0000120 09_20041207120119 accessed 24 August 2010).

Palmquist, R. (2005) Property value model, in K.G. Mäler and J.R. Vincent, eds., *The Handbook of Environmental Economics: Valuing Environmental Changes*, pp. 785–786, Amsterdam: North-Holland Publishers.

Patterson, D.W., Kluender, R.A., and Granskog, J.E. (2002) Economic feasibility of producing inside-out beams from small-diameter logs, *Forest Products Journal*, 52(1):23–26.

Patterson, D.W., and Xie, X. (1998) Inside-out beams from small-diameter Appalachian hardwood logs, *Forest Products Journal*, 48(1):76–80.

Patterson, T.M., and Coelho, D.L. (2009) Ecosystem services: Foundations, opportunities, and challenges for forest products sector, *Forest Ecology and Management*, 257(8):1637–1646.

Pearce, D.W., ed. (1994) *The MIT Dictionary of Modern Economics*, 4th ed., Cambridge, MA: The MIT Press.

Pearce, D.W., Atkinson, G., and Mourato, S. (2006) *Cost-Benefit Analysis and the Environment: Recent Developments*, Paris, France: Organization for Economic Co-Operation and Development.

Pearce, D.W., Groom, B., Hepburn, C., and Koundouri, C. (2003) Valuing the future: Recent advances in social discounting, *World Economics*, 4(2):121–141.

Pearce, P.H. (1990) *Introduction to Forestry Economics*, Vancouver, CA: University of British Columbia Press.

Penfield, P. (2007) 3 avenues to cost reduction, *Supply Chain Management Review*, 11(1):30–36.

Perman, R., Ma, Y., McGilvray, J., and Common, M. (2003) *Natural Resource and Environmental Economics*, 3rd ed., London, UK: Pearson Education Limited.

Peters, C.M., Gentry, A.H., and Mendelsohn, R.O. (1989) Valuation of an Amazonian rainforest, *Nature*, 339:655–656.

Pickens, J.B., Johnson, D.L., Orr, B.D., Reed, D.D., Webster, C.E., and Schmierer, J.M. (2009) Expected rates of value growth for individual sugar maple crop trees in the Great Lakes region: A reply, *Northern Journal of Applied Forestry*, 25(4):1345–147.

Pindyck, R.S., and Rubinfeld, D.L. (1995) *Microeconomics*, 3rd ed., Englewood Cliffs, NJ: Prentice-Hall.

Plott, C.R., and Zeiler, K. (2005) The willingness to pay – willingness to accept gap, the "endowment effect," subject misconceptions, and experimental procedures for eliciting valuations, *The American Economic Review*, 95(3).

Png, I., and Lehman, D. (2007) *Managerial Economics*, 3rd ed., Malden, MA: Blackwell Publishing.

Potter, J., and Sanders, S. (2012) Do economists recognize an opportunity cost when they see one? Dismal performance or an arbitrary concept? *Southern Economic Journal*, 79(2):248–256.

Poudyal, N.C., Hodges, D.G., Tonn, B., and Cho, S.-H. (2009) Valuing diversity and spatial pattern of open space plots in urban neighborhoods, *Forest Policy and Economics*, 11:194–201.

Pressler, M.R. (1860) Aus der Holzzuwachlehre (zweiter Artikel), *Allgemeine Forst- und Jagd-Zeitung*, 36. Reprinted as Pressler, M.R. (1995) For the comprehension of net revenue silviculture and the management objectives derived thereof, *Journal of Forest Economics*, 1(1):45–88.

Prestemon, J.P., Turner, J.A., Buongiaorno, J., Zhu, S., and Li, R. (2008) Some timber product market and trade implications of an invasive defoliator: The case of Asian Lymantria in the United States, *Journal of Forestry*, 106(8):409–415.

Price, C. (1993) *Time, Discounting and Value*, Oxford, UK: Blackwell Publisher.

Price, C. (2004) Hyperbole, hypocrisy and discounting that slowly fades away, in H. Pajuoja and K. Heimo, eds. *Proceedings of the Biennial Meeting of the Scandinavian Society of Forest Economics held in Vantaa*, Finland 12–15 May, Scandinavian Forest Economics No. 40 (https://www.academia.edu/79209477/Institutional_analysis_of_incentive_schemes_for_ecosystem_service_provision_a_comparative_study_across_four_European_countries_a_comparative_study_across_four_European_countries).

Puttock, G.D., Prescott, D.M., and Meilke, K.D. (1990) Stumpage prices in Southwestern Ontario: A hedonic function approach, *Forest Science*, 36(4):1119–1132.

Radeloff, V.C., Hammer, R.B., Stewart, S.I., Fried, J.S., Holcomb, S.S., and McKeefry, J.F. (2005) The wildland-urban interface in the United States, *Ecological Applications*, 15(3):799–805.

Ramasamy, V., Zuboy, J., O'Shaughnessy, E., Feldman, D., Desai, J., Woodhouse, M., Basore, P., and Margolis, R. (2022) *U.S. Solar Photovoltaic System and Energy Storage Cost Benchmarks, With Minimum Sustainable Price Analysis: Q1 2022*, Golden, CO: National Renewable Energy Laboratory, NREL/TP-7A40-83586. (https://www.nrel.gov/docs/fy22osti/83586.pdf).

Randall, A. (1994) A difficulty with the travel cost method, *Land Economics*, 70(1): 88–96.

Rideout, D. (1985) Managerial finance for silvicultural systems, *Canadian Journal of Forest Research*, 15:163–166.

Rideout, D. (1986) The trouble with benefit-cost ratios: Benefit-cost ratio maximization versus wealth maximization, *Canadian Journal of Forest Research*, 16(1):142–144.

Rideout, D.B., and Hesseln, H. (2001) *Principles of Forest & Environmental Economics*, 2nd ed., Fort Collins, CO: Resource & Environmental Management, LLC.

Riera, P., Signorell, G., Thienec, M., Mahieud, P.-A., Navrude, S., Kaval, P., Rulleaug, B., Mavsarh, R., Madureirai, L., Meyerhoff, J., Elsasserk, P., Notarol, S., De Salvo, M., Giergicznym, M., and Dragoin, S. (2012) Non-market valuation of forest goods and services: Good practice guidelines, *Journal of Forest Economics*, 18(4):259–270.

Roof, K., and Oleru, N. (2008) Public health: Seattle and King County's push for the built environment, *Journal of Environmental Health*, 71(1):24–27.

Rosen, S. (1974) Hedonic prices and implicit markets: Product differentiation in pure competition, *The Journal of Political Economy*, 82:34–55.

Rosenthal, D.H., and Brown, T.C. (1985) Comparability of market prices and consumer surplus for resource allocation decisions, *Journal of Forestry*, 83(2):105–109.

Ruddell, S., Sampson, R., Smith, M., Giffen, R., Cathcart, J., Hagan, J., Sosland, D., Godbee, J., Heissenbuttel, J., Lovett, S., Helms, J., Price, W., and Simpson, R. (2007) The role for sustainably managed forests in climate change mitigation, *Journal of Forestry*, 105(6):314–319.

Samuelson, P.A. (1976a) *Economics*, 10th ed., New York, NY: McGraw-Hill, Inc.

Samuelson, P.A. (1976b) Economics of forestry in an evolving society, *Economic Inquiry*, 14(4):466–492. Reprinted as Samuelson, P.A. (1995) Economic of forestry in an evolving society, *Journal of Forest Economics*, 1(1):115–149.

Sander, H., Polasky, S., and Haight, R.G. (2010) The value of urban tree cover: A hedonic property price model in Ramsey and Dakota Counties, Minnesota, USA, *Ecological Economics*, 69:1646–1656.

Scapra, R., Buongiorno, J., Hseu, J.-S., and Abt, K.L. (2000) Assessing the non-timber value of forests: A revealed-preference, hedonic model, *Journal of Forest Economics*, 6(2):83–107.

Schelly, C., and Letzelter, J.C. (2020) Examining the key drivers of residential solar adoption in upstate New York, *Sustainability*, 12:2552 (https://doi.org/10.3390/su120 62552).

Sendak, P.E. (1991) Re-expressing interest rates estimated from the exponential model. *Northern J. of Applied Forestry*, 8(4):172–173.

Sendak, P.E. (1994) *Northeastern regional timber stumpage prices: 1961–1991*. Res Pap. NE-683. USDA Forest Serv. Northeast Research Station, Broomall, PA.

Sendak, P.E., and Bennink, J. (1985) *The Cost of Maple Sugaring in Vermont*, Research Paper NE-565, Broomail, PA: US Department of Agriculture, Forest Service, Northeastern Research Station.

Sexton, W.T., Malk, A.J., Szaro, R.C., and Johnson, N.C., eds. (1999) *Ecological Stewardship: A Common Reference for Ecosystem Management*, vol. I–III, Oxford, UK: Elsevier Science Ltd.

Sharma, M., and Oderwald, R.G. (2001) Dimensionally compatible volume and taper equations, *Canadian Journal of Forest Research*, 31:797–803.

Short, W., Packey, D., and Holt, T. (1995) *A Manual for the Economic Evaluation of Energy Efficiency and Renewable Energy Technologies*, NREL/TP-462-5173, Golden, CO: National Renewable Energy Laboratory.

Siegel, W.C., Haney, H.L., Jr., and Greene, J.L. (2009) *Estate Planning for Forest Landowners: What Will Become of Your Timberland?* General Technical Report SRS-112, Asheville, NC: US Department of Agriculture, Forest Service, Southern Research Station (www.srs.fs.fed.us/pubs/31987 accessed 5 August 2010).

Silberberg, E., and Suen, W. (2001) *The Structure of Economics: A Mathematical Analysis*, 3rd ed., New York, NY: McGraw-Hill Irwin.

Simpson, R.D., Toman, M.A., and Ayres, R.U. (2004) *Scarcity and Growth in the New Millennium: Summary*, Resources for the Future Discussion Paper 04-01, Washington, DC: Resources for the Future.

Smith, A. (1776) *An Inquiry into the Nature and Causes of the Wealth of Nations*, ed. E. Cannan, Chicago: University of Chicago Press.

Smith, E.D., Szidarovszky, F., Karnavas, W.J., and Bahill, A.T. (2008) Sensitivity analysis, a powerful system validation technique, *The Open Cybernetics and Systemics Journal*, 2:39–56.

Smith, J.S., Narkowski-Lindsay, M., Wagner, J.E., and Kittredge, D.B. (2012) Stumpage prices in southern New England (1978–2011): How do red oak, white pine and hemlock prices vary over time? *Northern Journal of Applied Forestry – Field Note*, 29(2):97–101.

Smith, R.L. (1959) Conifer plantations as wildlife habitat, *New York Fish and Game Journal*, 5:101–102.

Smith, V.L. (1968) Economics of production from natural resources, *The American Economic Review*, 58(3):409–431.

Smith, W.B. (technical coordinator), Miles, P.D. (data coordinator), Perry, C.H. (map coordinator), and Pugh, S.A. (data CD coordinator) (2009) *Forest Resources of the United*

States 2007, General Technical Report WO-78, Washington, DC: U.S. Department of Agriculture – Forest Service Washington Office.

Smith, W.R. (1988) The fallacy of preferred species, *Southern Journal Applied Forestry*, 12(2):79–84.

Snyder, S.A., Butler, B.J., and Markowski-Lindsay, M. (2019) Small-area family forest ownership in the USA, *Small-Scale Forestry*, 18:127–147.

Sourd, F. (2005) Optimal timing of a sequence of tasks with general completion costs, *European Journal of Operational Research*, 165:82–96.

Spelter, H., and Alderman, M. (2005) *Profile 2005: Softwood sawmills in the United States and Canada*, 85 p, Research Paper FPL-RP-630, Madison, WI: U.S. Department of Agriculture, Forest Service, Forest Products Laboratory.

Spengle, E.S. (2011) A shift in the wind: The siting of wind power projections on public lands in the Obama era, *Indiana Law Journal*, 1 July:1185–1217.

Stednick, J.D. (1996) Monitoring the effects of timber water yield harvest, *Journal of Hydrology*, 176:79–95.

Stier, J.C. (2003) *What Is My Timber Worth? And Why?* Madison, WI: Forestry Facts University of Wisconsin Extension, University of Wisconsin, School of Natural Resources, Department of Forest Ecology and Management.

Stowe, B., Wilmot, T., Cook, G.L., Perkins, T., and Heiligmann, R.B. (2006) Chapter 7, Maple syrup production, in R.B. Heiligmann, M.R. Koelling, and T.D. Perkins, eds. *North American Maple Syrup Producers Manual*, 2nd ed., Wooster, OH: Ohio State University Extension, The University of Ohio.

Strange, N., Brodie, J., Meilby, H., and Helles, F. (1999) Optimal control of multiple-use products: The case of timber, forage and water protection, *Natural Resources Modeling*, 12:335–354.

Szantio, Z., Escobedo, F., Wagner, J., Rodriguez, J.M., and Smith, S. (2012) Socioeconomic factors and urban tree cover policies in a subtropical urban forest, *GIScience & Remote Sensing*, 49(3):428–449.

Tahvonen, O. (2007) *Optimal Choice Between Even-Aged and Uneven-Aged Forest Management Systems*, Working papers of the Finnish Forest Research Institute, No. 60 (www.metla.fi/julkaisut/workingpapers/2007/mwp060.pdf accessed 16 June 2010).

Tarp, P., Buongiorno, J., Helles, F., Larsen, J.B., and Strange, N. (2005) Economics of converting an even-aged *Fagus Sylvatica* stand to an uneven-aged stand using target diameter harvesting, *Scandinavian Journal of Forest Research*, 20:63–74.

Tasissa, G., Burkhart, H.E., and Amateis, R.L. (1997) Volume and taper equations for thinned and unthinned Loblolly pine trees in cutover, site-prepared plantations, *Southern Journal of Applied Forestry*, 21(3):146–152.

Thomas, G.B., Jr. (1951) *Calculus and Analytic Geometry*, Reading, MA: Addison-Wesley Publishing Company, Inc.

Tom, S.M., Fox, C.R., Trepel, C., and Poldrack, R.A. (2007) The neural basis of loss aversion in decision-making under risk, *Science*, 315:515–518.

Touza, J., Termansen, M., and Perring, C. (2008) A bioeconomic approach to the Faustmann-Hartman model: Ecological interactions in managed forest, *Natural Resources Modeling*, 21(4):551–581.

United States Department of Agriculture, Forest Service. (2006) *Forest Inventory and Analysis National Core Field Guide, Volume I: Field Data Collection Procedures for Phase 2 Plots Version 3.1*, Newtown Square, PA (www.fs.fed.us/ne/fia/datacollection/manual-ver3_1/index.html accessed 27 July 2007).

Uys, H.J.E. (1990) A new form of internal rate of return, *South African Forestry Journal*, 154:24–26.

van den Berg, A., Perkins, T., Isselhardt, M., Godshall, M.A., and Lloyd, S. (2015) Effects of sap concentration with reverse osmosis on syrup composition and flavor, *Maple Digest*, 54(3):11–33.

Varian, H.R. (1992) *Microeconomic Analysis*, 3rd ed., New York, NY: W.W. Norton and Company.

Vaughan, W.J., and Russell, C.S. (1982) Valuing a fishing day: An application of a systematic varying parameter model, *Land Economics*, 58(4):450–463.

Venkatachalam, L. (2004) The contingent valuation method: A review, *Environmental Impact Assessment Review*, 24:89–124.

Volk, T.A., and Luzadis, V.A. (2008) Willow biomass production for bioenergy, biofuels and bioproducts in New York, in B. Solomon and V.A. Luzadis, eds. *Renewable Energy from Forest Resources in the United States*, Oxon, UK: Routledge Press.

Wagner, J.E. (2009) Expected rates of value growth for individual sugar maple crop trees in the Great Lakes region: A comment, *Northern Journal of Applied Forestry*, 25(4): 141–145.

Wagner, J.E. (2012) *Forestry Economics: A Managerial Approach: Routledge Textbooks in Environmental and Agricultural Economics*, London, UK: Routledge Press.

Wagner, J.E. (2020) Ruminations of economic decision modeling of managing forests with a focus on family forest landowners, *Journal of Forestry*, 118(4):362–372.

Wagner, J.E., Canham, H., Bentley, W., Germain, R., and Davis, C. (2000) *Financial Feasibility Analysis of In-Woods Chipping to Supply Wood Chips for the Proposed Norbord Expansion*, A report to the Watershed Agricultural Council, Syracuse, NY: State University of New York College of Environmental Science and Forestry.

Wagner, J.E., and Choi, J. (1999) Economic assessment of recreation, wildlife, and timber resources on Niagara Mohawk power company's Moose River land holdings, in W. Porter and J.P. Gibbs, project directors, *Ecological Assessment of Niagara Mohawk Power Corporation Lands, College of Environmental Science and Forestry*, Syracuse, NY: State University of New York.

Wagner, J.E., and Holmes, T.P. (1999) Estimating economic gains for landowners due to time-dependent changes in biotechnology, *Forest Science*, 45(2):163–170.

Wagner, J.E., and Newman, D.H. (2013) The Simon-Ehrlich Bet: Teaching Relative vs. Absolute Scarcity. *The American Economist*, 58(1):16–26.

Wagner, J.E., Nowak, C.A., and Casalmir, L.M. (2003) Financial analysis of diameter-limit cut stands in Northern Hardwoods, *Small-scale Forest Economics, Management and Policy*, 2(3):357–376.

Wagner, J.E., Rahn, J., and Cavo, M. (2019) A pragmatic method to forecast stumpage prices, *Forest Science*, 65(4):429–438.

Wagner, J.E., and Sendak, P.E. (2005) The annual increase of Northeastern regional timber stumpage prices: 1961–2002, *Forest Products Journal*, 55(2):36–45.

Wagner, J.E., Smalley, B., and Luppold, W. (2004) Factors affecting the merchandising of hardwood logs in the southern tier of New York, *Forest Products Journal*, 54(11): 98–102.

Wagner, J.E., and Stehman, S.V. (2015) Optimizing sample size allocation to strata for estimating area and map accuracy, *Remote Sensing of Environment*, 168:126–133.

Walker, A., Lockhart, E., Desai, J., Ardani, K., Klise, G., Lavrova, O., Tansy, T., Deot, J., Fox, B., and Pochiraju, A. (2020) *Model of Operation-and-Maintenance Costs for Photovoltaic Systems*, Golden, CO: National Renewable Energy Laboratory, NREL/TP-5C00-74840 (www.nrel.gov/docs/fy20osti/74840.pdf).

Wear, D.N., and Newman, D.H. (1991) The structure of forestry production: Short-run and long-run results, *Forest Science*, 37(2):540–551.

Webster, C.E., Reed, D.D., Orr, B.D., Schmierer, J.M., and Pickens, J.B. (2009) Expected rates of value growth for individual sugar maple crop trees in the Great Lakes region, *Northern Journal of Applied Forestry*, 25(4):133–140.

West, G.G., Moore, J.R., Shula, R.G., Harrington, J.J., Snook, J., Gordon, J.A., and Riordan, M.P. (2013) Forest management DSS development in New Zealand, in J. Tucek, R. Smrecek, A. Majlingova, and J. Garcia-Gonzalo, eds. *Implementation of DSS Tools into the Forestry Practice*, Slovakia: Technical University of Zvolen, pp. 153–163.

White, A.E., Lutz, D.A., Howarth, R.B., and Soto, J.R. (2018) Small-scale forestry and carbon offset markets: An empirical study of Vermont current use forest landowner willingness to accept carbon credit programs, *PLOS ONE* (https://doi.org/10.1371/journal.pone.0201967).

Whitehead, J.C., Pattanayak, S.K., Van Houtven, G.L., and Gelso, B.R. (2008) Combining revealed and stated preference data to estimate the nonmarket value of ecological services: An assessment of the state of the science, *Journal of Economic Surveys*, 22(5):872–908.

Willis, K.G., and Garrod, G.D. (1991) An individual travel-cost method of evaluating forest recreation, *Journal of Agricultural Economics*, 42(1):33–42.

Wilmot, T. (2011) Pricing sap, *Farming – The Journal of Northeast Agriculture*, 14(3):49–50 (www.uvm.edu/~pmrc/wilmot_pricing.pdf accessed 19 April 2016).

Winston, W.L. (1994) *Operations Research: Applications and Algorithms*, 3rd ed., Belmont, CA: Duxbury Press.

Winston, W.L. (2004) *Operations Research: Applications and Algorithms*, 4th ed., Boston, MA: Cengage Inc.

Wunder, S., and Wertz-Kanounnikoff, S. (2009) Payments for ecosystem services: A new way of conserving biodiveristy in forests, *Journal of Sustainable Forestry*, 28(3):576–596.

Yin, R. (1997) An alternative approach to forest investment assessment, *Canadian Journal of Forest Research*, 27(12):2072–2078.

Yin, R., and Newman, D.H. (1997) Long-run timber supply and the economics of timber production, *Forest Science*, 43(1):113–120.

Yin, R., Pienaar, L.V., and Aronow, M.E. (1998) The productivity and profitability of fiber farming, *Journal of Forestry*, 96(11):13–18.

Yoo, S. (2012) *Measuring Environmental Amenity Values from Urban Open Space Using a Spatial Hedonic Approach*, Ph.D. Dissertation State University of New York, College of Environmental Science and Forestry, Syracuse, NY.

Zhou, M., J.J. Liang, J.J. and Buongiorno, J. (2008) Adaptive versus fixed policies for economic or ecological objectives in forest management. *Forest Ecology and Management*, 254:178–187.

Zio, E., and Pedroni, N. (2013) *Methods for Representing Uncertainty: A Literature Review, Apports de la recherché 2013–3, Risk Analysis*, Les cahiers de la securite industrielle, FONCSI (https://d-nb.info/1149639296/34).

Zudak, L.S. (1970) Productivity, labor demand and cost in a continuous production facility, *The Journal of Industrial Economics*, 18(3):255–274.

Index

Note: Page numbers in *italics* indicate a figure and page numbers in **bold** indicate a table on the corresponding page. Page numbers followed by "n" with numbers refer to notes.

Printed in the United States
by Baker & Taylor Publisher Services